to New York hardly belonged on the same plane. The Shuberts' musical version of "Tonight or Never," which they called "Night of Love," ran two weeks here and only one in New York, but in both cities public reception was of an identical nature. Its chief virtue lay in the indication that Marguerite Namara, a delightful example of the classic prima donna outlook, should find another and better opportunity for herself.

"Meet the People," the intimate homemade revue brought from the Pacific Coast by the Hollywood Theatre Alliance, won a degree of support out of proportion to its slender and naive material. It opened at the Grand Opera House in late September and kept alive for twelve mildly prosperous weeks, apparently because the people in the audience found all the performers charming and unspoiled.

With a single exception, the list of four plays seen in Chicago but not at all in New York forms an exceptionally undistinguished little catalogue. The exception is Ruth Chatterton's brilliant performance in George Bernard Shaw's "Pygmalion." With the assistance of Barry Thomson and Dennis Hoey, Miss Chatterton kept the experiences of Eliza Doolittle before the Chicago public for seven weeks instead of the anticipated two. Prior bookings made her move restlessly from one theatre to another, until she had experimented with the stage facilities of the Selwyn, the Erlanger and the Harris between late November and the middle of January.

Ruth Gordon, who was reported as having said privately that she "had to get the play out of her system," appeared in a revival of "Here Today," a comedy considerably less amusing now than when it had failed to attract favorable notice in New York eight years before. Two characteristic operetta revivals from the Shubert repertory—"Blossom Time" and "The Student Prince"—rounded out the list of Chicago plays which did not reach New York.

The total Chicago season consisted of 25 different attractions. The almost complete absence of serious dramas and the unusually large array of musical shows provided ammunition for the argument that the Broadway theatre has become mainly an escapist enterprise.

The season's complete record of professional productions in Chicago is as follows:

Non-musical plays: "The Male Animal" (11 weeks); "Ladies in Retirement" (4 weeks, in two separate engagements of 2 weeks each); "The Time of Your Life" (5 weeks); "Lady in Waiting"

(3 weeks); "Pygmalion" (7 weeks); "Here Today" (4 weeks); "There Shall Be No Night" (3½ weeks); "My Sister Eileen" (15 weeks to May 31; continued on into the Summer); "See My Lawyer" (4 weeks); "Arsenic and Old Lace" (8 weeks to May 31; continued until June 28); "The Man Who Came to Dinner" (2 weeks); "Twelfth Night" (4 weeks). Held over from 1939-40—"Life with Father" (total of 66 weeks, of which 51 weeks were in 1940-41 season).

Musical comedies, revues, et al.: "Hold On to Your Hats" (6 weeks); "Too Many Girls" (3 weeks); "Meet the People" (12 weeks); "Night of Love" (2 weeks); "New Pins and Needles" (16 weeks); "Du Barry Was a Lady" (11 weeks); "Blossom Time" (5 weeks); "The Student Prince" (4 weeks); Dante in "Sim Sala Bim" (3 weeks); "Boys and Girls Together" (4 weeks); "Cabin in the Sky" (4 weeks); "Hellzapoppin" (3 weeks to May 31; continued on into the Summer).

Not included in these official calculations is the Yiddish musical comedy, "Goldele dem Bekers," which spent a week at the Studebaker Theatre in May.

The Theatre Guild and American Theatre Society, operating jointly, offered the following six plays to their subscribers: "Ladies in Retirement," "The Time of Your Life," "Here Today," "There Shall Be No Night," "Twelfth Night," "Arsenic and Old Lace." The use of "Arsenic and Old Lace" as a Guild play was unprecedented; in the eighth and ninth weeks of the engagement the Guild, in apparent desperation, offered its subscribers the choice of tickets or a refund.

Chicago showed no more sign of potential local producing enterprise in 1940-41 than in any other season in recent years. "See My Lawyer" was the only locally produced professional play of the year, unless the two Shubert operetta revivals—to which the name of William Thannhausen, a member of the Grand Opera house staff, was given as producer—be included on a technicality. Meanwhile the semi-professional groups in Chicago accomplished little on behalf of the upper reaches of the drama. Wherefore Chicago still remains no more than one of the more prominent whistle stops along the Broadway right of way.

THE SEASON IN SAN FRANCISCO

BY FRED JOHNSON

Drama Editor, *The Call-Bulletin*

IT wasn't, as feared, the worst theatrical year in San Francisco since its first gold-rush theatre was built and its bay washed the site of its present financial district.

The year might have been so judged on the meager score of Broadway touring attractions. These were discouragingly few. And there were still fewer coast productions to fill the period of doldrums suffered by three yawning legitimate theatres.

But, oddly enough, there was consolation in the local paucity of entertainments conceived in Hollywood, their movie-player casts equipped with play material of dubious brand and seemingly dependent upon star names to entice a hearing.

There were, in fact, but two premières of this order, whereas in the season of 1939-40 there were three new plays and one revue of coast origin to make San Francisco their trying-out point—and learn the worst.

But if Eastern and original Hollywood offerings were fewer in the year just ended, there was a grease-paint species of balm in Gilead for the not quite moribund rialto.

It came in the form of revivals rather than original script ventures—and still Hollywood figured partly in their casting. The producer was Henry Duffy, whose coast-wide chain of theatres collapsed in the depression era. In the Spring he reopened the Alcazar Theatre, which had been the nucleus for his house expansion in the late twenties, with the promise at this writing of recapturing its old tradition—and saving it from wreckage, that its site might be used as an auto parking lot.

In lieu of its old stock policy, he began the new regime with a pair of revivals headed by stars and supporting players from Broadway and Hollywood that have had the merit of companies originating much further east. That these troupers may be seen at admission prices no higher than $1.25 has caused enthusiasm among old Alcazar patrons of the kitchen-sink period and even caused the limousine trade to take surprised notice.

Edward Everett Horton took four weeks' time off from his film assignments to reappear in "Springtime for Henry," in

which he had toured for two recent seasons, with a halt in the Summer theatres. Supported by Gordon Richards, Vivian Vance and Marjorie Lord, his success in rejuvenating the legendary house was so marked that he was loath to answer a summons for further motion picture chores.

Billie Burke followed Horton in a return to her rôle of the feather-brained matron in Paul Osborne's "The Vinegar Tree," with such competent associates as Paul Cavanagh, Charles Waldron and Leona Maricle. When her engagement of five weeks ended, Francis Lederer came in to resume his playwright rôle in "No Time for Comedy," supported by Rose Hobart in the Cornell part and Doris Dudley as the antagonizing influence. Lederer's appearance in the city for a second time in the same rôle saw no waning of his popularity and Miss Hobart won critical raves for her portrait of the embattled actress-wife.

With Russell Fillmore again in the director's chair, Duffy is also booking most of his productions into Hollywood's El Capitan Theatre. And later he was to present Miss Burke in "The Marquise" at the rehabilitated Blackstone Theatre in Chicago, where Otto Kruger in "Libel," a later San Francisco attraction, was to follow her.

The producer's further program included a coast revival of "Quiet, Please," a comedy of the Hollywood scene by F. Hugh Herbert and Hans Kraley and one of the four similar treatments of film colony life to be rejected by Broadway earlier this season. After that he was to present Mrs. Duffy (the Dale Winter of "Irene" fame) in a new staging of "First Lady."

Season's-end in the San Francisco Bay area was brightened, and consolingly, by three stage festivals—by the Players in Stanford University's fiftieth anniversary observance, by the Berkeley (home of the University of California) diamond jubilee of the city's founding, and by the fourth annual light opera festival shared between San Francisco and Los Angeles.

The Stanford birthday theatricals embraced plays from the masterpieces of modern drama and lighter stage literature, going back to Boucicault's "The Poor of New York" and ending with "Accent on Youth." Among the others were "Of Thee I Sing," Ibsen's "The Wild Duck," Shaw's "Saint Joan," Behrman's "Rain from Heaven" and Smetana's "The Bartered Bride."

In addition to Berkeley's dance and musical events, the seventy-fifth anniversary festival ended with two massive drama productions in Hearst Greek Theatre on the campus—"Saint

Joan" and "Twelfth Night," with casts made up of visiting and local talent.

In the title rôle of the first appeared Elena Miramova, Russian-born immigrant returning to the scene of her early schooling that was followed by her starring in the London production of "Grand Hotel."

The Viola of "Twelfth Night" was Lois Moran, former film and stage actress now living in San Francisco, with Barbara Horder, former English stage associate of Sybil Thorndyke, in the rôle of Olivia.

The two summer afternoon attractions inspired a new zeal for a return of the famous guest stars of Greek tragedies and other productions in the amphitheatre in its earlier days. There was also an enlivening of interest among the student players of University of California's Little Theatre, which has supplied a succession of recruits to the Broadway stage.

The civic light opera season of four weeks was the most brilliant and profitable in the four years of its career, with a repertoire of "Naughty Marietta," "Rio Rita," "The Chocolate Soldier" and "Cabin in the Sky," the Broadway importation with Ethel Waters, Todd Duncan, Rex Ingram and others of its original cast.

John Charles Thomas donned uniform as "The Chocolate Soldier," supported by Hope Manning, Irra Petina, of the Metropolitan and San Francisco grand opera forces, and Film Comedian Billy Gilbert.

Miss Petina and Walter Cassel, the tenor of "Rio Rita," were tabbed as the season's outstanding discoveries. "Rio Rita" also afforded Comedian Joe E. Brown his first essay in light opera to noisy audience acclaim. Suzanne Sten, a prima donna of Chicago and San Francisco opera seasons, was impressive in the same production and Francia White, a favorite coast soprano, was well received in "Naughty Marietta."

One of Hollywood's original contributions to meet disaster was George Seaton's "About Tomorrow," a unique treatment of death and its aftermath. Frank Craven and J. M. Kerrigan, as ghostly father and son, were found lingering on the scene of a trivial family problem, to discover that they had gone to much unnecessary bother. Sally Eilers made a return to the stage as Craven's married daughter, with Harry Joe Brown, film producer and husband of the actress, presenting the comedy-drama in association with Film Director Ralph Murphy. After a postponement of several days, due to Miss Eilers' illness after ar-

rival in San Francisco, the piece was given a run of but one and a half weeks and then shelved.

Lee Tracy combated play rewriters and indifferent playgoers in the second film colony offering, Milton Lazarus' "Every Man for Himself." Despite the poor response, Producers Arthur Hutchinson and Arthur Ripley, who had earlier presented Laird Cregar in "Oscar Wilde," made the ill-timed venture on Broadway of a fourth lampoon of assorted Hollywood characters.

Of the New York dramatic gifts, Gertrude Lawrence in "Skylark" was one of the chief bearers, rewarded with a four weeks' run; Tallulah Bankhead in "The Little Foxes" was another, for a fortnight's capacity business. The Lunts in "There Shall Be No Night" broke Curran Theatre records for their eleven days.

William Saroyan's first play to be presented in his home city was "The Time of Your Life," with Saroyan hidden in the gallery's back row and fleeing before the call of "author." With Eddie Dowling, Julie Haydon and others of the original cast, its picture of a Barbary Coast saloon was viewed by the local experts as being so realistic, when it wasn't purely fantastic, that the piece enjoyed a run of three and a half weeks.

Sell-out houses for most of its single week greeted the appearance of a group of Hollywood players in three of Noel Coward's "Tonight at 8:30" playlets, for British war relief. In the casts of "Family Album," "Ways and Means" and "Fumed Oak" were C. Aubrey Smith, Philip Merivale, Reginald Gardner, Dame May Whitty, Doris Lloyd, Gladys Cooper, Benita Hume and Brian Aherne.

Cornelia Otis Skinner had a banner week in her character sketches and Ruth Chatterton's scheduled fortnight in "Pygmalion" was extended for a half week.

"Meet the People," the Hollywood youth revue, did uniformly good business for nine weeks, en route to Broadway.

Flora Robson in "Ladies in Retirement" was successful in a brief engagement, but May Boland in a revival of "Meet the Wife" was less fortunate.

The Berkeley Playmakers, in its seventeenth year, doubled its membership and augmented its acting, directing and scenic departments. The 1941 program embraced production of sixteen short American folk plays, engaging 150 players. The plays were selected from a total of almost 400 scripts received in the last one-act national playwriting competition, cash prizes for which were headed by the George Pierce Baker award.

The Wayfarers Civic Repertory Theatre of San Francisco and

Photo by Hans J. Knopf, Pix, Inc.

"NATIVE SON"

From below the sound of the furnace rises. Bigger hears it. Briefly he hesitates, then kneels down, picks Mary up and starts for the door. "Ain't nothin' happened!" he repeats, hoarsely.

(*Canada Lee, Anne Burr*)

THE BEST PLAYS OF 1940-41

AND THE
YEAR BOOK OF THE DRAMA
IN AMERICA

EDITED BY
BURNS MANTLE

With Illustrations

DODD, MEAD AND COMPANY
NEW YORK - - - 1941

INTRODUCTION

(And a Good Deal About "The Beautiful People")

ONCE before in this series of Year Books of the Drama in America the editor was troubled as to the selection of the ten plays most worthily representative of the particular theatre season the record was compiled to cover. That was the issue of 1926-27 and the troublesome play was Bourdet's "The Captive."

"The Captive" was a good play on an ugly theme. It had been ruled off the stage by the civic authorities as being an immoral drama, after having played 160 performances. The record called for its inclusion. The preponderance of opinion was against it.

In that dilemma I polled nine leading New York drama critics for an opinion. Five voted for "The Captive" and four against. I asked for a vote from playgoers and play readers and they were strongly against the inclusion of the play in these pages. In the end I decided against the play as one of the selected ten.

This year the disturbing opus has been William Saroyan's "The Beautiful People," which is a controversial play on an appealing theme. The decision this time is not on moral or civic grounds. It rests entirely on the question of whether or not "The Beautiful People" is a "best play" judged by such standards as universally have been applied to acted plays, and such standards as have heretofore been applied to the ten selected plays in these volumes.

So far as my single opinion as editor of the series is concerned the decision is easy. To me "The Beautiful People" is an interesting series of fairly fanciful character sketches set upon the stage in the framework of a play. Such story as is told is lacking in both cohesion and dramatic purpose. The play's episodes are unrelated in the sense of building a cumulative interest in either a comic or a dramatic climax. There have been other plays, it is true, and notable plays, including those of the Chekhov series, that were as lacking in conflict and suspense as this one, but none of them, to me, has been as light-bodied or as deliberately defiant of play building conventions as the Saroyan opus.

"The Beautiful People" is a series of gentle and often tender recitals, respecting the individual lives and philosophies of its characters. Acted in the theatre by a carefully selected group

of sensitive and sympathetic actor personalities it takes on a quality of sentimental appeal that falls away completely, it seems to me, once a description or digest of the material is attempted.

For example, I could tell you that the first scene of the play consists of no more than a duologue inspired by a young boy's (Owen Webster's) attempt to explain to a little old lady (Harmony Blueblossom) the devotion which his older sister (St. Agnes of the Mice, they call her) has for the mice that overrun their rambling home. But I cannot reproduce for you the strangely appealing atmosphere created by this recital, despite its complete lack of dramatic substance and form.

"Are you fond of mice?" asks Owen.

"Not particularly. Are you?" whispers Harmony.

"Only insofar as they reveal still further the magnificence of Almighty God. There's a thousand of them at least—somewhere in the wood. (*Raising his voice.*) No rats, mind you, just little mice. Give them a chance. If God gave them a chance, we've got to give them a chance, too."

"I never looked at it in that way," admits Harmony.

"That's the way my sister looks at it, and the mice are grateful, too. They go all over looking for things for her."

"I don't believe it."

"It's the truth. The whole thing is practically a small religion. There's a heart beating in those little animals." . . .

Following which Owen relates an experience of having met one of the Webster mice on the cowcatcher of a streetcar. They exchanged glances. Probably, he says, the mouse was on its way down to the waterfront.

Now such a scene must sound highly fantastic in the telling, or in the reading, unless the person hearing or reading it has seen the play and is able to recapture something of the eerie atmosphere with which the actors invest it.

And so it is with all four of the scenes that make up the play. Each has its own moment of beauty, strengthened by one or two speeches. In the second scene, for example, Agnes is pathetically torn between two emotional adventures—one of her mice is missing and must be found, and she had met a strange boy who had held a library door open for her and she had liked him—

"He's not nearly what I thought I'd find, but I like him," says Agnes.

"Well, that's fine," answers Owen. "It's nice to like somebody. Anybody." But Agnes has put her hands over her eyes and is crying. "Hey! What are you bawling about?"

"I *like* him."

"Is that the way it makes you feel?"

"It makes me feel sick, like a whole world sick, and nothing to do about it, but to like him, more and more with every breath you take. . . . All we did is walk and talk. We didn't even talk sense. I came home, feeling pity for everything. Not love—*pity*."

That confession of the birth of love in the heart of a girl is tenderly spoken and moving. Later it is elaborated in a further tenderly naive confession to the father. But that is the last we hear of the boy, or the adventure, save a promise that the boy is to call next day.

So it is, too, with Jonah Webster, the father and the keystone of the Saroyan arch. "Jonah Webster, drunk, enters singing," read Mr. Saroyan's instructions. "There is a moment of silence. Jonah is a big, powerfully built man in his early sixties. There is something of the poet about him, and something of the fool—who is fool by choice. He seems young, almost boyish, simultaneously full of humor and love and anger."

Jonah is the street corner philosopher of "The Beautiful People." His religion is his own, and he is content. Jonah's philosophy and Jonah's statement of being largely make up the last scene of the play. He is telling Father Hogan why it was that Owen was sent by Agnes to Father Hogan's church to recover the lost mouse.

"Now, you and I know mice are insensible creatures and cannot respond to affection and kindness," says Jonah. "Well, it appears *she* did not know, and that they *did* respond—in a way."

"I don't understand," admits His Reverence.

"Father Hogan, if I do not encourage the imaginations of my children, I also do not hinder them. With her faith in the mice—grew her faith in herself. As that faith grew, intelligence and humanity grew, and with these things came a greater and deeper expectation of others, of all the living. And, naturally, the possibility of deep disappointment, which may eventually become disillusionment, or even contempt. I think I'll soon know, since only this afternoon she met a boy whose reality moved her to pity for the whole world. Which is, of course, the beginning of true humanity. Now—her brother sometimes puts flowers out for her, here on the floor, as though they were from the mice, and once when she was very ill, he stayed up all night, grumbling to himself. Actually he was praying for her. When she was better again, he told her the *mice* had prayed for her. Because

she had watched over *them.* It's no matter to me what pattern faith or humor may take." . . .

"I sometimes stand on the street corners and talk to people, as you do inside the church," continues Jonah. "My only disciple is Dan here, but he's a good one. But my *church* is the whole blooming universe, and mice are as much a part of its magnificence as men, if they only knew. We are alive with all other things alive, from the mite to the whale. Pole Star and Pyramid. I tell them the same things when I stand on the corners you tell them inside the church, but from my heart to the Pole Star is the straightest line in the world, and as the star moves, so moves my heart—and yours, and Dan's and everybody's. The image of the pyramid to the human mind is the image of our grace, as men. The slaves who built the pyramid—the thousands of them over the hundreds of years—did not know the majesty of the thing being made. But the *image* of that thing began where it ended—in the living human mind. The line goes from one to the other; from the heart to the star, and from the star to the pyramid, and from the pyramid *back* to the heart. From *one* thing to *all* things. They're all *one,* to be seen as a whole majesty, or not to be seen at all. I choose to see, since I am by nature a religious man."

In writing and characterization each of the Saroyan episodes, as I say, contains a haunting value of its own, but, to me, it is only by sight and contact that you accept these beautiful people, if beautiful they be to you, at Mr. Saroyan's full appraisal. Nor do their adventures, to me, add up to the stature of a play. Some who saw "The Beautiful People" walked out of the theatre, grumbling. Others immediately bought seats for future performances. I have heard playgoers curse the play as a cheat, and I have heard others bless it as a work inspired by the peculiar genius of its creator. Six of my critical colleagues, John Anderson, John Mason Brown, George Jean Nathan, Joseph Wood Krutch, Stark Young and Grenville Vernon, voted it the best play of the season. Out of respect to their judgment, and in fairness to Mr. Saroyan, I have given you this account of it.

So much for the most controversial of the year's plays. The season otherwise was no more inspiriting and no more depressing than the dolorous state of a worried and warring world would seem to justify. The plays generally were rather on the serious side, though the flashes of farce and comedy were frequently riotous.

The drama that Paul Green and Richard Wright fashioned

from Mr. Wright's novel, "Native Son," proved mildly sensational and definitely arresting as a modern problem drama. Dealing with a racial question of such vital concern to the social body that it must move steadily toward permanent rather than temporary adjustment, this is such a drama as the citizenry should, I think, seriously ponder. Orson Welles staged it without an intermission, which heightened the dramatic impact. I have included it because plays that, to me, are important to the people are of greater significance than plays that are chiefly important to the drama's critics.

Lillian Hellman's "Watch on the Rhine" brought the second World War close to the American home by stirring a natural human sympathy for the victims of Nazi oppression. It was emotionally the most moving of the season's dramas, and superbly played by Paul Lukas and a carefully chosen company.

Emlyn Williams' "The Corn Is Green" was the one outstanding drama imported from the European scene. It had been produced some time ago in London, but its theme is dateless and its appeal so broadly human that it will continue to be an appealing play long after the wars are over. With Ethel Barrymore to intensify this appeal the play ran for many months.

"Lady in the Dark" was the sensational entertainment success of the year, thanks to Moss Hart's intelligent and provocative use of the psycho-analysis theme and Gertrude Lawrence's perfect fitness both for the interpretation of the drama and the performance of its musical fantasy interludes. So long as it played there was not a single performance without standees in the audience.

"Arsenic and Old Lace" was another of the wonders of the year in the line of entertainment. Telling with completely disarming boldness a story in which insanity and murder furnish the pivotal themes, this Joseph Kesselring comedy so convulsed its sympathetic auditors, and so amused even its milder critics, that it ran through the Winter and Summer playing to a succession of capacity audiences.

Elmer Rice's "Flight to the West" was the most skillfully staged of the war dramas, and one of the most interesting. Its completely developed realism, in fact, brought the imminence of war so close to its audiences that many found it a disturbing item and resented its intrusion upon their complacency.

Rose Franken's "Claudia" proved one of the pleasanter of the escapist dramas, introducing its audiences to a family of decent, wholesome, likable folk involved in problems concerned with both

life and death, yet uplifting rather than depressing in contemplation.

"My Sister Eileen" was another of the happier comedies. Its heroines were the usual two who come to the big city in search of careers and suffer familiar Greenwich Village experiences before they are able to negotiate a fair start. Two of Hollywood's brighter young men, Joseph Fields and Jerome Chodorov, wrote it, and with it strengthened a Broadway hope that more and more good will yet come to the legitimate theatre out of scenarioland.

Owen Davis' adaptation of Frances and Richard Lockridge's novel, "The Norths Meet Murder," produced an amusing little murder play that was also concerned with the possible adventures of likable and recognizable humans. The Moss Hart-George Kaufman comedy extravagance, "George Washington Slept Here," fell off somewhat from their recent comedy average, but it was also considerably better than much of their contemporaries' best work.

The usual statistical record of the season as a whole is contained in the later pages of this volume, which is the twenty-third in the series of Year Books of the Drama in America. You may read that record and will naturally draw your own conclusions from it. So, I suspect, will the theatrical historians of a future day when there shall be neither wars nor rumors of wars to distress the world. Just now that seems at least a couple of eons away.

B. M.

Forest Hills, L. I., 1941.

CONTENTS

ILLUSTRATIONS

THE BEST PLAYS OF 1940-41

THE BEST PLAYS OF 1940-41

THE SEASON IN NEW YORK

THESE are not years upon which we are likely to look back lingeringly. They are years of transition in practically every activity, and that includes the theatre. We could all be pretty blue about what is happening in our own little circle of action if we put our minds to it. I prefer to think of these as years in which the theatre played a good part in keeping up and stimulating the morale of a people beset by depressions and tragedies of one kind and another.

It was the year the World's Fair closed its second and last season, and paid its creditors something less than fifty cents on the dollar. But that same World's Fair was the last of the great spectacles of our time. It was a year in which the production of plays sank to a new low statistically. But it also was a year in which the picture producers paid the play producers and play authors approximately two million dollars for the privilege of reproducing stage plays on the screen.

It was the year in which there were no more than half a dozen outstanding play successes, and most of these of lightweight quality in a literary sense. It was a year in which "Charley's Aunt," a forty-eight-year-old farce, was revived in the most competitive stage market in the world and played for a total of 230 performances. It was the year in which "Tobacco Road" finally was withdrawn, at least temporarily, after a continuous run extending over seven and a half years. So who will say that it was not an interesting year, or one boasting distinction—to which future historians may be able to point as significant if not inspiring?

In June, 1940, we started a new record for your theatre library and found a sizable dividend of leftover entertainment from the year before. "Hellzapoppin" was still poppin' at the Winter Garden, where it had passed its first thousandth performance and was heading for its second. A few weeks later the Messrs. Olsen and Johnson, who had started these didoes in September, 1938, withdrew from the cast to go to California and

record the show in celluloid for future generations to ponder. They were succeeded by two other comic fellows, Jay Flippen and Happy Felton, and "Hellzapoppin" continued, we were assured, to as much laughter as before.

"The Man Who Came to Dinner" was still with us, and with Monty Woolley still the irascible occupant of the invalid throne. "Life with Father," with the original Howard Lindsay and Dorothy Stickney in the leads, was approaching its second year with no sign of faltering. So, too, were "Louisiana Purchase," with Billy Gaxton and Victor Moore, Irene Bordoni and Zorina, and "Separate Rooms," with Alan Dinehart, Glenda Farrell and Lyle Talbot, salvaged from the cinema.

It is with no particular sense of grief that we record the withdrawal of "Tobacco Road," after seven and a half years of reproducing life along a dirt road in Georgia at the Forrest Theatre in New York. The final score was 3,182 performances, the closing May 31, 1941. It began in December, 1933, and however it lasted the way it did no one will ever be able to tell you exactly. There were, naturally, many contributing factors. The New York run advertised the road tours of three other companies. The road tours, in turn, frequently enlivened by police action or censor action against the play, served also to hold attention centered on the New York engagement. Reductions in box-office prices that brought the Caldwell-Kirkland drama into direct and favorable competition with the motion pictures also helped. But of course the real reason for the record-breaking achievement was the same as that which accounted for the previous adventure of "Abie's Irish Rose"—a great many thousands of playgoers liked the show. There were laughs in it, and cussing; there was a strong overlay of sex and there was that subtle satisfaction that stage misery breeds with audiences that are forever seeking human contrasts to build up their own feeling of superiority.

The summer months were barren of new entertainment. In August "Higher and Higher," a Rodgers and Hart musical comedy that had done fairly well with Jack Haley and Marta Eggert from April until July, was revived. In early September, William A. Brady and Grace George, who can stand idleness just so long, decided to revive "Kind Lady," the mystery drama with which Miss George had had renewed success in the barn theatres during the hot months. A week later Alfred Lunt and Lynn Fontanne resumed the run of Robert Sherwood's "There Shall Be No Night" and continued at the Alvin Theatre for an additional sixty-six performances, making the total for that fine drama 181

performances altogether.

About the same time a goateed grandee of the world of magic, one called Dante, came out of the nowhere of a disturbed Europe and staged such a show of magic as Broadway had not seen since Harry Houdini escaped from his last straitjacket. "Sim Sala Bim" Dante called his show, a title he picked up from a Danish nursery rhyme. It included practically all the mysteries that previously had been staged by Herrmann the Great, Kellar the Greater and Thurston the Magnificent. In addition to these items Dante introduced several of his own, and for a few weeks had large audiences going cheerfully back to their kid days and liking the experience. There was talk then of establishing Dante in a permanent Magic Theatre, but nothing came of it.

Al Jolson had been in Hollywood the better part of ten years when he decided to give the Broadway theatre another taste of his quality as an entertainer. He came back the second week in September in a revue called "Hold On to Your Hats." In this Al pretended to be the Lone Ranger of the air waves who had been summoned West to help the cowboys of a dude ranch round up a bandit. But mostly he sang songs, told stories and cracked wise in the intimate stage fashion he had much to do in developing. His engagement was successful, but his health was poor, and his wealth sufficient to permit him to close his engagement after 158 performances. He promised to resume later, but didn't.

Harry Wagstaff Gribble, who has had his years of experience in the theatre, found a play called "Johnnie Belinda." Elmer Harris was the author and Helen Craig was engaged to play the heroine, a deaf mute who speaks but one word during the entire performance. She makes amazing progress, however, with the sign language. "Johnnie Belinda" was pretty obvious theatre, but it had definite values as emotional melodrama. Several of the experts made fun of it, but the play continued through the season to fair returns.

The most resounding of the early season hits was that of Ed Wynn and his "Boys and Girls Together" revue. The perfect fool had been away from Broadway for three years. His welcome home was vociferous and continuous over a period of weeks.

The first serious disappointment came with the Playwrights' Company production of Maxwell Anderson's "Journey to Jerusalem." An earnest work, an eloquent text, a story built up from what is known of the pilgrimage of Joseph, Mary and the boy Jesus to Jerusalem the year Jesus was twelve—these were virtues sacrificed to a static drama that never managed to arouse its

audiences. Their interest in the older Biblical speculations seemed pretty torpid.

The Rockefellers obligingly rebuilt the stage of their Center Theatre a third time for the staging of a skating rink show called "It Happens on Ice." This was a combination ice carnival and revue, with Joe Cook dragging in his gadgets and his gags and a large troupe of professional skaters performing marvels in a series of ice ballets and comedy skits. Sonja Henie was a co-producer with Arthur Wirtz of Chicago, but she did not appear in the program. Hedi Stenuf and Skippy Baxter were the ice stars. Both town and suburban trade was good, and the Center had its best season since "The American Way" was the attraction.

Revivals continued an early season feature. "Charley's Aunt," with Jose Ferrer in skirts, proved popular enough to run through the better part of the season, proving that forty-eight years is really nothing in the life of a good farce. William Saroyan's prize-winning "The Time of Your Life," with Eddie Dowling, came back for a return engagement that was more exciting than the original run.

The first George Kaufman-Moss Hart comedy of the season was one called "George Washington Slept Here." It had been eagerly anticipated. With that title and the historical East to roam about in everybody was convinced that here would be a hit of hits. Another "You Can't Take It with You" at least. But, as frequently happens, the handicap of expectation, plus an unwarranted extravagance in farcical interludes, proved too great for the comedy to overcome entirely. "George Washington Slept Here" ran from mid-October to mid-March. Neither its authors nor their producing associates were ever very happy about it. Neither was audience-response what it should be. Yet, when Summer came, this comedy was the first selection of 90 per cent of the barn theatre impresarios as an opening bill, and one of the most popular bills of the summer season.

Ethel Waters, the colored comedienne, having won her star as a dramatic actress in "Mamba's Daughters," decided to compromise between her musical comedy past and her dramatic present. She became the heroine of "Cabin in the Sky," a musical fantasy in which the Lawd's General and Lucifer Jr. staged a contest for Ethel's soul and that of a gamblin' boy friend, Little Joe. With the aid of a couple of good songs, and a Jacob's ladder in technicolor effects, Ethel won salvation and a nice box office gross.

Then came Ethel Merman with "Panama Hattie" and there

was more rioting in the lobbies. To change her character pattern Ethel devoted this season to being one of the most virginal of the Canal Zone girls. Before she could marry a minor executive she had to win over his eight-year-old daughter, which she did by song and story. There was nothing prissy about either Ethel's performance or that of her hotter associates.

Now there were three Hollywood comedies in a row, and not a hit among them. Their play patterns were similar, their people were the familiar high-living, loud-talking, over-dressed, over-sexed, gossip-column set screen drama promoters appear to delight in presenting as representative of the picture colony. "Beverly Hills" was the first of them. Lynn Starling and Howard Green wrote it. It told of a good husband—at least a good Hollywood husband—who had to submit to the seductions of a picture-backing banker's wife in order to get a profitable writing assignment. It was withdrawn after twenty-eight performances.

The next was called "Quiet, Please," was written by F. Hugh Herbert and Hans Kraly and told of a bad Hollywood husband who, because he was married to a glamorous Class A star while he was only a handsome Class B ham, went in for collecting blondes. This aroused the jealousy of the glamorous one and she consoled herself with a handsome garage attendant. "Quiet, Please" closed after sixteen performances.

The third Hollywood scandal flown in from the coast was Florence Ryerson's and Colin Clements' "Glamour Preferred." Here was the story of a third Hollywood husband, a glamour boy and no mistake, who had married a former star of the silent screen, hoping to settle down with her while she became a good wife and mother. On a personal appearance tour in the East, however, he was picked up by a former flame and this meeting resulted in such complications that the glamour home was threatened right up to five minutes before curtain time. "Glamour Preferred," partly the victim of a Hollywood-play prejudice stirred up by "Beverly Hills" and "Glamour Preferred," lasted only eleven performances.

A good deal of bright dialogue and good character drawing had gone into these three comedies, and each of them was expensively and attractively staged. But such honesty as there was in them was completely smothered by their authors' insistence upon emphasizing Hollywood intrigue, scandal and wisecracking comedy.

The playgoing situation was brightened perceptibly in November by the arrival of Helen Hayes and Maurice Evans in a hand-

some revival of Shakespeare's "Twelfth Night," and the coming of Ethel Barrymore in Emlyn Williams' "The Corn Is Green." Not only did Miss Hayes' Viola express pertness and charm, but Mr. Evans, adding a Cockney touch to Malvolio, lifted the somewhat soggy comedy of the classic to a new level. Margaret Webster, who directed the revival, was also determined that some suggestion of sanity and acceptable romance should break through the farcical sheath of the play, and this helped.

"The Corn Is Green" proved the most distinguished and absorbing of the season's importations. It previously had had a London success. Miss Barrymore found in the heroine the best and meatiest rôle she had played in years, that of an English school teacher who moves into a Welsh mining town, starts a school for the under-privileged miners and, discovering a genius, coaches him through a triumphant bid for a scholarship at Oxford. Her following was quick to respond and her Winter was a happy one.

Mid-season was strewn with failures. "Romantic Mr. Dickens" tried desperately to revive interest in a new biography of the immortal novelist. It was built up by H. H. and Marguerite Harper from recently discovered letters relating his love affairs. It was interesting only because John Barrymore's daughter, Diana, played the heroine, and played her very well. Another, "Delicate Story," was a warmed-over bit of Ferenc Molnar which even Edna Best, returning from a long absence, could not save after four weeks. A third was "Every Man for Himself," which also had to do with a Hollywood scandal—the hero being a writer who comes out of a four-day drunk with a wife he does not recall having acquired. Lee Tracy played this one, and hard, but it barely lasted out its first week.

There was disappointment for many in the failure of Paul Vincent Carroll's "The Old Foolishness." The Irish playwright had done so beautifully with "Shadow and Substance" and "The White Steed" it did not seem likely he could so quickly fail to live up to his early promise. But he could, and did. John Van Druten, whose successful past ("Young Woodley," "There's Always Juliet," "The Distaff Side") frequently bobs up to plague him, was lucky in drawing Jane Cowl and Peggy Wood as his leading women in "Old Acquaintance." These two fine actresses did more for the Van Druten text, it seemed to me, than the text did for them. Graceful writing, but a little on the artificial side. The Misses Cowl and Wood played "Old Acquaintance" from December till Spring.

Now, around holiday time, theatre bills brightened. A rough and ratty musical comedy, "Pal Joey," dramatized with compelling honesty by John O'Hara from his *New Yorker Magazine* sketches, bounded away to a whirlwind start and did not slacken pace for months. It brought a new musical comedy comedian and dancer, Gene Kelly, to the featured billing that will probably make a star of him before long. The score and lyrics were by Richard Rodgers and Lorenz Hart; Louise Hovick, who has been Gypsy Rose Lee's sister so long she is sick of the classification, came into her own as a comedienne, and Vivienne Segal had fun playing a Chicago Gold Coast lady who bought herself a gigolo.

Following "Pal Joey" the day after Christmas came another *New Yorker Magazine* item, a dramatization of Ruth McKenney's "My Sister Eileen" stories. This one, prepared for the stage by Joseph Fields and Jerome Chodorov, was staged by George Kaufman, with Moss Hart looking on. This, naturally, made every wise Broadwayite insist that the Kaufman-Hart interest was more than casual and probably included several lines and numerous situations. Mr. Kaufman was quick to deny the charge, and to give the Messrs. Fields and Chodorov full credit. The comedy, relating the adventures of Ruth and Eileen Sherwood of Columbus, O., the time they came to New York with $40 and a jointly shared determination to conquer the Big City—Ruth as a writer and Eileen as an actress—was broadly and intelligently comic. The girls settle in Greenwich Village and for three acts fight off a variety of pests, both well-meaning and vicious.

The Playwrights' second production was Elmer Rice's "Flight to the West," an early season anti-Nazi drama that excited sizable groups of citizens. The setting was novel, being that of a Yankee Clipper plane in flight from Lisbon, and the story was tense, telling of the discovery and detaining in Bermuda of a Nazi spy. Digests of both "My Sister Eileen" and "Flight to the West" are included in this volume.

A third representative play included in this book is Joseph Kesselring's "Arsenic and Old Lace," which came in early in the New Year and played to consistently large audiences well into the Summer. It happens also that audience reactions were more definitely divided at this entertainment than at any other. The story, as you will see later, has to do with two smart but mentally unbalanced old ladies who decide that if they devote their lives to helping lonely old men escape from life they will be doing a

good work. Thirteen mercy killings is their final record. Insanity and murder have not previously been employed in the theatre with such riotous results, and each audience contained a protesting minority that laughingly, though none the less positively, resented the authors' liberty. Howard Lindsay and Russel Crouse organized a company of twenty-one friendly backers for "Arsenic and Old Lace," each subscribing a thousand dollars or more, and each, as it turned out, sharing in the royalties of the season's greatest farce comedy hit.

Again, in the case of a second milder and saner murder mystery, Owen Davis' "Mr. and Mrs. North," the *New Yorker Magazine* figured as source material for one of the year's best plays. The sketches from which this comedy was extracted by Mr. Davis were first written for the magazine by Richard and Frances Lockridge, Mr. Lockridge being the drama critic of the New York *Evening Sun.* The North sketches were later included in a novel, "The Norths Meet Murder." Produced in January the North mystery ran through till Spring and during the Summer became one of the most popular of stock company bills, particularly with acting couples returning from Hollywood in search of a chance to renew their ties with the living theatre.

In late January the most sensational of the season's hits was scored by Moss Hart, his first successful solo play, "Lady in the Dark," and Gertrude Lawrence, who gave this exceptional entertainment literally her all. It was agreed by the drama's critics in New York that Miss Lawrence was probably the one actress in all the world who could do as complete justice to this heroine as she does. As a result of the combined popularity of the actress and the play in 162 performances given before vacation time, "Lady in the Dark" never missed once playing to a full house, plus standees. By her contract Miss Lawrence was permitted to rest for five weeks during the Summer, and expected to resume her engagement in September.

The Theatre Guild produced a symbolical drama by Philip Barry with music by Paul Bowles. "Liberty Jones" was the title, and the fight for freedom the theme. As it turned out "Liberty Jones" was pretty well muddled in its symbolism, so far as audiences were concerned, and the Guild withdrew the play after twenty-one performances.

A first comedy by a young Pennsylvanian named Francis Swann, which he called "Out of the Frying Pan," was not a great success, but it did prove a pleasant surprise. With a little nursing it continued for 104 performances, and went from Broadway

into the barn theatres.

February was good for the book, and the season as well. Rose Franken, who had been away since her first play, "Another Language," proved the surprise hit of the 1931-32 season, came East with a new comedy made from her "Claudia" stories. Sensitively and brightly written, ever so wisely cast in its three main parts, with Dorothy McGuire playing Claudia, Donald Cook her husband, David, and Frances Starr her mother, "Claudia" made many friends quickly and held them well into the Summer. Miss McGuire was a newcomer and had a happy season with her first Broadway success.

The Playwrights suffered a second failure, or comparative failure, with S. N. Behrman's "The Talley Method." The dialogue sparkled with Behrman wit and was impressive with Behrman wisdom, the chief rôles were splendidly played by Ina Claire and Philip Merivale, but the play refused to jell emotionally. Thanks to the popularity of the co-stars, however, it lasted seven weeks and was then withdrawn.

Katharine Cornell, unable to find a new play in which she could star with complete satisfaction, decided this late in the season to revive George Bernard Shaw's "The Doctor's Dilemma." This she did, surrounding herself with a superior cast—Raymond Massey, Bramwell Fletcher, Cecil Humphreys, Colin Keith-Johnson, Whitford Kane, Clarence Derwent and Ralph Forbes being in her support, to name only the men folk. The result was a brilliant performance and 112 showings.

Another lull and then a resounding dramatic adventure with Paul Green's and Richard Wright's "Native Son," a dramatization of Mr. Wright's sensational novel of the same title. This was an unpleasantly realistic drama, but of such importance as social criticism, and so smartly staged by Orson Welles, that it left its early audiences fairly stunned. Mr. Welles elected to play the drama's ten scenes without an intermission. Once you were in the theatre, and the lights were dimmed, you were there for the duration. You followed Bigger Thomas, colored chauffeur, through a realistic experience of trying to adjust himself to the white man's laws and prejudices; you saw him fall victim to the conditioning of his environment and his own panicky fear; you followed him through the commission of an accidental murder; took part in his capture; sat through his trial and sentence to death. The experience left you pretty limp. The cast was racially mixed, Bigger being played by Canada Lee, a colored actor of convincing talent who previously has had some success

as a jockey, a prize fighter, a concert violinist and a band leader. The play ran for ninety-seven performances, wilting before the heat of June.

A week after "Native Son" came in, Lillian Hellman's "Watch on the Rhine" was produced. This tremendously forceful drama also set its audiences cheering, and thus the closing weeks of the season became much more interesting than the opening weeks. Miss Hellman's drama, though anti-Nazi in purpose and effect, escaped the charge of being inspired by an unbalanced prejudice and was greatly strengthened by the logic and fair reasoning of its author. Superbly cast and directed by Herman Shumlin it drew large audiences for many weeks.

After "Watch on the Rhine" the season drifted unexcitingly to its close. The unpredictable William Saroyan did create something of a stir by bringing his newest play, "The Beautiful People," to Broadway and backing it with his own money when banks and angels failed him. The play's production started the now familiar Saroyan controversy, one group of enthusiasts insisting that the play, however unconventional in form, was inspiringly fresh and original in content, and written with great compassion and human kindliness. A second group insisted that "The Beautiful People" was no more than a collection of fanciful character sketches strung loosely together with no rhyme and less reason and therefore was not to be considered a play at all in any accepted theatre sense. Six out of nineteen New York critics, however, voted it the best play of the season in their Circle's annual search for a play that was entitled to receive the award, which was given finally to "Watch on the Rhine." Public support was uncertain, but sufficient loyalists appeared to keep the play running for weeks.

At the season's end a group of enthused theatre patrons organized as Experimental Theatre, Inc., which had received the endorsement of Actors' Equity, the League of New York Theatre Managers, the Dramatists' Guild, the Stagehands' and Musicians' unions, produced three plays in the hope of stimulating interest in the acted drama and also in doing pioneer work in giving a Broadway chance to both young and untried dramatists and young and hopeful actors.

There was laughter when the first play chosen was Euripides' "The Trojan Women." This, mused the cynics, was certainly going a long way back to find an untried dramatist. The Experimentalists replied that a part of their plan was to prove to Broadway producers that classic revivals were something still

worth considering. They had added a modern prologue by Robert Turney, who wrote "Daughters of Atreus" a few years back, and this linked the destruction of Troy by the Greeks with that of Rotterdam by the German invaders.

A second Experimental Theatre production revealed "Steps Leading Up," a modern labor play that dealt with racketeering in unions. This confirmed an old conviction that there are good plays written on unpopular subjects from which commercial producers naturally shy away. A third play, done the following week, was called "Not in Our Stars." This was slightly reminiscent of Sean O'Casey's "Juno and the Paycock," but good enough to excite a couple of Broadway producers to talk of a commercial trial the coming Fall. George Harr, a member of the Milliners' Union in New Jersey, wrote "Steps Leading Up." "Not in Our Stars" was the work of George H. Corey, who had previously shown sufficient promise to earn him a Rockefeller Foundation fellowship.

Statistically there was nothing to cheer about in the 1940-41 record. Less than a hundred new plays and musical entertainments were staged in New York where a dozen years ago totals of two hundred and fifty or more new plays in a season were common. In quality the new plays were of a fair average. There were, fortunately, several outstanding individual performances. It does not require many fine plays during any one season to prove the superior quality of available actors and dramatists, and these will always win through in the end.

THE SEASON IN CHICAGO

By Cecil Smith

Dramatic Critic of the *Chicago Tribune*

ALTHOUGH frequent lamentations and outcries rose into the welkin on the theatre managers' favorite subject of bad business, the Chicago season of 1940-41 makes a favorable impression when its statistics are amassed. In sum total, the year between June 1, 1940, and May 31, 1941, consisted of 194½ playing weeks. When this figure is compared with the 1939-40 total of 179½ weeks, a gain of 15 weeks in theatre occupancy is discovered. But since all of this gain and more still must be chalked up to the credit of the Blackstone Theatre, an independent house, it is fairly easy to locate the Shubert office as the principal source of the complaining, for the Shubert playhouses were not quite as busy as in the preceding year.

Cold and lifeless real estate facts should not be allowed, however, to divert attention from the peculiarities of an exceedingly strange and unpredictable season. A few noteworthy attractions brought endless streams of customers to the ticket windows; chief among these were "Life with Father," "There Shall Be No Night," "Du Barry Was a Lady," "My Sister Eileen," and "New Pins and Needles" (which played at a dollar top). On the other hand, many equally worthy plays and musicals either evoked only a faint response or actually died on their feet. Helen Hayes and Maurice Evans, for instance, are entitled to say anything they like about the way in which the Chicago public stayed away from "Twelfth Night." Alexander Woollcott will probably avoid the city in his future travels, for his reception in "The Man Who Came to Dinner" was just plain disheartening. There was no telling, it seemed, which plays the public would accept and which ones it would spurn.

The record-breaking run of "Life with Father" was the brightest single achievement of the season. On February 19, 1940, the Chicago company, with Percy Waram as Father Day and Lillian Gish as Vinnie, reopened the shuttered Blackstone Theater. A good many calamity howlers asserted that no play, not even "Life with Father," could last long in a theatre a mile away from the main loop sector. These prophets of doom were wrong be-

yond all description, for "Life with Father" ran on and on, and then on and on some more. In February the company celebrated the completion of a year's engagement, with the end still nowhere in sight. Finally, with a second Summer in the immediate offing, the play closed on May 24, 1941. The run amounted to 66 weeks—an all-time record for Chicago, surpassing by one week the 65-week engagement of "Lightnin' " sixteen years earlier.

Personal opinions are highly fallible, of course, but to my mind the Chicago company of "Life with Father" was on the whole the best of the three casts gathered together by Oscar Serlin. Percy Waram's impersonation of Mr. Day projects with more vigor than Howard Lindsay's, and it is not distorted by the transparent laugh-getting devices employed by Louis Calhern. Lillian Gish is ideally suited to the part of Vinnie, both in temperament and in appearance, though a good case could be made in favor of the superior acting technique of her sister Dorothy, of the Boston-Philadelphia-Detroit company. In the subsidiary rôles, naturally, the acting was of variable quality throughout the three companies; the Chicago performance was homogeneous and effective, however, and the acting on the closing night was virtually as fresh as at the opening.

The enormous success of the second company of "Life with Father" gave impetus to an already growing tendency to send current New York hits to Chicago with alternate casts, in order to capture business while publicity in national magazines and New York newspapers was still valuable. In addition to "Life with Father," Chicago playgoers saw five other performances by road companies. The miracle is that all of these casts, except for a hopeless group in an equally hopeless farce called "See My Lawyer," were amply good enough to do justice to their material and to ward off all public objection to the notion of a road company.

"My Sister Eileen," which opened at the Harris in February and ran on through the Summer months, matched New York's Shirley Booth, Jo Ann Sayers and Morris Carnovsky with Audrey Christie, Marcy Wescott and Philip Loeb, and for good measure threw in Guy Robertson as the muscular professional football player. The managerial wisdom of such intelligent and painstaking casting made itself felt immediately, for Chicago liked "My Sister Eileen" from the start, and gave it the best business of any comedy except "Life with Father."

When Russel Crouse and Howard Lindsay undertook to form a Chicago company of "Arsenic and Old Lace" they were, un-

fortunately, a little too scrupulous. Business in April and May, when the play got its start, was too uncertain to make a salary list comfortable which included the names of Laura Hope Crews, Effie Shannon, Erich von Stroheim and Helen Twelvetrees. Less expensively but equally appropriately cast, the play might readily have become a satisfactory money-maker. This is not to say that Messrs. Crouse and Lindsay went into the red on the unexpectedly short Chicago engagement, but it is safe to say that their income from Chicago will not radically alter the complexion of their 1942 surtaxes.

The Alexander Woollcott performance of "The Man Who Came to Dinner" unfolded its charms at a rather slow pace, though there was a great deal of excellent and merry acting to be seen. Clifton Webb's 24 weeks in the Kaufman-Hart comedy during the season before seemed to have exhausted public interest in Sheridan Whiteside, anyhow, so that these two weeks became the saddest in the Erlanger Theatre's year.

The provincial version of "Hellzapoppin" was the last of the season's duplicate companies. It is hard to talk about "Hellzapoppin" in language that might apply to any other known form of theatrical entertainment. Suffice it to say that Billy House and Eddie Garr seemed to reach their Chicago audience in satisfactory terms, which means that the whole enterprise was automatically removed from the sphere of austere professional criticism. It was a mistake to book the show into the vast Auditorium Theatre for its first five weeks, but once the error was rectified by a move to the smaller Erlanger, "Hellzapoppin" hit and maintained its stride.

Three attractions, all musical, played in Chicago before venturing to New York. Al Jolson, with his lavishly staged musical comedy, "Hold On to Your Hats," gave the city its first Summer musical in several years. Raoul Pène du Bois' colorful settings and costumes were spick-and-span; Martha Raye achieved a popular success equal to Mr. Jolson's; it was a relief to see Catherine Littlefield directing musical comedy dances instead of unduly pretentious things at the Civic Opera House; all in all, therefore, "Hold On to Your Hats" turned into a big hit, and, if proper terms of comparison are employed, enjoyed considerably more of a triumph in Chicago than in New York. (It should be noted, too, that Mr. Jolson's offstage problems with Ruby Keeler gave the show the best heart interest publicity since the days of John Barrymore in "My Dear Children.")

The other two musicals which moved eastward from Chicago

EDITED BY

BURNS MANTLE

THE BEST PLAYS OF 1909-19
(*With Garrison P. Sherwood*)
THE BEST PLAYS OF 1919-20
THE BEST PLAYS OF 1920-21
THE BEST PLAYS OF 1921-22
THE BEST PLAYS OF 1922-23
THE BEST PLAYS OF 1923-24
THE BEST PLAYS OF 1924-25
THE BEST PLAYS OF 1925-26
THE BEST PLAYS OF 1926-27
THE BEST PLAYS OF 1927-28
THE BEST PLAYS OF 1928-29
THE BEST PLAYS OF 1929-30
THE BEST PLAYS OF 1930-31
THE BEST PLAYS OF 1931-32
THE BEST PLAYS OF 1932-33
THE BEST PLAYS OF 1933-34
THE BEST PLAYS OF 1934-35
THE BEST PLAYS OF 1935-36
THE BEST PLAYS OF 1936-37
THE BEST PLAYS OF 1937-38
THE BEST PLAYS OF 1938-39
THE BEST PLAYS OF 1939-40
THE BEST PLAYS OF 1940-41

THE BEST PLAYS OF 1940-41

Y0-EFZ-206

the Pasadena organization, made much indeed of the rôle, furnishing a commentary, at all times clever, upon the turmoil of the present as evoked by the author through the media of suggestion.

Most of the audiences remained puzzled as to what "Across the Board" was all about, although one suspects that at the close Mr. Saroyan simply casts an eye to the future, has boy meet girl, and decides that life must go on regardless. In other words, his theme is the perpetual necessity of procreation, no matter what the stress of the times. And naturally Mr. Saroyan will have a perfect right to deride this whole explanation.

Of the ten best plays cited by Burns Mantle for the 1940-41 season not a single one was given in Southern California. "George Washington Slept Here" was planned as the second production of the Pasadena Community Playhouse Festival, the Cycle of Modern American Comedy, but that is part of the 1941-42 season. Also "Mr. and Mrs. North" was proposed for the new Selznick summer theatre exploit.

The Mantle selections for 1939-40 were represented by "There Shall Be No Night," with Alfred Lunt and Lynn Fontanne, "Skylark" with Gertrude Lawrence, and "The Time of Your Life," with Eddie Dowling and Julie Haydon. These were leading touring attractions, along with "The Little Foxes," with Tallulah Bankhead, a Mantle choice of earlier vintage, "Ladies in Retirement" and "Pygmalion," starring Ruth Chatterton. Pasadena Community performed Paul Osborn's "Morning's at Seven" from the Mantle 1939-40 list.

Most successful were those plays which brought well-established stars to the Coast like Lunt and Fontanne, Miss Lawrence and Miss Bankhead. "The Time of Your Life," with Dowling and Miss Haydon, fared very well.

The light opera season, which has become a yearly affair, was the most successful yet. Presence of Joe E. Brown helped to liven up "Rio Rita," the opening revival. "The Naughty Marietta" delighted beholders with well-balanced company and splendid ensemble. John Charles Thomas, who has been a regular personality of these productions, caused the S.R.O. sign to be hung up for "The Chocolate Soldier." Then this municipally supported organization brought from the East "Cabin in the Sky" with Ethel Waters starred, to play a two weeks' engagement, another hit being registered. The reception was exceptionally spirited during the entire series, and as usual the light operas thrived partially because of a large subscription list.

In the light opera domain a surprising attempt was made by a group of foreigners to meet movie competition with a top price of 50 cents, the old Mason Theatre, home of road shows for years, being the setting. Their effort was really valorous, despite that financially it did not succeed in the long run. "Rosemarie," "The Merry Widow," and a novelty, "Victoria and Her Huzzar," were presented.

Another "Folies Bergère" had its fling, and was fairly popular, with the Wiere Brothers standouts in comedy. Earl Carroll as usual compensated his patrons of his restaurant theatre with the "world's most beautiful girls," and such stars of comedy as Bert Wheeler and Dr. Rockwell.

Henry Duffy was once more on the scene, joining with Jesse L. Lasky in the production of "Quiet, Please," which had a pretentious première. This play with Hollywood setting lasted but a little while when taken to New York, and did not draw as expected in Los Angeles. It was liked, though, by those who knew the "inside" on Hollywood, because much of it was more typical and genuine than most such plays. But its very actuality, and the weakness of the central plot, caused it to miss fire with the general audience. Jane Wyatt and Fred Niblo were prominent personalities.

Duffy late in the season was responsible for bringing Billie Burke back to the stage in "The Vinegar Tree," in which she scored a Coast ten-strike a decade ago. Again was she regarded with favor. Joe E. Brown was the star of another revival—"The Show-Off."

Miscellaneous goings-on in the theatre included resuscitations of "Desire Under the Elms," "Yes, My Darling Daughter," "Abie's Irish Rose," "Petticoat Fever." In the wake of "Meet the People," came such things as "Thank You, Columbus," "Laugh It Off," "I'd Rather Sing," etc., but none lasted long. The Hollywood Theatre Alliance itself, which produced "Meet the People" also essayed "Zero Hour," controversially dealing with labor and communistic issues, but this was not welcomed. The new "Pins and Needles" arrived on the road but also quickly disappeared. An English thriller of some merit, called "Gaslight" was briefly given. A Gene Lockhart (the stage and film actor) revue, for charitable ends, was given on a series of Sundays. "Not for Children" by Elmer Rice was produced by Eighteen Actors, Inc., at the Pasadena Community Playhouse.

"The Mission Play" came to life for a week at Riverside, where it was originally written by John Steven McGroarty.

"The Pilgrimage Play" had its summer session. And "The Drunkard" still goes merrily on in its ninth year, outdoing, and outdoing again, practically all rivals.

Pasadena Community Playhouse supplied a comprehensive impression of the writings of Sir James M. Barrie during its 1940 Midsummer Drama Festival, including in the repertoire "Quality Street," "The Professor's Love Story," "Dear Brutus," "The Little Minister," "Mary Rose," "A Kiss for Cinderella," "The Admirable Crichton" and "What Every Woman Knows." "The Professor's Love Story" elicited interest as a unique revival.

During the regular season the Playhouse did tricks with the Shakespearean theme in presenting first "The Merchant of Venice" and following it with "The Lady of Belmont," written by St. John Ervine, and dealing with developments in the lives of the principal characters in "The Merchant" in after years. Also première of "A-Lovin' an' A-Feudin'" by Erik Barnouw and Ethel Richardson supplied a take-off on "Romeo and Juliet," with Southern backwoods setting.

"Two on an Island" by Elmer Rice, "Design for Living" by Noel Coward and "Knickerbocker Holiday" by Maxwell Anderson, which had never reached the West Coast on the professional stage, were performed, other features of the season being "Of Mice and Men," "A Slight Case of Murder," "I Killed the Count," "All the Comforts of Home" (by William Gilette), "Margin for Error," "The Front Page," "Topaze," "Whistling for a Wind" by De Witt Bodeen, a rather remarkable study of England under fire; "Manana is Another Day" by Dwight Morris and Theodore Apstein.

If one is speaking of the theatre in Southern California it seems one's eyes must often turn these days to Pasadena, and also more and more to Santa Barbara. Unconcentrated Los Angeles—that is in a geographical way, and maybe others—doesn't seem to have time for aught but the neighborhood cinema and radio for the most part. It needs the flashiest sort of cast to insure any marked appreciation for the work of drama sponsors, or something that registers as the occasional freak hit, like "The Drunkard" or "Meet the People."

The Theatre Guild of Southern California, which was the organization accountable for the "Tonight at 8:30" resplendence, demonstrated the value of names. The luster of these may be gauged by the following list: Basil Rathbone, Gladys Cooper, Roland Young, Philip Merivale, Constance Bennett, Dame May Whitty, C. Aubrey Smith, Judith Anderson, Brian Aherne, Edmund Gwenn, Greer Garson, Douglas Fairbanks, Jr., Henry Stephenson, Binnie Barnes, Reginald Gardiner, Blanche Yurka, Herbert Marshall, Rosalind Russell, Joan Fontaine, Ralph Forbes, Margot Stevenson, Muriel Hutchison, Isabel Jeans, Dorothy Stone, Claire Trevor, Doris Lloyd, John Garrick, Paul Cavanagh, Freddie Bartholomew, Melville Cooper, Una O'Connor, Georges Metaxa, Elsa Maxwell, Montagu Love, John Loder and Cissie Loftus.

Not all of them are known for stage work; some chiefly for screen, but it is the sort of star roster to lure in the West.

The directors by the way included George Cukor, Margaret Webster, Robert Sinclair, Edmund Goulding, Peter Godfrey and Dudley Murphy. Godfrey won special economiums.

"Charlot's Revue" gathered together such people as Fanny Brice, Reginald Gardiner, who alternated with Alan Mowbray as master of ceremonies, Anna Neagle, Mary Parker and Billy Daniels, the dancers; C. Aubrey Smith, and in a number called "Cads" such people as Henry Fonda, Sir Cedric Hardwicke, Chester Morris, Rod La Rocque, George Sanders, the film director Mitchell Leisen, Charles Farrell, Mischa Auer, and one or two others already mentioned. Simone Simon, Rita Hayworth, Jackie Cooper, Bonita Granville and Mary Brian were among the other film figures in the presentation. Robert Edmond Jones designed the "Tonight at 8:30" series.

So let Southern California hopefully look to a theatrical future motion picture-attuned—provided its cinema lights will ever see fit to give the more venerable medium its just due.

NATIVE SON

A Drama in Three Acts

BY PAUL GREEN AND RICHARD WRIGHT

IT was late March before "Native Son" arrived. In fact, it was not until the theatre season was two-thirds spent that any drama of striking force or originality came to production in this particular year. There had been a healthy expectation built up for the dramatization of Richard Wright's novel. The fact that Paul Green, himself a Pulitzer prize winner with a drama that had to do with the colored race, "In Abraham's Bosom," was to work with Mr. Wright on the play heightened interest in it. The further fact that the staging had been placed in the hands of Orson Welles was also promising (of just what no one was prepared to prophesy, Welles being the No. 1 unpredictable genius of the theatre) but promising of good theatre at least. As to that everyone was agreed.

And that is the promise which came true. "Native Son," in the Orson Welles treatment, is as impressive a theatre exhibit as has been produced in years. The emotional impact is terrific in itself, but it has been immeasurably heightened by the staging.

The play is divided into ten scenes, and there is no intermission. Once seated in the theatre there is no escape from it, nor from the effect that Mr. Welles was intently determined to produce from the authors' material. The drama builds steadily through a series of theatrical climaxes, and though it may be argued that theoretically these are the common climaxes of a conventional melodrama concerned with the career of a tough Negro, criminally inclined, they take on a new stature in this particular case.

So, too, does the dramatization, although it has lost something of the novel's force in the opinion of many of the book's readers. "Mr. Wright's long and pulsing novel of a Negro boy's snarling rebellion against a white man's world was vividly subjective in expression. Particularly toward the end it poked into painful psychological details," wrote Brooks Atkinson in *The New York Times*. "In the drama Mr. Green and Mr. Wright work in a more objective style. Without the subjective background their defense of Bigger Thomas's ghastly crime in the court scene sounds like generalized pleading. It lacks the stinging enlightenment of the last third of Mr. Wright's novel. But that completes this column's bill of exceptions to the biggest American drama of the season."

As we come into the theatre with the authors of "Native Son" we are made conscious of a heavy wooden railing separating us from the space usually occupied by the orchestra pit. Within the railing, on a slightly raised floor, are two long tables, right and left, and these are surrounded by chairs.

As our eyes become accustomed to the dim light we see beyond the tables a black velvet curtain. As the lights grow brighter the figure of a man appears at the right side of the courtroom. This is David A. Buckley, State's Attorney, an earnest, fairly heavy-set man of forty. Buckley stands now in a full light. He is evidently in the midst of his closing remarks to the jury.

"In connection with this case we have heard criticism of the American nation and its method of government," he is saying. "That government is not on trial here today. I deplore that in these crucial times, to excuse a brutal and perverted murder, there have been dragged out once again the viperous issues of race and class hatred. I shall not lower the dignity nor the righteousness of the People's cause to answer the silly, alien, and dangerous ideas. I know of no better way to disown such thinking than the imposing of the death penalty on this miserable human fiend, Bigger Thomas."

From the distance the chimes of a great clock can be heard. Buckley is approaching the end of his plea.

"The law of this land is strong and gracious enough to allow all of us to exist in peace and not tremble for fear that, at this very moment, some half-human black ape may be climbing through the windows of our homes to rape and murder our daughters. We are waiting to hear that jungle law does not prevail in this city. We want to know that we need not load our guns and sharpen our knives to protect ourselves."

The angry buzz of an alarm clock can be heard. Darkness has again enveloped the scene. Now the velvet curtain has disappeared, and the brick wall of a sprawling tenement has taken its place. Through an opening piercing the wall the outlines of a one-room, poverty-stricken apartment begin to take shape. The apartment is somewhere on the South Side of Chicago. It is the home of the Thomas family—Hannah, the mother, middle-aged and careworn; Bigger, the older son, a dark, muscular young fellow of some twenty or twenty-one, with deep-set eyes and sensitive, heavy face; Vera, his sister, a slender, brown-skinned girl of sixteen, and Buddy, a dark, sober little fellow of twelve.

It is a bare room. Bigger and Buddy have been sleeping on a pallet that is rolled up and pushed under the bed once they are off of it. Hannah and Vera sleep in a rusty iron bed at the back of the room, near a small dresser with a dull mirror above it. A drop-leaf table, covered with oilcloth and pushed against the wall; a few chairs; a box to be used as a chair; a gas stove; a sink and shelves for groceries are visible. Over the bed there is a large colored lithograph of Christ and two angels. It is the picture of the Resurrection.

Hannah has quickly shut off the alarm clock and hustled Vera and Buddy out of bed. Bigger is the lazy one. Hannah has started to sing a morning song when Bigger wakes—

"Life is like a mountain railroad—
With an engineer that's brave—
We must make the run successful
From the cradle to the grave."

"How the hell can a man sleep with all this racket?" growls Bigger, getting clumsily to his feet.

"Who'd want to sleep when the rest of us have to work so hard?" snaps Vera.

"Yeah, start right in soon's I get my eyes open!" answers Bigger, covering his head with the comforter.

But there is no more sleep for Bigger. Vera is going good, now. Why shouldn't Bigger be getting up? Why shouldn't he be out hunting a job? Why isn't he asking the man he used to drive a truck for to give him another chance? Hannah would defend her son. At least he has his application in at the relief station.

Hannah is busy with the breakfast and still singing. Buddy is dressed and will be washed as soon as he can get into the one bathroom that serves the floor. Vera, too. And Bigger. Bigger is the rebellious one—

"If you was the kind of man Ma always hoped you'd be," sneers Vera, "you'd not have to wait for your turn to go to the bathroom. You'd be up early and get there first. But no—you'd rather hang around Ernie's place with Jack and that low-life gang and let us live on relief."

"Relief didn't say more'n forty people have to use the same

toilet every morning—lining up like women to see Clark Gable. It's the way the white folks built these old buildings."

"Now don't start cussing the white folks again," protests Vera.

"They what keep us alive right this minute," adds Hannah. Bigger has stomped into the hall.

"He gets more like a stranger to us every day," says Vera. "He ain't never got a smile for anybody. And there's that Clara woman he runs with. Here I try to make myself respectable and be somebody, and he—"

"Oh, Lord, I don't know," sighs Hannah. She has gone to the hall door and is calling after Bigger contritely. "Come on back, son." And then to Vera: "Let's try to eat in peace."

"Bigger says we ain't got nothing to smile about, says that's what wrong with the niggers—always smilin', and nothing to smile about," reports Buddy cheerfully.

"Shut yo' mouth, boy!"

It is a worried Hannah who finally gets her family to breakfast. And a nervous Hannah who tries to read to her children from the Bible: "I have trodden the winepress alone; and of people there was none with me—"

A thin, dry, rattling noise in the wall attracts the boys. "If that ol' rat stick his head out this time, I'm gonna scrush it for him," announces Bigger, staring viciously at the wall.

The reading goes on: ". . . for I will tread them in my anger and trample them in my fury; and their blood shall be sprinkled upon my garments, and I will stain—"

The noise in the wall is repeated. "That's him all right!" whispers an excited Buddy. Hannah has finished her reading and started a prayer; "Lord our Father in Heaven, we thank Thee for the food You have prepared for the nourishment of our humble bodies. . . ."

They have begun to eat when suddenly Bigger springs up with a shout, "There he go!" The hunt for the rat is on. Bigger has lunged across the room, thrown himself over the bed and is viciously jabbing in the corner. Now he has an old baseball bat. Buddy has grabbed the bread knife. The frightened women are on their feet and screaming. Bigger is stalking the rat, brought to bay behind a trunk with his hole in the corner stopped up. The women would have Bigger let the rat get back into his hole. Bigger grabs a flatiron and heaves it with a powerful throw. "You hit him, you hit him!" yells Buddy.

A few minutes later the rat is dead and held up by the tail

while Hannah and Vera shudder and cry out, holding tremblingly to each other. . . .

In the excitement "a smallish, young white woman, carrying a black portfolio in her hands," has come to the door. She is Miss Emmet, a social worker, and she has come to report on her efforts to get a job for Bigger. Miss Emmet doesn't like rats, and she doesn't like Buddy's report that he and Bigger call this one, the biggest of them, "Ol' Man Dalton." Miss Emmet reminds them that Mr. Dalton has been very kind to people of their race. She has come now because there are a few additional questions she would like to have Bigger answer as head of the house—

"We ain't got nothin' but this one room, and there ain't no head to it," Bigger tells her, with a little laugh.

"Yes. But as soon as we place you in a job, Bigger, you'll feel differently," Miss Emmet is convinced.

Mr. Dalton, she says, is interested in placing his jobless tenants, and it happens there is an opening just now with Mr. Dalton himself—the job of chauffeur. By the record Bigger is a first-rate driver. But there is the matter of a reform school record. Bigger had failed to mention that.

" 'Three months term, ending June 15, 1939,' " Miss Emmet repeats as she writes. " 'Metropolitan Home for the Detention of Juvenile Delinquents—theft—taking of three automobile tires from a colored garage—' Is that right?"

"Yessum, that must be about right," answers Bigger, with a faint touch of mockery.

"And you haven't had any other trouble since, Bigger?"

"No'm. . . ."

Miss Emmet has completed her report and gone her way.

Everybody's happy now. Hannah is thanking the Lord for His goodness. Buddy is giving an imitation of what Bigger is going to do to that old twelve-cylinders of Mr. Dalton's. Even Bigger is smiling.

"Maybe this is the real break," says Vera, stopping to give her brother's arm an affectionate squeeze on her way to the door. "We are all so glad, Bigger. And we can quit living in one room like pigs."

Vera has gone to her job. Buddy has started out to sell his papers. Everybody in the Thomas family is going to hustle from now on, according to Hannah. And Bigger is going to be the real head of the house, looking out for the protection of Vera and Buddy after their mother gets too old to work.

Hannah has fished out a sock from under the mattress and taken fifty cents from it. Bigger is to fetch her soap and bluing, starch and other things she will be needing for her day's washing. Slowly the optimism of Hannah's faith seeps into the brain of Bigger. After she has gone, he stands for a long moment before the picture of Christ on the wall.

" 'I am the Resurrection and the Life'— Uhm—"

He is getting into his leather jacket. Suddenly he stops to toss the half dollar Hannah has given him. "Heads I do, tails I don't!" he mutters, and sneers with disgust when "Heads" it is.

From the tenement well below there comes a shrill whistle. Bigger recognizes the signal and leans out the window to answer. "Okay, be right with you, Jack." He has pulled out a packing box from under the bed, unlocked it and taken out a revolver, holding it toward the picture. "Here's what you didn't have—but I got it!" he mutters to the picture on the wall as he stuffs the gun in his blouse.

Bigger is kicking the packing box under the bed when Hannah comes back into the room. She had forgotten her washboard. "What you up to, boy?" she wants to know.

There is no answer. Bigger picks up his cap and rushes out the door. "Bigger! Bigger!" calls Hannah. But Bigger is down the hall and away. The lights fade.

SCENE II

In the darkness the noises of a city's streets are heard. Church chimes that have been ringing die away. The roar of traffic, the occasional rattle of a heavy truck; the clanging of a streetcar bell; the occasional punctuation of a siren call, as either a squad car or an ambulance dashes through.

Now the lights are up and we face the door of Ernie's Kitchen Snack, somewhere on Indiana Avenue, near 47th Street. . . . "The gullet of a narrow alleyway leads back into the shadows." It is mid-afternoon.

Sporty Jack Henson, one of Bigger's buddies, is leaning against the wall as Bigger saunters in. His cap is pulled down and his coat collar turned up. Bigger and Jack are there to meet "G.H." Everything is set for an enterprise they have planned. Bigger has had a squint of old Blum sitting bent over his cash register with his back to the door, working on his books. They should get at least a hundred and fifty bucks from the job. But there's to be no gun, Jack warns. "Somebody get killed—then the hot seat! Jesus! No!"

Clara Mears, "an attractive, kindly young Negro girl," has come looking for Bigger. She missed him last night. She would see him tonight. They might go to a picture. They might, but Bigger isn't greatly interested. "Love 'em and leave 'em." That's Bigger. . . .

Gus Mitchell has arrived. "He is a small-sized Negro about Bigger's age and wears his cap turned round like a baseball catcher." Gus is in a playful mood. He and Jack have a game of telephoning—cupping their hands to mouth and ear and pretending to carry on an important conversation as between the President of the United States of America and his Secretary of State.

The President is calling a meeting of the Cabinet; he is thinking of sending another note to that old Hitler—at which point Bigger cuts in—

"Hello, Mr. President," calls Bigger, pantomiming in imitation of the others. "I just cut in from the sidelines and heard what you said. Better wait about that war business. The niggers is raising sand all over the country. You better put them down first."

"Oh, if it's about the niggers, Mr. Hoover, we'll wait on the war." This from Jack.

"Yes, sah," continues Bigger. "At a time like this, we Republicans and Democrats got to pull together!"

"Reckon we can do without you, Mr. Hoover," concludes Gus. This throws them all into gales of laughter.

Ernie, owner of the shack, has returned. He threatens to throw the three loafers out of the alley. Bigger's belligerency returns. He is eager to go on now. Eager to pop off a few white folks, including ol' man Blum.

The sight of a sign writer piloting an airplane across the sky lifts his mood and fires his imagination—

"Speed! That's what them white boys got! Go on, boys, fly them planes, fly 'em to the end of the world, fly 'em smack into the sun! I'm with you! Goddam!" He is staring into the sky, the sunlight on his face.

"Yessir!" echoes Gus, tauntingly doffing his cap in a mock bow to Bigger. "Yessir! If you wasn't *black* and if you had some money and if they'd let you go to that *aviation* school, you might could be with 'em."

They have gone into their pantomime game again. They're

flying now, with Jack at the controls, Bigger giving the orders. "G.H.," a darkish, heavy-set young Negro, has joined them with a mocking "Heil Hitler" salute, but they go on with their game, giving that crowd on Michigan Boulevard a dose of hot lead! Look at them white folks fall! Now they've bombed the ol' Tribune Tower—

"A direct hit, Sergeant!" Bigger is complimentary. "Look at the fires—things flying through the air—houses—people—streetcars—hunks of sidewalk and pavements. Goddam! Whoom—tracer bullets. Look out! There comes the fighter planes! (*In his excitement* BIGGER *draws the pistol from his belt and starts waving at the imaginary enemy. In doing so he turns with it on* G.H.) Cold steel! Watch the turn— Put it through the navel."

At the sight of Bigger's pistol the three boys spring back in fear. The spirit of play leaves them. But Bigger goes on, his excitement mounting with the fury of his imaginary attack—

"Bigger, for Christ's sake! Somebody'll see you!" protests G.H.

"I told you he's crazy! Now just look at him!" shrieks Gus.

"You son-of-a-bitch, don't you call me crazy—"

Bigger has put up his gun, drawn his knife and grabbed Gus by the collar. "Put your hands up! Way up!" he orders. "Shut them liver lips! Take it back! Say 'I'm a lying son-of-a-bitch!'" Bigger is pressing the knife against Gus' belly. "I'm —I'm a lying son-of-a-bitch!" blubbers Gus.

"Next time you whimper on me I'm gonna kill you," announces Bigger. "Now scat! You ain't gonna be in on this. I'll take your share of the haul!" One more lunge at Gus, and Gus is flying out of the alley.

Now Bigger is at the peak of his passion and eager to go. The roar of the street comes through. A tower clock booms the hour of three. That's zero hour for Biger, but Jack and G.H. have lost their interest in adventure. This isn't the way they planned it.

"So you all turn against me—huh?" Bigger is laughing hysterically. "I knowed you bastards was scared! I'll do it by myself—just watch. And when I do, don't nobody even speak to me, don't ask me for time to die, you hear?"

Ernie has come to the door of the shack. He would order Bigger away a second time. With a quick swish of his arms Bigger has grabbed Ernie and sliced off a piece of his vest—

"This is a sample of the cloth!" he yells, in triumph. "Wanta see a sample of the meat?"

"I'll get my gun! I'll shoot you!" yells Ernie.

Before he can carry out his threat Buddy Thomas has come running into the alley. He brings a message from the lady who was at the house that morning. Bigger slashes open the envelope—

"You all keep quiet while I read my mail," he advises Ernie. A moment later he is staring at them with shining, wondering eyes. "Good God and Gin! Old man Dalton wants to see me at my convenience—immediately if not sooner." He is shouting now. "Damn all of you now—you can all go to hell! I'm gonna be driving for a millionaire, and don't you speak to me, no more, none of you. Hear me? I spit in your slimy faces—a bunch of yellow cowards."

JACK—Is it a job for real, Bigger?

BIGGER—And when I go riding by, tip your hats—you'd better—yeah, you had— (*He turns on* ERNIE.) Yeh, get your gun, Ernie. I ain't afraid of it—I'm finished with all you cheesy little punks—I'm on my way now— Here, take this fifty cents and buy you some hash.

ERNIE—On his way now—

JACK—Yeh! On his way! Take more'n a job to cure what ails him!

G.H.—Come on, let's get something to drink, Jack.

JACK—And a nickel for some canned music.

G.H.—Old boogie-woogie take the pressure off.

ERNIE'S VOICE (G.H. *has stepped inside the diner and disappeared. We hear him put the coin in the juke box, as* JACK *follows him inside.*)—What'll you have?

"The record goes on. The piano beats out a boogie-woogie rhythm. The boys clap their hands and get in the groove. They start to Lindy hop from the one end of the diner visible to the audience and slowly disappear off stage. As they dance past the door they push it shut slowly and the lights fade out."

SCENE III

Gradually the boogie-woogie dies away. The lights are up revealing a sun-filled, spotless Dalton breakfast room. Through a triple window a view of the Dalton grounds may be glimpsed. The table in the center of the room is decorated with a vase of hothouse poinsettia, and a large cage in which there are many birds stands in front of the window. Mr. Dalton "is about fifty-five or sixty and wears a pair of pince-nez be-ribboned glasses on the bridge of his nose. Mrs. Dalton is middle-aged, thin, almost ascetic, and dressed in flowing white, with a knitted shawl draped loosely about her shoulders. . . . Her eyes are staring and blinkless." She is holding a white cat in the crook of her arm.

Peggy, the Irish cook and maid, is standing by the table. Britten, Mr. Dalton's private detective, is seated at one side of the room, reading. Bigger, in his old black leather jacket, is standing before Mr. Dalton and Miss Emmet with his cap in his hand. Dalton, holding an application form in one hand and a cup of coffee in the other, is reading in a hurried, slurring tone—

" 'Twenty years of age—grammar school education—poor student but learns quickly when he applies himself. Counted as head of the house—color complex—father killed in a race riot in Jackson, Mississippi, August 15, 1930.' (*He looks up approvingly at* MISS EMMET.) Quite a lot of background factors, Miss Emmet—right, Ellen?"

"Yes," answers Mrs. Dalton, quietly.

" 'Knows how to obey orders but is of unstable equilibrium as to disposition.' (*He looks at* BIGGER.) Never mind all these words, Bigger—part of the new social philosophy."

"What kind of a car did you drive last, boy?" demands Detective Britten.

"A truck, sir."

"Got your license?"

"Yessuh."

"Show it to Mr. Dalton."

"I can drive most any kind. I can handle a Duesenberg right off."

"Well, I have a Buick."

"Yessuh."

"Now, Bigger, about this reform school business, just forget it. I was a boy myself once, and God knows I got into plenty of jams."

"But, he's colored, Henry," interposes Mrs. Dalton, softly.

"I know, I know, Ellen."

So far as his investigation is concerned, Mr. Dalton is satisfied. He must go now. A rent strike is threatening over on Prairie Avenue. Mrs. Dalton will make the final decision as to Bigger. Peggy will show him around.

There is a buzz from the back wall. It is Mary Dalton's call for her breakfast in bed, but Mr. Dalton will have no more of that. It doesn't matter if Mary had been out late the night before—at the university. She can get up just the same.

The Daltons and Miss Emmet have gone. Britten has stopped to ask Bigger where he got his leather jacket. "From the relief," Bigger tells him.

Peggy, the maid, would be friendly to the still embarrassed Bigger. Offers him a roll and butter. Tells him a little about the house. The draft he hears, starting suddenly, is from the automatic furnace. One of his jobs will be to look after the furnace. Another will be looking after Miss Mary—

"Before I forget it," says Peggy, "Miss Mary's going to Detroit tomorrow. You'll have to come early in the morning and drive her to the La Salle Street Station."

"Yessum."

"Now Mrs. Dalton, you'll like her. She's wonderful."

"She—she can't see, can she?"

"She's blind," says Peggy, pouring herself a cup of coffee. "Went blind years ago when her second child was born. It died, and she's been blind ever since. Never talks much, but she loves people and tries to help them. Loves that cat and her piano and her flowers."

Mrs. Dalton has come back into the room, deftly feeling her way along. She is still carrying the white cat. "Bigger, we've decided to engage you," she says quietly. "This is your new start."

"Yessum."

"Now you are one of us—a member of the family— We'll do all in our power to help you find your way in this new life."

"Yessum. Thank you, ma'am."

Mrs. Dalton is standing, with her face tilted up to the sunlight. Her mood is reminiscent. "Bigger, I used to teach school," she is saying, "and I once had a colored boy in one of my classes who was so distrustful that he carried a knife and a gun."

"Huh!" The startled Bigger drops a glass of water he has been holding. The glass is shattered. "Oh—I'm sorry, ma'am. I broke one of your glasses."

"That's all right—accidents will happen," says Mrs. Dalton, quietly. "That is all, Bigger. You have the job. Your pay will be twenty dollars a week, which will go to your mother. There will be five dollars more for yourself. You will have every second Sunday off. (*There is no answer from* Bigger.) Is that clear?"

"Yessum."

"And if you're ever bothered about anything, come to me and we'll talk it over. We have a lot of books here in the library. You can read any you like."

"No'm. Yessum."

"You don't have to read them."

Bigger is alone. His curiosity is piqued. He picks up a silver knife and weighs it in his hand with a grunt of satisfaction. He slyly opens the top drawers of the sideboard and peers into them, closing them quickly when he hears someone approaching.

Mary Dalton comes into the room. She is wearing a flowing red robe, opened at the bosom. "It blows and trails behind her. Her hair is bunchy and tousled, and she is puffing a cigarette. Mary is a slender, pale-faced girl of some twenty-two or -three, with wide restless dark eyes. Her lips are rouged heavily, and her fingernails done to a deep vermilion. Her whole appearance denotes a sense of boredom and weary child-like disillusionment."

Mary notices and is amused when he seems a little awed by her approach. She has poured herself a cup of coffee, taken a couple of aspirin tablets from a little tin box in her pocket and gulped them down with her first swallow. Now she is ready to question Bigger. Is he the new chauffeur? Yes. Does he belong to a union? No.

"Better join a union or Father'll exploit your shirt off," warns Mary. "My name's Mary Dalton, and I've got the most God-awful hangover in the world. Did you ever get drunk, Bigger?"

"No'm." Bigger isn't too certain about this answer.

Mary—Has Mother hired you?

Bigger—Yessum.

Mary—Well, don't take the job. I mean it. You'd better keep away from us—from Mother. She'll try to give you a serious, ambitious soul—make you want to be something in the world. And you've got no chance to be anything. None of you colored people have—where do you live?

Bigger—Over on Indiana Avenue.

Mary (*facing him*)—You know, I'd like to meet some colored people, sometime. You know, Bigger, sometimes I drive down South Parkway, and I look at all those brick buildings crowded with black people, and I wonder what's going on inside of them. Just think I live ten blocks from you, and I know nothing about you. I've been all over the world, and I don't know how people live ten blocks from me.

BIGGER—Yessum.

MARY—Yessum—yessum—don't you work in this house. Do you hear me? They made a law-abiding punk out of Green. I'll have you meet Jan Erlone and some of our friends. We're going down tonight to hear Paul Max at the rally. Then we're having a celebration down at Nicky's Danceland. D'you know where it is?

BIGGER—Yessum.

MARY—You'll drive me down there—

BIGGER—Got to—got to stick to my job.

MARY—That's your job—to take me where I want to go. Have you got a girl, Bigger? (*She takes out a cigarette and looks around for a match.*) Match! (BIGGER *does not move.*) Match!!! (BIGGER *nervously looks through his pockets and finally finds a match.*) Light it! (*He lights the cigarette.*) Bigger, how do you colored people feel about the way you have to live? (BIGGER *is standing with the match still in his hands. She looks at it and motions to the small table above the settee.*) Put it there. (*He drops it in the ash tray.*) Do you ever get real mad? Why don't you talk? Oh, maybe I'm not saying the right things, but what are the right things to say? I don't know. Bigger—say something . . . How is it that two human beings can stand a foot from each other and not speak the same language? Bigger, what are you thinking about? What are you feeling? D'you think I'm crazy?

BIGGER (*backing away*)—No . . . No, ma'am! (*She holds out her cup.*)

MARY—And you won't be like Green, will you, with your hat in your hand? Get me another cup! Who knows, you might be a leader among your own people. And I'd have a part in it, yes, sir.

BIGGER (*pouring the coffee*)—Miss . . . ?

MARY—Mm . . . Black. Mother's little spoiled darling'd have a part in it. . . . Tonight, Bigger, you're going to meet people who can tell you things . . .

BIGGER—Yessum.

MARY—And I appoint you a committee of one to look after me—get me home. If I should happen to drink too much—Hell, I always drink too much.

BIGGER—Got to stick to my job.

MARY—Your job is to do what I tell you!

Peggy has come and gone, taking Bigger with her. She will show him about the furnace and the flowers. Upstairs someone is playing a sentimental piece on the piano. Mary shudders, lights a cigarette and stands gazing before her. "Yassum . . . Yassum!" she mutters as the lights fade.

SCENE IV

The piano has stopped playing. In the dim light the outlines of Mary Dalton's bedroom may be seen, "the bed draped in ghostly white and raised like a dais or bier . . . The walls of the bedroom are cold and dead, and the whole scene is bathed in the snowy city's pallid light which glimmers through the window."

Outside the door of the room, which stands open, Bigger's voice is heard pleading: "Please, Miss Dalton. Please stand up and walk. Is this your room?" And then Mary's answer: "A great celebration, Bigger. God, I'm drunk!"

Mary walks into the room. "Her hat awry, her hair hanging down, her eyes set in a frozen stare and her face masklike and dead."

"And you're drunk, too, Bigger. It's a victory, Bigger. Hooray for the rent strike."

"For Christ's sake!" Bigger's voice comes from the hall, a sort of moan of protest. "This ain't my job, Miss Dalton."

"It is your job to see me home—safe home," answers Mary, pulling Bigger into the room after her. His head is lowered, his face somewhat averted. Mary's red handbag hangs from his left arm, his chauffeur uniform hat is in his hand. "The people are strong, Bigger," Mary is muttering; "you and me—thousands like us— Poor Father— Gimme a drink. Why don't you give me a drink?"

"No'm."

"Yessum—yessum—" Mary's tones are mocking, her head is rocking from side to side. "My father—a landlord that walks like a man— And we had a big celebration, didn't we?"

"Lemme go, Miss Dalton." Bigger's head snaps back, as though he had heard someone. "I got to go—ain't my job—got to get out of here."

She is stuffing his pockets with pamphlets and chiding him

for pulling away from her. "What are you scared of? You don't frighten me, Bigger. I frighten you—now. See, it's all turned around. Crazy world, isn't it?"

"This your room, Miss Dalton? They kill me—kill me—they find me in here—"

"Know what I am?" Mary's tone is insistent. "I'm what the Russians call 'the penitent rich'—I feed the poor—" She tosses a handful of pamphlets in the air. "And I'm drunk—and I'm dead—drunk and dead—inside I am—" She has put out her hand and touched his hair. "Your hair is hard—like little black wires—I know— It has to be hard—tough—to stand it—"

"No— No!"

She has reached up and touched his cheek. Then her own cheek. She looks vacantly at her hand. "See—not shoe polish —it doesn't come off! There's a difference and there's not a difference—Bigger—what are you thinking—what are you feeling?"

"Lemme go!"

"Yes, that's what I want—to break through and find you—"

"Ain't my job—ain't my job," Bigger is repeating with pathetic insistence.

Mary has drawn him over to the window seat and pulled him down beside her. Mary wants to talk and she has nobody to talk to. "Mother and Father—they talk up to God in the sky —I talk down—way, way down to you at the bottom. Oh, I wish I was black— Honest, I do— Black like you—down there with you—to start all over again—a new life—you don't mind—"

Mary has tried to put her head on Bigger's shoulder, but, passing out, rolls off to the floor at his feet. Bigger kneels down to hold her up. When he tries to rise she pulls him down again. When he would get away she tries to strike him and rolls again to the floor. In maudlin tones she is singing "Swing low, sweet chariot, coming for to carry me home—"

Bigger is pleading again that she be quiet. She strikes at him and again passes out. He falls back against the window, still pleading with her to get up. Now he has knelt and lifted her to the edge of the bed. At that moment the voice of Mrs. Dalton comes from the hallway:

"Mary! Is that you, Mary?"

Mrs. Dalton comes slowly into the room. Bigger backs slowly away from the bed, standing motionless as Mrs. Dalton feels her way. "Mary. Where are you? Are you asleep?" She has noticed the odor of alcohol. "You've been drinking! You reek of liquor! My poor child! Why do I fail you?" She pauses. There is no sound. "Sleep—sleep then."

As she reaches the door Bigger sinks faintly to the edge of the bed. He is breathing audibly and Mrs. Dalton turns at the door. "What is it?" Mary twists and murmurs. Bigger quickly reaches for a pillow and covers her face with it. She kicks and strikes at him. He pushes the pillow down—harder and harder. "What is it, Mary?" Mrs. Dalton takes a step back into the room. There is no sound. "Good night, Mary! I'll call you early for your train."

Mrs. Dalton has gone into the hall. For a moment Bigger remains motionless, then he starts for the door. As he turns he stumbles. He stands for a moment. Mary does not move. Bigger kneels down and touches her hand, her head. He shakes her arm. His panic mounts—

"Naw—naw—naw—naw—naw—"

He has run to the door and back again to Mary. Now he kneels and lifts her head and shoulders from the bed and shakes her again—

"I didn't do it—I didn't, I tell you— Wake up, wake up! Miss Dalton, Miss Mary— Naw—naw, naw—I didn't do it—I didn't go to do it! Naw—ain't nothin' happened! Ain't nothin' happened!"

From below the sound of the furnace rises. Bigger hears it. Briefly he hesitates, then he kneels down, picks Mary up and starts for the door.

"Ain't nothin' happened!" he repeats hoarsely. The furnace sounds increase. Bigger whirls and starts through the door as the lights fade. The roar of the furnace increases.

SCENE V

The sound of the furnace draft gradually dies away, and is picked up by the ringing of the telephone. Behind transparent French doors, separating his study from the breakfast room, Mr. Dalton can be seen at the phone, with Mrs. Dalton standing by apprehensively. Bigger, coming into the study, overhears the telephoning and stops to listen.

The message is final. Mary did not go to Detroit, as she had planned. She had evidently been out with that Erlone fellow, who had called up from the station.

Detective Britten brings no news, except that strike conditions are getting worse. He had found nothing at the station; can't understand Peggy's car being left out front in the snowstorm that has raged all night and with the door open. The chauffeur has said that he brought Miss Dalton home about 2:30— Do the Daltons trust the chauffeur? They do. So does Peggy. Bigger is just like all colored boys, but he keeps his place—

Peggy has swung the doors between the study and the breakfast room open. Bigger starts to leave, but knows that he has been seen. A moment later Britten has called him into the room, and started the questioning—

At what time did Bigger take Miss Dalton from the house? About 8:30. And he drove her to the University? Bigger hesitates. After all he's just working there. Britten persists. No, Bigger admits, he had not driven Miss Dalton to school. When they got as far as the Park she told him to turn around and take her to the Loop. Why hadn't he told this before? Because she told him not to.

Where had he taken her in the Loop? To 16 Lake Street. How long had she stayed there? About half an hour. When she came out Jan Erlone, the Communist, was with her. After that Jan drove the car, at Miss Dalton's suggestion. They went to Ernie's Kitchen Shack. And how long did they stay there?

"Well, we must have stayed—"

"We? Didn't you wait outside in the car?"

"Naw, suh. You see, Mister, I did what they told me. I was only working for 'em."

"And then what did you do?"

"They made me eat with 'em." Mr. and Mrs. Dalton exchange glances. "I didn't want to, Mister," Bigger hurries to explain. "They kept worrying me until I went in and had a drink with 'em."

"A drink, eh? So they were drinking—"

"Farewell party and Christmas and all—"

"And then you brought them home here?"

"Yessuh."

"How intoxicated was Miss Dalton, Bigger."

"She—she couldn't hardly stand up—up—Ma'am."

Did Erlone help Miss Dalton to her room? Yes. Did Erlone tell him to leave the car outside? Yes. Bigger was to go along home, get his things and come back this morning. Was Erlone drunk? Bigger guesses he was.

Britten has found the Communist handbills in Bigger's coat in the basement. How did they come there? Miss Dalton had given them to him, Bigger explains, nervously. But he didn't read them. And he ain't no Communist. No, sir, he'd never known Erlone before he came to work for Mr. Dalton—

"Naw, suh, naw, suh—you got me wrong, sir," protests Bigger. "I ain't never fooled around with them folks. The ones at the meeting last night was the first ones I ever met, so help me God."

"Come on, give me the facts!" Britten has turned furiously and grabbed Bigger by the coat lapels, shaking him. "Tell me about Miss Dalton and that Erlone. What did he do to her?"

"Naw, suh, I ain't—I don't know— Naw, suh."

"That's enough, Britten," interposes Mr. Dalton.

Britten releases Bigger and steps away. He was just playing a little. But he soon returns to the attack. Erlone had told him (Bigger) to leave the car in the drive and then had helped Miss Dalton into the house?

"Yassuh. He helped her up the steps, suh, and—uh, she was just about passed out."

"And Erlone went with her into the house?"

"Yes, suh—"

There is a movement at the study door. Jan Erlone walks in. He is nervous and agitated. He wants to know what Bigger has been telling. And why. He also wants to know where Mary Dalton is. She was to go to Detroit to see her grandmother. If she didn't go, where is she?

At Britten's first question Erlone denies that he was with Mary the night before. Then he admits it. Admits that he was with Mary and Bigger Thomas at Ernie's Kitchen Shack. Denies that they were drunk, but admits they had been drinking.

"Mr. Erlone, we know my daughter was drunk last night when you brought her here," says Mr. Dalton. "She was too drunk to leave here by herself. We know that. Now, do you know where she is?"

"I—I didn't come here last night," stammers Erlone.

"But you were with her and she was drunk. Do you mean you left her in that condition?"

"Well, I came as far as the door with her," admits Jan, hesitantly. "I had to go to a meeting. I took the trolley. Had to hurry. Bigger, what are you telling these people?"

Bigger makes no reply. Peggy helps Mrs. Dalton toward her room. Britten has returned to questioning Jan Erlone, accusing him flatly of lying—

"You got Miss Dalton drunk, Erlone—you brought her here

early this morning. You told the boy to leave the car in the driveway. You went inside—"

"I didn't."

"—and went upstairs with her, and now she's disappeared. Where is she?"

"Listen, I told you all I know."

"Erlone, you and I don't agree on certain things," interposes Mr. Dalton. "Let's forget that. I want to know where my daughter is."

"I tell you I don't know, Mr. Dalton."

Mr. Dalton has gone. Britten's attack on Erlone becomes threatening. If he won't talk now, a way will be found to make him talk later. It is Britten's final word.

With Britten gone Jan turns threateningly. Bigger backs away. "Go on away from here, Mr. Jan. Go on away!" he mutters, warningly. From the street can be heard the singing of a Christmas carol.

"What's all this about, Bigger? Why did you tell those lies?"

BIGGER—You heard me.

JAN—I haven't done anything to you, have I? Where's Mary?

BIGGER—I don't want to talk to you.

JAN—But what have I done to you?

BIGGER (*mumbling*)—I don't want to talk to you. Get out!

JAN—Listen, Bigger. (*Steps toward* BIGGER *who backs up against the wall.*) If these people are bothering you, just tell me. Don't be scared. I'm used to this sort of persecution. I'll help you in your rights. I know their crooked law. Listen now. Tell me about it. Come on, we'll go out and get a cup of coffee and talk it over. (BIGGER *pulls out his gun, aims it at* JAN.) For God's sake, man, what are you doing?

BIGGER—Get out!

JAN—I haven't bothered you. Don't—

BIGGER—Leave me alone.

JAN—For Christ's sake, man!

BIGGER (*screaming*)—Get away from here! Now! Now!

Jan pauses without looking at the gun. He goes out the study door. Bigger follows him with the gun. The furnace below switches on and Bigger looks up. He puts the gun away. The music of the carol singers comes in as the lights fade.

SCENE VI

As the music of the carol singers melts away the sounds of a Negro spiritual service are faintly heard. The lights reveal Clara Mears' one-room kitchenette apartment. A sink and a table, a bed and a dresser, all more or less dilapidated. Bigger Thomas is sitting on the edge of the bed, partly dressed. Clara is before the dresser, fixing her hair. Neither is very happy.

Bigger is muttering to himself. Clara is trying to get him to tell her the cause of his moodiness. She can't understand him. For two days he stays away from her and when he does come there is no happiness in their love. It is as though Bigger was all the time thinking of other things.

When Bigger answers her it is with cursing and complaint. She knows he only comes because he can't help himself. Now he wishes he could. Doesn't he love her any more? Sometimes he does—but now it is as though she was always holding him down—

"I don't. I don't," wails the unhappy Clara.

"And it's your little soft baby-talk again—and then we get some liquor—and end up by kissing and going to bed." He has got up and walked to the window. "You all around me—can't see—can't think—Goddam, I hate it! I hate it!"

He has kicked a small whiskey bottle viciously against the wall and shattered it. "Wish it was different! Now I do!" he mutters. He has gone back to his dressing, viciously yanking his shirt off the back of a chair.

CLARA—Now! How come you keep saying "now" all the time? How come you laughing like that?

BIGGER—Yeh, I'm laughing—laughing at everybody—everybody in the whole damn world—laughing at you.

CLARA—Please, Bigger, Bigger—you talk wild—drunk like.

BIGGER—That little old bottle of whiskey? Hunh, didn't even feel it.

CLARA (*rising and standing by his side*)—Why don't you try to sleep some? I'll fix you supper. You tired. Your po' face all tight, and yo' eyes full of blood.

BIGGER (*starting to put his coat on*)—You love me, Clara?

CLARA—You know that. And it ain't things you give me and that money don't matter. It don't matter at all. (*She helps him on with his coat.*) Something hard in your coat, Bigger. You got a gun. (*He backs away.*) Is that why you got all that money? Rob somebody?

BIGGER—Maybe they give me something in advance on my job.

CLARA—Who? Old white gal I see you eating with, down at Ernie's last night?

BIGGER—Maybe.

CLARA—She's crazy. Her face says she's crazy.

BIGGER—Aw, don't worry 'bout her.

CLARA—Leave her alone, Honey. She'll get you in trouble.

Clara is interested in Bigger's new job with the Daltons—over there on Drexel Boulevard, where the rich folks live. That's where a girl was kidnaped a year ago and the kidnapers tried to get money from her folks. Kidnaping! That's an idea! It strikes Bigger all of a sudden—

"Tried to get money! Yeh, yeh, I remember!" He is up on his feet now, his eyes shining. "Money, Goddamit! Everybody talking about it—papers with headlines, telephones ringing. Yeh, let 'em ring—ringing all over America, asking, asking about Bigger. The bells ringing! They'll sound the sirens and the ambulances beat their gongs."

Bigger's excitement mounts as the idea expands. Clara senses that there is something wrong and presses him for an answer. All right, he'll tell her. He's gotta tell someone. If she'll stay with him, they'll work together, they'll get money, with money they'll be safe.

"Listen—this gal where I work—this Dalton gal—she crazy!" He has pulled Clara over to him and is talking excitedly. "Crazier'n hell, see. Father's a rich man—millionaire—millionaire—and she's done run off—always hanging around with them reds—maybe done run off with one of 'em."

"I told you."

"Nobody don't know where she's gone—so, they sit worrying. All day they been worrying. (*He starts pacing up and down.*) And that blind woman—holding them white flower hands together and crying out . . . 'Where's my daughter?' And that detective tromping about, mashing things down. 'Where is she?' they saying. They don't know. I know."

"Bigger, what you talking about? What you done?"

"I tell you. They think she's kidnaped. Yeh, them reds got her. I heard 'em say so. Gonna ask for money, see? Plenty."

"Maybe she'll show up, Bigger. She'll come back."

"Hey, money. They got plenty of dough. They won't miss it. And we get some of it. Why not? And then you and me—we's free. Goddamit, free! You hear me? Free like them. One of them old empty buildings over there— Yeh, 36 Place and Michigan—door open all the time. I'll write 'em a letter and we'll wait for 'em there."

"But you can't do that, Bigger. They'll catch you. They'll never stop looking. The white folks never stop looking—"

"Yeh, but looking for the wrong folks."

Clara is apprehensive. She is afraid the Dalton girl may show up. No chance of that. Bigger knows. But when Clara demands to know if he has done anything to the missing girl his anger flares and his manner is threatening. "Say that again and I'll slap you through the floor," he warns.

From across the street comes the sound of the song service. Bigger has rushed to the dresser and rummaged about for pencil and paper. When he finds them he drops to the floor and tremblingly begins the composition of the letter. Clara is leaning her head against the head of the bed and weeping—

"All you ever caused me was trouble," she wails; "just plain black trouble—I been a fool—just a blind, dumb, black, drunk fool; and I go on being a fool 'cause I love you—love you clean down to hell—ain't never had nobody but you—nobody in my arms but you, close against me, but you—"

"Shut up, now. I got to write. No. I'll print it—with my left hand. Yeh! I'll sign the note 'Red.' "

He continues to mumble his satisfaction as he prints the letter. Soon he'll have turned the whole world upside down. There'll be headlines in the papers, police running around like chickens with their heads cut off. And he and Clara watching and waiting to pick up the dough—and freedom with it—

"Twenty years, up and down the dark alleys, like a rat. Nobody hear us—" Clara has slid down to the floor beside him, pressing her head protectively against his shoulder. "Nobody hear you, nobody pay any attention to you, and the white folks walking high and mighty, don't even know we're alive—"

Clara's arms are around him, her face against the back of his neck.

"Now they cut the pigeon wing the way we say—like bars falling away—like doors swinging open and walls falling down—and all the big cars and all the big buildings and the finery and the marching up and down, and the big churches and the bells ringing and the millionaires walking in and out bowing low before their God—hunh—huh. It ain't God now, it's Bigger. Bigger, that's my name."

He starts printing the note with his left hand. "Sir—we got your daughter—say nothing—the ransom is—"

The lights have faded, leaving only the glow of the filament in an overhead bulb. As that, too, fades out the song service gets louder and the curtain falls.

SCENE VII

The song service is gradually fading out. In the Dalton furnace room Bigger Thomas is on his hands and knees, peering through the small opening in the door. The light of the fire is on his face. The outlines of the Dalton basement are hazy in the half light. The twisting pipes of the furnace are overhead; back by the wall an automatic coal feeder has chromium trimmings that catch and throw off the streaks of light. There is a landing on the stairway at back onto which both the door from the house and the door leading to the street open.

Bigger is still on his hands and his knees when Britten comes through the door from upstairs, holding an electric lamp in his hand. Bigger jumps to his feet. The light shines full upon his face. In the flash of Britten's lamp he is seen to have an ax in his hand.

Britten's greeting is cheerful. He is amused to find Bigger fixing the furnace—with an ax. But a lot of funny things are happening. Everybody's upset with this "Who shot John?" business going on. He pokes his light around the furnace.

"No wonder the house is freezing upstairs," says Britten. "A ton of ashes banked up in there."

There is a call from the street door. It is from a reporter. It is followed by other voices demanding that someone "Open up!" Bigger is getting busy with the furnace. Britten goes to the door, opens it, and orders the reporters away. They answer by brushing by him into the cellar. There are four of them, and two camera-men with their flash bulbs all set. They are on their way upstairs, if they can make it. Britten would stop them—

"Take it easy—now, listen here, boys. This is Mr. Dalton's home. And Mr. Dalton's got no statement to make."

"What's the dope?" "What's going on?" "How about that Red you picked up—Jan Erlone?" "Was she sleeping with him?" "Says he's got witnesses." "Says he didn't even come here last night." "Says you had him arrested because he's a Communist—"

The reporters' queries tumble one over another. Britten doesn't know a thing. "Not a goddam thing. . . . I only work here. For Christ's sake, give me a break!"

Mr. Dalton has appeared on the landing, coming from upstairs. He is weary and shaken and holds a sheet of paper tremblingly in his hand. Immediately the camera-men begin bombarding him with their flashes. He raises his hand in protest. Britten goes to his side.

"Please, gentlemen—just a moment," Dalton is saying. "I am ready to make a statement now." He moves down among them as the photographers try for another shot. "I want you to listen carefully— The way you gentlemen handle this will mean life or death to someone—someone very dear to me. . . . Gentlemen, I have just phoned the police and requested that Mr. Erlone be released immediately. I want it known and understood publicly that I have no charges to prefer against him. It is of the utmost importance that this be understood. I hope your papers will carry the story. Further, I want to announce publicly that I apologize for this arrest and inconvenience. Gentlemen, our daughter Mary Dalton—has been kidnaped."

The statement has been punctuated with the flash of the photographers' bulbs. When Mr. Dalton has finished, the surge of questions is rapid and a little confusing. How does he know his daughter has been kidnaped? When did it happen? How much do the kidnapers want? Has he had any word?

The answers are prompt. It happened, probably, early Sunday morning. The demand is for $10,000. It came in a letter from the kidnapers which he holds in his hand. It was pushed under the door about an hour ago.

"The instructions for the delivery of the money are here, and I have been cautioned not to make them public," says Mr. Dalton. "But you can say in your papers that these instructions will be followed and I shall pay the ransom."

"How is the note signed?"

"It's signed 'Red.' "

"Communists!" sneers Britten.

"No, no," Dalton protests.

"Do you think some Communist did it, Mr. Dalton?" asks one of the newspapermen.

"I don't know. I'm not positively blaming anyone, if my daughter is returned. I'll ask no questions of anyone. Now that's all, gentlemen—all."

Britten helps Mr. Dalton get away. He is back now trying to herd the newspapermen out the street door. Now he has followed the last of them out. Or thinks he has. One remains. He stands gazing in apparent idleness at Bigger Thomas, still in the shadow. He approaches Bigger.

"What's the matter, boy?"

"Nothing, suh—nothing, suh."

"Nervous, huh?"

"No, suh. No, suh—I ain't nervous."

The Reporter has reached up and turned on the bulb that hangs in the center of the room. It throws a light directly on Bigger's face. The sweat on Bigger's brow glistens. The Reporter pulls out a stool for Bigger to sit on and sits down beside him. He wants to talk to Bigger—

"How come you want to talk to me?" Bigger demands.

"Just a few questions. You know anything connected with this story is news. Say, what do you think of private property?"

"Suh? Nawsuh, I don't own no property."

"Sure, sure. Tell me, what do *you* think of Miss Dalton? I've heard she was sort of wild."

"Nawsuh, nawsuh. She was a mighty fine lady."

"Why do you say she *was?*"

"I—uh—I mean she was fine to me."

"Yes, the Daltons are all fine folks."

The Reporter has brought the talk around to Jan Erlone and the party. It's true, Bigger admits, that Erlone talked a lot about the rich and the poor; about there not going to be no more rich folk and poor folk one day; about the black man's getting a chance for a good job and stand up high and equal; about there not being any more lynchings.

"You know, Bigger," the Reporter is saying, "such things as this ought to be a warning to this country. Here was a happy family, living in peace, loving their neighbors, with one daughter, a beautiful daughter—you agree with that, don't you, Bigger?"

"Yessuh."

"Yes, it's a warning to us." The Reporter has unwrapped a piece of gum, rolled the wrapping between his fingers and tossed it in the direction of the furnace. Bigger's eyes follow it closely. "You might say she was a martyr, died to help us to see the error of our ways. We've got to learn to treat people better in this country—raise up the oppressed, give them a chance. From what I've heard, Mary Dalton thought like that, too. What do you think has happened to her?"

"I don't know, suh."

"Look, that cigarette's burning your finger!" Bigger drops

the cigarette like a hot coal and jumps to his feet. The Reporter is in front of him, offering another cigarette, holding a lighted match for him. The light flares into Bigger's face. "They must have killed her, don't you think?"

"They must've done it, sir."

"Who?"

"Them Reds, sir."

"And then write a note signing their name to it?" He has blown out the match. "You don't think that, do you, Bigger? Naw!"

"Nawsuh!"

"Naw— Just suppose you had killed her, Bigger—"

"Nawsuh, I didn't do it. I didn't do it!"

"I'm just imagining," the Reporter continues a moment later. "Where were we? Oh, she's murdered. So now, we've got to dispose of that body—no traces—nobody ever to know. Well, what about a trunk—ship it off somewhere? Nunh-unh, that wouldn't do. What about weights—sink her to the bottom of the lake? Nunh-unh, they always rise to the surface. Bury her? No, that's too difficult. Somebody see you. What is it that wipes away all traces, hm?"

"Dunno, sir."

"I'll tell you—fire. Yeh, that's what I'd do—I'd burn the body up. Wouldn't you, Bigger? (*Suddenly loud.*) Go ahead and shake the ashes down, like the woman said. Come on, now. Shake 'em down. Bet you two bits you won't."

Bigger is nervously pacing the basement now. To the furnace and back. Facing the Reporter and walking away from him. He eyes the ax that the Reporter casually removes from his reach. He picks up a shovel slowly and throws open the lower door of the furnace. The Reporter is playing idly with the ax. Bigger grabs the grate handle and gives it a shake. The ashes puff out into the room. The furnace starts to hum. There is a glad relief in Bigger's voice. "It's all fixed now," he cries. "Draws fine—everything be warmed up now! Listen at her sing! Going to town. Goddam! Goddam!"

"Sing on, boy. Sounds mighty good," shouts the Reporter.

Britten has come from the landing to face the Reporter. "What the hell are you doing down here?"

"Just poking around—looking for my story."

"Ain't found it, I reckon."

"Maybe—"

"Hell of a note. We just called up the jail and that Erlone fellow won't leave."

"Says this Bigger boy's been lying, don't he?" Bigger has been sweeping around with a broom. He stops quickly.

"How'd you know? That's just what he said."

"Here's an earring, Britten. Might interest you."

"Where'd you get it?"

"Just picked it up."

The Reporter has stepped over, close to Bigger. For a second Bigger stares at him, then, with an agonized cry, he drops his broom and bolts out the street door.

"Holy Smoke!" Britten is excited. "What's the matter with him—having a fit or something?"

"You'd better catch him. He killed Mary Dalton and burned her in that furnace," says the Reporter, quietly.

Britten stares at him dumbfoundedly, then, pulling a whistle, begins to blow vigorously as he dashes for the door. In the distance other whistles can be heard. The lights fade. The roar of the furnace increases as the curtain falls.

SCENE VIII

The sounds of the pursuit have died away. It is the next night. On the top floor of an abandoned house Bigger Thomas is crouching in a corner, deep in the shadows. A piece of torn blanket is pulled around his shoulders; his feet are wrapped in tow cloth. The creaking of a swinging, rusty sign is heard, and the flapping of a piece of tin, as though a part of the roof were being blown in the wind. From below the muffled roar of the city is heard. There are intermittent flashes of light, apparently from the sign, and the slow, sweeping flashes from an airplane beacon now and then stab the scene.

The sounds and the moaning of the wind worry Bigger. He paces the room from time to time, talking to himself to bolster his courage. "I ain't scared, naw. They all scared, feeling me in the night, feel me walkin' behind 'em. . . . And everywhere the bulls is searching them old nigger houses—Indiana, Calumet, Prairie, Wabash. Ha! But I ain't among the niggers."

Bigger is waiting for Clara. When she doesn't come it worries him. He takes to muttering again, and to visioning his escape. Soon that old "Sun-kissed Orange" sign will go out and he will be getting away. Soon he'll be in one of those orange groves with the sun on his back.

The beacon light reminds him of Lindbergh, and Lindbergh didn't quit. "Boiling icy water below him, the thunder and the lightning, the freezing and the hail around him. . . . Old Lindbergh—he made it—got home, safe home. He not scared! . . . Aw, I ain't scared, neither!"

The scream of a siren is heard in the street below. Bigger jumps to his feet. The piece of blanket falls from his shoulders. He is gripping a gun tightly in his hand and crouching down for a look over the sill of the window. The sound dies away. "Sure, nothing but an ambulance! Another fool white man done broke his neck somewhere."

Clara has come, bringing him food and a bottle of liquor. She doesn't think anybody has seen her. She had gone to a different delicatessen and come back under the El, the way he told her. She didn't bring the papers. He's mad at that. But she can tell him that they got his picture. There are big, black headlines. The section down by Ernie's is all surrounded. That pleases Bigger—

"Hah! Knowed it—dumb nuts! Yeah! They smart, them white folks. Yeh, they get the niggers. But maybe not too smart."

It is nearing one o'clock. Five more minutes, figures Bigger, and the sign will go out and he'll be off in the dark across the roofs and down the alley. He'll find someone with a car who'll take him as far as he wants to go—the gun is going to help with that part of the plan—and then he'll catch a train to the West—

"Bigger, you can't make it that way— You can't," wails Clara, but he is not listening—

"Jesus, won't that sign hurry and go off? . . . Damn snow quit falling hours ago— Roads be cleared up now!" He is by the window now. "Jesus, that blizzard—like it stopped all the traffic to keep me shut up here."

"You can't get away—you got to walk down—meet 'em—tell 'em how it happened—"

"And they believe me, huh?" He has faced her angrily. "Goddamit, I stick my head out that door, my life ain't worth a snowflake in hell. They shoot me down like a dog. . . . (*He steps toward her.*) Jesus, that tin keeps banging. (*He whirls swiftly, backing up against her.*) What the hell was that? Look at that light moving. But I ain't scared. . . . I'd begun to see something. Aw, Christ. It's gone again. I'm all mixed up, but I ain't scared now."

A new flash of light crosses the scene. That's frightening. Bigger is ready to make a run for it now. He don't need Clara no more. Anything that gets in his way now, he'll kill. . . .

The sign goes off. There is a second's darkness. Then the airplane beacon sweeps the room. When it has passed other lights appear—

"Goddam, they got a spotlight somewhere!" Bigger slides over to a window. "They found us! They seen you coming back!"

He has gone over to Clara, grabbed her angrily and thrown her to the floor. "I ought to kill you! You tell 'em!"

Clara is pleading piteously that she did not tell. He kicks her and runs across the room. She would crawl after him. "Don't you come toward me. I kill you!" he warns.

"Go ahead! Shoot me! Kill us both—and then, no more worry . . . no more pain. Do it, Bigger!"

From the window he can see his pursuers coming over the roof with sawed-off shotguns. A powerful searchlight breaks through the skylight. Bigger grabs Clara. "You set 'em on me, you bitch!"

The glass of the skylight crashes and falls around them. Bigger holds Clara between him and the skylight. Several shots ring out. Clara sags down in Bigger's arms. "We got him!" yells a voice from the roof. "Come on out of there, nigger!"

"Yeah, yeah, yeah— In front of me and they shot you—" Bigger is muttering. "All right, goddamit, I killed you!"

"Come on out if you're alive!" "Come on out, you black bastard!"

A larger spotlight has picked Bigger out. He is moving toward the front of the room. "Yeah, white boys, come on and git me! You ain't scared of me, is you? Ain't nobody but Bigger in here! Bigger! Bigger! Bigger! Standing against the lot of you! Against your thousand—two thousand—three thousand—"

The light goes off. Bigger continues to walk forward, toward the audience, firing. There are other shots, from right and left. Sirens start, increasing in pitch and volume. The curtain falls.

SCENE IX

The shriek of the sirens has faded into the noises of the street and then into those of a restless, muttering crowd. Revealing lights disclose the outlines of the court room. The Judge sits on a high bench facing the audience and separated from it by the railing that stretches across the apron of the stage. Below the railing, in the pit itself sit Paul Max, the attorney for the defense; Bigger Thomas and his family, Hannah, Vera and Buddy. At other tables are the Daltons and various court officers.

Flags of the United States and the State of Illinois are draped on poles at the sides of the Judge's bench, and in back of the Judge a rather tremendous portrait of one who might be Thomas Jefferson. In the foreground, between the attorney's table and the Judge, State's Attorney Buckley is addressing the court, though he faces the audience.

"The defendant, Bigger Thomas, pleads guilty to the charges of the indictment," Buckley is saying. "The rest is simple and brief. Punishment must follow—punishment laid down by the sacred laws of this Commonwealth—laws created to protect that society and that social system of which we are a part. . . ."

Buckley has turned to the Judge, pleading that as Bigger Thomas is a criminal who goes against the law, therefore the law must destroy him; "if a branch of the tree withers and dies it must be cut off lest it contaminate the rest of the tree." He concludes by demanding the death sentence for the prisoner.

Paul Max has risen to his feet. He is a large man, kind of face, a little sloppy as to dress, a little sad in expression, but of a deep, abiding conviction in the justice of the cause he pleads. Max stands for the moment looking at Buckley. Turning to the Judge he begins:

"Your Honor, I want the mind of the Court to be free and clear . . . and then if the Court says death, let it mean death . . . and if the Court says life, let it mean that too. But whatever the Court says, let it know upon what ground its verdict is being rendered."

He has turned back, and is facing Bigger Thomas across the table. "Night after night, I have lain without sleep trying to think of a way to picture to you, and to the world, the causes, the reason, why this Negro boy sits here today . . . and why our city is boiling with a fever of excitement and hate."

He has turned back to face the Judge. "I have pled the cause of other criminal youths in this Court as Your Honor well knows. And when I took this case I thought at first it was the same old story of a boy run afoul of the law. (*He crosses and turns back, looking at* BIGGER, *who is just below him.*) But I am convinced it is more terrible than that—with the meaning more far-reaching. Where is the responsibility? Where is the guilt? For there is guilt in the rage that demands that this man's life be stamped out! There is guilt and responsibility in the hate that inflames that mob gathered in the streets below these windows."

With mounting eloquence Max, standing now within the rail before the Judge, calls attention to those injustices that he feels have crept into the case; the prejudices that have been dragged in; the inflammatory acts of city and state authorities; resulting in the arrest of hundreds of members of suspect organizations; the raids upon union labor headquarters, etc.

Frequently Buckley arises to object; frequently the Judge sustains, but as frequently over-rules the objection. "I have no choice in this matter," Max is saying, and now he faces Bigger across the railing. "Life has cut this cloth, not *I*. Fear and hate and guilt are the keynotes of this *drama*. You see, Your Honor, I am not afraid to assign the blame, for thus I can the more honestly plead for mercy! I do not claim that this boy is the victim of injustice. But I do say that he is the victim of a wrong that has grown, like a cancer, into the very blood and bone of our social structure. Bigger Thomas sits here today as a symbol of that wrong. . . . And the judgment that you will deliver upon him is a judgment delivered upon ourselves, and upon our whole civilization. (*Steps toward Bench.*) The Court can pronounce the sentence of death, and that will end the defendant's life—but it will not end this wrong!"

Buckley is on his feet again to shout an objection. The Judge warns Max that the Court is waiting for him to produce mitigating evidence. On this suggestion Max is quick to act. He goes back into Bigger's childhood to trace the flight of the Thomases from the South after they had seen Bigger's father shot down by a Southern mob while he was trying to protect one of his own kind from the same brand of violence and hate the mob outside the court-house stands for today; of their arrival in the North only to find themselves hemmed in by the same poverty, idleness, economic injustice and race discrimination they had left behind—

"It is that way of life that stands on trial today, Your Honor, in the person of Bigger Thomas. Like his forefathers he is a slave. But unlike his forefathers, there is something in him that refuses to accept this slavery. And why does he refuse to accept it? Because through the very teachings exemplified by the flag that hangs here in this Courtroom, he was led to believe that in this country all men are free. . . . Out of confusion, fear was born. And fear breeds hate, and hate breeds guilt, and guilt in turn breeds the urge to destroy the symbols of that fear and hate and guilt! . . . Bigger Thomas is an organism which our social system has bred. He represents but a tiny aspect of a problem whose reality sprawls all over this nation. Kill him, burn the life out of him, and still this living death continues. (*He straightens up.*) You cannot kill Bigger Thomas. He is already dead. He was born dead. Born dead among the wild forests of our cities, and amid the rank and choking vegetation of our slums . . . in the Jim Crow corners of our buses and trains . . . in the dark closets and corridors and rest rooms in our Jim Crow army. . . . In our Jim Crow navy, even in the trenches when we send them to war . . . marked off by the fingers of the laws as Black against White. . . ."

He turns to the Daltons and, though his sympathy is strong for them, out of their testimony for the State he weaves a picture of Dalton as the owner of the block of tenements in which the Thomases lived—tenements for which the rents are the highest and the living conditions the worst of any in the city. Yet Dalton, as owner, is held in high esteem because from his profits he has contributed a little to Negro charities—

"It's bribery, and corpses cannot be bribed," shouts Max. "Such living corpses as Bigger Thomas here are warnings to us to stop it, and stop it now before it is too late."

Max has returned again to stand above the railing facing Bigger as he reaches the end of his plea—

". . . Night and day, millions of souls, the souls of our black people, are crying out: 'This is our country too. We helped to build it. Give us a part in it, a part free and hopeful and wide as the everlasting horizon.' And in this fear-crazed, guilt-ridden body of Bigger Thomas, that vast multitude cries out to you now in a mighty voice, saying: 'Give us our freedom, our chance, and our hope to be men.' Can we ignore this cry? Can we continue to boast through every medium of public utterance . . . through literature, newspapers, radio, the pulpit . . . and that this is a land of freedom and opportunity, of liberty and justice to all . . . and in our behavior deny all these precepts of charity and enlightenment? Bigger Thomas is a symbol of that double-dealing. (*He turns to the* JUDGE.) And for that reason, Your Honor, I beg you, not in the name of Almighty God, but in the name of ourselves, to spare the life of Bigger Thomas."

Paul Max pauses. His effort is over. He walks slowly toward the steps and down to the table where his client sits. The lights are fading as a deep-toned chime is heard and the curtain slowly falls.

SCENE X

The chimes fade out as the rising curtain reveals, first the bare brick wall of a prison and then the steel bars of a cell. A bunk is hung by chains from the rear wall. Through a side brick wall the steel door to the death chamber can be seen.

Bigger Thomas is standing near the head of the bunk when Paul Max comes down the corridor. Max carries a telegram in his hand, which he passes through the bars to Bigger—

"I've got some bad news. I'm sorry, son."

Bigger takes the telegram, reads it, crumples it in his hand and throws it on the floor. "I know you did all you could," he says, and then he adds as casually as he can: "They're going to change my looks tonight, Mr. Max."

Max tells him of Mrs. Dalton going to the Governor with him for the final plea. Bigger is sorry for that; wishes she hadn't. He's all right, he keeps insisting; there's nothing nobody can do—

"Mr. Max, I'm glad I got to know you before I go," says Bigger.

"I'm glad I got to know you, too. I'm sorry to have to part this way. But I'm old, son. I'll be going soon, myself."

BIGGER—Ain't nobody ever talked like you before. How come you do this—you being a white man? Goddamit. (*He crosses to the opposite corner by the bunk.*) You oughta let me alone. How come you want to help me in the first place—and me black and a murderer.

MAX—Bigger, in the work I'm doing I look at the world in a way that shows no whites and no blacks. The reason I spoke to you as I did is because you made me feel how badly men want to live in this world.

BIGGER—I was all set to die—maybe. I was all right—then you come and start talking, digging into me—opening up my guts.

MAX—I just wanted to understand you, Bigger.

BIGGER—Understand me—she said that!

MAX—She was trying to help you, wasn't she?

BIGGER—Naw—and I hated her—and I ain't sorry she's dead.

MAX—Take it easy, son.

BIGGER—I hated her.

MAX—Because she was white, Bigger?

BIGGER—She made me feel like a dog— Yeh—that's the way

all of them made me feel—in their big house I was trembling and scared.

MAX—Didn't you ever love anybody, Bigger?

BIGGER (*crosses back to* MAX)—Maybe I loved my daddy—long time ago. They killed him.

MAX—Didn't you love your mother and sister?

BIGGER—Reckon so . . . Goddamit! There you start again.

Bigger's emotions again threaten to get out of control, but he fights them back. He is all mixed up now. And troubled. Such talk makes him think, and thinking makes him afraid to go this way. He paces the cell and Max steps up to stand before him—

"You creep in on me . . . crowd me to the wall . . . smother me . . . and I want to breathe . . . right up till that lightning hits me," Bigger protests. "Go away, Mr. Max."

Max stands quietly, calmly urging Bigger to go on.

"Why the folks who sent me here hate me so?" demands Bigger. "Long before I ever did anything they hated me. . . . How come they hate me so? 'Cause I'm black?"

"No, that's not it, Bigger. Your being black just makes it easier to be signaled out in a white man's world. That's all. What they wanted to do to you they do to each other every day. They don't hate you and they don't hate each other. They are men like you, like me, and they feel like you. They want the things of life just as you do, their own chance. But as long as these are denied them, as long as a few people hold all the power in the world, and rule and regulate the lives of millions of their fellow-men . . . just as long as that, those millions will keep groping around . . . frightened, and lost, and angry—like you were."

Now the light has come again into Bigger's eyes. There is another thing he doesn't understand—

"When I killed that girl, Mr. Max, I didn't mean to kill her . . . You know that . . . I killed her 'cause I was scared and mad . . . like you say. . . . I had been scared and mad all my life . . . but after I killed her, I wasn't scared no more—for a little while! I was a man!" He is pacing the cell again. "Yah! I was a man after doin' the last thing I ever figured to do! Maybe it was 'cause they was after my life then . . . and I was fighting . . . that made me feel high and powerful and free!"

MAX—Bigger, no. . . . That wasn't what I . . . Don't you see—you weren't fighting the right way. . . .

BIGGER—Yeah . . . yeah . . . reckon so. . . . Mr. Max, in the court room when you was talking. You told them I was dead . . . a corpse. . . . But I ain't dead now, Mr. Max. I ain't no corpse . . . I'm more alive now than I ever was in my life. Goddamit. I'm alive now and they're going to kill me! I'm all right now, Mr. Max. (*He crosses to opposite corner.*) I'm all right . . . you go on now . . .

MAX—You want me to go, Bigger.

BIGGER—Yeah. You go on now. I'm all right. For real, I am, Mr. Max.

MAX—Mr. Bigger.

BIGGER—Tell Maw and the others I was all right . . . wasn't crying none. See?

MAX—Yes, Bigger.

BIGGER (*a long pause*)—Good-by, Mr. Max.

MAX (*shaking hands*)—Good-by.

"Bigger grasps the prison bars. He looks straight out holding on to the bars. Max turns away from him and walks down the corridor and off right. The lights start to fade. Bigger just stands holding on to the bars, looking straight out. The lights fade out completely."

THE CURTAIN FALLS

WATCH ON THE RHINE

A Drama in Three Acts

BY LILLIAN HELLMAN

IN the years when the theatre was booming along at its commercial if not its artistic peak the stronger dramas of a season were usually all in circulation by the time the December holidays were reached. September, October and November were the months for which the producers saved their hoped-for hits.

Those were the days when the sources of supply were much more generously stocked with good drama than they are today. Broadway had the call over Hollywood. The most promising plays were written through the Winter, sold in the Spring, rehearsed in the Summer and produced in the Fall. The success of the current season was both spur and guide and usually an inspiration for the productions being prepared for the season to follow.

Nowadays so limited is the crop of plays that the moment one of promise appears it is immediately bought and quickly rushed to the stage that its producer may take advantage of what has become a continuous shortage of better drama. Last season's "There Shall Be No Night" did not arrive until April 29, 1940. This season's "Watch on the Rhine" was not ready until late March and did not reach Broadway until April 1, 1941.

Bearing out the older showman's conviction that it is always a good time for a good play, the date of production does not appear to matter greatly. Both these fine dramas were successful over night. Morning newspaper reviews rang with praise of them and public response is still not checked.

Lillian Hellman, starting with "The Children's Hour" the season of 1934-35, has written four plays. Three have been tremendously successful with both the critical fraternity and the playgoing public. Many are ready to insist that "Watch on the Rhine" is the greatest drama of the three—"The Children's Hour" and "The Little Foxes" being the other two. Certainly there is common agreement that of all the anti-Nazi dramas that have sprung from the bitterness and prejudices of the second World War, Miss Hellman's play is at once the most soberly reasoned and the most convincingly written of the lot.

"It is an anti-Nazi play which differs from all the others as completely as it transcends them," wrote Louis Kronenberger in New York's *PM*. "It is a play about human beings and their ideological ghosts; a play dedicated to the deeds they are called upon to perform, not the words they are moved to utter. It is a play whose final crisis, though peculiar to one man's life, is yet central to our own."

There were those who were willing to debate the justification for his enthusiasm with Mr. Kronenberger, but their arguments were based usually upon the drama's structural rather than its dramatic weaknesses.

The Farrellys have lived for a good many generations in a large country house about twenty miles from Washington, D. C. Of this home Fanny Farrelly, widow of Joshua Farrelly, founder of the current branch, is the lively mistress.

It is a Wednesday morning in the late Spring when first we enter the Farrelly home. The French windows of the wide living room open upon a broad terrace on which in pleasant weather a good deal of the family congregating is done.

Four or five generations have furnished this room, and they have all been people of taste. "There are no styles, no periods; the room has never been refurnished. Each careless aristocrat has thrown into the room what he or she liked as a child, what he or she brought home when grown up. Therefore the furniture is of many periods: the desk is English, the couch is Victorian, some of the pictures are modern, some of the ornaments French."

As we enter we find Anise, "a thin French woman of about sixty, in a dark housekeeper's dress," sorting, and, in a way, sniffing the morning mail. Across the terrace at back, Joseph, "a tall, middle-aged Negro butler," wheels in a breakfast wagon. And now Fanny Farrelly herself has appeared. "She is a handsome woman of about sixty-three. She has on a fancy, good-looking dressing-gown."

Mrs. Farrelly is one who likes to stir things up. This morning she is mildly excited because folks are expected on the noon train and no one appears to be doing anything about it. What if it is only eight-thirty? Mr. David should be down. Let Joseph set the clock ahead to nine and ring the bell. Of course the bell will disturb people. That's what it's for. David should be at the station by eleven-thirty. The train might come in early. No Washington train ever has, but this one might.

Nervous? Of course Fanny is nervous. "It's been twenty

years," she reminds Anise. "Any mother would be nervous. If your daughter were coming home and you hadn't seen her, and a husband, *and* grandchildren—"

"I do not say that it is wrong to be nervous. I, too, am nervous. I say only that you are."

"Very well, I heard you. *I* say that I am." She has gone back to reading her letters. "Jenny's still in California. She's lost her lavallière again. Birdie Chase's daughter is still *faire l'amouring* with that actor. Tawdry, Jenny says it is. An actor. Fashions in sin change. In my day, it was Englishmen. I don't understand infidelity. If you love a man, then why? If you don't love him, then why stay with him? (*Without turning, she points over her head to Joshua Farrelly's portrait.*) Thank God, I was in love. I thought about Joshua last night. Three grandchildren. He would have liked that. I hope I will."

There is not much in the rest of the mail, Anise reports. Advertisements and legal things for Mr. David and what appear to be a great many requests for the payment of bills addressed to the Count and Countess de Brancovis, who are Mrs. Farrelly's guests.

"In the six weeks the Balkan nobility have been with us, they seem to have run up a great many bills," observes Fanny.

Joseph has been ringing the bell with considerable viciousness and the first results are apparent in the appearance of David Farrelly, "a pleasant-looking man of thirty-nine."

David is not feeling too well, what with the noise of the "air-raid alarm" and his mother's irritated insistence that he should be showing a great deal more interest in the arrival of his sister than he is showing. As for the Balkan nobility, he knows nothing of their plans or how long they expect to stay—

"It's been six weeks," says Fanny. "Now that Sara and her family are coming, even this house might be a little crowded—(*He looks up at her. Quickly.*) Yes. I know I invited them. I felt sorry for Marthe, and Teck rather amused me. He plays good cribbage, and he tells good jokes. But that's not enough for a lifetime guest. If you've been urging her to stay, I wish you'd stop it. They haven't any money; all right, lend them some—"

"I have been urging them to stay?"

"I'm not so old I don't recognize flirting when I see it."

"But you're old enough not to be silly."

"I'm not silly. I'm charming."

Marthe de Brancovis, "an attractive woman of thirty-one or

'hoto by Vandamm Studio.

"WATCH ON THE RHINE"

Sara (to Fanny): For almost twelve years Kurt went to work every morning and came home very night, and we lived modestly and happily— (Sharply) As happily as people could in a tarved Germany that was going to pieces—

Kurt: Sara, please. You're angry. I do not like it that way.

(Lucile Watkins, Mady Christians, Paul Lukas)

thirty-two," has come down. Her interest in David is apparent, and Fanny's consciousness of it is also quite plain. The situation is amusing to David. At the moment, however, he is more concerned with the prospect of standing on a station platform waiting for a sister he has not seen in years. He may be a little afraid she won't like him, though as children they had been very fond of each other—

"You know, I've never met Sara's husband," David is saying to Marthe. "Mama did. I think the first day Sara met him, in Munich. Mama didn't like the marriage much in those days—and Sara didn't care, and Mama didn't like Sara not caring. Mama cut up about it, bad."

"Why?"

"Probably because they didn't let her arrange it. Why does Mama ever act badly? She doesn't remember ten minutes later."

"Wasn't Mr. Müller poor?"

"Oh, Mama wouldn't have minded that. If they'd only come home and let her fix their lives for them— (*Smiles.*) But Sara didn't want it that way."

Teck de Brancovis, "a good-looking man of about forty-five," has appeared at a second wild ringing of the bell on the terrace, and David hurries away to appease his mother and stop the racket. The de Brancovises have stopped behind. Teck finds the accumulation of unpaid bills disturbing. He certainly would like to pay them if he could— "We have eighty-seven dollars in American Express checks," he tells Marthe. "That's all we have."

"Maybe something will turn up. It's due," she says.

"David?" inquires Teck, with a smile. As she turns quickly to look at him he continues: "The other relatives will arrive this morning?"

"Yes."

"I think Madame Fanny and Mr. David may grow weary of accents and charity guests. Or is the husband of the sister a rich one?"

"No. He's poor. He had to leave Germany in '33."

"A Jew?"

"No. I don't think so."

"Why did he have to leave Germany?"

"Oh, I don't know, Teck. He's an anti-Nazi."

"A political?"

"No, I don't think so. He was an engineer. I don't know. I don't know much about him."

Teck is planning to go to Washington. A friend at the German Embassy has invited him to take a hand in a poker game. Marthe does not like that. Under the circumstances she doesn't think Teck should be seeing these friends or be seen at the Embassy.

"You have political convictions now?" queries Teck.

MARTHE—I don't know what I have. I've never liked Nazis, as you know, and you should have had enough of them. They seem to have had enough of you, God knows. It would be just as well to admit they are smarter than you are and let them alone.

TECK (*looking at her carefully, after a minute*)—That is interesting.

MARTHE—What is interesting?

TECK—I think you are trying to say something to me. What is it?

MARTHE—That you ought not to be at the Embassy, and that it's insane to play cards in a game with Von Seitz with eighty-seven dollars in your pocket. I don't think he'd like your not being able to pay up. Suppose you lose?

TECK—I shall try not to lose.

MARTHE—But if you do lose and can't pay, it will be all over Washington in an hour. (*Points to terrace.*) They'll find out about it, and we'll be out of here when they do.

TECK—I think I want to be out of here. I find that I do not like the picture of you and our host.

MARTHE (*carefully*)—There is no picture, as you put it, to like or dislike.

TECK—Not yet? I am glad to hear that. (*Comes toward her slowly.*) Marthe, you understand that I am not really a fool? You understand that it is unwise to calculate me that way?

MARTHE (*slowly, as if it were an effort*)—Yes, I understand that. And I understand that I'm getting tired. Just plain tired. The whole thing's too much for me. I've always meant to ask you, since you play on so many sides, why we don't come out any better. I've always wanted to ask you how it happened. (*Sharply.*) I'm tired, see? And I just want to sit down. Just to sit down in a chair and stay.

TECK (*carefully*)—Here?

MARTHE—I don't know. Any place—

TECK—You have thus arranged it with David?

MARTHE—I've arranged nothing.

TECK—But you are trying, eh? (*He comes close to her.*) I

think not. I would not like that. Do not make any arrangements, Marthe. I may not allow you to carry them through. (*Smiles.*) Come to breakfast now.

For a moment after Marthe and Teck have disappeared on the terrace the room is empty. Then Sara Müller appears in the doorway, and comes slowly into the room, as if expecting to find somebody. "Behind her in the doorway are three children; behind them Kurt Müller. They stand waiting, watching Sara. Sara is forty-one or forty-two, a good-looking woman, with a well-bred, serious face. She is very badly dressed. Her dress is too long, her shoes were bought a long time ago and have no relation to the dress, and the belt of her dress has become untied and is hanging down. She looks clean and dowdy. As she looks around the room, her face is gay and surprised. Smiling, without turning, absently, she motions to the children and Kurt. Slowly, the children come in. Bodo Müller, a boy of nine, comes first. He is carrying coats. Behind him, carrying two cheap valises, is Joshua Müller, a boy of fourteen. Behind him is Babette Müller, a pretty little girl of twelve. They are dressed for a much colder climate. They come forward, look at their mother, then move to a couch. Behind them is Kurt Müller, a large, powerful, German-looking man of about forty-seven. He is carrying a shabby valise and a brief-case."

The children are worried. Is it right that they should come in without ringing the bell? The door has never been locked—never since she can remember, Sara tells them.

"You find it curious to believe there are people who live and do not need to watch, eh, Bodo?"

"Yes, Papa."

"You and I." Kurt is smiling.

"My goodness, isn't it a fine room? I'd almost forgotten—" Sara has moved from one thing to another; noticed the picture of her father, "the famous Joshua Farrelly," over the mantel, and the picture of her grandmother. There is a photo standing on the piano. It is autographed—To Joshua and Fanny Farrelly. With admiration. Alfonso, May 7, 1910."

"Alfons von Spanien?" Bodo asks. "Der hat immer Bilder von sich verschenkt. Ein schlechtes Zeichen für einen Mann."

"Mama told you it is good manners to speak the language of the country you visit," corrects Joshua. "Therefore, speak in English."

"I said he seemed always to give his photograph. I said that is a bad flag on a man. Grow fat on the poor people and give pictures of the face."

The picture of Alfonso recalls many things to Sara—"a big party and cakes and a glass of champagne." There was an ermine boa, too—such a grand boa as Sara would like to buy for Babette—

"You were born here, Mama?" Bodo asks.

"Upstairs. And I lived here until I went to live with your father. (*Looks out beyond the terrace.*) Your Uncle David and I used to have a garden, behind the terrace. I wonder if it's still there. I like a garden. I've always hoped we'd have a house some day and settle down—(*Stops nervously, turns to stare at* KURT, *who is looking at her.*) I'm talking so foolish. Sentimental. At my age. Gardens and ermine boas. I haven't wanted anything—"

"Sara. Stop it!" Kurt has come to her and taken her hand. "This is a fine room. A fine place to be. Everything is so pleasant and full of comfort. This will be a good piano on which to play again. And it is all so clean. I like that. Now, you shall not be a baby. You must enjoy your house, and not be afraid that you hurt me with it. Yes?"

"Yes, of course. It's strange, that's all. We've never been in a place like this together—"

"That does not mean, and should not mean, that we do not remember how to enjoy what comes our way. We are on a holiday."

"A holiday? But for how long? And what plans afterwards?"

"We will have plans when the hour arrives to make them."

And now Anise has come from the hall, and the Müllers are discovered amid great excitement and many exclamations of surprise and wonder. There are confused introductions and bewildered remembrances jumbled together until Anise finally recalls that they have not had breakfast—or seen Miss Fanny— It is important that they should see Miss Fanny— "She cannot bear not knowing things. Miss Fanny!" Anise reminds Sara.

And now Fanny has come and taken Sara in her arms, and held her off to stare wonderingly at her. "Sara! Sara, darling. You're here! You're really here. . . . Welcome! Welcome! Welcome to your house!" And then she adds, slowly: "You're not young, Sara."

"No, Mama. I'm forty-one."

"Forty-one. Of course. . . . You look more like Papa now. That's good. The years have helped you."

She has turned to welcome Kurt. "Welcome to this house, sir. . . . You are a good-looking man for a German. I didn't remember you that way. I like a good-looking man. I always have."

"I like a good-looking woman. I always have," echoes Kurt, smiling. The children are greeted, one by one, a little excitedly. Finally David is sent for and the presence of the de Brancovis is explained. "Do you remember Marthe Randolph?" Fanny is saying. "I mean, do you remember Hortie Randolph, her mother, who was my friend? Can you follow what I'm saying? I'm not speaking well today."

"Of course I remember Marthe and Hortie. You and she used to scream at each other."

"Well, Marthe, her daughter, married Teck de Brancovis. *Count* de Brancovis. He was fancy when she married him. Not so fancy now, I suspect. Although still chic and tired. You know what I mean, the way they are in Europe. Well, they're here."

Sara would know what David is like, but Fanny can't tell her that. "He's a lawyer. You know that. Papa's firm. He's never married. You know that, too—"

"Why hasn't he married?"

"Really, I don't know. I don't think he likes his own taste. Which is very discriminating of him. He's had lots of girls, of course, one more ignorant and silly than the other—"

Soon David has come to speak for himself. The greeting with his sister is affectionate and exciting, with family introductions following. There is much that Sara and David have to say to each other, much that they have to remember. And again Fanny must bring up the matter of David's flirting with Marthe de Brancovis for Sara's information.

"You are making nervous jokes this morning, Mama," David says, sharply. "And they're not very good ones."

"I tell the truth. If it turns out to be a joke, all the better," gaily answers Fanny.

The talk has turned to Kurt and to plans for the future. Fanny has that all arranged. There is to be a new wing for Kurt and Sara and the old turkey house is to be fixed up for the children and Anise. Sara admits that the planning is very kind, but she is afraid they had better not make plans for a little while—not until Kurt has had a good, long vacation—

"A vacation? You'll be staying here, of course. You don't have to worry about work— Engineers can always get jobs, David says, and he's already begun to inquire—"

"I have not worked as an engineer since many years, Madame."

"Haven't you? I thought— Didn't you work for Dornier?"

"Yes. Before '33."

It isn't an easy story to tell, but it must be told if Fanny's insistence is to be quieted. It is true that Kurt had worked in many places as an engineer; it is true that they moved very often; it is true that frequently they have had a very hard time. "I have no wish to make a mystery of what I have been doing," Kurt is saying; "it is only that it is awkward to place neatly. (*Smiles, motions with his hand.*) It sounds so big: it is so small. I am Anti-Fascist. And that does not pay well."

Sara does not enjoy her mother's probing, but Fanny will have the truth. "You had a bad time, just trying to live, didn't you?" demands Fanny. "That's obvious, Sara, and foolish to pretend it isn't. Why wouldn't you take money from us? What kind of nonsense—"

SARA (*slowly*)—We've lived the way we wanted to live. I don't know the language of rooms like this any more. And I don't want to learn it again.

KURT—Do not bristle about it.

SARA—I'm not bristling. (*To* FANNY.) I married because I fell in love. You can understand that.

FANNY (*slowly*)—Yes.

SARA—For almost twelve years, Kurt went to work every morning and came home every night, and we lived modestly, and happily— (*Sharply.*) As happily as people could in a starved Germany that was going to pieces—

KURT—Sara, please. You're angry. I do not like it that way. I will try to find a way to tell you with quickness. Yes. (SARA *turns, looks at him, starts to speak, stops.*) I was born in a town called Fürth. (*Pauses. Looks up, smiles.*) There is a holiday in my town. We call it Kirchweih. It was a gay holiday with games and music and a hot white sausage to eat with the wine. I grow up, I move away—to school, to work—but always I come back for Kirchweih. It is for me the great day of the year. (*Slowly.*) But after the war, that day begins to change. The sausage is made from bad stuff, the peasants come in without shoes, the children are too sick— (*Carefully.*) It is bad for my people, those years, but always I have hope. In the festival of August, 1931, more than a year before the storm, I give up that hope. On that day, I see twenty-seven men murdered in a Nazi street fight. I cannot stay by now and watch. My time has come to move. I say with Luther, "Here I stand. I can do nothing else. God help me. Amen."

SARA—It doesn't pay well to fight for what we believe in. But I wanted it the way Kurt wanted it. (*Shrugs.*) They don't like us in Europe; I guess they never did. So Kurt brought us home. You've always said you wanted us. If you don't, I will understand.

DAVID—Darling, of course we want you—

FANNY (*rising*)—I am old. And made of dry cork. And bad-mannered. Please forgive me.

SARA (*going quickly to* FANNY)—Shut up, Mama. We're all acting like fools. I'm glad to be home. That's all I know. So damned glad.

DAVID—And we're damned glad to have you. Come on. Let's walk to the lake. We've made it bigger and planted the island with blackberries— (*She smiles and goes to him. Together they move out the hall entrance.*)

FANNY (*after a silence*)—They've always liked each other. We're going to have Zwetschgen-Knoedel for dinner. You like them?

KURT—Indeed.

FANNY—I hope you like decent food.

KURT—I do.

FANNY—That's a good sign in a man.

The irrepressible Bodo assists in the introduction of Marthe and Teck de Brancovis. "My name is Bodo," he informs them. "It's a strange name. No?" And then to his father he reports: "Papa, this is the house of great wonders. Each has his bed, each has his bathroom. The arrangement of it, that is splendorous."

"You are a fancy talker, Bodo," says his grandmother.

"Oh, yes. In many languages," adds Kurt.

"Please to correct me when I am wrong," continues Bodo, seriously. "Papa, the plumbing is such as you have never seen. Each implement is placed on the floor, and all are simultaneous in the same room. You will therefore see that being placed most solidly on the floor allows of no rats, rodents or crawlers, and is most sanitary. (*To the others.*) Papa will be most interested. He likes to know how each thing of everything is put together. And he is so fond of being clean—"

"I am a hero to my children," says Kurt, laughing. "It bores everybody but me."

Teck de Brancovis is quite certain that he has met Kurt Müller before, but Kurt is as certain that he has not, though admittedly he has lived in many places. Of course he has read Teck's name in the newspapers.

Kurt and Fanny have gone to the terrace for breakfast. The de Brancovis have the room to themselves. Teck is frankly curious about the newcomers. Curious about their luggage, too. Why are all the larger pieces unlocked and a shabby briefcase very carefully locked?

"I am curious about a daughter of the Farrellys who marries a German who has bullet scars on his face and broken bones in his hands," adds Teck. And far from being impressed by Marthe's pointed suggestion that it is no business of his, he calmly instructs Joseph to take the de Brancovis luggage upstairs.

"Obviously it is more comfortable to look at baggage behind closed doors," he explains.

"What kind of a silliness is this now?" Marthe demands. "Leave these people alone—I won't let you—"

"What?" She has followed him to the door.

"I said I won't let you. You are not—"

"How many times have you seen me angry?" Teck has turned to face her a little savagely. "You will not wish to see another. Run along now and have lunch with something you call Sally Tyne. But do not make plans with David. You will not be able to carry them out. You will go with me, when I am ready to go. You understand."

His last words come trailing back as he disappears through the door. The curtain falls.

ACT II

It is ten days later, with evening approaching. In the Farrelly living room Fanny and Teck are playing cribbage. Near them Sara is sitting on a couch, crocheting, and at a small table young Bodo is wisely studying a slightly scrambled heating pad, while Anise watches anxiously. The pad had cost Anise ten dollars and so far as she can judge Bodo has made a ruin of it.

The talk has turned to the number of languages the children speak, either well or badly, and this interests Teck. "You seem to have stayed close to the borders of Germany," he says to Sara.

"Did Herr Müller have hopes, as so many did, that National Socialism would be overthrown on every tomorrow?"

"We have not given up that hope. Have you, Count de Brancovis?"

"I never had it."

"Then it must be most difficult for you to sleep," suggests Joshua, who has just come in from the terrace.

Sara reprimands Joshua, and explains that she is not offended by what Teck has said. She just doesn't like polite political conversations any more. There is too much talk. "By this time all of us must know where we are and what we have to do," she says. "It's an indulgence to sit in a room and discuss your beliefs as if they were a juicy piece of gossip."

Fanny and Teck have finished their cribbage game. Fanny still owes Teck eighty-five dollars, but he would have her let that go until the next day. Then she may give it to him as a going away token.

The de Brancovis going away? Fanny is surprised at that. Going where—and when? Teck is not sure. He only has a feeling there are too many refugees there. Perhaps the Müllers will be leaving, also. And at Sara's expression of surprise he adds—

"I thought perhaps you, too, would be moving on. Herr Müller does not give me the feeling of a man who settles down. Men who have done his work, seldom leave it. Not for a quiet country house."

The three children are a little startled at the thought, and their grandmother is quick to settle it—

"I don't know what you're saying," she says to Teck. "They shall certainly not be leaving—ever. Is that understood, Sara?"

"Well, Mama—" Sara would evade an answer.

"There are no wells about it. You've come home to see me die and you will wait until I'm ready."

"Really, Mama, that isn't the reason I came home."

"It's a good enough reason. I shall do a fine death. I intend to be a great deal of trouble to everybody."

Which reminds Anise of the time before Sara was born that Miss Fanny, being jealous of her Joshua's waltzing with a great beauty of that day, screamed out in the middle of a grand ball that she was in labor and had to be taken home. For three weeks thereafter she kept the patient Joshua anxiously catering to her every wish—but, Anise knows, Joshua knew all the time.

"Once he said to me, 'Anise, it is well that I am in love. This is of a great strain and her Great-uncle Freddie was not right in the head, neither,' " sharply answers Anise in self-defense.

Anise, according to Fanny, is a liar and it takes a good deal of pleading before Sara is able to quiet her mother and her mother's beloved companion. Finally apologies are exchanged. . . .

Fanny is busily planning a birthday party for Babette. There shall be a musical program and presents. Perhaps, thinks Teck, that is why Mellie Sewell, a gossiping neighbor, had seen Marthe and David at Barstow's. They might have been buying a bit of jewelry for Fanny—or Babbie.

David is irritated by Teck's suggestion, and particularly irritated that his mother should pay any attention to Mellie's deliberately extended reports of Washington gossip. But Fanny is not greatly impressed—

"Mellie Sewell told me," she is saying to Teck, "that she had heard from Louis Chandler's child's governess that you had won quite a bit of money in a poker game with Sam Chandler and some Germans at the Embassy."

Kurt, who has been idly playing the piano, stops abruptly at this, but, noticing that Teck is eyeing him intently, shortly resumes.

"It must have been a big game," ventures David. "Sam Chandler plays in big games. . . . Sam and Nazis must make an unpleasant poker game."

"I do not play poker to be amused," says Teck.

It develops that Sam's business is that of selling bootleg munitions, which convinces Fanny that Sam is running true to Chandler form—they're all scoundrels and always have been. . . .

The children are being herded upstairs by Anise. It is time for their baths. Kurt is again strumming at the piano, and humming an old soldier song—first the words as Germans sang them in Berlin in 1918: " 'We come home. We come home. Some of us are gone and some of us are lost, but we are friends: Our blood is on the earth together. Some day. Some day we shall meet again. Farewell.' "

And then the words the Germans fighting in Spain sang in 1936 as they marched in Kurt's Brigade: " 'And so we have met again. The blood did not have time to dry. We lived to stand and fight again. This time we fight for people. This time the bastards will keep their hands away. Those who sell the blood of other men, this time, they keep their hands away. . . ."

The music has died out. There is a moment's silence. "We

did not win," Kurt adds, gently. "It would have been a different world if we had."

"Papa said so years ago," says Sara. "Do you remember, Mama? 'For every man who lives without freedom, the rest of us must face the guilt.' "

"Yes. 'We are liable in the conscience-balance for the tailor in Lodz, the black man in the South, the peasant in—' " She turns to Teck, unpleasantly, "Your country, I think."

The first of the presents for Babette's birthday party have arrived. Marthe de Brancovis brings in a large dress box. There are new dresses for Babbie—and for Marthe and Sara as well. All from Savitt's. It was this way in the old days, Sara remembers, happily. Now that she has a new evening dress Kurt will have to take her into Washington, and, it may be, to a dance. But Kurt does not smile at the suggestion. Sara is afraid she has hurt him. "It isn't that dresses have ever mattered to me," she is quick to say, as she takes his arms; "it's just that—"

"Of course they have mattered to you. As they should. I do not think of the dress." He has drawn her to him and is looking into her eyes intently. "How many years have I loved that face," he mutters, and leans down to kiss her, as if it were important. That the others see this does not matter to Kurt or Sara. . . .

Kurt has been called to take a message over the long distance phone, leaving Teck and Sara staring after him wonderingly. Now Teck has turned to thank Fanny for her generosity to his wife. Perhaps it was she who gave Marthe a sapphire bracelet from Barstow's!

No. That was not Fanny. That was David, who is quick to admit it. David has been given to understand also that it is none of Teck's business. Yes, Marthe admits. She had told David that.

Teck does not take the statement gracefully. It is, he says, playfully, the sort of thing about which they used to play at dueling in Europe. David does not think they should be as musical comedy about it as all that, but if Teck would like to suggest taking action it is right to warn him that he might get hurt—

"That would not be my reason," says Teck, slowly. He turns to Marthe: "Your affair has gone far enough—"

MARTHE (*sharply*)—It is not an affair—

TECK—I do not care what it is. The time has come to leave

here. Go upstairs and pack your things. (*She does not move.* DAVID *turns toward her.*) Go on, Marthe.

MARTHE (*to* DAVID)—I am not going with him. I told you that.

DAVID—I don't want you to go with him.

FANNY (*carefully*)—Really, David, aren't you interfering in all this a good deal—

DAVID (*carefully*)—Yes, Mama, I am.

TECK (*to* MARTHE)—When you are speaking to me, please say what you have to say to me.

MARTHE (*comes to him*)—You are trying to frighten me. But you are not going to frighten me any more. I will say it to you: I am not going with you. I am never going with you again.

TECK (*softly*)—If you do not fully mean what you say, or if you might change your mind, you are talking unwisely, Marthe.

MARTHE—I know that.

TECK—Shall we talk about it alone?

MARTHE—You can't make me go, can you, Teck?

TECK—No, I can't make you.

MARTHE—Then there's no sense talking about it.

TECK—Are you in love with him?

MARTHE—Yes.

FANNY (*sharply*)—Marthe! What is all this?

MARTHE (*sharply*)—I'll tell *you* about it in a minute.

DAVID—You don't have to explain anything to anybody.

TECK (*ignoring him*)—Is he in love with you?

MARTHE—I don't think so. You won't believe it, because you can't believe anything that hasn't tricks to it, but David hasn't much to do with this. I told you I would leave some day, and I remember where I said it—(*Slowly.*)—and why I said it.

TECK—I also remember. But I did not believe you. I have not had much to offer you these last years. But if now we had some money and could go back—

MARTHE—No. I don't like you, Teck. I never have.

TECK—And I have always known it.

FANNY (*stiffly*)—I think your lack of affections should be discussed with more privacy. Perhaps—

DAVID—Mama—

MARTHE—There is nothing to discuss. Strange. I've talked to myself about this scene for almost fifteen years. I knew a lot of things to say to you and I used to lie awake at night or walk along the street and say them. Now I don't want to. I guess you only want to talk that way, when you're not sure what you can do. When you're sure, then what's the sense of saying it? "This is why and this is why and this—" (*Very happily.*) But when you know you can do it, you don't have to say anything; you can just go. And I'm going. There is nothing you can do. I would like you to believe that now.

TECK—Very well, Marthe. I think I made a mistake. I should not have brought you here. I believe you now.

Marthe will move into Washington, though David and Sara urge her to stay where she is for a while. Marthe reminds Fanny of her (Marthe's) marriage to Teck and of her mother's deliberate planning for it. It was, Marthe can see now, her mother's rather than her own wedding. "No, I'm not hard on her," she corrects Fanny. "I only tell the truth. She wanted a life for me, I suppose. It just wasn't the life I wanted for myself. (*Sharply.*) And that's what you have tried to do. With your children. In another way. Only Sara got away. And that made you angry —until so many years went by that you forgot."

"I don't usually mind people saying anything they think, but I find that—"

"I don't care what you mind or don't mind. I'm in love with your son—"

"That's unfortunate—"

"And I'm sick of watching you try to make him into his father. I don't think you even know you do it any more and I don't think he knows it any more, either. And that's what's most dangerous about it."

The de Brancovis have decided to go their separate ways. Kurt appears suddenly in the study door. His face is tense. He would at first make light of the long-distance message he has received, but is soon forced to admit that he will have to go to California for a few weeks.

"It is in the afternoon newspaper, Herr Müller," Teck says, pointing to the paper on the table. "I was waiting to find the proper moment to call it to your attention." He has picked up the paper and begun to read: "'Zurich, Switzerland: The Zurich papers today reprinted a despatch from the *Berliner Tageblatt*— on the capture of Colonel Max Freidank. Freidank is said— (SARA *begins to move toward him.*)—to be the chief of the Anti-Nazi Underground Movement. Colonel Freidank has long been an almost legendary figure. The son of the famous General

Freidank, he was a World War officer and a distinguished physicist before the advent of Hitler.' That is all."

SARA—Max—

KURT—Be still, Sara.

TECK—They told me of it at the Embassy last night. They also told me that with him, they had taken a man who called himself Ebber, and a man who called himself Triste. They could not find a man called Gotter. (*He starts again toward the door.*) I shall be a lonely man without Marthe. I am also a very poor one. I should like to have ten thousand dollars before I go.

DAVID (*carefully*)—You will make no loans in this house.

TECK—I was not speaking of a loan.

FANNY (*carefully*)—God made you not only a scoundrel but a fool. That is a dangerous combination.

DAVID (*suddenly leaping toward* TECK)—Damn you, you—

KURT (*suddenly pounds on the top of the piano, as* DAVID *almost reaches* TECK)—Leave him alone. (*Moves quickly to stop* DAVID.) Leave him alone! *David! Leave him alone!*

DAVID (*angrily to* KURT)—Keep out of it. (*Starts toward* TECK *again.*) I'm beginning to see what Marthe meant. Blackmailing with your wife— You—

KURT (*very sharply*)—He is not speaking of his wife. Or you. He means me. (*Looks at* TECK.) Is that correct? (SARA *moves toward* KURT. DAVID *draws back, bewildered.*)

TECK—Good. It was necessary for me to hear you say it. You understand that?

KURT—I understand it.

SARA (*frightened, softly*)—Kurt—

DAVID—What is all this about? What the hell are you talking about?

TECK (*sharply for the first time*)—Be still. (*To* KURT.) At your convenience. Your hands are shaking, Herr Müller.

KURT (*quietly*)—My hands were broken: they are bad when I have fear.

TECK—I am sorry. I can understand that. It is not pleasant. (*Motions toward* FANNY *and* DAVID.) Perhaps you would like a little time to— I will go and pack, and be ready to leave. We will all find that more comfortable, I think. You should get yourself a smaller gun, Herr Müller. That pistol you have been carrying is big and awkward.

KURT—You saw the pistol when you examined our bags?
TECK—You knew that?
KURT—Oh, yes. I have the careful eye, through many years of needing it. And then you have not the careful eye. The pistol was lying to the left of a paper package and when you leave, it is to the right of the package.
SARA—Kurt! Do you mean that—
KURT (*sharply*)—Please, darling, do not do that.
TECK—It is a German Army Luger?
KURT—Yes.
TECK—Keep it in your pocket, Herr Müller. You will have no need to use it. And, in any case, I am not afraid of it. You understand that?
KURT (*slowly*)—I understand that you are not a man of fears. That is strange to me, because I am a man who has so many fears.
TECK (*laughs, as he exits*)—Are you? That is most interesting.

Teck has left them. Kurt is trying to explain to the others what has happened. He is convinced de Brancovis knows who he is and what he carries. The phone call was from Mexico and told him that the Nazis had caught Ebber and Triste and taken Max in Berlin—

"I am a German outlaw," Kurt is saying. "I work with many others in an illegal organization. I have so worked for seven years. I am on what is called a desired list. But I did not know I was worth ten thousand dollars. My price has risen."

"And what do you carry with you?"

"Twenty-three thousand dollars. It has been gathered from the pennies and the nickels of the poor who do not like Fascism, and who believe in the work we do. I came here to bring Sara home and to get the money. I had hopes to rest here for a while, and then—"

"And I had hopes someone else would take it back and you would stay with us—"

Kurt does not feel that it is unwise carrying the money with him. It should have been safe in Sara's home. "It was careless of you to have in your house a man who opens baggage and blackmails," he counters Fanny's charge of carelessness. Anyway it's been done. Now Teck would sell him his secret for ten thousand dollars—or sell him to the Embassy, probably to

Von Seitz. He does not believe that Teck has told Von Seitz anything yet. But—

"You're a political refugee," David is saying. "We don't turn back people like you. People who are in danger. You will give me your passport and tomorrow morning I'll see Barens. We'll tell him the truth— (*Points to the door.*) Tell de Brancovis to go to hell. There's not a damn thing he or anybody else can do."

SARA (*looking at* KURT, *who is staring at her*)—You don't understand, David.

DAVID—There's a great deal I don't understand. But there's nothing to worry about.

SARA—Not much to worry about as long as Kurt is in this house. But he's not going to—

KURT—The Count has made the guess that—

SARA—That you will go back to get Ebber and Triste and Max. Is that right, Kurt? Is that right?

KURT—Yes, darling, I will try. They were taken to Sonnenburg. Guards can be bribed— It has been done once before at Sonnenburg. We will try for it again. I must go back, Sara. I must start.

SARA—Of course, you must go back. I guess I was trying to think it wouldn't come. But—(*To* FANNY *and* DAVID.) Kurt's got to go back. He's got to go home. He's got to buy them out. He'll do it, too. You'll see. (*She stops, breathes.*) It's hard enough to get back. Very hard. But if they knew he was coming— They want Kurt bad. Almost as much as they wanted Max— And then there are hundreds of others, too— (*She gets up, comes to him. He holds her, puts his face in her hair. She stands holding him, trying to speak without crying. She puts her face down on his head.*) Don't be scared, darling. You'll get back. You'll see. You've done it before—you'll do it again. Don't be scared. You'll get Max out all right. (*Gasps.*) And then you'll do his work, won't you? That's good. That's fine. You'll do a good job, the way you've always done. (*She is crying very hard. To* FANNY.) Kurt doesn't feel well. He was wounded and he gets tired— (*To* KURT.) You don't feel well, do you? (*Slowly. She is crying too hard now to be heard clearly.*) Don't be scared, darling. You'll get home. Don't worry, you'll get home. Yes, you will.

The curtain falls.

ACT III

A half hour later the Farrellys and the Müllers are still in the living room. David is pacing nervously up and down the terrace. Kurt is idly picking out tunes on the piano. Fanny is sitting quietly in a chair and Sara, on the couch, is trying desperately to compose her nerves.

The conversation still concerns Kurt's plans. He will, of course, get to Germany if he can and there try to buy his friends out of jail. It has been done. The Fascists are neither so honorable nor so clever as they have craftily led the world to believe. "They are smart, they are sick, and they are cruel," Kurt admits. "But given men who know what they fight for—You saw it in Spain."

Oncc, Kurt remembers, he and Freidank, with two old pistols, had raided a home of a Gestapo chief, helped themselves to what they wanted, and were over the border before the chief knew what had happened.

The tension increases. It is de Brancovis they are waiting for, and waiting is hard. Probably Teck is keeping them waiting deliberately. Kurt is eager to get away. Yes, he admits to David, he could find an excuse not to go.

"Each could have his own excuse," he says. "Some love for the first time, some have bullet holes, some have fear of the camps, some are sick, many are getting older. Each could find a reason. And many find it. My children are not the only children in the world, even to me. . . ."

Teck has come downstairs. He carries Kurt's briefcase. It has not been touched, he tells Kurt. "I brought it from your room for your convenience."

Fanny wonders Teck did not steal the case and David is peevish about his explanations, which leads Teck to insist that if there are any further interruptions from these two the price of his silence will go up. He will do his business with Herr Müller and no one else.

To Kurt Teck explains his curiosity regarding the Müllers from the day of their arrival, and of his growing suspicions concerning Kurt himself. One day he was able to obtain from Von Seitz one of the "desired lists." There were sixty-three names on it, with accompanying descriptions.

Studying these de Brancovis finally was able to single out the name of Gotter, and to fit, to his own satisfaction, the name and the history of the Gotter exploits against the Nazis to Kurt. "'. . . Age 40 to 45. About six feet. One hundred seventy pounds. . . . Thought to have left Germany in 1933, and to have joined Max Freidank shortly after,'" Teck reads from the "desired list." "'Worked closely with Freidank, perhaps directly under his orders. Known to have crossed border in 1934—February, May, June, October. Known to have again crossed border with Max Freidank in 1935—August, twice in October, November, January—'"

"The report is unreliable," protests Kurt, quietly. "It would have been impossible for God to have crossed the border that often."

"'In 1934, outlaw radio station announcing itself as Radio European, begins to be heard,'" Teck continues. "'Station was located in Dusseldorf: the house of a restaurant waiter was searched, and nothing was found. Radio heard during most of 1934 and 1935. . . . Early in 1939, informer in Konstanz reported Gotter's entry, carrying money which had been exchanged in Paris and Brussels. Following day, home of Konstanz Gestapo chief raided for spy list by two men'"— (KURT *turns to look at* FANNY *and* DAVID, *smiles.*) "My God, Herr Müller, that job took two good men."

"Even you admire them," angrily says Sara.

"Even I. Now I conclude a week ago that you are Gotter, Karl Francis—"

Fanny and David would again interrupt, but Kurt quiets them. "Fanny and David are Americans and they do not understand our world—as yet," Kurt is saying. And to them he explains: "All Fascists are not of one mind, one stripe. There are those who give the orders, those who carry out the orders, those who watch the orders being carried out. Then there are those who are half in, half hoping to come in. They are made to do the dishes and clean the boots. Frequently they come in high places and wish now only to survive. They came late: some because they did not jump in time, some because they were stupid, some because they were shocked at the crudity of the *German* evil, and preferred their own evils, and some because they were fastidious men. For those last, we may well some day have pity. They are lost men, their spoils are small, their day is gone. (*To* TECK.) Yes?"

TECK (*slowly*)—Yes. You have the understanding heart. It will get in your way some day.

KURT (*smiling*)—I will watch it.

TECK—We are both men in trouble, Herr Müller. The world, ungratefully, seems to like your kind even less than it does mine. (*Leans forward.*) Now. Let us do business. You will not get back if Von Seitz knows you are going.

KURT—You are wrong. Instead of crawling a hundred feet an hour in deep night, I will walk across the border with as little trouble as if I were a boy again on a summer walking trip. There are many men they would like to have. I would be allowed to walk directly to them—until they had all the names and addresses. (*Laughs, points his finger at* TECK.) *Roumanians* would pick me up ahead of time. *Germans* would not.

TECK (*smiling*)—Still the national pride?

KURT—Why not? For that which is good.

FANNY (*coming over, very angrily, to* TECK)—I have not often in my life felt what I feel now. Whatever you are, and however you became it, the picture of a man selling the lives of other men—

TECK—Is very ugly, Madame Fanny. I do not do it without some shame, and therefore I must sink my shame in large money. (*Puts his hand on the briefcase.*) The money is here. For ten thousand, you go back to save your friends, nobody will know that you go, and I will give you my good wishes. (*Slowly, deliberately,* KURT *begins to shake his head.* TECK *waits, then carefully.*) What?

KURT—This money is going home with me. It was not given to me to save my life, and I shall not so use it. It is to save the lives and further the work of more than I. It is important to me to carry on that work and to save the lives of three valuable men, and to do that with all speed. But—(*Sharply.*) Count de Brancovis, the first morning we arrived in this house, my children wanted their breakfast with great haste. That is because the evening before we had been able only to buy milk and buns for them. If I would not touch this money for them, I would not touch it for you. (*Very sharply.*) It goes back with me. The way it is. And if it does not get back, it is because I will not get back. (*There is a long pause.* SARA *gets up, turns away.*)

TECK—Then I do not think you will get back. You are a brave one, Herr Müller, but you will not get back.

KURT (*as if he were very tired*)—I will send to you a postal card and tell you about my bravery.

DAVID (*coming toward* KURT)—Is it true that if this swine

talks, you and the others will be—

SARA (*very softly*)—Caught and killed. Of course. If they're lucky enough to get killed quickly. (*Quietly, points to the table.*) You should have seen those hands in 1935.

FANNY (*violently, to* DAVID)—We'll give him the money. For God's sake, let's give it to him and get him out of here.

DAVID (*to* SARA)—Do you want him to go back?

SARA—Yes. I do.

DAVID—All right. (*Goes to her, lifts her face.*) You're a good girl.

KURT—That is true. Brave and good, my Sara. She is everything. She is handsome and gay and— (*Puts his hand over his eyes.* SARA *turns away.*)

DAVID (*after a second, comes to stand near* TECK)—If we give you the money, what is to keep you from selling to Von Seitz?

TECK—I do not like your thinking I would do that. But—

DAVID (*tensely*)—Look here. I'm sick of what you'd like or wouldn't like. And I'm sick of your talk. We'll get this over with now, without any more fancy talk from you, or as far as I am concerned, you can get out of here without my money and sell to any buyer you can find. I can't take much more of you at any cost.

TECK (*smiling*)—It is your anger which delays us. I was about to say that I understood your fear that I would go to Von Seitz, and I would suggest that you give me a small amount of cash now and a check dated a month from now. In a month, Herr Müller should be nearing home, and he can let you know. And if you should not honor the check because Herr Müller is already in Germany, Von Seitz will pay a little something for a reliable description. I will take my chance on that. You will now say that I could do that in any case—and that is the chance you will take.

Kurt is not sure that he can get back to Germany in a month. David would bargain for two months, but Teck is firm. He will take $7,500 in a check, $2,500 in cash. Convinced there is not that much cash in the house he settles for $1,500 or $1,600 cash, the rest in a check. Fanny and David have gone to get the money.

With the "new world" out of the room, Teck awkwardly admits that he feels better. As Europeans, he, Kurt and Sara were born to trouble and expect it. "We are like peasants watching the big frost," ventures Teck. "Work, trouble, ruin— But no need to call curses at the frost. There it is, it will be again, always—for us."

"You mean my husband and I do not have angry words for you. What for? We know how many there are of you. They don't, yet. My mother and brother feel shocked that you are in their house. For us—we have seen you in so many houses."

"I do not say you *want* to understand me, Mrs. Müller. I say only that you do."

"Yes. You are not difficult to understand."

Kurt has moved over to the decanter table. He would pour Teck a drink. Whiskey? No. Sherry? Yes, Teck will take a little sherry. Now Kurt has poured the sherry, talking quietly as he does so of the things that have happened and are happening to the experiment with National Socialism.

"I do not think Von Seitz would pay you money for a description of a man who has a month to travel," Kurt is saying. "But I think he would pay you in a visa and a cable to Kessler. I think you want a visa almost as much as you want money. Therefore I conclude that you will try for the money here, and the visa from Von Seitz."

He has crossed the room now and is about to put the sherry on the table.

"I cannot get anywhere near Germany in a month and you know it." The tones of his voice are harsher. "I have been bored with this talk of paying you money. If they are willing to try you on this fantasy, I am not. Whatever made you think I would take such a chance? Or *any* chance! You're a gambler, but you should not gamble with your life!"

As Teck turns to stare at him, Kurt drops the glass of sherry and hits Teck a short, sharp blow in the face. Before de Brancovis can struggle to his feet Kurt is on him, hitting him on the side of the head. At the fourth blow Kurt ceases to struggle.

The boy Joshua has come into the room and stands quietly, "as if he were waiting for orders." Kurt has picked Teck up and balanced the body across his shoulder. In German he asks Joshua to open the doors. Now Kurt and his burden have disappeared.

"There's trouble," says Sara, quietly.

"Do not worry. I will go up now," Joshua answers, as quietly. "I will pack. In ten minutes all will be ready. I will say nothing. I will get the children ready— (*He starts quickly for the hall, turns for a second to look toward the terrace doors. Then almost with a sob.*) This was a nice house."

"We're not going this time, darling. There's no need to pack."

"But, Papa—"

"Go upstairs, Joshua. Take Babbie and Bodo in your room, and close the door. Stay there until I call you. There's nothing to be frightened of, darling. Papa is all right. (*Then very softly.*) Papa is going home."

Fanny has returned with the money and is counting it out on the table. David brings the check. They are surprised at the disappearance of de Brancovis and Kurt, who, Sara explains, have gone outside. Sara goes to the telephone. She makes a reservation on a plane for Brownsville. The name is Ritter. The ticket will be picked up at the airport. For this action Fanny and David demand further explanation.

"For seven years now, day in, day out, men have crossed the German border," says Sara, solemnly. "They are always in danger. They always may be going in to die. Did you ever see the face of a man who never knows if this day will be the last day? (*Softly.*) Don't go out on the terrace, David. Leave Kurt alone."

FANNY—Sara! What is—

SARA (*quietly*)—For them, it may be torture, and it may be death. Some day when it's all over, maybe there'll be a few of them left to celebrate. There aren't many of Kurt's age left. He couldn't take a chance on them. They wouldn't have liked it. (*Suddenly, violently.*) He'd have had a bad time trying to explain to them that because of this house and this nice town and my mother and my brother, he took chances with their work and with their lives. (*Quietly.*) Sit down, Mama. I think it's all over now. (*To* DAVID.) There's nothing you can do about it. It's the way it had to be.

DAVID—Sara—

FANNY—Do you mean what I think you— (*Sinks slowly into her chair.*)

SARA—He's going away tonight and he's never coming back any more. (*In a sing-song.*) Never, never, never. (*She looks down at her hands, as if she were very interested in them.*) I don't like to be alone at night. I guess everybody in the world's got a time in the day they don't like. Me, it's right before I go to sleep. And now it's going to be for always. All the rest of my life. (*She looks up as* KURT *comes in from the terrace.*) I've told them. There is an eight-thirty plane going as far south as Brownsville. I've made you a reservation. In the name of Ritter.

KURT (*looking at her*)—Liebe Sara! (*Then he goes to the table at which* FANNY *is sitting. To* FANNY.) It is hard for you, eh? (*He pats her hand.*) I am sorry.

FANNY—Hard? I don't know. I—I don't—I don't know what I want to say.

KURT—Before I come in, I stand and think. I say, I will make Fanny and David understand. I say, how can I? Does one understand a killing? No. To hell with it, I say. I do what must be done. I have long sickened of words when I see the men who live by them. What do you wish to make them understand, I ask myself. Wait. Stand here. Just stand here. What are you thinking? Say it to them just as it comes to you. And this is what came to me. When you kill in a war, it is not so lonely; and I remember a cousin I have not seen for many years; and a melody comes back and I begin to make it with my fingers; a staircase in a house in Bonn years ago; an old dog who used to live in our town; Sara in a hundred places—Shame on us. Thousands of years and we cannot yet make a world. Like a child I am. I have stopped a man's life. (*Points to the place on the couch where he had been sitting opposite* TECK.) I sit here. I listen to him. You will not believe—but I pray that I will not have to touch him. Then I know I will have to. I know that if I do not, it is only that I pamper myself, and risk the lives of others. I want you from the room. I know what I must do. (*Loudly.*) All right. Do I now pretend sorrow? Do I now pretend it is not I who act thus? No. I do it. I have done it. I will do it again. And I will keep my hope that we may make a world in which all men can die in bed. I have a great hate for the violent. They are the sick of the world. (*Softly.*) Maybe I am sick now, too.

SARA—You aren't sick. Stop that. It's late. You must go soon.

KURT (*looking up at her*)—Maybe all that I have ever wanted is a land that would let me have you. (*Then, without looking away from her, he puts out his hands, she touches them.*) I am going to say good-by now to my children. Then I am going to take your car— (*Motions with his head.*) I will take him with me. After that, it's up to you. Two ways: You can let me go and keep silent. I believe I can hide him and the car. At the end of two days, if they have not been found, you will tell as much of the truth as is safe for you to say. Tell them the last time you saw us we were on the way to Washington. You did not worry at the absence, we might have rested there. Two crazy foreigners fight, one gets killed, you know nothing of the reason. I will have left the gun, there will be no doubt who did the killing. If you will give me those two days, I think I will be far enough away from here. If the car is found before then— (*Shrugs.*) I will still try to move with speed. And all that will make you, for yourselves, part of a murder. For the world, I do not think you will be in bad trouble. (*He pauses.*) There is another way. You can call your police. You can tell them the truth. I will not get home. (*To* SARA.) I wish to see the children now. (*She goes into the hall and up the stairs. There is silence.*)

FANNY—What are you thinking, David?

DAVID—I don't know. What are you thinking?

FANNY—Me? Oh, I was thinking about my Joshua. I was thinking that a few months before he died, we were sitting out there. (*Points to terrace.*) He said, "Fanny, the Renaissance American is dying, the Renaissance man is dying." I said what do you mean, although I knew what he meant, I always knew. "A Renaissance man," he said, "is a man who wants to know. He wants to know how fast a bird will fly, how thick is the crust of the earth, what made Iago evil, how to plow a field. He knows there is no dignity to a mountain, if there is no dignity to man. You can't put that in a man, but when it's *really* there, and he will fight for it, put your trust in him."

DAVID (*gets up, smiles, looks at* FANNY)—You're a smart woman sometimes. (SARA *enters with* JOSHUA. *To* KURT.) Don't worry about things here. My soul doesn't have to be so nice and clean. I'll take care of it. You'll have your two days. And good luck to you.

FANNY—You go with my blessing, too. I like you.

Kurt would not be able to cash a check, so Fanny insists that he take the cash. She, too, would like to contribute something to his work. . . .

The children have come. Babette and Bodo are in Kurt's arms. Joshua stands bravely at the side of his father's chair. "We have said many good-bys to each other, eh? We must now say another."

He is smiling at them, "slowly, as if it were difficult." This time, Kurt says, he is leaving them with good people to whom he believes they also will be good. To Joshua's gentle protest that he is talking to them as though they were children, he answers that he wishes they were children, and that he had not taken their childhood from them.

"We have had a most enjoyable life, Papa," insists Babette.

"You are a gallant little liar. And I thank you for it," her father answers.

He has, Kurt would tell them, done something bad this day. Fanny would stop him there and the children protest loyally. "You could not do a bad thing," says Bodo, stanchly. But Kurt shakes his head—

"Now let us get straight together," he says. "The four of us. Do you remember when we read about 'Les Miserables'? Do you remember that we talked about it afterwards and Bodo got candy on Mama's bed?"

BODO—I remember.

KURT—Well. He stole bread. The world is out of shape we said, when there are hungry men. And until it gets in shape, men will steal and lie and—(*A little more slowly.*)—kill. But for whatever reason it is done, and whoever does it—you understand me—it is all bad. I want you to remember that. Whoever does it is bad. (*Then very gaily.*) But you will live to see the day when it will not have to be. All over the world, in every place and every town, there are men who are going to make sure it will not have to be. They want what I want: a childhood for every child. For my children, and I for theirs. (*He picks* BODO *up, rises.*) Think of that. It will make you happy. In every town and every village and every mud hut in the world, there is always a man who loves children and who will fight to make a good world for them. And now good-by. Wait for me. I shall try to come back for you. (*He moves toward the hall, followed by* BABETTE, *and more slowly, by* JOSHUA.) Or you shall come to me. At Hamburg, the boat will come in. It will be a fine, safe land—I will be waiting on the dock. And there will be the three of you and Mama and Fanny and David. And I will have ordered an extra big dinner and we will show them what our Germany can be like— (*He has put* BODO *down. He leans down, presses his face in* BABETTE'S *hair. Tenderly, as her mother has done earlier, she touches his hair.*)

JOSHUA—Of course. That is the way it will be. Of course. But—but if you should find yourself delayed— (*Very slowly.*) Then I will come to you. Mama.

SARA (*turning away*)—I heard you, Joshua.

KURT (*kissing* BABETTE)—Gute Nacht, Liebling!

BABETTE—Gute Nacht, Papa. Mach's gut!

KURT (*leaning to kiss* BODO)—Good night, baby.

BODO—Good night, Papa. Mach's gut! (BABETTE *runs up the steps. Slowly* BODO *follows her.*)

KURT (*kissing* JOSHUA)—Good night, son.

JOSHUA—Good night, Papa. Mach's gut! (*He begins to climb the steps.* KURT *stands watching them, smiling. When they disappear, he turns to* DAVID.)

KURT—Good-by, and thank you.

DAVID—Good-by, and good luck.

KURT (*to* FANNY)—Good-by. I have good children, eh?

FANNY—Yes, you have. (KURT *kisses her hand.*)

KURT (*slowly turning toward* SARA)—Men who wish to live have the best chance to live. I wish to live. I wish to live with you.

SARA—For twenty years. It is as much for me today—(*Takes his arms.*) Just once, and for all my life. (*He pulls her toward him.*) Come back for me, darling. If you can. (*Takes brief-case from table and gives it to him.*)

KURT (*simply*)—I will try. (*He turns.*) Good-by, to you all. (*He exits. After a second, there is the sound of a car starting. They sit listening to it. Gradually the noise begins to go off into the distance. A second later,* JOSHUA *appears.*)

JOSHUA—Mama— (*She looks up. He is very tense.*) Bodo cries. Babette looks very queer. I think you should come.

SARA (*getting up, slowly*)—I'm coming.

JOSHUA (*to* FANNY *and* DAVID. *Still very tense*)—Bodo talks so fancy, we forget sometimes he is a baby. (*He waits for* SARA *to come up to him. When she reaches him, she takes his hand, goes up the steps, disappears.* FANNY *and* DAVID *watch them.*)

FANNY (*after a minute*)—Well, here we are. We're shaken out of the magnolias, eh?

DAVID—Yes. So we are.

FANNY—Tomorrow will be a hard day. But we'll have Babbie's birthday dinner. And we'll have music afterwards. You can be the audience. I think you'd better go up to Marthe now. Be as careful as you can. She'd better stay here for a while. I daresay I can stand it.

DAVID (*turns, smiles*)—Even your graciousness is ungracious, Mama.

FANNY—I do my best. Well, I think I shall go and talk to

Anise. I like Anise best when I don't feel well. (*She begins to move off.*)

DAVID—Mama. (*She turns.*) We are going to be in for trouble. You understand that?

FANNY—I understand it very well. We will manage. You and I. I'm not put together with flour paste. And neither are you—I am happy to learn.

DAVID—Good night, Mama.

As Fanny moves out,

THE CURTAIN FALLS

THE CORN IS GREEN

A Drama in Three Acts

By Emlyn Williams

THE Broadway stage was perfectly set psychologically for the arrival of Emlyn Williams' "The Corn Is Green." The play was imported in late November, and not a single drama of major importance had preceded it. The season had not only been backward, but downright depressing. The reviewers were ready and eager to start dancing in the aisles, and did.

This play had been a London success the year before and was still running successfully when war clouds began to roll up the Thames. When the bargaining for an American production began there were several bidders in the market, but because Mr. Williams demanded a stiffish advance, none of them was ready at first to take the risk. Finally Herman Shumlin stepped forward and a deal was made.

Happily, Ethel Barrymore was looking for a play about the same time. She, too, had been long without a modern rôle that combined sympathy and intelligence in proper measure to satisfy both a star and her audiences. Here again the conditions were most favorable for the discovery of a hit.

"The Corn Is Green" is said to embody in its story considerable auto-biographical data. Mr. Williams, also, was a Welsh worker in his youth, and it was through the kindly and sympathetic interest of one of his early teachers that he was enabled to secure an education. In England his career as a successful dramatist has extended over several years. He was previously known briefly in America as the author and chief actor of a horror melodrama called "Night Must Fall" which earned for him a *succès d'estime* but not much in the way of royalties.

Mr. Williams tells a story of teacher and pupil in "The Corn Is Green" with great simplicity and great dignity. It is not dramatically an exciting story, and yet there is a fine emotional response stirred by the definitely human reactions of its people. He has artfully avoided such situations as might have proved romantically effective, but must also have had a cheapening effect upon the drama as a whole.

The opening scene of the play reveals the living room of a

cottage in Glensarno, Wales. The time is a sunny afternoon in June in the latter part of the last century. It is a pleasant, somewhat cluttered room. Through a front door a small stone porch, faintly overgrown with ivy, may be seen. The floor is of stone flags, with a rug in front of the sofa. The wall paper is faded. The furniture is "a curious jumble of old Welsh and Victorian pieces" and includes "a large, serviceable flat-topped desk under a side window with a desk chair in front of it." . . . "The most distinctive feature of the room is the amount of books on the walls, of all sorts and sizes; some in open bookcases, others on newly built shelves, on practically every available space."

As we enter the room Mr. John Goronwy Jones and Miss Ronberry are taking the last books from a large packing case and arranging them on shelves. "She is a gentlewoman in her thirties, with the sort of pinched prettiness that tends to look sharp before that age, especially when it makes sporadic attempts at coquetry; she wears a hat. He is a shabby Welshman of forty, bespectacled, gloomy and intense; a volcano harmless even in full eruption."

Mr. Jones is also singing, and in Welsh, which is not only disturbing to Miss Ronberry, but is giving her, she says, an agonizing headache. Mr. Jones is singing a hymn about the fires of hell to cheer himself up, and would continue, despite Miss Ronberry, but for other interruptions. Idwal, a boy who has been working in the garden, and Sarah, the housemaid, pop in to report progress.

Mr. Jones is inclined to take things calmly, but Miss Ronberry is considerably fussed. This is a wild and barren part of Wales to Miss Ronberry, with the people mostly barbarians and not a caller for fifteen miles. "I can't think why a Colonel should elect to come and live in this place," she sighs, as she finds a place for the last of the books. "I do hope the curtains will not be too feminine. I chose them with such care. I am frightened of the spinning wheel, too, and the china; his own furniture is so distinctive. The desk. And the waste paper basket . . . So . . . so virile!"

"Are you hoping the Colonel will live up to his waste paper basket?" twits Mr. Jones.

"That is horrid," answers Miss Ronberry, with a toss of her head.

"And then you will have two on a string: him and the Squire—"

A knock on the door and the entrance of a liveried groom announces the arrival of the Squire, who follows close upon the announcement. "The Squire is a handsome English country gentleman in his forties, wearing knickerbockers and gaiters; a hard drinker, bluff, kind, immensely vain; and, when the time comes, obtusely obstinate."

The Squire is in hearty good humor, informally friendly with Jones and of a mind to tease Miss Ronberry about her hesitant spinsterhood and her blossoming chances of being the county's next stunning, blushing bride. Also he is interested in the new tenant, a funny sort of chap, evidently, considering all the books he's sent ahead.

Idwal, the boy from the garden, is in again. His report is to Mr. Jones and in Welsh. The Squire doesn't understand Welsh, for all he has spent half his life in the neighborhood. Idwal, Mr. Jones translates, has been told that the Squire wants to see him. And so the Squire does. Wants to know why Idwal, having turned thirteen, is not at work in the mines. Mr. Jones explains that Idwal "has one lung funny." The Squire is touched. He straightway gives Idwal sixpence.

Now the approach of the expected tenants is reported, and that is exciting. Shortly Bessie Watty and her mother have appeared at the door. Bessie "is an extremely pretty, plump little girl of fourteen; it is a moment before one realizes that her demureness is too good to be true. She wears her hair over her shoulders, is dressed very plainly, in a shabby sailor suit and hat, and carries brown paper parcels." Mrs. Watty is "a middle-aged Cockney servant, dressed for traveling, carrying a hamper in her arms. Her self-confidence is not so overwhelming as the Squire's, but it is quite as complete, and as kindly."

The Wattys have barely had time to take a quick look around before they are followed by Miss Moffat, who comes through the door wheeling a bicycle. "She is about forty, a healthy Englishwoman with an honest face, clear, beautiful eyes, a humorous mouth, a direct friendly manner, and unbounded vitality. . . . Her most prominent characteristic is her complete unsentimentality. She wears a straw hat, collar and tie, and a dark unexaggerated skirt; a satchel hangs from her shoulder."

Miss Moffat greets those in the room with a friendly "Good afternoon," turns her bicycle over to Watty, announces that she thinks she will have a look at the garden first and is gone. She is back in a moment to face a puzzled Squire and a completely flabbergasted Miss Ronberry. Because Miss Moffat had signed her letters with her initials only and had written on unscented stationery in a bold hand, they were expecting a man. The "M.A." after the "L. C. Moffat" was not a military title, it appears, but a college degree. A female M.A. is something of a shock to the Squire. His thorough disappointment in the discovery of Miss Moffat is quite apparent as he takes himself off. She finds her first introduction to the landed gentry, however, most interesting.

Miss Moffat has gone now to continue her inspection of the house, leaving Miss Ronberry and Mr. Jones still a little stunned. Nor is Mrs. Watty able to help them greatly in their understanding of the new tenant—

"Ain't she a clinker?" hoarsely whispers Mrs. Watty.

"She is unusual, is she not?" ventures Miss Ronberry.

"She's a clinker, that's what. Terrible strong-willed, o' course. Terrible. Get 'er into mischief, I keep tellin' 'er. Would bring me 'ere. I said no, I said, not with my past, I said."

"Your past?"

"Before she took me up. But what with 'er, and now I've joined the Corpse, it's all blotted out."

"The Corpse?"

"The Militant Righteous Corpse. Ran into 'em in the street, I did, singin' and prayin' and collectin', full blast; and I been a different woman since. Are *you* saved?"

"Yes, I am." Mr. Jones is positive in his declaration.

"So'm I, ain't it lovely?"

"But what was your past?" Miss Ronberry would know.

"Light fingers."

"Light fingers? You mean—stealing?"

"Everywhere I went. Terrible. Pennies, stockin's, brooches, spoons, tiddly, anything. Every time there was a do, everything went; and I always knew it was me!"

Miss Moffat's return from upstairs puts an end to the Watty confession, and sends the confessor to the kitchen. And now Miss Moffat would like to learn a little more about the situation she has moved into. She likes the house and the taste of the people who had lived there before her. And she already knows a good bit about Miss Ronberry and Mr. Jones—

"I used to meet friends of yours at lectures in London," she is saying to Miss Ronberry. "You live alone, you have just enough money, you're not badly educated, and time lies heavy on your hands."

Miss Ronberry—The Wingroves! How mean—I should never have thought—

Miss Moffat—Isn't that so?

Miss Ronberry—Not at all. When the right gentleman appears—

Miss Moffat—If you're a spinster well on in her thirties, he's lost his way and isn't coming. Why don't you face the fact and enjoy yourself, the same as I do?

Miss Ronberry—But when did you give up hope—oh, what a horrid expression—

Miss Moffat—I can't recall ever having any hope. Visitors used to take a long look at my figure and say: "She's going to be the clever one."

Miss Ronberry—But a woman's only future is to marry and—and fulfill the duties of—

Miss Moffat—Skittles! I'd have made a shocking wife, anyway.

Miss Ronberry—But haven't you ever—been in love?

Miss Moffat—No.

Miss Ronberry—How very odd.

Miss Moffat—I've never talked to a man for more than five minutes without wanting to box his ears.

Miss Ronberry—But how have you passed your time since—

Miss Moffat—Since I had no hope? Very busily. In the East End, for years.

Miss Ronberry—Social service?

Miss Moffat—If you like; though there's nothing very social about washing invalids with every unmentionable ailment under the sun. . . . I've read a lot, too. I'm afraid I'm what is known as an educated woman. Which brings me to Mr. Jones; the Wingroves told me all about you, too.

Mr. Jones—My conscience is as clear as the snow.

Miss Moffat—I'm sure it is, but you're a disappointed man, aren't you?

Mr. Jones—How can I be disappointed when I am saved?

Miss Moffat—Oh, but you can! You can't really enjoy sitting all by yourself on a raft, on a sea containing everybody you know. You're disappointed because you're between two stools.

Mr. Jones—Between two stools? On a raft?

Miss Moffat—Exactly. Your father was a grocer with just

'hoto by Vandamm Studio.

"THE CORN IS GREEN"

"Ready?"

Miss Moffat has placed the examination papers in front of him. She smiles as she skims the uplicate paper which she holds.

"Henry the Eighth," she mutters. . . .

(*Richard Waring, Ethel Barrymore*)

enough money to send you to grammar school, with the result that you are educated beyond your sphere, and yet fail to qualify for the upper classes. You feel frustrated, and fall back on being saved. Am I right?

MR. JONES—It is such a terrible thing you have said that I will have to think it over.

Miss Moffat has no objection to Mr. Jones' thinking it over, but meantime she would like to know more about the countryside. How many families of just ordinary people are there? About twenty in the village and fifteen on farms around, Mr. Jones thinks. And how many children, say up to sixteen or seventeen? After they're twelve, Mr. Jones explains, they're not children. "Then they are sent away over the hill to the mine, and one a week they are old men."

"I see. How many can read or write?"

"Next to none. Why do you ask?"

"Because I'm going to start a school for them," announces Miss Moffat. ". . . See these books? Hundreds of 'em, and something wonderful to read in every single one— These nippers are to be cut off from all that, forever, are they? Why? Because they happen to be born penniless in an uncivilized countryside, coining gold down there in that stinking dungeon for some beef-headed old miser!"

"That's right."

"The printed page, what is it? One of the miracles of all time, that's what! And yet when these poor babbies set eyes on it, they might just as well have been struck by the miracle of sudden blindness; and that, to my mind, is plain infamous!"

It is a little hard for Miss Ronberry to understand that Miss Moffat means "ordinary" children, but Miss Moffat does. She is going to start a school for them, next door in the barn, and Mr. Jones and Miss Ronberry are going to help her. She will pay Mr. Jones a shilling more a week than he is making as a solicitor's clerk. She will make it worth Miss Ronberry's time to shut up her house—except one room.

"I've been left a little money and I know exactly what I am going to do with it," announces Miss Moffat, with a note of exultation in her voice.

"But those children are in the mine—earning money—how can they—" Mr. Jones is worried.

"I'll pay their parents the few miserable pennies they get out of it," answers Miss Moffat. "And when I've finished with you (*to* Miss Ronberry) *you* won't have time to think of snapping up a husband, and *you* (*to* Mr. Jones) won't have time to be so pleased that you're saved. Well?"

Mr. Jones—I do not care if you are not chapel, I am with you.

Miss Moffat—Good! I have all the details worked out—I'll explain roughly. . . . Come along—(*Pulls* Ronberry—*flourished papers.* Jones *sits next to her on couch.*) my dears, gather round, children—gather round— Of course we must go slowly at first, but if we put our backs into it . . . Here we are, three stolid middle-aged folk, settled in our little groove and crammed with benefits; and *there* are those babbies scarcely out of the shell, that have no idea they are even breathing the air . . . Only God can know how their life will end, but He will give us the chance to direct them a little of the way—

Mr. Jones—We have the blessed opportunity to raise up the children from the bowels of the earth where the devil hath imprisoned them in the powers of darkness, and bring them to the light of knowledge—

Mrs. Watty (*coming in from kitchen*)—Here's the tea!

Miss Moffat—Each of us can take several classes, not only for the children, but their fathers and their mothers, and the older people too.

The curtain is down for a moment. At its rise six weeks have elapsed. It is a night in August. The window curtains are drawn and the lamps are lighted. The room has undergone some slight changes in decoration, and appears to have been used generously. Two small benches are conspicuous. The desk and much of the furniture is littered with books, exercise papers, etc.

On one of the benches five black-faced miners are seated. They are wearing caps and mufflers, their corduroy pants are grimy. They are humming quietly in harmony. The ringleader among them is Morgan Evans, "fifteen, quick and impudent." The others are a year or two older.

Miss Ronberry had told them to wait, Morgan explains, when Mrs. Watty discovers them. Presently Miss Moffat appears. She is not quite ready to see them. Meantime she wishes they would go to the pump in the yard and wash their hands.

"Please, miss, can I have a kiss?" smirks Morgan.

"What did you say?" Miss Moffat demands.

"Please, miss, can I have a kiss?"

"Of course you can," answers Miss Moffat, putting her foot on the bench, grabbing Morgan by the neck, turning him over her knee and smacking him soundly with a roll of blueprints that she carries. "Can I oblige anybody else?"

The boys are grinning and jabbering as Miss Moffat goes into the yard. Morgan is not inclined to take the situation too good-naturedly as the grinning miners lumber awkwardly into the yard.

Mr. Jones peeks in to find the way clear and with a sigh goes about his work. Young Bessie Watty wanders in with some intention of being sociable, but receives little encouragement. Miss Ronberry also has assumed her appointed tasks when Miss Moffat returns.

Negotiations for the lease of the barn for school purposes is not going too well, and the papers she has been examining are discouraging. Altogether Miss Moffat is not very happy.

"It's been a bit of a day," she admits, when Miss Ronberry notes that she looks tired. "A letter from the mine to say no child can be released above ground—that's all blethers, but still . . . A request from the public house not to start a school in case it interferes with beer-swilling and games of chance. A message from the chapel people to the effect that I am a foreign adventuress with cloven feet; a bit of a day."

Nor is the situation cleared when the Squire calls. The Squire has been dining with Sir Herbert Vezey, who owns the barn, and brings definite word that Sir Herbert has decided against its being used as a school.

"He implied in his first letter that he would be willing to sell," Miss Moffat recalls.

"Then some big wig must have made him change his mind, mustn't he?" The Squire grins.

MISS MOFFAT—You?

THE SQUIRE—I have not called on you, madam, because I have been eyeing your activities very closely from afar—it is with dis—disapproval and—er—dis—

MISS MOFFAT—It is unwise to embark on a speech with the vocabulary of a child of five.

THE SQUIRE—I am not going to have any of this damned hanky-panky in my village!

MISS MOFFAT—*Your* village!

THE SQUIRE—*My* village! I am no braggart, but I'd have you know that everything you can see from that window—and you haven't got a bad view—*I own!* Now, my dear madam—

MISS MOFFAT—And stop calling me your dear madam. I'm not married, I'm not French, and you haven't the slightest affection for me!

THE SQUIRE—Oh . . . First of all, I'm not one to hit a woman below the belt. If you know what I mean. Always be fair—to the fair sex. . . . All my life I've done my level best for the villagers—they call me Squire, y'know, term of affection, jolly touching—I mean, a hamper every Christmas, the whole shoot, and a whopping tankard of beer on my birthday, and on my twenty-firster they all got a mug—

MISS MOFFAT—Go on.

THE SQUIRE—They jabber away in that funny lingo, but bless their hearts, it's a free country! But puttin' 'em up to read English, and pot-hooks, and givin' 'em ideas—if there were more people like you, y'know, England'd be a jolly dangerous place to live in! What d'ye want to do, turn 'em into gentlemen? What's the idea?

MISS MOFFAT—I am beginning to wonder myself.

THE SQUIRE—Anyway, this buying 'em out of the mine is a lot of gammon. I own a half-share in it.

MISS MOFFAT—That explains a good deal.

THE SQUIRE—Why don't you take up croquet? Keep yourself out of mischief. (*To* MISS RONBERRY, *who comes out of the bedroom.*) Well, my dear lady, anything I can do to make your stay here a happier one—

MISS MOFFAT—Thank you.

THE SQUIRE—I must be getting back. If I know Sir Herbert—my best old port will be no more—

MISS MOFFAT—Wait a minute.

THE SQUIRE—Yes?

MISS MOFFAT (*rising*)—I know I shall be sticking a pin into a whale, but here are just two words about yourself. You are the Squire Bountiful, are you? Adored by his contented subjects, intelligent and benignly understanding, are you? I should just like to point out that there is a considerable amount of dirt, ignorance, misery and discontent abroad in this world, and that a good deal of it is due to people like you, because you are a stupid, conceited, greedy, good-for-nothing—addle-headed nincompoop, and you can go to blue blazes. Good night!

The Squire is flustered. He thinks Miss Moffat must have been drinking. Miss Ronberry is also perturbed as the Squire abruptly leaves them. What is Miss Moffat going to do? Miss

Moffat is going to sell the house and take this dream child of a ridiculous spinster and smother it. Let Miss Ronberry inform the trades people and the mine that they are giving up the school.

But first they will have to start straightening things up. There are, for one thing, a lot of grimy exercise books among Miss Moffat's papers. Where did they come from? They were brought, Miss Ronberry explains, by the miners who were there a moment ago. They are in answer to Miss Moffat's request that they write an essay on "How I would spend my vacation."

Miss Moffat is skimming through the first of them, discarding them as she goes. "If—I has ever holiday—I has breakfast and talks then dinner and a rest, tea then nothing—then supper then I talk and I go sleep." Miss Moffat reads so much laboriously. "From exhaustion, I suppose," she comments as she adds the book to the others.

Now she has found one that arrests her attention. "The mine is dark. . . . If a light come in the mine . . . the rivers in the mine will run fast with the voice of many women; the walls will fall in, and it will be the end of the world—"

Morgan and one of the other boys have come in from the garden as she is reading. They stand, listening awkwardly—

". . . So the mine is dark . . . But when I walk through the Tan—something—shaft, in the dark, I can touch with my hands the leaves on the trees, and underneath . . . where the corn is green."

"Go on readin'," says Morgan, as Miss Moffat pauses.

". . . There is a wind in the shaft, not carbon monoxide they talk about, it smell like the sea, only like as if the sea had fresh flowers lying about . . . and that is my holiday."

She glances at the name on the book, and then at Morgan as he starts for the door. "Are you Morgan Evans?" she asks.

"Yes, Miss."

Miss Moffat—Did you write this?

Morgan—No, Miss.

Miss Moffat—But it's in your book.

Morgan—Yes, Miss.

Miss Moffat—Then who wrote it?

Morgan—I dunno, Miss. (Miss Moffat *nods to* Miss Ronberry, *who patters discreetly into the study.*)

Miss Moffat—Did you write this?

Morgan—I dunno, Miss. . . . What iss the matter with it?

Miss Moffat—Sit down. And take your cap off. Spelling's

deplorable, of course. "Mine" with two "n's" and "leaves" l, e, s.

MORGAN—What wass it by rights?

MISS MOFFAT—A "v" to start with.

MORGAN—I never 'eard o' no "v's," Miss.

MISS MOFFAT—Don't call me Miss.

MORGAN—Are you not a Miss?

MISS MOFFAT—Yes, I am, but it is not polite.

MORGAN—Oh.

MISS MOFFAT—You say "Yes, Miss Moffat," or "No, Miss Moffat." M, o, double f, a, t.

MORGAN—No "v's"?

MISS MOFFAT—No "v's." Where do you live?

MORGAN—Under the ground, Miss.

MISS MOFFAT—I mean your home.

MORGAN—Llyn-y-mwyn, Miss—Moffat. Four miles from 'ere.

MISS MOFFAT—How big is it?

MORGAN—Four 'ouses and a beer-'ouse.

MISS MOFFAT—Have you any hobbies?

MORGAN—Oh, yes.

MISS MOFFAT—What?

MORGAN—Rum. (*Takes small bottle of rum out of pocket.*)

MISS MOFFAT—Rum? Do you live with your parents?

MORGAN—No, by my own self. My mother iss dead, and my father and my four big brothers wass in the Big Shaft Accident when I wass ten.

MISS MOFFAT—Killed?

MORGAN—Oh, yes, everybody wass.

MISS MOFFAT—What sort of man was your father?

MORGAN—'E was a mongrel.

MISS MOFFAT—A what?

MORGAN—'E 'ad a dash of English. 'E learned it to me.

MISS MOFFAT—D'you go to Chapel?

MORGAN—No, thank you.

MISS MOFFAT—Who taught you to read and write?

MORGAN—Tott?

MISS MOFFAT—Taught. The verb "to teach."

MORGAN—Oh, teached.

MISS MOFFAT—Who taught you?

MORGAN—I did.

MISS MOFFAT—Why?

MORGAN—I dunno.

MISS MOFFAT—What books have you read?

MORGAN—Books? A bit of the Bible and a book that a feller from the Plas kitchen nab for me.

MISS MOFFAT—What was it?

MORGAN—*The Ladies' Companion!* Can I go now, pliss—

MISS MOFFAT—No. Do you want to learn any more?

MORGAN—No, thank you.

MISS MOFFAT—Why not?

MORGAN—The other men would have a good laugh.

Morgan has never written anything before, he admits. No one has ever asked him to. He is pleased and a little suspicious of her praise of what he has written. "It makes me that I—I want to get more clever still," he admits. "I want to know what iss—behind of all them books . . ."

No, he can't come tomorrow. He'll be working. Tomorrow night? He might—but not before seven. There's a six-mile walk. At seven then.

"Are you the one I spanked?" asks Miss Moffat.

Morgan turns at the door, grins, and is gone. Miss Moffat calls a little excitedly for Miss Ronberry and Mr. Jones. They come running—

"I have been a deuce of a fool," Miss Moffat announces joyfully. "It doesn't matter about the barn; we are going to start the school— . . . in a small way at first, in this room. . . . And I am going to get those youngsters out of that mine if I have to black my face and go down and fetch them myself! Get Jonesy before he posts those letters, and tell those others I'll be ready for them in five minutes. We are going on with the school!"

Miss Ronberry has scampered into the study, her voice trailing after her as she echoes—"We are going on with the school!" Miss Moffat has gone back to the Morgan essay—

". . . and when I walk—in the dark . . . I can touch with my hands . . . where the corn is green . . ."

Outside the school bell is ringing. The curtain falls.

ACT II

It is an early evening in August, two years later. "The room is now a cheerful jumble of schoolroom and living room, and there is every sign of cheerful overcrowding." Every place there is room to squeeze one in, there is a school desk. Two or three in a row. One or two sitting out individually. "Charts, maps, an alphabet list are pinned up higgledy-piggledy over all the books;

a large world globe on the shelf; hat pegs have been fixed irregularly back of the doors."

The children are gathered at their desks. Back of them are several older people, mostly parents. Miss Ronberry, perched on a tiny stool, is conducting the group, which is singing the Welsh air, "Bugeilio'r Gwenyth Gwyn;" the children, "shrill, sweet and self-confident, reinforced by harmony from older boys and parents."

At one desk Mr. Jones is correcting exercise papers. Bessie Watty is there, "silent, bored and prettier than ever, though still dressed as a sober little schoolgirl." The miner boys are "clean and almost spruce." The song is sung through to the end. There is a good deal of chattering after that. Some of the pupils, slates and pencils poised, would have more lessons, but Miss Ronberry feels that they should keep to the curriculum, even if she isn't sure how to spell it.

They do a little additional work on the multiplication table and then school is dismissed. Again there is a good deal of chattering, mostly in Welsh now. Slowly the crowd trickles out. Now only Old Tom, "an elderly and distinguished looking peasant," is left. Old Tom (it was he who wanted to know how to spell "curriculum") has another question for Miss Ronberry:

"Where iss Shakespeare?" he demands.

"Where? . . . Shakespeare, Mr. Tom, was a very great writer."

"Writer? Like the Beibl?"

"Like the Bible."

"Dear me—and me thinkin' the man was a place." Tom is still muttering as he starts for the door. "If I iss born fifty years later, I iss been top of the class."

Miss Moffat has not appeared. For an hour she has been out under the pear tree "doing grammar with Form 2" and that should have been enough to have prostrated her, thinks Miss Ronberry. But now Miss Moffat appears. She is looking for a Greek book. "Morgan Evans is starting Greek this month," she reports.

That news is a little startling to Miss Ronberry. The decision has even been a little startling to Miss Moffat. She doesn't know much Greek herself. She will just have to keep a step ahead of Morgan. Bessie Watty also has her opinion of this "stuck-up teacher's pet" who is going ahead so fast. He may be clever, as Miss Moffat insists. "He always looks right through me, so I don't know, I'm sure," sniffs Bessie, trying incidentally to interest Mr. Jones in the new scent she has on her hands. As for Morgan and Miss Moffat, Bessie is pretty sure the teacher is riding for a fall. "All this orderin' 'im about. I've got eyes in my head, if she hasn't, and he's gettin' sick of it." That's Bessie's opinion. "I think a lady ought to be dainty. She's no idea."

Miss Moffat can be heard calling before she reappears at the top of the stairs. Presently Morgan comes from the yard. "He is now seventeen. He is dressed in a shabby country suit, and is at the moment the submissive schoolboy, very different from the first act. He carries a sheet of writing and a pen. Miss Moffat's attitude to him seems purely impersonal."

"Finished?" queries Miss Moffat.

"Yes, Miss Moffat."

"How many pages?"

"Nine."

"Three too many. Boil down to six. Have you got those lines of Voltaire?"

"Yes, Miss Moffat."

"It's just five—have your walk now, good and brisk . . ."

"Yes, Miss Moffat."

"But kill two birds and get the Voltaire by heart. If you can ever argue a point like that, you'll do. . . . Back in twenty minutes—and take your pen from behind your ear."

As Miss Moffat disappears into her bedroom Morgan takes the pen from behind his ear and throws it on the desk with some irritation. Bessie Watty, still waving her scented hands about, is pleased.

"Now turn a somersault and beg," suggests Bessie. "Can you smell scent?" Morgan isn't interested. He has grabbed his cap from its peg on the door and gone out, slamming the door behind him.

Bessie is humming softly to herself, and smiling mysteriously. Bessie knows a thing or two which Mr. Jones has little success worming out of her—except that she understands there has been a break in the regular routine of Morgan Evans.

"It's been lessons every night with teacher, hasn't it, since we left the mine? And long walks in between, to blow the cobwebs away. But the last week or two we've been breaking our journey, so we've heard."

"How do you mean?"

"A glass of rum next door at the Gwesmor Arms and then another, and then another!"

"Oh—whoever told you that?"

"A little bird. . . ."

Bessie's mother has been away, attending one of her prayer meetings. Bessie thinks Mrs. Watty may stop at Gwesmor Arms on her way home and peek over the frosted partition and see what she can see. Then they'll know what's goin' on.

Mrs. Watty is back before they know it, and full of her adventures. She has been made a Sergeant Major, no less, succeeding to the shoes of a deserter in the ranks. Mrs. Watty had also stopped at the tavern, as Bessie predicted, and had seen young Mr. Morgan havin' a good drink. But she won't have Bessie or anybody tellin' Miss Moffat of this discovery.

Presently Miss Moffat is with them, but she asks no embarrassing questions. She is glad if Mrs. Watty had a good meeting. And she isn't interested in a request from Bessie for money for a ticket to the Tregarna Fair. She had told Bessie once before that she could not go to the Fair in school hours. Now Bessie's protest against such treatment has taken on an aggravated form. Her voice grows shrill and her face red as she reports that she can't stand any more sittin' down. It's been goin' on for two years now and Bessie has heard that as much sittin' down as that results in everything rottin' away.

"My mummy said all these lessons is bad for my inside," reports Bessie.

"She told me they stop you eating sweets, but perhaps I am telling the lie," suggests Miss Moffat. "What's the matter with your inside?"

"It goes round and round through sittin' down," shrills Bessie.

" 'Adelphos, a brother,' " mutters Miss Moffat. "There's nothing to prevent you going for walks between lessons. You can go for one now, as far as Sarah Pugh Postman, to see if my new chalks have arrived. Quick march."

Bessie has turned at the door. "I'm not goin'," she shouts.

"What did you say?"

"I'm not goin'! Everybody's against me. . . . I'm goin' to throw myself off a cliff, an' kill myself. . . . It'll make a nice case in the papers, me in pieces at the bottom of a cliff! . . . I'm goin' mad, mad, and I'm goin' to kill myself, nothin' goin' to stop me—stone dead at the bottom of a cliff—ah—ah—ah—"

Bessie's voice has mounted steadily and grown increasingly hysterical. Calmly Mrs. Watty comes from the kitchen. She carries a glass of water which she dashes into her daughter's face.

"I made a mess of your rug, ma'am," Mrs. Watty apologizes to Miss Moffat, as Bessie gasps and stutters, "but it's worth it. She's got bad blood, this girl, mark my word."

"She'll catch her death!" protests Miss Moffat.

"Nothing like cold water, ma'am," continues Mrs. Watty. "I learnt that with her father. 'E was foreign, you know."

Mrs. Watty has returned to her kitchen. Bessie is still trying to wipe the water from her eyes.

"And how do you feel after that?" inquires Miss Moffat.

"I can't remember anything. I'm in a comma," answers Bessie.

It is Miss Moffat's decision that Bessie shall sit on her bed for an hour with the door locked, and next week she shall go away into service. "I must count her as one of my failures," Miss Moffat admits, as she follows Bessie out of the room. "Fish out of water, of course. Guttersnipe species—if there is such a fish. She'll be more at home in service. . . ."

Morgan is back. "He is disheveled and it is fairly apparent that he has been drinking. He is defiant and the door bangs behind him." Miss Ronberry hastily explains that Miss Moffat is having something to eat.

"And I have been having something to drink, so we are quits," sullenly declares Morgan.

MISS RONBERRY—I will tell her that you are back—

MORGAN—I don't want to see no Miss Moffat.

MISS RONBERRY—You mean "I don't want to see Miss Moffat." The double negative—

MORGAN—Now don't you start! . . . I like the double negative, it says what I want the way I like, and I'm *not* goin' to stand *no* interferences from *nobody!* Voltaire indeed . . . (*Crumples paper, kicks it.*)

MISS RONBERRY—Morgan, I've never seen you like this before!

MORGAN—You haven't, have you? Well, now I come to think of it, I haven't neither, not for two years, and I'm surprised by meself, and shocked by meself! Goin' inside one o' them public houses and puttin' me nice clean boots on that dirty rail, and me dainty lady-fingers on that detestable mucky counter! Pourin' poison rum down me nice clean teeth, and spittin' in a spittoon—what's come over you, Morgan Evans? You come back to your little cage, and if you comb hair and wash hands and get your grammar right and forget you was once the Middle-weight Champion of the Glasynglo Miners, we might give you a nice bit of sewin' to do. . . . Where's that Bessie Watty, sendin' her mother to spy on me, I'll knock her bloody block off . . .

MISS RONBERRY (*outraged*)—Morgan Evans, *language!* Don't you dare use an expression like that to me again!

MORGAN (*facing her*)—I got plenty of others, thank you, and they are all comin' out. I am goin' to surprise quite a few—

MISS MOFFAT (*coming in from kitchen*)—Have a good walk, Evans?

MORGAN—Yes, Miss Moffat.

MISS MOFFAT—Can you repeat the Voltaire?

MORGAN—Not yet.

MISS MOFFAT—It's very short.

MORGAN—Paper blowed away.

MISS MOFFAT—Oh. Copy it again, will you, and bring it to me.

MORGAN (*muttering*)—Yes, Miss Moffat.

MISS MOFFAT—Would you like a drink?

MORGAN—No, thank you.

Miss Moffat is not worried about Morgan. He has the most receptive mind she has ever encountered. She is worried, however, when Miss Ronberry announces the approach of the Squire, who has not been there since her last rather exciting encounter with him. She knows what has brought him back, and she knows that it is of vital importance that she make a proper impression upon him at this time. She must be helpless and clinging. She borrows Miss Ronberry's shawl and when she reappears to greet the Squire the shawl is draped across her shoulders and she is carrying a bowl of roses. She hopes Miss Ronberry will look after the flowers. They are rather a task when one has a splitting headache.

And then she sees the Squire! How good it is of him to come—considering the overwrought fashion of her behavior at their last meeting. She is especially interested in the Squire's recent activities. She had so wanted to hear his speech at the prize-giving that afternoon, after hearing he had done so well the week before at the Croquet. She is proud when he tells her that Griffith, the butcher, had nearly laughed his napper off on that occasion—proud because if it had not been for the school and the Griffith children learning English, the butcher never would have understood a word—

"Squire, you see before you a tired woman," admits Miss Moffat, putting her hand to her head. "We live and learn, and I have learnt how right you were that night. I have worked my fingers to the bone battering my head against a stone wall."

"But I heard you were a spiffing success."

"Oh, no—"

"It's fair of you to admit it, I must say," mutters the Squire.

"You see, in one's womanly enthusiasm one forgets that the qualities vital to success in this sort of venture are completely lacking in one: intelligence, courage and authority . . . the qualities, in short, of a man."

"Come, come, you mustn't be too hard on yourself, y'know. After all, you've meant well."

"It's kind of you to say that."

"What about this Jones chappie?"

"He's a dear creature, but—I have no wish to be fulsome, I mean a man like yourself."

"I see."

"One gets into such muddles! You'd never believe!"

"Well . . . I've never been on your side, but I'm sorry to hear you've come a cropper. When are you giving it up?"

"Oh . . . That again is difficult; I have all my widow's mite, as it were, in the venture—"

Morgan Evans has come from the study with his paper. Seeing the Squire he quickly excuses himself, being very polite and deferential about it. The Squire is quite impressed when he hears that Morgan used to be one of his miners. Miss Moffat is pleased. Morgan is the problem about which she has been impelled to ask the Squire's advice. It isn't that Morgan has got into any trouble. It's just that he is clever. Not at figures, as the Squire had hoped. But as a writer.

"This boy . . . is quite out of the ordinary," insists Miss Moffat.

"Sure?"

MISS MOFFAT—As sure as one of your miners would be, cutting through coal and striking a diamond without a flaw. He was born with very exceptional gifts. They must be—they ought to be given every chance.

THE SQUIRE—You mean he might turn into a literary bloke?

MISS MOFFAT—He might, yes.

THE SQUIRE—I'm blowed! How d'ye know?

MISS MOFFAT—By his work. It's very good.

THE SQUIRE—How d'ye know it's good?

MISS MOFFAT—How does one know Shakespeare's good?

THE SQUIRE—Shakespeare? What's he got to do with it?

MISS MOFFAT—He was a literary bloke.

THE SQUIRE—Ye-es. *He* was good, of course.

MISS MOFFAT—This little tenant of yours, Squire, has it in

him to bring great credit to you.

THE SQUIRE—Yes, he *is* a tenant of mine, isn't he?

MISS MOFFAT—Imagine if you could say that you had known—well, say Lord Tennyson, as a boy on your estate!

THE SQUIRE—Rather a lark, what? Though it's a bit different, y'know, Tennyson was at Cambridge. My old college.

MISS MOFFAT—Oh . . . Poor Evans. What a pity he was not born at the beginning of the eighteenth century!

THE SQUIRE—Beginning of the eighteenth century—now when was that . . .

MISS MOFFAT (*taking books from case*)—He would have had a protector.

THE SQUIRE—What against?

MISS MOFFAT—A patron. Pope, you recall, dedicated the famous "Essay on Man" to his protector.

THE SQUIRE—"To H. St. John Lord Bolingbroke." Mmm . . . I *have* heard of it, now I remember—

MISS MOFFAT—Isn't it wonderful to think that that inscription is handed down to posterity? (*Reading from the other book.*) "To the Right Honourable Earl of Southampton . . . Your Honour's in all duty, William Shakespeare."

THE SQUIRE—Oh.

MISS MOFFAT—I often think of the pride that surged in the Earl's bosom when his encouragement gave birth to the masterpiece of a poor and humble writer!

THE SQUIRE—Funny, I never thought of Shakespeare being poor, somehow.

MISS MOFFAT—Some say his father was a butcher. The Earl realized he had genius, and fostered it.

THE SQUIRE—Mmm! If this boy really is clever, it seems a pity for *me* not to do something about it, doesn't it?

MISS MOFFAT—A great pity. And I can tell you exactly how you can do something about it.

THE SQUIRE—How?

MISS MOFFAT—There's a scholarship going.

THE SQUIRE—Scholarship? Where?

MISS MOFFAT—To Oxford.

THE SQUIRE—Oxford?

MISS MOFFAT (*moving closer*)—A scholarship to Trinity College, Oxford, open to boys of secondary education in the British Isles. My school hardly comes under the heading of secondary education, and I wrote your brother at Magdalen; he pulled some strings for me, and they have agreed to make a special case of this boy, on one condition. That you vouch for him. Will you?

THE SQUIRE—My dear lady, you take the cake. . . . Can't he be just as clever at home?

MISS MOFFAT—No, he can't. For the sort of future he ought to have, he must have polish—he has everything else. The background of a university would be invaluable to him. . . . Will you?

THE SQUIRE—Well, the 'Varsity! Y'know, hang it all . . . mind you, he'll never get it.

MISS MOFFAT—I know, but he *must* have the chance—

THE SQUIRE—Still, y'know, even the mere prospect of one of my miners—

MISS MOFFAT—Think of Shakespeare!

THE SQUIRE—All serene. I'll drop a line to Henry next week. Rather a lark, what? I must be off—

MISS MOFFAT—I should be most obliged if the letter could be posted tomorrow. Would you like me to draft out a recommendation and send it over to the Hall? You must be so busy with the estate—

THE SQUIRE—I am rather. Polka supper tomorrow night . . . Yes, do do that. Good-by, dear lady!

MISS MOFFAT—Thank you so very much, Squire—

THE SQUIRE—Happier conditions, and all that! Glad you've come to your senses!

MISS MOFFAT—Thank you so very much, Squire!

THE SQUIRE—Not at all, I'm all for giving a writer-fellow a helping hand. Tell my brother that, if you like . . .

The Squire has gone and Miss Moffat is exultant. She has done all that she had hoped to do, she assures the astonished Miss Ronberry. "I've beaten you at your own game, my dear; at my age and with my looks I flirted with him! And he is going to write to Oxford; at least I am going to write to Oxford for him. Hallelujah! I am entering my little pit-pony for a scholarship to Oxford, child, Oxford University!"

"But they don't have miners at Oxford University."

"Well, they're going to. The lad is on this earth for eighty years at the most out of a few millions. Let the proud silly ones grovel and be useful for a change, so he can step up on their backs to something better! I was bursting to say that to the Lord of the Manor, so I must vent it on you. . . . Thank you for your shawl, my dear—and now you've served your purpose, you can go home—but you'd better watch out, I may beat you to the altar yet."

Miss Ronberry is still a little startled as Miss Moffat sees her through the front door. A moment later the desk is cleared, the papers neatly arranged and Morgan Evans has been called for a lesson. When he comes there is more than a suggestion of the defiant spirit he had shown before. He has his pen, books and papers, and has soon settled to answering Miss Moffat's questions.

"Is this your essay on the Wealth of Nations?"

"Yes."

"Say so and underline it. Nothing irritates examiners more than that sort of vagueness. (*Pauses. She hands him the exercise book.*) I couldn't work this sentence out."

" 'The eighteenth century was a caldron. Vice and elegance boiled to a simmer until the kitchen of society reeked fulminously, and the smell percolated to the marble halls above.' "

"D'ye know what that means?"

"Yes, Miss Moffat."

"Because I don't. Clarify, my boy, clarify, and leave the rest to Mrs. Henry Wood. . . . 'Water' with two t's . . . that's a bad lapse. . . . The Adam Smith sentence was good. Original, and clear as well. Seven out of ten, not bad but not good—you *must* avoid long words until you know exactly what they mean. Otherwise domino. . . ."

Now there is a break in the lesson. "Next Tuesday I am starting you on Greek," Miss Moffat has just said. "I am going to put you in for a scholarship to Oxford."

MORGAN—Oxford? Where the lords go?

MISS MOFFAT—The same. I've made a simplified alphabet to begin with. It's jolly interesting after Latin. . . . Have a look at it by Tuesday so we can make a good start—oh, and before we go on with the lesson, I've found the nail file I mentioned— (MORGAN *slams a book.*) I'll show you how to use it. I had them both somewhere—

MORGAN—I shall not need a nail file in the coal mine.

MISS MOFFAT—In the what?

MORGAN (*turning to her*)—I am going back to the coal mine.

MISS MOFFAT—I don't understand you. Explain yourself.

MORGAN—I do not want to learn Greek, nor to pronounce any long English words, nor to keep my hands clean.

MISS MOFFAT—What's the matter with you? Why not?

MORGAN—Because . . . because I was born in a Welsh hay-field when my mother was helpin' with the harvest—and I always lived in a little house with no stairs, only a ladder—and no water— And until my brothers was killed I never sleep except three in a bed. I know that is terrible grammar but it is true.

MISS MOFFAT—What on earth has three in a bed got to do with learning Greek?

MORGAN—It has—a lot! The last two years I have not had no proper talk with English chaps in the mine because I was so busy keepin' this old grammar in its place. Tryin' to better myself . . . tryin' to better myself, the day and the night! . . . You cannot take a nail file into the "Gwesmor Arms" public bar!

MISS MOFFAT—My dear boy, file your nails at home! I never heard anything so ridiculous. Besides, you don't go to the Gwesmor Arms!

MORGAN—Yes, I do. I have been there every afternoon for a week, spendin' your pocket money, and I have been there now, and that is why I can speak my mind!

MISS MOFFAT—I had no idea that you felt like this.

MORGAN—Because you are not interested in me.

MISS MOFFAT—Not interested in you?

MORGAN—How can you be interested in a machine that you put a penny in and if nothing comes out you give it a good shake? "Evans, write me an essay. Evans, get up and bow. Evans, what is a subjunctive?" My name is Morgan Evans, and all my friends call me Morgan, and if there is anything gets on the wrong side of me it is callin' me Evans! . . . And do you know what they call me in the Village? Ci bach yr yagol! The schoolmistress's little dog! What has it got to do with you if my nails are dirty? Mind your own business!

MISS MOFFAT—I never meant you to know this. I have spent money on you—I don't mind that, money ought to be spent. But time is different. Your life has not yet begun, mine is half over. And when you're a middle-aged spinster, some folk say it's pretty near finished. Two years is valuable currency. I have spent two years on you. Ever since that first day, the mainspring of this school has been your career. Sometimes, in the middle of the night, when I have been desperately tired, I have lain awake, making plans. Large and small. Sensible and silly. Plans, for you. And you tell me I have no interest in you. If I say any more I shall start to cry; and I haven't cried since I was younger than you are, and I'd never forgive you for that. I am going for a walk. I don't like this sort of conversation, please never mention it again. If you want to go on, be at school tomorrow. If not, don't.

MORGAN—I don't want your money, and I don't want your time! . . . I don't want to be thankful to no strange woman—for anything!

MISS MOFFAT—I don't understand you. I don't understand you at all.

Miss Moffat has taken her cloak from its peg on the door and gone out. Morgan, with a defiant smirk, produces a bottle and takes a drink. He is settling himself with folded arms when Bessie Watty appears. "She has put her hair half up and wears earrings."

"Hello!" Bessie calls, cheerily. Morgan does not answer. "Caught my knee climbin' down the rainpipe, ooh. . . ." She is clutching her leg and grimacing. Still no response from Morgan. "P'r'aps I'm invisible!" snaps Bessie and marches into the kitchen, gaily singing "Bell Bottom Trousers."

From some distance away there comes the sound of singing. It is the men returning from the mine. Bessie comes back. Her mother's gone out, she announces. Morgan pays no attention to her.

"Talkin' a lot, aren't I?" says Bessie.

"Yes!" snaps Morgan.

BESSIE—Well, I'm not deaf.

MORGAN—Been spyin'?

BESSIE—If people lock me in and take the key out of the keyhole, they can't blame me for listenin' at it. Oo, I think she's wicked.

MORGAN—Mind your own business!

BESSIE—I won't. I like to know about everything; I like doin' all the things I like. I like sweets. I don't care if it does make me fat, and I love earrings. I like to shake my head like a lady. . . . It's funny. . . . We never been by ourselves before. (*She begins to sing in Welsh. The tune is "Lliw Gwyn Rhosyn yr Haf." Sits on edge of table.*) Didn't know I knew Welsh, did you? . . . You like that song, don't you? That's why I learnt it.

MORGAN—You are different when you sing.

BESSIE—Am I? . . . What's this, medicine? (*Picks up rum bottle, drinks. He takes bottle from her, takes a drink and puts it in his pocket.*) Tastes like rubber. Nice, though. . . . You know—you was quite right to put her in her place. Clever chap like you learnin' lessons off a woman!

MORGAN—That's right. . . .

BESSIE—You don't 'ave to go to Oxford! Clever chap like you!

MORGAN—That's right. . . .

BESSIE (*going to him*)—What a man wants is a bit o' sympathy!

She has started singing again and backing tantalizingly away from him. He follows slowly. Impulsively he takes her in his arms and kisses her. The curtain falls.

It is a morning in November, three months later. It has been snowing and there are reports that the roads have been blocked. As this is the first day on which Morgan Evans is to sit for the Oxford scholarship the Moffat household is variously upset. The Squire is to be one of the official watchers. The storm may delay him. And it would be quite terrible if Morgan could not get through. Miss Moffat has not slept a wink all night. "I could 'ear her thinkin'," reports Mrs. Watty.

There is a letter from Bessie Watty, which reminds Miss Ronberry that Bessie has been away three months now. Her mother must miss her. "No," quickly answers Mrs. Watty. "I don't like 'er, you know; never 'ave."

"But, Mrs. Watty, your own daughter!"

"I know, but I've never been able to take to 'er. First time I saw 'er I said—'No.' With 'er dad being foreign, you see."

"But couldn't your husband have taken her abroad to his own family?"

"Oh, my 'usband was quite different. British to the core."

With that Mrs. Watty goes back to her kitchen. A moment later Miss Moffat comes slowly down the stairs. She is confident that nothing will keep Morgan away this day, or the Squire either. She is particularly pleased to assure Miss Ronberry that Morgan has been working hard. The night before she had had to take his books away from him at 10 o'clock.

"I hope he won't get wet—he must not be upset in any way," Miss Moffat continues. "What made you think he wasn't working well?"

MISS RONBERRY—Nothing, only—you remember the night you went for that long walk, when he might be going back to the mine?

MISS MOFFAT—Yes?

MISS RONBERRY—The next morning he started studying again, and yet it seemed so different.

MISS MOFFAT—How?

MISS RONBERRY—Almost strained . . . what a silly thing to say . . . I mean, as you did not say anything more about the mine—

MISS MOFFAT—He didn't say any more himself. He just turned up. I didn't embrace him on both cheeks, but I said "Righto." Since which time, he has never stopped working.

MISS RONBERRY—I *am* so glad . . . Oh, this arrived from the Penlan Town Hall! It must be his birth certificate—

MISS MOFFAT—Good. . . . I must send it off to the President of Trinity. Rather a nervous post mortem from him last night; two pages to ask if the youngster's legitimate; thank Heaven he is. And no conviction for drunkenness; references have been spotless. That will help, I hope.

MISS RONBERRY—Would it not be splendid if he . . . won!

MISS MOFFAT (*after a pause*)—Not very likely, I am afraid. The syllabus rather attaches importance to general knowledge of the academic sort. His is bound to be patchy—on the exuberant side—I have had to force it; two years is not enough even for him. If he checks himself, and does not start telling them what they ought to think of Milton, with fair luck he might stand a chance. He will have some pretty strong public school candidates against him, of course. Bound to. It depends on how much the examiners will appreciate a highly original intelligence.

MISS RONBERRY—But wouldn't it be *exciting!*

MISS MOFFAT—Yes, it would. People run down the universities, and always will, but it would be a wonderful thing for him. It would be a wonderful thing for rural education all over the country.

MISS RONBERRY—And most of all, it would be a wonderful thing for you!

MISS MOFFAT—I suppose so . . . It is odd to have spent so many hours with another human being, in the closest intellectual communion—because it has been that, I know every trick and twist of that brain of his, exactly where it will falter and where it will gallop ahead of me—and yet not to know him at all. I woke up in the middle of the night thinking of Henry the Eighth. I have a feeling there may be a question about the old boy and the Papacy. (*Taking book from shelves.*) I'll cram one or two facts into him, the last minute. . . . Oh, God, he must win it. . . . He must . . .

They have just caught sight of both the Squire and Morgan coming toward the house when Bessie Watty walks in the door. "She is shabbily dressed in a semi-gown of fashion and wears a cloak. Her manner is staccato, nervy and defiant." Mr. Jones is with her, but he did not bring her, he explains. She brought him.

She has not come to see her mother, Bessie explains. She has come to see Miss Moffat. Miss Moffat is not pleased. She can give Bessie just one minute of her time, and she can wait in the study. Bessie is not impressed.

"Morgan Evans is sitting for his Oxford examination here this morning," Miss Moffat explains.

BESSIE—Well, 'e needn't.

MISS MOFFAT—What do you mean?

BESSIE—Because he won't ever be goin' to Oxford.

MISS MOFFAT—Why not?

BESSIE—Because there's goin' to be a little stranger. I'm going to have a little stranger.

MISS MOFFAT—You're lying.

BESSIE—Doctor Brett, The Firs, Cheltenham. . . . And if you don't believe it's Morgan Evans, you ask 'im about that night you locked me up—the night you had the words with him!

MISS MOFFAT—I see . . . Why couldn't I have seen before! (*Turns to her.*) Does he know?

BESSIE—I've come to tell 'im! I was ever so upset, of course, and now I've lost me place—ooh, he was artful—he'll have to marry me, or I'll show him up, 'cause I must give the little stranger a name—

MISS MOFFAT—Stop saying "little stranger," if you must have a baby, then call it a baby! . . . Have you told anybody?

BESSIE—Mr. Jones, that's all—

MISS RONBERRY (*coming in*)—The Squire is coming up the road!

BESSIE—I'll wait here for him.

MISS MOFFAT—For the next three hours, he must not be disturbed. You are not going to see him.

BESSIE—You can't bully me, the way I am! 'Asn't sunk in yet, 'as it? I'm teaching *you* something, am I? You didn't know thinks like that went on, did you? Why? You couldn't see what was goin' on under your nose, 'cause you're too busy managin' everythin'! Well, you can't manage him any longer, 'cause he's got to manage me now, the way I am, he's got to—

MR. JONES (*poking his head round the study door*)—Morgan Evans has turned the corner up the hill—

MISS RONBERRY—So there isn't much time!

MISS MOFFAT (*to* BESSIE)—I'm afraid I am going to do a little managing now. You are going into the kitchen, where your mother will make you breakfast; you will then lie down, and as soon as this session is finished we will go upstairs and talk it all over when we are a little calmer. (*A knock at the front door.*)

BESSIE—He's here! I got to see him!

MISS MOFFAT (*stopping her*)—If you try and disobey me, I shall not answer for the consequences. (*Holds her wrist.*)

BESSIE—You wouldn't dare lay a finger on me—

MISS MOFFAT—Oh, yes, I would. If you attempt to stay in this room or to blab to anybody about this before we have had that talk—even your mother—I am in a pretty nervous state myself, this morning, and I shall strike you so hard that I shall probably kill you . . . I mean every word of that.

There is another knock. Miss Moffat opens the door to the kitchen and waits for Bessie to leave. "I don't mind," smirks Bessie. "Three hours'll go soon enough."

The Squire is shown in. He is wearing his Inverness cape and hat, and carrying several sporting periodicals. The Squire is cheerful and brings cheerful news. He has bought the barn from Sir Herbert. The whole school can be moved in there by March, and they can knock a door through from the cottage.

Miss Moffat is pleased, naturally, but just at the moment the examination is too much on her mind— A knock at the front door announces the arrival of Morgan. Miss Ronberry takes his cap, coat and muffler. He is very quiet, greeting them calmly, deferentially, receiving their best wishes gracefully. Miss Moffat hands him a card to memorize before she breaks the seal of the examination papers. It is a few facts about Henry the Eighth. Her last words of advice are: "Name and particulars to save time. And don't get exuberant. Or illegible—"

"But aren't you going to wish my little protégé good fortune?" beams the Squire.

"Good luck," says Miss Moffat, quietly.

"Thank you," answers Morgan.

"Ready?" Miss Moffat has taken the shears and cut the envelope, placing the examination papers in front of him. She smiles as she skims the duplicate paper which she holds. "Henry the Eighth" she mutters. She is looking toward the kitchen, and then at Morgan as the curtain slowly falls.

ACT III

It is an afternoon in July and seven months later. The Moffat living room has been cleared of most of its school paraphernalia since the school itself has been moved into the barn next door. But there are still a couple of desks and a blackboard there for individual class study.

At the moment Mr. Jones has Idwal and Robbart at work on an exercise. Near them sits Old Tom, who is also getting in a little extra study, and at one side is the Squire looking something like a student, but not much. The exercise on the blackboard reads: "Elizabeth, known as Good 'Q. Bess.'" A moment later, when Mr. Jones steps out of the room, Idwal rushes to the board and changes the inscription to read: "NO . . . GOOD . . . BESSIE."

Mr. Jones, on his return, is for making an example of whoever did that, but there isn't time. Idwal thinks perhaps it was somebody who would like to know what has happened to Bessie Watty all these months. Nobody seems to know anything about Bessie.

The Squire is waiting to hear something about Morgan Evans' arrival. The Oxford examinations are over. Morgan will be home shortly, but whether the results will be known before Miss Moffat gets them in the mail is not certain.

The school bell has rung and studies are over for the day. The town is reported as excited over the prospect of Morgan's return. The women are getting out their Sunday gowns, and the men are rounding up the grocer and his fiddle, the public with his cornet and Robbart with his mouth organ. Miss Ronberry thinks perhaps if they were all to repeat in unison: "Morgan Evans has won the scholarship!" it would help.

Miss Moffat has come from the school. She is amused when they tell her the Squire has gone out to see if there is any sign of Morgan's coming. "That man is really becoming a nuisance," she says. "He gave up Henley to be here this week."

"You do not appear nervous," suggests Mr. Jones.

"I am past being nervous," says Miss Moffat. "If he has won I shan't believe it. Flatly."

"And if he has lost?"

"If he has lost . . . we must proceed as if nothing had happened. The sun rises and sets every day, and while it does we have jolly well got to revolve round it; the time to sit up and take notice will be the day it decides not to appear."

Mr. Jones and Miss Ronberry have gone into the school to get their reports for the day. Miss Moffat is alone when the garden door opens suddenly and Morgan Evans appears. He had caught an early train, he explains. Fearing the townsfolk might all be watching for him he had left the train at Llanmorfedd and got a lift to Gwaenygam.

Morgan's English has "immensely improved and he expresses himself with ease." He has nothing to report as to the award. They had talked to him for an hour, and they had borne down heavily on the New Testament question, as Miss Moffat had thought they would.

"I spent five minutes explaining why Saint Paul sailed from a town three hundred miles inland," explains Morgan. And as for Parnell . . . Morgan smiles at the recollection. "I was going to stick up for the old chap," he says, "but when they started off with 'that fellow Parnell,' I told the tale against him for half an hour, I wasn't born a Welshman for nothing."

He spent a half hour with the President, but so did the other nine candidates, all of whom had impressed Morgan as being brilliant. He really had gained the impression that he had failed. The fact that the villagers have all got into their best clothes and are really expecting a holiday makes the thought of failure the harder to bear. He wishes they did not have to speak about it.

"But we must," insists Miss Moffat. "You faced the idea the day you left for Oxford—"

Morgan—I know, but I have *been* to Oxford, and come back, since then! I have come back—from the world! Since the day I was born, I have been a prisoner behind a stone wall, and now somebody has given me a leg-up to have a look at the other side . . . they cannot drag me back again, they cannot, they *must* give me a push and send me over!

Miss Moffat—I've never heard you talk so much since I've known you.

Morgan—That is just it! I *can* talk now! The three days I have been there, I have been talking my head off!

Miss Moffat—Ha! If three days at Oxford can do that to you, what would you be like at the end of three years?

Morgan—That's just it again—it would be everything I need,

everything! Starling and I spent three hours one night discussin' the law—Starling, you know, the brilliant one . . . The words came pouring out of me—all the words that I had learnt and written down and never spoken—I suppose I was talking nonsense, but I was at least holding a conversation! I suddenly realized that I had never done it before—I had never been *able* to do it. (*With a strong Welsh accent.*) "How are you, Morgan? Nice day, Mr. Jones! Not bad for the harvest." —a vocabulary of twenty words; all the thoughts that you have given to me were being stored away as if they were always going to be useless—locked up and rotting away—a lot of questions with nobody to answer them . . . a lot of statements with nobody to contradict them . . . and there I was with Starling, nineteen to the dozen. I came out of his rooms that night, and I walked down the High. That's their High Street, you know.

MISS MOFFAT—Yes, yes. . . .

MORGAN—I looked up, and there was a moon behind Magd—Maudlin. Not the same moon I have seen over the Nant, a different face altogether. Everybody seemed to be walking very fast, with their gowns on, in the moonlight; the bells were ringing, and I was walking faster than anybody and I felt—well, the same as on the rum in the old days!

MISS MOFFAT—Go on.

MORGAN—All of a sudden, with one big rush, against the moon, and against that High Street . . . I saw this room; you and me sitting here studying, and all those books—and everything I have ever learnt from those books, and from you, was lighted up—like a magic lantern—ancient Rome, Greece, Shakespeare, Carlyle, Milton . . . everything had a meaning, because I was in a new world—my world! And so it came to me why you worked like a slave to make me ready for this scholarship . . . I've finished.

MISS MOFFAT—I didn't want you to stop.

MORGAN—I had not been drinking.

MISS MOFFAT—I know.

MORGAN—I can talk to you too, now.

MISS MOFFAT—Yes. I'm glad.

Now there is more excitement. The Squire is back and startled to see Morgan standing before him. His greeting is almost effusive. Mr. Jones experiences a similar thrill. And Miss Ronberry. The suspense is growing—and there isn't much likelihood that they will know the result before the day after tomorrow.

They have taken Morgan into the kitchen to get him some food when the door opens and Bessie Watty appears. "She has completely changed; she might be ten years older. Her hair is up; she wears a cheaply smart costume, with a cape, and looks dazzlingly pretty in a loose opulent style. Her whole personality has blossomed."

Bessie's greeting of the Squire and Miss Ronberry is cheery and bold. She has read about the scholarship and she has come "to congratulate a certain young gent" in case he has won. Four weeks ago, Bessie is proud to admit, she had had a seven pound, thirteen ounce, baby—and they needn't any of them sneer at that. "If I had a wedding ring you'd think it was sweet," she tells Miss Ronberry, who considers the adventure disgusting.

Mrs. Watty has come from the kitchen. She is properly surprised at the sight of Bessie, and amused at Bessie's announcement that she has been turnin' her mum into a granny. Miss Moffat, however, is not amused. She tries to stop Bessie from telling the name of her child's father. Bessie is not to be stopped. "It's no good, Miss," she says, turning to the others. "It's Morgan Evans."

"I've been dreading this for months," admits Miss Moffat, as the others recoil from the news. "In a terrible way it's a relief."

"Bamboozlin' me every week he was in the gutter," sneers Bessie.

Miss Moffat—Lies, all lies, and I was glad to be telling them—

Miss Ronberry—I can't go on listening! I can't bear it? It all comes of meddling with this teaching—she was in my class—what *would* Papa have said? This horrible unnatural happening—

Miss Moffat—Don't talk nonsense, it isn't horrible, and it isn't unnatural! On the contrary, it's nature giving civilization a nasty tweak of the nose. The school-mistress *has* learnt a lesson, but it's a little late now.

Bessie (*rising*)—Where is he?

Mrs. Watty—Over my dead body, my girl—

Bessie—She's right, Mum, it's too late, I got a four weeks old baby, kickin' healthy and hungry, and I haven't got a husband to keep him, so his father's got to turn *into* my husband. That's only fair, isn't it?

The Squire (*rising*)—I'm sorry, Miss Moffat, but I'm inclined to agree—

Bessie—I'll call him—

MR. JONES—There is no need to call him!

THE SQUIRE—What's the matter with you?

MR. JONES (*taking a step forward*)—I am sorry to say that I have a strong feeling of affection for this young woman.

BESSIE—Oh, yes—I've got the face of an angel, haven't I?

MR. JONES—And I am willing to do my duty by rehabilitating her in wedlock (BESSIE *sits center of couch.*), and bestowing on the infant every advantage by bringing it up a Baptist.

THE SQUIRE—Are you serious?

MR. JONES—I am always serious.

BESSIE (*to* MISS MOFFAT)—You'd like that, wouldn't you?

MRS. WATTY (*crossing down right of couch*)—Now we're not pretendin' it's a windfall, but for a girl who's took the wrong turnin' it's a present! And you'd 'ave your way in everything—wouldn't she, sir?

MR. JONES—Of course—

MRS. WATTY—Well, will you?

BESSIE—No. I won't. I'd like to oblige . . . (*Laughs.*) but really I couldn't! (MR. JONES *turns away.*) Besides, my friend would be furious.

MRS. WATTY—Your friend?

BESSIE—Ever such a nice gentleman, sporting, quite a swell, owns a race-course. (WATTY *looks suspicious.*) You needn't look like that, I only met him ten weeks ago.

Bessie enjoys reciting the details of her adventure. She had gone to work as a barmaid when she met her new friend. He wants to marry her, but he won't have the baby. " 'E says it would be different if the father'd been a pal of his," reports Bessie. That, she thinks, is understandable.

Perhaps Mr. Jones would consider takin' the baby without her? What about mother love? Miss Ronberry would know. It may sound wicked, she admits, but she just hasn't got any. She can understand how Miss Ronberry would feel about it, but she isn't as old as Miss Ronberry. Life's just begun for Bessie—what does she want with a baby? However, she was careful to see that it was a nice baby and she wants it to have a good time. She could have left it on a doorstep, but she has come to Morgan Evans—

"You want to make him marry you, on the chance he will become fond enough of the child to ensure its future," charges Miss Moffat. "Your conscience will be clear and later you can go off on your own?"

"I shouldn't be surprised—"

"In the meantime, it's worth while to ruin a boy on—on the threshold of—"

"I don't know anything about that, I'm sure," says Bessie, going to the door and starting to call Morgan—

"Ssh!" interrupts Miss Moffat. "Wait a minute—wait. . . . There may be a way out . . . there must be—"

Miss Moffat has pulled Bessie back from the door. And now it is Mrs. Watty who is struck with an idea. Why shouldn't Miss Moffat adopt the baby? Bessie would agree to that and everything would be fine.

Miss Moffat is startled. The idea is ridiculous, even preposterous. The others are enthusiastic. "Oh, do, please, it'd put *everything* to rights," pleads Bessie. "I would know the baby was safe, Morgan Evans need never know a thing about it, I can marry my friend, and it will all be beautiful! He might grow like his father and turn out quite nice, and anyway I'm not really so bad, you know—and he's on the bottle now—and I could give all the instructions before I go—and you could have it straight away, see, because if it's going I don't want to have it with me any longer than I can help, see, because I'd only start gettin' fond of it, see—"

"Come on, Ma'am," urges Mrs. Watty. "You've been pushin' us about for three years, now we'll give *you* a shove!"

"But it's mad—I tell you—"

"Not as mad as takin' *me* in was, with my trouble! You've allus been like that, you might as well go on—"

"But I was never meant to be a mother—I'm not like Miss Ronberry—why, *she* is the one to do it—"

It is no use. One by one they batter down Miss Moffat's arguments until finally she gives in. She has Mrs. Watty's promise to stand by as the grandmother, and Bessie's promise never to breathe a word of the baby to Morgan Evans. Everybody is relieved. Now Bessie can go back to the pub and send her friend a wire.

"Are you going to take up a life of sin?" demands Mr. Jones glumly.

"I shouldn't be surprised," answers Bessie. "I'm only really meself with a lot of gentlemen round me, y'know, and a nice glass o' port will never come amiss, neither."

Bessie is no sooner gone than Morgan Evans comes quickly from the kitchen. The Squire has told him. Miss Moffat is distressed.

"He thought I knew," Morgan explains. "He said it was for

the best—that I ought to be told— It is funny. She and I, we do not know each other at all—it was a long time ago, and I never thought again about it—and neither did she, I know she didn't . . . and here we are. . . . It is funny, too, because if you and I had not made that bad quarrel, it would never have happened . . . It ought to make me feel older . . . but I feel more young than I have ever done before. . . . Oh, God, why should this happen. . . ."

"Steady."

"There is no need for you to upset yourself, my boy," comforts Mr. Jones. "Miss Moffat is going to take care of—of—"

"What?"

"I am going to adopt it," confirms Miss Moffat.

Morgan is angry. What the hell do they take him for? The baby is his problem. What will he do? He'll do the only thing any fellow with guts in him must do—he'll marry Bessie Watty. What else can he do? Beyond that he does not want to talk about it to anyone. "Bessie Watty and I are going to get married as soon as we can, and that's final," is Morgan's conclusion.

Sarah, the postmistress, has burst in with a telegram. It is, she suspects, another one for Bessie Watty from her friend. Mrs. Watty opens it and hands it to Miss Moffat. "Read it, ma'am; take your mind off things—"

Miss Moffat reads the telegram slowly. "You have won the scholarship," she says to Evans. " 'First, Evans; second, Fayver-Giles; third, Starling. Congratulations!' "

Sarah claps her hands and runs out through the door. Mrs. Watty offers a cheer and goes to lock the school door. Miss Moffat and Morgan are alone. She has walked over and stands facing him—

Miss Moffat—Look at me, Morgan. For the first time, we are together. Our hearts are face to face, naked and unashamed, because there's no time to lose, my boy; the clock is ticking and there's no time to lose. If ever anybody has been at the cross-roads, you are now—

Morgan—It is no good. I am going to marry her.

Miss Moffat—And I am going to speak to you very simply. I want you to change suddenly from a boy to a man. I understand that this is a great shock to you, but I want you to throw off this passionate obstinacy to do the right thing. . . . Did you promise her marriage?

Morgan—No, never—

MISS MOFFAT—Did you even tell her that you were in love with her?

MORGAN—No, never—

MISS MOFFAT—Then your situation now is the purest accident; it is to be regretted, but it has happened before and it will happen again. So cheer up, you are not the central figure of such a tragedy as you think—

MORGAN—That does not alter the fact that I have a duty to—to them both—

MISS MOFFAT—She has her own plans, and she doesn't want the child; and I am willing to look after it if you behave as I want you to behave. If you marry her, you know what will happen, don't you? You will go back to the mine. In a year she will have left you—both. You will be drinking again, and this time you will not stop. And you will enjoy being this besotted and uncouth village genius who once showed such promise; but it would not be worth it, you know.

MORGAN—There is a child, living and breathing on this earth, and living and breathing because of me—

MISS MOFFAT—I don't care if there are fifty children on this earth because of you! . . . You mentioned the word "duty," did you? Yes, you have a duty, but it is not to this loose little lady, or to her offspring either.

MORGAN—You mean a duty to you?

MISS MOFFAT—No. A year ago I should have said a duty to me, yes; but that night you showed your teeth . . . you gave me a lot to think about, you know. You caught me unawares, and I gave you the worst possible answer back; I turned sorry for myself and taunted you with ingratitude. I was a dolt not to realize that a debt of gratitude is the most humiliating debt of all, and that a little show of affection would have wiped it out. I offer that affection to you, today.

MORGAN—Why are you saying this to me now?

MISS MOFFAT—Because, as the moments are passing, and I am going to get my way, I know that I am never going to see you again. (*A pause.*)

MORGAN—Never again? But why?

MISS MOFFAT—If you are not to marry her, it would be madness for you to come into contact with the child; so if I am adopting the child, you can never come to see me; it is common sense. You have been given the push over the wall that you asked for.

MORGAN—But you . . . will be staying here—how can I never come back—after everything you have done for me?

MISS MOFFAT—D'you remember, the last six months, I've gone for a long walk over Moel Hiraeth, every morning at eight, like clockwork, for my health?

MORGAN—Yes?

MISS MOFFAT—There's one bit of the road, round a boulder—and there's an oak-tree, and under it the valley suddenly drops sheer. Every morning regularly, as I was turning that corner, by some trick of the mind, I found myself thinking of you working for this scholarship, and winning it. And I experienced something which must after all be comparatively rare: a feeling . . . of complete happiness. I shall experience it again. No, Morgan Evans, you have no duty to me. Your only duty—is to the world.

MORGAN—To the world?

MISS MOFFAT—Now you are going, there is no harm in telling you something. I don't think you realize quite what your future can become if you give it the chance. I have always been very definite about the things I wanted, and I have always had everything worked out to a T—p'raps that's the trouble with me, I dunno . . . I've got *you* worked out, and it's up to you whether it will come right or not—

MORGAN—Go on.

MISS MOFFAT—I rather made out to the Squire that I wanted you to be a writer—the truth might have sounded ridiculous; but stranger things have happened. You have brains, shrewdness, eloquence, and imagination; and Oxford will give you enough of the graces.

MORGAN—For what?

MISS MOFFAT—Maybe to become a great man of cur country. "If a light come in the mine" you said, remember?

MORGAN—Yes.

MISS MOFFAT—Make that light come in the mine and some day free these children. And you could be more, much, much more, you could be a man for a future nation to be proud of—Perhaps I'm mad, I dunno, we'll see. It's up to you.

Mr. Jones has come timidly from the kitchen. Will it be all right for him to ring the bell to announce a holiday for tomorrow? It will. He hurries away. Briefly again Morgan and Miss Moffat face each other. "I think that's all," she is saying.

"But—I—I—I do not know what to say."

"Then don't say it."

"I have been . . . so much time in this room—"

"And the lessons are over."

"I shall—always remember."

"Will you? Well, I'm glad you think you will—"

Idwal has rushed in to announce the band and the demand of the townsfolk that Morgan shall come to Penlan Town Hall that everybody may have a look at a "regular toff—"

"And please, Miss Moffat, Mr. Jones say is he to say school day after tomorrow, nine o'clock same as usual?"

"Nine o'clock. The same as usual. . . ."

She offers her hand to Morgan. "Good-by," she says. "And I had my heart set on coming up to London and having tea on the Terrace—"

There is the sound of voices mixed with singing from the distance. Morgan tries to say something and fails. He hurries into the study. Miss Moffat is at her desk when Mrs. Watty comes from the kitchen, looking cautiously about to be sure Morgan has gone. Bessie announces Mrs. Watty has sent a man over from the public-house with a paper for Miss Moffat—

"Tell him I can't see anybody," Miss Moffat is saying as Mrs. Watty hands her the paper. "What's this?"

"His birth certificate, ma'am."

"I had forgotten—all about that—"

"Come on, ma'am. You got to start sometime," says Mrs. Watty.

"Just coming," answers Miss Moffat.

Outside the singing and the cheering have increased. Miss Moffat is standing, looking down at the birth certificate, as the singing dies down.

"Moffat, my girl, you mustn't be clumsy this time. You mustn't be clumsy . . ."

The school bell rings clear and confident. She looks up, as she did once before, listening, smiling faintly. A vociferous burst of cheering in the village. She turns and walks towards the kitchen.

THE CURTAIN FALLS

LADY IN THE DARK

A Musical Drama in Two Acts

By Moss Hart

Music by Kurt Weill. Lyrics by Ira Gershwin

THE creation of "Lady in the Dark" began with an adventure of the author, Moss Hart, in the office of a psychoanalyst. It was there that the dramatic possibilities of a story involving the experience of a troubled heroine who should appeal to the mind probers for help occurred to him. Originally he saw the play as straight drama, and had mentally visioned Katharine Cornell in the rôle. But as the story developed in the writing it soon became apparent that the dream interludes were going to take on a fantastic and largely musical comedy background.

To this division of entertainment Gertrude Lawrence was for years an outstanding contributor. First in England, later in America. With her later growth as a dramatic actress, she became at once a first choice for the new play. Miss Lawrence, however, being particularly fond of drama and having, in a way, left her musical comedy past behind her, was not easily convinced that she should drop everything and become the heroine of Mr. Hart's dreams.

At one stage of the negotiations Irene Dunne of the motion picture group was mentioned as a possibility for the rôle, but before much was done about this Miss Lawrence had decided to play Mr. Hart's Liza Elliott, the lady who is cured of her confusions in the play. The wisdom of this choice was apparent from the beginning of rehearsals. By the time the play reached production in Boston, it was nationally known that here was to be observed a triumphant joining of actress and part.

"Lady in the Dark" arrived in New York in late January and immediately became one of the season's major theatre sensations. It is probably the only play in the history of the theatre that has consistently played not only to those capacity audiences so frequently quoted, but also to standees at every performance. Miss Lawrence's rôle is extremely exacting and she had taken the precaution of stipulating that she was not to play it during the hot weather. She was entitled by her contract to a three-month recess. She compromised on one of eleven weeks.

"Lady in the Dark" is the first play in many years to make effective use of the dream pattern, and the most intelligently written and soundly foundationed dramatically of any of which we have record. The Kurt Weill musical score fittingly complements the drama and Ira Gershwin's lyrics add definite value to the comedy interludes.

This neurotic heroine's evening begins in the office of Dr. Alexander Brooks, psychoanalyst, "a bright, cheerful, book-lined room. There are a desk, a couch, a few chairs, some pleasant pictures on the walls, a few plants of early Spring flowers on the window sill, and an air about the place that is distinctly unmedical."

The Doctor, himself, seated at the moment at his desk signing letters, "is a man in his middle forties, good-looking without being in any way handsome and, when he speaks, with an agreeable lack of the usual bedside manner."

Having finished the work in hand, being apprised of the time of day by a quick glance at his watch, Dr. Brooks rings for his secretary. Miss Bowers, "a jovial little woman, obviously wedded to her work, and clearly as efficient as the horn-rimmed spectacles she wears," responds.

The Doctor is ready to see the Miss Elliott who is waiting. A moment later, Miss Bowers has closed the door behind her and Miss Elliott has, with a slight show of hesitancy, taken the chair in front of the desk to which the Doctor has assigned her.

"Liza Elliott is a woman in her late thirties, plain to the point of austerity. She wears a severely tailored business suit, with her hat pulled low over her eyes. No single piece of jewelry graces her person and her face is free of make-up. There is an air of the executive about her, of a woman always in complete control, yet at the moment she seems to be fighting hard for a moment of calm before she can speak. The Doctor regards her silently, waiting. Their eyes meet. With an effort, she turns away and looks around the room."

She had, Liza admits, as she surveys the Doctor's office, expected something quite different. The sunlight and flowers are a surprise. Also the Doctor's Harvard accent.

"All—this—throws me off," says Liza. "I know very little about psychoanalysis, Dr. Brooks, but I do feel there should be a beard and a Viennese accent around some place."

"I'm all out of them at the moment," admits the Doctor, leaning forward a little. "Suppose you tell me about yourself, Miss Elliott."

The suggestion is disturbing. Liza nervously lights a cigarette. Does the Doctor know anything about her? A little, Dr. Brooks admits, but he would prefer to hear the story from her. He knows that she is the editor of *Allure,* the fashion magazine, and has been for ten years—

"I can't tell you what's the matter with me," blurts Liza, angrily. "I don't know. If I knew I wouldn't be here." She has risen and is pacing the floor. "I find this extremely humiliating."

"Why?"

"I have nothing but contempt for women who spend their days pouring out their frustrations at so much per hour. (*She turns and faces him directly.*) Let me get one thing straight, Dr. Brooks. There's nothing strange in my life. I have no queer twists. I am doing the kind of work I care most for and I am enormously successful at it. My love life is completely normal, happy and satisfactory. I wish there was some little phobia for you to gnaw at. But there isn't. (*She crushes out her cigarette and falteringly lights another.*) Sorry. I'll try to talk in a moment."

"Take all the time you want, Miss Elliott."

"I want to say something else. I don't particularly believe in psychoanalysis. Does that matter?"

"No."

"Dr. Carleton advised me to come here. There is nothing organically wrong with me whatever. That's—that's what's so maddening about it. I feel so ashamed to sit here whining about myself with a world at war. What difference does it make about the way *I* feel! But this isn't a question of happiness or unhappiness. I must make that clear. I'm here because everything in my life is imperiled—my work, all my relationships. I've turned to this in desperation, Dr. Brooks, because I've tried everything else. I've made every effort to pull myself out—and I can't."

"I don't think you need be ashamed, Miss Elliott. Can you tell me a little about the way you feel?"

Haltingly, with the help of the Doctor's gentle questioning, Liza's story is told: She seems to be going to pieces, and she can find no reason for that. Nothing is changed, nothing is different. Yet she finds herself in a constant state of terror and anxiety. She has nothing to be afraid of, yet every time the telephone rings she is filled with fear; she goes through each day in a kind of panic.

This has been going on for about six months, yet nothing that she can recall has happened to cause her alternate states of depression and gaiety. Recently the condition had been getting worse. Does she sleep? "As though I had taken ether," Liza insists. Frequently she has to fight to keep awake.

"You've kept working?"

"Two months ago I handed in my resignation. I felt that getting away from everyone and everything I ever knew might be the answer. And for a week I was well—though it was a kind of well-being that was actually painful. The fatigue disappeared. I would wake up in a state of intense excitement and go through the day in such high exhilaration that it was almost as hard to bear as the other thing. Then imperceptibly, the depression and the panic came back. So I've kept working. I've clung desperately to work to see me through the days—to try to steady myself. And now that's beginning to go. That's why I'm here. Something happened yesterday that—frightened me."

"What was it?"

"We had our usual weekly staff meeting. It's a thoroughly routine affair. The editorial staff meets weekly to discuss layout, space, general policy. Next month's cover—the Easter issue—was up for discussion; whether it was to be the regulation Easter cover or a painting of the circus. I vetoed the circus cover. Our advertising manager kept insisting on it. Suddenly I picked up a paper-weight from my desk and threw it at him. Afterward, I had a spell of weeping—I can't ever remember having cried before. I couldn't stop. This may seem trivial, Dr. Brooks, but it isn't. I have always been an enormously controlled person. That's why this—frightens me."

For twelve years Liza has been associated with the magazine. For ten years she has been its editor. She, in fact, started it—

"Kendall Nesbitt, the publisher, backed it for me," says Liza. Again she hesitates, and then rushes on: "It's ridiculous for me to be school-girlish about this. Mr. Nesbitt and I have been living together for a good many years. His wife refuses to divorce him."

"How do you feel about that?"

"I no longer think about it. We are quite happy together. Our arrangement is a very agreeable one. (*Impatiently.*) I've told you there is nothing strange in my life. It's a good deal more normal and successful than most. I've come to you because I know I am completely healthy in all other respects and this seems to be the only method of treating this—illness. Can you help me?"

"I don't know."

"What does that mean?"

"It's a little more complicated than my just saying 'Yes.' I don't know. It would be wrong for me to suggest that I know what your difficulty is, or how to help you. I can only advise that you embark upon a trial analysis—for a month, let us say. At the end of that time I should have enough data to at least make an honest diagnosis, and you, perhaps, may have a more complete picture of the essential trouble."

A month? Liza thinks she can manage that. She will be ready to start the following Tuesday. Dr. Brooks would prefer that she start immediately. Liza can't. There is too much to do. Dr. Brooks is insistent. Liza is determined. So, Dr. Brooks suggests, it probably would be wiser if she were to consult someone else.

Now Liza has agreed. What is she expected to do? "It's a simple procedure," the Doctor is saying. "It may even seem a little foolish to you. Just remove your hat, lie down on the couch, and speak any of the thoughts that come into your mind. Anything at all."

Liza flashes a quizzical smile at him. "You will get into your beard meanwhile, I trust," she says.

The Doctor has returned to his seat at the desk. Liza, tossing her hat onto a chair, lies down on the couch. For a moment neither speaks. Then Dr. Brooks says quietly, "I am listening—"

It is very curious, the first thought that comes into Liza's mind. "Out of all the millions of little pieces of which my life is made up, one silly little thing keeps going round and round in my mind. It's the first thought I had and it keeps turning."

It is a childhood song that Liza remembers—just bits of the tune, not the words. Yes, she has thought of the song before. Usually when she has been depressed, or when she is feeling panicky. She had remembered it just last night—

"I knew I was coming here this morning—and it frightened me. The song kept running through my head. Over and over. Then I fell asleep—and the song was in the dream, too. Now that I think of it, the song is always there when I dream. It changes—but the music is always there."

The dream? She cannot remember that. "It was one of those confused, fantastic dreams. I knew the people—they were the people I see every day—and yet they were not the people I knew at all. (*Her hands go to her eyes and cover them.*) I can't remember it."

"How did it begin?"

"With the song."

"Hum what you remember of the song. It doesn't matter about the words. Just hum the music."

Softly Liza begins to hum the song. The lights are whirling. Now the orchestra has taken up the song. As the music swells the lights grow dim, the room gradually disappears. Presently, as the lights brighten a little, a softly lighted bit of Park Avenue is to be seen, revealing the façade of a highly ornamental office building. There is a parade of twelve young men in faultless evening clothes. They are carrying lyres, and one has a banner reading: "New York Chapter—Liza Elliott Admirers."

Now the young men are singing, and quite lustily—

"We come to serenade the lovely lady we adore.
She occupies the seventeenth to twenty-second floor.
Our lady so seraphic
May not be very near us,
And with the sound of traffic
She may not even hear us—
But love is wrong without a song, so now as heretofore,
We come to serenade the lovely lady we adore."

The leader of the parade has stepped out for a solo:

"Oh, Fabulous One in your ivory tower—
Your radiance I fain would see!
What Melisande was to Pelléas,
Are you to me . . .

"Oh, Fabulous One in your ivory tower—
My heart and I, they both agree:
What Juliet was to Romeo
Are you to me . . ."

Now Sutton, Miss Elliott's maid, has appeared to sing her regrets that Miss Elliott is resting and cannot see them, though she would thank them for their song. The boys, in sweet sorrow, withdraw till tomorrow, when they promise to return to repeat their nightly serenade.

Again there is a turn of the scenery and we are in Liza's boudoir in which the color scheme is ever so blue. By messenger comes a sable coat for Miss Elliott. By messenger comes an enormous long-stemmed rose for Miss Elliott—from His Royal Highness, the French Pretender, no less.

Presently Beekman, Miss Elliott's chauffeur, bright in a canary yellow uniform, has appeared. He pauses long enough to agree in song with Sutton that—"When in silks out Liza goes, then, methinks, how sweetly flows the liquefaction of her clothes."

Now Liza has arrived. Her mood is glamorous and romantic, her hair is red, her gown gorgeous. Are there messages? Are there? Sutton sings a few—

"Huxley wants to dedicate his book to you
And Stravinsky his latest sonata.
Seven thousand students say they look to you
To be at the Yale-Harvard Regatta.
Epstein says you simply have to pose for him.
Here's the key to the Island of Tobago.
Du Pont wants you wearing the new hose for him.
Can you christen a battleship in San Diego?"

Liza dreamily makes a note of each of her idolaters and of her engagements—dinner at the Seventh Heaven with the Maharajah and two handsome men from Texas; the Toscanini broadcast; a party at the Harrimans'; the Skyscraper room—

"I'll probably motor to Bear Mountain to see the sun rise. You needn't wait up. Good night!"

The scene changes and there is Beekman standing at attention beside the Elliott car. He has changed to a blue costume to fit the evening's mood—

"I learned it would be blue tonight," explains Beekman, "so I'm driving the blue Duesenberg with the blue license plates and I've put the blue Picasso in the car."

"Very thoughtful, Beekman."

Beekman has started the Duesenberg and there is a flash of green lights, then red lights, and presently they are in Columbus Circle. Which reminds Liza that this is where she wanted to make a speech. Beekman gets her blue soap box from the car and helps her mount it. The crowd has gathered. Liza sings—

"There are many minds in circulation
Believing in reincarnation

In me you see
One who doesn't agree.
Challenging possible affronts,
I believe I'll only live once
And I want to make the most of it;
If there's a party I want to be the host of it;
If there's a haunted house I want to be the ghost of it;
If I'm in town I want to be the toast of it."

REFRAIN

"I say to me ev'ry morning:
You've only one life to live,
So why be done in?
Let's let the sun in
And gloom can jump in the riv'!"

When the singing speech is finished Liza and Beekman dance back into the car, there is a green traffic light and before you know it we are in the Seventh Heaven Night Club, which is certainly one of the handsomest in town. Several couples are dancing, but they stop when Liza makes an entrance, with Beekman carrying her coat.

"Words fail me," flutters Pierre, the propriétaire. "My little establishment which, I flatter myself, is the world's most exclusive night club since Louis the Fourteenth ran Le Petit Trianon, is only in the smallest degree worthy of your presence."

"You are sweet, Pierre."

Pierre has clapped for attention. "Miss Liza Elliott!" he announces. This brings everybody to attention. "Gentlemen—a toast! *The* toast! The toast of toasts! Liza Elliott!"

There is cheering from the crowd, and that is quite enough to set the gentlemen singing—"Girl of the Moment"—

"Oh, girl of the moment
With the smile of the day
And the charm of the week
And the grace of the month
And the looks of the year—
Oh, girl of the moment,
You're my moment
Ev'ry moment of the time."

That matter having been attended to a bugle call breaks suddenly upon the scene. And then another. Followed by the appearance of a Soldier, a Sailor and a Marine. They have come bearing a message to Miss Liza Elliott from the President of the United States. "The President requests . . . That for the National unity . . . For the furtherance of good will . . . And for the advancement of cultural and artistic achievement . . . Your portrait be painted and your likeness used on the new two-cent stamp!"

"How really lovely!" croons Liza. "Who is to paint me—and where?"

"I am to paint you—and here," answers the Marine. And does—with Liza posed in a throne-like chair produced for the occasion . . .

Now the portrait is finished and unveiled. It is pretty terrible, but it looks something as Liza looked in the Doctor's office—"austere, somewhat forbidding, entirely without glamor." One look is enough for Liza. She screams. She slaps the face of the Marine. She throws herself upon the throne-like chair and hides her face. . . .

The Marine tries to explain that he painted Liza! The crowd tries to sympathize, pointing first to the portrait and then to Liza— "If *she* is Liza! And *she* is Liza! What is Liza really like?"

Now their queries have merged with the tune of "Girl of the Moment" and they are demanding shrilly but rhythmically—"Oh, girl of the moment, where's the girl that was sublime?"

Again the lights are whirling as they were as Liza began the recital of her dream. The singers become "frozen" as the lights fade. The next moment we are back in the Doctor's office. Liza is stirring uneasily on the couch—

DR. BROOKS—You seem to have remembered a great deal of the dream.

LIZA—Yes.

DR. BROOKS—Did anything about the dream strike you as very strange?

LIZA—Why—only that it seems incredible—when I think of it in relation to myself.

DR. BROOKS—Yes, but you dreamed it. No one else did. You did. Fantastic as it may seem, it came from you. And a dream, you know, is merely a daydream at night. Doesn't it strike you as strange, Miss Elliott, that in your fantasy you are the complete opposite of your realistic self?

LIZA—I don't know what you mean.

DR. BROOKS—Well, in reality, you are obviously a woman who

cares very little for any of the feminine adornments most women use to enhance their attractiveness. In reality, you go to the opposite extreme—almost to the point of severity. Not only in dress, but in any form of rather innocent womanly guile. Yet, in your dream, the very opposite is true. In your fantasy you are the epitome of the glamorous woman—a woman using her femininity as a lure to all men—an enchantress. Doesn't it strike you as curious, too, that you, who have rejected beauty for yourself, in reality, at least, should spend all your days, in fact, dedicate your life to the task of telling *other* women how to be beautiful? That is the function of your magazine, isn't it?

LIZA (*slowly*)—Yes—yes, that's true. What does it mean?

DR. BROOKS—I don't know. Perhaps we shall find out. (*He rises.*) That will be all. Tomorrow at twelve-fifteen.

LIZA (*rises from the couch and slowly takes her hat from the chair. She looks at him for a moment, starts to speak, then checks herself*)—Good day.

DR. BROOKS—Good day, Miss Elliott.

Liza walks quickly to the door and goes out as the curtain falls.

Liza's office is a large, oak-paneled room, done in the Georgian manner—"an impressive room, as befits the editor of the most successful woman's magazine in the country."

Miss Foster, Liza's secretary, "a young girl of about twenty-five and very pretty" (and looking amazingly like Sutton, the maid of Liza's dream) tells a Mr. Nesbitt over the phone that Miss Elliott has not arrived and that she has several appointments as well as an engagement for lunch.

Miss Stevens, receptionist, "a tall, beautiful, willowy blonde girl," peeking in to make sure Miss Foster is alone, comes to report that the office is completely upset by the appearance of Randy Curtis, "the most beautiful hunk of man" Miss Stevens has ever seen. Mr. Curtis, it transpires, is a movie glamor boy who has come to pose for *Allure's* photographer.

When Liza arrives she goes briskly about the business of starting the day. She holds off seeing those who are waiting until she has had a few words with Maggie Grant, her fashion editor—"a good-looking woman in her early forties. A little on the acidulous side so far as humor goes."

To Maggie Liza reports her visit to Dr. Brooks. The treatment, she can see, is going to take some time. Which, at twenty dollars an hour, Maggie can understand. What does the Doctor do? Nothing. Also for twenty bucks an hour!

"I'm sorry," apologizes Maggie. "I know you're having a tough time, Liza, but this seems such a strange thing for you to be doing—it's so unlike you. I know that other people do it—but I wish you weren't. Digging down into yourself and bringing up stuff that'll frighten the hell out of you. God, *I* could give him an earful."

"I've got to try it, anyway," declares Liza. She does feel a little better, too. She could at least talk to Dr. Brooks.

The office routine is gathering speed. Alison Du Bois, one of the magazine's department writers—"a woman who could be any age between thirty and fifty, and positively alive with costume jewelry," has written a piece she would like to read to Liza. Russell Paxton, the magazine's photographer (who is as like Beekman, the chauffeur of Liza's dream, as a man could be) has come to add his slightly effeminate ravings to those of the girls who have seen Randy Curtis—

"Girls, he's God-like!" insists Russell, a little hysterically. "I've taken pictures of beautiful men, but this one is the end—the *end!* He's got a face that would melt in your mouth. . . . Liza, you've got to entertain him for a few moments. He asked to see you. I want to do one picture of him in color as Captain of the Coldstream Guards, and the damn costume hasn't arrived. He's been sitting in the studio for the last half hour in a cowboy outfit. Maggie, did you see him? Is he a creature out of this world or not? Liza, be charming to him—he's waited around like a perfect angel. He's heaven."

Russell has rushed out, but in a few minutes he is back with the God-like one in tow. "Tall, bronzed, sandy-haired, he is every woman's notion of what a good-looking man should be. There is none of the movie 'pretty-boy' about him. He is rugged, powerful, and as Miss Stevens so aptly phrased it, a beautiful hunk of man."

Mr. Curtis is a little embarrassed by this experience. He feels, in his cowboy outfit, that he should be leading a horse. Liza is quick to put him at his ease. Later she is a little surprised to have him tell her that not only had they met before—at a dinner—but that he had on that occasion taken her home. She is sorry. She would like to make amends now by having a little visit with him before he leaves. Randy is going to be too busy for that—but the next time he comes perhaps they can have dinner together.

There are covert smiles at this, and Charley Johnson, the advertising manager who has been waiting to see Liza, adds something to Randy's uneasiness by asking for his autograph. "I collect autographs of all the movie stars," says Charley, a little coyly. "I have them all in a big book and on rainy days I look at them."

Charley Johnson "looks and is slightly hung-over. In his rather dissipated face, there are still the remains of great good looks. To people who go for him, Charley is the charmer of the world." He stands now, after the others have gone, facing Liza, listening to her words of apology for her behavior of the day before.

"May I keep the paper-weight?" he asks, taking it from his pocket and tossing it up and down in the air. "Maybe I can tell the little ones some day what Grandpa was doing during the Second World War. Or do you think you'll want to throw it at somebody else?"

A moment later some act of Liza's has amused him and he has burst into a fit of laughter. "You kill me, Boss Lady," he chortles.

"Look here, Johnson!" Liza has slammed a paper cutter with which she has been toying down on the desk. "I don't like you. I never have. Your so-called charm has always eluded me, and I am repelled by what you consider amusing, such as that little episode with Mr. Curtis just now. You're here because you're excellent at your job and I have never allowed my personal dislikes to interfere with the magazine. (*The telephone rings.*) Yes? Send him right in. (*She hangs up and walks over to the fireplace, her back to* JOHNSON.) Suppose in the future you confine your remarks to your work. If you don't think you can do that perhaps you can make a pleasanter arrangement elsewhere."

"My, my!" He whistles irritatingly through his teeth. "Well, good morning."

Charley has practically bumped into Kendall Nesbitt as the latter comes through the door. "Be careful!" he warns Nesbitt. "Teacher's mad!"

Nesbitt "is a young fifty. A pleasant rich man's life has given him a polish that he wears with becoming elegance," but "his face, while a handsome one, has a soft weak quality."

Nesbitt's greeting of Liza is affectionate and solicitous. He has, he thinks, found the cause of her trouble, and its cure. Liza is troubled because of the unsatisfactory nature of their life together. This can now be adjusted. He has had a final conference with his wife and she has agreed to divorce him. Now he and Liza can marry.

The news comes as something of a shock to Liza. It takes her a moment to absorb it. She is, of course, pleased. Yet— "What is the matter with me?" she mutters.

"Liza, for God's sake, will you get out of this office and go home?" demands Nesbitt. "Why do you keep driving yourself when you're not well? Maggie can get out the magazine—you know very well she can. Why do you persist in this 'show-must-go-on' nonsense, when you're ill!"

"It's better for me here—really it is. Kendall, come to dinner tonight. We can talk then."

Miss Foster comes to announce that Randy Curtis is back and wants to see Liza. He has, Randy reports, had a three-day extension of leave. He would like to have that dinner with Miss Elliott tonight. Can't be done. Tomorrow night? Why, yes. Liza would be delighted. But he will have to pick her up at the office. It is press day and she will be working to the last minute.

Nesbitt, taking a hint that Liza wants to get on with her work, has tossed her a kiss from the doorway and disappeared. She rings for Miss Foster, asks her to summon Miss Grant and then changes her mind. She will not see anyone for the present, and she is not to be disturbed until she rings.

Now Liza has closed her door and turned the key in the lock. Slowly she walks over to the couch and flings herself upon it. She is lying on her back, her arm thrown across her face when suddenly she begins to hum again the song of her dreams. The lights dim into darkness. Through the darkness is heard the name of Liza, weirdly sung.

The singing, it appears as soon as the lights go up, is being done by a group of boys and girls dressed as High School graduates of a generation ago. They are singing a choral extolling the virtues and peculiarities of Liza Elliott.

They remember she was a cheer leader in her third year. They recall gathering in her room to read Dickens. They remember the house she used to live in and the way she used to sing. She was a whiz at tennis and the caricature she drew of M. D'Albert, the French teacher, was a scream. Now this Mapleton High School girl is going to be married—Liza Elliott is marrying Kendall Nesbitt.

First Kendall Nesbitt appears in a pool of light. Then Liza in a white gown. Now they have moved toward each other while the chorus sings of their buying the ring. The salesman is Charley Johnson. Instead of the ring Liza selects Charley proffers a small golden dagger, from which Liza recoils as both men disappear. Randy Curtis, "Flame of the Celluloid," takes their place. Randy is "a precious amalgam of Frank Merriwell, Anthony Eden and Lancelot," sings the chorus.

"Forty million women see him every week and forty million women love him," chorus the women. "In Kansas, in Patagonia, in Hollywood itself he is a man every woman wants."

Now Randy elects to sing of his love and draws Liza to him while he tells of their roaming through the Pleasure Dome of Kublai Khan. He had held her tight, also, in the gardens of Old Babylon. And now here she is, lost through the centuries, but found again.

"This is new—I was merely existing. This is new, and I'm living at last," sing Randy and Liza, ecstatically. "Head to toe, you've got me so I'm spellbound. I don't know if I'm heaven or hell-bound—"

But now it is getting a little mixed. Liza has left Randy's arms and is dancing with Charley Johnson. Six other girls have appeared, all wearing red wigs exactly like Liza's. Now Johnson has gone and Randy is back and Liza is frightfully upset. Now they've all gone and Liza alone is trying to straighten out her thoughts—

"What are you afraid of?" sings the chorus. "You should be happy. Every woman wants to be married. And this is the eve of your wedding day. What are you thinking of?"

"Take all the time you want, Miss Elliott." The voice of Dr. Brooks comes through the mist.

"How curious! How very curious! Of all the things I could be thinking of at this moment, a little school play I acted in when I was a child keeps running through my mind."

"We are all listening," intones the chorus.

"It was called 'The Princess of Pure Delight,'" Liza goes on. As she recites the story children appear representing the characters of a Prince in Orange and a Prince in Blue and a Prince whose raiment is of lavender hue— She tells how they had suffered and tossed at night for the neighboring Princess of Pure Delight—who was secretly in love with a Minstrel.

The King, her father, had settled that problem by bidding his Sorcerer propound a riddle that none could answer except the Minstrel, who eloquently made good his quest for his Princess' hand—

"The Princess then quickly came out of her swoon
And she looked at her swain and her world was in tune.
And the castle soon rang with cheer and with laughter
And of course they lived happily ever after."

Then Liza is suddenly back at her desk again, ordering the staff about, and being reminded by the impertinent Charley Johnson that this, Boss Lady, is her wedding day.

The wedding bells ring out. The procession is formed, led by Russell Paxton elaborately arrayed in morning coat, high hat and striped trousers, with all the boys and girls as bridesmaids and ushers trouping back of him. Liza is being dressed for the occasion and the scenery is being slowly turned into a church with a high stained glass window and a great wedding cake for an altar. Nesbitt has come to offer Liza his arm, the flower boys and girls are active and Randy is singing. Now Charley Johnson has become the minister and is intoning with warning voice—

"If there be any who know why these two should not be joined in holy wedlock let him speak now or forever hold his peace."

A Voice in the Chorus recites an answer to that—

"The murmurings of conscience do increase
And conscience can no longer hold its peace.
This twain should ne'er be joined in holy wedlock
Or e'en in secular board and bed-lock.
This is no part of heaven's marriage plan.
This woman knows she does not love this man."

"No, no! No, no! That isn't true!
I do! I do! I do! I do!"

"This woman at the altar
Is not the true Liza Elliott.
Tell them about yourself, Liza Elliott.
Tell them the woman you really want to be—
Longing to be beautiful
And yet rejecting beauty.
Tell them the truth.
Tell them the truth.
This is no part of heaven's marriage plan.

"No, no! It isn't true!

"This woman knows she does not love this man."

"I do! I do! I do! I do!"

Liza is backing away from the altar, her hands over her ears to shut out the accusing voices. Randy is still singing "This Is New" and the Chorus is offering as a counter melody "What a Lovely Day." "It all becomes a bizarre combination of oratorio and mysterious and ominous movement winding up in a cacophonous musical nightmare." The curtain falls.

Back in Dr. Brooks' office Maggie Grant is sitting in the chair opposite the Doctor's desk. Maggie has come to protest, or at least to find out, just what is happening to Liza.

"God knows I don't know anything about it," admits Maggie, "but you do hear the damnedest things! One person discovers he was frightened by cornflakes as a child, and another one finds out the only trouble with him is he can't stand Radio City. So what does he do about that?"

"It's not quite as bad as that, I hope, Miss Grant." Dr. Brooks is smiling. "Did Miss Elliott know you were coming to see me?"

"No, no—I just did this on my own. You see—we're very great friends. We've grown up with the magazine together—and I know Liza so well that the change in her these last few months scares me. She's going through some kind of hell—and the terrible thing is that even *I* can't seem to reach her. She seems to be sinking into herself more and more. Yesterday afternoon I got kind of a shock. I came back to the office after lunch and her door was locked. I had to pound to get in. She'd fallen asleep on the divan. I'd never known her to do anything like that before. She didn't make sense for a few minutes—she'd been dreaming. She hardly seemed to notice me. Then she started to cry. Couldn't stop. Then she seemed to get hold of herself and we started to work. But she couldn't work. She'd start and stop—pace the floor—light cigarettes—toss them away. Finally—she just walked out. And with the magazine going to press! You can't realize what a different Liza Elliott that is—she's been like a machine all the years I've known her. That's why I'm frightened, Dr. Brooks. Is she on the right track? Can you help her? Forgive my being skeptical—I'm very fond of her and very worried."

"I hope I can help her, Miss Grant. Analysis takes time and patience and courage—on Miss Elliott's part. I can't discuss

hoto by Vandamm Studio.

"LADY IN THE DARK"

Liza Elliott had been for ten years the editor of a fashion magazine called *Allure*.
(*Gertrude Lawrence*)

details with you—I'm sure you realize that. But for your own reassurance—I'm inclined to be hopeful. I can't say any more than that."

Liza has been waiting. She tosses her hat aside and goes quickly to the couch. Quietly Dr. Brooks directs her thought back to the end of their last conference. She was telling then of her panic when Kendall Nesbitt had told her of his divorce; of her flinging herself on the couch; of the dream that followed, and of Maggie's pounding on the door.

Dr. Brooks presses the fact of her reaction to Mr. Nesbitt's divorce. Liza feels that a decision must be made concerning her marriage, but she cannot make up her mind as to what it should be. Why can't Dr. Brooks help her? Does she want to marry Nesbitt? No. Does she want to be told not to marry him? No.

"I can only suggest again that we try to learn more about your present emotional state before deciding anything," Dr. Brooks advises. "You noticed, I presume, that in this dream, too, you are again the glamorous woman."

"Yes, yes. What of it?"

Dr. Brooks—Why do you think you continually dream this fantasy, and yet never attempt to act it out in your conscious life?

Liza—I don't know.

Dr. Brooks—Have you any reason that you give yourself for the austere way you dress, for instance?

Liza—Only the simple and valid one that I happen to like business suits and simple dresses.

Dr. Brooks—Do you think there is a chance that that may not be the real explanation?

Liza—Suppose it isn't? What earthly difference does it make?

Dr. Brooks—Have you always felt that way about clothes? As a child, for instance?

Liza—Yes, yes! As far back as I can remember.

Dr. Brooks—That's curious, isn't it? Children usually like pretty clothes.

Liza—Well, I didn't! And I was a perfectly happy, normal child!

Dr. Brooks—I see. Now, these men in the dream. They are the men you usually see every day?

Liza—Yes. All except Mr. Curtis.

DR. BROOKS—Oh, yes. And I think you told me you have an engagement with him for tomorrow night, didn't you?

LIZA—I intend to break it.

DR. BROOKS—Why?

LIZA—I only said "Yes" to get rid of him. He came in just after Kendall told me about—Kate. I wanted to get him out.

DR. BROOKS—Why do you intend to break the engagement?

LIZA—Because I can think of nothing I'd like to do less.

DR. BROOKS—Really? Why?

LIZA—It just wouldn't interest me, that's all. Do we have to go on with this forever?

DR. BROOKS—Do you think most women would feel that way? Don't you think most women would be delighted to spend an evening with a man as attractive as Curtis? They might even feel flattered at being seen with him.

LIZA—I wouldn't. Do you mind?

DR. BROOKS—There's a strange contradiction here, isn't there? Remember in your dream Mr. Curtis made love to you—held you in his arms. Yet here you savagely reject him. That's a curious denial, isn't it?

LIZA—Yes, yes, what of it?

DR. BROOKS—Bear with me a little further, Miss Elliott—it's important. Then, in your dream, you are suddenly a bride—but it is Kendall Nesbitt you find at the altar. Not Randy Curtis. And the mocking voices of other women make the ceremony a nightmare—turn it into a horror you cannot face. Yet your job is to make other women beautiful, isn't it?

LIZA—We've been over that before, haven't we?

DR. BROOKS—I wonder if your scorn and hatred of other women is because you are afraid of them. You make them beautiful to appease them, but the more beautiful you make them the more they continue to rob you, and your hate and fear of them grows. Perhaps the reason for the way you dress is that it is a kind of protective armor—with it you are not forced to compete. You don't dare.

LIZA—That's not true. I reject that—all of it. You forget Nesbitt.

DR. BROOKS—No. You see, Miss Elliott, even the man you have belongs to another woman. In a sense he is a man already taken—a man that you share. And the thought of having him alone sends you into a panic. You don't dare compete as a woman.

Liza (*after a pause* Liza *rises from the couch and faces him. Her voice sounds strange, as though she could not quite control it*)—I've had enough. I'm not going any further. Send me a bill for whatever this is. Good day.

Dr. Brooks (*rises but makes no move to detain her*)—Good day, Miss Elliott. (*She goes quickly out.*)

The curtain falls.

It is late the next afternoon. In Liza's office Russell Paxton is sprawled out on the couch, a lady's evening cape thrown across him as a coverlet, a rather outrageous lady's hat shielding his eyes. Alison Du Bois is slumped in a chair and Maggie Grant is nervously pacing the room. They have been waiting long for Liza. She has not come, nor have they been able to get in touch with her. Time is getting short. The magazine must be sent to the printers. What are they to do?

There are suggestions. Alison, learning of the psychoanalyst experiment, is certain if Liza had tried astrology she would have been all right. Russell is convinced Liza is cracking up. He knows women. "A career or a baby isn't always the answer," announces Russell. "Sleeping around isn't either," he adds, with a wicked glance at Alison. "None of you ever seem to realize that anything is wrong until you're in the middle of a blitzkrieg!"

"What do they call you at home, Professor? The Magic Bullet?" asks Maggie.

"Well, look around you, dear. You're all so messy—maybe that's why so much bitchery goes on."

They have about decided to go ahead without Liza when she arrives. She is no sooner in the office than orders begin to fly. "I'm sorry about this," she flings from her desk. "We'll have to work late. Russell, talk to Adams, will you? He's outside. See if he can hold the men at the shop. Alison, call Bergdorf's for me and see if they'll hold over until the next issue. Promise them anything. Maggie, wait here a minute, will you?"

"Darling, you look liverish—you ought to take a good physic," suggests Alison. "It's not very chic, but . . ."

"Come on, dear—move, move! We've been all through your upper colon many times." Russell has practically pushed Alison through the door.

To Maggie, Liza is willing to offer some sort of explanation. She tells her of Nesbitt's divorce announcement and of her strange emotional reaction. Since seven o'clock this morning she has been driving furiously about Long Island trying to compose her thought and subdue her nerves, but without success. She knows people must be talking—but she is sick—sick inside. And she has quit the analysis.

"Maybe the Doctor could have helped if you'd given him time," Maggie is saying. "You shouldn't have quit, Liza. You shouldn't!"

"I couldn't stand it, I tell you."

Mr. Nesbitt is announced. Better see him, Liza decides. Facing him can't be worse than what she is going through.

"I'll get things moving," promises Maggie. "Don't worry about the magazine—we'll get it out. Just try and decide about the Easter cover, will you?"

"All right. Thank you, Maggie."

There are explanations for Kendall, but they are not very satisfactory. The plain fact is that she does not want to marry him. Liza admits that. As to going on as they have been doing, she hasn't decided about that, either.

"I can't explain it," Liza admits, finally. "How can I make clear to you what I don't understand myself. There *is* no valid reason. I can't give you one. I've tried to think it out—you must know I have—but I can't. I'm ill, Kendall."

"I won't let you off this easy, Liza. I know you're ill—but you'll be well again. Other people go through these things, too. Meanwhile, you haven't the right to trifle with other people's lives, even with this as an excuse. I won't let you."

It is Kendall's decision that Liza should go through with their marriage. Her confusion will clear up after that. "I'm going to fight, Liza," he says, moving toward the door as Russell Paxton comes barging into the room, his arms full of trailing chiffon.

Russell wants Liza's okay on a picture he is posing—a knight in armor backed by four lovely models—one in a ski outfit, one in evening dress, one in an afternoon dress for Southern wear, and another in a negligee. It isn't very good, Liza thinks, but let it go.

Charley Johnson has come in during the posing. Now that the room is cleared he would state his business. First, he wishes his Boss Lady would decide on the circus cover for the Easter number. He can get a helluva tie-up with Ringling Brothers if she will. Second, he had hoped to make this Easter number big so that he could leave his job in a blaze of glory—

"This is what might be termed my resignation, Boss Lady," says Charley. "Please—no tears. Just a light kiss on the cheek, perhaps. Then a quick good-by. Hot dog!"
"Pretty thin-skinned, aren't you?"

CHARLEY—Me? You mean you think I'm tossing in the towel because you spanked me yesterday? No-oo! Just got a better offer—that's all.
LIZA—Where?
CHARLEY—*Town and Country.*
LIZA—I'll meet it.
CHARLEY—'Fraid you couldn't.
LIZA—I'll be the judge of that.
CHARLEY—Why? I annoy the pants off you, don't I?
LIZA—That has nothing to do with the way you do your job. I'll meet their figure. Does that settle it?
CHARLEY—Look—it has nothing to do with salary. I'm taking less. But I can get somewhere there that I can never get here. (*He pauses slightly.*) Your job. I'm afraid that's what I want.
LIZA—How nice of you to be so frank.
CHARLEY—Yah—I'm ambitious. Want to run the whole thing myself, some day. Never suspect it, would you? But I'm an eager lad, full of dreams. And there isn't a chance of that here. You married that desk years ago, Boss Lady, and you're never going to get a divorce. I know your kind.
LIZA—Do you really!
CHARLEY—Yep. You have magazines instead of babies. Maybe you're right. There's a lot like you.
LIZA (*quietly*)—Get out of here!
CHARLEY—Now, I didn't mean to be insolent. Honest.
LIZA—You're not only insolent. You're contemptible. I know your kind, too, Johnson. And I'm sick of that incredible side-show you put on under the guise of "the gay young man with a wicked tongue." It doesn't always excuse your being an ill-mannered boor, and I question whether that isn't the extent of your talent.
CHARLEY (*stung*)—Rage is a pretty good substitute for sex, isn't it?
LIZA (*exploding*)—Get out! (*She picks up a cigarette box from the desk and flings it at him.*)
CHARLEY (*dodging*)—Don't think it hasn't all been charming.

And if we ever need a good man over there, I'll make you an offer.

Charley strolls out, whistling. Liza crumples into her chair, her head on her arms, and is crying violently when Miss Stevens comes to announce the return of Randy Curtis. Liza barely has time to recover her poise before Randy is standing before her, resplendent in white tie and tails.

Seeing that Liza isn't dressed he suggests that it would be a lot more fun if she were to go just as she is. He is sick of glamour girls. Liza will not have it that way. She is going to dress. And, while he waits outside, she does dress—taking an attractive gown from the dummy model over which it is draped, a colorful evening cape from another, kicking off her shoes and getting into a new pair.

She is crying a little wildly as she dresses and is just fluffing out her hair when Maggie comes to demand another explanation. "Liza! What *is* this?"

"Advertisement! From *Allure!* Magazine of Beauty! Like the line? The most alluring women are wearing it."

"Liza, are you all right?" Maggie has taken Liza by the shoulders.

"I'm fine! Let me alone!" Liza has shaken Maggie off and dashed through the door. Maggie is staring after her as the curtain falls.

ACT II

Late the following afternoon Liza is in her office, studying layouts spread on her desk. Maggie, come to take her away, is disturbed by the increasing darkness. "It's as gloomy as a Willkie button in here," protests Maggie.

Liza will not leave. She insists that she must stay and work. Neither can she be moved by Alison Du Bois, who drops in on her way to the "21" Club. Liza was positively the sensation of the Stork Club the night before, when she walked in with Randy Curtis, Alison bubbles. "Nobody talked of anything else all night."

"Not even Hemingway?" queries the incredulous Maggie.

After they have gone Liza sits staring unseeingly at her desk for a time. Now she is up and pacing the room. A book on Astrology that Alison has left catches her eye. She picks it up and opens it. "Turning to Astrology, now, eh?" mutters an inner voice. "What will be next? Numerology?"

"Astrology! The stars! And you're clutching at it! Helplessly! You're clutching at anything!"

The voices are closing in upon her. She has gone back to the cover drawings on her desk. Again the voices begin to taunt her: "Can't make up your mind!" "Can't even decide on a cover!" Then the voices of Nesbitt and Charley Johnson and Randy Curtis come in to plague her.

"The circus cover or the Easter cover? Why can't you decide?" a voice is demanding. "Even this little decision frightens you now. It's getting worse. It's getting worse." "You must decide this now or you'll go mad! You can't leave here without deciding!" "The Easter cover or the circus cover?"

The lights fade out. When they are raised Liza is standing staring at an enlargement of the circus drawing at which she was gazing on her desk—"a brilliant picture of circus performers in full costume." The walls of the office have disappeared. From a distance circus parade music comes floating in. Now the paraders have appeared, stepping high and lively; and singing—

"The Greatest Show on Earth! It's full of Thrills and Mirth! You Get Your Money's Worth! Come one! Come all!"

Now the Ringmaster, who is really Russell Paxton grown very operatic, is calling the wonders of the show—

"Ladies and Gentlemen, I Take Pride in Introducing
The Greatest Show on Earth!
Liza Elliott's Gargantuan Three-Ring Circus
Featuring for the First Time
The Captivating and Tantalizing Liza Elliott . . .
The Woman Who Cannot Make up Her Mind!"

The Ringmaster has now called Liza Elliott to trial. The charges against her are numerous. Whereas, she cannot make up her mind about the Easter cover; whereas, she cannot make up her mind about marrying Kendall Nesbitt; whereas, she cannot make up her mind as to the kind of woman she wants to be, executive or enchantress—

"In a world where tumult and turmoil reign, these indecisions of Liza Elliott only add to the confusions of an already, as indicated, confused world—"

"Therefore be it resolved, That Liza Elliott be brought to trial and be made to make up her mind."

Charley Johnson is named "the death-defying trapese artist

and prosecuting attorney," and Randy Curtis "the thrilling bareback rider and attorney for the defense." The chorus sings lustily of their achievements.

Kendall Nesbitt, "peerless witness and lion tamer," is called. He confirms the Ringmaster's suspicions. He is divorcing his wife, expecting to marry Liza, but now she refuses to make up her mind. Sings the Ringmaster—

"The Mister who once was the master of two
Would make of his mistress his Mrs.
But he's missed out on Mrs. for the mistress is through—
What a mess of a mish mash this is!"

Randy, for the defense, would now call the jury's attention to the fact that while Liza gave Kendall her heart she did not give him her word, and "When a maid gives her heart but does not give her word, how on earth can that maid have betrayed him?"

Liza takes the stand to confirm this fact. When the attorney for the prosecution asks her if she can give the court any reasonable explanation as to why she cannot make up her mind she sings them the story of Jenny, who suffered variously because of her habit of making quick and lasting decisions.

Jenny, it appears, made her mind up when she was three that she herself would trim the Christmas tree. "Christmas Eve she lit the candles—tossed the taper away. Little Jenny was an orphan on Christmas Day." And so it goes. Jenny made her mind up at twenty-two to get herself a husband. "She got herself all dolled up in her satins and furs and she got herself a husband—but he wasn't hers." Jenny made her mind up at fifty-one to write her memoirs. "So she wrote 'em and she published all her loves and her hates and had libel suits in forty of the forty-eight States." Finally Jenny made her mind up at seventy-five that she would break all longevity records. "But gin and rum and destiny play funny tricks and poor Jenny kicked the bucket at seventy-six."

The saga of Jenny convinces the jury that Liza is right. It would be foolish for her to make up her mind. In the midst of the congratulations Charley Johnson again calls the attention of the jury to the circus cover, but Liza grabs the drawing from his hands.

"You see?" says Charley to the jury. Turning to Liza he adds dramatically: "You're afraid. You're hiding something. You're afraid of that music, aren't you? Just as you're afraid to compete as a woman—afraid to marry Kendall Nesbitt—afraid to be the woman you want to be—afraid—afraid—afraid!"

Now the crowd has turned on Liza again and is taunting her accusingly. The circus music has started and the parade is re-forming. Through the beat of the rhythm come the words: "Make up your mind, make up your mind, make up your mind!" The lights fade.

We are back in Dr. Brooks' office. Liza is pacing the floor. She is too nervous to lie down. She has been telling Dr. Brooks of the dream—the dream that was more than a dream, more like a kind of hallucination. Through it all she had the feeling of remembered emotion—as though she had experienced it all before. As a little girl she had felt that way constantly—"the bad feeling" she called it. She thinks she must have felt it first when she was very small—not more than three or four years old.

The lights are dimmed. Now they are brightened. Liza stands in a pool of light. A little distance from her is a group of people in such evening clothes as they wore in 1904. One woman of great beauty is Liza's mother. Presently her father joins the group. In his arms is Liza as a little girl. He has brought her to say good night and to sing a little song.

There are compliments for Liza and for her beauty, but her father just laughs them off. He and Liza's mother are reconciled to having a plain child, he says. Rather a relief, thinks Father. "One beauty in the family is enough, I can tell you," he says, patting his wife's cheek. "I couldn't stand two."

"She'll never be a beauty, Helen, no matter what you do, and I'm glad of it," insists Father over his wife's protests, as he pats his daughter's cheek. "Daddy's little ugly duckling, isn't she? Come, Liza! Sing us your song, and then a good-night kiss." Liza buries her face in his shoulder. When she looks up she is struggling against tears. Her father begins the song, but Liza has burst into tears and run from the room.

"I ran to the nursery and looked in the mirror," the grown Liza recalls, as the group fades out. "I felt ugly and ashamed. When my mother came in I hated her because she was so beautiful!"

Now a group of school-children has emerged from the darkness. Their teacher is rehearsing them in the singing of a Cinderella song. When they have finished, she names David Reed and Liza Elliott to play the Prince and Princess. Liza jumps up and down with joy. David scowls and announces that he doesn't want to be the Prince.

"Why can't we have a pretty Princess—like Barbara?" demands the pouting David. "A Princess ought to be beautiful, oughtn't she? Liza will spoil everything! I don't want to be the Prince if she's the Princess."

The teacher reprimands David and would go on with the play. But now Liza rebels, running from the room in tears. "I couldn't bear it," recalls the grown Liza. "I wanted to crawl away and hide."

Three years later the little Liza, sprawled on the floor munching an apple, is told of her mother's death by a sympathetic housekeeper.

"I wanted to cry. Yet somehow I couldn't," reports the grown Liza. "I loved my mother. But I could feel no grief. The tears wouldn't come."

The child Liza has run off into the darkness. When she returns she is wearing her mother's evening cloak. She is standing before a mirror humming a song when her father comes from her mother's room. He is shocked. He rips the cloak from the child and sends her to her room.

"But that feeling was gone," reports Liza. "I don't know why. It was gone. Until . . ."

A group of seventeen-year-olds are dancing, the girls in white with bow-knots in their hair, the boys in blue serge, with stiff collars. Ben Butler has asked Liza to dance. They are interrupted by an announcer.

"Listen, everybody! The votes are all in and counted. Want to hear the results? (*They yell: 'Yes! Yes!'*) Here you are: The Graduating Class of Mapleton High School votes Homer Adams the Boy Most Likely to Succeed (*Applause.*), Henry Conrad the Most Brilliant Student (*Applause.*), Barbara Joyce the Most Beautiful Girl (*Applause.*), Ben Butler the Handsomest Boy (*Applause.*), and Liza Elliott the Most Popular Girl!"

The winners are noisily congratulated. The dance goes on. Ben and Liza have a good look at each other. She doesn't think him the handsomest, nor does he think she is the most popular. They hadn't voted for each other. Now they seem to be seeing each other for the first time. Ben proposes that they sit out the rest of the dance; that they break their respective dates and go in to supper together. What about Barbara? Well, Ben hasn't exactly quarreled with Barbara, but he is beginning to have his opinion of a girl who flirts all the time.

"Maybe it took a girl like Barbara to make me see how nice you are, Liza," he says. "Who are you going on the boat ride with?"

"Homer Adams."

"Break it and come with me."

"Oh, I couldn't, Ben."

But finally Liza is persuaded. Ben kisses her impulsively. In her happiness Liza covers her face with her hands. She doesn't want to dance. She doesn't want to move. She just wants to sit there and be happy. His arm is around her waist and her head is on his shoulder.

Now Liza is singing the little song that she had not thought of in years. "My ship has sails that are made of silk— The decks are trimmed with gold— And of jam and spice there's a paradise in the hold—"

It's a song of a maid and her true love. Ben thinks it is lovely. "It's—it's just a song I've always known. But I never could remember all the words before," says Liza.

Barbara Joyce has strolled by. She laughs a little when she sees them. Barbara is blonde and very beautiful. She would like to talk with Ben for a minute. Liza excuses him. He will be right back.

Liza waits. And waits. But Ben does not come. Soon another boy appears to tell her that Ben and Barbara are in having supper. Liza is sitting with her face in her hands weeping as the lights fade out. . . .

"I'm afraid we have only a little time left today," Dr. Brooks is saying, as the office lights brighten; "so what I want to say I must say quickly. Shall I wait until tomorrow? I know this has been difficult for you."

Liza—No. I'm all right.

Dr. Brooks—Let me try to fit the pieces together, if I can. We can see the pattern more clearly now, I think. A little girl, convinced of her own ugliness, rejects herself as not as good as other little girls, and then is rejected by the world.

Liza—The world?

Dr. Brooks—Yes. That little episode in school was tragic. School and other children are a child's world, aren't they?

Liza—But why did that—"bad feeling"—disappear when my mother died? I don't understand that.

Dr. Brooks—Perhaps because that constant reminder of

beauty—of all that you were not and longed to be—was no longer there.

LIZA—And then?

DR. BROOKS—Then you blossomed as yourself until once again—and at a most crucial moment—a beautiful woman robs you. I think, then, that you withdrew as a woman. That you would no longer risk being hurt as a woman competing with other women. But the longing remained—and so did the rage and the deep sense of injustice. And what you are facing now is rebellion—rebellion at your unfulfillment as a woman.

LIZA—But that's not true! I did love Kendall. And I know he loves me. How can you answer that?

DR. BROOKS—I can't answer that yet, Miss Elliott. But there is an answer, I think, to that, too. (*He rises.*) Tomorrow at the usual time?

LIZA—Yes. Good day. (*She goes quickly out.*)

The curtain falls.

A week later, in Liza's office, four beauteous models are again assembled, together with Charley Johnson and Maggie Grant, waiting for a missing Liza to come and pass on the gorgeous evening clothes and wraps the girls are wearing.

Charley would take the models down to the drug store for a rich frappé, but Maggie objects. Charley is to stay right there until he has apologized to Liza, as he had promised. Charley's willing. He realizes that he has said things he should not have said. He knows that for six years he has furnished his share of Liza's causes for irritation. There's a reason for that. It's because he likes and admires Liza—

"I've always admired her—as a person," insists Charley. "As a woman she makes me sick. Let me tell you something, Maggie. It's not what I say or the way I behave sometimes that gets under her skin. It's because I see through the pose. The big executive pose. She can't stand that. It frightens her. She needs that authority she wears like a thick enamel—she's afraid without it, God knows why! I knew that from the first day I walked into this office—but I could never resist chipping bits of it off and seeing what was underneath. Because underneath it, she's a helluva girl."

Russell Paxton bursts into the office in a state of excitement. "That bitch," meaning Alison Du Bois, has crossed Russell again. And deliberately. Alison has calmly loaned his color plates to a friend. "Maggie, you of all people know that I've put up with

Alison in an absolutely God-like fashion. Now, either she goes or I do. And just before I leave I may tear out her entrails and photograph them in color."

Russell has stormed out and Alison has floated in. What has she done with Russell's color plates? "Darling, I didn't loan them. I dropped them and broke them—I haven't told him yet. . . ."

Liza and Randy Curtis have been to lunch. It was fun and Randy has proved so fascinating that he has made Liza late for all her appointments. He must take himself out of her life right this minute. But Randy, too, is fascinated—with Liza—

"You're about three different people, Liza," the glamorous one insists. "Today at lunch you were like someone I'd never met before—gay, and . . . I don't know—completely different from the other night. And the minute you walk into this office you're someone else again. If you want to talk about fascinating—*you're* the one!"

Randy can be very endearing sometimes, Liza admits, but now he must go. No, she can't possibly take the afternoon off for a walk through the park, with cocktails to follow. She has work to do.

"Liza . . . Tell me something." Randy has taken her hand and become quite serious. "It's not just the movie star you like, is it? Don't mind my asking that. It's because—sometimes I can't tell where the movie star leaves off and I begin. You see, I know people invite me around—not because they want *me*—they want a name and a face. And I find myself playing up all the time—giving 'em what they expect. Paying for my dinner. And it's not me at all. I get more and more lost in the shuffle. I didn't want it to be that way—with us."

"It's not, Randy."

"Come on—take the afternoon off, Liza! Let's get drunk."

The door opens and Charley Johnson appears. He realizes the intrusion and is ready to withdraw, but Liza wants to see him. It is Randy who must go.

For a moment Liza and Charley stand looking at each other. Invited to sit down, he pleads a pressure of business. "I thought Maggie was in here . . ."

"Never mind. This is Boss Lady speaking," answers Liza. "You see, it occurred to me, Johnson, that in all the years you've been here, in all those charming talks we've had together, *you've* always had all the answers. And now that you're leaving, I thought I'd like at least one little talk in which *I* had the answers."

Charley is not greatly interested. He continues poised and confident when Liza admits that a great change has come over her. She is no longer afraid of him, and she used to be terrified every time he came into her office. Now she is ready to meet him on new grounds.

"Would you come out into the open where *I'm* the boss, Miss Elliott?" Charley suddenly demands. "Just once? Dinner, cocktails—name it yourself. Any place away from that God-damned desk. I'll even make it my office and my desk. How about it?"

"It's the best offer I've had today. Only I like being boss, Johnson."

"I know that. But so do I."

"I know that. But so do I."

"Well, sir—here we are."

"Yes, sir—here we are."

They are still facing each other when Miss Foster comes in to announce Kendall Nesbitt, and Charley gracefully withdraws.

Kendall is in a state of mind. He takes Liza in his arms. He begs her not to leave him.

"Kendall, dear, it isn't you—it's me. I know that now. Something mixed up inside myself—something I'm only dimly beginning to understand—but it's like a searchlight playing over my entire life. So many, many things are suddenly clear. It's not you, darling, it's me."

"I need you terribly, Liza. I've been alone all my life except for you."

"Kendall—help me. I'm trying to fight my way out of the dark. Help me to do the right thing. For both of us. I can't bear to see you like this—we're bound together by years of kindness and affection—we always will be, Kendall. Always. I want so desperately for you to understand now. I must make you understand."

"It's over, Liza, isn't it? Nothing either one of us can do about that. It's over. I guess I've known for a long time, but I couldn't face it. I'm sorry— For just now. (*He takes her in his arms again.*) Perhaps I do understand, Liza—in my own way. Perhaps the thing that brings people together—that need they have of each other—is a very strange one. Love is just a label for it—a word. It's not as simple as that. It's love and fear and hiding and longing and all the little pieces that go to make up the mystery and wonder of a human being. I know—because I've had a battle of my own. It's what brought us together, Liza—each in our own separate way—and now it's tearing us apart. It's the way things happen. (*He kisses her gently.*) You'd do this, Liza. Fight your way through. Perhaps you'll be one of the lucky ones—the ones who come out of the dark into the sun. But some way—somewhere—find a place for me in your life, will you?"

"Always, Kendall. Always."

Kendall has gone, and with him a part of Liza's life, she tells Maggie. Liza realizes now that for the first time she is learning all about someone she never knew before—herself. "It's frightening—and wonderful," she says. "Somehow I'm going to find the courage to see it through."

"You've never run away from anything in your life, Liza."

"There are other ways of running away, Maggie. I think my whole relationship with Kendall was a flight from something I didn't dare face. And Kendall, too. He's like a lost child, really—this false front of strength that I have gave him the security he needed."

Now Randy Curtis is back, and in a state of excitement. He has come to ask Liza to marry him. Before Liza can overcome a normal surprise Randy has rushed into a confession. He realizes that Liza has known him only a week. He would like her to know that he doesn't care a hoot for acting. He fell into a Hollywood career by dumb luck and if he weren't doing that he would probably be running a gas station in Arizona. Now, suddenly, he has come to realize that he needs Liza—that of all the women he has known she is the only one who has ever given him a feeling of peace, and of courage—

"Maybe it goes back to when I was a kid. I was kicked out on my own at twelve—scared and desperate and needing someone to hang on to. And the funny thing is that still goes. I often think when I'm playing one of those big strong-man scenes and telling everyone where to get off—boy, if they only knew! Gee, this is a helluva love scene I've just played."

Liza finds Randy's proposal a little disturbing. She will want time to think it over. Yes, he may phone her later and hold the hope of taking her to dinner. . . .

Liza is standing at her desk, trying to collect her thoughts when Charley Johnson comes back. He, too, has reached a decision—

"I'm supposed to apologize for what I said the other day—

promised Maggie I would," Charley begins. "But I've been thinking it over quietly and I've decided I'm not going to. I'm sorry—I can't help it. It's just that you've had to be the boss—always—and something in me deeply resents that. I can't help it. I know I've been pretty rotten to you—and I've kicked myself for it afterward. But there's always been that secret battle between us—from the beginning—and I've always had to win—because, well, because I'm me, I guess. Anyhow, I want you to know—now that I'm leaving—that for all your Goddam shenanigans I think you're fine. (*He turns away.*) I've turned in the Hattie Carnegie layout to Paxton, so I guess that washes me up. Anything else?"

LIZA (*staring at him as though seeing him for the first time*)—Johnson—or, Charley—if I may—give me back that paper-weight and stay, will you?

CHARLEY—Huh?

LIZA—I know all your reasons for wanting to leave, but it appears that I'm slowly getting a divorce—from myself. I think you ought to stick around and see the fun. What do you say?

CHARLEY (*looking at her for a long moment*)—Sorry. It wouldn't work.

LIZA—You mean—two bosses?

CHARLEY—Roughly.

LIZA—You're right. But suppose we ran it together—I might even step aside after a while if you didn't get too drunk with power.

CHARLEY—You—you mean that?

LIZA—Yes. Only—I'd like the paper-weight now, as a token that you're going to stay. Because—I want you to stay—very much.

CHARLEY (*crossing to her after a slight pause*)—Here you are. Catch. (*He tosses the paper-weight to her, she catches it, goes behind her desk.*)

LIZA—Thank you.

CHARLEY (*suddenly turns after quite a pause*)—Now look—I'd like to change the format right away—I've been sick of it for years. Got a layout on your desk?

LIZA—Yes. The July issue.

CHARLEY—Here's what I mean. To hell with the title being on top. Put it over here. See what I mean? (MAGGIE *enters and stares amazed at the picture of the two of them present.*)

LIZA—Yes—yes!

CHARLEY—Then change the type—you suggested that yourself months ago.

LIZA—Change the size, too!

CHARLEY—Sure, sure. Look—let me show you something . . . !

LIZA (*as she looks up and sees* MAGGIE)—Maggie, be an angel and telephone Mr. Curtis at the Waldorf and tell him I can't see him tonight—I'll talk to him in the morning. But look, Charley, we can't do all that for the July issue, can we?

CHARLEY—Sure, we can! Listen—I've got a layout in my office—let me get it—be right back.

LIZA—Okay.

CHARLEY (*to* MAGGIE, *as he rushes out*)—Be nice to me, Wonderful. I'm your boss now.

MAGGIE (*acidly*)—Would you mind telling me, Miss Elliott, exactly what the hell goes on here?

LIZA—Oh, Maggie, Maggie, I almost made a great mistake! I almost twisted up my life all over again. I might have married Randy! He seemed a refuge—a tower of strength! Those parts he plays—and the way he looks! And you know what, Maggie? He's another Kendall. Frightened and insecure—seeing in me what Kendall saw in me—needing what Kendall needed. A mother—not a wife! I almost did the same thing all over again. And I'll tell you something else—I've suddenly seen Charley Johnson for the first time—and I think I know the reason why for a great many things. (*Gaily.*) Don't worry about me, Maggie! I'm going to be all right!

MAGGIE—Well, for God's sake!

CHARLEY (*dashing back, arms full of papers, going right to the desk and seating himself*)—Look—I made up this dummy just for fun a few weeks ago— See what it does to the whole magazine?

LIZA—Yes, yes . . . I like it.

CHARLEY—Now, look at this . . . The ads here . . . The color section here. What about that? It's dangerous—but if we can pull it off it can be great. (LIZA *has apparently not heard. Intent on the papers in her hands, she begins to hum. It is that song.* CHARLEY *suddenly sings.*) "And of jam and spice, there's a paradise in the hold."

LIZA (*looking at him—astonished*)—Why—do you know that song?

CHARLEY—Yeah—haven't heard it since I was a kid, though. Go ahead—do you know it all?

LIZA—Yes—I know all the words—now. (*She smiles, then slowly begins to sing.* CHARLEY, *as the remembered words come back to him, softly joins in.* MAGGIE *looks curiously from one to the other—then elaborately sinks into a chair and folds her hands in her lap.* LIZA *is singing gaily—happily. Oblivious of* MAGGIE *they half-smile at each other.*)

THE CURTAIN FALLS

ARSENIC AND OLD LACE

A Comedy in Three Acts

By Joseph Kesselring

IT was all of three years ago that Joseph Kesselring wrote the comedy that came to be called "Arsenic and Old Lace," and two years ago that the Messrs. Howard Lindsay and Russel Crouse bought it. "Bodies in Our Cellar" it was called originally and Mr. Kesselring had an idea that Dorothy Stickney (Mrs. Lindsay), who has been playing so successfully with her husband these last two seasons in "Life with Father," would be ideal in the rôle of one of the maiden aunts who are the comedy's chief characters.

Mr. Kesselring sent his script to Miss Stickney with this suggestion and Miss Stickney, being not only a dutiful but an admiring wife, having read and liked it, turned it over to Mr. Lindsay. Now Mr. Lindsay at the moment was up to his armpits in preparations for the production of that before mentioned "Life with Father" at the Summer theatre in Lakewood, which is near Skowhegan, Maine. He had no time to fool with another comedy, but the idea interested him and he sent it on to Crouse, who was at that time picking up a little extra cash writing scenarios in Hollywood. Mr. Crouse was also interested and so "Bodies in Our Cellar" became a Lindsay-Crouse property, to be staged if, as and when.

Another year passed before they got to work at it and six months after that before it was produced at the Fulton Theatre, New York, the night of Jan. 10, 1941. It proved an immediate comedy riot. "It is a noisy, preposterous, incoherent joy," Richard Lockridge wrote of it in the New York *Sun.* "You wouldn't believe that homicidal mania could be such great fun." These sentiments were pretty generously echoed by the Lockridge colleagues, and the playgoing public began flocking to the theatre. "Arsenic and Old Lace" ran through the remainder of the theatre season and continued into the Summer.

Naturally, there was a minority report submitted by those who still find it difficult to extract gusts of humor from either homicidal mania or harmless insanity, but it was a protest quickly and overwhelmingly voted down. The situations in "Arsenic and Old

Lace" are so frankly and completely idiotic it is practically impossible to stand against them. And these were also playgoing days when the "escape comedies" were especially popular.

The living room of the old Brewster home in Brooklyn, into which we are shown one late September afternoon, is "just as Victorian as the two sisters, Abby and Martha Brewster, who occupy the house with their nephew Teddy." Its distinguishing features are a long seat under the window at the right side of the room as we face it, and a stairway that, starting near the front door at the left rises to a landing and then turns and continues to a balcony that crosses the room at back. The balcony leads to bedrooms and, through an arch, to a stairway that continues to the top floor.

At the moment tea is being served by Abby Brewster, "a plump little darling in her late sixties." Seated at her left is the Rev. Dr. Harper, a conventional member of the cloth, and at her right the nephew Teddy, rather formal in frock coat and striped trousers. Teddy also conspicuously wears a pince-nez on a black ribbon and a fairly forbidding mustache.

Table talk is desultory, ranging from the excellence of Dr. Harper's last sermon to the prevailing catastrophes of war on the other side of the world. About the war situation Abby has practically arrived at a conviction. "It may not be charitable of me," she admits to Dr. Harper, "but I've almost come to the conclusion that this Mr. Hitler isn't a Christian."

Teddy would also have a good deal to say about the war, being convinced that America's danger lies in the Pacific and not the Atlantic, and especially around the Panama Canal, but Abby manages quietly to shut Teddy up. Dr. Harper is soon back on the paths of peace.

"I must admit, Miss Abby, that war and violence seem far removed from these surroundings," the Doctor is saying. "The virtues of another day—they're all here in this house. The gentle virtues that went out with candlelight and good manners and low taxes."

"It's one of the oldest houses in Brooklyn," says Abby, glancing about contentedly. "It's just as it was when Grandfather built and furnished it—except for the electricity. We use it as little as possible—it was Mortimer who persuaded us to put it in."

"Yes, I can understand that. Your nephew Mortimer seems to live only by electric light."

"The poor boy has to work so late. I understand he's taking Elaine to the theatre again tonight. Teddy, your brother Mortimer will be here a little later."

"Dee—lighted!" responds Teddy, revealing his teeth in a broad grin.

"We're so happy it's Elaine that Mortimer takes to the theatre with him."

"Well, it's a new experience for me to wait up until 3 o'clock in the morning for my daughter to be brought home."

Shortly it develops, a little to Abby's distress, that Dr. Harper is not altogether pleased with the thought of his daughter's suitor being a newspaper man, and, more than that, a dramatic critic. Dramatic critics, insists the Doctor, being constantly exposed to the theatre, are quite likely to develop an interest in it. As to that Abby is quick to allay the Doctor's fears—

"Not Mortimer!" she promises. "You need have no fear at all. Why, Mortimer hates the theatre."

"Really?"

"Oh, yes. He writes awful things about the theatre. But you can't blame him, poor boy. He was so happy writing about real estate which he knew something about and then they just made him take this terrible night position."

"My! My!"

"But, as he says, the theatre can't last much longer and in the meantime it's a living. (*Complacently.*) I think if we give the theatre another year or two—"

A knock at the door saves the theatre for the moment. Police Officers Brophy and Klein are calling. They are quick to salute Teddy. They have come, Brophy explains, for the toys for the Christmas fund. Teddy starts upstairs calmly enough, to fetch them, but as he reaches the landing he stops, draws an imaginary sword, cries out a lusty "Charge!" and continues the rest of the distance at double quick.

This rather startling exhibition, being apparently familiar to those in the room, excites no comment, nor does it interrupt the flow of conversation. Presently, when Abby has gone to get a can of beef broth for Officer Brophy to take to his ailing wife, Teddy suddenly reappears on the balcony with a bugle and blows a call.

"Colonel," protests Brophy, "you promised not to do that."

"But I have to call a cabinet meeting to get the release of those supplies," Teddy explains, wheeling and re-entering his bedroom.

"He used to do that in the middle of the night," Brophy explains to Dr. Harper. "The neighbors raised Cain with me. They're a little afraid of him, anyway."

"Oh, he's quite harmless."

"Suppose he does think he's Teddy Roosevelt," puts in Officer Klein. "There's a lot worse people he could think he was."

"Damn shame—a nice family like this hatching a cuckoo," adds Brophy.

"Well, his father—the old girls' brother—was some sort of a genius, wasn't he? And their father—Teddy's grandfather—seems to me I've heard he was a little crazy, too."

"Yeah—he was crazy like a fox. He made a million dollars."

"Really? Here in Brooklyn?"

"Yeah—patent medicine. He was kind of a quack of some sort. Old Sergeant Edwards remembers him. He used the house here as sort of a clinic—tried 'em out on people."

"Yeah, I hear he used to make mistakes occasionally, too."

"The department never bothered him much because he was pretty useful on autopsies sometimes, especially poison cases."

"Well, whatever he did, he left his daughters fixed for life. Thank God for that—"

"Not that they ever spend any of it on themselves."

"Yes," admits Dr. Harper, "I'm well acquainted with their charities."

"You don't know a tenth of it. When I was with the Missing Persons Bureau I was trying to trace an old man that we never did find— Do you know there's a renting agency that's got this house down on its list for furnished rooms? They don't rent rooms, but you can bet that anybody who comes here looking for a room goes away with a good meal and probably a few dollars in their kick."

"It's just their way of digging up people to do some good to," concludes Brophy.

Martha Brewster is home, after having taken some broth to an injured Mr. Benitsky. "Martha is also a plump sweet elderly woman with Victorian charm. She is dressed in the old-fashioned manner of Abby but with high lace collar that covers her neck."

Martha is pleased to greet the police officers and Dr. Harper, and a little peeved with Teddy when, having brought the toys, he refuses to let the officers have either his General Miles or his battleship *Oregon*. Teddy has retired General Miles, he reports, and he has promised Bob Evans that he would send the *Oregon* to Australia. On these obligations Teddy stands firm, and he carries General Miles and the *Oregon* with him when he again charges furiously up the stairs and into the blockhouse.

"The stairs are always San Juan Hill," Martha explains to Dr. Harper.

"Have you ever tried to persuade him that he wasn't Teddy Roosevelt?" asks the Doctor.

"Oh, no!" interposes Abby.

"He's so happy being Teddy Roosevelt," adds Martha.

"Oh, Martha, remember—once a long time ago we thought if he would be George Washington it would be a change and we suggested it to him."

"But he stayed under the bed for days and wouldn't be happy," remembers Martha.

Dr. Harper is agreed that Teddy's happiness is really all that is important. In fact he has brought certain papers he would have Teddy sign—papers in which Teddy commits himself to Happy Dale Sanitarium, should anything happen to his aunts. This is merely a precautionary measure taken by Martha to avoid unpleasant legal proceedings after she and Abby are gone.

"Give Elaine our love," calls Abby, as Dr. Harper is leaving. "And please don't think harshly of Mortimer because he's a Dramatic Critic. Somebody has to do those things."

This is the first time Martha and Abby have been alone and there are intimate reports to make. Martha has been worried about leaving Abby, but, Abby insists, everything has gone along fine. She has managed without any help, and is quite proud of that. They warn Teddy that he is going to Panama to dig another lock for the canal. This news pleases Teddy tremendously. As soon as he has gone to prepare for the ceremony, Abby takes Martha by the hand and leads her coyly toward the window seat. Just as she is about to lift the seat there is a knock at the door.

The caller is Elaine Harper, "an attractive girl in her twenties," who "looks surprisingly smart for a minister's daughter."

Elaine has come looking for Mortimer Brewster, who had asked her to meet him there. The news shocks Martha. But Elaine understands. "There's something about calling for a girl at a parsonage that discourages any man who doesn't embroider," she says. "After young men whose idea of night life was to take me to prayer meeting it's wonderful to go to the theatre almost every night of my life."

Not finding Mortimer, Elaine is about to dash back across the cemetery to say good-night to her father, but as she opens the door her young man walks in. Mortimer is of no particular type.

Just a dramatic critic. A lively, amiable, politely fresh young man, he slyly pats Elaine where he shouldn't as he passes her to greet his aunts.

With Martha and Abby retiring discreetly to do the dishes, Elaine promptly moves over to Mortimer to be kissed. She finds Mortimer preoccupied.

"Well, can't you take a hint?" pouts Elaine.

"No. That was pretty obvious. A lack of inventiveness, I should say," answers Mortimer, chucking her under the chin.

ELAINE—Yes—that's exactly what you'd say! (*She walks away ruffled.*)

MORTIMER (*not noticing the ruffle*)—Where do you want to go for dinner?

ELAINE—I don't care. I'm not very hungry.

MORTIMER—Well, I just had breakfast. Suppose we wait until after the show?

ELAINE—But that'll make it pretty late, won't it?

MORTIMER—Not with the little stinker we're seeing tonight. From what I've heard about it, we'll be at Blake's by ten o'clock.

ELAINE—You ought to be fair to these plays.

MORTIMER—Are these plays fair to me?

ELAINE—I've never seen you walk out on a musical.

MORTIMER—That musical isn't opening tonight.

ELAINE (*disappointed*)—No?

MORTIMER—Darling, you'll have to learn the rules. With a musical there are always four changes of title and three postponements. They liked it in New Haven but it needs a lot of work.

ELAINE—Oh, I was hoping it was a musical.

MORTIMER—You have such a light mind.

ELAINE—Not a bit. Musicals somehow have a humanizing effect on you. (*He gives her a look.*) After a serious play we join the proletariat in the subway and I listen to that lecture on the drama. After a musical you bring me home in a taxi and you make a few passes.

MORTIMER—Now wait a minute, darling, that's a very inaccurate piece of reporting.

ELAINE—Oh, I will admit that after the Behrman play you told me I had authentic beauty—and that's a hell of a thing to say to any girl. It wasn't until after our first musical you told me I had nice legs. And I have, too. (MORTIMER *stares at her legs for a moment, then walks over and kisses her.*)

MORTIMER—For a minister's daughter you know a lot about

life. Where did you learn it?

ELAINE (*casually*)—In the choir loft.

MORTIMER—I'll explain that to you sometime, darling—the close connection between eroticism and religion.

ELAINE—Religion never gets as high as the choir loft. Which reminds me I'd better tell Father please not to wait up for me tonight.

MORTIMER (*almost to himself*)—I've never been able to rationalize it.

ELAINE—What?

MORTIMER—My falling in love with a girl who lives in Brooklyn.

ELAINE—Falling in love? You're not stooping to the articulate, are you?

MORTIMER (*ignoring this*)—The only way I can regain my self-respect is to keep you in New York.

ELAINE—Did you say keep?

MORTIMER—No, I've come to the conclusion that you're holding out for the legalities.

ELAINE—I can afford to be a good girl for quite a few years yet.

MORTIMER—And I can't wait that long. Where could we get married, in a hurry—say tonight!

ELAINE—I'm afraid Father will insist on officiating.

MORTIMER—Oh, God! I'll bet your father could make even the marriage service sound pedestrian.

ELAINE—Are you, by any chance, writing a review of it?

MORTIMER—Forgive me, darling. It's an occupational disease. (*She smiles at him, lovingly, and walks toward him. He meets her halfway and they forget themselves for a moment in a sentimental embrace and kiss. When they come out of it, he turns away from her quickly.*) I may give that show tonight a good notice!

ELAINE—Now, darling, don't pretend that you love me that much.

MORTIMER (*looking at her with polite lechery*)—Be sure to tell your father not to wait up tonight.

ELAINE (*aware that she can't trust either of them*)—I think tonight I'd better tell him to wait up.

MORTIMER (*reassuringly*)—Darling, I'll telephone Winchell to publish the banns.

ELAINE—Nevertheless—

MORTIMER—All right, everything formal and legal. But not later than next month.

ELAINE—Darling. I'll talk it over with Father and set the date.

MORTIMER—Oh, no!—we'll have to consult the Zolotow list. There'll be a lot of other first nights in October.

Teddy has come from upstairs dressed in tropical clothes, topped by a solar topee. He is ready for Panama. On the way down he has time to greet his brother Mortimer, who assures him that, as the President, he has the country squarely behind him. Teddy expresses pleasure at the news and disappears through the cellar door.

Mortimer has always liked Teddy the best of his brothers, he tells Elaine. Jonathan, a brother who left Brooklyn very early—by request—was always a little difficult. "Jonathan was the kind of boy who liked to cut worms in two with his teeth," Mortimer explains. "He wanted to be a surgeon, like Grandfather, but wouldn't go to Medical School. His practice got him into trouble."

Elaine decides to skip across the cemetery again to say good-by to her father. "Before I go out with you he likes to pray over me a little," she explains to Mortimer. "Well," answers Mortimer, brightly, "if the prayer isn't too long, I'd have time to lead you beside the distilled waters."

Now Mortimer has confessed to his aunts that he is going to marry Elaine. They are properly thrilled. That is the way they have always hoped it would happen. They must have a little celebration. There is still some of Martha's Lady Baltimore cake left, and they will open a bottle of wine to go with it.

Mortimer is too busy to hear their plans. He has mislaid a chapter of a book he is writing on Thoreau and is making a search through the desk for it.

"Well, with your fiancée sitting beside you tonight I do hope the play will be something you can enjoy for once," sighs Abby, happily. "It may be something romantic. What's the name of it?"

"'Murder Will Out!'"

"Oh, dear!" Abby, quite shocked, disappears quickly and quietly into the kitchen. Mortimer, not hearing her go, continues talking. As he does so he moves toward the window seat. "When the curtain goes up the first thing you see will be a dead body," he is saying. He lifts the seat. What he sees startles him into dropping it quickly. He would move away, but is held fascinated to the spot. Again he lifts the seat, stares in wildly, and again drops it. He is about to go a little mad when Abby comes blithely back from the kitchen prepared to set the table for dinner. He calls to her—

MORTIMER—Aunt Abby!

ABBY—Yes, dear.

MORTIMER—You were going to make plans for Teddy to go to that sanitarium—Happy Dale.

ABBY—Yes, dear, it's all arranged. Dr. Harper was here today and brought the things for Teddy to sign. Here they are. (*She hands them to him.*)

MORTIMER—He's got to sign them right away.

ABBY—That's what Dr. Harper thinks— (MARTHA *enters from the kitchen, carrying a tray with the table silver. Throughout the scene the two sisters go ahead setting the table—three places.*) Then there won't be any legal difficulties after we pass on.

MORTIMER (*glancing through the papers*)—He's got to sign them this minute! He's down in the cellar—get him up here right away.

MARTHA—There's no such hurry as that.

ABBY—When he starts working on the Canal you can't get his mind on anything else.

MORTIMER—Teddy's got to go to Happy Dale now—tonight!

MARTHA—Oh, no, Mortimer—that's not until after we're gone.

MORTIMER—Right away, I tell you!—right away!

ABBY—Why, Mortimer, how can you say such a thing? Why, as long as we live we won't be separated from Teddy.

MORTIMER (*trying to be calm*)—Listen, darlings, I'm frightfully sorry, but I've got some shocking news for you. (*The sisters stop work and look at him with some interest.*) Now we've all got to try to keep our heads. You know, we've sort of humored Teddy because we thought he was harmless.

MARTHA—Why, he *is* harmless!

MORTIMER—He *was* harmless. That's why he has to go to Happy Dale—why he has to be confined.

ABBY—Mortimer, why have you suddenly turned against Teddy?—your own brother!

MORTIMER—You've got to know sometime. It might as well be now. Teddy's killed a man.

MARTHA—Nonsense, dear.

MORTIMER (*rising and pointing to the window seat*)—There's a body in the window seat!

ABBY—Yes, dear, we know.

MORTIMER—You *know?*

MARTHA—Of course, dear, but it has nothing to do with Teddy.

ABBY—Now, Mortimer, just forget about it—forget you ever saw the gentleman.

MORTIMER—Forget?

ABBY—We never dreamed you'd peek.

MORTIMER—But who is he?

ABBY—His name's Hoskins—Adam Hoskins. That's about all I know about him—except that he's a Methodist.

MORTIMER—That's all you know about him? Well, what's he doing here? What happened to him?

MARTHA—He died.

MORTIMER—Aunt Martha, men don't just get into window seats and die.

ABBY—No, he died first.

MORTIMER—But how?

ABBY—Mortimer, don't be so inquisitive. The gentleman died because he drank some wine with poison in it.

MORTIMER—How did the poison get in the wine?

MARTHA—We put it in wine because it's less noticeable. When it's in tea it has a distinct odor.

MORTIMER—You put it in the wine?

ABBY—Yes. And I put Mr. Hoskins in the window seat because Dr. Harper was coming.

MORTIMER—So you knew what you'd done! You didn't want Dr. Harper to see the body!

ABBY—Not at tea! That wouldn't have been very nice! Now you know the whole thing and you can forget all about it. I think Martha and I have the right to our own little secrets.

MARTHA—And don't you tell Elaine!

For a moment Mortimer is completely stunned. The Aunts, however, are quite unconcerned. They chatter along about this and that, agreeing that they should, among other things, take Mrs. Schultz's Junior to the movies again some day soon—but not, Martha insists, to another of those scary pictures.

Preparations for the evening meal call Abby and Martha again into the kitchen. Taking advantage of this absence Mortimer dashes to the telephone and phones his office. He wants to confirm the fact that he is really where he is. Suddenly his mind is made up. He leaps for the kitchen door and summons Abby and Martha. When they come hurrying back they are both amazed and worried by his excitement. What if Mr. Hoskins is there in the window seat? Why should Mortimer worry about that? And why is he so keen to have something done about it? Teddy is down in the cellar now, digging a lock—

"You mean you're going to bury Mr. Hotchkiss in the cellar?" demands the horrified Mortimer.

"Why, of course, dear. That's what we did with the others."

"Aunt Martha, you can't bury Mr.—" Suddenly the full import of what they are saying strikes Mortimer. "Others?" he shouts.

"The other gentlemen," sweetly explains Abby.

"When you say others—do you mean—others? More than one others?"

"Oh, yes, dear. Let me see, this is eleven, isn't it, Abby?"

"No, dear, this makes twelve." Mortimer backs up and sinks in a chair beside the telephone.

"Oh, I think you're wrong, Abby. This is only eleven."

"No, when Mr. Hoskins first came in it occurred to me that he would make an even dozen."

"Well, you really shouldn't count the first one."

"Oh, *I* was counting the first one. So that makes it twelve."

The telephone has rung. Still dazed, Mortimer answers. It is his office. Al, the City Editor, evidently fears that Mortimer might have been drinking. Mortimer hasn't, but he is glad Al has called. He wants to tell him to get someone else to cover the play opening that night. . . .

"Well, where were we?" inquires Mortimer cheerfully, when his telephoning is finished. Recollection follows with a shock—

"TWELVE!" Now he remembers.

"Yes, Abby thinks we ought to count the first one and that makes twelve," explains Martha.

MORTIMER—Now let me get this. . . . (*Grabs* MARTHA *and sits her in a chair.*) Who was the first one?

ABBY—Mr. Midgely. He was a Baptist.

MARTHA—Of course, I still think we can't take full credit for him because he just died.

ABBY—Martha means without any help from us. You see, Mr. Midgely came here looking for a room.

MARTHA—It was right after you moved to New York.

ABBY—And it didn't seem right that your nice room should go to waste when there were so many people who needed it.

MARTHA—He was such a lonely old man.

ABBY—All his kith and kin were dead and it left him so forlorn and unhappy.

MARTHA—We felt so sorry for him.

ABBY—And then when his heart attack came—and he sat dead in that chair, so peaceful—remember, Martha?—well, we decided then and there that if we could help other lonely old men to find that peace, we would.

MORTIMER (*immersed in their story for a moment*)—He dropped dead, right in that chair. How awful for you!

MARTHA—Not at all! It was rather like old times. Your grandfather always used to have a cadaver or two around the house. You see, Teddy had been digging in Panama and he thought Mr. Midgely was a yellow fever victim.

ABBY—That meant he had to be buried immediately.

MARTHA—So we all took him down to Panama and put him in the lock. (*Rising.*) You see, that's why we told you not to bother about it. We know exactly what's to be done.

MORTIMER—And that's how all this started—that man walking in here and dropping dead.

ABBY—Well, we realized we couldn't depend on that happening again.

MARTHA—Remember those jars of poison that have been up on the shelves in Grandfather's laboratory all these years—

ABBY—You know the knack your Aunt Martha has for mixing things. You've eaten enough of her piccalilli!

MARTHA—Well, Mortimer, for a gallon of elderberry wine I take a teaspoon full of arsenic, and add a half-teaspoon of strychnine and then just a pinch of cyanide.

MORTIMER (*appraisingly*)—Should have quite a kick.

ABBY—As a matter of fact, one of our gentlemen found time to say "How delicious!"

MARTHA—Well, I'll have to get things started in the kitchen. (*She starts out.*)

ABBY (*to* MORTIMER)—I wish you could stay to dinner, dear.

MARTHA—I'm trying out a new recipe.

MORTIMER—I couldn't eat a thing. (MARTHA *exits to kitchen.*)

ABBY (*calling after* MARTHA)—I'll come and help you. (*She turns to* MORTIMER, *relieved.*) Well, I feel better now. You have to wait for Elaine, don't you? (*She smiles.*) How happy you must be! I'll leave you alone with your thoughts.

When his aunts have gone Mortimer stands completely dazed for a minute. Suddenly he is aroused to action. One more look inside the window seat convinces him that action is indeed necessary. He pauses to take a drink of water—but suddenly remembers that poison comes in glasses and quickly puts the glass down. He is still staring at the window seat when there is a light knock at the door, followed by the return of Elaine. Mortimer does not hear her. Nor is he very cordial when he does.

Elaine would be very happy if Mortimer would let her. She has not only told her father about their plan to marry (that's what took her so long) but she has also told him not to wait up for her tonight.

If Mortimer hears her at all he is not impressed. He would have her turn around and go right back home and stay there. He will call her up when he can. The theatre? They are not going to the theatre. Something has come up. Something about which he is not free to talk. Married? Of course they will be getting married some day—Mortimer hopes. But right now there is something that has to be done and will she please go home? No, Elaine will not go home. Not at least until she has had some reasonable explanation of what has happened to Mortimer.

The phone is ringing. It is Mortimer's office. At the phone, with his hand over the transmitter, Mortimer makes one more plea—

"Elaine, you're a sweet girl and I love you. But I have something on my mind now and I want you to go home and wait until I call you."

"Don't try to be masterful!"

"When we're married and I have problems to face I hope you're less tedious and uninspired!"

"And when we're married, *if* we're married, I hope I find you adequate."

Elaine has run out of the room. Mortimer would call her back, but she disappears through the door. Al has hung up and Mortimer is busy trying to get him back when the doorbell rings. Abby waddles cheerfully to the door and lets in a very disgruntled old man. His name is Gibbs and he understands that there are rooms for rent there. Abby is immediately interested. She introduces herself and Martha. Won't Mr. Gibbs come in and get acquainted? Mr. Gibbs will.

At the phone Mortimer is still having trouble getting Al back. He hasn't paid much attention to the conversation with Mr. Gibbs, which has proceeded rapidly. Mr. Gibbs, Martha and Abby learn, is a lonely old man who has been living in a hotel. He hasn't any family, which convinces Abby that he certainly has come to the right place. Martha, too, is pleased. She has gone to the sideboard to fetch the elderberry wine.

On the phone Mortimer has finally made his connection and is in a row with Al as to who shall cover the night's opening. Surely there is somebody there—that bright office boy who wants to learn to write. Or one of the printers—especially the funny one that sets Mortimer's copy. Why not let him try it? You never can tell about printers.

Mortimer has just slammed the phone down and is ready to start drinking when he notices the elderberry wine bottle on the table.

"Do you have your own elderberry bushes?" Mr. Gibbs is asking.

"No, but the cemetery's full of them," answers Martha, smiling sweetly.

Mortimer has reached for the wine bottle when Martha sees him and promptly interposes a gesture of warning. That wine isn't for Mortimer. That is for Mr. Gibbs. Mr. Gibbs, in fact, is about to toss off a glass when Mortimer realizes what is happening.

"Hey!" he shouts. "Get out of here. Do you want to be killed? Do you want to be poisoned? Do you want to be murdered?"

Mr. Gibbs is on his way to the door before Mortimer has finished calling to him, and Mortimer is right on his heels, ready to slam the door after him.

"Now you've spoiled everything," pouts Abby, as Mortimer leans weakly against the door.

"You can't do things like that!" he warns them. "I don't know how I can explain this to you. But it's not only against the Law, it's wrong. It's not a nice thing to do. People wouldn't understand. *He* wouldn't understand."

"Abby, we shouldn't have told Mortimer."

"What I mean is . . . well . . . this has developed into a very bad habit."

"Now, Mortimer, we don't try to stop you from doing the things you like to do. I don't see why you should interfere with us."

"ARSENIC AND OLD LACE"

Mortimer (shouting): Hey! Get out of here! Do you want to be killed? Do you want to be poisoned? Do you want to be murdered?

(*Allyn Joslyn, Josephine Hull, Jean Adair, Henry Herbert*)

Photo by Vandamm Studio.

The telephone is ringing again. It is Mortimer's editor calling back. Mortimer will have to go to the theatre. There is no one else. All right, Mortimer agrees to go. He will see the first act —and "pan the hell out of it." Mortimer must see a lawyer.

Mortimer is ready to leave for the theatre, but before he goes he extracts a promise from Abby and Martha. They are not to do anything—they are not to let anyone in the house—and they are to leave Mr. Hoskins right where he is while Mortimer is gone.

It isn't easy for the aunts to promise, especially as they had planned to hold services—Methodist services—for Mr. Hoskins before dinner. But they will agree to wait if Mortimer will join them later. Mortimer will enjoy the services, especially the hymns, they're sure of that.

Mortimer has found Teddy's commitment papers in the desk, and taken them, as well as some extra paper, with him. (*He may get a chance to write his review of the play on his way to the theatre.*)

Abby and Martha are relieved at Mortimer's going, but they can understand his distraction. Probably becoming engaged always makes a man nervous. What Mortimer needs is a long vacation for his honeymoon.

There is a ring of the doorbell. That's disturbing, seeing the aunts had promised not to let anyone in. They will pretend that there is no one at home. By peeking from the window on the landing they can see two men who evidently have arrived in a motor car standing in front of the house.

The doorbell ring is followed by a knock. Then the door is thrown open and a tall man walks into the room. He is assured and easy, as though he were familiar with the premises, and takes a long look around in all directions save at the stairs, where Abby and Martha are huddled, too frightened to speak. "There is something sinister about the man—something that brings a slight chill in his presence. It is in his walk, his bearing and his strange resemblance to Boris Karloff."

The intruder has turned and called out the door to someone he addresses as "Doctor." Presently the Doctor is revealed as Dr. Einstein, a small man, "somewhat ratty in appearance, whose face wears the benevolent smirk of a man who lives in a haze of alcohol. There is something about him that suggests the unfrocked priest." Dr. Einstein speaks with an accent that is faintly German. He stands, "timid but expectant," just outside the door as the first comer, who is Jonathan Brewster, explains that this is the home of his youth.

"As a boy I couldn't wait to escape from this house," says Jonathan. "And now I'm glad to escape back into it."

"Yah, Chonny, it's a good hideout," agrees Dr. Einstein.

"The family must still be here," Jonathan goes on. "There's something so unmistakably Brewster about the Brewsters. I hope there is a fatted calf awaiting the return of the prodigal."

"Yah, I'm hungry," agrees the Doctor, at the moment catching sight of the wine bottle on the table. "Look, Chonny! Drink!"

"As if we were expected! A good omen."

They are approaching the table when Abby demands to know who they are, and what they are doing there. Jonathan? Neither Abby nor Martha is to be taken in by that claim. Jonathan doesn't even look like Jonathan. And the other one isn't Dr. Einstein, either.

"I see you're still wearing the lovely garnet ring that Grandma Brewster bought in England," says Jonathan, indicating the ring on Abby's hand. "And you, Aunt Martha, still the high collar—to hide the scar where Grandfather's acid burned you."

Now Abby and Martha think maybe the voice is the voice of Jonathan. His explanation that Dr. Einstein is a plastic surgeon who has altered the Jonathan face would be convincing if it didn't look so much like a face Martha has seen recently in the movies.

That can be explained, too. Dr. Einstein has given Jonathan three different faces in the last five years. The last one he altered just after they had themselves been to the movies. The Doctor admits he was a little "intoggsicated" at the time.

Abby and Martha are apprehensive. They would like to suggest that Jonathan and his friend continue on their way, but they don't know just how to do it. Jonathan, for his part, has no intention of moving on. It is good to be back in Brooklyn; good to find his aunts looking not a day older, and quite as sweet and charming and hospitable as they always were. Jonathan had promised Dr. Einstein they would be like that. And how is his dear brother Teddy? Did Teddy go into politics? Jonathan has seen Mortimer's picture at the head of his newspaper column so he knows about his younger brother. "He's evidently fulfilled all the promise of his early nasty nature," says Jonathan.

Seeing that Jonathan apparently has no intention of leaving, Abby and Martha make an excuse to get into the kitchen for a further consultation. Left to themselves Jonathan and Dr. Einstein also do a bit of conferring.

"Well, Chonny, where do we go from here?" Dr. Einstein

would know. "We got to think fast. The *police!* They got pictures of that face. I got to operate on you right away. We got to find some place—and we got to find some place for Mr. Spenalzo, too."

"Don't waste any worry on that rat."

"But, Chonny, we got a hot stiff on our hands."

"Forget Mr. Spenalzo!"

"But we can't leave a dead body in the rumble seat! You shouldn't have killed him, Chonny. He's a nice fellow—he giffs us a lift—and what happens—" He gestures strangulation.

"He said I looked like Boris Karloff. That's your work, Doctor. You did that to me."

"Now, Chonny—we find a place somewhere—I fix you up quick."

"Tonight?"

"Chonny, I got to eat first. I'm hungry. I'm weak."

Abby and Martha have returned from their kitchen conference. They are very happy, they announce, that Jonathan has remembered them and taken the trouble to call, but their lives have been very peaceful since he left them and they are hoping he will leave them again.

Jonathan, on his part, remembers with regret the trouble he caused them as a boy, and would not think of imposing himself upon them again if it were not for Dr. Einstein. For a long time he had been promising Dr. Einstein what to expect when he met his dear aunts, and especially when he (the Doctor) tasted some of Aunt Abby's home cooking.

Abby is pleased, but of no mind to be influenced by Jonathan's palavering. Aunt Martha thinks, perhaps, seeing there is a good-sized pot roast cooking, the least they can do—

"Thank you, Aunt Martha. We'll stay to dinner," says Jonathan, quickly. And Abby, a little reluctantly, agrees.

Jonathan and the Doctor are sent upstairs to freshen up. They can use the washroom in Grandfather's laboratory. Everything is there, just as Grandfather left it. And that gives Jonathan a great idea. With Grandfather's laboratory, a perfect operating room, an attic ward with ten beds—what an ideal setting for Dr. Einstein's talents!

"You don't know this town, Doctor," Jonathan enthuses. "Practically everybody in Brooklyn needs a new face."

As for their not being invited to stay, Jonathan will take care of that. They have been invited to dinner—the rest will be easy.

"It's like comes true a beautiful dream," sighs Dr. Einstein, taking a swig from his flask. "Only I hope you're not dreaming. It's so peaceful."

"Yes, Doctor, that's what makes this house so perfect for us. It's so peaceful."

At that moment Teddy comes from the cellar, pauses to blow a blast on his bugle, marches to the stairs and starts up. At the landing he stops to sound a clarion "Charge!" and sweeps on through the balcony door.

Jonathan watches him curiously. Einstein, staring after Teddy, hastily takes another swig from his flask. The curtain falls.

ACT II

It is after dinner. The dishes have been removed and the room set in order. Jonathan, in the most comfortable chair, is enjoying an after dinner cigar. Dr. Einstein is relaxed and happy. The attitude of Abby and Martha is that of people "who wish their guests would go home."

Jonathan has been telling his aunts something of his experiences as a globe circler, skipping much that Dr. Einstein would put in but which Jonathan is convinced would not interest Abby and Martha. It was in London that Jonathan met Dr. Einstein. Before that, Jonathan had been in South Africa, and then in Amsterdam at the diamond market. "I wanted to go back to South Africa and Dr. Einstein made it possible for me," says Jonathan.

"A good job, Chonny," recalls the Doctor. And then to the aunts: "We take off the bandages. He look so different the nurse had to introduce me."

"I loved that face," muses Jonathan. "I still carry the picture with me."

The picture, shown to the aunts, is more like the Jonathan they used to know, but not much. At the moment Abby and Martha are more interested in getting Jonathan and the Doctor started on their way than they are in the pictures. By this time, however, Jonathan is in no mood to go any farther that night. Before he can assert his intentions Teddy has come dashing up from the cellar.

Teddy is greatly excited. He has just found the biography of his life as President. In it is a picture of himself and Dr. Einstein just as he said—a picture carrying the caption: "President Roosevelt and General Goethals at Culebra Cut." When the Doctor fails to recognize himself Teddy explains that, of course, the picture hasn't been taken yet. They hadn't even started work on Culebra Cut.

Now Teddy would have General Goethals accompany him to Panama for an inspection of the new lock. Abby and Martha would stop this expedition if they could, but Teddy is obdurate. Not even Jonathan's order that Teddy go to bed has any effect. By way of compromise Jonathan agrees to the inspection.

Again the question of Jonathan and Dr. Einstein's moving on is brought up. This time Jonathan is even more firm than before—

"Dr. Einstein and I need a place to sleep," he says, firmly. "This afternoon, you remembered that as a boy I could be disagreeable. It wouldn't be pleasant for any of us if—"

"Perhaps we'd better let them stay here tonight," agrees a frightened Martha.

It can't be for more than the night, Abby insists. She and Martha need the rooms for their lodgers. Jonathan, however, is plainly convinced that he and Dr. Einstein will be staying on—

"When Dr. Einstein and I get organized—when we resume practice—I forgot to tell you—we're turning Grandfather's laboratory into an operating room. We expect to be very busy."

"Jonathan, we're not going to let you turn this house into a hospital."

"A hospital—heavens, no!—it will be a beauty parlor!"

Dr. Einstein has returned excitedly from the cellar. What he has seen! The Panama Canal! Dug to fit Mr. Spenalzo exactly —four feet wide and six feet long! Could it be the aunts were expecting them? That *would* be hospitality!

It will be a good joke on the aunts, thinks Jonathan—sleeping in a house with a body buried in the cellar. He and the Doctor will bring Mr. Spenalzo in through the window after the others have gone to bed. They will go now to put their car in the yard.

Abby and Martha would not have it that way. It interferes with their plans for the services for Mr. Hoskins, but they are forced to accept. When Teddy comes from the cellar they tell him there has been another yellow fever victim; that he is in the window seat, and that he should be taken to the canal as soon as the lights are out. Neither should anyone be told, especially not General Goethals. It will have to be a state secret. So long as it is a state secret Teddy is agreeable.

Now there is a conflict as to who shall go to bed first. Jonathan is determined to stay up. So are Abby and Martha. The matter is finally compromised when Jonathan again becomes threatening and the aunts protestingly disappear. A moment later Jonathan and Dr. Einstein have taken their luggage to their room.

With the house dark, the cellar door opens softly and Teddy peers cautiously about. Finding everything safe he switches on the cellar light, goes to the window box and opens it slowly to minimize a very definite creaking at the hinges. A moment later Teddy, with a burden, is seen crossing the room and disappearing through the cellar door.

Now Jonathan and Einstein have appeared at the door of their room on the balcony. Jonathan lights a match to help them find the way downstairs. Jonathan goes outside to hand Mr. Spenalzo through the window. The Doctor, approaching the window in the dark, stumbles and all but falls into the open seat. A moment later the first of Mr. Spenalzo appears. Dr. Einstein takes hold and pulls energetically, and finds himself left with one of Mr. Spenalzo's shoes in his hand when he slips on a rug and Mr. Spenalzo falls. At that moment there is a knock at the door. This is followed by hurried action at the window seat, followed by the creak of the cover.

Now the front door is quietly opened and, by the light of a remote street light, Elaine is revealed. Cautiously she moves into the room, calling to Abby and Martha. Back of her the slam of the front door is heard and Elaine turns to face a menacing Jonathan.

There are mutual exclamations of surprise. Elaine has come in search of Miss Abby and Miss Martha. Who is Jonathan? Jonathan and his friend, Dr. Einstein, just now turning on the lights, are living there, Jonathan explains. He himself is Jonathan Brewster. Having learned that much Elaine would return home. She had only come over because she thought she had seen someone prowling about the grounds. That probably was Jonathan, too—

Jonathan has grabbed her by the arm. So she saw someone prowling about the grounds? Just how much did she see? Elaine struggles to get away. Dr. Einstein takes her other arm and holds her firmly while Jonathan's questioning goes on. What did she see? And who?

Teddy has dashed up from the cellar. He is surprised at what he sees, and a little disappointed. He had understood this was to be a private funeral.

"Teddy! Teddy! Tell these men who I am!" pleads Elaine.

"That's my daughter, Alice!" answers Teddy, continuing on

his way across the room to the stairs.

"No. No. Teddy—Teddy—" Elaine is still struggling to get away from Jonathan.

"Now, Alice, don't be a tomboy," cautions Teddy. "Don't play rough with the gentlemen!" He dashes up the stairs. At the landing he pauses to draw his imaginary sword and deliver his "Charge!" before disappearing into his room.

Before Jonathan can stuff a handkerchief in her mouth Elaine has emitted a healthy scream. This brings Abby and Martha to the balcony, but not before Jonathan and Einstein have pushed Elaine into the cellar entry, Einstein holding her there while Jonathan answers the aunts.

Abby and Martha are dressed for Mr. Hoskins' funeral—black dresses, black hats and gloves. They turn on the lights from the balcony. What is going on? Jonathan tells them that he and the Doctor have just caught a sneak thief. No need to call the police. They have already attended to that. Let Abby and Martha go back to their rooms immediately.

Again there is a rattling of the door knob, followed by a knock. Abby starts for the door. Elaine, escaping the clutches of Dr. Einstein, dashes in from the cellar. Abby manages to get to the door and unlocks it to let Mortimer in. Elaine rushes into his arms—

"Oh, Mortimer, where have you been?"

MORTIMER—To the Nora Bayes Theatre—and I should have known better. (*He sees* JONATHAN.) My God, I'm still there!

ABBY—This is your brother Jonathan—and this is Dr. Einstein.

MORTIMER (*surveying* JONATHAN)—I know this isn't a nightmare, but what is it?

JONATHAN—I've come back home, Mortimer.

MORTIMER (*looking at him and then at* ABBY)—Who did you say that was?

ABBY—It's your brother Jonathan. He's had his face changed. Dr. Einstein performed the operation on him.

MORTIMER—Jonathan, you always were a horror, but do you have to look like one?

EINSTEIN—Easy, Chonny! Easy!

JONATHAN—Mortimer, have you forgotten the things I used to do to you? Remember the time you were tied to the bedpost—the needles—under your fingernails. I suggest you don't ask for trouble now.

MORTIMER—Yes, I remember. I remember you as the most

detestable, vicious, venomous form of animal life I ever knew. (JONATHAN *gets tense and takes a step toward* MORTIMER.)

ABBY (*stepping between them*)—Now don't you boys start quarreling again the minute you've seen each other.

MORTIMER—There won't be any fight, Aunt Abby. Jonathan, you're not wanted here, so get out!

JONATHAN—Dr. Einstein and I have been invited to stay.

MORTIMER—Oh, no—not in this house.

ABBY—Just for tonight.

MORTIMER—I don't want him anywhere near me.

ABBY—But we did invite them for tonight, Mortimer, and it wouldn't be very nice to go back on our word.

MORTIMER (*reluctantly giving in*)—All right, tonight—but the first thing in the morning—out. Where are they sleeping?

ABBY—We put them in Jonathan's old room.

MORTIMER (*picking up his suitcase and starting for the stairs*)—That's my old room. I'm moving into that room. I'm here to stay.

MARTHA—Oh, Mortimer, I'm so glad.

EINSTEIN (*to* JONATHAN)—Chonny, we sleep down here.

MORTIMER—You bet your life you'll sleep down here.

EINSTEIN—You sleep on the sofa—I sleep on the window seat.

MORTIMER (*stopping suddenly, as he remembers* MR. HOSKINS)—The window seat! Oh, well, let's not argue about it. That window seat's good enough for me tonight. I'll sleep on the window seat.

EINSTEIN—Chonny—all this argument—it makes me think of Mr. Spenalzo.

JONATHAN—Spenalzo. (*He starts looking around.*) Well, Mortimer, there's no real need to inconvenience you. We'll sleep down here.

MORTIMER—Jonathan, this sudden consideration for me is very unconvincing.

EINSTEIN—Come, Chonny, we get our things out of the room, yes?

MORTIMER—Don't bother, Doctor.

JONATHAN—You know, Doctor, I've completely lost track of Mr. Spenalzo.

MORTIMER—Who's this Mr. Spenalzo?

EINSTEIN—Just a friend of ours Johnny's been looking for.

MORTIMER—Don't you bring anybody else in here.

EINSTEIN (*on the stairs*)—It's all right, Chonny. While we pack I tell you about him. (JONATHAN *goes up.*)

ABBY—Mortimer, you don't have to stay down here. I could sleep with Martha and you could have my room.

JONATHAN (*on the balcony*)—No trouble at all, Aunt Abby. We'll be packed in a few minutes, and then you can have the room, Mortimer.

Jonathan and Einstein have gone on upstairs. Briefly and excitedly Elaine tries to tell Mortimer of her experience with Jonathan. That he is some kind of a maniac she is convinced. She is trembling in Mortimer's arms.

It is nearly 12 o'clock. TWELVE! That brings everything back to Mortimer. Now he flies into excited action. Elaine must go home right away. The aunts can be fixing coffee and sandwiches if they want to, but let them hurry. And now Elaine rebels. What's going on in this house, she wants to know.

"You were supposed to take me to dinner and the theatre tonight," she protests. "You called it off. You asked me to marry you . . . I said I would . . . five minutes later you threw me out of the house. Tonight, just after your brother tries to strangle me, you want to chase me home. Now, listen, Mr. Brewster . . . before I go home, I want to know where I stand. Do you love me?"

MORTIMER (*going to her*)—I love you very much, Elaine. In fact, I love you so much I can't marry you.

ELAINE (*drawing away*)—Have you suddenly gone crazy?

MORTIMER—I don't think so—but it's just a matter of time. (*Seats her on the sofa.*) You see, insanity runs in my family. (*He looks toward the kitchen.*) It practically gallops. That's why I can't marry you, dear.

ELAINE—Now wait a minute, you've got to do better than that.

MORTIMER—No, dear—there's a strange taint in the Brewster blood. If you really knew my family—well—it's what you would expect if Strindberg had written "Hellzapoppin."

ELAINE—Now just because Teddy . . .

MORTIMER—No, it goes way back. The first Brewster—the one who came over on the *Mayflower*. You know in those days the Indians used to scalp the settlers—he used to scalp the Indians.

ELAINE—Mortimer, that's ancient history.

MORTIMER—No, the whole family! Take my grandfather—he tried his patent medicines out on dead people to be sure he wouldn't kill them!

ELAINE—He wasn't so crazy. He made a million dollars.

MORTIMER—And then there's Jonathan. You just said he was a maniac. He tried to kill you.

ELAINE—But he's your brother, not you. I'm in love with you.

MORTIMER—And there's Teddy. You *know* Teddy. He thinks he's Roosevelt.

ELAINE—Even Roosevelt thinks he's Roosevelt.

MORTIMER—No, dear, no Brewster should marry. I realize now that if I had met my father in time I would have stopped him.

ELAINE—Now, darling, all of this doesn't prove you're crazy. Just look at your aunts. They're Brewsters, aren't they—and the sanest, sweetest people I've ever known.

MORTIMER (*glancing at window seat and moving toward it*)—Well, even they have their peculiarities.

ELAINE (*walking away from him*)—Yes, but what lovely peculiarities!—kindness, generosity, human sympathy! (MORTIMER *lifts the window seat to take a peek at* MR. HOSKINS *and sees* MR. SPENALZO.)

MORTIMER (*to himself*)—There's another one!

ELAINE (*turning to* MORTIMER)—There are plenty of others! You can't tell me anything about your aunts.

MORTIMER—I'm not going to! (*Crossing to* ELAINE.) Elaine, you've got to go home. Something very important has just come up.

ELAINE—Come up from where? We're here alone together.

MORTIMER—Elaine, I know I'm acting irrationally, but just put it down to the fact that I'm a mad Brewster.

ELAINE—If you think you're going to get out of this by pretending you're insane, you're crazy! Maybe you're not going to marry me, but I'm going to marry you. I love you, you dope!

It is no good. Mortimer is not to be won over. If Elaine loves him she will get the hell out of there. When he fails to respond to her good-by kiss, which is really a "production number," Elaine is through.

"Oh, you—you—critic!" she cries, flouncing through the door and slamming it after her.

Mortimer is still too busy to be greatly concerned. He calls Abby from the kitchen. He demands to know what she and Martha mean by not keeping their word. They told him they would not let anyone in the house while he was gone, and here is this stranger in the window seat—

Stranger? Abby knows nothing about any stranger. She looks and is quite peeved. Who can that be? It is getting so anybody thinks he can walk into their house! Well, if this impostor thinks he is going to be buried in their cellar, too, he's mistaken.

"We've always wanted to hold a double funeral," admits Abby, "but we're not going to read services over a perfect stranger."

"A stranger. Aunt Abby, how can I believe you? There are twelve men in the cellar and you admit you poisoned them."

"Well, I did," admits Abby, drawing herself up proudly. "But do you think I'd stoop to telling a fib?"

Mortimer is pacing the room restlessly when Jonathan appears on the stairs. Mortimer turns on him. Mortimer has decided that Jonathan is going to get out of that house as quickly as possible. Jonathan, however, is of a different mind. It is, says he, Mortimer who is leaving. The two men are facing each other threateningly when the aunts come in from the kitchen. Abby has brought Martha to have a look at the stranger in the window seat.

At that suggestion Jonathan and Mortimer both throw themselves on the seat, barring Martha's way. Then Mortimer as quickly changes his mind. He springs up from the seat and faces his brother—

"Jonathan, let Aunt Martha see what is in the window seat," he says sweetly. "Aunt Abby, I owe you an apology. I have very good news for you. Jonathan is leaving. He's taking Dr. Einstein and their cold companion with him. (*He walks to* JONATHAN.) You're my brother, Jonathan. You're a Brewster. I'm giving you a chance to get away and take the evidence with you. You can't ask for more than that. (JONATHAN *doesn't move.*) All right. In that case, I'll have to call the police."

"Don't reach for that telephone. (*Crosses slowly toward* MORTIMER.) Are you still giving me orders after seeing what's happened to Mr. Spenalzo? . . . Remember, what happened to Mr. Spenalzo can happen to you, too."

There is a knock at the door. It is Officer O'Hara. He had noticed the lights on and wanted to make sure everything was all right. The aunts introduce him to their nephews. O'Hara has a feeling he has seen Jonathan somewhere before, but Jonathan, making for the stairs, doesn't think that likely.

"I'd hurry if I were you, Jonathan," calls Mortimer, tauntingly. "You're all packed anyway, aren't you?" Jonathan hurries upstairs without replying.

O'Hara thinks he will be going, too, but that is not as Mortimer would have it. He insists O'Hara should stay. There will be coffee and sandwiches in a minute. O'Hara is still wondering where he has seen Jonathan's face before.

"He looks like somebody you've probably seen in the movies," suggests Mortimer.

"I never go to the movies," snaps O'Hara. "I hate 'em. My mother says the movies is a bastard art."

"Yes, it's full of them," admits Mortimer.

Now it transpires that O'Hara's interest in the theatre stems from the fact that his mother had been an actress. Peaches Latour was her stage name and she had had a long season with "Mutt and Jeff." When he learns that Mortimer also has his theatre connections, that he is, in fact, the Mortimer Brewster who is a dramatic critic, Officer O'Hara is stirred with enthusiasm. That puts them both in the same business. O'Hara is really a playwright. The police force is just temporary. He's been on it twelve years, collecting material for a play.

"I'll bet it's a honey," bets Mortimer.

"Well, it ought to be," agrees O'Hara. "With all the drama I see being a cop. Mr. Brewster, you got no idea what goes on in Brooklyn."

"I think I have."

Jonathan and Einstein have come from upstairs with their suitcases. Mortimer and Abby are glad to bid them good-by. It will be all right for O'Hara to be going, too, if he likes. But O'Hara has no intention of going now. He wants to talk with Mortimer about the play. They are going to write it together, promises O'Hara, and he is not going to leave the house until he has told Mortimer the plot.

In that case Jonathan thinks he and Dr. Einstein will be running along. Not until they are prepared to take everything with them, Mortimer insists, with anxious glances in the direction of the window seat. He will take O'Hara into the kitchen to talk about the play.

"I might have known you'd grow up to write a play with a policeman," sneers Jonathan.

"Get going, now—all three of you!" commands Mortimer, following O'Hara out.

Jonathan's face is alive with hatred. This affair between him and his brother has to be settled. He and the Doctor will take Mr. Spenalzo down and dump him in the bay. Then they will come back, and if Mortimer tries to interfere—

Einstein is worried. He knows Brooklyn isn't a good place

for "Chonny," but he is afraid to stand against him. He takes the suitcases into the cellar.

Jonathan is on his knees on the window seat, opening the window for Mr. Spenalzo's exit, when Einstein come back from the cellar greatly excited. That hole in the cellar he had told Jonathan about—it's occupied!

"We got an ace in the hole!" chuckles Dr. Einstein.

Jonathan has disappeared down cellar to confirm the news when Mortimer comes in from the kitchen. He sees the window open, but finds Mr. Spenalzo still in the window seat. He is leaning out the window calling Jonathan softly, when Jonathan answers quietly from the cellar door.

"Yes, Mortimer!"

MORTIMER (*turning around and seeing* JONATHAN)—Where have you two been? I thought I told you—

JONATHAN—We're not going.

MORTIMER—Oh, you're not. You think I'm not serious about this, eh? Do you want the police to know what's in that window seat?

JONATHAN—We're staying here.

MORTIMER—All right! You asked for it! This gets me rid of you and O'Hara both at the same time. (*He goes to the kitchen door.*) Officer O'Hara!

JONATHAN—If you tell O'Hara what's in the window seat, I'll tell him what's down in the cellar.

MORTIMER (*closing the door swiftly*)—The cellar?

JONATHAN—There's an elderly gentleman down there who seems to be very dead.

MORTIMER—What were you doing down in the cellar?

EINSTEIN—What's *he* doing down in the cellar?

O'HARA (*off-stage*)—No, thank you, ma'am. I've had plenty! They were fine!

JONATHAN—Now, what are you going to say to Officer O'Hara?

O'HARA (*walking in*)—Say, your aunts want to hear it too. Shall I get them in here?

MORTIMER (*pulling him toward the door*)—No, O'Hara. You can't do that now. You've got to ring in.

O'HARA—The hell with ringing in. I'll get your aunts in and tell you the plot.

MORTIMER (*stopping him*)—No, O'Hara, not in front of all these people. We'll get together alone some place, later.

O'HARA—Say, how about the back room at Kelly's?

MORTIMER (*hurrying him toward the door*)—Fine. You go ring in and I'll meet you at Kelly's.

JONATHAN—Why don't you two go down in the cellar?

O'HARA—That's all right with me. (*Starts for cellar door.*) Is this the cellar?

MORTIMER (*grabbing him*)—No. We'll go to Kelly's. But you're going to ring in on the way, aren't you?

O'HARA—All right, that will only take a couple of minutes.

MORTIMER (*getting his hat*)—I'll ditch this guy and be back in five minutes. I expect to find you gone. Wait for me. (*He exits, closing door.*)

JONATHAN—We'll wait for him, Doctor. I've waited a great many years for a chance like this.

EINSTEIN—We got him where we want him. Did he look guilty?

JONATHAN—Take the bags back to our room, Doctor.

When Abby and Martha come from the kitchen they are surprised to find Jonathan and Einstein still there. Mortimer won't like it if he finds them when he gets back. "He's gotta like it," observes the Doctor, with a satisfied grin.

Jonathan thinks his aunts had better be getting them something to eat while he and the Doctor take Mr. Spenalzo into the cellar. Mr. Spenalzo is going to like it down there with Mr. Hoskins whatever the aunts may think about it.

What they think is that they will not have it. They do not allow strangers in their cellar. Besides there isn't room enough. There are already twelve graves down there, and that makes it a little crowded. What room there is left they will be needing.

"You mean you and Aunt Martha have murdered—" Jonathan is mightily astonished.

"Murdered! Certainly not!" Abby flouts such a suggestion. "It's one of our charities."

"What we've been doing is a mercy," adds Martha.

"You've done that—right in this house—and buried them down there!"

"Chonny, we been chased all over the world— They stay right here in Brooklyn and do just as good as you do." The Doctor must smile at the thought.

Jonathan isn't pleased. Besides his record is thirteen. "There's Mr. Spenalzo. Then the first one in London. Two in Johannesburg—one in Sydney—one in Melbourne—two in San Francisco —one in Phoenix, Arizona—"

"Phoenix?"

"The filling station— The three in Chicago, and the one in South Bend. That makes thirteen."

"But, Chonny, you can't count the one in South Bend. He died of pneumonia."

"He wouldn't have got pneumonia if I hadn't shot him."

"No, Chonny, he died of pneumonia. He don't count."

"He counts with me. I say thirteen."

"No, Chonny. You got twelve. They got twelve. The old ladies are just as good as you are."

"Oh, they are, are they?" storms Jonathan. "That's easily taken care of! All I need is one more—that's all—just one more."

Mortimer has opened the door, come hastily into the room and stands facing them.

"Well—here I am!" says Mortimer.

Jonathan turns and looks at him "with the widening eyes of someone who has just solved a problem." The curtain falls.

ACT III

The room is empty. From the cellar come sounds of a sizable row. Martha and Abby can be heard protesting volubly that whatever is being done cannot be done. This is their house, and they forbid it. The idea of burying a good Methodist with a foreigner! Wait until Mortimer hears!

At that moment Mortimer returns. He has been over to Dr. Gilchrist's and he has got Teddy's commitment papers all signed. Now he wants to find Teddy. When Teddy has signed, Mortimer will be ready for Jonathan. The aunts are puzzled by that statement.

"You had to go and tell Jonathan about those twelve graves," Mortimer explains. "If I can make Teddy responsible for those I can protect you, don't you see?"

Abby and Martha are still puzzled. They pay taxes to have the police protect them, and that is where they are going now —to fetch the police.

But if they tell the police about Mr. Spenalzo, the police will find Mr. Hoskins, too, and probably all the other gentlemen. Martha and Abby cannot understand such reasoning. "We know the police better than you do," says Abby. "I don't think they'd pry into our private affairs if we asked them not to."

"But if they found your twelve gentlemen they'd have to

report to headquarters."

"I'm not so sure they'd bother," says Martha. "They'd have to make out a very long report and if there's one thing a policeman hates to do, it's to write."

Again the aunts are determined to go for the police, and again Mortimer works feverishly to hold them back. Finally they agree to let him work in his own way—but—Jonathan and Mr. Spenalzo will have to be out of the house by morning. Mortimer promises that much and hurries to Teddy's room.

Now Jonathan has come from the cellar. After warning him of Mortimer's promise to have him out of the house by morning, the aunts go to their rooms. And now Dr. Einstein appears, dusting himself off and admiring the fit of Mr. Spenalzo's shoes, which he has appropriated. Everything has been fixed up in the cellar, reports the Doctor, "smooth like a lake." The Doctor is tired and thinking eagerly of bed. But, Jonathan reminds him, they still have Mortimer to take care of, no matter how dead for sleep the Doctor may be. Nor will this be a quick job. Jonathan finds no aesthetic satisfaction in haste in these matters. Haste leaves nothing to remember.

Jonathan has gone to the cellar to get Dr. Einstein's instrument case and the Doctor is standing in the doorway, still protesting that he is in no condition for a long and terrible operation, when Teddy appears suddenly on the balcony with his bugle. Mortimer is at his heels. This proclamation is a secret to fool Japan, Mortimer explains. It is no time to summon the Cabinet. Teddy, mollified, goes back to get into his signing clothes.

Mortimer has come downstairs. He finds Einstein alone and excited. The Doctor would have Mortimer get away quickly and at once. Mortimer can't go. He is waiting for something important. But he would advise Dr. Einstein to go. There's going to be trouble in that house, any minute now—

"Chonny is in a bad mood," pleads Einstein. "When he is like dis—he iss a madman!—things happen—terrible things!"

"Jonathan doesn't worry me now," answers Mortimer.

EINSTEIN—Ach! Himmel! Don't those plays you see teach you anything?

MORTIMER—About what?

EINSTEIN—At least, people in plays act like they got sense.

MORTIMER—Oh, you think so, do you? You think people in plays act intelligently. I wish you had to sit through some of the ones I have to sit through. This little opus tonight—for instance. In that play there's a man—(JONATHAN *enters from the cellar, carrying an instrument case. Pauses in the doorway, watching* MORTIMER.)—he's supposed to be bright. He knows he's in a house with murderers—he ought to know he's in danger. He's even been warned to get out of the house. Does he go? No, he stays there. I ask you—is that what an intelligent person would do?

EINSTEIN—You're asking me!

MORTIMER—He didn't even have sense enough to be scared—to be on guard. For instance, the murderer invites him to sit down.

EINSTEIN—You mean, "Won't you sit down?"

MORTIMER—Believe it or not, that one was in there, too.

EINSTEIN—And what did he do?

MORTIMER—He sat down! Mind you—this fellow is supposed to be bright. (*Pulls chair towards him and sits.*) There he is —all ready to be trussed up. And what do they use to tie him with?

EINSTEIN—What?

MORTIMER—The curtain cord. (JONATHAN *snatches at the idea, draws his knife, goes to the window and cuts the curtain cord.*)

EINSTEIN—Well, why not? A good idea. Very convenient.

MORTIMER—A little too convenient. When are playwrights going to use some imagination? (JONATHAN *has coiled the curtain cord and is moving behind* MORTIMER.) The curtain cord!

EINSTEIN—He didn't see him get it?

MORTIMER—See him? He sat there with his back to him. That's the kind of stuff we have to suffer through night after night. And they say the critics are killing the theatre. It's the playwrights that are killing the theatre. So there he sat—the big dope—this guy that's supposed to be bright—waiting to be tied up and gagged. (JONATHAN *is now behind* MORTIMER *with the curtain cord looped and ready to drop over his shoulders.* JONATHAN *drops loop over* MORTIMER'S *shoulders and pulls it taut and ties it behind the back of the chair. Simultaneously* EINSTEIN *leaps to* MORTIMER, *pulls* MORTIMER'S *handkerchief out of his pocket and gags him with it.* JONATHAN *steps to* MORTIMER'S *side.*)

EINSTEIN—You're right about that fella—he wasn't very bright.

JONATHAN—Now, if you don't mind, Mortimer—we'll finish

the story. (MORTIMER *is making unintelligible sounds.* JONATHAN *goes to sideboard and brings candelabra down and lights candles.*) Mortimer, I've been away for twenty years. But never—my dear brother—were you out of my mind. . . . In Melbourne one night—I dreamt of you. . . . When I landed in San Francisco—I felt a strange satisfaction— Once again I was in the same country with you. (JONATHAN *turns out lights and goes to cellar door, picks up instrument case and sets it down on table between the candelabra.*) Now, Doctor—we go to work.

EINSTEIN—Please, Chonny—for me—the quick way—eh?

JONATHAN—Now, Doctor, this must be an artistic achievement! After all, we're performing before a very distinguished critic.

EINSTEIN—Chonny—

JONATHAN (*flaring*)—Doctor—

EINSTEIN—All right. Let's get it over with!

The Doctor has taken off his coat and is rolling up his sleeves. From his instrument case he takes a long probe and measures Mortimer's face with it. Then another. Suddenly he feels faint and demands a drink. His flask is empty. He finds Aunt Abby's bottle of wine on the sideboard. He pours two drinks, splitting with Jonathan all there is left.

"One moment, Doctor, please," Jonathan is saying. "Where are your manners?" He turns to face Mortimer. "Yes, Mortimer. I realize now that it was you who brought me back to Brooklyn. We drink to you! (*Raises glass.*) Doctor—to my dear brother—!"

As they raise their glasses Teddy again appears on the balcony. He is formally dressed. He blows a terrible blast on his bugle. Jonathan and the Doctor are so startled they drop their glasses and spill the wine. Mortimer writhes with disappointment.

Dr. Einstein, realizing, as Jonathan warns him, that now they will have to dispatch Mortimer the quick way, has returned to the job. There is a knock at the door. Jonathan and Einstein have barely time to get between Mortimer and the door when Officer O'Hara appears. The bugle has brought him, and there is going to be hell to pay in the morning. Teddy had promised the neighbors not to do that any more.

"It's all right, Officer. We're taking the bugle away from him," says Jonathan.

"I better speak to him myself," says O'Hara, crossing the room to turn on the lights. He has started up the stairs when he hears Mortimer mumbling through his gag.

"Hey, you stood me up," protests the officer, coming back to Mortimer. "I waited an hour at Kelly's for you." And then, to Jonathan and Einstein: "What happened to him?"

"He was explaining the play he saw tonight," explains Jonathan. "That's what happened to the fellow in the play."

"Did they have that in the play you saw tonight?" demands O'Hara, incredulously. "Gee, you can't trust nobody. They practically stole that from the second act of *my* play. In the second act just before— I'd better begin at the beginning. It opens in my mother's dressing room, where I was born—only I ain't born yet. (MORTIMER *mumbles and stamps his feet.*) Huh? Oh, yes. (*Goes to* MORTIMER *and starts to remove the gag.*) No! You've got to hear the plot."

O'Hara has found the telephone stool and placed it at Mortimer's feet. He sits on it and begins the story.

"Well, she's sitting there making up, see—when out of a clear sky the door opens—and a man with a black mustache walks in —turns to my mother and says: 'Miss Latour, will you marry me?' He doesn't know she's pregnant." The curtain comes slowly down.

O'Hara has talked the night through. Daylight is streaming in at the windows. Mortimer, still tied to the chair, is no better than semi-conscious. Jonathan is asleep on the couch. Einstein, pleasantly intoxicated, is listening to O'Hara, who has taken off his coat and loosened his collar. He has just reached the most exciting scene of his play—

"—there she is lying unconscious across the table—in her longeray—the Chink is standing over her with a hatchet (*he takes a pose*)—I'm tied in a chair just like you are—the place is an inferno of flames—it's on fire—great effect we got there— when all of a sudden—through the window—in comes Mayor La Guardia."

Mortimer is startled into a second's consciousness, but collapses again. Einstein pours himself another drink. O'Hara also has one (it's his flask), and plunges ahead with the story. There is a knock at the door. From the window on the landing Einstein sees who it is. He tries to arouse Jonathan, finds he can't, and skips upstairs. O'Hara has reached a point in the play where he, as the hero, pulls a gun, faces a door and yells, "Come in!" The door opens and in walk Officers Klein and Brophy.

"Hey, Pat, what do you know," calls O'Hara in greeting. "This is Mortimer Brewster! He's going to write my play with me! I'm just telling him the story."

"Did you have to tie him up to make him listen?" demands Klein, busy getting Mortimer out of his bonds.

The whole force, it appears, has been searching for O'Hara. Klein and Brophy were also detailed to stop in and warn the aunts about Teddy and his bugle blowing. There's hell to pay about that, too. The Lieutenant has said that Teddy will have to be put away. With that conclusion Mortimer is agreed.

Officer Brophy is at the telephone reporting the finding of O'Hara when Jonathan wakens in time to hear—

"Mac?—Tell the Lieutenant he can call off the big man hunt. We got him. . . . In the Brewster house. . . . Do you want us to bring him in? . . . Oh, all right—we'll hold him right here."

Jonathan has jumped to his feet and stands between the two policemen. "So, I've been turned in, eh? All right, you've got me! I suppose you and my stool-pigeon brother will split the reward."

"Reward!" Both Klein and Brophy grab Jonathan.

JONATHAN—Now I'll do some turning in! You think my aunts are charming, sweet old ladies, don't you? Well, there are thirteen bodies buried in their cellar!

MORTIMER (*quietly but swiftly slipping upstairs*)—Teddy! Teddy!

KLEIN—What the hell are you talking about?

BROPHY—You'd better be careful what you say about your aunts—they happen to be friends of ours.

JONATHAN—I'll show you! I'll prove it to you! Come down in the cellar with me! (*He starts to drag them.*)

KLEIN—Wait a minute! Wait a minute!

JONATHAN—Thirteen bodies—I'll show you where they're buried!

KLEIN (*refusing to be kidded*)—Oh, yeah?

JONATHAN—Oh, you don't want to see what's down in the cellar!

BROPHY (*to* KLEIN)—Go on down in the cellar with him, Abe.

KLEIN—I'm not so sure I want to be down in the cellar with him. Look at that puss. He looks like Boris Karloff. Hey, what the hell! Hey, Pat! (JONATHAN, *at the mention of* KARLOFF, *grabs* KLEIN *by the throat.*)

BROPHY—What d'you think you're doing?

KLEIN—Get him off me. (BROPHY *swings on* JONATHAN *with*

his nightstick. JONATHAN *falls, unconscious.*) Well, what do you know about that? (*There is a knock on the door.*)

O'HARA—Come in! (LIEUTENANT ROONEY *bursts in. He is a very tough, driving, dominating police officer.*)

ROONEY—What the hell are you men doing here? I told you *I* was going to handle this.

KLEIN—Well, sir, we was just— (KLEIN'S *eyes go to* JONATHAN.)

ROONEY—What happened? Did he put up a fight?

BROPHY—This ain't the guy that blows the bugle. This is his brother. He tried to kill Klein.

KLEIN (*feeling his throat*)—All I said was he looked like Boris Karloff.

ROONEY—Turn him over!

BROPHY—We kinda think he's wanted somewhere.

ROONEY (*taking a look at* JONATHAN)—Oh, you kinda *think* he's wanted somewhere? If you guys don't look in the circulars we hang up in the station, at least you could read *True Detective*. Certainly he's wanted! In Indiana! Escaped from the Prison for the Criminal Insane—he's a lifer. For God's sake, that's how he was described—he looked like Karloff!

KLEIN—Was there a reward mentioned?

ROONEY—Yeah—and *I'm* claiming it.

BROPHY—He was trying to get us down in the cellar.

KLEIN—He said there was thirteen bodies buried down there.

ROONEY—Thirteen bodies buried in the cellar? And that didn't tip you off he came out of a nuthouse?

O'HARA—I thought all along he talked kinda crazy.

This is the first time Rooney has seen O'Hara. He is quick to tell the playwright that he's suspended. The news doesn't matter greatly to O'Hara but he would like to come over sometimes and use the station typewriter.

"No wonder Brooklyn's in the shape it's in, with the police force full of flatheads like you," the Lieutenant is saying. "Thirteen bodies buried in the cellar!"

"But there are thirteen bodies in the cellar," insists Teddy, who has come running down the stairs.

"Who are you?" demands Rooney.

"I'm President Roosevelt."

"What the hell is this?"

"It's the fellow that blows the bugle," explains Brophy, as both he and Klein salute Teddy. . . .

Mortimer has told the Lieutenant of the commitment papers. Teddy is going to Happy Dale. As for the thirteen bodies buried in the cellar—"Do you think anybody would believe that story?" Mortimer asks.

"You can't tell," admits the Lieutenant. "Some people are just dumb enough. You don't know what to believe sometimes. A year ago, a crazy guy started a murder rumor over in Greenpoint and I had to dig up a half-acre lot, just to prove—"

There is a knock at the door. It is Elaine with Mr. Witherspoon, "an elderly tight-lipped disciplinarian." Mr. Witherspoon is the superintendent at Happy Dale and he is looking for Teddy. Teddy, for his part, does not intend to put up with anything like insubordination, but when Mortimer explains that his presidential term of office is over, and that he can now start on his hunting trip to Africa, with Mr. Witherspoon as guide, Teddy is quite happy. "Bully! Bully!" he ejaculates, and starts off to get his equipment together.

Abby and Martha, however, are not pleased. No one shall take Teddy from them. If Teddy disturbs the neighbors they will promise to take his bugle away from him, but if Mr. Witherspoon takes him to Happy Dale then he will have to take them, too.

"It ain't only his bugle blowing and the neighbors all afraid of him, but things would just get worse," explains Lieutenant Rooney. "Sooner or later we'd be put to the trouble of digging up your cellar."

ABBY—Our cellar?

ROONEY—Yeah—your nephew is telling around that there are thirteen bodies buried in your cellar.

ABBY—But there are thirteen bodies in our cellar.

MARTHA—If that's why you think Teddy has to go away—you come down to the cellar with us and we'll prove it to you.

ABBY—There's one, Mr. Spenalzo—who doesn't belong there and is going to have to leave—and the other twelve are our gentlemen.

MORTIMER (*standing in front of the cellar door to head them off*)—I don't think Lieutenant Rooney wants to go down in the cellar. He was just telling me that last year he had to dig up a half-acre lot—weren't you, Lieutenant?

ABBY—Oh, he doesn't have to dig. The graves are all marked. We put flowers on them every Sunday.

ROONEY—Flowers! (*He thinks things over and then turns to*

WITHERSPOON.) Superintendent. Don't you think you can find room for these ladies?

WITHERSPOON—Well, I—

ABBY—You come along with us and see the graves.

ROONEY—I'll take your word for it, lady—I'm a busy man. How about it, Super?

WITHERSPOON—They'd have to be committed.

MORTIMER—Teddy committed himself. Can't they commit themselves? Can't they sign the papers?

WITHERSPOON—Certainly.

MARTHA—Oh, if we can go with Teddy we'll sign the papers. Where are they?

The papers are found and signed. The detail of having a physician attest the commitments is taken care of when Dr. Einstein, passing through the room and heading for the door, is pressed into service by Mortimer. The Doctor is a little nervous about signing, and more nervous when he hears Lieutenant Rooney repeat his description as Jonathan's accomplice as it is being telephoned from headquarters. But happily for the Doctor the Lieutenant stares at Dr. Einstein without any sign of recognition, and the Doctor is quick to bid them all good-by and hurry out.

Now Mortimer, as next of kin, is asked to sign the papers committing Abby and Martha also to Happy Dale. This causes a hurried conference on the aunts' part, followed by a rather momentous confession—

ABBY—We're really very worried about something.

MORTIMER—Now, Aunt Abby, you're going to love it there.

MARTHA—Oh, yes, we're very happy about the whole thing! That's just it!—we don't want anything to go wrong.

ABBY—Will they investigate those signatures?

MORTIMER—Now, don't worry—they're not going to look up Dr. Einstein.

MARTHA—It's not his signature, dear, it's yours.

ABBY—You see, you signed as next of kin.

MORTIMER—Of course. Why not?

MARTHA—It's something we've never wanted to tell you, Mortimer. But now you're a man—and it's something Elaine should know, too. You see, you're not really a Brewster. (MORTIMER *stares.*)

ABBY—Your mother came to us as a cook—and you were born

about three months afterward. But she was such a sweet woman—and such a good cook—and we didn't want to lose her—so brother married her.

MORTIMER—I'm—not—really—a—Brewster?

MARTHA—Now don't feel badly about it, Mortimer!

ABBY—And you won't let it make any difference, Elaine?

MORTIMER—Elaine! Did you hear—do you understand?—I'm a bastard!

Sharing Mortimer's exultation Elaine has thrown herself into his arms. A moment later, when breakfast is mentioned, she has dragged him toward the door. "Mortimer's coming to my house," says Elaine. "Father's gone to Philadelphia and Mortimer and I are going to have breakfast together."

Mortimer and Elaine have gone happily on their way. Teddy has appeared with his equipment, including a canoe paddle for Mr. Witherspoon to carry. Lieutenant Rooney is about to take Jonathan, handcuffed to Klein and Brophy, to the station.

"He's going to Indiana," the Lieutenant explains to the aunts. "Some people out there want to take care of him the rest of his life."

Jonathan, in connection with his farewells, has one last suggestion: Now that the old house is seeing the last of the Brewsters, why don't they turn the property over to the Church. "After all, it should be part of the cemetery," says Jonathan. And, as he prepares to go, he adds: "Well, I won't be able to better my record. But neither will you. At least I have that satisfaction. The score stands even—twelve to twelve."

"Jonathan always was a mean boy," pouts Aunt Martha, as her nephew is led away. "Never could stand to see anyone get ahead of him."

"I wish we could show him he isn't so smart," muses Abby. Her eyes fall upon the somewhat dolorous Mr. Witherspoon standing by the window. "Mr. Witherspoon, does your family live with you at Happy Dale?"

"I have no family."

"Oh—"

"Well, I suppose you consider everyone at Happy Dale your family."

"I'm afraid you don't understand. As head of the institution, I have to keep quite aloof."

"That must make it very lonely for you."

"It does. But my duty is my duty."

"Well, Martha—" begins Abby. Martha has already started for the sideboard to get the wine bottle. "If Mr. Witherspoon won't have breakfast with us, I think at least we should offer him a glass of elderberry wine."

"Elderberry wine?"

"We make it ourselves," says Martha.

"Why, yes! Of course, at Happy Dale our relationship will be more formal, but here— (*He sits, as* MARTHA *brings the wine to the table with one wine glass.*) You don't see much elderberry wine nowadays. I thought I'd had my last glass of it."

"Oh, no—"

"Here it is!"

Martha is handing Mr. Witherspoon the glass of wine. As he starts to toast the ladies and lifts the glass to his lips

THE CURTAIN FALLS

MY SISTER EILEEN

A Comedy in Three Acts

BY JOSEPH FIELDS AND JEROME CHODOROV

IN his introduction to the Random House book version of "My Sister Eileen" George S. Kaufman, who directed the play, intimates that the authors of the dramatization, Joseph Fields and Jerome Chodorov, were definitely threatened by a mild insanity when he first encountered them struggling with their working life in Hollywood. Their escape and complete recovery was due in large part, Mr. Kaufman believes, to their discovery of a book of sketches called "My Sister Eileen," written a few years back by Ruth McKenney for the *New Yorker Magazine.*

The Messrs. Fields and Chodorov decided that there was a play in the sketches and told Miss McKenney so. Miss McKenney replied that they were absolutely right; she knew there was a play in "My Sister Eileen" because she had written it in collaboration with Leslie Reade. But no one would produce it.

Undismayed by this news the Messrs. Fields and Chodorov asked if they might try their hand at a second stage version and Miss McKenney said they might, and welcome. The play was written, Moss Hart read it, called it to the attention of Mr. Kaufman and Max Gordon, the producer, and a production was agreed upon, with Mr. Kaufman directing. The result added greatly to the cheer in New York at Christmas time, 1940.

In the theatre program Miss McKenney explains that while the stories were actually inspired by the early experiences of the McKenney girls in New York, she naturally permitted her own fancy to take a few extravagant flights in their retelling, and later approved, for the good of the play, certain additional flights taken by the playwrights and their director.

A touch of tragedy shadowed the production when news reached New York just a week before the play's showing that Eileen McKenney had been killed in an automobile accident in California.

"There is a warming and friendly quality about the play," wrote Richard Lockridge in the New York *Sun,* "and a believable sense of the wonder, the laughter, the touch of amiable insanity and the air of camping out, which, those who have graduated from life in Greenwich Village tell us, were the stuff of life in that fascinating sector of metropolitan existence." And this is a true statement.

The authors of "My Sister Eileen" invite you, the particular summer evening of the play's opening, to meet them and their friends "in a one-room basement studio in Greenwich Village, near Christopher Street. It is a large room and far from cheerful, but there is an air of dank good nature about it that may grow on you. The walls are sandy tan-color plaster, with a few interesting streaks of darker hue here and there."

Over a painfully obvious imitation fireplace at the back of the room is an arched and grated window. Through the window, which is open, a glimpse may be had of the sidewalk of the street above, of the lower section of a lamp-post at the curb and of the lower extremities of such persons as pass by from time to time.

Within sight, and almost within reach, are a door leading to a small bathroom and a curtained alcove hiding a kitchenette. "The room itself is furnished in that curious fashion that may be seen only in the darker purlieus of the Village." There are two very hard-looking day beds and scattered chairs. Over one of the beds hangs "a large, impressionistic oil that has a vague pastoral implication," and over the other "a hanging bookcase whose open shelves are loaded with bric-a-brac that attests to somebody's good aim with three shots for a nickel."

The room is fairly lighted from the street light, but as Mr. Appopolous opens the door to usher in two prospective renters he quickly switches on a ceiling light that adds dimly to the scene. Mr. Appopolous "is a squat, powerfully built man. . . . He has a heavy shock of hair, bushy eyebrows and is a complete bully whenever he feels it is safe. . . . He speaks with an indefinite foreign intonation—possibly East Side, possibly Greek—a lingual bouillabaisse."

"Here you are! Come in, my dear young ladies! Enter!" Mr. Appopolous is followed into the room by two young women —Ruth Sherwood, "a well-built girl with a frank, good-natured face and intelligent eyes," and her sister, Eileen, with "a lovely face and swell figure. . . . There is no question about who is the beauty in the family. Eileen is not self-conscious about her good looks, accepting them naturally, just as she does the leadership of her sister in all worldly things." Ruth is carrying a portable typewriter and Eileen an overnight bag. "They both seem very tired and hot in their summer dresses."

"Aha! Isn't it just what you've been dreaming about?" Mr. Appopolous demands, with the air of the eager salesman.

"Yes, it's very nice. Only we're not sure—" Ruth gets no farther.

"Let me tell you, my dear young ladies, this is the best value for your money you can get in New York!" Mr. Appopolous' gestures are sweeping. "Look around! Look around! Note the exquisite imitation fireplace—the magnificent bookshelves—and these big comfortable day beds . . . (*He pats one of the beds, a hard solid slab, then covers up with a discreet cough.*) Just look at this interesting and exciting dormer window . . . (*At this moment a man passes the window.*) Look! Life passes up and down in front of you like a regular parade! What more could a young person with a typewriter want? (*Indicates the portable with a patronizing wave.*) Am I wrong in presuming that you are authors?"

"Haven't you something higher up?"

"Higher up? Higher up? My dear young ladies, why don't you let me show you the place before you raise a lot of objections?"

Ruth is for bargaining. Eileen is for staying—even if it is only for a few days, until they see— Eileen is very tired. She already has one shoe off. Mr. Appopolous continues his argument persuasively. The apartment is the coolest in the building; they can have it for forty-five dollars a month; if they don't like it one hundred per cent at the end of their first month he will give them their money back.

More than that he will send right now for their baggage, which they have left at the bus station. Ruth is still trying to voice a gentle protest. It is no use. Jensen, the handyman, is told to go for the baggage.

This means, Jensen explains, that he will have to quit work on the water pipes, and that is going to cause a lot of hollering—

"Never mind the hollering," shouts Mr. Appopolous, angrily. And then to the astonished girls he quickly explains: "There has been no hollering at all! He's crazy!" He has pushed Jensen out the door and turned again to the girls. His manner is now gentle and conciliatory. "Now, my dear young lady—sit down. (RUTH *faces him defiantly.*) Go ahead, sit down! (*She wilts under his gaze and sits.*) Now I will tell you why I have wasted so much of my time taking a personal interest in you two girls.

(*Points to a painting over the bed.*) Do you see that landscape? (*The girls glance at it and wince a little.*) That's from my blue-green period."

"You mean *you* painted that?" Ruth is amazed.

"Years ago. Now you understand why I reach out a sympathetic hand to you neophytes . . ."

"After having scaled the heights yourself." Her sarcasm is lost on Appopolous. He beams.

"Painting is just one of my interests. I also write epic poetry and epic drama. These studios are merely a hobby—a sanctuary for struggling young artists. . . ."

Ruth finally gives in. It may not be what they wanted, but—Eileen just has to get to bed. Ruth has found her pocketbook and is reluctantly counting out the first month's rent. She is up to forty-four dollars when an earth-shaking "Boom!" is heard from the cellar. "The room quivers and the windowpane rattles dangerously. The girls become rigid with fright. Appopolous snatches the money from Ruth's hand."

APPOPOLOUS—This will be enough!

EILEEN—My God!

RUTH—What—what was that?

APPOPOLOUS (*turning to them innocently*)—What was *what?*

RUTH—That noise—the whole room shook.

APPOPOLOUS (*giggling*)—That just goes to show you how you'll get used to it. I didn't even notice it.

EILEEN—Get used to it? You mean it happens all the time?

APPOPOLOUS—You won't even be conscious of it. A little blasting—the new subway . . . (*He indicates the floor with a casual wave. The girls stare at him in horror.*)

RUTH—You mean they're blasting right underneath us?

APPOPOLOUS—What are you worrying about? Those engineers know how much dynamite to use.

EILEEN—But does—does it go on all the time?

APPOPOLOUS (*cheerfully*)—No—no—they knock off at midnight and they don't start again until six in the morning.

RUTH—Six in the morning!

EILEEN (*picking up the overnight bag.* RUTH *grabs her typewriter*)—We can't live here!

APPOPOLOUS—Listen—in New York you either live, A, over a subway, or B, where they are building a subway, or C, you don't live in New York!

RUTH—Stop double-talking the alphabet and give us our money back!

APPOPOLOUS—What are you getting hysterical about?

RUTH—I'm not getting hysterical—*yet*. All I want is my money back!

APPOPOLOUS—Be honest—be fair to yourselves. Don't rush in and out of things. Sleep on it tonight and see how you feel in the morning.

RUTH (*rushing after him, angrily*)—You can't do this to us! Give me my money!

APPOPOLOUS (*with vast dignity*)—I said I'd give you your money back and I will—(*The girls look at him hopefully.*)—if at the end of a month you are *still* dissatisfied . . . Good night, ladies. Sleep tight. (*He goes, closing the door behind him. There is another terrific boom from below.*)

RUTH (*slowly turning to* EILEEN, *fixes her with a baleful eye.* EILEEN *drops her head and turns away sheepishly. Sweetly*)—Yes, Eileen, sleep tight, my darling. (*Then bitterly.*) You were in such a hell of a hurry to get to bed. (*A woman and dog cross in front of the window. The dog starts to take a nasal inventory of the iron bars.*) Oh, get away from there!

EILEEN—How did I know they were blasting underneath us?

RUTH—I had an instinctive feeling the moment I saw this place . . . But all a man has to do is tell you how beautiful you are, and your ping changes to a purr! (*In a sudden burst of angry energy, Ruth crosses to the kitchen alcove and glares in.*) Model kitchenette! Eileen, promise me you'll never go in there! (RUTH *throws the bathroom door open and looks in with disgust.*) And look at that! Thank God we took a bath before we left Columbus!

EILEEN (*pathetically*)—Oh, Ruth, what are we going to *do?*

RUTH (*grimly*)—We're going to do thirty days!

Ruth has taken off her dress and hung it in the closet. Eileen is still biting her nails and wondering. Wondering how much of a mistake they have made coming to New York. Wondering if their last $49.71 will last until one of them gets a job. Wondering what Billy Hunneker is thinking now. Wondering about Aunt Carrie—

"Gee, we've got to make good—if it's only to spite Aunt Carrie," decides Eileen.

"Nuts with Aunt Carrie—we've got to spite practically everybody in Columbus!" says Ruth.

They agree that they probably had better send Mother and Dad a wire—collect—and would, if the telephone had not been discontinued—

"We ought to have it connected in the morning so we can start calling up for jobs," ventures Eileen.

"You don't call up for jobs, dear, you go out and look for them. (*She sits on the bed tentatively, then groans.*) Boy! What Bernarr Macfadden would give for these beds!"

"Gee, I hope we land something soon so we can start paying Pop back."

"Don't worry, darling, we will. We've *got* to. It's a cinch Dad can't help us any more."

"It doesn't seem fair. Poor Pop works so hard all his life and what's he got to show for it?"

"You'd be amazed at all the things that aren't fair, Eileen. (*Rises, goes to the door and bolts it.*) I hope some fresh air gropes its way in here. It's stifling."

Ruth has switched off the light, but the light from the lamp post still floods the apartment. She would pull down the shade—but there is no shade. She thinks perhaps closing the window might help. A dog could chase a cat through that window. But if they close the window they'll suffocate. So they try to go to sleep and forget.

There's a moment's quiet and then a small boy dashes by the window, running a stick across the iron bars and giving a very good imitation of a machine gun in action. A second later he is back, going the other way. The girls have jumped from their beds in fright. Ruth is clutching her head in her hands in despair, and Eileen is staring at her miserably. But there is nothing to be done. They go back to bed.

Now two men have stopped outside the window. Visible from their waists down, they are arguing loudly and are obviously plastered. One wants to go back. The other has had enough. The first one is insistent. The second disgusted, especially with the broads that have been offered for his entertainment.

"You go away from there, you drunken bums!" shouts Eileen, sitting up in bed, holding the bedclothes before her.

"Ah! A dame!" shouts the First Man, delightedly.

"You go 'way from there or we'll call the police!" echoes Ruth.

"*Another* dame! Look, Pete! There's *two* broads—one for you, too! (*The* SECOND MAN *squats beside him and peers in.*

They leer at the girls drunkenly. The FIRST MAN *points to* EILEEN.) That one's mine!"

"Okay. Mine ain't so bad."

"You get away from here," calls Ruth.

"Hello, cutie!"

"Go 'way, go 'way, go 'way!" screams Eileen.

"What's your apartment number, Marlene?" the First Man wants to know.

"Yeah, we'll be right in!"

" 'Fit as a fiddle and ready for love!' "

Ruth has gathered her bedclothes around her and has grabbed a window pole, threatening to beat the hands off the man who is trying to interfere with her closing the window. Suddenly "a huge pair of feet and legs encased in a blue uniform come up to the window. A nightstick moves in between the two men."

LONIGAN—What's goin' on here? Come on! Break it up! Break it up!

FIRST MAN—Just a social visit, officer.

SECOND MAN—We was just goin' . . . good night.

LONIGAN—Go on—get outa here! Go on! (*The men go off hastily. The cop bends down and peers into the window at* RUTH. *He smiles wisely.*) Oh, I get it!

RUTH—I'm awfully glad you came, officer.

LONIGAN (*heavily*)—Yeah—I'll *bet* you are.

EILEEN—Officer, do you think you could do something about the lamp post? It shines right in here.

LONIGAN—Sure, I'll put a shade on it . . . You're new in this neighborhood, ain't ya?

RUTH—We just moved in today.

LONIGAN—Well, if you're smart you'll move out tomorrow. I don't go for this stuff on my beat . . . I'm warning you! (LONIGAN *scowls at them and walks off.*)

RUTH (*staring after cop, stunned*)—Did you—did you hear what he said, Eileen?

EILEEN—Yes, I did . . . Ruth, I'm afraid.

RUTH—It's all right, darling. (*She closes the window, and goes to* EILEEN'S *bed, slipping in beside her.*) It'll be all right. (*A church clock somewhere in the distance starts to strike the hour. The girls lie on their backs, staring at the ceiling, helplessly, in a kind of stupor. There is a peaceful, gentle lull, broken suddenly by a tremendous explosion from below. A lamp falls to*

oto by Lucas Studio.

"MY SISTER EILEEN"

Appopolous: Painting is just one of my interests. I also write epic poetry and epic drama.
(*Morris Carnovsky, Shirley Booth, Jo Ann Sayers*)

the floor with a crush. The girls throw their arms around each other, terrified.) Oh, my God!

Eileen wails softly on Ruth's shoulder as the curtain falls.

It is again afternoon, a few weeks later. There have been a few slight changes in the apartment. Books have been added, there are new bed covers "and indications of a woman's hand around the room, but it hasn't helped much."

Eileen is in the kitchenette stirring something on the small stove. She comes out when she hears a booming voice singing lustily, "I'm a rambling wreck from Georgia Tech, and a helluva engineer."

The voice belongs to "a powerfully built man of about twenty-seven, with an amazing growth of chest hair. This latter is perfectly apparent at all times, since his habitual costume is a pair of basket-ball shorts, sneakers without socks and a narrow cotton jersey. He is good-looking in a completely blank way, and is usually a bit glazed from a steady and quiet diet of straight gin." But for that he might have made the All-American.

The man's name is Ted Loomis, but his friends call him The Wreck. He introduces himself to Eileen; announces that he lives upstairs; sniffs appreciatively at the spaghetti and meat balls Eileen is cooking; asks for Ruth; finds she is out and departs. Later, he calls back, he and Helen, his wife, want to have a talk with Eileen and Ruth about something—

Ruth is home and wearied by a day of being snubbed by office boys. Nothing encouraging to report. Nothing encouraging in the mail, either. Just another batch of returned manuscripts.

Eileen, however, has news. Eileen reports meeting a man in the Theatre Guild office, a newspaper reporter named Chic Clark, and he gave her his number and wants Ruth to call him up.

Mr. Appopolous has called. They have been looking for him. They want Mr. Appopolous to do something about a spot on the wall where a leak of some kind is soaking through. Also he should do something about a curtain for the window. And about the back door lock. And the day beds— "It's like sleeping in an iron lung," protests Ruth, with feeling.

Mr. Appopolous is not interested. He is all excitement about a one-man exhibit of his paintings covering all the Appopolous art, and will be wanting to borrow the painting above Ruth's bed. This will be all right with them— "I'll hang the Sunday funnies there," says Eileen.

"You must excuse Eileen, Mr. Appopolous," explains Ruth, before the landlord has time to take offense. "I keep telling her not to confuse the artist with his personality, but she still thinks you're a louse." The compliment leaves Mr. Appopolous unmoved.

With their landlord gone, Ruth thinks she will take a cold shower and go to bed. She can't do that because Eileen has invited a man to dinner; a Frank Lippencott who manages the Liggett drugstore in Forty-fourth Street.

"Gee—since I've been in New York I've only met one man—and he said, 'Why the hell don't you look where you're going?' " sighs Ruth, staring at Eileen in honest admiration.

EILEEN—Well, Frank's a very nice boy, and, besides, he hasn't let me pay a single lunch check since I've been going in there.

RUTH (*going into the bathroom*)—Why don't you wander into Schrafft's some day?

EILEEN—I wanted you to meet him. Then, whenever you're in the neighborhood, you can have your lunch there, too.

RUTH—I have a feeling that before long the Forty-fourth Street branch of Liggett's is going to be under new management.

EILEEN—Well, it comes in handy . . . I'll finish cooking—you take it easy, darling. (*Elaborately casual.*) Oh, Ruth, we ought to have something for dessert. You're dressed. Would you mind running down to the bakery . . .

RUTH (*coming out of the bathroom, very resigned*)—You know, it's wonderful the way you manage with only one maid.

EILEEN—As long as you're going the back way, you might as well cash in those six milk bottles.

RUTH—Anything else?

EILEEN—No, that's all. Just use your own judgment about the dessert. Get something nice.

RUTH—Well, I've got a nickel and six milk bottles, I can run riot! (*She goes up the back stairs.*)

EILEEN (*gets out a dress from the closet and starts to the bathroom. There is a knock at the door. She turns anxiously*)—Frank? (*The door opens and a very good-looking young man with an erect military carriage enters. He smiles pleasantly.*)

MAN—Hello.

EILEEN (*uneasily*)—Yes?

MAN—Hot, isn't it?

EILEEN—Yes. Is there anything . . . ?

MAN—Mind if I sit down? (*Without waiting for a reply, he

sinks comfortably into a chair and stretches out.)

EILEEN (*with growing apprehension*)—I think you're making a mistake. What apartment do you want?

MAN (*stretching his legs*)—Is Violet home?

EILEEN—You've got the wrong apartment.

MAN (*reassuringly*)—It's all right. Marty sent me . . . over at the armory.

EILEEN (*firmly*)—I don't know any Marty. You'll have to get out of here.

MAN—Don't be like that. I'm a good fella.

EILEEN (*angrily*)—I don't care what you are! Will you please go!

MAN (*thoughtfully, as he looks her over*)—Are you sure Violet Shelton doesn't live here?

EILEEN—If you don't get out of here I'm going to call the police!

MAN (*laughing*)—They can't arrest me. I'm a Captain in the United States Army.

EILEEN—All right, you asked for it—now you're going to get it! (EILEEN *rushes to the door, throws it open and yells lustily. The* CAPTAIN *smiles after her.* RUTH *starts down the back stairs.*) Mr. Loomis! Mr. Loomis! (*Turning to him.*) You'd better get out of here. A big, husky friend of mine is coming down here in a minute.

CAPTAIN—Glad to see him. (*He lights a cigarette.*)

RUTH (*entering through the back door, box in hand*)—I got some banana shortcake. That ought to make him feel at home.

EILEEN—Ruth!

RUTH (*cordially*)—Oh—how do you do?

CAPTAIN—How do you do?

EILEEN—Don't "How do you do" him, Ruth! He's nobody!

RUTH (*bewildered*)—You mean he isn't Liggett's?

EILEEN—Of course not!

RUTH—Then who *is* he?

EILEEN—I don't know. He just walked in and he won't go 'way. (*She goes behind* RUTH.) Make him go 'way, Ruth!

RUTH (*stepping forward valiantly, then stopping*)—Now you go 'way! And stop bothering my sister.

CAPTAIN (*flatly*)—No.

EILEEN (*as* RUTH *advances a few steps*)—Be careful—he's a soldier.

THE WRECK (*dashing in from the front door menacingly*)—What's the trouble, girls? (*The* CAPTAIN *rises.*)

EILEEN—This man walked in and he won't go 'way!

THE WRECK (*looking him over and then advancing on him, threateningly*)—What's the idea of crashing in on these girls?

CAPTAIN—Now don't get yourself excited—it's just a mistake.

THE WRECK—You bet it was a mistake. Now get movin'!

CAPTAIN (*pleasantly*)—Very well . . . (*To the girls.*) Good evening. (*He goes to the door and pauses at the steps, looking* THE WRECK *over thoughtfully.*) You are the hairiest madame I *ever* saw.

The Captain has disappeared hurriedly up the stairs. The Wreck is able to clear up the Violet matter. There was a girl named Violet who had the studio before the Sherwoods took it.

Now The Wreck's wife has joined them. Helen Loomis is "a cute little girl of about twenty-two, with a wide-eyed view of life and a rather phlegmatic brain." Her husband calls her "Sugar," and Sugar is plainly nervous. There is something that has to be settled and The Wreck was supposed to have told Ruth and Eileen what it is. Now it comes out. It seems the National Broadcasting Company has sent for Helen's mother to appear on the Hobby Lobby program. Helen's mother builds things out of matchsticks. It took her fifteen years to make the Flatiron Building and now she is just finishing Radio City.

Naturally Mother wants to save hotel expense, and is preparing to move in with her daughter. Unfortunately, Helen's mother doesn't know about The Wreck.

"You mean she doesn't know that you're married?" asks Eileen.

"Well, you might go a little deeper than that—she doesn't even know we're engaged," says The Wreck.

"We're going to get married as soon as the professional football season starts," adds Helen, quickly.

It is The Wreck's hope that while Helen's mother is in town Ruth and Eileen will let him sleep in their kitchen—

"He wouldn't be in your way—really," promises Helen. "You'd feel a lot safer with The Wreck around—and he's awfully handy. He can clean up and he irons swell."

"But no washing—that's woman's work," adds The Wreck.

The girls are worried by the prospect, but sympathetic. They're pretty crowded as it is, but—perhaps, thinks Eileen, they could do it for one night. Before Ruth can register doubt the Loomises have dashed out of the door and upstairs to get The Wreck's things.

"Something tells me you weren't quite ready to leave Columbus," says Ruth.

"Oh, well—he's practically married," says Eileen, with a shrug.

A knock at the door announces the arrival of Frank Lippencott. Eileen rushes for the kitchen to change her dress. Ruth opens the door and Frank, not noticing the steps, stumbles into the room. "Frank is a mild-mannered boy of about 25, with a somewhat prissy air. A few pencils and pens are clipped neatly into the breast pocket of his white linen suit."

Ruth has some little difficulty keeping up a conversation with Frank, but Eileen soon relieves her. Frank is plainly impressed with Eileen's freshness and beauty. It is for her that he has brought a bottle of California red wine to go with the spaghetti. "It's a special we're running this week," he explains. "So's our spaghetti," Ruth assures him, putting him quite at his ease.

"Gee, this is great!" says Frank, looking around him admiringly. "I always wanted to live in the Village, in a studio like this . . ."

"What stopped you?"

"Well, in my position in the drugstore, you've got to keep up appearances."

"I see. Where the Liggetts speak only to Walgreens and the Walgreens speak only to God."

"What?" Frank is puzzled, but this time there is no one to help him out. Eileen has discovered that Mr. Appopolous has forgotten to bring a table. She and Frank will have to go and get one.

It is while Ruth is alone that Chic Clark barges through the half open front door. Chic is "a pouchy, red-faced man in his middle thirties. He wears a badly wrinkled suit. He is perspiring freely, his shirt is open at the collar and his tie is hanging loosely."

Chic is looking for a party named Sherwood—Eleanor Sherwood. He has written the address on the inside of a matchbook cover, but he is quick to recall that the name really is Eileen. He is also glad to meet Eileen's sister, though a little surprised by the contrast.

The return of Frank and Eileen with the table is followed by introductions that explain a lot. Mr. Clark is the newspaper man who has promised Eileen that he will help her sister, and he stands by that promise. But just at the moment he would like to send Ruth and Frank Lippencott to a night ball game. He is plainly disappointed when he discovers that it is Eileen, not Ruth, that Frank has come to see.

To cover the situation, Ruth is quick to suggest that they all have a drink. Frank is as quick to uncork his bottle of wine. He has passed the glasses, and Ruth has offered a toast—

"Here's to us, and Burgundy, California!" Suddenly there is another blast from the subway below. Frank starts back in fear, spilling his drink all over his nice white suit.

"For Crissake—what was that?" shouts Chic, springing to his feet. Eileen has rushed to Frank and is trying ineffectually to wipe the wine from his coat.

In the midst of this excitement The Wreck appears at the back door with a folded army cot and pillow under one arm and an assortment of bedclothes under the other. He is closely followed by Officer Lonigan who is poking him into the center of the room with his nightstick.

"What the hell do you think you're doin'—runnin' around in your drawers?" demands Lonigan.

"Lay off me, will ya?" pleads The Wreck, turning to the girls. "Will you tell this big clown I'm okay?"

RUTH—Yes, he's all right.

EILEEN—Yes.

LONIGAN—I found him in the alley, with all these bedclothes. I think he's some kind of a sex nut!

THE WRECK—You're crazy! I'm going to live here!

RUTH—It's all right, officer!

EILEEN—Yes—we know him . . .

LONIGAN (*staring at them in recognition, his manner becoming grim*)—Oh, it's you two! I thought I warned you about openin' up on my beat!

RUTH—Why, you—you old . . .

EILEEN—How dare you say things like that?

THE WRECK—Say, listen . . .

CHIC—Look here, officer—you're sniffin' up the wrong tree. I'll vouch for these girls!

LONIGAN—Oh! (FRANK *pops behind the closet curtains, as* LONIGAN *advances on* CHIC.) That makes it all right—and who are you?

CHIC—I'll tell you who I am—I'm . . . (*The door is kicked open and a mammoth Cossack in full costume comes down the steps. Draped in his arms is the limp unconscious form of* VIOLET SHELTON, *a very luscious blonde of indeterminate years. She wears an evening gown.*)

COSSACK—I am doorman at Russian Kretchma—she pass out. (*He carries her to a bed and puts her down.*)

THE WRECK—It's Violet.

RUTH—Violet!

EILEEN—But she doesn't live here!

COSSACK (*coldly*)—Please—this is not the first time I have take her home. Good night! (*Clicks his heels, bows, and exits.*)

CHIC (*admiringly*)—Colder than Kelcey!

LONIGAN (*looking at his watch*)—She's early tonight!

RUTH (*taking a long and resigned look at* VIOLET)—Well, for a place with a bad location, and no neon sign, we're doing a hell of a business!

The curtain falls.

ACT II

One afternoon ten days later Ruth is at her typewriter while The Wreck finishes a batch of ironing. It is a jovial occupation with him. His defiant theme song, "I'm a rambling wreck from Georgia Tech, and a helluva engineer," rolls lustily from his throat. Now and again he stops to take a healthy swig of gin from the flask in his pocket. It is also apparent that he takes pride in his work.

"Which way do you want these pleats turned?" he asks Ruth, indicating a skirt on the board.

"Toward Mecca," answers Ruth, returning to her writing. The fact that she is writing a story intrigues The Wreck. He wishes she would write one about him and Helen and the way they met. The Wreck was peddling vacuum cleaners in those days. Helen was his first client. They fell in love during his first demonstration and he never did get back to the office.

"What happened to the vacuum cleaner?" asks Ruth.

"It's upstairs," says The Wreck. "We still hear from the company."

Ruth has gone out to mail a manuscript. The Wreck is taking another drink from his flask when a "small birdlike face appears at the window." The Wreck turns wrathfully. "What are you lookin' at, you old bat?"

The face disappears, but the next minute Helen comes rushing in to report that the lady was her mother, and that Mother is excitedly insisting that she has been cursed at by a naked man.

To Helen the situation grows dangerous. What if her mother should discover the truth? And she might if The Wreck continues to hang out around there. Helen doesn't like the idea of The

Wreck's being so close to Eileen, anyway. If they only had a couple of dollars he could go to the "Y" till Mother leaves. The Wreck is looking for something to pawn when he spies the Appopolous picture on the wall. He couldn't get a nickel on that, but the frame is pretty fancy. He will have a try with that. . . .

Eileen and Ruth are home, and The Wreck is back, when Helen's mother barges into the Sherwood apartment. There is fire in her eye as she orders her daughter out of the place—

"I will not have you associating with these depraved women and their—consort!" snaps Mrs. Wade.

"What?" Ruth and Eileen have turned indignantly.

"Who's a consort?" demands The Wreck.

"If you dare address me, I will call the police!"

"Please, Mother—he's—he's just a—friend of theirs . . ."

"What!"

"Yes, just a friend of ours," Ruth adds, sadly.

"Not another word!" storms Mrs. Wade. "You're moving out of this place at once! Now get upstairs!" With an imploring look at the girls Helen dashes out the door. Mrs. Wade has turned to face the girls. "Don't you dare talk to my Helen again! You're not fit to associate with decent people!"

Ruth and Eileen gaze helplessly at each other. The Wreck is still staring at the door Mrs. Wade has just slammed. "I'm going to wait until Mother's Day and then sock her," declares The Wreck, with feeling. "Gee, you kids were swell not to give us away—Helen and me—and I'll never forget it."

"Oh, that's all right, Wreck."

"No, I appreciate it. Well, I got to go around the corner a minute and tend to some business. Then I'll pack my stuff and get outa here."

"Don't forget your ironing board," cautions Eileen.

"I won't. Thanks again. I had a very nice stay here." The Wreck has gone. A minute later the lower half of him can be seen passing the window stealthily. He is carrying the Appopolous picture.

Things are beginning to look a little more promising for the Sherwoods. Ruth has met the editor of *The Manhatter* and left him some of her stories, which he has promised to read, and Eileen has been assured by Chic Clark that his city editor, Mr. Bains, has promised to give Ruth a trial assignment any day now.

They have a caller. It is Violet Shelton, the girl who used to live there, and who "dropped in on them the other night." Violet wants to apologize, and she would also like to help them if she can. She thinks she might get Eileen a job—

"Ever take 'em off?" Violet asks.

"What?" demands the startled Eileen.

"Take 'em off—strip," explains Violet.

"No."

"You don't, huh? Well, I'll see what I can do, anyway. So long!"

"So long!"

"Too bad you don't strip, though—they're always looking for new faces."

Violet has left a package of her new cards with them. Many of her old friends will no doubt be wondering where she is living now. Ruth thinks they might have the cards scattered over New York from a plane.

Eileen also reports a second experience. She had stepped into a Food Show and gathered together a bag of samples of breakfast food. At the Okay Chewing Gum booth she had met a young man who offered her a job passing samples of the gum out on the street. If she will see him Sunday he thinks he can arrange to give her the West Side of Times Square. But Eileen isn't sure she will be interested now that she has made up with Frank and everything is all right at Liggett's again. . . .

Mr. Appopolous has come for his picture. He is about to open his one-man show and he wants his blue-green opus. Where is it? Neither Ruth nor Eileen has the slightest idea what could have become of the picture—but they had warned him several times about the lock on the back door.

"I don't think you realize what this so-called disappearance means," soberly protests Mr. Appopolous. "That painting was the last existing canvas from my blue-green period!"

"What happened to the others? Termites?" asks Ruth. Mr. Appopolous storms out in disgust. . . .

Now Mr. Bains has called Ruth from the City Room of Chic's paper and given her an assignment. She is to go to Pier 63, Sands Street, Brooklyn, and get a story about a Brazilian training ship that is in with a crew of young coffee millionaires from Brazil. Ruth is wildly excited. So is Eileen. The next minute they have exchanged stockings—Eileen taking the one with a run in it that Ruth was wearing. Now Ruth is ready—but hasn't carfare to get to Brooklyn! She will have to cash in a carton of milk bottles. She has started up the stairs when she realizes that she doesn't even know where Brooklyn is. "You can't miss it!" shouts Eileen. And as Ruth is disappearing she calls: "Remember a coffee millionaire is as good as a job!"

Eileen has turned away from the window when Robert Baker, "a good-looking young man of about thirty," appears there. He bends down and is examining an address book when Eileen turns. He smiles politely and tips his hat.

"I beg your pardon. This is 233, Apartment 1-A, isn't it?"

"Yes, it is."

"Thank you very much." Mr. Baker rises and disappears. The Wreck has just come down the back stairs.

"Is that you, Wreck?" calls Eileen.

"Uh-huh. I'm just getting my things together." He pulls the kitchen curtains closed.

"I just wanted to know. I may need you," warns Eileen, as there is a knock at the front door.

Mr. Baker introduces himself. No, Marty didn't send him. And he is not looking for Violet. He is looking for Miss Ruth Sherwood. He is an associate editor of *The Manhatter*. He has read some of Eileen's stories. He thinks she is a clever writer and he is hoping that Mr. Cross, *Manhatter's* editor, will be interested in her work. When a moment later he also expresses interest in Eileen's ambition to become an actress, and thinks perhaps he can help get her at least into a producer's office, Eileen is all smiles—

"Ruth was right, Mr. Baker," she says, sweetly. "You're one of the nicest persons I've met in New York, too."

"You're very kind, but I don't suppose you've met many people since you've been here." Mr. Baker is smiling, too.

EILEEN—Oh, yes! We've met quite a few! And the things they say about New York aren't so. Folks go out of their way to try to help you. I know everybody's just lovely to me.

BAKER (*looking her over thoughtfully*)—I think I can understand that. . . . Look, why don't we go somewhere and have a cool drink while we're waiting for your sister?

EILEEN—Oh, I'd love to. I'll get my hat.

BAKER—We can go right down the street—there's a bar at the Parrot's Cage.

EILEEN (*going to the bathroom*)—Oh, that'll be swell, because Ruth won't be back for quite a while yet.

BAKER—Oh, fine.

EILEEN—Excuse me a moment. I'll put my hat on.

BAKER—Certainly. (*Two men in work clothes roll a large barrel past the window.*)

First Workman—Watch it, now. Watch it.
Second Workman—O.K. I got it.
Baker (*grinning*)—Interesting studio.
Eileen (*from bathroom*)—How's that?
Baker—I say it's—an interesting studio.
Eileen—Well, it's all right for just the two of us.
Baker—Yes, I suppose for two girls living alone. . . . (The Wreck *crosses from the kitchen to the front door in his basket-ball trunks, his trousers neatly pressed and draped over his arm.* Baker *stares at him open-mouthed.*)
The Wreck (*waving casually*)—Hi! (Eileen *emerges from the bathroom and just catches a glimpse of the departing* Wreck.)
Eileen (*going to* Baker, *helplessly*)—Oh! Our back-door lock is broken and sometimes people happen to pass through. . . . (*The curtain is lowered for a few moments to denote the passing of an hour. When it comes up again we hear voices in the hall.*)
Eileen (*from the hall*)—That's a charming little place, Mr. Baker. I had a lovely time.
Baker—So did I—I'm glad you like it.
Eileen (*coming in*)—Won't you come in for a few minutes?
Baker—Thanks—if we're going out to dinner, I'd better give you a chance to change. I'll drop back later.
Eileen—We're not dressing, are we?
Baker—Just as you like.
Eileen (*sighing with relief*)—Let's not. Wouldn't you rather go to some quiet little place?
Baker—I'd much rather.
Eileen—So would I.
Baker—See you later . . .
Eileen (*extending her hand*)—Good-by!
Baker—Good-by! (*He starts to go.*)
Eileen—Thanks for the Cuba Libres!
Baker—Good-by. (Baker *goes.* Eileen *looks after him a moment, an ecstatic expression on her face. She hums as she tosses her hat on the bed and goes to the closet.* Baker *appears at the window.*) I won't be long.
Eileen—I'll be ready!

Eileen has picked up her dress and started for the bathroom when Chic Clark appears from the kitchen, carrying a highball in either hand and grinning broadly. Chic has evidently come to stay and nothing Eileen can say discourages him. She tries to thank him for speaking to Mr. Bains about Ruth. He just follows her around the room with the highballs. She tries to tell him of her date with Mr. Baker, but he promises to fix that by throwing Baker out when he comes. She asks him to excuse her, but he is not interested—

"Excuse ya? After I went and fixed it to get ya alone without that eagle-eyed sister of yours around!"

"What! That call Ruth got *was* from the editor, wasn't it?"

"What are ya worryin' about? I'm handlin' it, ain't I?"

"It wasn't the editor! It was *you!*"

"Look, it's gonna work out the same way. I'm gonna hand the story to the city desk as a sample of what she can do. . . ."

"You sent Ruth over to Brooklyn on a wild-goose chase."

"Wild-goose nothing! I'm letting her cover my assignment. What kind of a heel do you think I am?"

"Of all the dirty rotten tricks!"

"What are you yelpin' about? I'll slip her a couple of bucks for her trouble . . ."

Eileen is on the verge of tears, Chic would put his arm around her comfortingly. Again she backs away to avoid him and the pursuit is renewed. Suddenly Eileen has an inspiration. She goes to the phone and begins dialing. She will call Chic's City Editor and tell him the whole story. She has the connection and has called the City Editor when Chic gives in.

"Wait a minute. You win . . . You double-crosser! A fine little sneak you turned out to be!"

There is a blast from the subway below. "I look forward to the day when the Bronx Express runs right through this room!" yells Chic, and slams out the door.

Eileen is dashing about in her slip looking for a dress when Frank Lippencott appears at the window and hurries down. Eileen is helpless. She gets into the bathroom in time to change.

Frank has brought Eileen a box of candy and is nervously struggling with a great idea. He has been thinking about it all night. Frank has discovered that he has been wasting his life. He isn't trying to propose marriage, but— It has occurred to Frank that he and Eileen might have each other and still have their freedom.

"Frank Lippencott! How dare you suggest such an outrageous thing?" demands Eileen, her eyes flashing.

"I don't see why it's so outrageous," insists Frank. "After all *you* ought to understand these things. After what I saw right in the room!"

"What does that mean?"

"Well, you and your sister aren't exactly puritans—are you?"

"Oh, no? What *are* we?"

"Well—you know—Bohemians . . ."

"We are *not* Bohemians! We're a couple of girls from Columbus, Ohio, who came here to make a living! And that's all we came here for! So if you know what's good for you—*get out!*"

Eileen has followed the flustered Frank to the door and shut it after him. She has run again to the bathroom only to be called back by another knock. Still it isn't Mr. Baker. This time it is Mr. Appopolous. He has come to face the Misses Sherwood with a pawn ticket that has been "*sub rosa* slipped under his door." It is a ticket for the Appopolous blue-green picture and he is pretty indignant. But the more he looks at Eileen the more mollified he becomes. Now, with a gleam in his eye, Appopolous is controlled by an idea. He is sure he and Eileen could understand each other.

"Miss Sherwood—Eileen—you are both a beautiful and desirable young lady . . ." Mr. Appopolous is following Eileen about the room, and she is trying her best to avoid him. "From the first night you came here I admired you. Not only for your charming build and wholesome personality, but I felt we were kindred spirits that would both enjoy the same things."

"Yes . . . Well, we can talk it over some time . . . I'm expecting a friend in a few minutes and I've got to change . . ."

"Women have never played a disturbing rôle in my life. I am creative enough without women . . . I am able to express myself . . . (*He looks at her reproachfully.*) *Please,* Miss Sherwood, stand still while I am talking to you."

"You really *must* excuse me now, Mr. Appopolous . . ."

He has caught up with her now, and is holding her as she struggles to get away from him.

"This is—this is against the law," breathlessly protests the struggling Eileen. "You've got to get out of another person's apartment when they tell you to!"

"There is a higher law—the law of nature," declares Mr. Appopolous, raising his hand to heaven.

The phone is ringing. By a Herculean effort Eileen manages to get away from Appopolous and reach the phone. He follows her and she has no more than recognized Mr. Baker's voice when Appopolous tears the phone from her hand and, with a rough "Call back later!" slams the receiver down. Eileen slaps him soundly. Appopolous is rubbing his face and mumbling. "You struck me!"

"You bet I struck you, and if you don't get out of here, I'll hit you over the head with this phone!"

"I assure you, young lady, that will not be necessary. I should have known better. Life is for idiots! A man like me in this position! Believe me, the gods must be laughing, indeed!"

Appopolous strides majestically from the apartment. Eileen stares after him for a moment. The phone rings again. This time it is Mr. Baker. He'll be right over. And Eileen will be ready . . .

Eileen has barely disappeared in the bathroom when the sound of hearty masculine laughter is heard outside the door. A moment later Ruth slips through the door and turns quickly to close it on the first of six very handsome young navy officers. Ruth cannot shut the door and a moment later the six young men have filed into the room after her. "Their dark skins contrast brilliantly with their immaculate tropical white uniforms." They represent the Brazilian Navy, and the louder Ruth bids them good-by the more determined they appear to be not to understand her.

"Good-by! Au revoir! Auf Wiedersehen!" yells Ruth.

"Ah! Agora nao podem fugir—nos!" . . . "Depors de virmo toda esta distancia," answer the Admirals.

"Eileen! Eileen!" screams Ruth.

"What's going on?" demands Eileen, running out of the bathroom.

"The Fleet's in."

Now the Admirals are struck by the appearance of Eileen, and are ready for a new attack. Eileen is intrigued, but Ruth is furious. If she only knew how to say "Get the hell out of here!" in Portuguese, that might help. But she doesn't. She is standing before them now, pointing to the door and shouting "Go!" No good.

"What did you bring them *here* for?" Eileen wants to know.

"Bring them! They've been on my tail ever since I left the Brooklyn Navy Yard. There was another dozen when we started out, but they got lost in the subway."

The Admirals are laughing loudly, and edging a little closer to Eileen.

"What do they want, anyway?" demands Eileen, a little frightened.

"What do you *think* they want?"

"My God! We've got to get them out of here!" Eileen is now really alarmed.

But the more Eileen pleads with the boys to go away, the closer they cling to her and to the idea of staying. She tries, in pantomime, to explain that she has a date to do a little eating. They think she is inviting them to dinner. She tries to pretend that she is sick with a stomach ache and must lie down. The minute she tries that there is such a rush of Admirals toward the couch she is forced to shriek and jump up in horror.

"For God's sake! Don't let them get any wrong ideas!" warns Ruth.

Now the Admirals have gone into a huddle, each taking a coin from his pocket to toss. "What are they tossing for?" Eileen wants to know. "I don't know, but I've got a hunch it's not for *me!*" answers Ruth.

The tossing is over. The five losers are slapping the back of the winning sixth in congratulation. He, smiling broadly, advances on Eileen and bows gallantly—

"Minha querida prima Americana, ganhei voce en temo los admirado toda a noite. Dar me is grand prager fantai consigo esta tarde."

"It's a romantic language, isn't it?" Ruth's sarcasm is not appreciated.

FIRST ADMIRAL (*to the others*)—Que tal foi?

ALL ADMIRALS—Muito bom . . . Aquilo for bom!

EILEEN (*to her suitor, desperately*)—No understando—no spikee Portugeese . . .

RUTH—My sister means "Elle ne parle pas Portugeese."

FIRST ADMIRAL (*offering his arm to* EILEEN *courteously*)—Bom. Sim, señorita.

EILEEN (*backing away*)—No! I don't know what you won, but you're not going to collect from me! (*There is a sudden explosion from below. The* ADMIRALS *start with surprise, cross themselves, and rush for the door.*)

ADMIRALS—Deus men! Que foi isso!

EILEEN (*with sudden inspiration, dashes for front door, throws it open and urges the men out, excitedly*)—Earthquake! Earthquake! Run for your lives! (*The* ADMIRALS, *however, are by this time fully recovered and they grin at her.*)

RUTH—What a performance! Helen Hayes couldn't have done it better!

EILEEN (*facing the men angrily*)—Stop grinning at me—you big dopes!

FIRST ADMIRAL (*discovering the phonograph and crossing to it, turns it on. A Conga blares forth loudly.*) Musica! Musica!

ALL ADMIRALS—La Conga! La Conga! (*They throw their hats in the air. The* FIRST ADMIRAL *grabs* EILEEN, *another* RUTH, *and the dance is on with great gusto, despite the girls' protests.*)

RUTH—Leave me out of this. I can't even dance the rhumba!

SECOND ADMIRAL—Linka Conga! (*He grabs* EILEEN *by the hips from behind, and the others quickly line up in back of him —going into the dance, deserting* RUTH. *Propelled against her will,* EILEEN *finds herself leading them around the room, the men laughing and shouting excitedly. The Conga is definitely their dish.*)

EILEEN—Ruth! Ruth!

RUTH (*shouting over the clamor*)—Eileen! Listen! I've got an idea! (*She backs in front of* EILEEN, *leading her in the direction of the back door.*) Lead 'em out the back door—and run like hell for the front and I'll let you slip in!

EILEEN (*slapping at the* ADMIRAL *who holds her in a vise-like grip*)—You do it and I'll let *you* slip in!

RUTH—They won't follow me! *You're* the one they want!

EILEEN (*as she leads the men out the back door*)—You better *be* there! (*They go out with much conga crying and general hilarity.* RUTH *stares after them a moment. As she is watching them off,* BAKER *enters through the front door.* RUTH *turns and sees him. She is taken completely by surprise.*)

BAKER—Good evening, Miss Sherwood. . . .

RUTH (*wets her lips, opens her mouth, but nothing comes out.* BAKER *looks at her in surprise*)—Oh—oh . . . Hello—Mr.—Mr. Baker . . . (*Suddenly the conga line appears at the window, headed by* EILEEN. *They are crouched over and shuffling gaily.* BAKER *goes to the window, staring in amazement. As the line passes, we notice that three little street urchins, one a dusky brown, have joined onto the end of the line.* RUTH *deliberately avoids looking, as she tries gracefully to edge to the door to fulfill her part of the bargain.*)

BAKER—What's going on?

RUTH—Nothing at all . . . Just some friends of Eileen's . . . They're from Brazil . . . They just happened to . . . (*At this moment* EILEEN *leads the line into the room again, trying to close the door behind her desperately. A crowd has collected at the window, staring in and yelling excitedly as* LONIGAN, *the cop, comes running down the back stairs blowing his whistle.*)

EILEEN—Ruth, where the hell were you?

"As Eileen reaches Baker a blank look of horror spreads over her face. She tries to shake hands with him. The conga line's direction suddenly shifts and Baker follows along, making a valiant attempt to talk to her as the curtain falls."

ACT III

The studio is empty next day when Mr. Appopolous and his handyman, Jensen, let themselves in with the Appopolous pass key. They have come to bring back the blue-green painting. The one-man show has been a disappointment. Even with the promise of "Free Iced Tea" nobody came. Mr. Appopolous is greatly discouraged.

Jensen has started to work on the back door lock when Ruth arrives. She is wearing the official "Okay" costume—"a short red skirt with ruffles, a red top with cross straps, a high wicker red hat. Over her shoulders is hung a display box built like a drum filled with sample 'Okays.' "

Ruth realizes that this is the last day of the Sherwood lease, but she is too tired to talk about it. Unless, perhaps, Mr. Appopolous is ready to give them back their month's rent—seeing they're still dissatisfied.

Mr. Appopolous can't remember anything about that, but he is full of promises looking to their renewal of the lease, if Ruth has finally got a job. With the help of Violet, the former tenant, Mr. Appopolous is finally edged out.

Violet has come to check up. She has a new lead for Eileen—a job in a nude ranch show. "All you gotta do is wear a G-string and play volley ball," promises Violet. But Ruth is afraid Eileen doesn't play volley ball.

At the moment, it appears, Eileen is still in court—the magistrate's court in Twelfth Street. "I hope she doesn't come up before Dooley," says Violet. "He passes out thirty days like they were peanuts."

"Thirty days!" Now Ruth is anxious. "They can't do that to you just for kicking an officer . . . Can they?"

"It all depends on how hard she kicked," says Violet.

Robert Baker calls from the window before he comes in. He has been to the magistrate's court and has news. Due to certain peculiar ramifications of the case Washington has ordered Eileen to be held. It has something to do with Pan-American relations—

"But I'm sure it's going to be all right," adds Baker, quickly. "Now, don't worry. And listen, I've read your stories and I think they're swell! And what's more, I've done something about it!"

RUTH (*excitedly*)—You have?

BAKER—Yes, I've passed them on to his highness! (*Biting it out.*) Mr. Ralph Spencer Cross! Editor of *The Manhatter*.

RUTH—Gee, then you actually liked them.

BAKER—I certainly did. You really ought to have a little more faith in yourself.

RUTH—I should?

BAKER (*softly*)—Yes—you definitely should.

RUTH—Thanks. I'm beginning to . . . (*There is an awkward pause. They smile at each other.*)

BAKER—It's almost three o'clock. I'll give him a ring and see if he's read them yet. May I?

RUTH—May you! (BAKER *dials.*) You're getting terribly involved in our troubles, Bob . . . It doesn't seem fair . . .

BAKER—I enjoy it . . . My plan is to . . . (*Into phone.*) Oh, hello . . . Miss Leeds, please.

RUTH—Who's she?

BAKER—His right hand. My plan is to see if he won't put you on the staff.

RUTH—The *staff?*

BAKER—Why not? (*Into phone.*) Hello, Miss Leeds? Baker . . . How does it look? Yeah?

RUTH—Has he read them?

BAKER—It looks all right. He's reading it with his feet out the window.

RUTH—What?

BAKER—That's always a good sign. (*Into phone.*) Let me speak to him, darling . . . (*To* RUTH.) I'll introduce you over the phone.

RUTH—Oh! I don't think you'd better.

BAKER—Ralph? Bob . . . Did you read that stuff I sent you? Ruth Sherwood . . . (*Nods and smiles.*) How'd you like it? (*His face hardens.*) Yeah, well, in my opinion your *opinion* stinks! Well, I don't think you know a story when you see one. . . . I don't know why you need a staff at all . . . I'll be right up. (*He hangs up and picks up his hat.*) Well, what do you think of that?

RUTH—Bob, maybe he's right. Maybe they're not as good as we think they are.

BAKER—Of course they are. He's just a pompous ass, that's all!

RUTH—But, Bob, I don't want you to get into any trouble . . .

BAKER—Don't worry about me. I've been meaning to have it out with that Stork Club Pulitzer for years!

Baker has gone and Ruth, utterly miserable, has thrown herself across the bed. There is a knock on the door. Ruth doesn't even look up, but in response to her weary "Come in," Walter Sherwood enters. "He is a good-looking man in his late forties, with a gently humorous point of view, soft-spoken and immensely likable." He is staring around the room expectantly when Ruth spies him—

"Dad, darling!" The next second she is in his arms, and explanations are running wild. Everything is all right at home. Everything's all right with Ruth and Eileen, too. Her get-up? Oh, that's only a fill-in job; a healthy job, too; keeps Ruth out in the air all day long. Eileen? Oh, Eileen's doing fine, too—

At which moment Officer Lonigan appears at the window and raps on the bars. "Oh, good afternoon, Officer!" calls Ruth, heartily. "Kinda quiet here today—so far!" answers Lonigan, with vast meaning. "Yes, isn't it? Oh, this is my father." "Uh-huh . . ." "Well—thank you for looking in." "Don't mention it. So long, *Daddy!*"

Lonigan continues his beat and Ruth is at some pains to explain to her father that the officer's familiarity means nothing, really. "That's just a part of Fiorello's courtesy campaign," she explains.

"I see," answers Mr. Sherwood, continuing a casual inspection of the room, and looking in at the kitchen distastefully. "Tell me, Ruth—don't you ever get a little homesick for Columbus?"

RUTH—Oh, no—not yet, anyway.

SHERWOOD—I just wondered what you'd think of maybe—coming back?

RUTH—Back?

SHERWOOD—Columbus looks a lot better after you've been away.

RUTH—Oh, I couldn't go back—now.

SHERWOOD—Why not?

RUTH—Oh, I just couldn't, that's all.

SHERWOOD—Any special reason?

RUTH—Well . . . The truth is, Dad—I—I've met someone.

SHERWOOD—Oh!

RUTH—For the first time in my life, I've met someone.

SHERWOOD—Why, I'm very happy, Ruth. Who is he?

RUTH—He's a magazine editor. I want you to meet him. He's an awfully nice fellow.

SHERWOOD (*delighted*)—Well! This is a surprise, Ruth! When are things going to happen?

RUTH (*hastily*)—Oh, it's nothing like that—yet—I've only met him a couple of times.

SHERWOOD (*quizzically*)—Oh! You've only met him a couple of times?

RUTH—Uh-huh.

SHERWOOD (*grinning*)—You sound like your sister Eileen.

RUTH (*self-consciously*)—Now that I think of it, I do.

SHERWOOD—Well, I'll go down and get the bus tickets and wire Mother that I'm bringing you home.

RUTH—No, Dad! You can't do that!

SHERWOOD—Now, why not, Ruth?

RUTH—We've signed a three months' lease!

SHERWOOD—Three months' lease? On this?

RUTH—Well, we got a special price of—forty dollars.

SHERWOOD (*staring*)—Special . . . ?

RUTH—You've really got to live here, Dad, to appreciate its charm.

SHERWOOD—Yes, I suppose so.

RUTH—Well, I guess the charm is a bit subtle, but—but it was just what we wanted and—and we were afraid of losing it, so—

A knock at the door, followed by the abrupt entrance of Mr. Appopolous, stops her. Mr. Appopolous has come to show a prospective tenant the apartment, a proceeding that is pretty puzzling to Mr. Sherwood. The prospect, "woman of about thirty, thin and sharp, with a very crisp, businesslike air," is not impressed. As for the bed, "I wouldn't lie on that—in the morgue," says she. The dormer window, "It's Alcatraz without a view of the bay!" Even for thirty-five dollars the apartment to her would still be a "calcimined catacomb." Finally, when the subway workers let go with one of their biggest and best explosions, she is ready to run. "I wouldn't live here if you paid me thirty-five dollars a month! And threw in Tyrone Power!" is her parting shot.

Father Sherwood's experiences are not ended. Mr. Appopolous and his prospect have no sooner disappeared than The Wreck and Helen come gaily down the stairs, The Wreck bellowing his theme song, "I'm a rambling wreck from Georgia Tech, etc." They are a little high, and have come to announce their marriage. They decided not to wait for the football season, after Helen had been to the doctor's, and they are about to start on their honeymoon. "I'm goin' upstairs and break the news to Helen's old lady before I sober up!" announces The Wreck . . .

The legs of the six Admirals, walking two abreast, can be seen at the window. A moment later they march into the room, followed by Eileen and "a distinguished little man in a cutaway and striped trousers." At sight of her father, Eileen, after a moment's apprehensive hesitation, rushes into his arms. The Admirals, wearing their dress uniforms but no hats, are drawn up stiffly at attention.

The little man, it transpires, is the Brazilian Consul. He has come, he explains, to right a most disastrous wrong and—

"Oh, that's all right," Ruth assures him, with an anxious glance at her father.

"Señorita, *you* are as generous as—as *she* (*indicates* EILEEN) is beautiful," agrees the Consul, bowing low. "But I must apologize on behalf of the Brazilian Government. So wild, so impetuous, these young boys . . . They beg for your forgiveness."

At the Consul's command the Admirals have mumbled their apologies. Now he would insist in the name of his government in making reparations. After all Eileen did spend the night in jail. That is worth at least $5. In addition to which he bestows upon her the ribbon of the order of St. Christopher—Second class!

The Admirals have recovered their hats, which Ruth had parked for them, and filed out. Explanations as to how they happened to be there in the first place are going to be extremely simple, Eileen assures her father, but before any can be made Mr. Sherwood has made his decision—

"You girls are coming home with me tonight. If you have any

explanations, you can make them on the way back to Columbus," says he. "I'll be right back and I want you to be ready to go."

The girls are shocked and depressed. What will people in Columbus say? The more they think of that the more determined they become. "I'm not going back," announces Ruth, firmly. "Not now—not when I'm just beginning to find out something about myself!"

"Find out what?"

"Well, for one thing—I think differently—I feel differently. I am stronger than ever—as though I really knew myself for the first time! That's why I'd hate to go back. I may never feel this way again!"

"You're right, Ruth! I don't care what Dad says—I'm not going back either . . . I'm going to have a career— Dammit!"

Chic Clark comes through the kitchen. He has news. His City Editor has read Ruth's Brazilian story and thinks "it's the absolute nuts." Eileen doesn't believe it. Chic Clark's an awful liar. Didn't he frame the whole thing? The Wreck comes back just in time to help the girls give Mr. Clark the bum's rush.

Now Ruth has lost her courage. They might as well give in and start packing. If either of them had only landed a job they might have stayed. But—

There is a new complication, too. Ruth, mentioning the encouragement she felt after her talk with Bob Baker, hears the story of what happened while she was out with the Brazilians. Hears, too, that Eileen also is convinced that Bob is the nicest man they have met in New York—

"He's really the first boy I've met who seemed to care what happened to me—how I got along—and everything," reports Eileen.

"I know."

"Oh, well!"

"We're going home anyway, so it doesn't matter about Bob," sighs Ruth. The catch in her voice is revealing. It brings Eileen up with a turn—

"Gee, Ruth—I never dreamed. You mean—you like him, too?"

"Strange as it may seem."

"Why, I never had any idea . . ."

Neither Eileen nor Ruth is very happy when Bob Baker does come. Nor is he greatly cheered. He had had his meeting with Mr. Cross and Mr. Cross had fired him—

"Oh, Bob! That's terrible! It's all my fault!"

"No, it isn't! I'll get something—and so will you—just see if you don't!"

"Yes, only we're going back home tonight."

"Home? You mean for a visit?"

"No, I'm afraid we're just going home."

The phone is ringing.

Chic Clark has appeared at the window again. Before Jensen can chase him away he has time to shout a warning that it probably is the City Editor who is on the wire. And it is—

"Yes, Mr. Wilson . . . Oh, thanks so much, Mr. Wilson. . . . Oh, that's wonderful! . . . What? . . . Yes, Mr. Wilson!" Ruth hangs up excitedly. "I've got a job! I start Monday morning!" she cries.

"See! That's what I've been tryin' to tell yuh!" yells Chic from the window, and this time, though Jensen is after him, he is not chased away. Ruth is too happy to allow that.

Everybody's happy now. Bob Baker has an idea that they should all go to dinner. He's just about saved enough in ten years for that. But—Ruth, wanting Eileen to go, thinks she had better wait for her father. And Eileen, determined that Ruth shall go, remembers suddenly that she has a date.

"Say! What is this mad rush to go out with me?" demands the puzzled Baker.

"Eileen's just being silly, Mr. Baker!" insists Ruth. "It's all settled. Because I just have to talk to Dad. Really—about some things—" She has gone to the bathroom to change her dress. Baker is staring after her, a little hurt.

"What's the matter with Ruth?"

"Oh, she's—she's just excited, I guess—she—"

Frank Lippencott has appeared at the window, the usual package under his arm. He asks to come in and is a little overwhelmed by Eileen's sudden cordiality. He is also considerably surprised when, a moment later, she is reminding him of their dinner date. He rises to the occasion, however, If they are really going to dinner he will stop back at the store and check the ice cream—the pistachio must be running pretty low—

"It looks as if you're stuck with me, Ruth. Like it or not," says Baker, taking her hand.

"Yes, it looks that way, doesn't it?" answers Ruth, looking at Eileen, affectionately. . . .

Baker has gone, to be back in twenty minutes, when Mr. Appopolous reappears. He comes bearing good news. He has a letter from the city. The subway blasting is all over. Now he can make each of his studios "a haven of beauty and repose. New furniture! New paint! A-1 stoves and plumbing! Reduced rents—"

"Reduced rents?" Eileen is interested.

"How much reduced?" Ruth is skeptical.

"This place will be given away for thirty dollars on a lease . . ."

"Thirty dollars . . ."

"And you are really going to do all those things?"

"Certainly."

"And you are sure about the blasting?"

"In black and white." He points to the letter and the signature, "Robert Moses."

There is nothing that Mr. Appopolous is not ready to promise. The lease will be for six months, on a perfectly friendly basis. Everything will be fixed, including the spot on the wall. The girls are still suspicious, but Ruth signs the lease just as her father comes through the front door. He stares anxiously at them as he realizes they are just as he left them.

SHERWOOD—Aren't you getting ready, girls? The bus leaves in forty minutes!

RUTH (*happily*)—We're not going, Dad!

SHERWOOD—What?

EILEEN—Isn't it wonderful! Ruth sold a story! And she's got a job on a paper!

APPOPOLOUS (*grabbing* SHERWOOD'S *hand*)—You are the father? Congratulations! You've got a pair of brilliant daughters!

SHERWOOD (*dazed*)—But wait a minute . . . !

RUTH—Oh, it's all settled, Dad—we've just signed a six months' lease!

SHERWOOD—Six months' lease!

APPOPOLOUS—Good-by! Good-by! (*He starts out. There is a sudden burst of fire from what seems to be a nest of machine guns directly under the floor. The din is terrific and keeps going for a moment. The girls and* SHERWOOD *stand spellbound.* APPOPOLOUS *listens calmly, nodding to himself. Finally silence is restored.*)

EILEEN—For God's sake!

RUTH—What was that?

APPOPOLOUS (*cheerfully*)—I *told* you. The blasting is over.

Now they are starting to drill! Good-by! Good-by! (*Suddenly the floor cracks open and a grimy workman, a pneumatic drill in his hands, pushes his head through the floor and looks at them with a start.*)

MAN—What the . . . ? (*Yells down.*) Hey, Pete, it looks like we didn't judge the distance right . . . !

"The drilling comes over again" as

THE CURTAIN FALLS

FLIGHT TO THE WEST

A Drama in Three Acts

By Elmer Rice

ELMER RICE'S determination to keep the playgoing world thinking seriously of current world problems resulted in his bringing "Flight to the West" to production this season. It came to Broadway at a favorable moment, there having been nothing resembling a thoughtful play produced since Emlyn Williams' "The Corn Is Green" had stimulated theatre interest five weeks before.

It was Mr. Rice's idea to make up a passenger list for a Yankee Clipper plane flying out of Lisbon for New York—a list that should reasonably and truly be representative of various international citizen groups. The thought and actions of these selected passengers were to be motivated by both the history shaking events of the day, and also by the racial heritages of each.

Both argument and action are naturally somewhat cramped in the physical setting of the play. Mr. Rice manages, however, to keep his story development following an ascending scale, and to create both a healthy theatrical suspense and an intelligent argument. "Frankly it [the play] gives wings to a debating society, lifting its members to what is physically, at any rate, a new altitude," wrote John Mason Brown. " 'Flight to the West' is the most absorbing American drama of the season," countered Brooks Atkinson.

The drama was given seventy-two performances at the Guild Theatre, under the sponsorship of the Playwrights' Company. It was then withdrawn and turned over to a newly formed corporation which presented it at popular prices for a run extending into the early Spring.

It is about 10 in the morning of a July day in 1940 when we join the passengers and crew of the Pan-American Airways transatlantic clipper in "Flight to the West." The clipper is lying alongside her landing pontoon at Lisbon. The passengers are about to embark for the flight to America. Three sections in the middle of the flying-boat are exposed—the lounge, about twelve feet square, which serves as a sitting-and-dining salon, and smaller compartments on either side of it.

Across the lounge the entrance door of the plane is swung open. There is a sort of gangplank leading up to it, and, inside the plane, portable stairs lead down to the floor of the deck. Along the side-walls of the partitions between the lounge and the compartments are sofas that at night can be made up into berths. A narrow aisle runs the length of the ship, dividing the sofas into two sections, and leading to other sleeping compartments in the rear, as well as to the flight deck forward. The solid partitions between the compartments have been cut away to improve visibility.

There are small windows in the lounge fitted with Venetian blinds. The furnishings are rich but extremely simple. "The design is strictly functional, everything being planned solely for use. . . . The whole interior suggests the living quarters of a small, but very modern yacht, rather than the inside of an airplane."

It is near sailing time. Two Portuguese mechanics in white overalls, with "P.A.A." embroidered on their chests, are struggling with a heavy mat on the pontoon. Inside the ship Richard Banning, a junior flight officer, is busy with last minute instructions, both to the Portuguese and to the clipper's two natty stewards who are bringing in an assortment of luggage.

The first of the passengers to come aboard is Edmund Dickensen, a blind man in his middle forties. He wears a black velvet bandage over his sightless eyes. The stewards are particularly careful with Mr. Dickensen and the stairs. Marie Dickensen, his wife, and Lisette, a 12-year-old daughter, follow. Mrs. Dickensen is thirty-five, a small, nervous, intense person. She is anxious now about a basket the steward Tom carries behind her. In the basket is her three-weeks-old son, James, asleep. The Dickensens are shown to the forward compartment, to wait there until after the take-off.

The other passengers follow in groups. They include Louise Frayne, "an aggressive, self-confident woman, rather mannishly dressed"; Col. Archibald Gage, "a tall, angular, elderly man, with a Southwestern accent"; Count Paul Vasilich Vronoff "fifty-odd, stoutish, with a neatly trimmed beard"; Frau Clara Rosenthal, "a woman of forty-five, soberly dressed," and Dr. Herman Walther, "stout, bald, clean-shaven, in his middle fifties; he carries a leather dispatch case which he never relinquishes."

These have been given seats in the lounge or the compartments. It doesn't matter where they sit for the take-off. They will be shown their quarters later.

And now Howard Ingraham, "quiet, intellectual, in his forties," and the Nathans—Hope, "a fair girl of twenty-two," and Charles, her husband, two years older, "dark and good-looking," enter. These three are more excited over the adventure than the others. The whole thing seems a little incredible to them. A rear compartment which the stewards call the "bridal suite," has been reserved for the Nathans, somewhat to their surprise.

"We start in about two minutes now," Banning is warning the passengers. The Portuguese boys have taken the outside gangplank away. The door to the plane is closed and locked and the inside steps removed. The motors have begun to race.

"Now, if you'll please all fasten your seat belts," Banning is saying. "And no smoking, please, until we are up in the air."

He sits beside little Lisette Dickensen and straps her in with him, which is exciting for Lisette. They are all a little tense by this time and busy asking questions. The ship is loaded with about forty tons, reports Steward Gus, as he passes the chewing gum. No, he can't tell about the weather, but he doesn't anticipate anything worse than a light headwind, which may delay them a little.

Now the roar of the motors has increased and the dash of foaming water past the windows obscures the view. "We're off!" announces young Mr. Nathan, a little exultantly.

"Yes, there goes Europe. I wonder if I'll live long enough to see it again," muses Ingraham.

"I wouldn't care much if I never did," declares Hope Nathan. ". . . Oh, look! We're off the water!"

The roar of the motors has diminished to a faint drone. The splashing water at the windows has given way to a view of a blue sky. The stewards have loosened the seat belts. The lounge buzzes with conversation, which is stilled momentarily as Gus, standing in the middle of the lounge, gives the passengers their routine instructions—

"Now, ladies and gentlemen, you can move around or do whatever you like. Only please remember, no smoking allowed, except right here, in the lounge. If you want something—some cigarettes or a cup of coffee or a drink—just ask for it. The berths are all made up, in case you want to take a little nap. Ladies' powder room aft on the left. Gentlemen's room, forward on the right."

From a slip of paper Gus reads off the numbers of their berths and asks that they follow him. As the Nathans stand watching their fellow travelers, one of them puzzles Hope. Count Vronoff —where has she seen that Russian before? Somewhere—she is sure of that.

Charles has disappeared in the passage. Hope starts to follow and then turns back for a word with Howard Ingraham. She wants to thank him for recommending a doctor to her in Lisbon. When he inquires solicitously as to her health she assures him with a smile that everything is quite all right. Even a little better: She is going to have a child. She is terribly happy about that, but she hasn't told Charles—

"You see, I thought it would be nicer to save it as a surprise until we get home," says Hope. "So please don't let anything slip about the doctor or anything, will you?"

"No, I certainly won't! I can't tell you how delighted—"

Charles is calling. Hope goes to join him but is gone for only a minute. She comes back to ask Banning please to give the "bridal suite" to the Dickensens. It will be much nicer for them. Charles is agreed to that, too, and Mrs. Dickensen is tremendously grateful. Banning is the surprised one. The crew had been instructed to be especially nice to the Nathans, which, Charles explains, is due to the fact that his father-in-law is in the diplomatic service.

Presently Charles and Ingraham find themselves alone in the lounge. To Charles this presents an opportunity he has been waiting for. He long has wanted to have a talk with Ingraham—

". . . As I started to tell you yesterday, at the hotel, you've had a deep influence on my thinking," Charles is saying. "As a matter of fact, you're even indirectly responsible for my marriage."

INGRAHAM—Well, that certainly is news! How was that?

CHARLES—Well, the first time Hope and I met was at a very dull reception in Paris, about a year ago. We sort of got off in a corner and she happened to mention that she'd known you most of her life and that you had greatly influenced her mental development, too. That was a good basis for a beautiful friendship, and before we knew it, we were engaged.

INGRAHAM—That might have happened if I had never written a line.

CHARLES—Well, you may be right. But I don't exaggerate when I say that your books were a sort of Bible to my generation. We read them and mulled over them and discussed them —especially *The Betrayal of Democracy*. You taught us how some old men in Paris made America trade away the Fourteen Points to get the League of Nations and then how some old men in Washington shut us out of the League—and then what happened afterwards. And it made us resolve that no old men were ever going to lead us down the path of war. So we joined up with something called the youth movement. We had the red tag pinned on us, though most of us weren't reds at all, but just young people who wanted the right to lead lives in which going to war had no part. Some of us even got into rather heated arguments with our families. For example, me. You see, the American tradition runs pretty strong in my family. My mother's folks claim descent from Haim Solomon, who was mixed up in the American Revolution, and my paternal great-grandfather lost a leg at Antietam, and father himself went overseas in 1917. Well, you get the picture.

INGRAHAM—Yes, it's a pretty familiar one. And what follows?

CHARLES—What follows is that a year ago, three months ago, in fact, I knew exactly where I stood and why on this question of war and peace. But there's been Finland and Norway and Holland. And I've seen Paris bombed and France defeated. And these past weeks, I've lived among refugees and listened to them. It's done things to me, and the result is that now I don't know where the hell I stand. And I was hoping you could help me out.

INGRAHAM—That's very flattering, but I'm in about the same fix you're in. You see, I'm having a hell of a time right now trying to get straightened out myself.

CHARLES—You mean you've changed your point of view, too?

INGRAHAM—Well, a man doesn't readily throw overboard the convictions of a lifetime. For twenty years I've devoted myself to decrying war and the war makers, agitating for disarmament, for a world commonwealth. But, more and more, I began discovering to my horror that my facts and my arguments were being used in ways that I had certainly never intended, by the rabid isolationists, by the critics of democracy, even by the Nazi propagandists. And I tell you, it's knocked the props from under me. I'd been deluding myself with the belief that I was a clear thinker with a constructive program, but now as I look at myself, all I see is another confused liberal.

CHARLES—Well, my God, I'm certainly glad I talked to you—because if you feel that way, you can imagine the state I'm in. I see all this going on around me and I get the feeling that I should be doing something about it. I've even been playing with the idea of training to be an army pilot.

INGRAHAM—Why?

CHARLES—I don't know why. It's completely irrational—something that's just bobbed up out of this inner turmoil of mine. I certainly have no appetite for fighting in a war or even learning to fight. But I feel that I should be doing something a little more relevant than settling down to the practice of law.

Charles admits that he has not discussed his state of mind with Hope. Nor does he intend to until he has made more sense out of it himself. He has a feeling that as a married man he may be exempted, should there be conscription, and he is not sure he wants to be exempted. Neither does he consider any thought of raising a family immediately important. There will be plenty of time for that. He asks that Ingraham be particularly careful not to say anything to Hope about their talk. . . .

Hope is completely happy. To think that she and Charles will be home tomorrow is almost too much for one girl to bear. Something will have to be done in the way of a celebration—a night out at a movie, perhaps. And to think—in the new home there will be bathtubs, too!

"Oh, Charles, that beautiful word!" exclaims Hope. "You know, all my life, I've been hearing superior people in Europe and Asia sneering at us for our bathtub civilization. But when you've lived in some of the places I've lived in, you no longer believe that dirt is romantic and that if it doesn't smell, it isn't culture."

All Hope wants, all she dreams of, "is a big shiny bathtub with a home built around it." The thought of being anchored to a stay-at-home husband contentedly settled down to a nice steady law practice is positively thrilling.

Suddenly Hope is conscious of a change in Charles. He has become grave and preoccupied. She fears that she may have said something wrong. She would not have him think that she is selfishly thinking of herself and her happiness exclusively. Perhaps she should have stayed with her father and mother. Maybe—but Charles is quick to assure her that what she has done and what she is doing, are entirely to his liking. . . .

Marie Dickensen has come into the lounge. She would, if she could find words, thank the Nathans again for their kindness in giving up their compartment to her and her family.

"It's really nothing, Mrs. Dickensen," Charles is quick to assure her. "We've been sleeping mostly in barns and along the roadside, these past few weeks."

"That is how my baby was born—along the roadside in a deserted gasoline station," says Marie.

HOPE—You mean just like that—without a doctor or anyone to help you?

MARIE—Yes, madame. We were in a motor lorry, fifteen or twenty of us, running away from the Germans—for how many days I can't tell you. Then my pains began to come and I couldn't stand it, any longer, jolting along on the rough country roads. So they put us down, by the side of the road—my husband and Lisette and I.

HOPE—They left you there like that—all by yourselves!

MARIE—You must not blame them. They were not bad people. Just frightened, that's all. And thinking of their own lives and their own babies. My husband helped me, as best he could; and Lisette, too. And after a while, some other people came along and took us with them. It's nothing unusual. Many people are entering the world now—and leaving it—under such conditions.

HOPE—I don't see how you lived through it. I'm sure I never could have.

MARIE—We never know what we can do, until we must.

CHARLES—What part of France are you from?

MARIE—I come from Belgium. My husband is American. But I—I am Belgian. This is not my first exile. I come from Louvain.

HOPE—Louvain! Where the famous library is!

MARIE—Where the famous library was! Twice I have seen it destroyed and each time a part of my life was destroyed with it.

CHARLES—I've often heard my father speak of the library. He saw it when he was a boy—the old one, I mean.

MARIE—I grew up in it. My father was librarian there in nineteen fourteen. Then they came through. They shelled, they burned, they slaughtered. And that wonderful, beautiful building fell in ruins and all those priceless books went up in smoke. My mother was killed in the attack and my older sister.

HOPE—Oh, no!

MARIE—Then, after the war, the Americans rebuilt the library. Do you know they collected pennies from the school children in America to rebuild the library in Louvain?

HOPE—No, I didn't know that. Did you, Charles?

oto by Vandamm Studio.

"FLIGHT TO THE WEST"

Frau Rosenthal: I understand how you feel. . . . It is only natural that you should wish to have child. But you must not.
Hope: Why? I don't see why?
Frau Rosenthal: No, you must not, please! . . . To bring into the world a Jewish child, that is great sin, because now, for the Jews, there is only misfortune.

(*Eleanore Mendelssohn, Betty Field*)

CHARLES—Yes, I've read about it.

MARIE—It was a beautiful thing to do. Ever since then, I have loved everything American. When I was nineteen, I went back to Louvain, and there I met my husband. He had come over to help in the rebuilding and they invited him to stay on the staff. You know, when the new building was dedicated, they were going to have an inscription that said: "American generosity has rebuilt what German barbarism has destroyed"—or something like that. But somebody was afraid it would hurt the feelings of the Germans, so they didn't put it up. (*She laughs harshly.*) It's really quite funny, isn't it? They didn't want to hurt their feelings!

CHARLES—Yes.

HOPE (*going impulsively to* MARIE)—You have your family.

MARIE—Yes, I have my family. All except my ten-year-old son, who was killed by a bomb—the same bomb that blinded my husband and crushed Lisette's arm.

HOPE—It will be different in America. All these things that have happened to you—you'll be safe from all that. You'll begin a new life, all of you.

MARIE—What kind of a life? We have absolutely no money. Everything we had left went to pay for the aeroplane fares. The doctors told me a long sea voyage might be fatal to my husband. He must have weeks and weeks of rest and quiet. What shall we do? How shall we live?

CHARLES—Hasn't your husband any family in America?

MARIE—His parents live on a small farm in Ohio. We will go there, I suppose, because we have nowhere else to go. But what then? Will we become farmers? A blind scholar and a little girl with one arm and a woman of thirty-five, who has lived always in towns and no longer wants to live at all? No, it would be much better if we were all dead. Only before I die, there is one thing I would like to do. I would like to do to them what they have done to us: burn down their houses, kill their babies and their old people, put out their eyes, and cut off their arms. Oh, if I only had the power to do that! Even to one of them!

HOPE—But what good would that do? That wouldn't help anybody or anything.

MARIE—I don't want to help anybody! I only want to make them feel what I have felt. (*Suddenly breaking off.*) Please excuse me! I know I shouldn't talk like that. But I can't help it! I can't help it! (*She begins to cry.*)

HOPE—Why don't you try to get some rest, Mrs. Dickensen?

The baby will get sick, if you don't.

MARIE (*rising*)—Yes, I will try. The last two nights I haven't slept at all. But first I must see the steward about some food for my husband. (*She exits abruptly.*)

The passengers are beginning to circulate. Business Man Gage has come into the lounge, and Louise Frayne, the newspaper columnist. Captain McNab, who is in charge of the flight, is there, too. The conversation is general, and quite complimentary to Miss Frayne. Both Mr. Gage and Captain McNab are regular readers of her column. So, for that matter, is the German diplomat, Dr. Walther, who has joined the group.

Now Mrs. Dickensen, returning from the ship's kitchen, finds Dr. Walther standing in her way in the aisle. She hesitates until Charles calls Walther's attention to the blockade. The Doctor moves back with a quick apology. Marie's face, on hearing Walther identified, becomes transfigured by hatred. "She pauses for a moment, almost unable to move, then crosses swiftly, her fists clenched and her lips compressed."

"Is there anything I can do for you?" Louise asks.

"No. No, thank you. Nothing!"

Marie has moved quickly on. Dr. Walther has seated himself, hardly conscious of her.

"That woman's face! If I only knew how to put that into words!" Louise is saying, as the curtain falls.

By mid-afternoon the clipper's passengers have settled down. At the moment in one compartment Louise, McNab and Gage are playing rummy, with Vronoff looking on. In the other compartment Dr. Walther is studying the color plates in a large book on butterflies. Butterflies, it appears, are one of Dr. Walther's minor passions. At the rear of the lounge Frau Rosenthal is writing a letter.

Charles Nathan, coming from the forward part of the ship, and Hope, returning from her berth, meet in the lounge. Hope has not found it easy to sleep, and suddenly her early excitement over the trip has disappeared. That she can explain—

"When we got on I felt such a sense of relief because I thought that, at last, we were leaving all that European mess behind us," says Hope. "But here we are—carrying it right along with us. Those poor Dickensens and that German woman with the tragic eyes, just sitting, hour after hour, writing and writing and never saying a word. And as if that weren't enough, that old smoothie of a Nazi diplomat! Every time he and Mrs. Dickensen come near each other, I can just feel the electric sparks."

Charles admits that probably they are all a little jittery. But —tomorrow they will be in New York. Let Hope concentrate on that. And let her get the idea out of her head, too, that he is keeping anything from her, which is another of Hope's current worries.

Count Vronoff has stopped for a few words with the Nathans. The Clipper is nearing the Azores. Soon they will land at Horta, and the thought is pleasant to Vronoff.

"The outermost frontier of Europe," he is saying. "Then I shall be able to expel the foulness of the Old World from my lungs and fill them with the fresh air of the New."

Count Vronoff is on his way to California. He has been holding the chair of Slavonic Literature in the University at Zurich and he is to have a similar post in the University of California. He feels that he already knows California pretty well—through the books of Jack London and John Steinbeck. He has gone on to take a seat in the compartment with Dr. Walther, leaving Hope to wonder again where it is she has seen him before. A moment later she has it—

"I met him at a party at the French Consulate in Jerusalem, about five years ago," Hope exclaims in some excitement. "He wouldn't remember me, of course. I was only about seventeen and very much of a backfisch."

"He told me he'd been teaching at Zurich," puts in Louise Frayne, who has come in with Captain McNab.

"Yes. Slavonic literature. That's what placed him for me," Hope goes on. "He used to teach at the British Near-Eastern College. I remember being tremendously impressed because I was deep in Dostoievski. And then I was so disillusioned a few months later when I heard that he'd got into some kind of trouble with the British authorities and had to leave Palestine. Only I'm sure he had a different name. Something beginning with an A."

"Excuse me, but this has the smell of news about it. What kind of trouble with the British authorities could a professor of Slavonic literature get into?"

"I really don't know. All that interested me was that a romantic illusion had been punctured. But I definitely remember hearing my father talk about his getting into trouble."

Louise's news sense is expanding rapidly. How can she get in touch with Hope's father? By radiogram to the Hotel Splendide in Marseilles? Good. The message written and ready to send, Louise is free to join the others in the drinks Charles has ordered. . . .

The islands of the Azores are beginning to come rapidly into view. Most of the passengers are at the windows. Frau Rosenthal has quit her writing to join them. In the side compartment Dr. Walther speaks quietly to Vronoff without raising his eyes from his butterfly book—

WALTHER—What instructions did you receive when you left Zurich?

VRONOFF—Only to consult you.

WALTHER—You have a British passport?

VRONOFF—A forged one.

WALTHER—But why? My information is that you have been a British subject since 1928.

VRONOFF—Yes, that is true. But I was obliged to leave Palestine several years ago and, at that time, the British authorities revoked my passport. I am an unfortunate individual, Dr. Walther—a propertyless man, and without a country.

WALTHER—Let us not wander from the subject, if you please. Your passport was not questioned by the American Consul in Zurich when you obtained your visa?

VRONOFF—No.

WALTHER—Good. Then there is nothing to fear from the American immigration authorities.

VRONOFF (*with a warning gesture, as he sees* LOUISE *approaching from the lounge*)—Later!

WALTHER—Have you ever climbed the Matterhorn, Count Vronoff?

VRONOFF—No, no! I am very subject to vertigo. Even when I ride up in a lift, I become a little dizzy.

LOUISE—Oh, steward.

GUS (*entering from the galley*)—Yes, ma'am?

LOUISE—I'd like to get this radiogram off, as quickly as possible.

GUS (*taking the message*)—Right away.

The general movement of the passengers is toward the lounge. Walther and Vronoff join them. Colonel Gage has wandered in. Louise, who has been writing, is there in time to hear Dr. Walther call attention to the clearness of the view.

"You seem to know these islands quite well, Dr. Walther,"

ventures Louise. "I suppose you'll soon be establishing air bases here."

"I do not think so, Miss Frayne. Our present task is to complete the pacification of Europe."

"Pacification?" echoes Howard Ingraham, joining the group. "That's a curious way of describing what's going on back there."

"No, very accurate, Mr. Ingraham," persists Walther. "For the first time since the dissolution of the Roman Empire, we have the promise of a Europe that is unified, organized and at peace. It may, perhaps, seem unfortunate that this colossal task can be accomplished only by the use of force. But, after all, force is the fundamental law of nature. In the struggle for existence, the strong must conquer the weak."

"That's the philosophy of gangsterism," puts in Louise.

"Miss Frayne, I am aware that you are not sympathetic to the government which I represent," answers Walther, with some spirit. "Nevertheless—"

"Whoa! Wait a minute! It will be a better argument if we just don't all get excited," intervenes Colonel Gage.

They are all quick to insist that they are not excited, but the Colonel insists they are. Besides, he would like a chance to say his two cents' worth if they'll let him—

"Oh, sure, go ahead—" prompts Louise.

"Well, I'm a feller in the oil business that lays awake nights, trying to figger out how he can make an honest dollar or two," reports Colonel Gage. "Not that it does me much good, because as fast as I figger how to make it, some feller down in Washington is figgering how he can take it away from me."

INGRAHAM—I think you're getting off the subject, Colonel.

GAGE—All right, I'll get right back on again. What I want to say is that my business takes me around quite a good deal, and, one time or another, I've met all the dictators—Hitler, Mussolini, Franco—every one of them. Never did get to see Stalin. He was always busy playing hide-and-go-seek in the Kremlin. But when you get to know these fellers, you soon find out that they're all just folks—just like you and me. Take Goering. I went out shooting with him, four or five months ago, on that big country place of his. And there he was, laughing and making jokes and showing me what makes everything tick. You'd have thought he was a big kid, playing with a lot of new toys.

LOUISE—Charming!

GAGE—Or take even Hitler. He once postponed a date with

me because he wanted to go hear some opera by that German composer. What's his name?

WALTHER—Richard Wagner.

GAGE—Wagner, that's it! And all the while I was talking to him, he was humming tunes from the opera.

LOUISE—Maybe we could get him over to America on a concert tour.

GAGE—Mind you, he's done a lot of things I don't like. So has Stalin. So has Musso. But I could mention some things that go on in Washington that I don't like, either.

INGRAHAM—Are you suggesting that we might just as well have Hitler in Washington?

GAGE—No, of course I'm not. What's more, I don't believe he's got any interest in Washington. I agree with Dr. Walther here, that the Nazis have got plenty to do in Europe, without bothering us—that is, providing we don't coax them into it. Matter of fact, I had that right from Hitler himself.

LOUISE—Well, of course, that settles it!

GAGE—No, I think he means it. Anyhow, I don't see that sticking out our necks is going to get us anywhere. Seems to me it's much smarter to talk business with Hitler and get our share of world trade than to get ourselves blown to bits, fighting Europe's battles.

LOUISE—In other words: let's play ball with Hitler, is that it?

GAGE—Well, when you come right down to it, I'd rather play ball with him, than fight him and get licked.

LOUISE—I'll be God-damned if I would! Oil contracts or no oil contracts, I'd rather die fighting for freedom than live in a Hitler-dominated world.

CHARLES—Well, if it came to that, so would I!

HOPE—Let's hope it never comes to that!

GAGE—Of course it won't! Seems to me you folks are all just out gunning scarecrows. Live and let live, is the way I look at it. Just like I said: I think Hitler and the rest of 'em have got a lot to learn from us—I told Hitler that right to his face, but all the same, I can see where we might learn something from them.

INGRAHAM—What?

GAGE—Well, a lot of things. How to get things going, without a lot of debating and palavering, back and forth—

INGRAHAM—Yes, I've heard that before. Every local Chamber of Commerce has some vest-pocket Hitler or Mussolini—an ambitious fellow who hasn't very much use for democracy and feels that what we need is a strong hand at the helm—his own hand, preferably. Let's concede that the democratic method isn't always the quickest and the most efficient. But what of it? What's the use of having the trains run on time, if the passengers' minds have stopped running altogether? No, our trouble has never been that we've had too much democracy, but that we've had too little. Social injustice—that's what makes us vulnerable—because it breeds resentment and weakens loyalty. Millions of youngsters who've never been able to get jobs; millions of adults out of work in a country that boasts of being the richest and the most progressive in the world; millions of our black citizens subjected to daily humiliations. And certain individuals talking and acting as if they owned America, merely because they happen to have got hold of its wealth. No, Colonel Gage, I happen to believe not only that our democracy is worth defending but that the best way to defend it is to make it work. And if we can't do that, we'd better change our tune from "God Bless America" to "God Help America!"

Colonel Gage resents any reflection upon his Americanism. His kin had fought in the American Revolution and he, himself, had commanded a regiment in the A.E.F. But the Colonel does not think that Americanism means the country should be run for the benefit of misfits and no-accounts. It isn't the cranks and idealists who have developed America. So far as Colonel Gage knows there weren't any labor agitators on the *Mayflower,* or any red flags flying over the covered wagons of the pioneers. As for the Jews—

"Nobody's got anything personal against the Jews," insists the Colonel. "All anybody asks is that they don't try to run the whole show. Isn't that so, Dr. Walther?"

"But, of course!" answers Dr. Walther. "These are matters of biological theory, not of the hatred of individuals. To prove my point, I need only tell you that my first wife was a Jewess."

"Yes, I heard about that, from one of the Washington correspondents," snaps Louise. "You divorced her, the month after Hitler came into power, and two weeks later, she committed suicide."

"That is a shamefully false imputation!" Dr. Walther has risen. "I must ask you to excuse me."

"No, please! I'll go!" Louise, too, has risen and is moving away. "I'm entirely at fault. Flying always plays hell with my nerves and I've had too many highballs. Please excuse me—all of you!"

The atmosphere is still at a tension as Charles Nathan feels that he should also take a hand in the discussion. This is the first time Charles has ever met a representative of the Nazi government and he would like to ask Dr. Walther how, in his opinion, "any philosophy of life or any political theory can justify what your nation has done to the Dickensens and millions of unoffending people like them?"

Dr. Walther does not answer. It is a subject he does not care to discuss with Charles. Why? Because Charles is a Jew? Again Walther does not answer and Charles, growing belligerent, would carry the issue further if Ingraham did not interfere, practically forcing him into a seat.

"Dr. Walther, do you mind if I speak frankly to you?" Ingraham is asking.

"Why, certainly not, Mr. Ingraham," answers Walther. "We Germans admire frankness. Frankness and realism—those are qualities on which we pride ourselves."

"Yes, I know you do. That's what prompts me to speak. And I want to make it clear that I have no personal grievance against Germany. On the contrary, I was a graduate student at Heidelberg, just before the World War. Some of the happiest days of my life were spent wandering through the Schwarzwald and the Harz Mountains with a few kindred spirits—keen, eager young men, full of ideas and ideals. And I learned to love the literature of Goethe and Schiller and Lessing—and Heine, too! And the music of Bach and Beethoven and Schumann. But where are they today? That's what I want to ask you. Where are they and the spirit that animated them? Is it their Germany that lends itself to pogroms and the mutilation of children? Do they stand guard with the jailers of Prague and Paris? Are we to search for them in the crumbling ruins of Dutch and Norwegian villages—in the rubble heaps of Louvain? In all sincerity, Dr. Walther, I ask you what madness has driven your country to this frenzy of annihilation that threatens to wipe the earth clean of every vestige of intelligence and culture? Can you answer that?"

"You yourself have answered those questions admirably, Mr. Ingraham, in your excellent books, particularly *The Betrayal of Democracy!*"

"But—!"

"Allow me, if you please! In those books you have ably exposed the machinations of the munition makers and the Entente propagandists. The story of today is the story of 1914—a conspiracy of the plutocracies to imprison us in our narrow borders until we die for want of air. While you were a student at Heidelberg, I was already studying for my doctorate in Entomology at Leipzig. But I was also a reserve lieutenant of artillery and when Russia mobilized against us and there was no course open except to hurl ourselves against France before the iron jaws closed, I had to abandon my studies and join my regiment. We had no quarrel with the Belgians—then or now. But we were fighting for our existence, and they shut their gates and turned their guns against us. They were the aggressors, not we. You have spoken of Louvain. My battery stood before Louvain, and each time I gave the order to fire, I prayed that the beautiful library would be spared. And when, at last, we entered the city and I saw the building in ruins, my eyes filled with tears. Why didn't they let us through? What did they gain by resisting? What—"

Marie Dickensen has come in quietly from her compartment. For a moment she stands listening to Walther. No one has noticed her. Suddenly "she is unable to restrain herself, and rushing into the lounge, she throws herself at Walther and seizes him by the throat," screaming—

"Murderer! Assassin! You murdered my mother! You murdered my son!"

For a second everything is confusion. Ingraham and Charles finally succeed in pulling Marie away from Walther, who rises angrily to straighten his collar and tie. The roar of the engines has increased as the plane glides toward a landing.

"All right, Mrs. Dickensen! All right! Everything is all right," Charles is protesting.

"Ah, non, non! Je ne veux pas! Je ne veux pas! Laissez-moi!" Marie is protesting, hysterically, as Charles forces her off.

"We are landing in a minute! Sit down, please, and fasten your belts!" the steward Gus is saying. "Are you all right?" he inquires of Walther.

"It's nothing," answers Walther, wiping his face with his handkerchief. "I'm sorry for the poor woman! These Latins are all alike. They have no emotional stability!"

"Boy, that sure was a pretty landing!" announces Colonel Gage, as the spray dashes over the windows and the plane taxies through the waves. The curtain falls.

ACT II

Late that afternoon Hope Nathan is sitting in the left lounge when she is joined by Howard Ingraham. The other passengers are scattered variously about the ship, some in the lounge, some in the right compartment. Her husband, Hope reports, has gone to lie down. Like everybody else, the Nathans had been terribly upset by what had happened before—

"I'm beginning to think I don't know much about my own country," says Hope. "When I heard Colonel Gage going on, I was shocked speechless. You see, all these years, while I've been wandering around from one troubled country to another, I've been consoling myself with the thought that some day I'd go back home where things are different. Just my congenital optimism, I guess. I was born in 1918, a few days after the Armistice, and they called me Hope, because they thought a new day was dawning. Awful name, isn't it?"

"I've always thought it suited you very well."

"I think it's dreadful. Something out of the bottom of Pandora's box. When war broke out last September, I was going to change it to False Hope, but Charles wouldn't hear of it."

"Damned unreasonable fellow."

Count Vronoff and Dr. Walther are evidently maneuvering for a further chat, but there is too much interference. First, Lisette Dickensen has found the Doctor's butterfly book and is looking at the pictures. Then Gus, the steward, gets into the conversation. Gus admits to having been German born, but, after being sixteen years in America, and an American citizen for ten years, he insists that he has little use for what he remembers of Germany.

Now Lisette's mother has come to drag the child away, and slap her for not minding when she was told to keep away from that *"sale boche!"*

"She shouldn't hit the poor child," protests Hope, as the Dickensens disappear. "She didn't mean to do anything wrong."

"I know just how she feels about it," counters Louise. "If I'd been through what she has, I'd want to go and beat out the brains of our Teutonic friend, myself."

"Yes, that is how it is in the world today," says Frau Rosenthal. "Hatred makes hatred and cruelty makes cruelty. When I heard those two men talking—Dr. Walther and Colonel Gage—I couldn't listen, any longer."

Louise has an answer to her radiogram. Hope's suspicions are confirmed. It is evident that Count Vronoff is on his way to America to engage in similar activities. That something should be done about this Hope and Louise are agreed. But what?

Alone in the right compartment Walther and Vronoff, convinced that they cannot be overheard, continue their confidences. Walther has instructions for Vronoff. When he gets to Berkeley he is to select living quarters at a certain number on South Elm Street. He is to avoid the society of all Germans, including members of the faculty. He is to pose as a disinherited man whose heart bleeds for unhappy Russia. Thus will he excite sympathy, especially among the women students. But— Let him also remember that "in American academic circles sexual irregularity is regarded with even more disfavor than unorthodox political views." Vronoff knows. Hadn't he lived fifteen years in England?

As for his duties, it will be possible and reasonable for Professor Vronoff to invite a few students to his room from time to time. Among those who come one may arrive early, or stay until after the others have left—

"In this way you will receive reports of the utmost significance," Walther informs him. "San Francisco is the largest port on the Pacific Ocean. It is also a center of shipbuilding and airplane manufacture. In other words, you will be at one of the focal points for the gathering of intelligence."

As for the manner in which this intelligence is to be transmitted, Walther has also worked that out. He has invented a new code, simple and flexible, which is associated cleverly with the butterfly book—

"Each week you will receive by post, a copy of some publication containing an article that deals with butterflies. The first five specific names mentioned in the article will constitute the key for that week. For example, let us suppose the first mention is of Aphantopus hyperanthus. Looking in the check list, we find that it appears as number twelve. Now since the twelfth letter of the English alphabet is L, we substitute L for A, M for B, N for C, and so on, for the first word of the code. Now suppose that the second mention is of Pieris napi—"

Captain McNab has appeared suddenly. The Walther-Vronoff conference is quickly ended. Presently Louise has found Captain McNab in the lounge and shown him the radiogram. The Captain is startled. Something, he agrees, should be done. But what? Maybe Louise had better radio the Department of Justice.

"As far as we know, they'd have no legal proof of what his intentions are in coming to America," says Louise. "If you ask me, the best thing would be never to let him get to America at all."

McNab admits the logic of her suggestion, but is still doubtful as to his right to take action. After all, there is only the radiogram to go on. Of course, if Louise could get him official confirmation from the British Intelligence Office, then it would be a different story. Louise thinks she can.

Vronoff has come into the lounge. "What time tomorrow morning do we arrive in New York, Captain McNab?" he asks.

"About ten, unless this head wind gets worse," answers the Captain.

"Good."

"Here's hoping it blows a gale!" adds Louise. Vronoff disappears. The curtain falls.

It is ten o'clock at night. The lights are on, the windows dark. Charles and Captain McNab are playing chess and Louise is reading in the left compartment. In the lounge Hope and Vronoff are reading and Frau Rosenthal is writing letters. Walther and Gage are playing pinochle in the right compartment.

The pinochle game breaks up with Gage $30 ahead. On this victory the Colonel thinks he will sleep comfortably. Steward Tom has brought Louise an answer to her radiogram. That breaks up the chess game. The Captain has work to do.

Presently Frau Rosenthal, gathering up her writing things, finds herself alone with Hope in the lounge. It is because her family is so widely separated that she must write so much, Frau Rosenthal volunteers. She has a sister in Germany, married to a German; her daughter is living in Palestine and her own husband is in Cuba. It is because she hopes to find the money to send for her husband that she is going to America. Before Hitler came, the husband had been one of the best known art dealers in Berlin and her son-in-law a successful German painter.

"Excuse me, when I see you sitting there, I just think it's my daughter," Frau Rosenthal is saying. "She has white skin and blue eyes like you. Would you allow me to ask you a question?"

"Why, of course."

FRAU ROSENTHAL—You are not a Jewish girl?

HOPE—No, I'm not. Why?

FRAU ROSENTHAL—And did you meet your husband in Palestine?

HOPE—Heavens, no! Charles and I met in Paris, about a year ago.

FRAU ROSENTHAL—And you knew he was Jewish?

HOPE—Well, yes, I suppose I did. I can't remember that we ever discussed it. Neither of us is very religious. Especially not I. You see, I'm the granddaughter of a missionary.

FRAU ROSENTHAL—I don't speak of religion. Only of race. You did not think about that, before you got married?

HOPE—No, of course not! Why on earth should we? I really don't understand all this talk. What difference does it make what race a person belongs to?

FRAU ROSENTHAL—Yes, so we Jews talked in Germany. Race counts for nothing—only nationality; and so we thought of ourselves only as Germans. To us, we thought, nothing can happen; like peasants who build their villages on the sides of a volcano, where smoke comes out of the top. Then one day, comes not only smoke, but fire and boiling lava that flows over the houses and burns the sleeping people alive.

HOPE—Yes, I know. But I just can't believe it will ever be like that in America.

FRAU ROSENTHAL—Who knows what it will be in five years or ten years? Ten years ago in Germany, we laughed at Hitler. We said he is a foolish fellow with a Napoleon complex, that only stupid shopkeepers can take seriously.

HOPE—Well, if a Hitler ever did come to life in America, I'm sure only the worst elements would listen to him.

FRAU ROSENTHAL—It was these elements in Germany that became the Storm Troopers and made Hitler Chancellor. And then the others followed—the educated and the respectable people, they followed—even the artists! My husband, for years, gave help to young German artists. When they asked for advice or assistance, he never refused. But after Hitler, it was different! They denounced him as an enemy of German culture. They broke open his beautiful gallery and smashed and made dirty everything. And on the outside, they wrote with yellow paint: "The Jews are our misfortune!" Yes, even when you have seen it all, it is hard to believe. That's why I talk this way to you. (*Impulsively, going to* HOPE.) Please, you will not be angry if I give you some advice?

HOPE—Why, no, of course not!

FRAU ROSENTHAL—It is only to say that you must not have children.

HOPE (*shocked*)—Why do you say that?

FRAU ROSENTHAL—Yes, I understand how you feel. A young wife, filled with happiness, it is only natural that you should wish to have a child. But you must not.

HOPE—Why? I don't see why!

FRAU ROSENTHAL—No, you must not, please! You must not think only of your own happiness, but of the child, too. To bring into the world a Jewish child, that is a great sin, because now for the Jews there is only misfortune.

HOPE—I understand how terrible it's been for you.

FRAU ROSENTHAL—Not only for me. For millions in Germany, in Austria, in Czechoslovakia, in Poland. And now in Italy and France and Holland, too. You think in America it will be different—

HOPE—Yes, I do!

FRAU ROSENTHAL—So we thought in Germany. So they thought in all the other countries. But it is not so. You heard this Colonel Gage, how he talked. It means that even in America, this danger exists, too. For the Jews in all the world now, there can be only suffering and persecution. Do you wish to have a child who will be beaten and insulted by the other children? Who must wear a Jewish dress and cannot play in the schoolyard? A child who cannot study at the university and who is permitted to work only on the roads and to live only in a ghetto? Can a mother wish such a life for her child? No, it is better to ache in your heart for the child you do not have, than to ache for her unhappiness in a world where she cannot find a place.

Hope's distress is so apparent Frau Rosenthal regrets having spoken, and yet she still feels the truth should be told and faced. Frau Rosenthal has gone to her berth when Charles rejoins Hope. He is excited about the radiogram that has come to Louise and the confirmation of their suspicions about Vronoff. He is glad, too, for another reason: This Vronoff incident has helped him make up his mind about his own problem. Now he has decided that it is his duty to learn to be an air pilot, that he may be able to fly a bomber some day, if that should be necessary. When Hope protests Charles is quick to remind her that he is an American who feels that America is in danger and is worth defending.

"There are millions of unmarried men," protests Hope. "They won't need you."

"Maybe they won't. But I need them," answers Charles. "Because I feel that I have a big stake in America. What are fellows like me going to do? Sit back behind our legal exemptions and go complacently about our little private businesses, while the enemy creeps inside the gate? Or crouch in a corner and wring our hands in despair? No! If we let America go by default, we have only ourselves to blame."

"You've just got yourself emotionally unstrung, that's all.

Just because that Nazi insulted you this afternoon, you think you have to—"

"That's not true! Maybe that's what made up my mind for me. But I've been thinking about it for a long time—ever since the day Paris was bombed. There I was, sitting on the *terrasse* of the Café d'Harcourt on the Boul' Mich' having a coffee, between sessions of my exams, when the raid started, and I went into the street and stared up at the sky, listening to the distant detonations of the bombs and praying to God they weren't falling anywhere near where you were. Then when it was over, I rushed in to phone you, and all the while I kept thinking: 'What the hell am I doing, anyhow, puttering around with a fool examination in international law, when those bloody bastards in the sky are systematically making all law obsolete?' "

Charles' determination still persists through all Hope's arguments, even through her vain dream of finally finding peace and happiness in her own home. She will one day come to see the situation as he does, Charles is confident of that. True, as she charges, there was a time just a little while ago when he believed none of the things he believes now—

"Suppose I told you that I'm going to have a baby—what then?" Hope suddenly asks.

"Hope, you don't mean it!"

"Yes, I do."

"But, darling, why haven't you told me? How long have you known it?"

"A few weeks. Just before we left Paris."

"Why didn't you tell me?"

"Because I knew we had a long hard trip ahead of us. And I didn't want to be coddled and made a fuss over. Anyhow, I wasn't absolutely sure until I went to see a doctor in Lisbon."

"You should have told me."

"Yes, I suppose I should. But I wanted to wait until we got home and then give you what I thought would be a happy surprise. But I guess I was fooling myself about that, too—especially after listening to Mrs. Rosenthal, just now."

"Mrs. Rosenthal? What's she got to do with it?"

She tells him what Mrs. Rosenthal has said. Charles resents the tactlessness of such a statement, but is free to admit its truth. He, too, has thought of that. "It's a great responsibility today, bringing a child into the world," he says. "It's not just our own happiness that's involved. You have to think of the child's future, too."

But he would not have Hope think that, as she insists, she has made a mess of her life, of her marriage and everything. He doesn't want her to give way to the hysteria that is threatening. He asks only that she be reasonable. But—Hope doesn't want to be reasonable. Right now she doesn't want to talk any more to anybody about anything. She just wants to be by herself. Charles cannot stop her as she hurriedly leaves him. . . .

Captain McNab has a second radiogram. He has sent for Louise Frayne. Also for Officer Banning. He lets Louise read the radiogram, but "not for publication." To Banning he suggests that perhaps it would be wise for them to land at Bermuda, even if they have got an excellent reserve load of fuel in the tanks. Banning is reading the telegram. Dr. Walther, on his way to his berth, passes them—

"Well, gentlemen, while the ship goes flying through space at the rate of a hundred and fifty miles an hour, here you are, calmly smoking your cigarettes," chirps Walther, with heavy jocosity. "It's wonderful."

McNab—We got a couple boys up there, keeping their eyes on things.

Walther—I see. Everything under control, eh?

McNab—Yes, I think so.

Walther—Then I think I'll confidently go to bed. Good night.

The Others—Good night.

Walther (*as he crosses the left compartment*)—Good night, Mr. Nathan. (Charles *looks up without replying, as* Walther *exits.*)

Banning (*giving the radiogram back to* McNab)—I'll go up and tell the boys about Bermuda.

McNab—No use telling the passengers until we're ready to land. Only gives them something to worry about.

Banning—Right. (*He exits to the flight deck.*)

McNab—When you've got passengers, it's better not to take any chances on anything.

Louise—That's a damned good policy—on land, sea, or in the air.

Tom (*entering with a drink*)—Rye and plain water, Miss Frayne.

The curtain falls.

ACT III

Early the next morning Charles is the first one in the lounge. He has been up since sunrise, and is now sipping his coffee. Presently Hope is with him. She had not slept well. She is surprised to hear that they are coming down at Bermuda. The official explanation is that they have to refuel, Charles explains, but Vronoff is undoubtedly the real cause. Vronoff is supposed to be a British subject.

Hope is of no mind to talk over her last interview with Charles. So far as she is concerned there is nothing to be straightened out. He has made it very plain what he wants to do, and how he feels about things, says Hope, and as for herself, she will just have to figure out some sort of adjustment.

Dr. Walther is in for his coffee shortly, and eager to know what time the ship will arrive in New York. None of the crew can enlighten him. Colonel Gage, too, is anxious. To the Colonel the ship appears to be flying mighty low. Why they should be down to 3,000 feet with a 10,000 foot ceiling is more than he can understand. And besides that, they're still dropping.

Presently Officer Banning arrives. He wants all the passengers rounded up in the lounge, and with their passports. No, not because they are already in New York, but because they're stopping at Bermuda and will be there in less than ten minutes.

"For what reason?" Dr. Walther demands. "It was my understanding that we flew direct from the Azores to New York."

"Yes, that's our schedule. But that's a pretty long hop, you know. And when there's a head wind, we don't take any chances with our fuel reserve."

"This seems to me to be carrying caution to a ridiculous extreme."

"Well, sir, it's not P.A.A.'s policy to run any risks when the safety of passengers is concerned."

Steward Gus has been around lowering the French shades over the windows. British military regulations are very strict in Bermuda. When Count Vronoff appears he is white and nervous, and takes a seat in the left compartment. The Count had been specifically informed in Lisbon that there would be no stop in Bermuda, he protests. They tell him it is the weather that is responsible.

A moment later, when he is alone in the compartment, Vronoff takes a revolver from his pocket and slips it under the seat in front of him. Marie Dickensen, coming along the passageway, is in time to see this, but when Vronoff looks up suspiciously she gives no indication that she is at all aware of his presence. A moment later Banning has arrived and helped her fasten her belt. Marie is excited. This delay is bad for her husband. Every hour is important to him.

The clipper is down now to a smooth landing. Banning would have them all unfasten their belts and step into the lounge. Officers will come aboard presently to inspect the passports. No one will be allowed ashore, and he asks all passengers please to be careful about raising the window blinds. They will be there just long enough to take on fuel and go through the routine formalities.

Now Captain Arthur Hawkes, a British officer in the intelligence service, accompanied by two non-commissioned officers, comes down the stairs from the flight deck. He is carrying a portfolio and is followed by Captain McNab. A calm, affable person Captain Hawkes takes a seat in the right compartment, greets Officer Banning amiably and asks that Miss Frayne be the first passenger sent in. He asks to see the interesting radiograms she has received and thanks her for the privilege of keeping them. She has, he feels, done them a service. He is grateful to her, and to Mrs. Nathan, too.

Howard Ingraham is the next called, and is quickly dismissed. Then Frau Rosenthal. She is not an American citizen, Frau Rosenthal explains, but she has her quota number and her immigration visa, and these are quite in order. Neither is she carrying any firearms, as an inspection of her handbag confirms.

"We don't allow anyone to bring firearms on board, Captain," McNab explains.

"I'm aware of that—but there is always the possibility that some passenger may be a little absent-minded," answers Captain Hawkes, handing the relieved Frau Rosenthal back her bag and dismissing her.

The Nathans are called next and quickly passed. "We're indebted to you, Mrs. Nathan," says Captain Hawkes.

"I didn't do a thing, except happen to remember a rumor I heard, years ago. Miss Frayne did all the rest."

"She's just been giving you all the credit. You Americans are a modest lot, evidently."

"I never heard that before," laughs Charles.

Colonel Gage is next, and a little pompous in his friendliness. He would like Captain Hawkes to come down to Texas one day and have a game of golf with him. And then Count Vronoff is called.

The Count approaches the inquisitors with an affected calmness. He is, he protests, a British subject. His name is Russian, yes, because he is an unfortunate victim of the Bolshevik revolution, but he is a British subject by naturalization. No, he has no firearms—a fact that Captain Hawkes is careful to have his corporal confirm. Captain Hawkes also orders his assistants to fetch both the Vronoff and the Walther hand luggage from their berths.

"Is that all?" Count Vronoff would know.

"Not quite. There'll be a few questions that you'll have to answer, I'm afraid."

VRONOFF—What kind of questions?

HAWKES—Well, about this passport, for one thing. It's a forgery.

VRONOFF—You are making a mistake, Captain. I assure you, upon my honor, that you are making a great mistake.

HAWKES—No, I don't think so, Count Vronoff. According to my information, you formerly held a British passport in the name of Leonid Pavlich Arenski. But in 1935 you were expelled from Palestine because you had been selling intelligence of a military nature—to a foreign government. And at the same time, your passport was revoked.

VRONOFF—No, no, Captain! This is really laughable. I am a scholar—an authority on Slavonic literature. And my name is Count Paul Vasilich Vronoff—a collateral descendant of the famous Golitzin family. You are surely confusing me with someone else. I can easily prove it to you.

HAWKES—Well, you'll be given every opportunity to do so. Do you mind just sitting down, for a moment, while I finish with the others?

VRONOFF—But, Captain, I swear to you, by the soul of my sainted mother—

HAWKES—Blasphemy won't help you, Count Vronoff. Next, please!

BANNING—Dr. Walther. (*The* SECOND CORPORAL *motions* VRONOFF *to a seat, as* WALTHER *enters the right compartment.*)

HAWKES—Dr. Hermann Walther?

WALTHER—That is correct.

HAWKES—German passport—is that right?

WALTHER—A diplomatic passport. I am attached to the German Embassy in Washington.

HAWKES—Yes. (*He signals to the* SECOND CORPORAL, *who, without a word, proceeds to search* WALTHER *for weapons.*)

WALTHER (*furious*)—What is the meaning of this?

SECOND CORPORAL (*to* HAWKES, *ignoring* WALTHER)—Nothing, sir.

WALTHER—This is inexcusable!

HAWKES—Just hand over that attaché case, will you please?

WALTHER—No! I refuse! (*But the* SECOND CORPORAL *has already taken the dispatch case out of his hand.*) I protest against this! I am a diplomatic officer, traveling under the protection of the American flag!

HAWKES—There's no better flag in the world to travel under, sir.

McNAB—You said it!

WALTHER (*to* McNAB)—Captain McNab, I formally protest against this violation of my rights.

McNAB—I'm sorry, Dr. Walther, but there's just nothing I can do about it. We're under British military control, as long as we're in port here.

The British corporals have reappeared with the Vronoff and Walther luggage and are told to take it ashore. Walther and Vronoff are asked to sit down while Captain Hawkes finishes his inspection.

Marie Dickensen is the last to be called. The Dickensens, Captain McNab explains, are all on one passport. The husband and two children are in the bridal suite. Marie, too, is quickly dismissed. She hopes now they will be able to go, but Captain Hawkes is not reassuring. There is still considerable questioning to be done, he explains, indicating Vronoff and Walther. Further delay is plainly displeasing to Marie.

At first Dr. Walther refuses to accompany Captain Hawkes ashore, but the actions of the corporals is rather persuasive and the Doctor soon realizes the uselessness of physical resistance. He again warns Captain McNab, however. "Your company and your damned Yankee government will have reason to regret this," declares Walther as the corporal leads him away.

There is not much for those who are left to do. The post bags have been taken off for censorship, which will probably consume several hours. Colonel Gage decides the only thing left to them is to shoot a little bridge. They are arranging a table in the lounge when Marie Dickensen comes back to the left compartment. "With a sudden, swift movement she stoops and gropes under the seat for the revolver that she has seen Vronoff conceal there. She rises, with the revolver in her hand. Gus catches a glimpse of her just as she turns away."

"Are you looking for something, Mrs. Dickensen?" asks Gus, coming into the compartment.

"No, no! Nothing!" answers Marie, concealing the revolver in her handbag.

She goes quickly back the way she has come. Gus looks after her suspiciously and then returns to the lounge. The bridge game is just getting under way as the curtain falls.

Several hours later the plane is again in flight, as indicated by the raised window shades and the low even hum of the motors. Hope, Louise, Gage and Ingraham are still at the bridge table in the lounge. Dr. Walther is writing at a desk in the right compartment. Marie Dickensen has just appeared at the left, clutching her handbag. Seeing Banning coming down the stairs from the flight deck, Marie sinks into a seat in the left compartment. When Gus appears a moment later she asks that he get her a drink of brandy.

Now the bridge game has broken up, with Colonel Gage some nine hundred points in the lead. Charles has joined the group and the talk naturally turns to the probable future of Count Vronoff. Colonel Gage doesn't think the British will hang him. Probably only keep him interned in Bermuda for the duration. Which doesn't strike Charles as being an awful fate.

Louise would like to have Officer Banning tell her whether any tie-up between Vronoff and any other passenger on the plane was discovered during the examination, but Banning is not inclined to talk about that. Both Louise and Charles, however, are convinced that Walther is in on the play in some way, and why the British didn't hold him in Bermuda, too, is more than they can understand. That, explains Colonel Gage, would have led us right straight into war.

"When Hitler is ready to make war on us he'll make it, no matter what we do," prophesies Louise.

"If you ask me, he'd much rather do business with us than make war on us," ventures Gage. "And I'm not so sure that that wouldn't be the smart thing for us to do."

"Colonel Gage, do you really think we can avoid this thing that threatens us by refusing to face it, or by huddling under the umbrella of appeasement?" asks Howard Ingraham. "Don't you see that what we're dealing with is a poison of the mind, a corruption of the spirit, that no compromise, no gesture of conciliation can protect us from? And no ocean barrier, either, for it travels on the wind. Take us, all of us here, Americans and Europeans alike, flying through space to imagined security and carrying with us, all the while, the same corrosive elements that have destroyed security everywhere. Like a homing pigeon, flying from a plague-stricken land and yet bearing in its very wings the germs of the infection."

"Yes, that's so!" agrees Hope. "We're all trying to escape something that there's no escape from."

Colonel Gage refuses to be drawn into another argument. In the left compartment Marie has taken her drink of brandy from Gus. When she is alone again, as the others scatter, or go back to their reading, she takes the revolver from her bag and slips into the lounge.

Captain McNab has come into the right compartment at Dr. Walther's request. The Doctor has prepared a statement for the State Department and his own Government of the Bermuda incident and demands that Captain McNab supplement this with a similar statement. To do that, the Captain explains, he would have to have instructions from someone higher in authority. His job is to get the ship from New York to Lisbon and back. That's all.

In that case Dr. Walther demands that Captain McNab send a radio message to his company requesting that some person to whom he can present his demand meet the ship at the New York airport. "Please bear in mind that I speak as a representative of the Third Reich," concludes the Doctor. "Well, sure, I'll send the message if you want me to," agrees Captain McNab. "But if you'll take my advice, Dr. Walther, you'll drop the whole thing. They've got a right to question passengers and examine mail and baggage, while we're in port there, and if your government is going to kick up a fuss about it, they may not stop at that, next time."

"I did not ask for your advice, Captain McNab, nor am I interested in receiving it," answers Dr. Walther, with mounting anger. "We have had enough American meddling in our affairs and our patience is beginning to be exhausted. As long as your government keeps up this fiction of neutrality and continues to maintain diplomatic relations with us, it is our intention to insist upon our full rights under international law and to protest against these disgraceful unneutral acts." Captain McNab would interrupt if he could, but Dr. Walther stops him and hurries on. "One moment, if you please! I did not fail to observe the rapport that exists between you and these British officers. You work hand-in-glove with your dear British cousins, don't you? Well, we shall put an end to that! Before long, we shall teach the British their proper place in the world and when that is done, we may find it necessary to teach you Yankees a few lessons, too!"

Walther's voice has risen to a shout. All the passengers in the lounge are listening. Marie, trembling violently, clutches the revolver as she rises uncertainly to her feet. McNab has sharply agreed to send the message and started for the flight deck. Walther, shaking with rage, stands looking after McNab and muttering imprecations in German. Marie has leveled the revolver. Charles Nathan, seeing what has happened, throws himself toward her, shouting, "No! No! Don't do that!"

"Assassin! C'est ton tour!" shrieks Marie and fires.

Charles falls to the deck as McNab rushes back to the lounge. Hope is on her knees by Charles' side. McNab pulls her away. The curtain falls.

Two hours later the plane is nearing New York. In the left compartment the lower berth has been made up and Charles is lying in it, very still. Hope sits beside the berth watching her husband anxiously. Louise and Gage are in the lounge. Walther is by himself in the right compartment, trying to read.

Officer Banning has come to announce that they will be in in about twenty minutes. Everything has been arranged. There will be an ambulance at the field and it is only ten minutes from there to the hospital. Everything, he assures Hope, is going to be all right.

Little Lisette Dickensen is anxious, too. Both about Charles and about her mother. What will they do to mama? Will they send her to prison?

"She didn't mean to do it," says Lisette. "She liked him. She told papa what a kind man he is."

"Yes, I know, dear. We'll do whatever we can, Lisette." Hope would console the child. Lisette runs back to the Dickensen compartment.

Captain McNab has appeared with a message for Dr. Walther. There will be a Department of Justice man awaiting him at the airport. For what purpose? McNab doesn't know, but he has a suspicion that Vronoff has done some talking in Bermuda.

As the passengers settle and begin to adjust their seat belts Howard Ingraham pauses beside Dr. Walther. "I hope you won't think me impertinent if I ask you a personal question," he says.

"No, of course not."

INGRAHAM—Well, it's just that I'm curious about your reaction to all this.

WALTHER—My reaction? Excuse me, but I do not quite understand.

INGRAHAM—I mean to the fact that you owe your life to a member of a race which you profess to despise—a man, who in the terms of your philosophy, is your inferior and your enemy. How does that affect you? In a human way, I mean.

WALTHER—I do not understand why it should affect me, at all, Mr. Ingraham.

INGRAHAM—You mean that you feel nothing at all? No sense of gratitude? No inner intimation that you may have been guilty of an injustice, that your doctrines may need a little overhauling and revising?

WALTHER—I am afraid we do not speak the same language, Mr. Ingraham. I am by training a man of science. And a scientist who has arrived at certain conclusions upon the basis of observed facts does not allow his conclusions to be disturbed by personal and irrelevant accidents.

INGRAHAM—And the human equation means nothing to you? You reject generosity, tolerance, self-sacrifice, brotherliness—all those unscientific qualities that create decent relationships between human beings and make life bearable?

WALTHER—It is just as I have said: we speak different languages. I am a scientist and a realist. You are a sentimentalist and a romanticist. I speak for a young, vigorous, and determined race, which clearly understands the rôle it is destined to play in human history and which rejects the whining beatitudes and the weak slave morality of your dying Jewish-Christian culture.

INGRAHAM—And what would have become of your own magnificent personal destiny, if Charles Nathan hadn't stepped between you and that bullet?

WALTHER—You really surprise me, Mr. Ingraham. That a man of education and experience should permit himself such banalities is quite incomprehensible. It is one more example of the mental debilitation that results from overexposure to liberalism and democracy. Surely you don't really believe that there is anything admirable in risking one's life to save an enemy! Such an action seems to me quite atavistic, or perhaps I should say devolutionary—a form of biological retrogression. The healthy organism is concerned first with survival and second with domination.

INGRAHAM—We seem to have succeeded in astonishing each other.

WALTHER—Yes, I have no doubt. To those who have not been disciplined in clear thinking, the most obvious truths always seem incredible. But please allow me to go further and repudiate your romantic suggestion that Mr. Nathan was actuated by a desire to save my life. That is really laughable. His action was entirely unmotivated—it was nothing more than a muscular reflex. If he had had a moment for thought, he would have taken good care not to intervene.

And, concludes Dr. Walther, if Charles' mind had been trained to function logically, "instead of being warped by the corrosive philosophy of liberalism and the insidious poisons of Jewish mysticism," he would not have needed so much as a moment's thought to have halted his action.

Ingraham has crossed the lounge to the left compartment. Hope is still keeping her anxious vigil. And, she says, "trying to remember what the world was like yesterday, when we stepped onto this plane." It has made her pretty moody. Especially the remembrance that, when Frau Rosenthal had told her she had no right to bring a Jewish child into the world, and Charles had told her that he had decided to become an army pilot, that she acted "like some hysterical little nit-wit." "Charles, darling, please get well and forgive me," she cries.

Ingraham would be reassuring. It was natural and human for her to act as she did and he hopes she will go ahead and have her child. "Good Lord, if people like you and Charles don't have children, the human race may just as well go out of business altogether," he says.

"Well, I don't know about that," answers Hope. "But I do know that I *am* going to have the baby—no matter what happens. I've decided that, while I've been sitting here and watching him. Because I want so very, very much to have it—and nothing will ever convince me that it's wrong. (*Impulsively.*) Mr. Ingraham, this may sound like a crazy thing to say, but somehow, what

Charles did this afternoon and what happened to him seems to have given me the courage and the strength to face whatever the future holds. Does that make any sense at all?"

INGRAHAM—Yes, it does! It makes a lot of sense. I understand perfectly what you mean. Because the same thing has happened to me mentally that has happened to you emotionally.

HOPE—Oh, how? Tell me, please. This is awfully important to me.

INGRAHAM—Well, when I came aboard this plane, I was in a state of confusion and bewilderment—filled with a sense of defeat and frustration. But now my faith and my sense of values have been restored—by what Charles did and by a very illuminating talk I've just had with Dr. Walther.

HOPE—Well, that I don't understand at all! How could talking to Walther make you believe in anything but the certainty of universal destruction?

INGRAHAM—No! That's what I've learned on this plane—that it's not their way of life that will win in the end, but ours. I see clearly now something that I only sensed before. It's just this: that rationality carried to its ruthless logical extreme becomes madness, because man is a living and growing organism and not a machine, and in all the important things of life, a sane man is irrational. Do you see what I mean?

HOPE—Yes. Yes, I think I do! You mean what Charles did—!

INGRAHAM—Yes, exactly. An impulsive act that goes beyond reason and self-interest. That's how sane people live—illogically, instinctively, intuitively. Thinking with their feelings, rather than with their minds. Reaching out to each other, trusting each other. That means flexibility, and in flexibility there's strength and the potentiality of growth. But the other thing is rigid and in the end there's no strength and no growth in that—only brittleness and sterility. That's the issue: rational madness against irrational sanity. It sounds paradoxical but it's true. And, in the long run, madness will lose; because madness is disease and sanity is health and, if disease wins, it means the end of the world and no healthy man can believe in that.

HOPE—Yes, that's it! Oh, thank you so much for saying it for me. Because I believe it—I really do!

INGRAHAM—And never stop believing it! Bring your child into the world with that belief—a faith in the future and in the eventual triumph of sanity and decency. Because your faith and your courage will help make it come true.

HOPE—I will! I promise you I will!

Charles is stirring. Hope bends over him. He is not feeling any too good, he admits. But there are a few things he wants to say before they start doping him up again.

"What have they done with Mrs. Dickensen?" Charles wants to know.

"She's forward, in the crew's wardroom," Ingraham tells him. "I'll see that everything possible is done for her and her family. I've got to go and throw some things into a bag."

Ingraham has gone. Charles turns his eyes toward Hope. "Hello, Mrs. Nathan!" he says. "Kind of funny, isn't it, my turning out to be a bodyguard for that Nazi bastard?"

HOPE—I don't think it's a bit funny. And stop talking, please.

CHARLES—All right, I will, if you'll just let me say one thing.

HOPE—What?

CHARLES—Just that I'm very happy about the baby.

HOPE—Oh, thank you, darling! It's what I've been waiting to hear you say. Because I was afraid you didn't want it. That's what made me so miserable. But I'm not any more. Only, darling, please get well in a great hurry, so you can help make this world a clean and decent place for a nice child to grow up in. You will, won't you?

CHARLES—Don't worry about that. I intend to live, if it's the last thing I ever do.

"The motors swell to a roar as the plane descends to its final destination."

THE CURTAIN FALLS

CLAUDIA

A Comedy in Three Acts

By Rose Franken

ROSE FRANKEN had been nine years away from the Broadway theatre when "Claudia" brought her back in February, 1941. At least it had been nine years since Miss Franken's first comedy, "Another Language," had proved so positive a late season hit that it ran through the Summer of 1932 and well into the Winter following. After that it toured the country, became a stock company favorite and is still much in demand by amateurs and Barn theatre producers during the vacation months.

Nine years away, and yet Miss Franken was always in pretty close touch with Broadway. She was writing scenarios, short stories and novels in California. From two of her most successful novels she took the characters of Claudia and David Naughton and put them into a play. The play, concerned with the gradual awakening of Claudia as a child-wife, to maturity and the responsibilities of marriage and motherhood, gave Miss Franken a good deal of trouble in its casting. She must have interviewed a hundred prospective Claudias before she selected Dorothy McGuire for the rôle. Both her patience and judgment were happily rewarded. There was almost as much written about Miss McGuire's fitness for the rôle as there was about the play. With Frances Starr playing Claudia's mother, and Donald Cook the husband, David, the comedy proved an actors' triumph.

Like its Franken forerunner, "Another Language," the comedy of "Claudia" achieved a great popularity with women audiences. The heroine's consuming curiosity regarding her sex appeal, her definite mother fixation, her reluctance to grow to full stature as a wife—these familiar feminine characteristics helped to keep the matinees crowded, even well into the hot weather months. But "Claudia" also won positive acclaim from many of her gentlemanly critics—"The best new American play of the season is, by all odds, Miss Rose Franken's 'Claudia,'" wrote Richard Watts in the New York *Herald Tribune*. "I was more deeply touched at last night's première of Rose Franken's new play, 'Claudia,' than I have been by any theatrical presentation since the beginning of the season," echoed Sidney Whipple of the

World-Telegram. If the other reviewers were less definite in their enthusiasms they were all at least friendly.

It is an early Fall evening when we first meet the Naughtons, David and Claudia. They are sitting in their living room at Stillbrook, which is about seventy miles from New York. It is a "low-ceilinged living room of a skillfully restored 1760 house, with which judicious liberties have been taken." While it is not richly furnished, "it is informed with beauty and taste, lacking all flavor of the suburban."

David Naughton, deeply interested at the moment in the stock market page, "is a clean, good-looking, virile thirty." Claudia, going over her checkbook and vouchers at her desk, "is very young and full of voltage. She is dressed in a one-piece wool frock, and her hair-do is simple and childlike."

Mrs. Brown, Claudia's mother, is sitting on the sofa, knitting. "She is in her fifties—a gentle woman, with an unexpected dash of humor and a code of robust contempts."

Mrs. Brown is expecting David to take her to the station for a train back to New York, and she hopes that he is paying attention to the time. Claudia is not interested. She considers it quite foolish of her mother even to think of going home. For the moment, however, Claudia is more seriously concerned with the discovery that the bank has made a mistake of a hundred and two dollars and two cents in her account.

"Banks don't make mistakes," calmly suggests Mrs. Brown.

"They can't make mistakes, I've told you that a dozen times," adds David.

"Go ahead. Take their part against your wife," protests Claudia. "And anyway, why can't they, I'd like to know? Are they God?"

"They use adding machines."

"What does that prove? We use a washing machine and look at your shirt last week."

"You talk to her, Mother. You gave birth to her."

"You married her. She's yours now."

Claudia goes on with her letter to the bank demanding that she be credited with the hundred and two dollars. She doesn't intend to be the victim of any such racket. Neither does she trust David's judgment too much. He's always selling stocks that immediately thereafter go up, or buying stocks that as promptly go down. But she is quick to bring her checkbook and her figures to him when he offers to help.

David has quite a time with Claudia's accounts. It is difficult to tell the difference between her 3s and her 5s, for one thing, and though she is sure of both her addition and her subtraction she still is pretty firmly convinced that nine from thirteen leaves six, until she counts it out on her fingers. Still, David cannot discover just where Claudia has made her mistake.

Again the question of Mrs. Brown's going back to town comes up. Why won't she stay for the week-end? Because, says Mrs. Brown, with a smile, she is tired being under her daughter's thumb. Even Bertha, the housekeeper ("a plump middle-aged European, with the proverbial heart of gold"), and a promise of more of Bertha's exceptional cooking, including fresh, home-made bread, fail to deter Mrs. Brown.

Her interest in Bertha, and Fritz, Bertha's husband, however, is keen. For one thing they have been with the Naughtons two weeks now, and that is something of a record. For another, they came without references, after having been out of work for a long time, and that isn't too promising.

"I still say it's dangerous to take people off the streets—"

"We didn't, we took them out of the paper," Claudia is quick to explain. "We advertised in the Connecticut paper and they were our only answer. And only ninety a month for the whole couple. It's enough to make you believe in God."

"Claudia, that's sacrilege."

"Don't be silly, God doesn't just connect with important things. He has His nose in everything. . . ."

Mrs. Brown has gone to her room to pack. At her mother's disappearance up the stairs Claudia has become suddenly quiet. When she speaks there is an anxious look in her eyes—

"David, I don't think she looks awfully well, do you?"

"I don't wonder with you for a daughter."

CLAUDIA (*fear tightening in her throat*)—No, I mean it.

DAVID—I thought she looked fine, dear.

CLAUDIA—Really, did you? But I wonder why she won't stay over until Monday? Couldn't you sort of tell her that—

DAVID—Mother doesn't need me to tell her that I like having her here.

CLAUDIA—I know. You've been so sweet to her. And I adore you for it.

DAVID—I bet that was one of the reasons you married me.

Because I was good to your mother.

CLAUDIA—It was. That, and the back of your neck.—David, do try to find out what's taking her into town tonight, won't you?

DAVID—God, but you're a curious devil. (*Pulls her to him—kisses her.* FRITZ *appears at the dining-room door, wearing a leather jacket and carrying his cap. Like* BERTHA, *he has strength and dignity, and a basic quality of deep suffering akin to beauty. At moments, however, the tragedy in his face gives way to a flash of humor.*)

FRITZ—Good evening. (*Proudly withdraws a mammoth egg from his pocket.*) Just now I found it in the henhouse. A double yolk.

DAVID—Wow!

CLAUDIA—Did one of ours lay that?

DAVID—The rooster.

CLAUDIA (*coldly*)—If a rooster ever laid eggs, they wouldn't be bigger than marbles— This is practically an omelet! Let me take it up to show Mamma.

DAVID (*rising to look for something on desk*)—Been out to the barn, Fritz? (*Digresses to* CLAUDIA.) Claudia, did you see my pipe scraper?

CLAUDIA—What does it look like?

DAVID—You know that little flat piece of metal I scrape my pipe with?

CLAUDIA (*stopping short. Intelligently*)—Like a sort of a little can opener?

DAVID (*eagerly*)—Yes, where is it?

CLAUDIA (*going on her way*)—I didn't see it. (DAVID *looks after her, frustrated.*)

FRITZ (*clearing his throat. Sotto voce*)—I wanted to talk to you about the cow—

CLAUDIA (*pausing on the stairs*)—Majesty?

DAVID (*to* FRITZ)—Is she coming in?

CLAUDIA (*curiously*)—Coming from where? Was she out?

FRITZ (*to* DAVID)—I thought I would let the plowing go, and take her in the morning.

DAVID—By all means.

CLAUDIA (*coming down a couple of steps*)—What is all this? Where are you taking her?

DAVID—To the bull.

CLAUDIA (*intrigued*)—Is there a particular time?

DAVID—Fairly particular.

CLAUDIA—How do you know when it is?

DAVID—A little birdie tells us.

CLAUDIA (*the sophisticate*)—In other words, she's going to start having a calf again.

DAVID—We hope.

CLAUDIA—But it's inhuman, she just had one. What happens if you don't bother her with the bull?

DAVID—She doesn't consider it a bother.

FRITZ (*explaining with simple directness*)—If she didn't have a calf, Mrs. Naughton, she wouldn't give milk.

CLAUDIA—What a lot of shenanigans. (*As she reaches top stair.*) There ought to be a simpler method—

DAVID (*calling after her*)—You think one up, and let us know about it!

It is plain to Fritz that Claudia is new to farm life, and quite as evident that David is not. David inherited his love of the farm. If he had his way he would quit being an architect and just settle down to raising pigs.

Fritz is worried about another thing. He and Bertha have never been as happy in any place before. They are ever so eager to stay, but they feel they will have to leave. There is something in Fritz's past that David doesn't know, but that he should know—

But David has made his own investigations. He knows all about Fritz. "I couldn't very well leave Mrs. Naughton up here all day alone, with people I couldn't check up on," explains David.

"But you let us come . . . ?"

"Why not? You can't go on paying for a mistake forever. You have to begin fresh sometime. Besides, there seemed to be a little doubt about your part in the whole thing."

"Yes, but it does not matter. It is over now. Only in a way, it is not over. We could not get a job afterwards, because always I said where I was. And people, always they were sorry, but they would not have us. Then we saw your advertisement. We were up in Bridgeport, a couple's job, where I told the lady, and she was afraid to keep us. She was nice about it. She said she was getting her old gardener back, but we knew, Bertha and I. And Bertha said, 'Better keep our mouths shut, next time.' "

"Well, I'm glad you didn't. I'm glad you told me. It makes

"CLAUDIA"

Claudia: We advertised in the Connecticut paper and they (the servants) were our only answer. And only ninety a month for the whole couple. It's enough to make you believe in God.

Mrs. Brown: Claudia, that's sacrilege.

(Dorothy McGuire, Donald Cook, Frances Starr)

Photo by Vandamm Studio.

everything all right."

Fritz's gratitude is all but overwhelming. He is practically inarticulate when he tries to express his thanks.

There is a long distance phone call from Julia. Julia is David's sister-in-law. She is asking if she can stop off at the Naughtons' the next day. She is driving Darushka, the opera star, to Boston for a concert. They will be there for lunch. . . .

The affairs of Claudia are resumed. David has not yet found the mistake of the checkbook. Now he must tell her that they probably are going to lose Fritz and Bertha. Fritz had been in jail. He signed the wrong signature to a check. Of course they couldn't keep a man who has been in prison! Or could they?

They are grinning sheepishly at each other as David lifts Claudia to a sitting position beside him on the arm of the chair. "We're so subtle!" David is saying.

"Darling, you're not subtle," insists Claudia.

"Oh, I suppose you are."

Claudia—At least I wasn't trying to appear hard-boiled with Fritz thanking me all over the place. (*Pleased.*) David, we have beautiful souls, do you know it?

David (*bleakly*)—Or maybe we're just hanging on to a good couple. He is a damn good farmer. He does the work of two men, he's out in the barn at five every morning.

Claudia—I don't wonder. It's a job in itself, keeping all the animals pregnant.

David—Bred's the word.

Claudia—It's the same principle.—A farm is really a very sexy place, isn't it, David?

David—Should be, if it's a good farm. I wish I knew where you put that pipe scraper.

Claudia—I didn't take it, so how could I put it any place—David, let's talk about sex for a minute.

David—Why talk about it?

Claudia—Don't be silly. Look. Take Majesty. She doesn't have to have any personal magnetism. Nature does it for her. But Nature doesn't do one thing for a woman but make it harder. You let a woman go without a girdle like a cow and see what happens.

David—You don't wear a girdle.

Claudia—But have I got sex-appeal?

David (*weighing it*)—You have a nice spirit.

CLAUDIA—Why did you marry me, if I'm not attractive!

DAVID—There were other things about you. You don't smoke; you don't drink—

She has picked up the prize egg to hurl at him just as Mrs. Brown comes downstairs with her traveling bag and puts a stop to the sport. . . .

The phone has rung. It is three rings in place of the two Naughton rings, but Claudia tiptoes to the phone just the same. She is listening now, in spite of the continued protests of her mother and husband, who refuse to be shushed, and she is amused by what she overhears.

"Some day you'll listen once too often, and you'll hear something you don't want to hear," warns David.

"Listening over the phone is as dishonest as cheating," adds Mrs. Brown. And then, her curiosity aroused: "What was so gorgeous you were hearing?"

"Who is Ring Three anyway?" puts in David, succumbing.

They are just a couple of back yard gossips to Claudia, but finally she tells them. The voice she has heard belongs to somebody new, and is very English. "'I say, Mary, old bean, did you find *Sad Ecstasy?*'" imitates Claudia. "'It was in your files, Mr. Jerry! And how are you gettin' along up there all by yourself?'"

And now she knows who the newcomer is. The butcher told her. He's a writer, and he rented the little brown house on the river road. "He sounds like a first-rate pansy to me," says David. . . .

Claudia has gone to see what Bertha is doing about that fresh bread and jelly she promised, which gives her mother and David a chance for confidences.

Is there anything wrong, as Claudia suspects, David wants to know. Mrs. Brown is worried by that thought and a little evasive.

"David, that child's worse than a detective. I never have been able to fool her."

"She's certainly got herself an overdose of mother image."

"I wish she didn't," says Mrs. Brown, unhappily.

"I wish she didn't, too," admits David.

"That's why I was so glad when you bought the place out here."

"The only thing she doesn't like about it is leaving you in New York."

"It's the best thing could have happened to all three of us."

"You know what it's all about, don't you?" queries David, with a kind of quizzical respect.

"I ought to. I had the same kind of attachment to my mother. And it didn't make for an easy marriage."

"Good old umbilical cord, eh? (*A little grimly.*) It looks like it's going to take more than moving to the country to break it with Claudia. She's got a grip like a truck driver."

"She has to learn to let go of the people she loves. To hold close with open hands."

"That's a pretty big order. But she'll learn."

Mrs. Brown is hoping that David will be patient with Claudia and David has promised. He loves Claudia, he is sure, more than he loves himself. But he has had his moments of perplexity—

"Know what she said to me on the night we were married?"

"Enough."

"Enough is right; it almost ruined me. No, but the thing she said that struck out at me was, 'David, you couldn't be more darling to me if you were my own father. . . .' And the damnedest part of it was, I felt like her father."

Their talk has returned to Mrs. Brown and the urge that is calling her home. In the morning she has an appointment to have some X-ray pictures taken. There will be consultations. She doesn't want anyone to go with her. She is seeing a famous specialist. There will probably have to be an operation. "On the other hand, it might be—just a mistaken diagnosis."

"Certainly. They're all a bunch of alarmists," says David, pretending to be convinced.

"No, David," answers Mrs. Brown, after a moment's pause. "No use our fooling each other. But don't tell Claudia—yet."

"I won't; and I'm not going to believe it myself either until those pictures are developed."

Claudia is back from the kitchen, a little suspicious of the long conference. She still can't understand why her mother has to go back to town. Because she has a dentist's appointment, insists Mrs. Brown. A loose bridge— And she dutifully opens her mouth for an inspection—

"Good-by, Mrs. Naughton!"

"Good-by, Mrs. Brown!" Claudia is shouting after them as they disappear. "Drive carefully, for heaven's sake! And, David— Bring me a pickle!"

Bertha and Fritz are in to set the living room right. Claudia has orders for the lunch next day. They will all have to be very proper—

"I want you both to feel that this is your home—and nobody remembers what happened before you came here."

There is a ring at the bell. "That's Mamma back again, they were too late for the train, I'll go!" cries Claudia, rushing to the door.

The bell ringer is not Mother or David. It is Jerry Seymoure, "a tall good-looking young man, somewhat older than David, with a small mustache and an unmistakable air of the world. He is dressed in sports clothes, and has distinction and experience—charming to old ladies and children, even though they bore him."

Jerry has begged the use of a phone that he may call for help. He has a flat. He wants to get in touch with the nearest garage. He tries and discovers they are all closed. He can't fix a flat himself. There isn't a jack in the car. What to do?

Claudia has an answer. Let Fritz fix it. Fritz thrives on flat tires. While Fritz works the conversation is rambling and bright, including sort of an exchange of social and domestic references. "I say, you sound very much like a bad novel," Jerry finally submits. "The sort where all the characters are either very precocious or very whimsical."

"There isn't a grain of whimsy in my make-up," Claudia insists, pertly. "My husband wouldn't put up with whimsy."

"Good Lord—you're not married?" Jerry is plainly astonished.

"What would I be doing here if I weren't?"

"I haven't the vaguest notion. You see, I thought you were your daughter."

"Now who's whimsical?"

"I'm just confused," admits Jerry.

Claudia tells him of how they came by the farm; of how Jerry loves it and farms it quite seriously and of the perfectly huge egg they got that very morning, which she proudly displays—

"It would discourage me enormously if I were a hen," says Jerry.

"If I were a rooster, it would give me an inferiority complex," admits Claudia.

They compare an interest in dogs and cats and their respective animal possessions. When they get back to the farm and Claudia, Jerry suspects Claudia is altogether domestic, and when she practically forces a glass of milk on him he is sure of it. Claudia doesn't approve of men keeping house by themselves and when he would know how she has learned so much about him she frankly admits that she has listened in when he was talking with Mary. They are, she explains, on the same party wire, and she (Claudia) is a listener—

"I'm not proud of it. I try to overcome it," says Claudia.

"I have never listened over a party wire in my life," announces Jerry, righteously.

"My husband's the same way!"

"He sounds frightfully well-behaved in every respect."

"Oh, no, it's just that he can't stand little crimes like reading somebody's newspaper over their shoulder—or taking a spoon out of a hotel. But give him an out-and-out scoundrel, and he takes his hat off to him."

"Then I'm his man. I haven't a scruple."

"I thought you said you never listened over a party wire in your life?"

"I haven't. This is my first acquaintance with a party wire. I do read other people's letters, however. I enjoy them immensely. And I have no hesitancy when it comes to other men's wives."

"Not any?" Claudia is frankly incredulous.

"Not any."

Fritz has come to tell Jerry the tire is fixed. Jerry is not alone grateful, he is definitely impressed. Claudia's admitted devotion to Fritz changes all his plans—

"Forget what I said about other men's wives—it doesn't go here," says Jerry, as he lifts Claudia's hand to his lips "with a gesture of real decency and relinquishment."

"Why doesn't it?" a vulnerable Claudia wants to know.

"Let's say it's because your husband was good enough to fix my tire for me. Good-by and good luck."

Jerry disappears quickly, even as Claudia is still looking after him and echoing—"My husband!" It takes her a moment to realize Jerry's mistake.

A moment later David's whistle is heard from the yard. Now he is in the room bidding her catch the pickle he has brought her. But Claudia is not in a playful mood at the moment.

"David, I have a face like a baked potato!" she says quite tragically.

"No, dear, baked apple."

Claudia—Well, anyway, you were right, I have no more sex than a guinea hen! Fritz was the only man in the house and he was upstairs and I began talking about a fly like a fool, and he thought he was my husband.

DAVID—Who? The fly or Fritz?

CLAUDIA—Jerry!

DAVID—Who's Jerry?

CLAUDIA—The man I listened to over the phone. He just this minute left.

DAVID—What was he doing here?

CLAUDIA—He had a flat tire. Fritz fixed it for him.

DAVID—Why didn't he fix it himself?

CLAUDIA—He's not the type to carry a jack.

DAVID—What type is he?

CLAUDIA—He's not only English, he's British. And miles taller than you, David.

DAVID—I don't like him.

CLAUDIA—He was lovely about it when I told him I listened. He said he had no scruples, either.

DAVID—Glad to know it.

CLAUDIA (*joyously*)—You're jealous!

DAVID (*pooh-poohing the idea*)—Who, me? I just don't want him hanging around here using Fritz.

CLAUDIA (*bitterly*)—So that's your worry! Using Fritz. I wish I could make you eat those words. I wish I could make you so jealous you'd want to kill him!

DAVID (*aping her with enjoyment*)—With my bare hands.

CLAUDIA—If any man ever insulted me, the way he insulted you, I wouldn't sit there grinning about it!

DAVID (*continuing to clown*)—How'd he insult me?

CLAUDIA—First he said, "I enjoy reading other people's letters, and I have no hesitancy when it comes to other men's wives."

DAVID (*his good nature vanishing*)—So? . . .

CLAUDIA (*scathingly*)—Oh, you don't have to get all blown up about it. In the next breath he said it didn't apply in my case, and walked himself off!

DAVID—The fellow has more sense than I gave him credit for.

CLAUDIA—But doesn't it occur to you, if I'm good enough for you to be in love with, I'm good enough for other men to be in love with?

DAVID—Not necessarily. I'm just easy to please. You say yourself you're not beautiful. God knows you're not bright, you've got no sex-appeal, and yet I'm a simple fellow; you're all the woman I want.

CLAUDIA (*tensely*)—But if nobody else wants me, how long will you want me?

DAVID (*pulling her down to sofa*)—That's how long— (*Grinds it out against her lips in a passionate kiss.*)

CLAUDIA (*emerging for air. Enchanted*)—You make me feel like a bad woman.

Now David would hurry up with the examination of Claudia's checkbook and get to bed. Claudia is still a little dazed, but she dutifully reads off the numbers and amounts of her canceled checks and the accounts for which they were drawn. When they come to one for $100 which went for a lime spreader the mystery is solved. Claudia had forgotten to enter that one. . . .

David has turned to another of his worries: Is Claudia completely happy on the farm? Claudia thinks she is. Of course she worries sometimes and sometimes she wishes—

"That Mother would live here with us." David finishes the thought for her. "Then it would be perfect for you, wouldn't it?"

"I'm not asking for it. I realize perfectly well how unfair it would be to you, David."

"Unfair to you, too, dear."

"I know. It's not good. Someday when I'm an old woman, I'll develop a twitch in one eye and you'll hike me to a doctor and he'll say it's because I had an attachment to my mother. (*Moves restlessly to desk and picks up egg.*) Life becomes complicated the minute you're born, doesn't it? An egg doesn't know how lucky it is."

"But an egg misses a lot of fun."

"That's right," cries Claudia, cheerily; "an egg doesn't have you, an egg can't snuggle up to you in bed. Let's go up, quick!"

She has started to tear up her vouchers to expedite matters, and that irritates David. After all, vouchers might come in handy in tracing income tax deductions.

"I just marvel how grown men can be so scared of a little tax," says Claudia. "Why don't you just ignore the whole thing for once, and see what happens?"

The telephone has rung. Claudia is excited. It is late. Who can it be? David knows the signs. Claudia is immediately possessed of a fear that something has happened to her mother! "Listen, darling, when are you going to stop being a Mammababy?" he demands. "You're a married woman now. You've got a husband who loves you."

"I'm sorry, David. She's on my mind. I don't know why— Oh, please let me answer."

She has gone to the phone. The call is for Fritz. That's a

little funny, seeing neither Fritz nor Bertha has any friends near— It's a man's voice. Rather nice, too—

Bertha has come to answer for Fritz. She is talking in Hungarian, and with considerable agitation. She will call Fritz and let him answer on the kitchen phone.

"David, we've got a right to know what's going on," says Claudia, sidling toward the phone when Bertha has gone. When David does not object she gently lifts the receiver to her ear. A second later she hangs up.

"Not really, we haven't," she says. "I couldn't understand them, anyway—such jibberish." Claudia wouldn't want to appear too noble.

"You're a nice girl—I like you," says David, as he catches her to him and cups her face in his hands.

"That's not very exciting—just to like me," says Claudia, a little tremulously.

"Don't you believe it. When you like the person that you love—that's marriage— And it's exciting."

He has picked her up and carried her to the stairs. He has switched the room into darkness and started up as the curtain slowly falls.

ACT II

Early afternoon the following day Claudia and her two guests have finished lunch and are moving into the dining room. Claudia is wearing a simple sweater and skirt but Julia, her sister-in-law, "distinctly Back-Bay, is expensively and conservatively groomed," and Mme. Daruschka, a successful opera star of Russian origin, is more showily gowned. Daruschka is "essentially peasant, with china-blue eyes, pink skin and flaxen hair. She is given to sudden impulses of clowning, a little like an overgrown Newfoundland dog, and her speech is robust, joyful and chronically redundant."

The luncheon, by unanimous agreement of the guests, has been delicious. The Naughton farm, as Julia finds it, has been immensely improved. Daruschka, too, is quite charmed with the farm. Wants to buy it, in fact. Furniture and all. How much would it cost? She offers $15,000. That doesn't interest Claudia. Anyway, it's David's—

"What price does he put on the place?" Daruschka demands.

"I offered him $30,000 last night, and he said it was a deal," says Claudia.

Daruschka is a little startled, but she would be businesslike.

She offers $25,000. After a look around and a burst into song that proves to her the air agrees perfectly with her voice, she settles for $30,000. Claudia still thinks Daruschka is joking, but Daruschka isn't. Even now she is out looking over her property.

"But David doesn't want to sell the place; he loves it," protests Claudia to Julia. "Where would we go? What would we do?"

"When you get almost a hundred per cent profit in less than six months you don't ask so many questions," counsels Julia.

"Almost a hundred per cent profit is quite good, isn't it?"

"Not bad."

"But it wouldn't be fair. The poor thing doesn't know what it's all about. She says herself she's an ignoramus."

"She's the smartest ignoramus you'll ever meet."

Claudia is still trying to make up her mind. Of course a hundred per cent profit— That would be something with which to startle a person who thinks you haven't got enough sense to balance a checkbook. And, of course, living in the country does mean that you're far away from everyone— It's a lovely farm— But—Claudia never before realized how much she did want to sell—

Daruschka is back and bursting with enthusiasm. "Listen, everybody! I have been a fool not to buy a farm in the country before!"

"Where've you been?"

"All over the place! What a garden! What a kitchen!" She turns on Claudia. "I would like to move in right away, because I am going to Hollywood for all winter next week. How soon can you get out?"

"You're only joking, aren't you?" Claudia is pleading for sanity.

"Joking? I will show you if I am joking." Daruschka has crossed quickly to Claudia's desk and is writing out a check. It is for $500. "Here! This deposit arranges everything. And my lawyer will call your husband on Monday."

Claudia is still confused, but helpless in the sweep of the Daruschka enthusiasm. Even Julia is powerless to drag the singer back to their car that they may resume their journey. As an excuse to linger Daruschka doesn't want to go now until she has seen Claudia try on some gift pajamas that Julia has brought her. Let Claudia try on the pajamas, add her (Daruschka's) earrings, and a dash of perfumery and see what a change there will be. "And do something nice with your hair, for

God's sake," calls Daruschka, as Claudia starts upstairs.

Now Daruschka is at the window looking out over her new possessions. As she crosses to the terrace her excitement mounts— "Oh, what do you think? A car just drove up. And it is David . . . He is getting out. He is going in the garage! Look! He has turned back again. I can see his face. He is handsome! And tall! (*Waves.*) Yoohoooo! (*To* JULIA.) He thinks I am a crazy woman! (*Calls.*) Hurry up! Come in quick, I have just bought your house! (*To* JULIA.) He is *very* handsome."

There is more helloing and yahooing and then Jerry Seymoure appears at the terrace door—

"I do not blame Claudia for being madly in love with you," bubbles Daruschka, quite oblivious of her mistake. "I could fall in love with you myself. Come in, come in."

Fritz has brought in Daruschka's and Julia's wraps. Jerry is startled as he notices Fritz's white serving jacket. Daruschka promptly misreads his astonishment—

DARUSCHKA—You are surprised you have no house any more? You are surprised I bought it?

JERRY—You could knock me over with the proverbial feather. (*Recovers himself.*) I found your jack on the running board of my car last night, Fritz. I left it in the garage on the shelf.

FRITZ—Thank you, sir. I was looking for it. (*Exits.*)

DARUSCHKA (*with a nod to* JULIA)—Introduce me to the poor man. He doesn't seem to know who I am.

JERRY (*unaware of* JULIA, *who has withdrawn to fireplace to await developments*)—You underestimate your fame, Madame Daruschka.

DARUSCHKA—Listen to him, he is delightful! But just the same you are a terr'ble liar, you knew I was coming—I shall call you David, no?

JERRY—I've always been very fond of the name of David.

JULIA (*deciding he has gone far enough*)—I'm Claudia's sister-in-law, Julia Naughton. You're Jerry Seymoure. I met you at the Riddles' a few weeks ago.

JERRY (*not at all disconcerted*)—But of course! (*Shakes hands.*)

JULIA—I didn't know you lived up here.

JERRY—I don't. I've rented a little week-end shack to finish a novel.

DARUSCHKA (*outraged*)—Wait a minute, wait a minute!

Somebody is making a fool of me! Why did you pass yourself off as Claudia's husband?

JERRY—I didn't. You jumped to conclusions. (CLAUDIA *appears on the stairs, completely transformed into a seductive and glamorous young woman.*) As a matter-of-fact, I jumped to a few myself. Hello!

Now Claudia is confused, though she manages an answering "Hello." Daruschka, however, is positively excited. She scents romance and refuses to accept anything less. They have all been trying to fool her, but she knows. For one thing, she knows that this Jerry knows all the entrances and exits. And as for Claudia—

"Innocent . . . Bust or no bust, you have danced circles around us! Come now, confess."

"I don't know what you're talking about," answers Claudia, with complete simplicity.

"She doesn't know what we are talking about," Daruschka repeats to Julia, with "divine lewdness."

"It does look strange, darling," Julia admits. "He doesn't write very good novels, but he's extremely attractive. Why didn't you tell us about him?"

"Because I don't even know him."

They have gone now, completely disbelieving the story of Jerry's trouble with a flat tire. Even astrologically the signs are against them, in Daruschka's imagination. Claudia was born in December, the sign of the goat, and must be "all feelings and impulses." Jerry admits to Taurus, the sign of the bull. That makes it perfect.

There is an awkward silence for a moment, which Jerry refuses to cover with small talk. He feels that he has been made a monkey of; he has been robbed and that's all there is to it. He is leaning over the sofa ready to kiss Claudia. She would put him off, but he is not to be put off this time.

"You're tantalizing," insists Jerry, advancing firmly.

"Tantalizing?" Claudia is both mollified and agreeably astonished.

JERRY—And you're desirable. Utterly desirable.

CLAUDIA (*in sudden misgiving*)—And just what—

JERRY (*interrupting*)—Just what you think it means.

CLAUDIA—Oh. (*Reaches out for something else to talk about.*)

JERRY (*forestalling her again*)—And I don't want a glass of milk.

CLAUDIA (*surprised*)—How did you know I was going to ask you that?

JERRY—You had that look.

CLAUDIA (*hopefully*)—Are you sure you wouldn't like some?

JERRY (*firmly*)—I was never surer of anything in my life. . . . It's a lovely day. Run get a wrap. My car's outside.

CLAUDIA (*debating it*)—In the middle of the afternoon?

JERRY—What better time?

CLAUDIA (*deciding against it*)—I don't think so. David'll be home any minute. We can all three go for a nice long ride some evening.

JERRY—Hey!

CLAUDIA—What's the matter?

JERRY (*hoarsely*)—I don't like it.

CLAUDIA (*solicitously*)—Why, your forehead's perspiring!

JERRY—I'm not surprised.

CLAUDIA (*obligingly*)—I'll open a window.

JERRY—That won't help.

CLAUDIA (*abruptly*)—You know, I'm almost tempted to go for that ride. It might do David good to come home and find me gone.

JERRY (*weighing the implications a little dubiously*)—Is he the jealous type?

CLAUDIA (*bitterly*)—I wish he were.

JERRY (*relieved*)—Oh. So he's not in love with you.

CLAUDIA—He is! (*Adds lamely.*) But differently. (*Moodily.*) He likes my spirit.

JERRY (*putting the wrong two together*)—Good God. He sounds like a— (*Finds it difficult to vocalize.*)

CLAUDIA (*abstractedly*)—First-rate pansy? . . . (JERRY *stares at her in amazement.* CLAUDIA *smiles pleasantly.*) That's what he called you, last night.

JERRY (*grimly*)—Oh, he did, did he? Let's go.

Claudia has thought of another excuse. Her mother's coming. Jerry cannot understand that. He has a mother, too, but he doesn't care particularly about seeing her. His father was different. His father was real—

"So that's what's wrong with you," Claudia decides. "You've got a father image. And that's just as bad as a mother image.

You know, it's apt to upset your whole sex life if you're not careful."

"There's nothing the matter with my sex life," snaps Jerry. To prove it he catches Claudia to him and kisses her passionately. For a moment Claudia is startled. "Well, that's a funny business . . ." she says. ". . . Would you mind doing it again, please?"

"Why?" Jerry is a little distrustful.

"Because the most wonderful feeling shot right through me . . ."

"You uninhibited darling!"

Completely enchanted, Jerry has drawn her to him again.

"Not too much of a one, please."

"You'll take what you get and like it," answers Jerry, somewhat disgruntled. . . .

David's whistle is heard from the yard. Claudia is trying to pull away and Jerry, "with male dominance," has no intention of letting her go.

David is standing in the front door. "The smile fades from his face. He makes no sound. Only the waxy look around his nostrils and his utter stillness reveal that his world is toppling. Jerry wheels. His arms drop to his sides. Claudia moves toward David. She is a little self-conscious, but shows neither guilt nor guile."

"Hello, dear!" calls Claudia. She turns to Jerry. "This is my husband. I don't know your last name. . . ."

JERRY (*over a closing throat*)—Seymoure.

CLAUDIA (*to* DAVID)—This is Mr. Seymoure, David—(*Breaks off apprehensively.*) You're white as a ghost, is anything wrong?

DAVID (*pushing her aside. His eyes on* JERRY)—Get out.

CLAUDIA (*smartly*)—I won't get out, why should I? (*Her fears focusing.*) Why didn't Mamma come?

DAVID (*in the same ominous tone*)—Get out! (*Moves her forcibly from his path.*)

JERRY (*not enjoying any of it*)—Hold on a minute, there's another side to this story—

CLAUDIA (*impatiently*)—David, for heaven's sake, stop wiggling your nostrils like that, you look silly!

DAVID (*with a control that augurs no good*)—Do you want to go by yourself, or do you want me to carry you?

CLAUDIA (*drawing herself up with offended dignity*)—*Please.*

DAVID (*his fingers brutal against her arm*)—I'll give you just five seconds to go upstairs and take off that masquerade costume! (*Adds in breaking fury.*) And wash that stuff off your face!

CLAUDIA (*stunned and affronted*)—How dare you talk to me like that! (*The enormity of the breach sweeps over her.*) In front of a perfect stranger, too! I'll never forgive you until you beg my pardon! (*She flies up to her room, leaving them to face a completely unexpected reversal of the situation—herself in the rôle of the outraged wife, and* DAVID *in the position of erring husband. For a moment, there is a small, fleet silence, while* DAVID *seeks to readjust himself. It serves to lower their emotions an octave toward the normal.* JERRY *is the first to find his voice.*)

JERRY—Incredible. You come in and find her in the arms of another man, and you should beg her pardon. (*Curiosity surmounting strain.*) Look here, are you going to?

DAVID (*steadily*)—I might. After I get to the bottom of this.

JERRY (*with a kind of astonished reverence*)—That's love. (*Hastily, as* DAVID *advances.*) You don't have to throw me out. I'm going.

DAVID—Not so quickly. (*Makes a move to block his path.*)

JERRY (*reasonable, but agitated*)—Now hold on a minute, I don't blame you for wanting to take a crack at me, but in the name of justice, listen to my side of it— (*For an instant "his side of it" eludes him, but he manages to continue with mounting indignation.*) By God, I ought to take a crack at *you!* You oughtn't to let her loose without a keeper, she's a menace to a man's sanity. I don't think she even knows what it's all about. . . .

DAVID (*fists clenched*)—She doesn't. And if you weren't such a bastard you'd have realized it.

JERRY (*hoarsely*)—But how was I to know? She acts like she does, she talks like she does— She's led me one hell of a dance. I'm shot. (*Sinks into a chair.*) Believe me, I'm the nearest thing to mopping my forehead I've ever been in my life. And by God, I'm going to do it! (*Takes out his handkerchief and mops.*)

DAVID (*fists slowly unclenching*)—I know that feeling.

JERRY (*elliptically*)—I suppose you thought I was the—same sort I thought you were?

DAVID (*shortly*)—More or less.

JERRY—Extraordinary, how she did it.

DAVID—Want a drink?

JERRY (*looking up as if he hadn't heard correctly*)—Thank you. (*Adds in deep gratitude.*) Straight.

Jerry is embarrassed. He gulps his drink. He hopes that David will understand the situation. It was quite difficult for him to accept Claudia's naïveté, but, being such a sweet kid, he thought he ought to know.

Claudia comes upon them during Jerry's hesitant explanations and apologies. She notes David's puzzled but apparently complaisant attitude—

"Why don't you two kiss each other?" she blurts.

"I could do a lot worse. And so could you, young lady," answers Jerry.

"I resent that remark. And I don't like to be called 'young lady' in that tone of voice."

"I'm sorry. I'm sorry about a lot of things. Forgive me. Both of you. Au 'voir."

Now Jerry has left them. Claudia is petulant. David, she charges, has poisoned Jerry's mind against her, just as everything was going beautifully. Why did she let Jerry kiss her? She didn't. It was Jerry's idea.

David can understand that. "You're young. You're lovely," he says.

"Why didn't you ever tell me that before?"

"Was it necessary?"

"Yes. It was. It does things for you, when a man thinks you're desirable."

Now Claudia is convinced that David is jealous and that pleases her. But if he is, why didn't he do something about it. He could have knocked Jerry down at least—

"Don't you know you could have smashed something very fine and beautiful between us?" David is saying.

"Smashed it? Why, I built it up! I only did it for your sake," insists Claudia.

DAVID (*slowly*)—I think you really believe that.

CLAUDIA—But it's no fun to be in love with a woman no other man would give house room to! Oh, David, you should have seen me. Once I got going, I simply sizzled!

DAVID—Suppose you tell me about it. (*Finding it hard.*) Did you—like it when he kissed you?

CLAUDIA (*enthusiastically*)—The most wonderful feeling shot clear through me, from my eyebrows to my toes. And then what do you think happened?

DAVID (*the knife twisting in him*)—I don't know.

CLAUDIA—Instead of the feeling going to Jerry, it shot right back to *you*. (DAVID *looks at her. She seems a little lost.*) You don't get it.

DAVID (*starkly*)—No. I don't get it.

CLAUDIA (*urgently*)—But it's perfectly clear! Kissing Jerry made me more in love with you. I even asked him to kiss me again, to make sure. And the same thing happened.

DAVID—What same thing?

CLAUDIA (*with all her heart*)—I was crazy about you. . . . Can't you understand the way it worked?

DAVID (*after a moment*)—Come to think of it—it happened to me once like that, too.

CLAUDIA (*her heart stopping*)—Oh.

It was a girl sitting opposite him in the subway who had stirred David. But that experience only sent him home loving Claudia the more. Claudia is relieved to hear that. ". . . Marriage is a sort of rebirth of two people," she concludes, finally. "Getting born once is hard enough. Getting born twice is a terrible job." . . .

Now Claudia has a new worry. David is expecting an important call that may take him into town. That might mean that he has heard something from Claudia's mother. Perhaps her engagement with the doctor— Claudia is worried. She has a feeling her mother's life of late has been lonely—

"Mother's had a lot of happiness, too, dear," says David, his voice deepening. "And if she's a little lonely now—well, maybe loneliness is a lesson we all have to learn."

"Don't say that!"

"But it's true. You might as well face it. You're going to lose one of us first. Mother or me. Take your choice."

"Neither!" answers Claudia, passionately.

"Look, darling; when are you going to start real work on this marriage of ours? Grow up to be a big girl?"

"Is it too much to ask for everything to be just the way it is now—always?"

"Yes, dear," says David, quietly. "It's too much to ask. Life won't give it to you."

Claudia is threatened with tears. "How did we get on this subject anyway?" she demands. "Kiss me. Hold me tight."

She is in David's arms now. "His eyes, looking off into space, are grave. With effort he lifts himself from the sober thoughts which claim him."

David manages to lift his mood by pretending to be highly offended by the perfumery Claudia is using. She smells, he says, like a little tart. And the earrings! And the pajamas! She had better be getting rid of all of them. Which reminds Claudia—

She has sold the farm!

That's a good joke, too, David agrees, but finally Claudia manages to convince him that she means it. The deal with Daruschka has been made—

"She wants to buy everything," Claudia explains, a little breathlessly; "even the furnishings and the livestock—but we can always get new furniture, and after all, what could we do with a cow in New York— And don't interrupt, what do you think she's paying—you can't guess. Thirty thousand dollars!"

David won't believe it. The whole thing's preposterous. And now Claudia is the angry one—

"Oh, stop treating me like a half-wit!" she exclaims. "Won't you ever learn a lesson? First you thought I had no sex, and look what I did to a perfectly strange man! You thought I couldn't even balance a checkbook, and I've made you almost a hundred per cent profit on an investment! The trouble with you is, you don't appreciate me, that's the whole thing in a nutshell."

"Nutshell is right!"

"There you go."

"But I tell you, it's a lot of nonsense! You'll never hear from her again."

"Does this look like we'll never hear from her again?"

There's the check that binds the bargain, and that puts another complexion on the situation. Now David is worried. He can't believe that Claudia really wants to sell the farm.

Claudia is a little evasive. Of course twelve thousand dollars is a lot of profit. They could go to a hotel for a couple of days and then get an apartment. After all, aren't they a little young to bury themselves in the country?

"Why don't you tell me the truth about it, dear?" David has suddenly checked the flow of excuses. "You've given me every reason but the real one. You want to be near Mother, is that it?"

"But, David, you just can't wave away twelve thousand dollars. It isn't *sensible!*"

Claudia finally extracts a compromise acceptance of the situation from David, though there is not much joy in the prospect for him. He has left her now to explain to Bertha that Daruschka will want them to stay, but even as she calls Bertha Claudia is conscious of a new complication. She has suddenly grown faint and must steady herself against a chair. She remembers that she woke up that morning feeling a little funny. Perhaps it was the hot bread she ate, or the pickle.

Bertha, looking very wise, decides that it was nothing that she had eaten that accounts for Claudia's condition. It is just a little morning sickness—

"Bertha . . . Are you sure?" . . . Claudia is breathlessly excited.

"I bet you twenty cents. I told Fritz already."

"I never dreamed . . . Could it really be?"

"With my first baby it was three months before I knew," says Bertha.

David is coming and Bertha must be sent away. This is a very private time in a woman's life. David must be told. She manages the telling, after a good deal of playful fencing, and David is as excited as she, though he would try hard not to appear so.

"This scene is all wrong," Claudia concludes. "Aren't you happy? Don't you want a baby?"

"Not now." David is leaving much unsaid.

CLAUDIA—Why, David?

DAVID—You're too young.

CLAUDIA (*mercuric as always*)—But I want to have children young. With the proper management I can be a grandmother at forty!

DAVID—That's just dandy.

CLAUDIA (*with depths*)—Darling, don't feel like that. I'm old. Inside of me, I'm old. As if I'd lived before.

DAVID—Sometimes I think that's true.

CLAUDIA—It's going to be all right, really. Let it happen when it wants to.

DAVID—There's quite a little wisdom in that.

CLAUDIA—Unless you're not as happy about it as I am. Remember what you said before? About two people having to want the same thing, or it's no go?

DAVID (*spending a moment in heaven*)—I want it. (*Suddenly aware that he's been swept off his feet.*) Say, wait a minute. How do you get that way?

CLAUDIA (*demurely*)—You should know.

DAVID—In words of one syllable, why didn't you tell me you were going to have this child before I went upstairs?

CLAUDIA (*parroting him*)—In words of one syllable, I did not know I was going to have twins before you went upstairs.

DAVID—Then it all happened while I was washing my hands?

CLAUDIA—Yes.

DAVID—*What* happened?

CLAUDIA—I was dizzy.

DAVID—I'm dizzy too, but that doesn't make me pregnant!

CLAUDIA—This was a special kind of dizziness. Bertha said so.

DAVID—Bertha said so? And you take Bertha's word for it, you crazy cluck!

CLAUDIA—But I know it's true. I have feelings when things are so.

DAVID—I wish you didn't have so damn many feelings.

CLAUDIA—I think I must have felt it when I sold the house to Daruschka.

DAVID (*trying to find the right words*)—But, Claudia, doesn't the thought of having children make you want to keep the farm?

CLAUDIA—Oh, I know; milk fresh from the cow, and eggs a minute old, and all that sort of thing. But just think how much we're going to *need* that extra money now.

DAVID—But money isn't everything. We've got enough to scrape through on.

CLAUDIA—You still don't want to sell it, do you?

DAVID—Now less than ever.

CLAUDIA (*slowly*)—And with me—it's—more than ever.

DAVID (*quietly*)—That's not so good. (*They look at each other.*)

CLAUDIA (*in a small, miserable voice*)—But it's natural for a girl to want to be near her mother when she's having her first baby? (*Compelling his eyes.*) Isn't it, David? Tell me if it isn't. Please.

DAVID (*after a long moment. A little thickly*)—I guess it is, darling. Quite natural. And normal.

CLAUDIA (*softly*)—I'm glad. I love you, David. (*With a sudden genuine impulse.*) Darling, let's go outside before the sun goes down. I suddenly know that feeling you had about being close to the land.

DAVID—You go ahead. I want to make out Fritz's check first.

CLAUDIA—All right, I'll meet you at the barn. I want to talk to Majesty. Majesty and I have quite a lot in common now.

Claudia drifts toward the terrace, "surrounded by an almost palpable cloak of happiness." David opens the door for her. "There is a kind of beauty in the gesture, surpassing chivalry."

David stands for a moment looking after Claudia. He turns then to the phone. Before he can find a number Claudia's mother is calling. Being assured that Claudia is not in the room she talks freely. For a moment David listens, his face wearing a serious, troubled expression. Then he insists that he will come right in. Claudia thinks he has an engagement with a client anyway. Then suddenly he changes his mind—

"Hold on a minute, though, I'll have her on my tail. She said something about going along to have a visit with you. . . . I tell you what; you lie down and rest a while, and catch the six-ten out here. . . . Because I say so. This is no time for you to be alone. . . . No, I won't tell her. She won't know anything until you want her to know it. . . . Now look here. If you don't come out, I'm coming in, and that's final. (*Hesitates.*) Unless, of course, it's too much for you after a rotten day. (*He shakes his head at her answer, in a kind of wonderment.*) Well, Mrs. Brown, I take my hat off to you, that's all I can say. I hope when my time comes I can take it like that. . . . (*Smiles a little.*) Boloney, yourself. . . . (*Clears his throat.*) Good. We'll meet you. . . . Of course I won't. Not a word. (*With robust assurance.*) Sure I can carry it off. Don't you worry. . . . So long, Mother. (*He hangs up the receiver, his face graven in lines of grief. He takes out his pipe, using the scraper on it half-heartedly, and then puts it down without filling it. He turns swiftly as the doors of the dining room open, and* CLAUDIA *stands in the threshold. One glance at her stricken, staring eyes and it is obvious that she knows. But* DAVID *nevertheless attempts to dissemble.*) That was Mother on the wire, she's coming out on the six-ten . . . (*He falters, aware of the futility of trying to soften the blow. He moves slowly toward her, his whole heart going out to her in a single whispered challenge to her courage.*) Claudia? . . ."

Claudia speaks "as if breath were at a premium within her: 'I heard the phone. I came back. You always said I'd listen . . . once too often—' "

"Oh, my darling . . ."

"With a small cry of pity, David tries to draw her to him,

but she stands, numb and still, in his embrace, and he realizes that in this deep moment of her bereavement, he is but an alien, an intruder. Slowly, out of his vast love and understanding, he withdraws from her, permitting her the dignity of meeting alone the supreme test of an approaching womanhood. With the slight, almost imperceptible lifting of her closed, still face, the curtain slowly falls."

ACT III

Later that evening, after the lights are on, Bertha is taking a tray supper to Mrs. Brown, who has arrived on an earlier train and gone directly to her room.

David and Claudia have been walking. Now they are back and David is helping Claudia off with her coat with something akin to paternal solicitude. Claudia "is bloodless, and stony, taut with a control that has not yet given way to tears."

All of life has been changed for Claudia in just a few hours, nor does David's philosophy that "everything's always changing" lessen her misery. "Maybe I'll die before Mamma," she says, with a kind of bitter hope.

"All right, and I might die before either of you. Or all of us be destroyed by hurricane, or flood, or war," counters David.

CLAUDIA (*turning away*)—You're trying to tell me that losing your mother isn't really very important against all the other dreadful things that are happening in the world.

DAVID (*his hands on her averted shoulders*)—No, I'm not. Because it is important. Birth and death—that's the whole cycle of life; and whatever happens beyond that cycle, is just so much embroidery. (*With a short laugh.*) There's a lot of embroidery these days, I'll admit. But if you can take this, darling, you can take anything.

CLAUDIA (*turning in passionate rebellion*)—I can't take it, I won't take it! It isn't right for her to die!

DAVID—Who's running this universe? You or God?

CLAUDIA—There isn't any God.

DAVID—Hey, wait a minute. He's given you a home, a husband, a baby—

CLAUDIA—Don't fool yourself. (*In bleak disillusion.*) Nothing—and no one—really belongs to anyone.

DAVID—If you've learned that, you've learned a lot, my dearest.

CLAUDIA—Then what's the sense of pouring your heart and

soul out in what you don't possess and never can possess?

DAVID—Because a loan carries a greater obligation than a gift.

CLAUDIA—I'll lend you a baby and take back your mother, is that it?

DAVID—Something like it.

CLAUDIA—No, thank you. I don't want children on those terms. I'm sorry I even went to the doctor.

DAVID—But he didn't give you the baby; I'm the guy that pulled that trick.

CLAUDIA (*on a little whimper of anguish*)—Oh, David, don't try to be gay. (*Sinks to sofa.*) There's so much pain inside of me.

DAVID (*kneeling beside her*)—Then make friends with it, darling, and it'll stop hurting you.

CLAUDIA (*in a whisper*)—Make friends with pain? As if a person could.

DAVID—Mother has, all these weeks. And it's made her strong and quiet inside.

CLAUDIA—But why must it be!

DAVID—There's a reason behind it all.

CLAUDIA—It sounds like you're the one that believes in God all of a sudden.

DAVID (*simply*)—All of a sudden, I think I do.

CLAUDIA (*harshly*)—Then let him work one of his miracles.

DAVID—It mightn't be the miracle you're asking for.

A moment later Claudia's torrent of grief is loosed in heartbroken, gulping sobs, and in David's arms she finds a moment's release. When she has recovered her poise, and has learned from Bertha that her mother is already there, she quickly tries to remove the traces of her tears.

Perhaps when they tell Mother about the baby, that will help. Bertha had told Mrs. Brown that she should stay on, all the time, with her daughter, but Mrs. Brown did not agree. She had told Bertha that she was going on a trip—

"She said the country is too quiet for her; she wants to treat herself to a nice time in Florida," reports Bertha. "But, of course, when she hears about the baby she will not want to go away, that is sure. . . ."

Claudia's doubts are clearing. They will all go on just as they are. "Bertha's asking Mamma to come here to live with us made everything clear all at once," says Claudia. "That's the way it ought to be, that's what a home is for. It holds you when you need it. It's a place to be born in and to die in. We have no right to give it up. I was wrong, David."

"But there'll be memories."

"Memories can't hurt you. You said you could make friends with pain. Then you can make friends with memories too."

At the top of the stairs, Mrs. Brown stands for a moment looking down at them, as if trying to gauge the situation that lies before her. "She has changed to a simple gray silk dress. Perhaps it is merely the softness of her gown, or the stillness within her that lends her a subtle quality of remoteness in place of her usual crisp efficiency."

There is "a barely imperceptible moment of struggle," and then Claudia has plunged into the give and take that has always marked her relationship with her mother. There is a good deal of good-natured banter about the cat that Bertha had told Mrs. Brown David and Claudia had gone to visit. When that white lie is exploded they are at particular pains trying to stir her curiosity about the coming of the twins.

"Did Dr. Morrison say he'd charge the same price for twins, David?" Claudia asks, quite matter-of-factly.

"You can have up to five," answers David.

But Mother is not to be baited. Twins, they would do well to remember, run in families. And she continues knitting almost furiously on the sweater she is finishing for Claudia. It is not until Claudia has been sent upstairs for another ball of yarn that David is able really to convince Mrs. Brown that a grandchild is on the way. For a moment she is anxious for Claudia. Is the doctor a good doctor? Is Claudia all right?

"It'll be so hard to tell her now," she says, after a long pause. "I'm a coward, David."

"When it comes to Claudia, I guess you are. You haven't got the guts to let her do her own suffering."

"She's not disciplined to pain. Life's been gentle with her up to now."

"And you'd like to go on taking all the hard knocks for her. Leave her only the easy ones."

"Wouldn't you?"

"Sure. Only I know I can't. I know I don't have to. She'll meet life on its own terms. She wouldn't be your daughter if she couldn't."

They get around after a while to telling Mother about Daruschka having bought the farm. And they add the exciting item of David walking in and finding Claudia being passionately kissed by a British Englishman. Neither of these events proves greatly exciting to Mrs. Brown. Now Fritz has come to tell her that Bertha is making apple strudel and if she wants to see how they are rolled she had better come to the kitchen . . .

It has come to Mrs. Brown's notice that Fritz and Bertha have a son; that it was to help that son that they needed an advance on their wages. She, Mrs. Brown, feels that something should be done to help Fritz and Bertha with this problem—

"If that boy's in bad company, and Fritz and Bertha are worried about him, I'd offer him a job right here on this farm—digging potatoes, clearing the woods, I wouldn't care what," says Mrs. Brown. "You can use two men outdoors, you've said so yourself."

"But, my dear lady, be reasonable," pleads David. "Suppose this lad's done something wrong, something actually wrong?"

"Like forging a check or something," adds Claudia.

"When you were a little girl you stole a dollar right out of my pocketbook. Big as life," says Mrs. Brown, as though blurting out a family scandal. "And did I put you in a reform school? No. I just tried to show you that nice little girls didn't steal."

"You're a marvelous old duck, Mrs. Brown," declares David, with an emotion he takes pains to hide. "Allow me to tweak your nose."

"And if it's the extra salary you're worried about," says Mrs. Brown, smartly slapping down David's hand and returning furiously to her knitting— "You don't have to worry about money."

"She's going to leave us a million dollars," almost shouts Claudia.

"How'd you guess it?"

"That's why we're so nice to you. To keep on the right side of you."

"I wouldn't put it past you. (*Rises.*) I've left my glasses in the kitchen."

Fritz has come and David has gone into the matter of his son. They would like him to go to an agricultural college, Fritz reports, but he knows that Bertha will be very happy at Mr. Naughton's suggestion that he come and work around the farm. Fritz feels that they had made a mistake about the boy. He had been headstrong, but he did not know what he was doing and when he got into trouble Fritz took the crime on himself. Now he knows he should have let his son take the punishment. It would have been better. . . .

David's sister Julia is back from Boston. She is impressed

with the happy family scene she has come upon. She decided against the Boston week-end after she got there and heard from her husband. She has stopped by on her way back to advise them against selling the farm. She's glad to hear that David is sending back Daruschka's check.

It is when Claudia is taking Julia to the door that Mrs. Brown tells David she is convinced Claudia knows their secret.

"Yes, Mother, she knows," David admits. A silence falls between them.

MRS. BROWN—And she's let me go . . .

DAVID (*quietly*)—I think so.

MRS. BROWN (*like a prayer*)—It makes all the difference, David.

DAVID (*with a profound humility of wanting to know*)—Does it, Mother?

MRS. BROWN—Yes, it's like a miracle. It's just as if she were the mother, and I were the child.

DAVID—Maybe that's the way it ought to be. If it's right.

MRS. BROWN—It's right, David. Suddenly, I'm quite sure of that.

DAVID (*gruffly*)—Just the same, I'll miss you a hell of a lot around here. I guess you know that, don't you?

MRS. BROWN (*with all her love for him behind her words*)—You can't get rid of me so easily. I'll be sticking my two cents in every so often, you wait and see.

DAVID (*humorously, but as if, inside, he wants desperately to believe*)—How'll I know?

MRS. BROWN—I'll tweak your nose.

DAVID (*huskily*)—You do that.

CLAUDIA (*entering*)—Julia's very sweet.

DAVID—Yes, she was really almost human tonight. After ten years I'm beginning to see why Hartley married her.

MRS. BROWN—I wonder how you talk about me behind my back?

CLAUDIA (*abruptly*)—Hey!

MRS. BROWN—What's the matter?

CLAUDIA—How long before you begin to feel life? . . .

MRS. BROWN—Four and a half months. Why?

CLAUDIA—That's ridiculous, I just felt it.

DAVID—Lady, that wasn't life, that was bread and jelly.

MRS. BROWN—If that kind of talk is going to begin again, I'm going upstairs. (*Gathers up her knitting.*)

CLAUDIA—I'll have Bertha bring you some hot milk—with an egg in it.

MRS. BROWN—You'll do nothing of the kind.

CLAUDIA—It'll make you sleep.

MRS. BROWN (*crisply*)—I don't need anything to make me sleep, thank you.

CLAUDIA (*coming close to her for a brief, fleeting moment*)—Will you really rest well?

MRS. BROWN (*in full answer*)—Like an infant . . . with not a worry in my heart. (*Starts up the stairs.*)

DAVID—Pleasant dreams, Mother. (*He moves to* CLAUDIA *and puts his arm around her.* CLAUDIA *slips her hand in his. Together, they stand there, looking up at* MRS. BROWN.)

CLAUDIA (*softly*)—So long, Mrs. Brown. . . .

MRS. BROWN (*with a little smile*)—So long, Mrs. Naughton. . . .

"Fritz, in his rough jacket, has come to the terrace door with an armful of wood, which he has brought in from outdoors. Slowly, as he pulls off his cap,"

THE CURTAIN FALLS

MR. AND MRS. NORTH

A Comedy in Three Acts

By Owen Davis

(Based on a novel by Frances and Richard Lockridge)

THIS story was told about the time Owen Davis was putting a novel called "The Norths Meet Murder," by Frances and Richard Lockridge, into play form: The Lockridges have a place near Brewster, N. Y. Mrs. Lockridge has a garden. Last Spring her irises were lovely—but—not as lovely as those in a neighbor's garden. That, her friends told her, was because the neighbor, who happened to be Rex Stout, had a lot of money with which to promote his garden. He got the money by writing mystery stories. All right, Mrs. Lockridge would write a mystery story. And with Mr. Lockridge's co-operation she did. She wrote a mystery story about the Norths, who previously had been the leading characters in a series of sketches Mr. Lockridge had sold to the *New Yorker Magazine.*

Mr. Davis had the play finished and ready for a Broadway trial last Fall, but unfortunately its arrival was delayed until January. Which gave another murder play, the sensationally popular "Arsenic and Old Lace," a chance to beat it to Broadway by two days. With two murder plays for the playgoers to talk about, one fantastic and sensational, the other believable and simple, naturally the more exciting exhibit had the better of the contrast. "Mr. and Mrs. North," however, fared handsomely at the hands of the critics, and grew steadily in popular esteem during the next several weeks.

There is a pleasantly unforced realism in the telling of Mr. and Mrs. North's experience with murder. Their contacts with cadavers and constables may take somewhat extravagant turns now and again, but generally they are such experiences as it is easy for one young married couple to think of another young married couple having had. Being exceptionally normal and charming, the Norths provide their friends with a pleasant evening.

Their apartment in Greenwich Village, New York, definitely represents a modern trend in apartments, but is neither extravagantly contrived or furnished. Looking across the living room the door letting into the front hallway is at your right. There is a wide central archway at back, to which two low steps lead. Back of the archway is a shallow dining room, and between the living and dining room a fairly conspicuous closet in which the Norths keep their liquor supply. There is a large and inviting sofa in the living room, with a coffee table in front of it, a desk alongside the left wall, and a familiar assortment of easy chairs and casual tables.

It is a sunny apartment this October afternoon, and empty. But presently a fumbling with a key is heard at the door. Mr. North, a small, eager, earnest young man in his thirties, lets himself in. He is carrying a suitcase, a brief case and a bunch of flowers in florists' green paper.

Mr. North puts his things down, calls inquiringly for "Pam!" decides that there is no one at home and is prepared to settle and wait when a loud knocking at the door is followed by the appearance of Mr. Buono, a fat and jolly Italian janitor.

Mr. Buono is the bearer of a large framed portrait that has been left for delivery when the Norths should return home. It is probably something Mrs. North knows about. If Mr. North would leave a key with Mr. Buono when he and Mrs. North are going out—

But Mr. North has had his own trouble with keys. So far he has had four made for Mrs. North, who has promptly lost them all and is frequently found waiting on the landing for Mr. North to come home and let her in.

There is also something else on Mr. Buono's mind. The day before, when he was working in the Clarks' apartment below, he had heard Mr. North come in. Shortly after, he had heard a cry and a fall. The Clarks' chandelier had been badly shaken. Mr. Buono, being worried, had run up the stairs and knocked on the North door, calling to Mr. North. But no one answered him. Why did no one answer?

No one answered, Mr. North is convinced, because there was no one there. He was in Philadelphia and Mrs. North had taken the car and gone to her mother's. It may have been Pete, the cat, that Mr. Buono heard. Or it is possible Mr. Buono had been drinking.

"Pete is a very smart cat, Mr. North," Mr. Buono agrees, "but he don't speak good English like I hear. Anyway, Mrs. North brought Pete down to Mrs. Buono before she go."

"Well, this window was open. I guess it was the wind."

"Very bad wind. It come in the house and blow something down that shake Mr. Clark's chandelier—then it come in some more and—puff—blow everything up just like it was before."

An auto horn is heard outside the window. Mrs. North has arrived.

The embrace of the Norths—Pam and Jerry—is mildly exuberant. They have missed each other, even though it was just for one night. Especially did Pam, a small, pert, fascinatingly unconventional person, miss Jerry on the ride back from her mother's.

"That doesn't mean that you needed me, does it?" quickly inquires Jerry, as any husband might ask of any wife whose driving was like Pam's.

"Of course it doesn't," answers Pam, with assurance.

NORTH—No troubles? No little incidents?

PAM—Not a thing happened.

NORTH—Oh!

PAM (*smiling*)—I do wish I could think of something. I know you'd like me to think of something, but it was just as though you had been driving yourself, except, of course, there was the flipper.

NORTH—The what?

PAM—The flipper.

NORTH—I am afraid you've got me there.

PAM—I always think of it as the flipper, probably you think of it as something entirely different.

NORTH—I'm afraid I must. What would it be—the "flipper"?

PAM (*taking off hat and coat*)—That thing on the side of the windows. You know, that glass thing. It sticks out like a sort of an ear. Well, one of them came loose.

NORTH—It's a good thing you were standing still.

PAM—Oh, but I wasn't. I just pulled it off and put it behind the seat. Of course, the apple made it a little bit harder.

NORTH (*questioningly*)—Apple?

PAM—I was eating it, and it sort of got in the way.

NORTH—Look! The—flipper—came loose—you pulled it off while you were eating an apple and without stopping—

PAM—But I did stop.

NORTH—I should think you would—my God!

PAM—Yes. I had to stop. The road ended in a lot of men.

NORTH—Men?

PAM—It seems I was on the wrong road. The road ended there and the men were adding some more to it.

NORTH (*worried*)—A good thing you had space to stop and turn around.

PAM—Oh, I didn't have to turn around. You see, the road was sort of wet and the car just skidded—and then, I just drove back! (*The doorbell rings.* NORTH *admits* BUONO.)

BUONO—Excuse me, Mrs. North.

PAM—Oh, Mr. Buono.

BUONO—I no can put your car in the garage. There is no gas. I try to make her go, but she no go. She don't even got a little drop of gas.

NORTH—No gas?

PAM (*cheerfully*)—I knew there wasn't much left. The little red marker was clear down to the bottom.

BUONO—That's all right, Mrs. North, just so long as you know. I fix it for you. I make a push and she goes right in the garage.

PAM—Thank you, Mr. Buono, I was sure you could do it.

BUONO—It's a pleasure. (BUONO *exits.* PAM *turns and looks at* NORTH, *who is standing in deep thought.*)

NORTH—Do you know, this is the most amazing thing I ever heard of.

PAM—What?

NORTH—How far did you drive?

PAM—Why, about 90 miles, I think.

NORTH—And you drove 90 miles and you ran out of gas right at your own doorstep!

PAM—I don't see that's so strange. I thought I'd probably run out of gas somewhere, so I bought a gallon.

NORTH—Why just one gallon?

PAM—I only had 20 cents.

NORTH—That makes it a miracle. You go out and drive 90 miles with 20 cents, and you buy a gallon of gas with it, and you have just exactly enough gas to get you to your own doorstep!

PAM—Well, I don't see anything so miraculous in that. That's as far as I wanted to go.

NORTH (*kissing her with amused resignation*)—You're wonderful!

Jerry has started to cross the room when he notices a lady's gold compact on the floor. He picks it up and passes it to Pam.

It isn't hers. So far as she knows she has never seen it before. Which reminds Jerry of Mr. Buono's story about hearing someone in the Norths' apartment the afternoon before. Perhaps—

But that idea is silly to Pam. The compact must belong to Dorothy, the maid, although it's funny Pam hadn't seen it when she straightened up the room after Dorothy had left. Maybe—

There is a ring at the door. Claire Brent and Louis Berex are calling—she an attractive young matron, he a pleasant, rather serious escort. It is evident that Claire is worried and eager to talk with Pam, and also that she is greatly surprised to find Jerry home. She thought he was in Philadelphia. And so he was until a few hours ago. And what is all this whispering about? What are the girls hatching? Jerry wants to know.

Little by little the story is revealed. Claire had asked Pam to help her with a certain matter, and Pam had agreed. The certain matter concerned Stan Brent, Claire's husband. Pam was going to see Stan and sort of argue with him—

"North, I don't know how much you know about all this," Louis is saying. "But Stan Brent is—do you ladies want to go somewhere—while I tell North what Brent is?"

"I know something," admits Jerry. "Pam *tells* things. And I'd like to help, but I won't have Pam mix herself up in it. That sort of thing never works. You thought if Pam talked to him—as an outsider, coolly, she might persuade him to give you a divorce, Claire, wasn't that it?"

"Well—"

"Well, mightn't it help? You say yourself you want to help, so why wouldn't you want me to?"

"Because I don't think it would help, really. I think he'd merely resent an outsider coming in, and be—harder to handle than ever. I think, however they feel, outsiders should stay outside."

"That's right. If I were married to Claire I'd feel the same way. We'll work it out. Things are going to be all right."

"But things aren't going to be all right, Louis," cries Claire, desperately. "You just say that, but things are all wrong. I didn't want to drag Pam in—but she offered it and—she was a straw to clutch at." She is trying to regain lightness. "You don't mind being a straw, do you, Pam?"

"Of course not, Claire." She turns to Jerry. "I just wanted to see Stanley Brent and talk to him. Can't I see people and talk to them without everybody getting in a stew? It's just like seeing anybody and talking to them—and, Jerry, I told you last week I was going to do it."

But Claire has changed her mind. She is convinced that she and Louis should go right now down to Stan's office. And Louis agrees. They are moving toward the door when Jerry again notices the gold compact on the table. It isn't Claire's, is it? No, it isn't Claire's. And with more apologies Claire and Louis are gone. . . .

Pam has discovered the wrapped picture. Of course they don't have to keep it. Mr. Lacey had sent it out on approval. Before Jerry is fully aware of what is happening, he has unwrapped the picture and stood it on the mantel. It is the likeness of a white-bearded man with an old-fashioned black stock, white collar and clothes of the period of the 1890's.

"You know, Jerry, I always did like a dull gold frame," enthuses an enraptured Pam.

"Who is it?" Jerry wants to know.

"It's a picture. It gives the room depth. The room needs depth."

North—Look. This is not just a picture. It's a picture of someone. *Whom* is it a picture of?

Pam—That doesn't matter.

North—Listen, if we're going to hang it up we'll have to know who it is. You can't hang just any strange man over the mantel.

Pam—Wouldn't you hang a Sargent? Wouldn't you hang a Rembrandt?—if somebody gave it to you for saving their life, or something?

North—You're not arguing that this is a Rembrandt, are you?

Pam—Well, I should say not. The idea of your insisting it's a Rembrandt—Jerry! (*She straightens the picture.*)

North (*somewhat upset*)—Steady, boy, steady. All I'm trying to say is that we can't hang a portrait of somebody we don't know, unless, of course, it was by an artist that everybody knows. Now there are portraits that are pictures and when people look at them they are surprised and delighted and say maybe "My God," and then there are other kinds and people say "Who is it?" This is a "Who is it?"—and you can't hang a "Who is it?" in a room unless you know who it is!

Pam—Oh, Jerry, I don't think that makes a particle of difference. (*She gathers wrapping paper and string.*)

North—People would think it was an ancestor. We can't be all the time explaining.

to by Vandamm Studio.*

"MR. AND MRS. NORTH"

am: That's the point! Nobody named Edwards has lived here since we have. Don't you see Edwards is the murderer's name? He put his name in the slot over the letter box so the man vas going to kill would see it and ring the bell.

(Philip Ober, Millard Mitchell, Peggy Conklin, Albert Hackett)

PAM—Oh, don't be silly. How could anyone possibly think that funny old man is our ancestor!—Anyway, we've just got it on approval.

Jerry has sat down beside Pam on the sofa, and put his feet comfortably on the coffee table. Now he would like to know just what Pam did while he was gone. She had gone to her mother's, he knows that, but evidently she did not go until quite late. What was she doing before that? Well, Pam had been shopping. For stockings, mostly. But not finding any stockings she liked she bought a couple of volumes of Felicia Hemans' poetry—all calf, 25 cents. Then she—

The doorbell rings. Jane and Ben Wilson and Clinton Edwards are calling. They are on their way to the Tompkins' cocktail party. They have come to pick up the Norths. The Norths had forgotten all about the Tompkins' party and certainly are not in any state of dress to go now, but Pam doesn't see why they can't pretend they haven't come home at all and are still on the move.

It is while Pam is in the bedroom brushing up that Jerry mentions the Clinton Edwards' party of the night before. He is sorry that he had to miss it. Edwards was sorry, too, but so long as Mrs. North was there—that was some help.

"But she didn't—I mean she drove out to her mother's, didn't she?" asks Jerry, in some surprise.

"I believe she did, later, but she stayed with us until about 10 o'clock," answers Edwards.

Jerry has no time to worry about this before Pam has dashed back into the room to report that somebody has certainly been in her bedroom since she was there. The things on her dresser have been disturbed. Now the Norths, Jane Wilson and Edwards have followed Pam back into the bedroom. Ben Wilson, about to follow them, notices the gold compact on the table. He stops suddenly, picks it up and is plainly angry. He slips the compact into his pocket just as the others return.

Pam North is excitingly sure that they have had a burglar. No one but a burglar would have moved her hand mirror from the left to the right side of her powder box and left it glass-side up. So she knows. The burglar idea sends Jerry to his desk to see if anything there has been disturbed. It hasn't. But he still wants to have a look around the house, so the Norths give up the idea of going on to the cocktail party.

When the others have gone Jerry would take up with Pam

the question of when and how she got to her mother's, seeing she had forgotten to speak of having been at the Edwards' party.

Pam's explanation is a little halting, but filled with detail. First there was a long delay at her hairdresser's. Then there was a little trouble with the car, because the—you know—wouldn't work. Then there was the shopping. So, being late, Pam decided she'd be a little later, and had stopped in at the Edwards' party—

". . . just for a minute—I'd given him my lobster receipt and I wanted to see if he'd ruined it," runs the explanation. "And he had. It was terrible. So I took just one cocktail—I like to have a cocktail before I start driving—it gives me confidence."

"Well, darling, you give me a cocktail now—I need confidence," says Jerry.

"You poor dear," gurgles Pam, kissing him. "Of course you do! I'll get you one right away." She is moving toward the living room.

"No gin out there," calls Jerry.

"I'll get a new bottle," says Pam, stopping at the liquor closet.

As she opens the door the body of a well-dressed man falls toward her.

At the sight of the body Pam gives a loud cry and shrinks back. Jerry jumps forward just in time to catch the body and let it down on the steps. Pam is in his arms now, trembling with fear.

North—All right—all right, kid, all right—

Pam (*shuddering*)—Jerry!—I'm—

North—Steady!

Pam—Jerry!

North—Just a minute!

Pam—What are we going to do?

North—Call the police, I guess. Do you know I've never called the police. I never really thought I would.

Pam—Well, this is a good time. (North *turns and goes quickly out. As he leaves the room* Pam *looks at the dead body with some apprehension and draws away from it.*) Oh, dear!

North (*outside, calling loudly*)—Buono! Oh, Buono! the police! Quick! Get a policeman. Quick, Buono! Someone has been murdered!

Pam—Jerry, Jerry—this is awful!

North (*grimly*)—Yes.

Pam—I've always wondered how people felt when they discovered a murder, and even now I'm not quite sure.

NORTH—I am.

PAM (*looking with dread at the body*)—But it isn't as if we knew him, of course.

NORTH—No—but it's bad enough.

PAM—Come, Jerry, let's get out of here.

JERRY—I'm sorry, dear, but I'm afraid we can't do that until the police come.

PAM—Darling—you know—they'll think we did it. They always do.

NORTH—People who find bodies—yes, they do. Usually—say, Pam, you didn't see it—(*He looks at the body.*) him—I mean, before you left here yesterday—

PAM—No—I'd have mentioned it. (*Sound of running footsteps on stairs.*)

NORTH—Steady! It's the police! (*He starts for the door.*)

PAM—Jerry!

NORTH—Yes?

PAM—Do I look all right?

NORTH—Now don't be nervous, Pam.

The arrivals are Mr. and Mrs. Brooks, a young couple from upstairs. He is in his shirtsleeves and she is wearing a dressing gown. Immediately they are a part of the excitement, and there is a good deal of excited questioning and answering. Now Buono has arrived, and the excitement mounts. Buono thinks perhaps Mr. North hit the intruder too hard—

"We never so much as saw him before!" indignantly protests Mr. North.

"We didn't know him," adds Mrs. North. "We came home and Jerry said open a new bottle of gin and—and I did—I don't mean I opened the gin—I—just opened the door and he—he fell out!"

"Good! That's good! When the police come you say it *just* like that!"

The first policeman to arrive is Officer Cooper, a burly fellow and officious. He wants to know what is going on and who they are—

"Gerald North; this is my apartment; this is my wife," explains Jerry, nervously. "We found this man here, like this, when we came home!"

"Do you want to make a charge against these two?" demands

Cooper, making a gesture in the direction of Mr. and Mrs. Brooks.

"Peter!" yells Mrs. Brooks, and dashes out the door, followed by her husband.

"Not them. They live upstairs. They just come in. They don't do nothing!" explains Buono.

"Well, somebody seems to have done something, all right," says Cooper.

A moment later Lieutenant Weigand of the Homicide Squad has arrived and taken charge. He is handsome, interested, less officious than most of his kind. His assistant is Detective Mullins, a typical stage detective, with hat. He would keep the hat on if Lieutenant Weigand did not ask him to take it off.

The Lieutenant's questioning is to the point and a little frightening to the Norths. They try to tell him that they have no idea who the dead man is; that they never had seen him before; that they found him in the liquor closet—

"We keep all sorts of things in there," Pam explains, though the explanation is not altogether satisfying.

"Well, there's a lot here I don't understand. You've got a lot of explaining to do," warns the Lieutenant.

Detective Mullins, who has been examining the body, can find nothing. The pockets are empty and the tailor's tag has been cut out of the coat. The Lieutenant returns to his questioning. What does Buono know? Buono knows that Mr. North is a very fine tenant, but he thinks he should tell the Lieutenant about the voices and noises he (Buono) had heard in the North apartment the day before.

Jerry is quick to deny that he knows anything about the noises Buono reports. He was in Philadelphia and can prove it. However, he knows now that there had been someone in the apartment. Pam knows, too—someone who moved her mirror to the other side of her powder box. And, recalls Jerry, there was the woman's gold compact they had found.

The Lieutenant would like to see the compact, but when Jerry goes to the table for it it isn't there. He can't understand it. Pam can. She had picked it up and taken it into the bedroom. She'll get it.

"Sure this compact couldn't have been an old one that was kicking around the house," suggests the Lieutenant.

"My wife never had a gold one," says Jerry.

The compact that Pam brings back is not gold. It is large and black. But she insists it is the same. The Lieutenant is puzzled. "Is this the one, North? It's important, you know!" The Lieutenant is very stern.

"Of course it is," chirps Pam.

"I asked *Mr.* North!"

"Well, I'm *Mrs.* North. I always help him in every way I can. This is the one we found, isn't it, Jerry?"

"Why—sure—this is the one all right," agrees the puzzled Jerry, reluctantly.

"I'll take care of it," says the Lieutenant, putting the compact in his pocket.

The questioning is resumed. Pam thinks it would be nice if the Lieutenant would let her and Jerry help him solve the murder. The Lieutenant thinks so, too. So they all go over the story again—about Mr. North being in Philadelphia, and Mrs. North at her mother's, and neither of them in the apartment for twenty-four hours. They had only been back about half an hour. Yes, there were callers. Some people had wanted to take them to a cocktail party, Pam explains. Mullins takes the names of the callers.

Nobody else had been there, so far as Pam can remember, except Western Union, who got the wrong house. Is Pam sure Western Union went away? Oh, sure. She heard the door slam—

"Did you *see* the Western Union boy?"

"No—oh, you mean—"

"One of them had to get in some way and let the other in, and he would have needed a key to get from the vestibule to the hall. Right?" The Norths nod. "He'd try ringing somebody's bell, probably, and pretend to be looking for somebody and then pretend to go out by slamming the door from the inside."

PAM—But I was in here then!

LIEUTENANT—How long?

PAM—About five minutes; just before I went out.

MULLINS—They could have gone up a flight—

LIEUTENANT—That's right—and watched until you went out—as soon as you'd gone, he picked that door lock or used a key.

NORTH—The murderer?

LIEUTENANT—Or the victim. Either could have got in first.

PAM—I'm sure the man I heard was the murderer.

LIEUTENANT—Why?

PAM—Because of the trouble. He had to go to all the trouble

of planning how to get in, and then getting in, so of course it was the murderer.

MULLINS (*rising*)—I don't get that.

PAM—It's perfectly obvious. Nobody is going to that much trouble to get murdered, but if you are going to murder somebody you expect to go to a lot of trouble. I would.

LIEUTENANT—Mullins, go and ask the janitor if he let any strangers into the house yesterday, and then come back.

MULLINS—O.K., Loot!

LIEUTENANT—Now, this window wasn't open, you say?

PAM—No, it wasn't!

NORTH (*offended*)—We said that.

LIEUTENANT—Right—but maybe there was just a few little things you haven't said. (*He goes to the window.*) Say!

NORTH—Yes.

LIEUTENANT—Look!

MULLINS (*entering and closing the door*)—The janitor says "no." He didn't let anybody in, front door or back.

LIEUTENANT—What do you make of this, Mullins? (*They all look closely at the window ledge.*)

NORTH—Looks like tracks or something.

MULLINS—Yeah, soot marks.

PAM—Pete! See, there's a paw mark and there's his—where he sat down! I took him down to Mrs. Buono, she lives in the basement; and Pete missed me and came up the fire escape; he often does, only I was gone by that time— Oh!

LIEUTENANT—What?

PAM—I'd closed the window but see—one paw mark is just inside—only one—the window had been opened and Pete was coming in—then something *frightened* him and he jumped back. Jerry! Pete saw the murder!

MULLINS—That's screwy, Lieutenant.

LIEUTENANT—I don't know. It was probably Pete all right, and the murderer had arrived in time to open the window—that was—?

PAM—Between 3:30 and 4 o'clock. But Pete wouldn't come straight up here. He always goes up to the roof and smells around a bit, and it would take him a minute or two to make up his mind to come in. That's it, Jerry! Pete saw the murder and it scared him—poor kitty.

LIEUTENANT—Seems to me as if it were about 4 o'clock, a little before or after. It isn't final, but it is something to go on, right? (*The policeman* COOPER, *on guard at door, now calls to someone on the stairway.*)

COOPER (*in hall*)—O.K.! Bring it up.

PAM (*alarmed*)—Bring what up?

LIEUTENANT—The basket. (*He looks at* NORTH *doubtfully.*)

PAM (*happily excited*)—The basket! Jerry, they're going to bring up the basket!

NORTH—Yeah, but they're going to put him in it!

PAM—Oh!

The curtain falls.

Between 8 and 9 o'clock that evening the Norths are busy reading the late editions of the evening newspapers. They are full of the murder and all sorts of conjectures, including one that North himself may have been the murderer. Pam is loath to contemplate what her mother is going to think when she reads them.

Jerry is still a little worried about the compact. Why did Pam substitute her old black compact for the gold one they found? Pam would evade the subject if she could, but seeing she can't she admits that she has a reason. It has nothing to do with the murder, but—she thinks she knows who owns the gold compact and if she's right, its discovery might get a friend of theirs into a lot of trouble. She can't tell Jerry who the friend is, because that is the kind of secret a man can never keep. A gossip secret.

There is a ring at the door. It is the Fuller Brush Man, a voluble talker and a persistent salesman. Jerry would send him away, but Pam thinks if they are going to camp as soon as the murder is solved, they will be needing a new broom. There are several kinds of brooms. Some are stiff and some aren't so stiff. Some are fiber brooms, patented, and some are not. The Brush Man is sorry he hasn't a sample with him. The day before, he tells them, he did have a sample. But when he knocked they wouldn't let him in. This statement fairly startles Jerry—

"Yesterday afternoon? What time yesterday?"

FULLER BRUSH MAN—About four o'clock. I could hear you talking so I rang a couple of times but you wouldn't answer.

NORTH—You heard voices, but you didn't hear anything that was said, did you?

FULLER BRUSH MAN—No.

NORTH—Or *see* anyone?

FULLER BRUSH MAN—No.

NORTH—It's important, there's been—well—there's been a little trouble here. It might be a big help if you had seen any stranger trying to get out of this house.

FULLER BRUSH MAN—Well, I didn't, but after I left the house I met a man on the steps who was trying to get in.

PAM—You did?

FULLER BRUSH MAN—He'd been ringing one of the bells, but nobody answered, and he asked me if I had a key, but of course I didn't.

PAM—Take his name, Jerry. This may be very important! (*To salesman.*) We may want you to swear that the man you met trying to get into this house wasn't my husband.

FULLER BRUSH MAN—Who's your husband?

NORTH—I am.

PAM—And you can just swear it wasn't he.

FULLER BRUSH MAN—Well, I don't know—it looked a lot the way he does. (*He looks doubtfully at* NORTH.)

PAM—Oh!

FULLER BRUSH MAN—Bigger than him maybe, but a feller has got to be careful what he swears to.

NORTH—This man spoke to you, you said?

FULLER BRUSH MAN—Yes.

NORTH—Careful now! Did you ever hear my voice before?

FULLER BRUSH MAN—Yes, sir.

NORTH—When?

FULLER BRUSH MAN—You said we ought to get a control so we would know what was stiff and what wasn't. I remember it because it sounded sort of nutty.

Jerry takes the Brush Man's name, against the possibility that the police will want to send for him. He is Albert Talbot of 101 East 158th St., and he will be glad to meet the police. They are mostly married men and their wives use brushes.

Lieutenant Weigand and Detective Mullins are there a few minutes later and are glad to hear about Mr. Talbot. The Lieutenant is even more interested in Pam's announcement that she knows the murderer. He had left his card and Pam found it in the mailbox. At least Pam had found a small, narrow card bearing the name of "Edwards" in the mailbox when the postman opened it for her, because she had forgotten her key. She had gone right back upstairs and got the manicure tweezers and then downstairs to pick up the card without touching it. She goes now to fetch the card, with the tweezers, so Lieutenant Weigand can see it.

"Did anyone named Edwards ever live here?" asks the Lieutenant.

"That's the point," says Pam. "Nobody named Edwards has lived here since we have. Don't you see—that Edwards is the murderer's name? He put his name in the slot over the letter box so the man he was going to kill would see it and ring the bell."

LIEUTENANT—Wait a minute! The murderer came about—what did we say? 3:30 or about that. Before that he had rung your bell and pretended to be Western Union! (*They nod.*) Then he must have already made an appointment with the man he was going to kill—and given the man your address and a false name.

PAM (*dubiously*)—Why false?

LIEUTENANT—Nobody would use his own name. The murderer talked to this other man by telephone probably, perhaps around noon Monday. He *said* he was Edwards, which means, of course, that the victim knew somebody named Edwards, who might possibly call him up and arrange an appointment. Right so far?

PAM—Right.

LIEUTENANT—The murderer—

PAM—Call him X. People always do.

LIEUTENANT—So X telephoned the victim Brent—

PAM—Brent!

LIEUTENANT—Brent was his name. We identified him all right. Nothing on his clothes or in his pockets, but we traced him through some dental work. He's a lawyer at 25 Broad Street—Stanley Brent.

PAM—Claire Brent's husband!

MULLINS (*startled*)—Say!

LIEUTENANT (*sternly*)—You said you didn't know him!

PAM—We don't know him. I wanted to, but Mr. North wouldn't let me, so we really don't know him at all, do we, Jerry?

NORTH—Yes.

LIEUTENANT—What's that?

PAM—We know his wife, Claire Brent, that's all, isn't it, Jerry?

NORTH—No.

LIEUTENANT—Here! Wait a minute!

NORTH—Sure I know him! Of course I did.

PAM (*shocked*)—Why, Jerry!

NORTH—If he was a lawyer I knew him. I just thought of it.

The Lawyer Brent Jerry knew had been the attorney for the plaintiff in a suit a woman author had brought against Jerry, charging that he had stolen the idea for a story from her. He (Brent) had called Jerry a "literary termite"—Pam remembers that. Jerry had just as soon she would forget it.

It is all very interesting to Lieutenant Weigand, and the fact that both the Norths knew Claire Brent very well, yet didn't know her husband, interests him even more. He thinks they had better ask Claire over and break the news of her husband's death to her there. If Mrs. North would phone Claire—

Pam has gone into the bedroom to phone. "Stanley Brent had quite a practice," Lieutenant Weigand explains to Jerry. "I've been down at his office going through his books. Everything seemed to be all right down there—money enough, and plenty of insurance. His wife will get $100,000 worth." He is holding the card slip firmly with the tweezers and reading it searchingly. "Do you know anybody named Edwards?"

"Edwards? Let me see—I know three people—one of them is a laundryman, and then there's Dr. Richard Edwards—"

"And then there was one of them here."

"That's Clinton Edwards."

"We haven't looked him up yet. But Mullins will check up those names between now and morning. . . ."

When Claire Brent comes, and the news of her husband's murder is told her, as gently as possible, her reaction to the shock is emotional but controlled. He had not been at his office since Monday, she had learned, and she had wondered about that. Edwards? Yes, they had known several "Edwardses," including Clinton. Her husband had had business relations with Clinton, but she knew nothing more than that. She had not seen Stan Brent since Monday morning, and only for a few minutes then. She had driven to their country place and then to the Danbury Fair, where she had spent the day painting. She is a little faint now, but refuses a drink—

"It isn't what you probably think," she says. "I don't want to put on an act about it. It's been all over with Stanley and me long ago—but—he was my husband."

Pam has come back and brought Louis Berex and Clinton Edwards with her. Louis is anxious about Claire. He is willing to answer any of Lieutenant Weigand's questions, but he would like to take Claire home. Yes, Stanley Brent was his attorney. Not his friend. Just his attorney. Louis is something of an inventor, dabbling in the transmission of telephotos and that sort of thing. But it was in a matter of stocks and bonds that Brent had been his attorney. . . .

Clinton Edwards lends himself amiably to Lieutenant Weigand's questioning. He had known the Brents socially; been to their parties and had them to his; but that was all. He had heard gossip that Brent had had a night-club mix-up with a Benjamin Wilson, because of Mrs. Wilson, but— He knows no more. The card? With his name printed on it? That was a distressing thing for someone to have done—to try to throw suspicion on him— He thinks it fortunate that Edwards is a common name. He had, Edwards admits, had some little trouble with Brent. They both had served Louis Berex as advisers. Once Berex had quit him (Edwards) and gone to Brent. Edwards didn't like that.

The Norths have returned and are immediately interested in the examination of Edwards. Pam, especially—

LIEUTENANT (*interrupting*)—I wonder, Mr. Edwards, if you'd mind giving me an idea of where you were and just what you were doing on Monday afternoon.

EDWARDS—Why—

LIEUTENANT—Just routine.

PAM (*pleasantly*)—For the record, you know.

EDWARDS—Why, I—I was out of town Sunday and part of Monday morning. I changed and went to my office; then I returned to my apartment. I was having a small buffet supper for some friends Monday night.

PAM—It was really very pleasant.

EDWARDS—I spent the afternoon making some preparations, and giving directions to Kumi. Kumi is my Japanese servant. Aside from him, I live alone and very simply—but very simply, as Mrs. North will tell you.

LIEUTENANT—You stayed in your apartment all the afternoon?

EDWARDS—Yes. I was trying my hand at cooking. You may perhaps regard that as, how shall I say, an odd activity for a man.

LIEUTENANT (*exchanging looks with* MULLINS)—No, I wouldn't think anything about that particularly. Were you alone there all the afternoon?—with Kumi?

EDWARDS—Yes.

LIEUTENANT—Kumi was there when you came home, of course.

EDWARDS (*smiling*)—Yes, he was. I'm afraid you wouldn't think all this as very much of an alibi. Perhaps if you would be a little more definite about the time when the murder was committed—

PAM—Between 3 and 4:30.

EDWARDS—Between 3 and 4:30—about then I must have been preparing the lobsters and Kumi was probably cleaning upstairs.

LIEUTENANT—It's all just for the record, you know.

EDWARDS—And you have no other questions to ask of me?

LIEUTENANT—At present, no.

EDWARDS (*rising*)—Then I really think I must be going along, if it's all right, Lieutenant.

LIEUTENANT—Quite.

EDWARDS—Good night, Mrs. North. Good night, Mr. North. (*He shakes hands with the* NORTHS, *his back for a moment to the* LIEUTENANT, *who signals* MULLINS. *The latter slides a nickel watch across the rug past* EDWARDS' *foot. As he turns toward the door,* EDWARDS *sees watch and stoops to pick it up. He turns with it to the* NORTHS.) Oh. Did you drop this watch?

LIEUTENANT—Thanks.

EDWARDS—Oh, it's yours. (*Hands watch over.*) And now, good night. Good night, all.

LIEUTENANT, PAM, NORTH (*simultaneously*)—Good night, Mr. Edwards. (EDWARDS *exits.* MULLINS *rises and crosses eagerly to right of* LIEUTENANT, *and* PAM *hustles over to left of* LIEUTENANT. *All three look curiously at back of the nickel watch.*)

NORTH—What is it?

PAM (*now wise in the lore of detection*)—Don't be stupid! We got his fingerprints!

The Lieutenant and Mullins react delightedly. The curtain falls.

ACT II

In the Norths' apartment at 10 o'clock next morning, Jerry North is worrying over the household accounts at his desk while Pamela North is trying to entertain Detective Mullins. Mullins is drinking highballs and Pam is chattering. First she is chattering about the wink, which she is convinced is a lost art. Nobody winks nice and friendly like any more, but only suggestively, like truckmen.

Pam is stopped for a minute while Jerry straightens out a bill. It appears that she has been buying a set of "Pranklets." She thinks perhaps "Pranklets" is a trade name, like "Roughies" or "Shaggies." Or "Pranklets" may be a game. They finally discover that it was merely a matter of writing. What had been written was "p—r—anklets." That would mean a pair of anklets, and Pam remembers those. She wears them in the country. Detective Mullins is greatly entertained.

Now Lieutenant Weigand has arrived. He wants to check a few things with Mullins. He wants to have another look at the fire escape, and he wants to have another talk with Louis Berex and Claire Brent. He thought they might be willing to come here.

The Norths are reluctant to bother Claire Brent again, but they decide it may be best. As for Detective Mullins' checks—he has looked up the other Edwardses mentioned. Edwards, the laundryman, was a Jew named Goldstein. The Edwards name just went with the laundry. Goldstein admitted he didn't like Brent, but he didn't kill him.

Mullins has also been investigating Clinton Edwards' man, Kumi. Nothing there, either. Kumi reports that Mr. Edwards spent all Monday afternoon, from about 3 to 5, in the kitchen getting ready for his party. Kumi had been upstairs the whole time, but when he came down there was a mess of Spanish lobster on the stove.

Pam admits that, with her recipe—or receipt—it takes hours to fix Spanish lobster, and it was her receipt—or recipe—that Edwards used. There was no litter of lobster shells, the Jap explained, because he had tossed them all down the incinerator.

Then there is another item that has been giving the Lieutenant a lot of trouble. On the card marked "Edwards" he has discovered another mark. It is a part of a letter cut down the center—an "X" or a "K." He doesn't get very far with that investigation, but he sends the card to headquarters for further fingerprint examinations.

Mullins has checked the "Western Union" clue. The company insists no boy had been sent to the Norths' address on Monday. The door keys have been checked, too. Pam had only lost three of her own. Then she borrowed Jerry's and lost that. And of course if she knew where she lost them they wouldn't be lost.

They have got back to Louis Berex and Claire Brent again. Pam is worried about them and the Lieutenant thinks he knows why—

"... It has just occurred to her that 'X' is the last letter in Berex' name," he explains to Jerry.

"But it could be a 'K'—and anyway it's absurd to think that a nice man like Louis Berex could—oh, dear."

LIEUTENANT—Somebody did it, you know.

PAM—Well, I just know he didn't! Why should he? What earthly reason would he have had?

LIEUTENANT—Well—let's see—Mrs. Brent has told us she and her husband hadn't hit it off very well for a long time.—Brent had always given his wife plenty of money—Berex couldn't do that because he hasn't got it to give—only in case of Brent's death, and he did die, she gets one hundred thousand dollars life insurance. Motive? One hundred thousand dollars!

PAM—I don't suppose you can help talking like a detective, only I really do wish you wouldn't, anyway we know the time of day Mr. Brent was murdered—thanks to Pete—and Claire and Louis Berex were up in Danbury at the Fair, so that's all right.

NORTH (*putting ice cubes in shaker*)—Alibis, you know, all a person has to do is tell you where they were Monday afternoon between three-thirty and five o'clock.

LIEUTENANT—Sure, that's all, and by the way—where were *you?*

NORTH (*startled*)—Me?

LIEUTENANT—Yes—you?

NORTH—Oh!

LIEUTENANT (*coldly*)—No reason why you shouldn't tell me, is there?

NORTH—NO—no reason.

LIEUTENANT (*sternly*)—Where were you Monday afternoon, Mr. North? At your office, I suppose?

NORTH—Why, yes—yes—at my office—of course I was—I—ah, darn it all—I wasn't either!

PAM—Why, Jerry!

NORTH—I was at a reception for one of our authors at the Ritz, from about five o'clock on— (*Hesitates.*) Well, that's the trouble. As a matter of fact I left the office about three.

LIEUTENANT—And?

NORTH—Took a walk.

PAM (*sadly*)—Oh, Jerry!

NORTH (*firmly*)—I just took a walk in Central Park. I didn't see any reason why I shouldn't. A man's got a right to take a walk, I guess. How did I know there was going to be a murder about the time I was feeding pigeons?

PAM (*soothingly*)—There! There! I'm sure he believes you. It's just a coincidence really. You're going to be perfectly all right.

NORTH—Of course I'm going to be all right. It isn't even a coincidence. It isn't anything at all—of all the— (PAM *is giggling.*) O.K., kid, O.K. Have your games.

LIEUTENANT—Games?

NORTH—She's trying to kid me, don't you see?

LIEUTENANT (*coldly*)—No, I don't.

PAM—Nonsense. Of course I'm not trying to kid you.

NORTH—But I tell you, I was walking in Central Park.

PAM (*to* LIEUTENANT)—People do, you know!

NORTH—Of course I was.

Jerry has decided to make them all a drink. It being pretty early in the morning Pam votes for something light—a "stinger" perhaps. Jerry has gone to make it. It is funny about Jerry, Pam thinks—how guilty he looked when the Lieutenant was questioning him. Certainly the Lieutenant would never think that either she or Jerry—

"There's a time, lady, in every case we are on when the Loot just naturally suspects everybody," chips in Mullins.

"Oh, I wouldn't say I let myself get excited or went chasing off on false scents," protests the Lieutenant. "For example, Mrs. North, I have a letter here. (*Takes a letter from his pocket.*) I wasn't going to mention it until I knew a little more about what's going on—but perhaps I might as well. The day before Brent was murdered you wrote him this letter."

"Oh!" Pam is plainly afraid.

"In this you asked Brent to come here to see you; here to this apartment."

"About Claire. I thought he was treating her dreadfully and I wanted to persuade him to let her get a divorce."

"Rather a serious matter, Mrs. North," continues the Lieutenant, gravely. "This note asks him to— (*He reads.*) "'Call to see me on a personal matter almost any afternoon before five o'clock.' Why before five o'clock, Mrs. North?"

"Because Jerry told me not to write Stanley Brent and I didn't want to disobey him," promptly answers Pam.

It was perfectly silly of her to write the letter, agrees Pam, but it was even sillier for Lieutenant Weigand to suspect that it might mean anything it doesn't mean.

Jerry is back with the drinks. He has ice wrapped in a towel and a mallet to crack it with. He is giving the ice a couple of resounding whacks with the mallet when the Lieutenant suddenly has a burst of vision. The District Attorney has been demanding to know what sort of blunt instrument the murderer used on the dead Brent! And there it is, right in Jerry's hand—the heavy ice mallet!

A second later Jerry and Pam have caught the twinkle in the Lieutenant's eye and the smirk on his face, and they are both indignant. Yet, when Jerry puts the ice in the shaker with the brandy and crème de menthe and begins shaking vigorously his whole body shakes with him. That also impresses Weigand. He thinks he will take the mallet with him and see what the Medical Examiner thinks of it. . . .

The Norths have gone to change their clothes. Nice people, the Lieutenant agrees, but, as he tells Mullins, they have more on the Norths than any other of the suspects—

"How about the Claire Brent dame? Could she of?" Mullins wants to know.

"Have? Could have," corrects the Lieutenant.

"That's what I said, could she of? Or that Berex guy, or there's Ben Wilson, Mr. Edwards told us about, or even Edwards, although his fingerprints don't fit into anything. Or this Jap you sent for—lots of angles, Loot. Or the janitor here, Bono. I don't like that bird. He smells of garlic. Any of 'em—could they have of?"

"Why not the Norths? How do you figure them so out of it?"

"Oh, just by watching people, the good ones and the bad ones. Motives are O.K. sometimes, and so are the alibis, but some guys have got murder in 'em and some ain't."

Ben Wilson is at the door. He has come looking for the Lieutenant before the Lieutenant starts looking for him. Wilson knows that sooner or later his relations with Brent will come out and he wants to forestall any wrong impressions. It is true that he (Wilson) has had trouble with Brent; plenty of it. It's true Brent was making a play for Mrs. Wilson, but it isn't true that he had any success. Mrs. Wilson didn't want any part of that affair. Anything that the Lieutenant hears to the contrary is a lie. And if Weigand gets to thinking that Wilson killed Brent, that will be a lie, too.

"Brent was killed we think, as a matter of fact we're pretty sure, sometime between 3:30 and 5 o'clock Monday afternoon."

"I was in and out of my office. You can check up on that, if you want to."

"Right. And your wife? Do you happen to know where she was about that time?"

"She was shopping. I got home rather early and she came in a few minutes later. The taxi driver had to help her carry her packages."

The door has closed after Ben Wilson no more than a minute before Buono, the janitor, comes dashing in to report a big clue. Detective Mullins had put the Fuller Brush Man in the hall to spot the fellow he had seen trying to get into the North apartment the day of the murder and the Brush Man has just picked Ben Wilson.

"Jeez—it's tough when you can't get no clues to work on," explodes Mullins; "but it's hell when you get too many."

Officer Cooper, bringing the Edwards card back from the Medical Examiner, reports that Claire Brent and Louis Berex are waiting. They are shown in now and Lieutenant Weigand has handed Louis the Edwards card—

"Take a look at this, will you, Mr. Berex? It's all right, it's been photographed."

"It looks as if it came out of a mailbox or something."

LIEUTENANT—Yes, it did. What do you know about it?

LOUIS—Me—what would I know about it?

LIEUTENANT (*sternly*)—I think you cut it off the top of a letterhead of your own and I think you printed the name "Edwards" on it and stuck it in the slot beside the bell downstairs in the hall.

LOUIS—I never saw it before.

CLAIRE—Why should he? What reason could he have for doing any of these things?

LOUIS—You're not by any chance thinking *I* killed Brent?

LIEUTENANT—I think you prepared that slip of paper. I think it was cut off the top of one of your letterheads, and I think this little mark here on the edge of the slip was part of the x which happens to be the last letter of your name, Berex, and I think you've slipped up a little because I think you signed this slip without knowing it.

LOUIS—No, I see what you mean—but I never saw it before. I think you're the one that slipped up yourself. I think that if you try to prove that I know anything about Brent's murder, you're working yourself into trouble.

CLAIRE—Now, Louis, don't get excited. He hasn't *said* anything about *murder.*

LOUIS—I don't know how it works in, but you think the murderer wrote the name of Edwards on this slip of paper and used it somehow, in killing Brent. Maybe he did, for all I know, but you see I'm not the murderer. I never saw this slip before, so what do you do next?

LIEUTENANT—I've got this report from headquarters. (*He shows the letter.*) According to them this little smudge here shows very clearly your fingerprints. I got your fingerprints from a piece of stationery you'd been handling in your office. And there's no doubt about it at all.

LOUIS—That isn't possible.

LIEUTENANT—They've developed them down at headquarters. You can see the fingerprints clearly. (NORTH *and* PAM *come down to table, and look at the little smudge on the slip.*)

PAM—Yes, but look, they're on the wrong side.

LIEUTENANT—What's that?

CLAIRE—What do you mean, Pam?

PAM—The prints are upside down. Nobody could possibly have put this slip into that slot downstairs if they'd hold it that way. You'd have to hold it like this— (*She turns the slip around in her hand and shows it to* LIEUTENANT.) Don't you see?

NORTH—And there are no fingerprints on that end of it.

PAM—Gloves—they often do! Or manicure tweezers.

LIEUTENANT—That's a point, Mrs. North, but it's not conclusive.

LOUIS—You've got a slip of paper there cut from a piece of my office stationery, and it has my fingerprints on it.

LIEUTENANT—Yes.

LOUIS—Wait a minute. I don't know what that spells to you, but I know what it spells to me! Whoever murdered Stanley Brent is out to hang it on me, he's figured me to be the goat.

Lieutenant Weigand has something more than the fingerprints to go on. He has been investigating Claire Brent's alibi. The day she said she had been at the Danbury Fair painting there wasn't any Fair. It had closed the day before!

Claire admits she had lied. She had planned going to the Fair. And with Louis. They were to meet at the railroad station in Brewster and drive to the Fair. After they had started the day was so fine they just drove around. Once they had got out of the car and sat for a while on a hill looking down over the Croton Valley. Claire hadn't told about that because of the suspicions she feared it would arouse in the Lieutenant's mind, and the fear that the story would get into the newspapers.

"We've got to get the facts, you know, and among the facts there is one that is growing to be very interesting to me," the Lieutenant is saying.

"What one?"

LIEUTENANT—That you and Mrs. Brent are what is rather commonly known as lovers.

LOUIS (*rising menacingly*)—Being a cop you probably don't know that there's a difference between being a woman's lover and a man's being in love with a woman.

LIEUTENANT—Listen. I don't *give* a damn. Your habits are nothing to me. I *am* a cop. I've things to find out. You're just another fact to me.

CLAIRE (*insolently*)—Well—what about it?

LIEUTENANT—You haven't *denied* that there is an affair between you and Mr. Berex?

CLAIRE—I don't have to deny it. It's up to you. You'll have to prove it, won't you? You can't just guess about it.

LIEUTENANT—I'm about through guessing! I want action now! You two wanted to get rid of Brent—well, I guess you did all right. The slip in the letterbox was made from a letterhead of yours, Berex, your fingerprints are on it! Never mind whether they are upside down or not! You lied, both of you, about where you were at the time of the killing, and innocent people don't have to lie. I arrest Berex on suspicion of the murder of Stanley Brent and I arrest you, Mrs. Brent, as an accessory to that murder!

CLAIRE—No! You can't do that!

LOUIS—Don't get excited, Claire.

MULLINS (*grasping* LOUIS *by the arm and looking at* CLAIRE) —How about her?

LIEUTENANT—No, I'll take care of her.

PAM—Please, Lieutenant.

NORTH—Take it easy, Pam.

LOUIS—It's all right, Mrs. North—don't get into a panic, Claire. (*He turns to* LIEUTENANT.) The District *Attorney* won't hold us.

LIEUTENANT (*smiling*)—That depends.

LOUIS—That depends on what he thinks of our story, but he isn't going to hear our story until we get someone to advise us.

LIEUTENANT—Come on!

CLAIRE (*to* LOUIS)—Must I?

LOUIS—It's a gag! (*He looks at* LIEUTENANT.) He's got to take somebody down town to get his picture in the papers. (*He turns to* PAM.) Don't worry, Pam, I'll get her out of this all right.

PAM—I hope so.

MULLINS—Come along!

After the officers and their prisoners have gone the Norths are in a state of nerves. Pam is ready to scram. Jerry insists, over her protest, upon reciting the possibilities of Louis Berex having bludgeoned Stanley Brent to death—right there, in the Norths' apartment. He has just reached the climax of his story when the door buzzer rings violently and Pam screams.

Now they are shouting at each other, Pam insisting that she wants to move. She can't live in that apartment any longer. She can't wait until November, even if their rent is paid. She wants to get out. It's like living with ghosts—

The curtains in the arch before the dining room begin to stir. Why? Nobody has opened a window. Suddenly a black cat jumps out between the curtains! There's someone in that room! Jerry is ready to investigate, but not too eager. Finally he gets to the door. After all, it is his apartment! And—

The door is opened. There is no one in the dining room. Let Pam come and see for herself. But Pam has sunk weakly on the couch. She wants Jerry to come and sit with her. She doesn't like being alone. She is sobbing now—but her nerves—her nerves are getting better—all the time—

A knock at the door sets her off again, but she regains control a moment later. Jerry goes to the door. It is Timothy Barnes, their postman and an old friend.

Mr. Barnes, middle-aged and round-shouldered, is also a little excited. He doesn't want to sit down. He has just come to tell them something he knows about the murder. Timothy knows who did it!

BARNES—The police asked me if I could give them any help about this murder and I said no, I couldn't. But a kind of funny thing just now happened and now I can.

PAM—What is it?

BARNES—It was only a few blocks from here, just now, there was a crowd on the sidewalk and I bumped into somebody going the other way. I looked up to say "excuse me" and it was a man—at first I thought he was mad at me for running into him—but he wasn't—he was afraid!

PAM—Afraid?

BARNES—I got a funny feeling, sort of, the way he looked at me, and after I went on I looked back, and he was following me, and when I looked again I couldn't see him and then I remember—I'd seen him before and he'd seen me, and he saw me in that crowd and he *recognized* me, and he was afraid, because I met him in the hall, downstairs here, about four o'clock this Monday afternoon.

PAM (*startled*)—Timothy!

BARNES—It was my four o'clock delivery. I only had a letter or two for this house and I was slipping them into the boxes, when I heard footsteps on the stairs. I looked up expecting to say "hello" or something—but it wasn't anybody I knew—it was a stranger.

PAM—Not the man who was following you on the street just now.

BARNES—Yes.

PAM—Then you did see the murderer!

BARNES—And I want to get his name quick because I know he's following me. I'll go to the police as soon as you tell me who he is. I've seen him with you and Mr. North. I'm sorry but I'm afraid he's a friend of yours.

PAM—I don't care who he is. It's terribly important to me to have him arrested! I'll tell you something, Timothy, that even Mr. North doesn't know! I'm really to blame for the murder!

BARNES—No!

PAM—Yes. I invited Mr. Brent to come here and he did, and he was murdered. (*Rises.*) Now I'll get Mr. North and you describe this man to us, then we'll telephone the police. Now I'll get you a bottle of beer—

BARNES—Oh, no, I'll get it, Mrs. North. I know where it is.

PAM—Of course you do, Timothy. You go and get it. I'll be right back. (*She exits into the bedroom and closes the door after her.* BARNES *goes through dining room. We hear a thud and a muffled cry from the dining room, then another thud. There is a pause, and* PAM *and* NORTH *enter from the bedroom.*)

NORTH (*entering*)—Well, Timothy!

PAM (*following him in*)—He went into the kitchen for a bottle of beer. (*She looks into the dining room.*) Jerry. There's a chair turned over in there! I'm frightened!

NORTH—Nothing to be frightened of—I— Wait a minute. (*He crosses into dining room—for a moment,* PAM, *in terror, stands looking after him—then she cries out.*)

PAM—Jerry—Jerry!

NORTH (*coming back.* PAM *reads in his face the horror of his discovery*)—Timothy's dead, Pam—someone's killed him. Just exactly as Stanley Brent was killed. He's—he's out there—in the kitchen. There—there isn't anything we can do—he's—he's dead!

PAM—Someone followed him on the street, Timothy said—someone followed him *right* to this apartment. Oh, Jerry.

NORTH—Don't cry, Pam, I'll—take care of everything.

PAM—Oh, I'm so terribly afraid.

NORTH—Stop that! Behave yourself!

PAM—Yes, Jerry!

NORTH—Just leave everything to me! (*He crosses firmly to the telephone and dials the operator.*) Hello! Get me Police Headquarters, please. This is Spring 7-3017. (*After a pause.*) Hello, Police Headquarters? This is Gerald North, 95 Greenwich Place. Yes—a man has been murdered in my house—yes—what? Yes! God damn it, another!

The curtain falls.

ACT III

It is Friday afternoon. The janitor, Buono, has come to the Norths' apartment to put up bookshelves. His house is getting a bad name with all these murders, and he wishes the Norths would have them somewhere else, but if there are going to be more photographs taken of the place he wants it to look swell.

Jerry North, troubled and trying to work out a list of possible suspects from among his friends, doesn't want to be bothered with bookshelves. Let Buono get out. Jerry doesn't even want to be bothered with Pam. He wishes she would get out, too. And she would go, but just then she thinks of an excuse to stay. She wants to help Jerry figure everything out. For which pretty show of interest she gets herself hugged.

Jerry has made out a list of the North friends—Louis Berex, Claire Brent, Edwards, Ben Wilson, Jane Wilson. One of them must have committed the murders, because it must have been someone who knew the Norths would be away Monday. He has asked them all to come over for another check-up. Claire and Louis had been released by the magistrate as soon as he heard of the murder of Timothy Barnes. . . .

Lieutenant Weigand and Detective Mullins are back. Something else has happened. Cooper, the officer left in charge of the hall, has disappeared. The District Attorney and Inspector O'Malley are greatly excited about it.

The Norths know nothing of Cooper. He was at the door when they went out at about 11 that morning. He wasn't there when they came back, that's true. But they didn't think anything of that.

Presently Inspector O'Malley arrives. The disappearance of Cooper has put an edge on his temper. He wants to know what has become of Cooper. The Norths wouldn't know about that.

"Now, be reasonable, Inspector," protests Pam. "You put Cooper out there in the hall to take care of us—we're not supposed to take care of Cooper."

"Two men killed right here, no witness in either case—all we know is that you and Mrs. North reported you found the bodies," continues O'Malley, turning to Jerry.

"We had to tell someone about it; we didn't want them," says Pam.

And now, as a further proof of something, O'Malley has Mrs. North's letter to Stanley Brent. That should mean something to the District Attorney. He will be taking Lieutenant Weigand and Detective Mullins back with him to consider that letter. And he will leave Gordon, another cop, to watch over the Norths until he gets back. Their friends may come in, but the Norths can't go out. . . .

Pam's letter is news to Jerry, too. What about it? Pam's explanation is both weak and halting. Jerry is persistent—

"And what did you write to Stanley Brent about?"

"Nothing really—I was so anxious to help Claire—I—I just asked him to come here."

"You just asked him to come here and be murdered?"

"Jerry, how can you say a thing like that?"

"You wrote Brent to come here and the police have your letter?"

"Yes, Jerry—I'm afraid you think that makes things look pretty bad for us—don't you, dear?"

"I'm afraid that makes things look pretty God damned bad for us," answers Jerry, with emphasis.

"Well, in a way it's a judgment on you! You shouldn't have told me what I couldn't do."

Louis Berex has come. He is still excited about the possibilities of the case. He and Claire are free for the moment, but there is no telling when they may be involved again. The police are a pretty stupid lot. Item by item Jerry and Louis go over the known facts. Louis' fingermarks on the card—they were plainly intended to involve him. The murderer wanted to be rid of both Louis and Timothy Barnes, the postman. That's plain. Someone who hated Louis.

It couldn't have been Ben Wilson. Or Jane. Or Claire. Or the Norths. Or Clinton Edwards.

Then there is the clue of the gold compact. What about that? Can Pam explain that? Pam can, but she doesn't want to. Not right now. Perhaps later—if she has to. Pam, says Jerry, is evidently trying to shield some woman.

A ring of the doorbell saves Pam for the time being. It is Jane Wilson and Clinton Edwards. They had met in the hall. Shortly Claire Brent and Ben Wilson appear. The Wilsons evidently have had a spat. Nobody is in a very good temper. Pam thinks it would help matters if they were all to sit down and talk about something pleasant. Jerry thinks so, too. So, with a good deal of muttering, they find places.

North—Now—what's pleasant?

Claire—Personally, I'm in a foul temper. When I got home I found my apartment full of detectives. They'd been into everything; the whole place was turned upside down.

North—Do you know what they were looking for?

Claire—They made me give them a full description of the things Stan always carried with him—his watch, his cigarette lighter, cigarette case, keys, pocketbook, everything. It seems they still think they are going to find them.

Louis—But suppose they don't find them?

North—They'll never find that stuff. We can't just sit around and wait, can we? Now, we've all got to work out this thing among ourselves, but we can't get anywhere if anyone here tries to keep important facts secret.

CLAIRE—Of course we can't!

LOUIS—We might work this out if each one of us was willing to tell the absolute truth.

EDWARDS (*rising from desk*)—We must. It's absolutely necessary!

JANE—Yes, all of us!

PAM—You don't mean tell all the truth, absolutely all of it, at one time?

NORTH—She just doesn't like to waste it.

PAM—Well—then I'll start.

NORTH (*alarmed*)—Here! Wait a minute!

PAM—Oh, no, Jerry, I'm not ever going to try to keep another secret. Some women can and some can't—it's like wearing blue.

EDWARDS—What *is* your secret, Mrs. North?

PAM—Well—I wrote a note to Stanley Brent and asked him to come here to see me—and he came—and somebody killed him! (*The others move restlessly.*) Then I told Timothy Barnes to go in the dining room there to have a bottle of beer while I went into the bedroom to get Jerry—and he did—and somebody killed him, too. (*The apprehension of the others becomes greater.*) Oh, don't worry—nobody's going to kill you—I don't think.

WILSON—Brent wouldn't have paid any attention to your asking him to come here.

NORTH (*turning to* WILSON)—Now, Ben, I want to ask you one question. The Fuller Brush Man said you made an attempt to enter this apartment on Monday afternoon, shortly before the murder. What was your purpose, and why did you come here?

WILSON—I think you'd better ask Pam.

PAM—I wrote him a note!

NORTH—Another note!

WILSON—She did. Thursday is Jane's birthday. She was going to help me pick out a bracelet for her.

PAM—So I wrote him to come for me Monday and then—I just forgot all about it.

That explains that. Now, who else can reasonably be suspected? Ben Wilson thinks Louis Berex knows more than he has told. Louis resents that and is willing to make something of it if Wilson says any more. What, for that matter, had Wilson and his wife been rowing about? Stanley Brent, wasn't it? Wilson is ready to fight at that suggestion. Jerry quiets them. As a matter of fact, says Jerry, he is the chief suspect in the eyes of the District Attorney and Inspector O'Malley.

"You of all people!" protests Claire, and the others join her. "You're a square guy and everybody knows it." "We're your friends. You have our absolute confidence." "It's just fantastic!"

"It's swell to know you folks all have faith in me and I'm afraid I'm going to need all my friends," says Jerry, taking a gold watch from his pocket. "I figure the Inspector will be back here looking for trouble in—in just about ten minutes."

"Why, Jerry! Where did you get that watch?" demands Pam.

"Watch?"

"That isn't yours!"

"Why, no—it's better than mine," admits Jerry, examining it.

"That's Stan's watch! He carried it the day he was murdered!" exclaims Claire.

Jerry drops the watch on the table. When he picks it up again and shakes it the broken works rattle against the case.

"Now it isn't as good as mine," he says.

"Jerry! Where did you get it?"

"That's what we all want to know?" Ben Wilson's voice is stern.

"I didn't get it! What I mean is I—I've just got it!"

"Where did you find it?"

"In my pocket. Pam and I went out this morning and I changed my suit when I came back. You don't suppose I'd be carrying it on purpose, do you? I just put my hand into my pocket and—oh, my God—"

From his pocket Jerry, in shocked surprise, now brings forth Stanley Brent's cigarette case, his keys, his wallet and a mechanical pencil—

What does it mean, Wilson and Berex want to know. Bit by bit they drag back the evidence against Jerry—his admission that he had had law trouble with Brent; his admission that he hated Brent. It looks bad, admits Wilson.

"So that's it? My friends! I was a 'square guy.' You all had faith in me! I might have known it! 'The rats deserting a sinking ship.'" Jerry's anger is mounting.

"Oh, Jerry! That isn't worthy of you! That's a terribly bad simile." Pam has gone to Jerry to show her sympathy and confidence.

"Why is it? They are rats, aren't they?"

"Of course they are—but you're not a sinking ship."

Jerry has sent for Buono. He means to get to the bottom of things now. "That junk," he says, pointing to the pile on the table, "was put into my pockets by the man who murdered Brent. His first plan was to throw suspicion on Berex, and when that fell down he started after me. But this time he's slipped up. He's got me sore! He only planted one clue against you, Berex, but look at the mess of clues he planted on me!"

Buono is puzzled. Why should Mr. North worry because somebody has given him so many fine things? But North is both worried and mad. Somebody else has been in that apartment while he and Pam were out that morning. That settles it. The Norths are moving—just as soon as the police will let them the Norths are getting out, and all their friends can go to hell.

"You can't trust nobody these days," laments Buono. "Here you live all these years, nice and comfortable, then you pack up and go 'way the first time a couple of little things goes wrong!"

"I'll go pack our bags right now," says Pam. "I'll take one for you and one for me and we'll take Pete and the manuscript of your novel. Wait. I'll get it for you—"

Pam has gone to the closet door. As she opens it Officer Cooper, bound with two towels and gagged with a third, starts to fall out. Pam and Jerry scream, just as Inspector O'Malley, Lieutenant Weigand and Detective Mullins come in the front door.

"Now, this is going a little too far!" shouts Jerry.

"It's Cooper!" cries the Lieutenant.

"Well, I'll be damned!" This from O'Malley.

They get the bandages off Cooper and hear his story. After the Norths had gone out he had taken the key and come up to have a look around the apartment. He had heard a sound in the kitchen, gone to investigate and had been soaked—probably by Mr. North, and probably with a mallet!

Now O'Malley has found the watch and other things on the table. Where did they come from? Jerry only knows there had been someone in there while he and Pam were out. O'Malley isn't satisfied. He will have to arrest Jerry—and does. This, so far as he is concerned, ties up the case. If Weigand and Mullins hadn't been a couple of lunkheads it would have been solved three days ago. "Take him down town and lock him up, then report to me, both of you, at headquarters."

O'Malley leaves them. Reluctantly Mullins puts handcuffs on Jerry. Pam isn't going to have that. They must know Jerry couldn't have done murder. Why not arrest the rest of them? Any or all of them?

Lieutenant Weigand is sorry, but they may yet have to do that very thing. They had traced the compact Pam gave them and discovered it belonged to her. Pam will have to be held as a material witness. The compact is a bad bit of evidence against Mrs. North—

"It isn't evidence at all," shouts Pam. "We did find a gold compact, and I'll tell you now who took it. I saw Claire Brent looking at it and I think she took it."

CLAIRE—I didn't take it. It was Jane Wilson's compact. I had seen it on my husband's dressing table.

EDWARDS—When we were here Tuesday afternoon, I saw Ben Wilson take that compact.

WILSON (*takes compact from his pocket*)—Yes, I took it. Jane said she left it at her mother's, and I found it here in this room, over there.

JANE—All right. Stan and I did go dancing Saturday night, and I left my compact on the table. Stan must have picked it up and put it in his pocket.

PAM—So you see Jerry didn't have anything to do with the compact or the murder. It's all silly and stupid and I'm not going to let you put him in jail because, well, because—he's the sort of man who wouldn't like it at all!

LIEUTENANT—Sorry, Mrs. North. Come on, Mullins.

PAM—No. No! Louis—Mr. Edwards, can't you do something?

LOUIS—We'll do what we can, Mrs. North.

EDWARDS—He'll have his chance in court. He may be able to explain everything.

PAM—Explain? What do you mean by that?

EDWARDS—There is some question about his alibi, as I understand it. I really know nothing about it.

PAM—That's a mean thing to say. Once you were all our friends but not one of you has said a word to help Jerry, and you dare to insinuate that he wasn't taking a walk in Central Park.

EDWARDS—I simply meant—

PAM—You meant to be mean, because you are mean! Louis Berex told us about your taking advantage of him about money, and you're mean in plenty of other ways! I saw that at your party Monday night! You served bottles of American champagne with lots of napkins wrapped around them, and you served cheap butter, and you made your Spanish lobster out of canned lobster!

LIEUTENANT—What?

NORTH—Canned lobsters?

PAM (*rattling on at* EDWARDS)—I was at the grocer's today and I saw some canned lobster and I remembered how your canned lobster tasted.

NORTH—Pam!

MULLINS—Say—Mrs. North!

LIEUTENANT—Please, Mrs. North.

MULLINS—Stop her, will you?

NORTH—Pam!

PAM (*unheeding*)—I should have known it—a mean person is always mean—six live lobsters would cost about four dollars and two cans of lobster would cost about eighty cents.

NORTH—Wait, Pam—

LOUIS—What is it?

LIEUTENANT—Mrs. North! Mrs. North!

PAM (*turning on the* LIEUTENANT)—Well, what is it?

MULLINS—Mrs. North. There goes his alibi!

PAM—What?

MULLINS—Canned lobster!

PAM (*her face lighting up*)—Why, of course—with canned lobster it wouldn't take you five minutes and you had plenty of time to come here and murder Stanley Brent!

EDWARDS—Absurd! What motive would I have had?

LIEUTENANT—Just a minute! What's this, Mr. Berex, about Edwards here having taken advantage of you in business matters?

LOUIS—Why do you ask?

LIEUTENANT—Among Brent's papers we found this contract with the Reliance Electric Company. Edwards acted with power of attorney.

LOUIS—Drawn when I was in South America.

LIEUTENANT—It represents a surprisingly large amount.

LOUIS—A surprisingly small amount considering what the company is making.

LIEUTENANT—How much, exactly?

LOUIS—$3,000 a year.

LIEUTENANT—Now we've got it. Edwards, you've been drawing $30,000 a year.

LOUIS—Then for the past three years you've robbed me of—

MULLINS—Eighty-one thousand dollars!

LIEUTENANT—And Brent must have known it.

NORTH—And you killed Stanley Brent and Timothy Barnes and you planted all this junk in my pockets to try to lay the blame on me!

LIEUTENANT—It was easy for you to get a letterhead of Louis Berex' with his finger prints on it. Mrs. North scattered door keys wherever she went and you stole one. You had the means and the motive and the opportunity.

EDWARDS—Brent tried to ruin me. It was his life or mine. My alibi was perfect—until she started to babble about the canned lobster. The police could never have broken it down—nothing could have broken it down, except the chatter of this bungling little bitch! (NORTH, *handcuffed, grasps a bowl of flowers from the coffee table, as if he would heave it at* EDWARDS.)

PAM—Oh!

MULLINS (*seizing* EDWARDS)—I've got him, Loot!

LIEUTENANT—Good work, Mullins. (LIEUTENANT *and* MULLINS *take* EDWARDS *out.*)

PAM—Jerry! Did you hear what he called me?

NORTH—Why—yes—

PAM—Why didn't you hit him? (NORTH *shows handcuffed wrists.*) Oh, Jerry. Just wait. I'll get a key. (*Crosses to telephone and dials operator. A pause.*) Hello! Give me Police Headquarters! Please. This is Spring 7-3017. (*Pause.*) Hello—Police Headquarters? This is Mrs. Gerald North, 95 Greenwich Place— Oh— (*She turns to* NORTH, *radiant.*) Jerry, they're sending the reserves!

THE CURTAIN FALLS

GEORGE WASHINGTON SLEPT HERE

A Comedy in Three Acts

BY GEORGE S. KAUFMAN AND MOSS HART

GREAT expectations were rife, not to say rampant, when announcement was made that George S. Kaufman and Moss Hart, the most consistently successful of present day playwriting collaborateurs, had finished a comedy of country life called "George Washington Slept Here." The title itself was pregnant with promises of humor and satire, particularly in the Eastern country where our native amateur historians ride high horses and frequently suffer comical falls. Furthermore it was suspected that material for the comedy had been freshly gathered by the playwrights. "As property owners in Bucks County, Pa., George S. Kaufman and Moss Hart are now putting their country estates to work," reported Brooks Atkinson in the introduction to his review of the play, providing confirmation for the earlier suspicion.

It was reasonably to be expected by those wise in such theatre situations that some measure of disappointment would follow the production of the comedy. The Kaufman-Hart promise had automatically oversold itself. This disappointment, however, while it was definitely in evidence the first few days of the engagement, was not shared by the greater play-supporting public. "George Washington Slept Here" was not the "smash" success that those former Kaufman-Hart triumphs, "The Man Who Came to Dinner" and "You Can't Take It with You" had been, but it was a substantial success compared with what Broadway usually and inelegantly refers to as a "flop." It ran for five months and was a popular choice with the Summer stock companies.

It is the playwrights' pleasure to expose, a little exaggeratedly, the experiences of a typical city "sucker" who falls into the clutches of yokel "slickers" when he buys a place in the country. If they have applied the technique of broad farce to what might more effectively have been treated as a straight comedy subject, they have at least extracted a good deal of fun from situations that will be easily recognized as fundamentally both plausible and human.

The first scene of the first act of "George Washington Slept Here" takes us into what evidently was the living room of an abandoned farmhouse somewhere in Pennsylvania—"Bucks County, to be precise," as the authors slyly put it. It is probably the most thoroughly abandoned farm house in the country, going back to Revolutionary days. "The plaster has come off the wall in great patches; one window has been roughly boarded up, and it is clear that no one has lived there for quite some time."

The only piece of furniture left in the room is a decrepit rocking chair. Part of an old rusty plow can be seen in the corner, and an old Socony oil can has been tossed into the wide open fireplace.

"Outside it is evidently a fine Spring day, for the sunlight is streaming in through the dirty panes of the remaining window."

There is the sound of a motor car driving up. A moment later a key is inserted in the lock of the door, the door swings creakily open and a man enters. "His name is Mr. Kimber. He looks like the caretaker of an abandoned farm, and that is what he is."

Kimber is followed by another man—"a smallish man—the kind of average man you meet every day in the week. His name is Newton Fuller." It is plain to be seen that Mr. Fuller is greatly pleased with the house just as he finds it. A moment later he has gone to the door to summon Annabelle—"an attractive woman in the forties, and no fool, to say the least." Annabelle is Mrs. Fuller, and it is equally plain that she does not share her husband's enthusiasm for this particular adventure.

Annabelle fails to rise to Mr. Fuller's enthused reaction to the sight of the fireplace, or the beams, or the funny old door. She is even able to restrain her emotions when she is told that the house is probably two hundred years old.

"Just think, Annabelle!" Mr. Fuller is saying. "George Washington slept here! George Washington!"

"Martha wasn't a very good housekeeper," calmly observes Annabelle.

"This whole countryside is tied up with American history," continues Mr. Fuller, his eyes shining. "That road we came along—that's the old York road. The Continental Congress used it, going to Philadelphia. Washington crossed the Delaware

oto by Vandamm Studio.

"GEORGE WASHINGTON SLEPT HERE"

Uncle Stanley is seen to be hale and hearty, "a good-looking man in his sixties, with all the surance that is bred by success. When he speaks, others listen; when he cracks a little joke the ughter is general. In short—Uncle Stanley is that rich relative—and how well he knows it."

(Jean Dixon, Dudley Digges, Kendall Clark, Ernest Truex)

only a little ways from here. Don't you get a kind of a thrill, Annabelle?"

"What's the matter with you, Newton? You knew you were in America."

"I know. But I get a kick out of these things. That old graveyard we just passed—full of Colonial soldiers. My! Think of what happened right around here! Maybe right in this very house. Say, if only these walls could talk."

"Oh, if they could there'd probably be a commercial with it. . . . Now, come on—we ought to get going."

But Newton is not ready to go. He wants daughter Madge to see it. And Madge's friend, Steve. Sensing at least a little sympathy in their attitude he goes into further flights of enthusiasm for the fireplace and the old Dutch oven, the twenty-inch stone walls and the hand-pegged floor—

Madge and Steve are reasonably impressed, but Annabelle is still restless. "Newton, you buy me a book on American history and I'll read it on West Ninety-seventh Street," says she. "Right now I'm hot and hungry."

"Annabelle—" Newton's great moment has arrived.

"Newton, we have *seen* the house."

"Annabelle—I've bought it!"

Annabelle, on her way to the door, is stopped in her tracks. "What was that?"

"I said I've bought this place. It's—it's yours."

"Why, Dad? You mean it?" Madge is a little thrilled.

"Just a minute, Madge." Annabelle has turned to her beaming husband. "I heard you correctly, Newton? You have bought this outhouse?"

"It's all ours."

Annabelle just can't believe her ears. That Newton should have deliberately taken what little money they had and, without consulting anybody, had done this thing is beyond her. He must have lost his mind. Besides he knows she hates the country. Why did he do it—*why?*

"Well—well, I've had this feeling that—I wanted something I could hang onto," Newton explains. "A home, and a piece of land—that's real. That lasts as long as anything lasts. Look at this house. It was standing here when this country started and it's standing here today. And the way things are now it's pretty wonderful to come back to a thing like this. That's why I wanted it. I wanted it for all of us. Annabelle, don't be angry. Say you're not angry, *please.*"

"Angry? I could spit from here to Mount Vernon."

Madge and Steve have had a look at the upper floor—after Mr. Kimber has warned them to be careful—some of the floors had fallen in last winter—and report the rooms small but with a lovely view from every window. By knocking out a partition they could get two lovely rooms out of the four.

The very thought of rebuilding, of fixing everything up just as they want it, is still thrilling to Mr. Fuller. He and Mr. Kimber have talked it over and Mr. Kimber is going to superintend everything.

"And have you been here two hundred years, too?" sweetly asks Annabelle. Mr. Kimber doesn't quite get it.

Now Madge and Steve think they'll have a look at the barn, but again Mr. Kimber would warn them about the walls. One, at least, is caving in. And is that the dining room? Annabelle would know, pointing through another door. It is, and it isn't, Newton explains. Right now it is the tool shed, but it will be the dining room eventually.

And is there a kitchen? Oh, indeed there is. A great big kitchen. One of Mr. Kimber's cows is occupying it at the moment, but Annabelle is sure there will be room for all of them. She has gone to see.

"Well, Mr. Kimber, here we are," beams Newton. "Quite a surprise, wasn't it?"

"Yes, sir. Have you figured out yet what you're going to do about water?"

"Water? What water?"

"Well, what you're going to do about getting water."

"Getting water? We've got water."

"No, you ain't, Mr. Fuller."

"Why, of course we have. What about the well? Mr. Henderson said the well was the deepest in the whole county."

"Yeah, it's deep all right, but there ain't no water in it."

"Well, I'm certainly going to speak to—" Before he can finish Annabelle has returned from the kitchen and started determinedly up the stairs. "Look, Mr. Kimber—let's not say anything to Mrs. Fuller about—the water."

"Yes, sir. But she's going to find out as soon as she wants a drink of water."

Of course there's the brook, but water would have to be carried up a bucket at a time. Mrs. Fuller might not like that. No, Mr. Kimber agrees, there's nothing to stop them from digging another well. Newton's enthusiasm is bubbling again. He wishes he could go right out and dig the well himself.

"Ah, Mr. Kimber, you don't know what this does to a man. You've lived in the country all your life, but I tell you, when you've been cooped up in the city ever since you were born—just the feel of walking on your own piece of land—why, I *own* all this, Mr. Kimber! I own every bit of it! Those trees, and the brook, and this house—I can hardly believe it. I want to learn all the things that *you* know, Mr. Kimber—the names of trees, and birds. I want to see the seasons change, right with my own eyes. I want to find out for *myself* that Summer is here, instead of getting a cold from the air cooling at the Music Hall. Gosh, I can see myself coming down my road on an Autumn night, the smell of the leaves burning—coming in and lighting that fire, and maybe it's raining outside—I tell you, Mr. Kimber, this is the finest thing that ever happened to me."

"You're going to need a cesspool too, Mr. Fuller."

"Go ahead and get one, Mr. Kimber," enthuses Newton, rhapsodically. "You see, that's just what I mean, Mr. Kimber. Whatever you put into a place, whatever you do to it, why, it's yours! Gives you something to work for. Yes, sir, Mr. Kimber, I can see myself ending my days right here. I can hear 'em saying: 'There's the old Fuller place—right up the road there. Ever meet Old Man Fuller? Couldn't meet a nicer old codger—been here for thirty-five years. Don't know what we'd do without him. Yes, sir!' "

"Excuse me, Mr. Fuller. My cow is trying to get into your car. Get away from there, Bossie. Get away."

Mr. Kimber has gone to drive Bossie out of the yard. Newton is still beaming pleasantly at the thought of growing old on what is to become the old Fuller place when Annabelle comes down the stairs. Her mood is still critical. George Washington may have slept there, but he certainly did not have any place to hang his clothes. She couldn't find a single closet. And he apparently never had to go to the bathroom.

"Oh, I forgot to tell you, Annabelle—there aren't any just yet," explains Newton.

"What are we supposed to do—run back to the apartment?" Annabelle would know.

Madge and Steve are back from the barn. They have found a lot to be enthusiastic about. The barn will be perfect for a studio. A little smelly, perhaps, but perfect. And Steve is sure the brook can be dammed up for a swimming pool. He is going to bring out his surveying instruments and fix that right up.

"See, Annabelle?" beams Newton. "Why, I can hardly wait to get to work on it. Let's take these boards down right now." With a mighty tug he pulls off a board—and cuts his finger on a nail. But what's a cut finger to Newton Fuller! He has gone back to the fireplace. "Boy, can you imagine that fireplace with a big roaring fire." He has stuck his head in with the intention of looking up the flue. Down comes a cloud of soot, closing both eyes and smudging his face.

"Oh, Dad, that's a shame," sympathizes Madge, trying to wipe her father's face. Steve offers his handkerchief and between them they lead the half-blinded Newton to the rocking chair. He sits in it and it collapses under him. Newton is floundering dazedly to his feet as the curtain falls.

A month later the Fullers are moving in. The room has been cleaned up, the missing panes have been supplied for the window and the plow and the oil can have disappeared. The plaster, however, is still hanging in strips from the walls.

There is a mess of furniture in the center of the room, flanked by piles of books and barrels of chinaware. Newton and Annabelle, Madge and Steve are all hard at work. Newton is in overalls. Annabelle has a dust cloth around her head. Madge is wearing an old pair of slacks. Everybody is getting in everybody else's way. Nobody knows where anything goes. Everybody is a little on edge and given to short answers. Steve is attaching a radio, but getting nothing but static.

Newton is doing a little better than the others. Newton, in fact, is pretty peppy. He thinks it probably is the country air. With a hammer and chisel he attacks a barrel of china and—crash! The chisel goes practically all the way through. If Newton would only sit down Annabelle would be greatly pleased.

"You've done enough," she insists. "Made us give up the apartment—had to get out here by June fifteenth—'everything will be ready.'—Everything except bedrooms, bathrooms, dining room, kitchen, floors, walls, ceilings—"

There is a blast of static from the radio. It doesn't look to Steve as though the reception was going to be any too good on the farm. Annabelle is sure of it.

Newton, however, refuses to be discouraged. There are bound to be little annoyances, but— If they will listen right now they can hear the soft notes of the yellow-breasted barn swallow—

"Has a triple call," Newton explains. "It'll come three times.

Now listen. . . . Sssh!"

They listen, and it comes. "But it is not the barn swallow. It is the horrible thumping sound of a well drill crashing through stone."

"That's not the same bird, is it, Newton?" sweetly asks Annabelle.

Reports from the well are at least promising. Mr. Kimber is sure they are going to strike something this time. Meanwhile, the soft air is laden with heavenly odors and Newton is happy. He stands in the doorway, inhaling with enthusiasm and thumping his chest proudly. Now he has returned to unpacking the books. He thinks he had better attend to putting up the bookshelves himself. Meantime, he dips into one or two at random. There's "A Study in Scarlet" by A. Conan Doyle. Newton hasn't read that in years. . . .

Katie the cook comes from the kitchen to announce that she is leaving. Nobody could work in that kitchen. Katie's scared. She just opened the door and a horse walked in. But that, Annabelle assures her, won't happen after the new wall is finished. Won't Katie please make the best of things for a few days? Katie isn't sure.

It now appears that work on rebuilding the Fuller place has been temporarily stopped because Neighbor Prescott needed all the men who are helping Mr. Kimber. It also appears that Neighbor Prescott is not all a neighbor might be. Madge had met him that morning and talked with him. At least Mr. Prescott had talked with her—

"He said," reports Madge, "'You are trespassing on my property and I will thank you to get off.' So we got off."

There is also the question of commuting which isn't particularly encouraging. Most of the good trains seem to have been taken off for some strange reason. For example, it will be necessary for Steve to stay overnight, or get back around midnight. But Annabelle is sure Newton will be able to work out a schedule.

"Of course you'll get to the office at a quarter to seven in the morning," explains Annabelle sweetly; "take a Pullman out here at night to get some sleep. You won't see much of the double-breasted swallow, Newton, but you can commute."

Mr. Kimber is in to report on the well. They're down four hundred and twenty feet now, and luckily they've struck mud. Annabelle is thrilled. A nice, big pitcher of iced mud will certainly be refreshing in an August hot spell.

And there is the matter of gravel. They are going to need another load, Mr. Kimber reports, and the price has jumped. The price has jumped on lime, too. And the trees will have to be sprayed. If the trees aren't sprayed the elms are likely to get the elm blight, and the oaks by the brook are likely to get the oak bore. The big willow already has a canker in it, and they'll have to be looking out for tent caterpillar and the measuring worm. Then the Japanese beetle will be along the first of July.

"Let me understand this, Mr. Kimber," demands Annabelle. "Every tree has to be sprayed—is that right?"

"Yes, ma'am."

"Well, who runs through the woods and sprays all *those* trees, Mr. Kimber? *They* seem to be doing all right."

"I don't know, ma'am. All I know is trees have got to be sprayed."

"Annabelle, if Mr. Kimber says the trees have to be sprayed, why, he knows."

"If he knows, let him answer my question. Who sprays the trees in the woods, Mr. Kimber?"

"What else was there, Mr. Kimber? We'll talk about the trees later."

"*He* ought to be sprayed, if you ask me," Annabelle mutters to herself.

Mr. Kimber is not at all disturbed. There are a few other items he is prepared to mention. They will be needing a couple more truck loads of manure, and that's up to $45 a load now, indicating to Annabelle that Mr. Kimber must have got in on a sale. And they will be needing probably six more truckloads of dirt—

At that Annabelle rebels. If there is one thing they have got it's dirt. They may be without water, but to discover that they haven't any dirt, either, that's too much. Newton is at some pains to save the situation by explaining that what Mr. Kimber has in mind is a special kind of dirt. And Mr. Kimber would also add a bit of cheer to the situation.

"The seventeen-year locusts, they don't come along till August," says he; "so we don't have to worry about them."

"The seventeen-year locusts too, h'm?" But what Annabelle is about to say about them is lost on Mr. Kimber. He leaves abruptly.

"Well, they only come every seventeen years, Annabelle," points out Newton.

ANNABELLE—Yes, I can just imagine them talking the whole thing over last year. One locust saying to another: "Only a year more, and then Newton Fuller will buy that place, and up we go. We'll all meet at Newton Fuller's place—us, and the Japanese beetle, and the tent caterpillar, and the measuring worm—we'll all gang up and have a hell of a time!"

NEWTON (*making a stand*)—Annabelle, sometimes I just don't understand you. Here you are, face to face with the most wonderful thing in the world. Nature. And all you see is a few insignificant little—trivialities. Why, you've got a grandstand seat at the greatest show in the world—the whole panorama of nature going on right before your eyes. Insect against insect, worm against worm—all the complicated forces that make locusts stay down in the ground for seventeen years, and Japanese beetles come up right on July first—why, you ought to be struck with wonder at the very privilege of being able to watch it.

ANNABELLE—Why, that's the greatest love scene you've played in twenty-two years.

NEWTON—Well, it makes me mad all through to have you stand there and complain about buying a little bit of spray.

ANNABELLE—That's all very fine, Newton—you and the insects—but when the honeymoon is over, where is the money coming from to pay for all this?

NEWTON—Oh, it's not going to be so much. You always have to do things like this in the beginning. Take gravel, for instance. You heard what Mr. Kimber said—we won't need any gravel for another two years.

ANNABELLE—Oh, as far as gravel is concerned we're all set. I was just thinking of little things like eating. Because when manure costs more than a sirloin steak, Newton, it kind of makes you stop and think. (*The sound of the pump again, pounding away.*) Makes you feel like the Emperor Jones.

Another of the neighbors has called. She is Mrs. Douglas, a pleasantly conventional sort, and she comes bearing a gift of flowers for Annabelle to bid the Fullers welcome. It is always nice, she thinks, to have new neighbors. The flowers are right out of the Douglas garden. It is a very old garden. In fact the Douglas house goes back to the seventeen hundreds, they think.

"I was born in that little house," reports Mrs. Douglas, with a touch of pride. "I've lived here all my life."

"Think of that, Annabelle." Newton is quite thrilled. "Tell me—do you know anything about this house, Mrs. Douglas? When did George Washington sleep here?"

"Well, I know there is a legend that Mr. Washington slept here, but I'm afraid that isn't true, Mr. Fuller."

"What? He never slept here at all?"

"No. As a matter of fact we investigated, and we discovered George Washington never slept here. It was Benedict Arnold. Perhaps you'd like to have an old map of the place, with all the original boundaries. You see, I'm president of the County Historical Society. I think it might be interesting to you."

"Say, I certainly would, if it wouldn't be too much trouble, Mrs. Douglas."

"Why, not at all."

A roll of thunder warns Mrs. Douglas that she had better be starting home. Because of the threatened storm she is afraid she will have to use the road instead of driving across the fields. Why she should not use the road is a mystery to the Fullers. But Mrs. Douglas has a reason. She knows that Mr. Prescott does not like to have people using it.

"After all, it's Mr. Prescott's road, you know," she smiles.

"Why, no, it isn't. It's our road," corrects Newton. "It leads to his house too, but it's our road."

"Oh, I'm afraid you're mistaken, Mr. Fuller. It's Mr. Prescott's road. Didn't they tell you that when you bought the place?"

"My husband, Mrs. Douglas, bought this place by radio-photo."

"But, Mrs. Douglas—"

"Just a minute, Newton," interrupts Annabelle. "Just how do we get to our house, Mrs. Douglas—jump?"

"Well, your right-of-way is actually through the woods. I suppose in time you'll just have to build a road through, because after a heavy rain it's quite impassable."

There is another crack of thunder and Mrs. Douglas hurries out. Flashes of lightning outside and in. Annabelle is trying to figure just how Newton could have been so completely dumb as to buy the house and accept it without even making the ordinary inquiries. In the midst of which Mr. Kimber is in with a further report about the well. Looks dubious now. They've struck a cemetery. And a man has just left a paper for Mr. Fuller. It is a bill for taxes—road tax, school tax, an extra assessment for the County Poorhouse—

"Let's pay that and move right in," suggests Annabelle.

The storm has started in earnest now, with a terrific crash of thunder. Steve and Madge come running into the house. They had been at the brook when they saw the storm coming. It's dark as pitch outside, and the rain is coming down in torrents. Newton is worried lest something be hurt by the storm.

"What can it hurt? That room where Benedict Arnold slept?" Annabelle wants to know. To further relieve her taut nerves she has started singing lustily: "Wintergreen for President—da de da de da de—Wintergreen for President!"

Outside, as Newton leans peering through the window, a car is stopping. Clayton Evans and his wife, Rena Leslie, are seeking shelter for a few minutes. Driving got so bad they couldn't go on.

Mr. and Mrs. Evans, it transpires, are actors, in the country for a summer's engagement at the Playhouse, where they are to open in "The Firebrand" shortly. They are on their way to rehearsal. Madge is thrilled to recognize Mr. Evans. She has seen him on the stage many times.

Mrs. Evans' feeling for the country is quite on a par with that of Annabelle, but Mr. Evans is inclined to take things as they come. "What do you expect of a summer theatre, anyhow?" he demands of the complaining Rena.

"Not a great deal, Clayton," says she. "I would just like to have them take the pigs out before they put the hams in, that's all."

The thunder has come again. And the lightning. And the rain. Upstairs there is a clatter of doors and shutters banging in the wind. Now Steve comes rushing down the stairs to report a leak in the roof. Madge discovers the rain coming in the windows. And under the door. Newton thinks they had better be getting rags from the kitchen. His handkerchief is hardly enough to stem the tide.

"Newton! It's raining, Newton! Right in our little nest!" Annabelle calls, sweetly, as the water begins to drop from the ceiling. "You know, I think they just put the roof on while you signed the deed, Newton, and then took it right away again."

Newton has found a bucket to catch the plop, plop, from the ceiling. Now he thinks he had better light a fire, a nice, big fire. And he does. But it doesn't stay lighted long. Suddenly great clouds of smoke begin to pour into the room, starting a general epidemic of coughing.

"You know, Newton, I've got a name for this place: Wuthering Heights," announces Annabelle.

At which moment, with the thunder and lightning building to a terrific crash, Mr. Kimber bursts through the door to report that the Big Tree has just blown down. That's "Bingo!" as far as Annabelle is concerned.

Now another crash of thunder and the lights go out. "They'll come on again," insists Newton, cheerfully, as a vivid flash of lightning illumines the room. The thunder is rolling deafeningly as the curtain falls.

ACT II

The following August, late on a Friday afternoon, we are again in the Fuller's living room. "Either local labor has come through or else Annabelle has gone to work, for the room has undergone a complete transformation. It is now an attractive, tastefully furnished and livable room. . . . In short it looks like that place in the country that Newton Fuller dreamed about."

However, from the outside there is still the familiar sound of the well drill, and Annabelle's expression is not altogether happy as she comes from the garden carrying "a couple of puny radishes," which she promptly tosses into the waste basket.

It is hot. Annabelle has turned on the electric fan. She stands before it for a moment and then drops onto the sofa and would try for a few moments' rest if it were not, first, for the pounding of the well drill and, second, the harsh clicking of a lawnmower which the industrious Mr. Kimber is pushing across the lawn.

Annabelle has some trouble stopping Mr. Kimber. He has to cut the grass sometime, he insists. If he doesn't do it now it will just keep on growing. He does finally stop and Annabelle returns to the sofa. But now it is the flies. First one, which is successfully pursued with a fly swatter, and then another, which gets away, though in the chase Annabelle does succeed in smashing a small china figure on the table.

Mr. Kimber has been going to get at the screens since the first of July. But even if he had found time he doubts if it would have done any good. Every time anybody goes in or out the door some flies are bound to get in.

Hester, the maid, furnishes the next irritation. Hester would like the night off. Her fellow is driving over from Hatboro and this will be the only night she can see him. But, as it happens, the Fullers are having guests, as Hester knows. It is the Fullers' first week-end party and Hester will simply have to put off seeing her young man until some other night, or even until next week. But Hester can't see her young man next week. He's getting married.

"Getting married?" echoes Annabelle. "Well, then he isn't your young man, Hester."

"He is till he gets married," persists Hester. "That's why I got to see him tonight."

The only possible compromise seems to be Annabelle's offer to let Hester go right after dinner; as soon as she has turned down the beds and seen that there is water in all the rooms. Hester is pretty sulky about it, but apparently accepts the situation.

Madge has come tripping gaily down the stairs and headed for the door. She knows, as her mother reminds her, that the expected guests are her friends; but she'll be back.

Hester presents another proposition: Would it be all right if Annie, the cook, serves the dessert? It would not. Annabelle is firm about that. Hester, a little sulkier than before, has gone back to the kitchen when a voice, coming apparently from nowhere, is heard to mutter—

"Hester is going to have a baby!"

The next moment a boy about fourteen or fifteen has rolled out from under the divan. He is Raymond, a curiously aggravating young snip, and he is flush with information.

"You're awful dumb, Aunt Annabelle," continues Raymond. "I knew about Hester three weeks ago."

Annabelle looks at Raymond a little helplessly. "I cannot believe that you are my brother's child," she sighs.

RAYMOND—Say, who knows? . . . I wonder how Mama's doing in Reno with the cowboys. I'll bet you she's in there pitching all the time.

ANNABELLE—Look here, Raymond, you are going to be here another month, until the divorce is over. So we may as well have an understanding. In the first place, you have been stealing my little chalk figures and selling them to the Quaker House Antique Shop.

RAYMOND—Me?

ANNABELLE—Now, don't deny it—I know you have.

RAYMOND—Aunt Annabelle, how can you call your own nephew a thief?

ANNABELLE—And if you don't stop I am going to murder you in your bed some night, so help me God.

RAYMOND—You know I nearly killed Mama once. They

stopped me just in time. Of course I was just a kid then.

ANNABELLE—You know, Raymond, you kind of fascinate me.

RAYMOND—You'll get used to it. . . . O-o-oh! Here comes that actress. Can she stink up a theatre. (*As* RENA *comes into sight.*) Hel-lo, Miss Leslie. (*Holding the screen door for her.*) And how are *you* this afternoon?

RENA (*entering*)—Out of my way, rat.

RAYMOND—Boy, are you a lousy actress! (*And on this note of charm he goes.*)

RENA—You know, I can't decide whom Raymond resembles—Leopold or Loeb.

ANNABELLE—Well, another month and the divorce is over. The only thing that's holding it up now is the custody of Raymond. Neither one of them will take him. . . .

Rena Leslie has come to visit a bit, and also to convey a warning. She is glad to hear that Mr. Fuller is still enjoying his country life experiment and that he still thinks Benjamin Franklin makes up for the Japanese beetles. She, too, is becoming reconciled to life as a Summer actress—

"I'm playing that maid again this week," reports Rena. "Last night the scenery fell over right in the middle of the second act. Didn't make a damned bit of difference—it was just as good. You know, I don't understand the theatre. These hams come down here, work their cans off for a dollar-eighty a week, live in places that a cockroach would turn up his nose at—and for what? Just to *act*. So help me God, actors will act *any*where, *in* anything, and *for* anything—all they want to do is *to* act."

How did she get into acting? Well, Rena married one. Her Clayton is one of those he-charmers there is no resisting when he really sets his mind to charming. "Now that I'm cured it's kind of fun to sit in the bleachers and watch Clayton bat that ball around," says Rena. "I say to myself: 'My God, is that what I fell for.' But I did."

And that leads naturally to the purpose of Rena's visit. She has come to warn Mrs. Fuller about Clayton and Madge.

"Now look, Mrs. Fuller," Rena is saying. "This is not the jealous wife speaking—it's just that I like you, and I think you ought to know what's going on."

"Going on?"

"You don't know anything about it, then?"

"No, I don't."

"Well, it's just that Clayton and Madge have been seeing a

great deal of each other, and if I know the signs I'm afraid she is in for a bad time. Ordinarily I don't interfere, but your daughter's too nice a girl, Mrs. Fuller. Anyhow, now you know, and you can do what you want about it."

Rena is sure that this particular romance is in its early stages and is really no more than one of those Summer things. She meets Newton coming in as she goes out and there is a hearty exchange of greetings in the yard. Newton comes laden with more parcels than he can get through the door without considerable maneuvering. It's part of the fun of owning a country place, he insists, the experience of going into a store and knowing that you need practically everything you see.

"Know what this is, Annabelle?" Newton is saying. "Little Miracle Chicken Feed."

"You'd better take a spoonful, because I've got some news for you," advises Annabelle.

"Bad news? Mr. Kimber quit?"

"No, we've still got Mr. Kimber. But your daughter, Mr. Fuller, is having a little romance with a married man."

"What do you mean, Annabelle? Who?"

"Clayton Evans. That's what Miss Leslie was here about."

"Madge and Mr. Evans? I don't believe it."

"Now, don't just toss it aside, Newton."

"Honestly, you women! Always seeing the worst in everything. Why, when I was just out of college I was so crazy about Maxine Elliott that I used to go to the theatre four times a week, just to see her. But I didn't break my engagement to you and marry Maxine Elliott, did I?"

"No, you didn't, Newton."

"Well, even so, it's just too silly, Annabelle. I wouldn't even talk to her about it. Silly thing like that . . ."

Newton also has news. He has asked Uncle Stanley out for the week-end. Annabelle can hardly credit her hearing. Uncle Stanley—of all people! And why? Well, Newton just couldn't help himself. This was the only week-end Uncle Stanley would have. He is on his way to visit another niece and nephew—

"Uncle Stanley. Old windbag!" Annabelle mutters disgustedly. "Have to be quiet till he gets up, and when he takes his nap in the afternoon, and close the windows because there's a draft, and everybody sit around and listen while he tells how he made his money, as though we hadn't heard it seven hundred times before. Madge's friends will have a wonderful time."

"Oh, they're young people—they'll be outside all the time."

"Well, all I can say is, if we ever get that money, we've earned it. Twenty-two years of 'take *my* chair, Uncle Stanley—it's more comfortable.' 'Here's the white meat for *you,* Uncle Stanley.' 'Why, look, Madge, what Uncle Stanley has brought you. A package of chewing gum. Say thank you to Uncle Stanley.' "

"Well, we've gone this far, Annabelle—we can afford to be nice a little longer."

Annabelle is forced to admit the logic of that conclusion and is shortly making plans to get all the Uncle Stanley pictures on display, and see to the ordering of the favorite dishes. When she has gone to attend to these matters Newton has a chance for a confidential talk with Mr. Kimber. Expenses are rather piling up on Newton. Everything has cost so much more than he has counted on he finds that he will have to take things easy for a while. Even the next payment on the threshing machine, due Monday, is going to present a problem. And when Annabelle comes back to remind him that he has not given her a check to cover Hester's and Annie's wages, and the things she had bought in the village, Newton is plainly worried.

At this moment an irate Neighbor Prescott, dressed impeccably in sports clothes, and holding Raymond lightly by the arm, strides into the room. It appears that Raymond has been entertaining himself at Mr. Prescott's expense. Raymond has just thrown a dead skunk in Mr. Prescott's swimming pool. The day before he had pasted Roosevelt stickers all over the Prescott garage. Mr. Prescott wants Raymond kept off his property, and he hopes he has made himself understood. With that warning Mr. Prescott strides out.

"Raymond, I'm warning you," warns Newton. "The next thing you do, I am going to throw you across my knee and give you the hiding of your life."

"I'd like to see you try it, you old poop. Didn't even know enough to buy a farm with water—that's how dumb you are."

Raymond has dashed out, it may be to greet Uncle Stanley, the sound of whose car horn is heard. There is a rush now to set the scene for Uncle Stanley. The pictures are distributed just in the nick of time.

Uncle Stanley, accepting Newton's effusive greeting, is seen to be hale and hearty; "a good-looking man in his sixties, with all the assurance that is bred by success. When he speaks, others listen; when he cracks a little joke, the laughter is general. And he has come to expect it. In short, *Uncle Stanley* is that rich relative, and how well he knows it."

Newton and Annabelle are both ever so glad to see Uncle Stanley, and say so. Say so several times in fact. And pleased almost beyond words that he has not forgotten to bring another of his pictures. Annabelle knows just where that should go. Uncle Stanley is certainly looking wonderful. Annabelle, in fact, has never seen him looking healthier. And they are both at great pains to make Uncle Stanley comfortable.

For his part Uncle Stanley is pleased to approve the little house, when his attention is called to it, though he does make a suggestion or two about the placing of the furniture. Uncle Stanley has always been a great one to notice things like that. "I remember when I was a little shaver—"

This, as Newton and Annabelle well know, leads into the one about that time his mother took Uncle Stanley shopping in Pittsburgh when he was 7. It still runs along about as it did before. Whenever there is a change Annabelle is able to prompt Uncle Stanley and get him back into the main thread of his reminiscence. It was the linoleum, not the rug, department of Horne's. And they were blue, not red, squares that prompted Uncle Stanley's comment. He is not, however, able to finish the story this time. Madge's friends have arrived.

There are four of the week-enders and they are full of chatter and interesting intimacies as they barge in. They are given pause when they run into the older generation, but only for a moment. With introductions taken care of Annabelle shoos them all up to the third floor. The girls are to have the big room with the strawberry wallpaper and the boys the little blue room down the hall.

Uncle Stanley is sorry he didn't know the Fullers were having company this week-end, or he wouldn't have come. Newton should have told him. Yes, Newton should, Annabelle agrees—but she is going to see that he gets his Sunday roast duck just the same.

"Annabelle, I'll tell you something," beams Uncle Stanley. "Of all the girls my nephews married, I always thought you were the nicest. And you know what? (*He gives her a shrewd wink.*) Well, never you mind, Annabelle. But Uncle Stanley doesn't forget . . . Now I think I'll go up to my room and freshen up a bit."

"I'll bring your bags up and help you unpack," says Newton, grabbing the heavier of the luggage.

"Thank you, Newton . . . Damn it, I knew I'd forgotten something. I forgot to bring out any cigars."

"Ah-ha-ha! We think of everything, Uncle Stanley. Look what we've got here. (*He triumphantly exhibits a box of cigars.*) Corona Coronas!"

"Now, Newton, you shouldn't have done that."

"And here are those little candies you like, to take the taste of the cigar out of your mouth."

"You certainly make a person feel at home, Newton . . . Well!"

They are part way upstairs when Newton reminds Uncle Stanley that he did not finish his story about the shopping trip. Uncle Stanley resumes at the point of going to the rug department.

"Linoleum," prompts Annabelle from below.

"What happened then, Uncle Stanley? Tell us what you said and how the salesman looked when you said it," suggests Newton, swinging on ahead with the heavy bag. The curtain falls.

The following Sunday afternoon the Fuller living room is a sight. The Fullers and their guests are spread all about. Outside it is raining furiously. It has been raining for two days, and everybody is bored stiff. Uncle Stanley is sleeping in the only comfortable chair, and under Uncle Stanley are the Sunday papers. He has been sitting on them since 9 o'clock.

At the window Newton is looking for, and seeing, a bright patch in the sky. He thinks perhaps it is going to clear up. Annabelle is not impressed. Newton has been seeing that same spot for two days.

Raymond is missing at the moment, but Annabelle doesn't think anyone should go searching for him. Why trifle with their luck? Sue, one of the week-end guests, is agreed. The night before, just as they were going to sleep, Sue reports, a voice from under the bed had called: "These things are highly over-rated." That was Raymond, too.

Uncle Stanley is awake now. He's afraid he must have dozed off, and he is also afraid he feels a draft. "Reason I'm fussy about drafts," Uncle Stanley explains, "when I was a little shaver—couldn't have been more than eight or ten—my seat in school was right next to the window, and I kept getting colds. Well, one day it suddenly occurred to me that if I put a piece of wood in the window pulley they couldn't open the window. So you know what? That's what I did, and they never could open that window again."

"What do you know, Uncle Stanley!" Newton, at least, is

appreciative. Suddenly from somewhere comes the terrible sound of a raspberry.

"What's that?" roars Uncle Stanley.

"Come out of there, Raymond," commands Annabelle. And Raymond rolls out from under the divan.

"Boy! If you didn't have any money would you have trouble with those stories!" comments Raymond, smiling at Uncle Stanley.

Uncle Stanley leaps from his chair with a bellow of rage, but nothing comes of it. Raymond eludes him and at that moment Newton really does discover the sun. The next minute the room is flooded with sunlight and the atmosphere undergoes a decided lift. Everybody cheers up and all the week-enders start for the swimming pool.

With the sun out, Newton thinks it would be nice if he and Uncle Stanley were to take a little walk, but Uncle Stanley had rather rest—if the young people outside don't make too much noise. He still hasn't read the Sunday papers, either, and takes those with him.

"I hope that draft rushes right upstairs and hits him in the right place," hopes Annabelle. And she can't understand Newton's anxiety to take Uncle Stanley for a walk. Can't he see enough of him in the house?

And now Mr. Kimber rushes in, all excitement. They've struck water, and no kidding. Forty gallons a minute!

Their joy is short-lived. On the heels of Mr. Kimber comes Mr. Prescott, shouting—

"Mr. Fuller, you have just put down a well on *my* property. You are drawing *my* water."

NEWTON—What? Why—Mr. Kimber!

MR. KIMBER—No, we ain't. That well is on our property.

PRESCOTT—Don't tell me—look at your deed. Your property ends at the brook. Why don't you look at your deed first, instead of having a man go out and dig wells wherever he wants to.

ANNABELLE—Look, Mr. Prescott, can't this be adjusted? We've been trying for three months to get water. Now even though the well *is* on your property, couldn't you allow us to use it?

PRESCOTT—Madame, this well that you have put down has tapped *my* spring—you are taking all *my* water. I just tried to fill our swimming pool and there was no water. There is no water anywhere in the house. Now is that clear to you?

ANNABELLE—Yeh. No wonder we got forty gallons a minute.

PRESCOTT—Well, Mr. Fuller? Do you plug it up or do I have *my* men do it and send you the bill?

NEWTON (*quietly*)—Better go out and tell the men, Mr. Kimber.

MR. KIMBER—Yes, sir. (*He goes.*)

PRESCOTT (*savagely*)—Thank you very much.

ANNABELLE—And thank you, Mr. Prescott. Now since you're so fussy about private property, suppose you get the hell off ours.

PRESCOTT—I'll be glad to, Mrs. Fuller. It may interest you to know, by the way, that I am on the board of directors of the bank that is foreclosing this property, and that I will take great personal pleasure, on Tuesday, in escorting *you* off it. Good day. (*He goes.*)

ANNABELLE (*a moment's pause*)—What did he say, Newton?

NEWTON—I didn't quite—understand him, Annabelle.

ANNABELLE (*calmly*)—Come on, Newton, I want the truth. (NEWTON *hesitates a second, then realizes the jig is up. Slowly he draws a letter from his coat pocket; hands it to her without a word. She reads it, then looks at him.*)

NEWTON—I'm sorry, Annabelle. I just didn't have the heart to tell you.

ANNABELLE—That's all right, Newton. Just kind of a shock, that's all. Foreclosing.

NEWTON—It's just that—everything cost so much more than I figured. I had enough money at the beginning, but it just melted away.

ANNABELLE—Why didn't you tell me, Newton? Why did you carry it all yourself? I would have understood.

NEWTON—Oh, I was the one who got us into it, and—I knew how you felt about it, and—somehow I just couldn't.

ANNABELLE—Do you know something, Newton? I was beginning to like it, too. I was beginning to like it a great deal.

The mortgage is for $5,000. They might raise something on Newton's insurance policies, suggests Annabelle. They might, if Newton hadn't already done that. Newton has been going nearly crazy the last few days. And now there are but two days before the foreclosure. Uncle Stanley is their only chance—and a fine chance he is! Still Newton refuses to give up hope. After all, the money is coming to him some day. Why shouldn't he ask for some of it now?

"Just $5,000 to save the house. He ought to be willing to do that," says Newton.

"That's true, Newton. Oh, if only he would. Suppose we both tackle him. I'll come in on it too. You'll see some of the finest buttering since the Spring of 1912. We *must* get it, Newton. We *must*."

Just now, however, there are a couple of other things to think about. For one, Madge comes barging through the door in a state of emotional excitement and dashes upstairs, looking neither to the left nor the right. She is followed by friend Steve in a state of temper which he manages to control. Steve takes one look at Madge as she disappears, turns around and leaves the house.

" 'There's a hell of a situation up in Yale, up in Yale; there's a hell of a situation up in Yale,' " the precociously observing Raymond can be heard singing lustily outdoors.

"Stop that singing! Don't you ever think of anybody except yourself?" shouts Uncle Stanley from his window.

"No, you old bull-face! Do *you?*" shouts back Raymond, resuming his musical announcement concerning Yale.

"I'll tend to you!" promises Uncle Stanley, closing his window with a bang. The next minute he is rushing down the stairs and would continue on through the door if Annabelle and Newton did not stop him.

Uncle Stanley is furious. Also he is packing up and leaving. There are some things he will not stand another minute. And now the buttering begins. Both Annabelle and Newton think Uncle Stanley is a perfect saint to have stood what he has stood, and they are prepared to help him forget everything. There is his favorite chair. The door is closed so there shall be no draft, and Annabelle is even prepared to start laughing all over again when she thinks of that last story about the piece of wood in the window. Now Newton has found a cigar for Uncle Stanley and Annabelle is slipping in a sly reference to the roast duck with chestnut dressing. Not to mention a surprise dessert—

"Uncle Stanley," Newton is saying, as the old gentleman settles back in restored comfort and seems in a softened mood; "there was a fellow in our office—I don't know, about fifteen years ago—and he had an aunt that was going to leave him a whole lot of money, and this fellow got in some trouble or other, and he finally had to go to his aunt and ask her if she'd—give him some."

"She was a damned fool if she did it," says Uncle Stanley.

ANNABELLE (*deciding to take over the reins*)—Uncle Stanley, Newton is trying to tell you something. Uncle Stanley, we're going to lose this house if we don't get five thousand dollars by tomorrow. Will you give it to us?

UNCLE STANLEY—Five thousand dollars?

ANNABELLE—We wouldn't ask you if we were not absolutely desperate—we both felt that if Newton could have just that much of his inheritance *now,* why, it wouldn't be too much to ask.

NEWTON—You see, Uncle Stanley, this house means a great deal to both of us. We've never had anything that was really ours before—

ANNABELLE—It would just break Newton's heart to lose it—I know it would. Will you do this for him, Uncle Stanley?

NEWTON—It would be wonderful of you.

UNCLE STANLEY—That's all very well, Annabelle, but people shouldn't go about buying things they can't afford to pay for.

ANNABELLE—But surely, Uncle Stanley, a man of your means—

UNCLE STANLEY—That has nothing to do with it. You go ahead and do this thing and then expect me to pull you out of it.

NEWTON—I'm sorry, Uncle Stanley. Maybe I shouldn't have. But this can't mean very much to you and it means an awful lot to me. I think you ought to do it.

UNCLE STANLEY—This is quite a shock to me, Newton—I'm surprised at you. You're the first one of my nephews that ever asked me for money. And since you've gone ahead on this thing without consulting me, as a lesson to you I've got to say NO.

NEWTON—Uncle Stanley, I'm not going to let you say No. That money would mean more to me *now,* if I could keep this house, than—anything you might leave me afterwards. I think if you won't do this for me—why—*please* say Yes, Uncle Stanley. It means just everything to me.

UNCLE STANLEY (*stopping to look at both of them*)—Newton—Annabelle—I'm going to tell you something. (*He stops and looks at them again.*) I haven't got a God-damned cent.

Newton and Annabelle are shocked. They can't believe it. Uncle Stanley must be joking. But facts are facts. Uncle Stanley, as he tells them, had gone broke in 1929—lost every cent he had accumulated. True, the factory in Pittsburgh still stands and the firm name of Stanley Menninger and Company is still upon it. Uncle Stanley gets all his mail there. But the factory has belonged to the bank since 1929. Uncle Stanley gets a hundred dollars a month for the use of his name. He's terribly anxious that they should not say anything to the other nieces and nephews about this—

"But why did you do it? Why did you go on fooling everybody all these years?" Annabelle wants to know.

"Well, Annabelle, I'll tell you. When I walked out of that broker's office that day, I didn't have a cent. I said to myself, 'You know what you're going to be the rest of your life? You're going to be a poor relation. No more white meat, no more comfortable chairs, no more Corona Coronas!' And I didn't like it a bit. So I said to myself, 'Look—if you can keep them thinking you're rich, why, you can have a wonderful life.' Winters in Florida, Spring in California, Summers in Maine with the rest of my nephews—I was very pleased when you bought this house, Newton—it kind of filled in some open time. Now, wouldn't I have been a fool to give all that up?"

"Gosh!" This from Newton.

"That is the dirtiest trick I have ever heard of in my life," says Annabelle.

"Well, now look at it the other way, Annabelle," begs Uncle Stanley. "Look at all the happiness I've given you—thinking about that money you thought you were going to get. Meanwhile it hasn't done anybody any harm, and I've had one hell of a time. Now, is that so terrible, Annabelle? (ANNABELLE *just looks at him. He turns and starts out.*) Five thousand dollars, huh? Listen, if I had five thousand dollars, do you think I'd be here. I'd be over at the Stork Club."

So that's that. For a moment there is still another problem to take the Fullers' minds off their mortgage. First Steve bursts in to ask that he be excused from dinner. He finds he will have to hurry back to town. Then Rena Leslie arrives, also in something of an emotional state, with an explanation. The thing that she feared has happened: Her husband and Madge Fuller are running away together. Madge isn't upstairs, she is sitting with Clayton Evans with her suitcase all packed at the Colonial Inn just across the river.

"Think we can still catch them, Miss Leslie?" asks Newton, moving over to the fireplace and taking down the old flintlock that hangs above it. "I know how to handle this."

"For God's sake, Mr. Fuller!" shrieks Rena.

"We're crossing the Delaware, too!" announces Newton. "Come on!"

They are all following him as he rushes out the door and the curtain falls.

ACT III

The next morning Raymond is the first one to put in an appearance. He apparently is in a vicious temper. This is partly assuaged by the sight of Annabelle's bag, which she has left on the sofa. Raymond pounces on the bag and, making sure he is not being watched, rifles it thoroughly. Ten cents in the purse is the extent of his loot. When Hester appears he magnanimously offers her the dime. Let it be "for the baby" suggests Raymond.

"Baby? I don't know what you're talking about," says Hester.

"Well, then you're in for a hell of a surprise," Raymond assures her.

Mrs. Douglas has called. She, too, is a neighbor and is eager to see Mr. Fuller. Mrs. Douglas has discovered an old map which she is sure Mr. Fuller will be interested in seeing. It is from the original deed, and unless she is mistaken, it shows both the road and the well on the Fuller rather than the Prescott property.

The idea is even exciting to Raymond. The road and the well on the Fuller property—he bets Mr. Prescott would give anything to get his hands on that map. Raymond will take charge of it, if Mrs. Douglas likes, and see that his Uncle Newton gets it. Mrs. Douglas has a feeling, however, that she should see Mr. Fuller personally—

"Oh, Uncle Newton is sick in bed—didn't you know, Mrs. Douglas?" lies Raymond, glibly. "He's got some kind of blood disease."

"Oh, dear!"

"Aunt Annabelle has to be with him all the time, and I sort of look after things down here, the best I can."

"Oh! What a comfort you must be to your aunt, Raymond, at a time like this.—Well, I'll come back tomorrow—maybe Mr. Fuller will be better and I can give him the map then."

"Oh, I heard them say, Mrs. Douglas, that if he isn't any better—why, they may quarantine the house. Why don't you let me take it up to him, Mrs. Douglas? Maybe this good news'll make him feel better. I can tell him just what you told me."

"You're a fine boy, Raymond. You will be careful of it, won't you? It belongs to the Museum. Tell Mr. Fuller that I hope he feels better, and I'll stop by tomorrow. Good-by, I wish I had a boy like you."

Mrs. Douglas is no more than through the door before Raymond is on the phone calling Mr. Prescott, whom he advises craftily not to hang up. But he has no more than mentioned the map and assured Mr. Prescott that if he is smart he'll buy it, when Uncle Newton comes down the stairs. Raymond thinks he will take a walk. It is much too nice to stay indoors. Raymond's gentle attitude is a little alarming. "All sweetness and light," mutters Newton. "Huckleberry Capone."

Mr. Kimber has called. He feels pretty bad about Mr. Fuller's losing the house and he is worried about what is to become of everything. "There is a two-year supply of gravel on hand, and a lot of manure. The cow's just starting to give milk, too."

"That's good," agrees Newton. "I'll come outside after a while, Mr. Kimber, and we'll go over everything."

"Yes, sir. . . . Well, it'll be a long time before them real estate people find another sucker," cheerfully prophesies Mr. Kimber as he disappears.

Uncle Stanley has a couple of new ideas. "Sometimes, if you write to Mrs. Roosevelt the darnedest things happen," suggests Uncle Stanley. And when the Fullers (ANNABELLE *having come in from bidding the Japanese beetles good-by.*) explain that there isn't time, Uncle Stanley springs a second inspiration—

"Ed and Julia still think I've got a lot of money—why don't you sell them your share of what they think I'm going to leave? You not only get the five thousand to save the house, but maybe make a little on the side. We can split it three ways. Damned good business proposition, Newton."

"Why, Uncle Stanley, you're as crooked as a corkscrew," charges Newton.

Uncle Stanley has gone for a stroll down to the store to get himself a couple of White Owl cigars. Newton and Annabelle are silent for a moment, and then their talk turns logically to the problem of breaking up.

Newton thinks he will give the cow to Mr. Kimber, and Annabelle agrees. It would be pretty cramped in the two rooms they are going to live in. There are other things, too, but Newton can't put his mind on them right now.

"Funnily enough, Newton," Annabelle is saying, a dreamy expression creeping into her eyes, "there are a lot of things I'm going to miss about this place. Just—little things. Walking upstairs to bed at night—that feeling of a house you get when you walk up a flight of stairs. Puttering around the place, and —I don't know, the whole feeling that it's yours, inside and out.

You know, one night last week I couldn't sleep, and I came down and went out in the kitchen and got an apple, and then I came in here and sat for a minute—just by myself—and then I wandered outside and took a little walk around, just looking at things, and for the first time, Newton, I knew what you meant. About—coming back here, and having a place like this, and—what it does to you. I began to feel very grateful to those old boys who—fought around here. Yes, sir—Life, Liberty and the Pursuit of the Japanese Beetle—I'm going to miss it."

"By gosh, Annabelle—it makes me awful happy to hear you say that. You know what? Let's save up every penny we can, and maybe in five years or so we can get another little place. Because that's what we both want now. We'll get another little place."

"Only with water."

"Sure. Sure. Only—I wish we could keep this place, water or no water."

"Well, we can't, Newton. And now I don't know what *you're* going to do, but I'm going to have a drink. I need it." She is going to the cabinet.

"At ten o'clock in the morning, Annabelle?"

"Yes, and I suggest you have one, too. It'll make us both feel better."

They have poured their drinks and lifted their glasses to "the new place." Then Madge comes down. She is contrite and unhappy because she had made a fool of herself, and pretty miserable thinking she probably never will see Steve again. But she will not take a drink—even to drown Mr. Evans.

Annabelle favors another little drink for the Fullers. And Newton agrees. After all it must be well past 10 o'clock by now. They are both feeling a lot better. When Hester comes to inquire about lunch they decide they'll not have any. Also they decide they had better tell Hester about their leaving tomorrow, though they hate to give her such short notice—

"Oh, that's all right," agrees Hester, reassuringly. "I'm getting married anyhow."

"Oh, that's fine, Hester—you got your young man after all."

"Well, not him. He got married to the other girl. Yesterday."

"Oh! Then I don't understand."

"Well, he brought his brother along to talk me out of it, and the way it ended up I'm going to marry his brother."

"I see. But what about the baby?"

"Well, his brother—it's all in the same family."

That takes care of Hester. But what about Raymond? Annabelle thinks they might move out quietly and just leave him there. That inspiration calls for another drink. Another drink and in bigger glasses. Little glasses are such a nuisance. It's easier, too, if each one has his own bottle—

When Uncle Stanley comes back with another idea, they give him a drink. Also a bottle. "Well, you've got the right idea," agrees Uncle Stanley. "This is what pulled us through in 1929."

"I remember I used to say to myself," remembers Uncle Stanley, "every Christmas why not give all the nieces and nephews great big wonderful presents—make it a real Christmas. Then I'd say to hell with 'em."

"Here's to Uncle Stanley!"

"Here's to Uncle Stanley! I don't know why!" echoes Annabelle.

"Well, I was a good fellow when I had it."

"The hell you were!" says Newton.

Rena Leslie has arrived, and Rena must have a drink—and a bottle. She will have to do a little catching up, but she thinks she can make it. Rena is glad to meet Uncle Stanley. She's heard so much about him. And what an actor he is—playing that rich uncle all these years!

Mr. Kimber also reappears. Mr. Kimber must also have a drink—and a bottle.

"Bring in the Japanese beetles, too, Newton," suggests Annabelle.

Each drinks by himself now. It takes too long to organize an excuse. Uncle Stanley is convinced that he feels a draft, but Newton doesn't mind any more. Let him go right on feeling it.

Suddenly from his corner Mr. Kimber breaks into song. "I'll never smile again unless I smile at you," promises Mr. Kimber. He looks as though he meant it.

Everybody is comfortably high by now. Rena Leslie has arrived at a decision. She is through with the Summer theatre. "I don't mind an occasional rustic touch," says Rena; "but when you walk into your dressing room and find that a couple of birds have built a nest in your brassière—it's time to go back to the city."

Everybody's leaving. That makes it pretty sad. Mr. Kimber is mad, too. He had met Mr. Prescott's caretaker just before he came in and the caretaker had told him that Mr. Prescott was prepared to buy in the Fuller place at the foreclosure. Mr. Prescott doesn't propose to have any more trouble about people using the road and digging wells and things.

"Certainly is wonderful," muses Annabelle. "Our working like dogs around here and then Mr. Prescott gets the whole thing."

"That's the way it is. If the second payment is not made, we lose the property. 'Shall revert to the owners in its original condition, or be subject—' "

" 'In its original condition.' " The phrase sticks in Annabelle's mind. "And Mr. Prescott gets it, huh? Well, let's revert it to its original condition."

"What?"

"Let's leave this place just as it was when we walked in here."

"Hooray!"

"Whoopee!"

"Mr. Kimber, bring in that plow and a couple of old oil cans."

Annabelle has picked up a paper weight from the table and thrown it through the window. Newton decides that's a wonderful idea and throws another. Now Newton has moved on to the bookcases and dumped a row of them on the floor. And crashed a couple of vases to the floor.

Uncle Stanley, insisting on his right to join in, decides to go upstairs and break every goddam window in the place.

Mr. Kimber, bringing in the plow and the oil cans, is sent back for the garbage and the gravel.

"Was there gravel here when you first came?" asks Rena.

"There was everything here when we first came," answers Annabelle. "And bring a saw and a pick-ax, Mr. Kimber! And some hatchets—"

From upstairs is heard the frequent crash of glass. Uncle Stanley is doing his work.

Newton has pulled down a couple of window curtains and stuffed them up the chimney to make the room good and smoky. Mr. Kimber is back with the saw and hatchets. It is Annabelle's suggestion that Uncle Stanley, who is through with the upstairs windows, take the saw and a pick-ax and make the roof leak good.

Newton has dumped the gravel in the center of the floor and sent Mr. Kimber for a load of manure. "And put the cow in the kitchen!" Annabelle calls after him. And now, while Newton amuses himself by tossing armfuls of kindling into the air, Annabelle and Rena are hacking away at the stair balustrade with their hatchets—Rena lustily singing, "Oh, the monkey tied his tail around the flagpole, around the flagpole, around the flagpole," as she works.

The destruction is at its height when the door bursts open and in barge Madge and Steve.

"Come on—grab an ax. We're restoring this place to its original condition," yells Newton.

Steve and Madge stand amazed at what they see. Then they leap to action.

"Listen—the place is saved!" roars Steve.

"What? What are you talking about?" Newton and Annabelle shout back, practically in chorus.

"It's Raymond!"

"Raymond! What's happened?"

"Plenty."

"Raymond fell down the well and we got there just in time."

"Raymond fell down the well? Where is he now?"

"He's still down there," reports Madge.

"I pushed him back again," admits Steve.

"We got there and Raymond was swimming around, holding the map out of the water."

"Map? What map?"

"This map. The old map of the place that Mrs. Douglas brought you this morning."

"Let me see it."

"It shows that we own the road and the well and everything, and he was going to sell it to Mr. Prescott without your knowing anything about it."

"My God!" From Newton.

"I knew it!" From Annabelle.

"We got my surveying instruments and went over the whole thing," Steve hurries on. "Your property goes sixty-four and a half feet into the Prescott place."

"The whole road is ours, and so is his well."

"All this and Raymond, too," adds Rena.

Now there is great rejoicing. Miracles still happen. Everybody happy—until Uncle Stanley comes joyfully from upstairs. "I chopped a hell of a hole in the roof!" reports Uncle Stanley.

They start to tell him what has happened, but are quickly interrupted by Neighbor Prescott. He has come over to warn them that he has stood about all he can, and the next time any of them trespass on his property he is going to set the dogs on them.

His property! Newton will have him know that even the dogs are on the Fuller property and he would thank Mr. Prescott not to use the road, either. Mr. Prescott is startled but not stunned.

After all the property will be his tomorrow. There may have been a mistake about the boundaries, but there is to be a foreclosure and the Fullers haven't got $5,000. Let them think that over.

Uncle Stanley has sneaked back upstairs. Also, warns Mr. Prescott, if they do any further damage to the house they will be taken into court. Furthermore—

From outside comes the sound of a particularly loud and insistent automobile horn. Followed by the voice of Uncle Stanley shouting greetings. Where is everybody? Had they forgotten him? He has come with the $5,000 they wrote him about. He flew down with the check, just to surprise them.

It takes Newton and Annabelle a minute to get it, but when they do, they play up to Uncle Stanley beautifully. Mr. Prescott is the embarrassed one.

"I'm Stanley J. Menninger," Uncle Stanley informs Mr. Prescott; "the Menninger Ball Bearing Works, Pittsburgh, Pennsylvania. My card."

It is one of those engraved cards. Mr. Prescott is impressed. Naturally, he doesn't want any trouble. He wouldn't, for example, think of letting Mr. Menninger send for a staff of lawyers—

"I—ah—I think this whole thing can be adjusted in a neighborly fashion. Suppose—oh—why don't you and Mr. Menninger come up and see me this afternoon, Mr. Fuller—have a little chat?"

Uncle Stanley is agreeable—but, of course, such a meeting would be entirely up to his nephew. He thinks perhaps he should give Newton the check and let him handle the matter himself—

"Thank you, Uncle Stanley, and I won't forget how generous you've been," says Newton.

Raymond, who has come sneaking through the door in a bedraggled state, and has been hidden by Annabelle's skirts, suddenly realizes that there is still a chance for blackmail—

"Hey, wait a minute," Raymond calls. "He hasn't got—"

But he gets no further. Rena, with one firm swish of the stair balustrade she is holding, brings it down on Raymond's head, and Raymond "goes out like a light."

"Why, what's the matter? What happened?" calls Mr. Prescott.

"Oh, poor Raymond has fainted," explains Rena. "It must be the heat."

And they carry him off.

"As far as your indebtedness at the bank is concerned," Mr. Prescott is saying to Newton; "don't bother Mr. Menninger for his check. I'll be happy to lend it to you. Meanwhile, if you want water, Mrs. Fuller, I'll have my caretaker run a pipe from that well you drilled. Will that be all right?"

The Fullers take the suggestion under advisement. Newton is inclined to hesitate, but Uncle Stanley urges him to accept.

"All right—I'll go," agrees Newton. "We'll be there, Mr. Prescott. Four o'clock—sharp."

PRESCOTT—Thank you. Thank you very much. Thank you, Mrs. Fuller.

MR. KIMBER (*coming in*)—Mrs. Fuller! Mrs. Fuller—I got two wheelbarrows full of manure right here, Mrs. Fuller. What'll I do with 'em?

ANNABELLE (*her eye on* MR. PRESCOTT)—Well, we won't need them now, Mr. Kimber. Thank you.

PRESCOTT—Well, I'll—see you gentlemen later, then. Good day, everybody. (*A nervous smile all around, as he goes. Not a soul moves as* MR. PRESCOTT *goes out. From outside we hear the sound of a heavy object overturning, then* MR. PRESCOTT'S *voice: "God damn it!"*)

MR. KIMBER (*peering out*)—Look out for those wheelbarrows, Mr. Pres— (*He shakes his head.*) Oh, oh, all over him. (*Exits.*)

NEWTON (*bubbling over*)—Uncle Stanley!

MADGE—Oh, Uncle Stanley, you were wonderful.

NEWTON—Folks, this calls for a drink.

ANNABELLE—Uncle Stanley, I want your picture. And this time I really want it.

STEVE—Uncle Stanley, you almost had *me* believing it. That's how good you were.

RENA—You ought to be with Warner Brothers.

NEWTON—You didn't do a bad job yourself, Miss Leslie.

RENA (*caressing the very spindle*)—Why, it was nothing at all. I loved it.

STEVE (*as he hands each a glass*)—Here you are, Mrs. Fuller, Madge—Miss Leslie.

NEWTON—Uncle Stanley, you deserve a double one.

UNCLE STANLEY—I've got it.

RENA—The stage is set, Mr. Fuller. All ready for your entrance.

NEWTON—Well—I bought this house because coming back here meant something to me. Not just to have a roof over our heads, but—something bigger. This place stands for something —for everything that seems to me to be worth while. So—here's to this house and what it stands for. That's all I want to say. (*They raise their glasses to drink, and as they do so,* MR. KIMBER *enters.*)

MR. KIMBER—Mr. Fuller—Mr. Fuller. That hurricane—it's headed right this way. (*All hell breaks loose. That summer storm has come up again—thunder, lightning, torrential downpour. It comes right through the roof that* UNCLE STANLEY *has so obligingly chopped a hole in, and sweeps in through the broken windows. With a shriek they are all over the place. "Get buckets!" "Close the doors!" "Go upstairs!" "It's coming in here!" "The windows are broken!" "The roof's leaking!"*)

Newton and Annabelle have finally got that place in the country.

THE CURTAIN FALLS

THE PLAYS AND THEIR AUTHORS

"Native Son," a drama in ten scenes by Paul Green and Richard Wright, from Mr. Wright's novel of the same title. Copyright, 1940, 1941, by the authors. Copyright and published, 1941, by Harper & Bros., New York and London. Rights reserved by Paul Reynolds & Son, New York.

Paul Green was a Pulitzer Prize Winner with "In Abraham's Bosom" in 1926. He has done considerable playwriting since his college days in the University of North Carolina, devoting a good deal of time and thought to the one-act folk play. He was born near Lillington, N. C., in March, 1894; was farm reared and entered the University in 1916, after two years at the Buie Creek Academy. The World War took him away from his studies, but he returned to them in 1919, was graduated in 1921, did some work at Cornell the next year and has been a member of the faculty of his alma mater since then.

Richard Wright was born on a plantation near Natchez, Miss. His father was a sharecropper in the South and his mother taught in the country schools. Richard ran away from home when he was 15, batted about the country the next few years and finally landed on the WPA Federal Writers' Project in Chicago in the early thirties. His first novel, "Native Son," stems from his Chicago experiences. He is writing a second book, is married, and lives in Brooklyn, N. Y.

"Watch on the Rhine," a drama in three acts by Lillian Hellman. Copyright, 1941, by the author. Copyright and published, 1941, by Random House, Inc., New York.

Lillian Hellman has written four plays, three of them notably successful—"The Children's Hour," "The Little Foxes" and the current "Watch on the Rhine." These three have been included in the "Best Play" volumes, and "The Little Foxes" led the voting when the New York Drama Critics' Circle failed to make a choice of the season's best play the season of 1938-39. Miss Hellman was born in New Orleans and is in her middle thirties.

She has been a book reviewer, a play reader, a writer of short stories, and a successful scenarist in Hollywood.

"The Corn Is Green," a drama in three acts by Emlyn Williams. Copyright, 1938, by the author. Copyright and published, 1941, by Random House, Inc., New York.

Emlyn Williams is a Welshman and proud of it. He spoke no word of English until he was 6, but learned rapidly after that, winning a scholarship in French that took him to Paris for a year, and a second scholarship in English that won him free tuition at Oxford. He might be described as a late starter, seeing he had not seen an acted play until he was 17. Soon after that he became an active member of the Oxford Dramatic Society and persistently a playwright. He wrote a piece called "Glamour," one called "A Murder Has Been Arranged" and made the English adaptation of "The Late Christopher Bean." "Night Must Fall" was one of his popular stage contributions and in London he played his own hero in "The Corn Is Green" with great success until the second World War interfered. The story of this play, he has said, has intimate touch with his own experiences as a boy. He has acted in America in "And So to Bed," "Criminal at Large" and "Night Must Fall." He is hoping to come again, when Britain has been given her "V" for Victory.

"Lady in the Dark," a musical play in two acts by Moss Hart, with music by Kurt Weill and lyrics by Ira Gershwin. Copyright, 1940, by the author. Copyright and published, 1941, by Random House, Inc., New York.

Moss Hart makes his first solo appearance in the "Best Play" books with "Lady in the Dark." Previously he has been represented rather frequently with his favorite collaborator, George S. Kaufman—first the season of 1930-31 with "Once in a Lifetime," again in 1934-35 with "Merrily We Roll Along," in 1936-37 with "You Can't Take It with You" and two seasons ago with "The American Way." He is New York born, caught stage fever in the office of Augustus Pitou, play producer, whom he served as a precocious office boy, and has enjoyed his Broadway adventures greatly.

Kurt Weill, German born, was studying piano at 8 and writing musical compositions at 12. In Berlin he both wrote and produced opera with Bert Brecht. His introduction to America was through the score of Paul Green's "Johnny Johnson," followed by his success with Maxwell Anderson and "Knickerbocker Holiday."

Ira Gershwin, for so many years the successful lyricist working with his gifted brother, the late George Gershwin, has had previous introduction in this series of stage records as the lyricist sharing honors with George Kaufman and Morrie Ryskind in writing the book for "Of Thee I Sing" the season of 1931-32. He is New York born and thought he would be a doctor when he left school.

"Arsenic and Old Lace," a comedy in three acts by Joseph Kesselring. Copyright, 1941, by the author. Copyright and published by Random House, Inc., New York.

Joseph Kesselring (Otto is a middle name but he doesn't use it) had a hard time convincing folks that he really had written "Arsenic and Old Lace" following the resounding hit of that comedy on Broadway. It was produced by Howard Lindsay and Russel Crouse and backed by twenty-one of their friends following the success of the Lindsay-Crouse "Life with Father." Practically everybody credited that team with building the play from an idea furnished by Mr. Kesselring. With the help of Mr. Lindsay and Mr. Crouse, however, Mr. Kesselring was finally able to convince playgoers and readers that he not only wrote "Arsenic and Old Lace," which was first called "Bodies in Our Cellar," but that he had previously had two plays produced—one called "There's Wisdom for Women" and the other "Cross-Town." True, neither succeeded, but there they were. Now he is at work on another comedy which he hopes will settle the matter for all time, even if it should turn out not to be quite as sensationally funny as "Arsenic and Old Lace." Mr. Kesselring, born in New York in 1902, was a boy soprano in New York churches for seven years before his voice changed. After that he did a little teaching, both English and music, and a good deal of writing—short stories for the cheaper magazines and a play he sold unproduced to the movies. He says he got the idea for "Arsenic and Old Lace" trying to imagine the most fantastically impossible thing his dear old grandmother could do. That turned out, in his imagination, to be murder. Hence the comedy.

"My Sister Eileen," a comedy in three acts by Joseph Fields and Jerome Chodorov. Copyright, 1941, by the authors. Copyright and published, 1941, by Random House, Inc.

Joseph Fields, eldest son of the late Lew Fields, old-time Weber and Fields comedian, and Jerome Chodorov, brother of Edward Chodorov, playwright and producer, stand as this season's strongest refutation of the feeling that nothing good can really come out of Hollywood—nothing good, that is, for the legitimate theatre. (If it is really good, the conviction is strong, Hollywood wolves will pounce upon it). After a modest success with scenarios they wrote a comedy based on certain character sketches Ruth McKenney had extracted from her own and her sister Eileen's experiences when first they came to New York in search of careers. These sketches had been published, first in the *New Yorker Magazine,* and later in book form. The Messrs. Fields and Chodorov turned them into a play and turned the play over to George Kaufman, who agreed to stage it for Max Gordon. New York immediately loved it—both because it was a smart comedy smartly staged, and also because it stemmed from that dear old Greenwich Village that is tied in with so many romantic adventures and memories in the New York mind. Both Fields and Chodorov were born in New York (Fields in 1895, Chodorov in 1911), and attended her public schools. Fields thought he would stick to the law when he was going to New York University, but changed his mind. Chodorov had no fixed ambitions and a variety of High School superintendents interfered with those he did have. In the World War Fields helped write and stage the Navy shows. Out of the Navy he wrote sketches for several revues, including Ziegfeld's. Chodorov went in for newspaper work and was with the New York *World* when it folded. They found each other in Hollywood.

"Flight to the West," a drama in three acts by Elmer Rice. Copyright, 1940, 1941, by the author. Copyright and published, 1941, by Coward-McCann, Inc., New York.

This will be Elmer Rice's fourth appearance in these year books. He was first chosen for his "Street Scene" in 1928-29, was represented by "The Left Bank" in 1931-32 and by "We, the People" in 1932-33, the same year his more popular "Counsellor-at-Law" was also a contender for honors. Born in New

York in 1892, and started on a lawyer's career, he rebelled in 1914 and was fortunate in scoring a success with his first play, "On Trial." He is one of the four producer-playwrights who make up the Playwrights' Company and has devoted a good deal of time to the staging of that firm's recent output. He threatens frequently to quit playwriting and play producing, and even occasionally to leave Broadway for good and all. Fortunately he has been lured back each time. And that is a good thing for the theatre.

"Claudia," a comedy in three acts by Rose Franken. Copyright, 1941, by Rose Franken Maloney. Copyright and published, 1941, by Farrar & Rinehart, Inc., New York.

Following the success of her play, "Another Language," which brought her into this record in 1931-32, Rose Franken went back to Hollywood and to short story writing. Among her stories were several concerned intimately with the adventures of an engaging young person named Claudia. These finally found their way into book form and were also made into a play by Claudia's creator and best friend. Miss Franken had tried her hand at playwriting before "Another Language" surprised both its author and producer by running through the Summer of 1931, but her earlier efforts did not meet with encouraging success. Miss Franken was born in Dallas, Texas, and is the mother of three children.

"Mr. and Mrs. North," a comedy in three acts by Owen Davis, founded on a novel, "The Norths Meet Murder," by Frances and Richard Lockridge. Copyright, 1940, by the authors.

Owen Davis began writing plays a good many years ago, and has kept at it pretty steadily ever since. His first successes were gained in the popular-price theatre with melodramas of the "Bertha the Sewing Machine Girl," "Confessions of a Wife," type. He moved to Broadway when the movies took over the business of the cheaper theatres and wrote "The Wedding Ring," "Lola," "Sinners," "The Family Cupboard," "The Detour," "The Nervous Wreck" and other successes. The season of 1922-23 he won the Pulitzer award with "Icebound." In 1935-36 he and his son Donald won success with "Ethan Frome," after having dramatized Pearl Buck's "The Good Earth" the season before.

The Lockridges, Richard and Frances, are newspaper folk. It was Mr. Lockridge who began writing "Mr. and Mrs. North" sketches for the *New Yorker Magazine* some years ago. These same characters Mrs. Lockridge later worked into the mystery novel plot from which Mr. Davis extracted the comedy. The Lockridges are from the Mid-West, were working on rival newspapers in Kansas City when they met and married. Mr. Lockridge, after a varied and successful newspaper career, is now drama critic on the New York *Sun.* Mrs. Lockridge stays home, cultivates a flower garden and thinks up mystery stories.

"George Washington Slept Here," a comedy in three acts by George S. Kaufman and Moss Hart. Copyright, 1940, by the authors. Copyright and published, 1941, by Random House, Inc., New York.

George Kaufman began contributing to "The Best Plays" with his earliest success, that of "Dulcy," which he wrote with Marc Connelly in 1921. Something of his has been included in practically every volume since then. Moss Hart joined up ten years later when he and Mr. Kaufman wrote the best of the Hollywood satires, "Once in a Lifetime." Jointly they have been represented by such popular hits as "You Can't Take It with You" and "The Man Who Came to Dinner." Mr. Kaufman came to New York from his birth town, Pittsburgh, Pa. Mr. Hart didn't have to come from any farther than the Bronx. Mr. Kaufman learned to write as a reporter and drama editor on *The New York Times.* Mr. Hart started as a producer's office boy, as is related elsewhere in these pages. Mr. Kaufman is married, Mr. Hart isn't. They both own farms in Bucks County, Pennsylvania. Recently they have been doing a bit of acting in Summer theatres just for the fun of the experience. In a Bucks County Playhouse production of "The Man Who Came to Dinner" Mr. Kaufman played Sheridan Whiteside, the irascible hero, and Mr. Moss took the rôle of Beverley Carleton, the English comedian. They were supported by Harpo Marx, the pantomimist of the Marx family, Harpo speaking lines for the first time in twenty-five years.

PLAYS PRODUCED IN NEW YORK

June 18, 1940—June 15, 1941

(Plays marked with asterisk were still playing June 15, 1941)

HIGHER AND HIGHER

(First engagement, 84 performances. Return, 24. Total, 108)

A musical comedy in two acts by Gladys Hurlbut and Joshua Logan from an idea of Irvin Pincus'; lyrics by Lorenz Hart; music by Richard Rodgers. Returned by Dwight Deere Wiman to the Shubert Theatre, New York, August 5, 1940.

Cast of characters—

Hilda O'Brien....................Eva Condon
Byng....................Robert Chisholm
Dottie....................Billie Worth
Miss Whiffen....................Hilda Spong
Sandy Moore....................Shirley Ross
Zachary Ash....................Jack Haley
Mike O'Brien....................Lee Dixon
Minnie Sorenson....................Marie Nash
Scullery Maid....................Marie-Louise Quevli
Three Nursemaids....................{ Peggy Stewart / Jane Richardson / Hollace Shaw }
Soda Jerker....................George Griffith
Ladies' Maid....................Jane Richardson
First Cop....................Robert Shanley
Cops....................{ Joe Scandur / Richard Moore }
Couturier....................Jack Whitney
Footman....................Carl Trees
Patrick O'Toole....................Leif Erickson
Ellen....................Janet Fox
Truckmen....................{ George Griffith / Joe Scandur }
Snorri....................Fin Olsen
Sharkey....................Himself
The Handyman....................Frederic Nay
The Cat....................Ted Adair
The Frog....................Lyda Sue
The Bat....................Sigrid Dagnie
Coachman....................Frederic Nay
The Gorilla....................Joseph Granville
Purity....................Jane Ball

Al Goodman's Orchestra.

Act I.—Scene 1—Section of Ballroom, New York Hotel. 2 and 4—Kitchen, Drake Mansion, New York. 3—Deborah Drake's Bedroom. Act II.—Scene 1—The Kitchen. 2—Zacky's Room. 3—The Old Carriage House. 4—Ballroom.

Staged by Joshua Logan; dances by Robert Alton; settings by Jo Mielziner; costumes by Lucinda Ballard.

"Higher and Higher" opened at the Shubert Theatre, New York, April 4, 1940, and continued until June 15, 1940, with 84 performances. The return engagement of 24 performances began August 5, 1940, with several changes in cast. Marie Nash succeeded Marta Eggert as Minnie Sorenson.

(Closed August 24, 1940)

KIND LADY

(107 performances)

A drama in three acts by Edward Chodorov; adapted from a story by Hugh Walpole. Revived by William A. Brady at the Playhouse, New York, September 3, 1940.

Cast of characters—

Mr. Foster....................John Robb
Mary Herries....................Grace George
Lady Weston....................Ivy Troutman
Rose....................Marie Paxton
Phyllis Glenning....................Joan Wetmore
Peter Santard....................Melchor Ferrer
Henry Abbott....................Stiano Braggiotti
Ada....................Dorothy McGuire
Doctor....................Wylie Adams
Mr. Edwards....................Oscar Stirling
Mrs. Edwards....................Elfrida Derwent
Aggie Edwards....................Grace Dougherty
Gustav Rosenberg....................Clarence Derwent

Acts I, II and III.—Living Room of Mary Herries' Home in Montague Square, London.

Staged by Felix Jacoves; setting by Watson Barratt.

"Kind Lady," dramatized by Edward Chodorov from Hugh Walpole's "The Silver Mask," and tightened up by George Haight, was tried first the Summer of 1934 at Southampton, L. I. It was brought to Broadway in April, 1935, and ran for 102 performances. The above revival followed Miss George's frequent employment of the play in the Summer theatres.

(Closed November 30, 1940)

THERE SHALL BE NO NIGHT

(First engagement, 115 performances. Return, 66. Total, 181)

A drama in three acts by Robert E. Sherwood. Returned by The Playwrights' Company in association with The Theatre Guild to the Alvin Theatre, New York, September 9, 1940.

Cast of characters—

Dr. Kaarlo Valkonen....................Alfred Lunt
Miranda Valkonen....................Lynn Fontanne
Dave Corween....................Richard Whorf

Uncle Waldemar..............................Sydney Greenstreet
Gus Shuman..Ralph Nelson
Erik Valkonen..................................Montgomery Clift
Kaatri Alquist.....................................Elisabeth Fraser
Dr. Ziemssen...................................Maurice Colbourne
Major Rutkowski.................................Edward Raquello
Joe Burnett...Charles Ansley
Ben Gichner..Thomas Gomez
Frank Olmstead...............................William Le Massena
Sergeant Gosden...................................Claude Horton
Lempi..Phyllis Thaxter
Ilma..Charva Chester
Photographer..Donald Fox
Photographer...John O'Connor

Acts I and II.—Living Room of the Valkonens' House in Helsinki. Act III.—Scene 1—Dave Corween's Rooms, Hotel Kamp, Helsinki. 2—Classroom in School House near Viipuri Bay. 3—The Valkonens' Living Room, 1940.

Staged by Alfred Lunt; settings by Richard Whorf; costumes by Valentina.

"There Shall Be No Night" opened at the Alvin Theatre, New York, April 29, 1940, and continued until August 9, 1940, with 115 performances. The return engagement of 66 performances began September 9, 1940, with several changes in the cast. Ralph Nelson succeeded Brooks West as Gus Shuman. See "Best Plays 1939-40."

(Closed November 2, 1940)

JUPITER LAUGHS

(24 performances)

A drama in three acts by A. J. Cronin. Produced by Warner Brothers under the management of Bernard Klawans at the Biltmore Theatre, New York, September 9, 1940.

Cast of characters—

Dr. Richard Drewett..............................Reginald Mason
Dr. George Thorogood...............................Carl Harbord
Dr. Paul Venner..................................Alexander Knox
Matron, Fanny Leeming...........................Edith Meiser
Dr. Edgar Bragg......................................Philip Tonge
Dr. Mary Murray....................................Jessica Tandy
Jennie...Mary Orr
Gladys Bragg ....Nancy Sheridan
Albert Chivers.....................................Charles Jordan
Martha Foster.....................................Esther Mitchell

Acts I, II and III.—The Doctors' Common Room at Hopewell Towers.

Staged by Reginald Denham; setting by Raymond Sovey.

Dr. Paul Venner, a cynical agnostic, is on the track of a serum that will cure most of the nerve disorders of the day. To Hopewell Towers Sanitarium, where he works and studies, comes Dr. Mary Murray, who is lovable and sympathetic. For Dr. Mary Dr. Paul gives up his mistress, who happens to be the wife of the superintendent. The mistress, jealously embittered, blows up Dr. Paul's laboratory, hoping to destroy his secret formula. Dr. Mary, rushing in to save the papers, is killed. Dr. Paul thereupon decides to go to China and carry on the work that Dr. Mary had hoped to do as a missionary.

(Closed September 28, 1940)

SIM SALA BIM

(54 performances)

A mystery spectacle in two parts conceived by Dante. Produced by Harry A. Jansen (Dante) at the Morosco Theatre, New York, September 9, 1940.

The cast of characters headed by the magician Dante and his assistant, Moi Yo Miller, included 35 performers in a program consisting of transformations, transfigurations, illusions, magic, novelty and comedy.

Driven out of Europe by the war Dante played an engagement in New York preparatory to sailing for South America. So hearty was his reception he changed his plans and organized a tour of the United States.

(Closed October 20, 1940)

HOLD ON TO YOUR HATS

(158 performances)

A musical comedy in two acts by Guy Bolton, Matt Brooks and Eddie Davis; lyrics by E. Y. Harburg; music by Burton Lane. Produced by Al Jolson and George Hale at the Shubert Theatre, New York, September 11, 1940.

Cast of characters—

Sierra....................Margaret Irving
"Slim"....................Gil Lamb
"Lon"....................George Church
Pete....................Jack Whiting
Mamie....................Martha Raye
1st Dudette....................."Jinx" Falkenburg
2nd Dudette....................Joyce Matthews
3rd Dudette....................Thea Pinto
Sheriff....................Lew Eckles
Fernando....................Arnold Moss
Lone Rider....................Al Jolson
Radio Announcer....................John Randolph
"Shep" Martin....................Joe Stoner
"Old Man" Hawkins....................Marty Drake

"Concho"....................Bert Gordon
Sound Effects....................George Maran
"Dinky"....................Russ Brown
Shirley....................Eunice Healey
Luis....................Sid Cassel
Pedro....................Will Kuluva
Rita...................."Jinx" Falkenburg
The Tanner Sisters....................Martha Tanner, "Mickey" Tanner, Betty Tanner
The Radio Aces....................Marty Drake, Lou Stoner, Joe Stoner
The Ranchettes....................Margie Greene, Anita Jakobi, Iris Wayne, Janis Williams

Act I.—Scene 1—Route "66." 2 and 7—Sunshine Valley. 3, 4, 5, and 6—Nationwide Broadcasting Co. Act II.—Scene 1—Lounge, Alamo Hotel, Mexico. 2 and 6—Sunshine Valley Rancho. 3—El Marihuana Café. 4—Street Scene. 5—Broadcast (Sunshine Valley).

Staged by Edgar MacGregor; supervised by George Hale; dances by Catherine Littlefield; music directed by Al Goodman; settings by Raoul Pene Du Bois.

The Lone Rider of the radio drama finds himself in a spot when a posse of cowboys come in from the West looking for the brave man to go West and round up the notorious bandit, Fernando. The Lone Rider has several narrow escapes, but finally sings his way out of trouble.

(Closed February 1, 1941)

* JOHNNY BELINDA

(312 performances)

A drama in three acts by Elmer Harris. Produced by Harry Wagstaff Gribble at the Belasco Theatre, New York, September 18, 1940.

Cast of characters—

Att'y General McKnight....................Bram Nossen
Clerk of the Court....................Blaney Harris
Defense Counsel McVail....................William Chambers
The Judge....................Henry Mowbray
Mountie....................Beau Tilden
Matron....................Vickey Delmar
Belinda McDonald....................Helen Craig
Dr. Jack Davidson....................Horace McNally
Mrs. Lutz....................Leslie Bingham
Floyd McGuiggan....................John Delmar
Fergus McGuiggan....................Frank Delmar
Jimmy Dingwell....................Ralph Cullinan
Reverend Tidmarsh....................Jack Lynds
Mrs. McKee....................Bertha Belmore
Grace Peters....................Valentine Vernon
Locky McCormick....................Willard Parker
Stella Maguire....................Jane Bancroft
Pacquet....................Jules Epailly
Black McDonald....................Louis Hector
Maggie McDonald....................Clare Woodbury
Andy McPhearson....................Beau Tilden
Hector McGuffy....................Edward Craig
Lizzie Gordon....................Margaret Cherry

Act I.—Scene 1—Street in Souris East, Prince Edward Island, off the coast of Nova Scotia. 2 and 3—A Grist Mill. Act II.—Scenes 1, 2 and 4—Black McDonald's Kitchen. 3—A Bedroom. Act III.—Scenes 1 and 2—Kitchen. 3—The Courtroom, Charlottetown.
Staged by Harry Wagstaff Gribble; settings by Frederick Fox; lighting by Feder.

Belinda McDonald, left deaf and dumb at the age of one year, following an attack of fever, is roughly brought up by her father, Black McDonald, following her mother's death. The community knows and treats her as "the dummy." She has few defenders until Dr. Jack Davidson arrives from Montreal. Dr. Jack has had some experience with the deaf and dumb. He teaches Belinda the sign language and falls in love with her during the process. When she gives birth to the child of a village tough who had seduced her Dr. Jack defends her. When she kills the child's father when he tries to take the infant from her Dr. Jack is her best witness. Following her acquittal they are married.

THE TIME OF YOUR LIFE

(32 performances)

A comedy in three acts by William Saroyan. Revived by The Theatre Guild, Inc., in association with Eddie Dowling at the Guild Theatre, New York, September 23, 1940.

Cast of characters—

Newsboy	Blackie Shackner
Drunk	John Farrell
Willie	Ross Bagdasarian
Joe	Eddie Dowling
Nick	Leo Chalzel
Tom	Edward Andrews
Kitty Duval	Julie Haydon
Dudley	Henry Jones
Harry	Fred Kelly
Wesley	Reginald Beane
Lorene	Nene Vibber
Blick	Grover Burgess
Arab	Houseley Stevens, Sr.
Mary L.	Celeste Holm
Krupp	William Bendix
McCarthy	Tom Tully
Kit Carson	Arthur Hunnicutt
Nick's Ma	Ann Brody
Sailor	Seymour Gross
Elsie	Marylin Monk
A Killer	Evelyn Geller
Her Side Kick	Frances McHugh
A Society Lady	Eva Leonard Boyne
A Society Gentleman	Ainsworth Arnold
First Cop	Seymour Gross
Second Cop	John Farrell

Acts I and III.—Nick's Pacific Street Saloon, Restaurant and Entertainment Place at Foot of the Embracadero, San Francisco. Act II.—Scenes 1 and 3—Nick's Saloon. 2—Room in New York Hotel, Around the Corner.

Staged by Eddie Dowling and William Saroyan; supervised by Theresa Helburn and Lawrence Langner; dances by Gene Kelly; settings by Watson Barratt.

"The Time of Your Life" was awarded both the New York Drama Critics' plaque and the Pulitzer prize as the best drama of American authorship produced during the season of 1939-40. (See "Best Plays of 1939-40.") It ran originally from October 25, 1939, to April 6, 1940. It was resumed September 23, 1940, for a preliminary engagement of two weeks in New York, which was extended to four weeks.

(Closed October 19, 1940)

THE LYRIC OPERA COMPANY

(24 performances)

A repertory of Gilbert and Sullivan operettas sponsored by Joseph Daltry and Herman Levin at the 44th Street Theatre, New York, September 30, 1940. Musical direction by Joseph S. Daltry; stage direction by Charles Alan; settings by Samuel Leve; dances arranged by Felicia Sorel.

THE GONDOLIERS

(September 30, 1940)

The Duke of Plaza Toro.........................Frank Kierman
Luiz...Walter Tibbetts
Don Alhambra Del Bolero.............................Paul Reed
Marco Palmieri.................................Allen Stewart
Giuselle Palmieri..............................William Geery
Antonio...James Pease
Francesco.................................Frederick Loadwick
Giorgio..Ernest Eames
Annibale..Robert Eckles
The Duchess of Plaza Toro......................Catherine Judah
Casilda...Marjorie King
Gianetta..Miriam Bentley
Tessa...Kathleen Killcoyne
Fiametta..Janet Webb
Vittoria...Anne Dawson
Giulia...Carol Wolfe
Inez...Jean Handzlik

Act I.—The Piazzetta. Act II.—Palace of Barataria.

MIKADO

(October 3, 1940)

Mikado..Walter Tibbetts
Nanki-Poo...................................Charles Latterner
Ko-Ko..Frank Kierman
Pooh-Bah..Robert Eckles

Katisha.......................................Catherine Judah
Pish-Tush.....................................Leonard Stocker
Yum-Yum.......................................Miriam Bentley
Pitti-Sing....................................Dean Gehring
Peep-Bo.......................................Mary Roche
Act I.—Courtyard of Ko-Ko's Official Residence. Act II.—Ko-Ko's Garden.

TRIAL BY JURY

(October 7, 1940)

The Learned Judge.............................Frank Stone
Foreman of the Jury...........................Paul Reed
Defendant.....................................Allen Stewart
Counsel for Plaintiff.........................Leonard Stocker
Usher...Ernest Eames
Plaintiff.....................................Mary Roche
Scene—A Court of Justice.

THE PIRATES OF PENZANCE

(October 7, 1940)

Major General.................................Frank Kierman
Pirate King...................................Walter Tibbetts
Samuel..Sydney Morton
Frederick.....................................Carlton Bentley
Sergeant......................................Robert Eckles
Mabel...Janet Webb
Edith...Miriam Bentley
Kate..Kathryn Lewis
Isabel..Ellen Merrill
Ruth..Anne Dawson
General Stanley's Daughters, Pirates, Policemen, Etc.
Act I.—Rocky Shore on Coast of Cornwall. Act II.—A Ruined Chapel.

(Closed September 30, 1940)

"The Mikado" was presented 11 times, "The Gondoliers," 7, and "Trial by Jury" and "Pirates of Penzance," 6.

BOYS AND GIRLS TOGETHER

(191 performances)

A revue in two acts by Ed Wynn and Pat C. Flick; lyrics by Jack Yellen and Irving Kahal; music by Sammy Fain; orchestration by Hans Spielac; arrangements by Russell Bennett and Don Walker. Produced by Ed Wynn at the Broadhurst Theatre, New York, October 1, 1940.

Principals—

Ed Wynn
Dave Apollon
Walter Long
Jerry Cooper
Al Baron
Jack Connover
Iris Marshall
Dell Parker
Kay Paulson
Mira Stephans

Tony and Renee de Marco
Lucienne and Ashour
The Six Willys
Jane Pickens
Marjorie Knapp
Edna Sedgwick
Sally Craven
Florence Foster
Phyllis Colt
Dorothy Koster
Lynn Lawrence
Ione Smith
Drucilla Strain
Paul and Frank La Varre
Dot and Dick Remy

Staged by Ed Wynn; dances directed by Albertina Rasch; music by John McManus; choral numbers by Al Siegal; settings by William Oden Waller; costumes by Irene Sharaff and Veronica.

(Closed March 15, 1941)

JOURNEY TO JERUSALEM

(17 performances)

A drama in three acts by Maxwell Anderson. Produced by The Playwrights' Company at the National Theatre, New York, October 5, 1940.

Cast of characters—

Marius....Arthur L. Sachs
The Greek Woman....Fay Baker
Herod....Frederic Tozere
The Soothsayer....Joseph V. De Santis
Mira....Alice Reinheart
Joseph....Horace Braham
Jacob....Ronny Liss
Miriam....Arlene Francis
Jeshua....Sidney Lumet
The Beggar....Joseph Wiseman
Shadrach....Charles De Sheim
Cassia....Terry Harris
Reba....Jeannette Chinley
Jesse....Edwin Vail
Zebulon....Alan Manson
The Centurion....Karl Malden
Ishmael....Arnold Moss
The Robber....Paul Genge
The Scribe....Henry Lascoe
The Porter....Walter Kapp
Gennesareth....David Leonard
Malachi....Joseph Kramm
Abbas....Charles Ellis
Chorazim....George Fairchild
Hanan....Byron McGrath
The Dove Woman....Juliet Talbot
The 1st Money Changer....Arnon Ben-Ami
The 2nd Money Changer....Joseph Wiseman
The Pharisee....Henry Walden
The Fruit Seller....Joseph Blanton
The Matzoth Seller....Katherine Cody
Flaccus....Paul Genge
Festus....James Gregory

Act I.—Scene 1—Court of Temple at Jerusalem. 2—Roof of Palace of Herod Antipas, Tiberias, Galilee. 3—Joseph's Home, Nazareth. 4—Desert Place Below Jericho. 5—Before City Gates of Jerusalem. Act II.—Scene 1—Inner Room of Temple. 2—Court of Temple. Act III.—Scene 1—Roof of Herod's Palace. 2—Joseph's House.

Staged by Elmer Rice; settings by Jo Mielziner; costumes by Millia Davenport.

Jeshua (Jesus) has been taken by his parents, Miriam (Mary) and Joseph, on a pilgrimage to Jerusalem for the Passover. Jeshua is 12, a fine, sensitive lad, spiritually detached from his relatives and friends, but unaware of his holy mission. On the way to Jerusalem the party is stopped by Ishmael, an outlaw from the mountains who is carrying on the rebellion against the Romans started by Judah. Ishmael is drawn to the boy Jeshua, discovers him as the Messiah, and saves him from the Roman soldiers at the gates of Jerusalem, where Herod Antipas has ordered that all children of 12 be stopped. Jeshua afterward meets the wise men in the temple and confounds them with his logic. Ishmael, protecting him a second time from the soldiers, is killed. Jeshua, believing now in his mission, carries on.

(Closed October 19, 1940)

IT HAPPENS ON ICE

(First engagement, 180 performances. Return 96. Total, 276)

A revue in two acts assembled by Sonja Henie and Arthur Wirtz; lyrics by Al Stillman; songs by Vernon Duke, Fred E. Ahlert and Peter de Rose. Produced by Sonart Productions at the Center Theatre, New York, October 10, 1940.

Principals engaged—

Joe Cook	Hedi Stenuf
Jo Ann Dean	Gene Berg
Jack Kilty	Buster Grace
Joan Edwards	Caley Sisters
Mary Janes Yeo	Edwina Blades
Dr. A. Douglass Nelles	Felix Knight
Le Verne	Geoffe Stevens
Lloyd Baxter	General Senna
Four Bruises	The Buccaneers

Staged by Leon Leonidoff; choreography by Catherine Littlefield and Robert Linden; music directed by Erno Rappe and conducted by David Mendoza; setting, costumes and lighting by Norman Bel Geddes.

The first engagement of "It Happens on Ice" closed March 8, 1941, and the return engagement started April 4, 1941.

(Closed June 14, 1941)

BOYD'S DAUGHTER

(3 performances)

A comedy in three acts by St. John Ervine. Produced by Copley Productions (W. Horace Schmidlapp and Joseph M. Gaites) at the Booth Theatre, New York, October 11, 1940.

Cast of characters—

Andy Haverson.......................................Walter Kelly
Andrew Boyd..Whitford Kane
Agnes Boyd...Helen Trenholme
Miss McClurg.......................................Grace Mills
John Haslett.......................................William Post, Jr.
Mrs. McBratney.....................................Estelle Reilley
Mrs. Clotworthy....................................Bernice Vert
Miss Logan...Esther Mitchell
Rev. Ernest Dunwoody, M.A..........................Hiram Sherman
William Henry Doak.................................Truman Smith
Carrie...Eda Heinemann
Rev. Arthur Patterson..............................J. P. Wilson

Act I.—Scene 1—Boyd's Shop in Donaghreagh, an Ulster Village Northern Ireland. 2—Living Room Behind the Shop. Act II.—Living Room. Act III.—The Shop.

Staged by Hiram Sherman; settings and lighting by Johannes Larsen.

Andrew Boyd runs the village grocery in Donaghreagh, Ireland. Being a kindly and expansive soul, Andrew attracts the gossips of the town to his shop. His daughter Agnes is his attractive assistant. Both John Haslett, who has come to open a rival shop across the street, and Rev. Ernest Dunwoody, who hopes to succeed the aging Rev. Arthur Patterson as the head of the local church, are bent on marrying Agnes. She favors the Rev. Ernest until John Haslett's store burns down. Then she knows that her heart has belonged to him all along.

(Closed October 12, 1940)

BLIND ALLEY

(63 performances)

A drama in three acts by James Warwick. Revived by Marie Louise Elkins and Clarence Taylor at the Windsor Theatre, New York, October 15, 1940.

Cast of characters—

Doris Shelby.......................................Lila Lee
Fred Landis..Richard Sisson
Dr. William A. Shelby..............................James Todd
Agnes..Dodee Wick
Teddy..Michael Artist
Nora...Aline McDermott
Hal Wilson...Roy Hargrave
Mazie Stoner.......................................Bernardine Hayes
Buck...Jay Adler
Nick...Jack Lambert
Officer Thorne.....................................Thomas Hume

Acts I, II and III.—The Living Room of Dr. Shelby's Home.

Staged by J. B. Daniels; setting by Frederick Fox.

"Blind Alley" was first produced in New York September 24, 1935, following a successful trial in the Summer theatres of

Carmel and Millbrook, N. Y. The story of Hal Wilson, a gangster who moves his mob into the Summer home of Dr. William A. Shelby, a professor of psychiatry, and is finally mentally and physically whipped by the professor, enjoyed an original run of 119 performances. Roy Hargrave played the gangster in both productions.

(Closed December 7, 1940)

CHARLEY'S AUNT

(233 performances)

A farce comedy in three acts by Brandon Thomas. Revived by Day Tuttle and Richard Skinner at the Cort Theatre, New York, October 17, 1940.

Cast of characters—

Jack Chesney....................Thomas Speidel
Brassett....................Harold deBecker
Charles Wykeham....................J. Richard Jones
Lord Fancourt Babberley....................Jose Ferrer
Kitty Verdun....................Mary Mason
Amy Spettigue....................Phyllis Avery
Col. Sir Francis Chesney....................Arthur Margetson
Stephen Spettigue....................Reynolds Denniston
Farmer....................Richard Cowdery
Donna Lucia D'Alvadorez....................Nedda Harrigan
Ela Delahay....................Katherine Wiman
Maud....................Mary Francis Heflin

Act I.—Jack Chesney's Rooms, St. Olde's College, Oxford. Act II.—Garden Outside Jack Chesney's Rooms. Act III.—Drawing Room of Mr. Spettigue's House.

Staged by Joshua Logan; settings and costumes by John Koenig.

"Charley's Aunt" was originally produced in London in 1892, with a popular comedian, W. S. Penley, playing the title rôle. It ran for years and has been revived twenty-nine times in England, mostly at Christmas time. The first American production was in 1893, with Etienne Girardot (who died in 1939, aged 83) as the Aunt from Brazil. After a three-year run in New York and on tour the farce went to the stock companies. In 1906 Girardot revived it and played it for another two years. In 1925 Herman Lieb restaged the play in New York, but it ran for only eight performances. The story and stage direction of "Charley's Aunt" have furnished a pattern for a countless number of similar plays since.

(Closed May 3, 1941)

GEORGE WASHINGTON SLEPT HERE

(173 performances)

A comedy in three acts by George S. Kaufman and Moss Hart. Produced by Sam H. Harris at the Lyceum Theatre, New York, October 18, 1940.

Cast of characters—

Mr. Kimber....................Percy Kilbride
Newton Fuller....................Ernest Truex
Annabelle Fuller....................Jean Dixon
Madge Fuller....................Peggy French
Steve Eldridge....................Kendall Clark
Katie....................Grace Valentine
Mrs. Douglas....................Mabel Taliaferro
Clayton Evans....................George Baxter
Rena Leslie....................Ruth Weston
Hester....................Paula Trueman
Raymond....................Bobby Readick
Uncle Stanley....................Dudley Digges
Leggett Frazer....................David Orrick
Tommy Hughes....................Edward Elliott
Sue Barrington....................Marian Edwards
Miss Wilcox....................Toni Sorel
Mr. Prescott....................Richard Barbee

Acts I, II and III.—Farm House in Pennyslvania.
Staged by George S. Kaufman; setting by John Root.

See page 337.

(Closed March 15, 1941)

BIG WHITE FOG

(64 performances)

A drama in three acts by Theodore Ward. Produced by The Negro Playwrights Company, Inc., at the Lincoln Theatre, New York, October 22, 1940.

Cast of characters—

Ellen Mason....................Hilda Offley
Juanita Rogers....................Maude Russell
Caroline Mason....................Eileen Renard
Phillip Mason....................Bertram Holmes
Mrs. Brooks....................Louise Jackson
Lester Mason....................Kelsey Pharr
Wanda Mason....................Alma Forrest
Victor Mason....................Canada Lee
Percy Mason....................Roburte Dorce
Claudine Adams....................Muriel Cook
Dan Rogers....................Edward Fraction
Count Strawder....................P. Jay Sidney
Count Cotton....................Andrew Walker
Brother Harper....................Robert Creighton
Sister Gabrella....................Trixie Smith
Black Cross Nurses....................Bertha Reubel, Almeina Green
Nathan Piszer....................Jerry Grebanier
Marx....................Stanley Prager

Caroline..Valerie Black
Philip..Carl Crawford
Bailiff..Stanley Prager
Police Sergeant..Lionel Monagas
Police Lieutenant..Ted Thurston
Members of mob: Harry Sangigian, Ken Renard, William Korff, Jay Raskris, Clyde Gooden and Frank Silvera.
Acts I, II and III.—Home of the Masons on Dearborn Street, Chicago, Ill., 1922 to 1932.
Staged by Powell Lindsay; setting by Perry Watkins.

Victor Mason is an educated Negro living in Chicago in 1922. Victor Mason is also an idealist and comes to believe that Marcus Garvey's promise to build a new republic for Negroes in Africa is the best chance his race has of overcoming the handicaps the enveloping white race puts upon it. Mason invests his savings with Garvey, loses both his money and his faith. His daughter turns prostitute, his son turns communist, his wife and mother-in-law turn against him and he is killed in a brush with the law when the authorities seek to evict him from his home.

(Closed December 14, 1940)

CABIN IN THE SKY

(156 performances)

A musical fantasy in two acts by Lynn Root; lyrics by John La Touche; music by Vernon Duke. Produced by Albert Lewis in association with Vinton Freedley at the Martin Beck Theatre, New York, October 25, 1940.

Cast of characters—

Georgia Brown..Katherine Dunham
Dr. Jones..Louis Sharp
Brother Green..J. Rosamond Johnson
Lily..Georgia Burke
Petunia Jackson..Ethel Waters
Lucifer, Jr..Rex Ingram
"Little Joe" Jackson..Dooley Wilson
The Lawd's General..Todd Duncan
Fleetfoot..Milton Williams
John Henry..J. Louis Johnson
Dude..Al Moore
First Henchman..Earl Sydnor
Second Henchman..Earl Edwards
Third Henchman..Maurice Ellis
Devil's Messenger..Al Stokes
Messenger Boy..Wilson Bradley
Domino Johnson..Dick Campbell
Imps: Archie Savage, Jieno Moxzer, Rajah Chardieno, Alexander McDonald.
Katherine Dunham Dancers: Claude Brown, Talley Beattey, Rita Christiana, Lucille Ellis, Lawaune Kennard, Roberta McLaurin, Alexander McDonald, Jiene Moxzer Harris, Rajah Chardieno, Evelyn Pilcher, Carmencita Romero, Edith Ross, Archie Savage, Lavinia Williams, Thomas Woosley, J. Emanuel Vanderhans, Candido Vicenti.

J. Rosamond Johnson Singers: Wilson Bradley, Rebecca Champion, Helen Dowdy, Clarence Jacobs, Ella MacLashley, Fradye Marshall, Arthur McLean, Louis Sharp, Eulabel Riley, Al Stokes, Laura Vaughns.

Act I.—Scene 1—Exterior of the Jacksons' Home Somewhere in the South. 2—Little Joe's Bedroom. 3—The Jacksons' Backyard. 4—The Head Man's Office in Hades. 5—The Jacksons' Front Porch. Act II.—Scene 1—The Jacksons' Backyard. 2—Exterior of John Henry's Café. 3—John Henry's Café. 4—At the Pearly Gates.

Staged by George Balanchine; dialogue directed by Albert Lewis; music directed by Max Meth; settings and costumes by Boris Aronson.

Petunia Jackson, sitting mournfully by the bedside of Little Joe, who is dying, prays earnestly to the Lord that her bad boy husband be given another chance. The Lord, knowing Petunia as a good worker in the church, listens and agrees. Joe is to have six months in which to redeem himself. Thereafter representatives of Heaven and Hell in the persons of The Lawd's General and Lucifer, Jr., fight for Joe's soul. Lucifer is about to win. Joe backslides and shoots Petunia in a dancehall. But again the Lord is friendly and helps Petunia squeeze Little Joe through the pearly gates.

(Closed March 8, 1941)

'TIS OF THEE

(1 performance)

A revue in two acts by Alfred Hayes, sketches by Sam Locke; music by Alex North and Al Moss; additional music and lyrics by Peter Barry, David Gregory and Richard Levine. Produced by Nat Lichtman at Maxine Elliott's Theatre, New York, October 26, 1940.

Principals engaged—

George Lloyd	Esther Junger
Jerry Munson	Jane Hoffman
Mervyn Nelson	Sherle Hartt
Van Kirk	Laura Duncan
Jack Berry	Vivian Block
Daniel Nagrin	Virginia Burke
Paul Roberts	Arno Tanny
Alfred Hayes	Ray Harrison
Jan Zerfing	Saida Gerard
Bram Vandenberg	Susan Remos
Alfred and Reese	Cappelo and Beatrice

Staged by Nat Lichtman; music directed by Alex Saron; choreography by Esther Junger; settings by Carl Kent.

(Closed October 26, 1940)

SUZANNA AND THE ELDERS

(30 performances)

A comedy in three acts by Lawrence Langner and Armina Marshall. Produced by Jack Kirkland at the Morosco Theatre, New York, October 29, 1940.

Cast of characters—

Sister Mary Lamb.....Lois Hall
Sister Abigail Adams.....Drina Hill
Sister Flavilla Ford.....Rosemary Carver
Sister Olympia Herring.....Mary Boylan
Sister Hannah Plunkett.....Kathryn Grill
Sister Amanda Perkins.....Bettina Cerf
Sister Clarissa Marshall.....Frances Harrison
Sister Suzanna Leeds.....Haila Stoddard
Patience Kent.....Jane Seymour
Brother Tom.....Lloyd Bridges
Reverend Abner Owen.....Philip Coolidge
Charles Owen.....Paul Ballantyne
John Adam Kent.....Morris Carnovsky
Brother McIntosh.....Royal Beal
Brother Tupper.....Howard Freeman
Brother Birdseye.....Ralph Wordley
Brother Plunkett.....Hale Norcross
Brother Stafford.....Charles Furcolowe
Brother Lemuel.....Richard Clark
Brother Longhorne.....Theodore Newton
Brother Galusha.....Tom Elwell
Mike Lenihan.....Ross Hertz

Acts I, II and III.—Communal Hall of Community House at Harmony Heights.
Staged by Worthington Miner; settings by Stewart Chaney.

Sister Suzanna Leeds had been reared in a colony devoted to an experiment in Christian Socialism at Harmony Heights in the early eighteen hundreds. There is no marriage or giving in marriage at Harmony Heights, but there are biological experiments in race improvement. The elders select and mate hopeful mothers and fathers. When Charles Owen sees Suzanna he joins the colony and hopes to win Suzanna as a mate. She sticks to the rules of the colony and is assigned to another. Rebellion flares. Charles finally wins Suzanna as his wife.

(Closed November 23, 1940)

* PANAMA HATTIE

(267 performances)

A musical comedy in two acts by Herbert Fields and B. G. De Sylva; music and lyrics by Cole Porter. Produced by B. G. De Sylva at the 46th Street Theatre, New York, October 30, 1940.

Cast of characters—

Mrs. Gonzales.....Conchita
Mac.....Eppy Pearson
Skat Briggs.....Pat Harrington
Windy Deegan.....Frank Hyers
Woozy Hogan.....Rags Ragland
Chiquita.....Nadine Gay
Fruit Peddler.....Linda Griffith
Tim.....Roger Gerry
Tom.....Roy Blaine
Ted.....Ted Daniels
Ty.....Lipman Duckat
Hattie Maloney.....Ethel Merman
Leila Tree.....Phyllis Brooks
Mildred Hunter.....Elaine Shepard
Kitty Belle Randolph.....Ann Graham
Nick Bullett.....James Dunn
Florrie.....Betty Hutton
Geraldine Bullett.....Joan Carroll
Vivian Budd.....Arthur Treacher
Pete.....Al Downing
First Stranger.....Hal Conklin
Second Stranger.....Frank DeRoss
Mike.....Jack Donahue
Whitney Randolph.....James Kelso

Act I.—Scene 1—Santa-Ana Plaza, Panama City. 2—Bar of Tropical Shore. 3—Street in Panama. 4—Yard of Nick's Cottage, Canal Zone. 5—Esplanade. 6—Patio of Admiral Tree's Home. Act II.—Scene 1—Santa-Ana Plaza. 2—Room in Barn Outside Panama City. 3 and 6—Street in Panama City. 4—Yard of Nick's Cottage. 5—Control House, Canal Zone. 7—Patio of Admiral Tree's Home.

Staged by Edgar MacGregor; dances by Robert Alton; settings and costumes by Raoul Pene DuBois.

Hattie Maloney had been known as "Panama Hattie" when she was one of the Canal Zone girls. When she reformed she became engaged to Nick Bullett, of the Philadelphia Bulletts. Nick was divorced and the custodian of an 8-year-old child. Hattie insisted that he send for the child before they were married. She wanted the child's endorsement of her as a prospective stepmother. Young Geraldine arrives and laughs right in Panama Hattie's face. Later they become buddies and everything is friendly by 11 P.M.

RETURN ENGAGEMENT

(8 performances)

A comedy in three acts by Lawrence Riley. Produced by W. Horace Schmidlapp and Joseph M. Gaites at the Golden Theatre, New York, November 1, 1940.

Cast of characters—

Mrs. Autumn Hetherington.....Evelyn Varden
George.....William Leicester
Bob.....Peter Garey
Patsy Tomkins.....Augusta Dabney

Eddie....................................Alexander Nicol
Eloise Hubbard....................................Ruth Lott
Ruth Conway....................................Audrey Christie
Mrs. Carlotta Faulkner....................................Leona Powers
Geneva Faulkner....................................Caryl Smith
Bill Gardiner....................................Thomas Coley
Elizabeth Emerson....................................Mady Christians
Geoffrey Armstrong....................................Bert Lytell
Baldy Bemis....................................Lewis L. Russell
Albert....................................Warren Clarke
Geneva's Maid....................................Helen Reid

Acts I, II and III.—Terrace of the Stockton Playhouse on the Estate of Mrs. Carlotta Faulkner, Near Stockton, Conn.

Staged by Frank Merlin and Rowland Leigh; setting by Johannes Larsen.

Elizabeth Emerson and Geoffrey Armstrong, as young players, had been married and divorced. Ten years later they are summoned to play guest star rôles at the Stockton Summer Theatre in Connecticut. During this engagement Geoffrey, always the great lover, flirts with the lady backer of the enterprise and is finally exposed as a pompous fraud. Elizabeth, however, discovers that she still loves the old ham and a reunion is promised.

(Closed November 7, 1940)

BEVERLY HILLS

(28 performances)

A comedy in three acts by Lynn Starling and Howard J. Green. Produced by Laurence Schwab and Otto Preminger at the Fulton Theatre, New York, November 7, 1940.

Cast of characters—

Lois Strickland ....Helen Claire
Della ....Enid Markey
Jose ....Peter Goo Chong
Art Browder ....Robert Shayne
Pedro ....Frank Chew
Miss White ....Doro Merande
Leonard Strickland ....Clinton Sundberg
Jean Harding....................................Ilka Chase
May Flowers....................................Violet Heming
A. Trumbull Eastmore....................................William J. Kelly
Mrs. Burnside....................................Effie Afton
Ted Farlow....................................William Talman
Policeman....................................Fred De Cordova
Geraldine Smith....................................Lea Penman

Acts I, II and III.—Leonard Strickland's Home, Beverly Hills.

Staged by Otto L. Preminger; settings by Donald Oenslager.

Lois Strickland is tormented by Leonard, her gifted but unambitious scenario-writing husband. She wants desperately to push him ahead. When she learns that her old friend, May Flowers, is married to a big producer with an important assignment to give out she begs May's help to get the job for Leonard. May, man-crazy, tosses herself into Leonard's arms, as the price of the job, but he eventually is able to stand up and assert himself. Which promises something, but not much, for Lois.

(Closed November 30, 1940)

QUIET PLEASE

(16 performances)

A comedy in three acts by F. Hugh Herbert and Hans Kraly from a story by Ferdinand Reyher. Produced by Jesse L. Lasky and Henry Duffy at the Guild Theatre, New York, November 8, 1940.

Cast of characters—

Tony....................Paul Marion
Betty....................Nina Clemens
Mr. Fitzgerald....................Michael Ames
Trude....................Trude Wyler
Bill Brady....................Bruce Macfarlane
Minnie....................Evelyn Wall
Jack....................Ralph Douglas
Bob Canfield....................Fred Niblo
Henry Dakin....................Anthony Kemble Cooper
Gloria Weston....................Ann Mason
Murphy....................Carl Chapman
A Tourist....................Oza Waldrop
Fred Mathews....................Arthur Hughes
Miss Gurney....................Bunty Cutler
Jim Faraday....................Herman Lieb
Carol Adams....................Jane Wyatt
Roland Pierce....................Donald Woods
Joe Manheim....................Fred Sears
Alice....................Judith Elliott
Jane....................Nancy Preston
Michael Kilmer....................Gordon Jones
An Electrician....................Charles McClelland
Bill....................Charles Martin
Julius....................Adolph Tews

Grips, Prop Men, Juicers, Sound Men, Extra Men, Ushers, Assistant Camera Men, Stagehands, Tourists.

Act I.—Scene 1—Theatre Set—Sound Stage 18, Imperial Studios, Hollywood, Calif. 2—Carol's Bungalow Dressing Room on the Lot. Act II.—Boudoir of Carol's Bungalow Dressing Room. Act III.—Scene 1—Carol's Bungalow Dressing Room. 2—Sound Stage 18.

Staged by Russell Fillmore under supervision of Henry Duffy; settings by Everett Burgess.

Carol Adams, a popular screen star, is married to Roland, who ranks no better than Class B. Roland would be a playboy. When he goes fishing he fishes for blondes as well as fish. Carol thinks she will be even. When Michael Kilmer, a handsome garage attendant with a college degree, returns the Adams car Carol prevails upon him to stay the night. Roland, back from his fishing, is properly suspicious and threatening, but finally forgiving. Michael reluctantly returns to the garage.

(Closed November 21, 1940)

GLAMOUR PREFERRED

(11 performances)

A comedy in three acts by Florence Ryerson and Colin Clements. Produced by Brock Pemberton at the Booth Theatre, New York, November 15, 1940.

Cast of characters—

Amanda Beckett....Helen Harmon
Loula....Elsie Mae Gordon
Webster....Henry Vincent
Angela Vaughn....Irene Corlett
Max Musick....Loring Smith
Lynn Eldridge....Flora Campbell
Two Silver-Fish Exterminators.... { Charles Rains / Thomas Babcock }
Jeff Potter....Lex Lindsay
Kerry Eldridge....Glen Langan
A Strange Girl....Elaine Perry
Bernard C. Goldwater....Louis Sorin
Nicholas Jorga....Stefan Schnabel
Mrs. Florinda Mott Pengilly....Maidel Turner
Lady Bonita Towyn....Betty Lawford
Homer Cox....James O'Rear
Henry....Haskell Coffin
Karl Reinbeck....Henry Levin
Sir Hubert Towyn....Robert Craven
Officer Hanan....James Gregory

Acts I, II and III.—The Eldridge Ranch House, San Fernando Valley, California.
Staged by Antoinette Perry; setting by John Root.

Kerry Eldridge, glamour boy of the screen, making a personal appearance tour of the East, bumps into Lady Bonita Towyn, with whom he played around before he married Lynn. Bonita, tired of a titled English husband, follows Kerry back to Hollywood and tries to take him away from his wife. Lynn promptly sends for Bonita's husband, Sir Hubert, who doesn't like Bonita very much, either, but is willing to help out the Eldridges.

(Closed November 23, 1940)

TWELFTH NIGHT

(129 performances)

A comedy in two acts by William Shakespeare; incidental music by Paul Bowles. Revived by The Theatre Guild and Gilbert Miller at the St. James Theatre, New York, November 19, 1940.

Cast of characters—

Orsino, Duke of Illyria....Wesley Addy
Curio....George Keane
Valentine....Philip Huston
Viola....Helen Hayes
Sea Captain....Anthony Ross
Sir Toby Belch....Mark Smith
Maria....June Walker
Sir Andrew Aguecheek....Wallace Acton
Feste....Donald Burr
Olivia....Sophie Stewart
Malvolio....Maurice Evans
Antonio....Ellis Irving
Sebastian....Alex Courtnay
Fabian....Raymond Johnson
Attendant to Olivia....June Brehm
Officer....Irving Morrow
Soldier....Anthony Ross
Sir Topas....William Hansen
A Page....Osbert Chevers

Act I.—Scenes 1, 4 and 8—Orsino's Palace. 2—Sea Coast. 3 and 7—Kitchen of Olivia's House. 5—Room in Olivia's House. 6 and 9—Street. 10—Olivia's Garden. Act II.—Scenes 1 and 5—Olivia's Garden. 2 and 4—Street. 3—Prison.

This version staged in two acts and fourteen scenes. The last notable revival of "Twelfth Night" was made by Jane Cowl in 1930. Previous American Violas have included Viola Allen, Julia Marlowe, Annie Russell, Margaret Anglin, Eva Le Gallienne and Vera Allen in Chicago.

(Closed March 8, 1941)

HORSE FEVER

(25 performances)

A farce in three acts by Eugene Conrad, Zac and Ruby Gabel. Produced by Alex Yokel at the Mansfield Theatre, New York, November 23, 1940.

Cast of characters—

Mrs. Drum....Zamah Cunningham
Virgo....Marietta Canty
Frank Drum....Joseph Pevney
Milly Flynn....Sara Seegar
Joe Flynn....Millard Mitchell
Janet Deering....Judy Parrish
Horatio Drum....Arthur Allen
Orville....Ezra Stone
Murphy....Clancy Cooper
Mr. Hilton....Neil Moore
Labor Day Green....Bobby Mitchell
Trilby....Herself
Maid....Kay Loring
Lucky Sam....Lou Lubin

Dr. Terganoff....................Daniel Ocko
Hotel Manager....................Seldon Bennett
City Marshall....................John L. Kearney
Photographer....................Jack Arnold
A Race Track Steward....................Peter Cusanelli
Jocky Lane....................Leslie Barrett
Messenger Boy....................Mitchell Kowal

Act I.—Living-Room, Drum House, Near Aqueduct. Act II.—A Hotel Room. Act III.—A Stable at Belmont Race Track.

Staged by Milton Stiefel; settings by Louis Kennel.

Orville Drum, an inventive youth, having read that experiments at Cornell have successfully treated animals through psychiatry, determines to reform a race horse the Drums have inherited. The horse has developed a complex against breaking at the post. Orville smuggles the horse into a hotel in a piano box, stables it in the bathroom for several weeks, gives it daily treatments and finally gets it ready for the Derby. The treatments are successful, but the horse loses the race.

(Closed December 14, 1940)

* THE CORN IS GREEN

(236 performances)

A drama in three acts by Emlyn Williams. Produced by Herman Shumlin at the National Theatre, New York, November 26, 1940.

Cast of characters—

John Goronwy Jones....................Rhys Williams
Miss Ronberry....................Mildred Dunnock
Idwal Morris....................Charles S. Pursell
Sarah Pugh....................Gwyneth Hughes
A Groom....................George Bleasdale
The Squire....................Edmond Breon
Mrs. Watty....................Rosalind Ivan
Bessie Watty....................Thelma Schnee
Miss Moffat....................Ethel Barrymore
Robbart Robbatch....................Thomas Lyons
Morgan Evans....................Richard Waring
Glyn Thomas....................Kenneth Clarke
John Owen....................Merritt O'Duel
Will Hughes....................Terence Morgan
Old Tom....................Sayre Crawley

Boys, Girls and Parents: Julia Knox, Amelia Romano, Betty Conibear, Rosalind Carter, Harda Norman, Joseph McInerney, Marcel Dill, Gwilym Williams, Tommy Dix.

Acts I, II and III.—Living-Room of a House in Glansarno, a Small Village in a Remote Welsh Countryside. Latter Part of Last Century.

Staged by Herman Shumlin; setting by Howard Bay; costumes by Ernest Schrapps.

See page 94.

FLEDGLING

(13 performances)

A drama in three acts adapted by Eleanor Carroll Chilton and Philip Lewis from a novel by Eleanor Carroll Chilton. Produced by Otis Chatfield-Taylor at the Hudson Theatre, New York, November 27, 1940.

Cast of characters—

Grace Linton....................................Norma Chambers
Andrew Linton...............................Frederick Bradlee
Barbara Linton...................................Sylvia Weld
Hugh Linton......................................Ralph Morgan
John Forbes...Walter Coy
Stella Berrick.......................................Lora Baxter
Kenneth Brede................................John Hoysradt
Bartholomew......................................Harry Hanlon
Miss Harper..................................Margaret Clifford
Richard Dennis.....................................Tom Powers
Acts I, II and III.—Living-Room of the Linton House in Connecticut.
Staged by Heinrich Schnitzler; setting by Richard Whorf.

When Grace and Hugh Linton eloped they agreed upon a life of service to humanity that should have for its motto, "Light in dark places." Though Grace had been brought up a Catholic the Lintons held successfully to their ideals and brought up their two children as religious liberals. When the children are grown Grace is stricken with a form of creeping paralysis that works steadily toward heart and brain. The daughter, Barbara, tortured by her mother's condition, decides upon a mercy killing and adds poison to her medicine. Finding no relief for a stricken conscience, and no help from her agnostic father; learning that her mother had gone back to the church a year before, Barbara also makes way with herself.

(Closed December 7, 1940)

ROMANTIC MR. DICKENS

(8 performances)

A drama in three acts by H. H. and Marguerite Harper. Produced by John Tuerk at the Playhouse, New York, December 2, 1940.

Cast of characters—

Martha...Emily Lorraine
Dora Spenlow (Later Dora Winter)................Gertrude Flynn
Marianne Leigh...................................Mary Heberden
Henry Kolle...................................Lawrence Fletcher

Charles Dickens.....................................Robert Keith
Timmy.....................................Lackland Campbell
Mr. Spenlow.....................................Marshall Bradford
Mrs. Charles Dickens.....................................Zolya Talma
Georgina Hogarth.....................................Elwyne Harvey
Mr. Twilling, the Vicar.....................................Roland Hogue
Baroness Burdett-Coutts.....................................Thais Lawton
A Girl.....................................Marita Sylva
A Lady-of-the-Evening.....................................Cathleen Cordell
Caroline Bronson.....................................Diana Barrymore
Queen's Lacky.....................................Tom Bate

Act I.—Scene 1—Charles Dickens' Lodging in London. 2—Library at Tavistock House, Dickens' London Home. Act II.—Tavistock House. Act III.—Scene 1—Tavistock House. 2—Green Room of Auditorium in the Gallery of Illustration.

Staged by Arthur Sircom; settings by Watson Barratt; costumes by Ernest Schraps.

Charles Dickens as a young man presumably fell in love with the Dora Spenlow who afterward became the heroine of "David Copperfield." When Dora was torn from his arms by her irate father Dickens moped but finally married. His home life was unhappy and he turned again to Dora, also married, until the day he met her and discovered she had put forty pounds on her person and added practically nothing to her mind. He then turned to a pretty young actress, Caroline Bronson, but was forced to give her up to avoid a scandal.

(Closed December 7, 1940)

DELICATE STORY

(29 performances)

A comedy in two acts by Ferenc Molnar; English text by Gilbert Miller. Produced by Gilbert Miller and Vinton Freedley at the Henry Miller Theatre, New York, December 4, 1940.

Cast of characters—

Mary Cristof.....................................Edna Best
Mrs. Lacroix.....................................Katherine Grey
Oliver Odry.....................................John Craven
Tony.....................................Alfred Etcheverry
Frank.....................................Milton Neil
Baron.....................................Arnold Korff
Mrs. Gola.....................................May Thomas
Henry Cristof.....................................Jay Fassett
Pip.....................................Norman Tokar
1st Cristof Child.....................................Howard Sherman
2nd Cristof Child.....................................Norma Clerc
3rd Cristof Child.....................................Haldor deBecker
Mrs. Benard.....................................Carlotta Nillson
Summons Server.....................................Leslie King
Little Girl.....................................Patsy O'Shea
Police Captain.....................................Harry Gribbon
Office Attendant.....................................Gordon Nelson
Laborer.....................................Thomas Brown
College Girl.....................................Natalie Thompson
Mrs. Clermont.....................................Florence Fair

Servant Girl....................................Jacqueline Clarke
Physician...Harry Irvine
Act I.—Scenes 1 and 2—Cristof's Delicatessen Store, Switzerland. 3—Police Captain's Office. Act II.—Scenes 1 and 3—The Delicatessen Store. 2—Room in the Cristof Flat.
Staged by Gilbert Miller; settings by Raymond Sovey.

Mary Cristof fancies that she has a mission. The wife of the proprietor of a delicatessen shop in Switzerland Mary sees so many lonesome, frightened, homesick young men start away to war that she thinks if she can be kind to them before they are called she will help them. With the first six she mothers romantically everything works as she planned it. But with the seventh she falls in love and there is trouble. Mary and Oliver Odry go for an automobile ride, are witnesses to an accident, are summoned by the police and have to do a lot of explaining—both to Mary's husband and to the police. Then it appears that Oliver had been engaged to another all the time.

(Closed December 28, 1940)

MUM'S THE WORD

(12 performances)

An entertainment in a prologue, ten numbers and an epilogue as imagined by Jimmy Savo. Produced by Jimmy Savo at the Belmont Theatre, New York, December 5, 1940.

The Sketches—

Swedish Idyll	Old-Fashioned Girl
Singsong Mother Goose	Bourgeois Gentilhomme
The Emergency Call	Engagement at Sea
Washerwoman in Love	Chestnut Man
Deep South Fever	When Jokes Were Young

Verbal annotations were by Hiram Sherman.
Staged by Al Webster.

The favor with which he had been received as a featured specialist in many revues convinced Jimmy Savo that he should join the ranks of the monologists who were billed as monodramatists. He assembled a bill of his favorite sketches, sweetened it with a few that were new and made the experiment. After twelve appearances he withdrew the program for revision.

(Closed December 14, 1940)

EVERY MAN FOR HIMSELF

(3 performances)

A farce in three acts by Milton Lazarus. Produced by Arthur Hutchinson and Arthur Ripley at the Guild Theatre, New York, December 9, 1940.

Cast of characters—

Al....................Murray Alper
Wally Britt....................Lee Tracy
Sneeden....................David Hoffman
Elizabeth....................Kay Linaker
Mel....................Charlie Williams
Janey....................Beryl Vaughan
York....................John Gaullaudet
Helen....................Margaret Tallichet
Mrs. Rumsey....................Jeanne Seel
Man....................Martin Myers
Woman....................Geneva Keenan
Rittenhoff....................Wally Maher
Grogan....................Charles A. Hughes
Humphrey Harrison....................Grant Richards
Dr. Lane....................Richard Bartell
Mrs. Lane....................Gerry Brent
Little Boy....................Billy Curtis
Officer....................Carl Payne
Dolan....................Edgar Roland Murray
Wally's Uncle....................George Roberts

Acts I, II and III.—Living Room of Wally Britt's Home in Hollywood Hills.
Staged by Arthur Ripley; settings by Ernest Glover.

Wally Britt, a successful Hollywood scenarist, goes on a four-day binge and wakes up in dinner clothes and a mental fog. He cannot remember bringing home the young woman who is wearing his pajamas. He cannot remember the story he has sold to a big shot producer for $10,000. He cannot remember inviting the sound effects man from the studio, with his wife and others, to come and live with him. When a New York gangster moves in and tries to marry the heroine things get pretty complicated, but Mr. Britt has the advantage. He had married her already.

(Closed December 11, 1940)

RETREAT TO PLEASURE

(23 performances)

A comedy in three acts by Irwin Shaw. Produced by Group Theatre, Inc., at the Belasco Theatre, New York, December 17, 1940.

Cast of characters—

Frances Galligan....................................Helen Ford
Peter Flower..Leif Erickson
Chester Stack.......................................John Emery
Eugene Makofske.....................................George Matthews
Norah Galligan......................................Edith Atwater
Lee Tatnall...Hume Cronyn
Mr. Ordway..Fred Stewart
Franklin Diederich..................................Art Smith
Lenore Trilling.....................................Florence Sundstrom
Husband...Joseph F. Foley
Wife..Marie Adels
Gretchen Tatnall....................................Dorothy Patten
Girl in Bathing Suit................................Barbara Beech
Lady at the Bar.....................................Ruth Nelson
Bartender...John McGovern

Act I.—Apartment of the Galligans. Acts II and III.—Florida.
Staged by Harold Clurman; settings by Donald Oenslager.

Norah Galligan had been working with the WPA in Ohio as a minor executive. When the government ordered 10,000 workers off the rolls Norah had considerable difficulty trying to rationalize her own conclusions. Returning to her home in New York she finds three men waiting for her—a young idealist without a job, a rich industrialist and a handsome but idle playboy. Trying to make up her mind which to accept she goes to Florida with the industrialist to ponder her problems. The playboy and the idealist follow after. Still she is uncertain and finally decides not to take any of them.

(Closed January 4, 1941)

CUE FOR PASSION

(12 performances)

A drama in three acts by Edward Chodorov and H. S. Kraft. Produced by Richard Aldrich and Richard Myers at the Royale Theatre, New York, December 19, 1940.

Cast of characters—

Vivienne Ames.......................................Doris Nolan
John Elliott..George Coulouris
Elsie...Clare Saunders
Bellboy...Bert Conway
Dave Herrick..Thomas Coley
Ann Bailey..Claire Niesen
Reporters .....Fred Sears, Melchor Ferrer, John Neilan, Ellen Love
Photographers...................Philip Faversham, Leonard Keith
Frances Chapman.....................................Gale Sondergaard
Paul Albert Keppler.................................Oscar Karlweis
General Escobar.....................................Wilton Graff
Clifford Gates......................................Ralph Locke
Herbert Lee Phillips................................Lauren Gilbert
Maitre d'Hotel......................................Roland Hogue
Marvin A. Mallett...................................Clay Clement

Doctor ....Albert Bergh
Mr. Clark..Guy J. Sampsel
Commissioner.....................................Edward Butler
Medical Examiner..............................Russell Morrison
Detectives.............Edwin Gordon, Edward Forbes, Scott Moore
Harkrider...Whitner Bissell
Florist...Harold Grau
Waiters...............................Peter Gregg, Leonard Keith
Ilsa Keppler..Lili Valenty
Hughes, D.A.....................................Douglas Gilmore
Acts I, II and III.—Living Room of Hotel Suite in City Between New York and Washington on a Night in September.
Staged by Otto Preminger; setting by Herbert Andrews.

John Elliott was a mean man but a brilliant writer. Developing a passion for the stage he is about to make his debut the night he is shot and killed. John Elliott's wife is also a brilliant writer, and only a shade less unpleasant than John. Motivated by vanity she seeks to make John's death appear to have been a suicide. All the suspects agree with her except Ann Bailey, a young girl who happens to have been the last one to have seen the dead man alive. She spills the beans in the last scene.

(Closed December 28, 1940)

THE OLD FOOLISHNESS

(3 performances)

A comedy in three acts by Paul Vincent Carroll. Produced by John Golden at the Windsor Theatre, New York, December 20, 1940.

Cast of characters—

Mrs. Sheeran....................................Margery Maude
Peter..Roy Roberts
Mike..Vincent Dcnehue
Mrs. Dorian (Ole' Contrairy)...............Grace Francis Findlay
Dan Dorian...Walter Burke
Maeve McHugh..Sally O'Neil
Phelim Fitzfagan..............................Laurence O'Brien
Rosemaryanne Fitzfagan.......................Guerita Donnelly
The Canon.....................................St. Clair Bayfield
Francis..Sean Dillon
Acts I and III.—Kitchen of the Sheeran Farmhouse, in a Glen at the foot of the Mourne Mountains, County Down, Ireland. Act II.—Scene 1—The Sheeran Kitchen. 2—Ruins of Ancient Castle atop a Neighboring Mountain.
Staged by Rachel Crothers; settings by Donald Oenslager.

Maeve McHugh has been living with Francis Sheeran in Dublin. When he leaves her Maeve seeks out the Sheeran family in County Down, not to complain about Francis, but to ask the family to help him. There are two other Sheeran boys living at home—Peter, the substantial head of the family, and Mike, a studious, poetical type. Both fall in love with Maeve. She cannot decide between them. When Francis returns and the Church takes a hand to complicate the matter further, Maeve takes to the road to puzzle things out for herself.

(Closed December 21, 1940)

OLD ACQUAINTANCE

(170 performances)

A comedy in three acts by John van Druten. Produced by Dwight Deere Wiman at the Morosco Theatre, New York, December 23, 1940.

Cast of characters—

Katherine Markham....................................Jane Cowl
Rudd Kendall..Kent Smith
Deirdre Drake.....................................Adele Longmire
Sabrina...Anna Franklin
Mildred Watson Drake..............................Peggy Wood
Susan..Edna West
Preston Drake.....................................Hunter Gardner

Acts I and III.—Katherine Markham's Apartment in the Washington Square District of New York City. Act II.—An Apartment on Park Avenue.

Staged by Auriol Lee; settings by Richard Whorf.

Katherine Markham is a novelist, rather on the intellectual side. Her oldest friend is Mildred Watson Drake, also a novelist, but definitely on the lighter or best-seller side. Katherine has carried on a bit, having an affair or two. Mildred has married, had a daughter and divorced her husband. Now comes Mildred's daughter, Deirdre, to take Katherine's latest affair, Rudd Kendall, right out from under her nose. This serves to strain but not to break the friendship of the old acquaintances.

(Closed May 17, 1941)

MEET THE PEOPLE

(160 performances)

A musical revue in two acts by Henry Myers; music by Jay Gorney and George Bassman; sketches by Ben and Sol Barzman, Mortimer Offner, Edward Eliscu, Danny Dare, Henry Blankfort, Bert Lawrence, Sid Kuller, Ray Golden, Milt Gross, Mike Quin and Arthur Ross. Produced by the Hollywood Alliance at the Mansfield Theatre, New York, December 25, 1940.

Principals engaged—

Jack Gilford	Robert Nash
Doodles Weaver	Virginia Bryan
Nanette Farbares	Fay McKenzie
Elizabeth Talbot-Martin	Marie DeForest
Jack Williams	Jack Boyle
Peggy Ryan	Robert Davis
Eddie Johnson	Louis Paul
Jack Albertson	Angus Hopkins
Barney Phillips	Beverly Weaver
Marion Colby	Sue Robin
Ted Arkin	Norman Lawrence
Dorothy Roberts	Beryl Carew
Jack Boyle	Kenneth Patterson
Patricia Brilhante	Michael Doyle
Josephine Del Mar	and others

Staged by Danny Dare; sketches directed by Mortimer Offner; orchestra directed by Archie Bleyer; settings by Frederick Stover; costumes by Gerda Vanderneers and Kate Lawson; lighting by Roy Holmes.

(Closed May 10, 1941)

* PAL JOEY

(198 performances)

A musical comedy in two acts by John O'Hara; music by Richard Rodgers; lyrics by Lorenz Hart. Produced by George Abbott at the Ethel Barrymore Theatre, New York, December 25, 1940.

Cast of characters—

Joey Evans	Gene Kelly
Mike Spears	Robert J. Mulligan
Gladys	June Havoc
Agnes	Diane Sinclair
The Kid	Sondra Barrett
Linda English	Leila Ernst
Valerie	Amarilla Morris
Albert Doane	Stanley Donen
Vera Simpson	Vivienne Segal
Terry	Jane Fraser
Victor	Van Johnson
Ernest	John Clarke
Max	Averell Harris
The Tenor	Nelson Rae
Melba Snyder	Jean Casto
Waiter	Dummy Spelvin
Ludlow Lowell	Jack Durant
Briefcase	Vincent York
Commissioner O'Brien	James Lane
Assistant Hotel Manager	Cliff Dunstan

Specialty Dancer: Shirley Paige.

Dancing Girls: Claire Anderson, Sondra Barrett, Alice Craig, Louise de Forrest, Enez Early, Tilda Getz, Charlene Harkins, Frances Krell, Janet Lavis, Amarilla Morris, Olive Nicolson, Mildred Patterson, Dorothy Poplar, Diane Sinclair, Mildred Solly, Jeanne C. Trybom, Marie Vanneman.

Dancing Boys: Adrian Anthony, John Benton, Milton Chisholm, Stanley Donen, Henning Irgens, Van Johnson, Howard Ledig, Michael Moore, Albert Ruiz.

Act I.—Scenes 1, 3 and 5—Night Club in Chicago's South Side. 2—Pet Shop. 4—Vera's and Joey's Rooms. 6—Tailor's Shop. 7—Joey Looks into the Future. Act II.—Scenes 1 and 3—Chez Joey.

2 and 4—Joey's Apartment. 5—The Way Things Looked at Dinner Time.
Staged by George Abbott; dances directed by Robert Alton; settings and lighting by Jo Mielziner; costumes by John Koenig.

Joey Evans is a tough hoofer of the night clubs. Vain, boastful, handsome, Joey is attractive to women. He picks up Linda English, an innocent; leaves her for Vera Simpson, a rich Gold Coast matron who finances a night club for him; tires of Vera and proceeds on his way toward other questionable adventures.

* MY SISTER EILEEN

(200 performances)

A comedy in three acts by Joseph A. Fields and Jerome Chodorov based on the stories of Ruth McKenney. Produced by Max Gordon at the Biltmore Theatre, New York, December 26, 1940.

Cast of characters—

Mr. Appopolous....Morris Carnovsky
Ruth Sherwood....Shirley Booth
Eileen Sherwood....Jo Ann Sayers
Jensen....George Cotton
A Street Arab....Eric Roberts
Lonigan....Tom Dillon
The Wreck....Gordon Jones
Another Street Arab....Robert White
Captain Fletcher....Charles Martin
Helen Wade....Joan Tompkins
Frank Lippencott....Richard Quine
Chic Clark....Bruce MacFarlane
Cossack....Benson Spring
Violet Shelton....Effie Afton
Mrs. Wade....Helen Ray
Robert Baker....William Post, Jr.
Walter Sherwood....Donald Foster
A Prospective Tenant....Eda Heinemann
The Consul....Joseph Kallini
Six Future Admirals: Michael Ames, Alan Brixey, Peter Knego, Paul Marion, Mel Roberts, Paul Seymour.
Acts I, II and III.—Basement Apartment in Greenwich Village.
Staged by George S. Kaufman; dance sequence staged by Paul Seymour; setting by Donald Oenslager.

See page 204.

ALL IN FUN

(3 performances)

A musical revue in two acts by Virginia Faulkner and Everett Marcy; music and lyrics by Baldwin Bergerson, June Sillman, John Rox, Irvin Graham, Will Irwin, Pembroke Davenport and S. K. Russell. Produced by Leonard Sillman at the Majestic Theatre, New York, December 27, 1940.

Principals engaged—

Bill Robinson	Imogene Coca
Red Marshall	Pert Kelton
Wynn Murray	Rosita Moreno
Paul Gerrits	Marie Nash
David Morris	Anita Alvarez
Walter Cassel	Bill Johnson
William Archibold	Maxine Barrat
Don Loper	Candido Botelho

Staged by Leonard Sillman; sketches directed by Edward Clarke Lillie; dances by Marjorie Fielding; settings by Edward Gilbert; costumes by Irene Sharaff; orchestra directed by Ray Kavanaugh.

(Closed December 28, 1940)

THE FLYING GERARDOS

(24 performances)

A comedy in three acts by Kenyon Nicholson and Charles Robinson. Produced by Edward Choate at the Playhouse, New York, December 29, 1940.

Cast of characters—

Doc Vermillion....................................Harlan Briggs
Art....................................Jack Sheehan
Opal....................................Josephine Evans
Donna....................................Lois Hall
Ozzie....................................John Call
Eadie....................................Darthy Hinkley
Pearl....................................Iris Whitney
Chick....................................Lyle Bettger
Hassan....................................James Marriott
Mama....................................Florence Reed
William Wentworth....................................Richard Mackay
Mrs. Wentworth....................................Suzanne Jackson
Dr. Jellicoe....................................Charles Francis

Acts I, II and III.—Top Floor of Doc Vermillion's House in Brooklyn.

Staged by Kenyon Nicholson; setting by Horton O'Neil; costumes by Helene Pons.

Donna, the baby of the Gerardo family of circus aerialists, and important to the act as a performer, meets William Wentworth, a graduate student at Columbia University, and becomes fascinated by his learning. Donna buys herself a book and starts absorbing knowledge. When Mama Gerardo threatens to throw William to the lions, or at least out of the house, Donna counters by threatening to quit the Gerardos. Being of age Donna wins, but a compromise is effected. The learned William goes with the act as a clown.

(Closed January 18, 1941)

FLIGHT TO THE WEST

(136 performances)

A drama in three acts by Elmer Rice. Produced by The Playwrights' Company at the Guild Theatre, New York, December 30, 1940.

Cast of characters—

Richard Banning....................Kevin McCarthy
1st Portuguese Mechanic....................John Triggs
2nd Portuguese Mechanic....................Harald Dyrenforth
August Himmelreich....................Rudolph Weiss
Thomas Hickey....................Paul Mann
Edmund Dickensen....................Don Nevins
Marie Dickensen....................Lydia St. Clair
Lisette Dickensen....................Helen Renee
Louise Frayne....................Constance McKay
Colonel Archibald Gage....................James Seeley
Count Paul Vasilich Vronoff....................Boris Marshalov
Frau Clara Rosenthal....................Eleanora Mendelssohn
Dr. Hermann Walther....................Paul Hernried
Howard Ingraham....................Arnold Moss
Hope Talcott Nathan....................Betty Field
Charles Nathan....................Hugh Marlowe
Captain George McNab....................Karl Malden
Captain Arthur Hawkes....................Grandon Rhodes
1st Corporal....................John Triggs
2nd Corporal....................Harald Dyrenforth

Acts I, II and III.—Aboard a Pan-American Airways Transatlantic Clipper on Two Successive Days in July, 1940.
Staged by Elmer Rice; settings by Jo Mielziner.

See page 236.

(Closed April 26, 1941)

THE LADY WHO CAME TO STAY

(4 performances)

A drama in seven scenes by Kenneth White, based on the novel by R. E. Spencer. Produced by Guthrie McClintic at the Maxine Elliott Theatre, New York, January 2, 1941.

Cast of characters—

Katherine....................Beth Merrill
Emma....................Mady Christians
Sadie....................Mrs. James Thornton
Milly....................Mildred Natwick
Phoebe....................Evelyn Varden
Ann....................Augusta Dabney
Roy....................Horton Heath
Roger....................Dickie Van Patten
Doctor....................Morton L. Stevens

The Scene is the Upstairs Sitting Room of the Garvis Home.
Staged by Guthrie McClintic; setting by Donald Oenslager.

Emma, Milly and Phoebe are three weird sisters living in a somber old mansion. With them is Katherine, their widowed sister-in-law. Because they resented their dead brother's marrying Katherine the three sisters, and especially Phoebe, are taking their revenge out on Katherine. Phoebe dies. So does Katherine. Thereafter they haunt the house. Emma carries on the revenge motive, torturing Katherine's two children. In the end insanity conquers and Emma burns the house down.

(Closed January 4, 1941)

FIRST STOP TO HEAVEN

(8 performances)

A comedy in three acts by Norman Rosten. Produced by Margaret Hewes at the Windsor Theatre, New York, January 5, 1941.

Cast of characters—

Eva Golden	Alison Skipworth
Carl Golden	Taylor Holmes
Mailman	Willard Cary
Checkers	Stanley Ackerman
KK	Frank Maxwell
Ruth	Elena Ryerson
Borgman	Eduard Franz
Richard	Erik Walz
Tony	William Challee
Mrs. Parsons	Frances Brandt
Building Inspector	James Bell
Alter	Joe E. Marks
Salesman	Douglas Rowland
Policeman	Robert K. Adams
Jerry	James Hayes
Mike	Edward Jurist

Acts I, II and III.—Lower Floor of Old Furnished Rooming House Set Among the Skyscrapers on Sixth Avenue, New York City.
Staged by Robert Henderson; setting by Louis Kennel.

Eva Golden is renting rooms in a Sixth avenue house that has been violating building laws. Her husband Carl has been trying to get her to sell the house and buy a chicken farm. Eva holds on to the house, and mothers a variety of roomers, until the house is condemned for subway construction.

(Closed January 11, 1941)

EIGHT O'CLOCK TUESDAY

(16 performances)

A drama in two acts by Robert Wallsten and Mignon G. Eberhart. Produced by Luther Greene and James Struthers at the Henry Miller Theatre, New York, January 6, 1941.

Cast of characters—

Ivan Godden....................................McKay Morris
Marcia Godden....................................Celeste Holm
Beatrice Godden....................................Pauline Lord
Dr. Graham Blaikie..............................Cecil Humphreys
Robert Copley....................................Herbert Rudley
Verity Copley................................Margaret Douglass
Ancill..Philip Tonge
Jacob Wait................................Bramwell Fletcher
Lieutenant Davies..............................Clancy Cooper
Sergeant Cassidy....................................Don Shelton
Gallaway Trench..................................James O'Rear

Acts I and II.—The Godden Library.
Staged by Luther Greene; setting by Lemuel Ayers.

On a certain Tuesday, at 8 in the evening, Ivan Godden is found dead in his library. Marcia, his wife, and Beatrice, his sister, share the discovery. Next door at the Copleys' a dinner party is being given. It would have been possible for any of the guests to have had contact with the dead man. Several of them did not like him any more than did his wife and sister. It takes two hours and more to ferret out the murderer, who turns out to be an old lover of Sister Beatrice.

(Closed January 18, 1941)

NIGHT OF LOVE

(7 performances)

A musical play in three acts adapted by Rowland Leigh from a play by Lili Hatvany; music by Robert Stolz; orchestration by George Lessner. Produced by the Messrs. Shubert at the Hudson Theatre, New York, January 7, 1941.

Cast of characters—

Cleo De Francine....................................Sally Evans
Madi Linden....................................Martha Errolle
Rubero....................................Frank Hornaday
Rudig....................................Harrison Dowd
Call Boy....................................George Spelvin
Count Albert De Gronac..........................Robert Chisholm
Nella Vago....................................Helen Gleason
Andor....................................Jack Blair
Lisel....................................Melissa Mason
Marchesa Sangiovani..........................Marguerite Namara
The Young Man....................................John Lodge
Tilly....................................Jann Moore
Waiter....................................Noel Cravat

Act I.—Nella's Dressing Room, Lucerne Opera House. Act II.—Scene 1—Corner of a Public Dining Room, Hotel Royale. 2—Sitting Room of the Marchesa's Suite—Hotel Royale. Act III.—Scene 1—Nella's Dressing Room—Opera House. 2—Foyer of Opera House. 3—Nella's Home.

Staged by Barrie O'Daniels; settings by Watson Barratt, costumes by Ernest Schraps.

Nella Vago and Madi Linden are rivals for better opera jobs within the gift of Count de Grisac. Both are talented, but while Nella is cold, Madi is warm. Seeking a romantic adventure that will release her emotional inhibitions, Nella makes up to a Young Man she thinks no more than a handsome gigolo. Nella is not only completely released, but the young man turns out to be a scout for the Metropolitan Opera in New York. As "Tonight or Never," a straight comedy, the original Hatvany opus ran for 232 performances in New York in 1930.

(Closed January 11, 1941)

* ARSENIC AND OLD LACE

(181 performances)

A comedy in three acts by Joseph Kesselring. Produced by Howard Lindsay and Russel Crouse at the Fulton Theatre, New York, January 10, 1941.

Cast of characters—

Abby Brewster.......................................Josephine Hull
The Rev. Dr. Harper.......................................Wyrley Birch
Teddy Brewster.......................................John Alexander
Officer Brophy.......................................John Quigg
Officer Klein.......................................Bruce Gordon
Martha Brewster.......................................Jean Adair
Elaine Harper.......................................Helen Brooks
Mortimer Brewster.......................................Allyn Joslyn
Mr. Gibbs.......................................Henry Herbert
Jonathan Brewster.......................................Boris Karloff
Dr. Einstein.......................................Edgar Stehli
Officer O'Hara.......................................Anthony Ross
Lieutenant Rooney.......................................Victor Sutherland
Mr. Witherspoon.......................................William Parke

Acts I, II and III.—Living Room of Brewster Home in Brooklyn.
Staged by Bretaigne Windust; setting by Raymond Sovey.

See page 165.

MR. AND MRS. NORTH

(163 performances)

A comedy in three acts by Owen Davis dramatized from stories by Frances and Richard Lockridge. Produced by Alfred de Liagre, Jr., at the Belasco Theatre, New York, January 12, 1941.

Cast of characters—

Mr. North.......................................Albert Hackett
Buono.......................................Tito Vuolo
Mrs. North.......................................Peggy Conklin
Claire Brent.......................................Barbara Wooddell

Louis Berex....................................Owen Davis, Jr.
Jane Wilson....................................Joan Marlowe
Ben Wilson....................................Lex Lindsay
Clinton Edwards....................................Lewis Martin
Cooper....................................Wylie Adams
Mrs. Brooks....................................Catherine Lawrence
Mr. Brooks....................................Gordon Duff
Lt. Weigand....................................Philip Ober
Detective Mullins....................................Millard Mitchell
Jenkins....................................Carter Blake
Ass't Medical Examiner....................................William Barry
Jones....................................Don Haggerty
Ross....................................Harold Grau
Fuller Brush Man....................................Horace Cooper
Inspector O'Malley....................................Stanley Jessup
Timothy Barnes....................................Frank Wilcox

Acts I, II and III.—The Norths' Apartment on Greenwich Place, New York City.
Staged by Alfred de Liagre; setting by Jo Mielziner.

See page 301.

(Closed May 31, 1941)

CRAZY WITH THE HEAT

(First engagement, 7. Return, 92. Total, 99)

A musical revue in two acts by Sam E. Werris, Arthur Sheekman, Mack Davis, Max Liebman and Don Herold; music and lyrics by Irvin Graham, Dana Suesse and Rudi Revil. Produced by Kurt Kasznar at the 44th Street Theatre, New York, January 14, 1941.

Principals engaged—

Willie Howard	Luella Gear
Richard Kollmar	Gracie Barrie
Carl Randall	Marie Nash
Don Cummings	Betty Kean
Philip King	Hildegarde Halliday
Ted Gary	Harriet Clark
Bobby Busch	Luba Rostova

Staged by Kurt Kasznar; sketches directed by Edward Clarke Lilley and Arthur Sheekman; settings by Albert Johnson; costumes by Lester Polakov and Marie Humans; choreography by Catherine Littlefield.

"Crazy with the Heat" was withdrawn by its original producers after seven performances. The production was then taken over by Ed Sullivan, newspaper columnist, restaged by Lew Brown and reopened January 30 with the addition of Mary Raye and Naldi, adagio dancers; Diosa Costello, night club chanteuse; Tip, Tap and Toe, dancers, and Carlos Ramiriz, South American tenor.

(Closed April 19, 1941)

THE CREAM IN THE WELL

(24 performances)

A tragedy in two acts by Lynn Riggs. Produced by Carly Wharton and Martin Gabel at the Booth Theatre, New York, January 20, 1941.

Cast of characters—

Bina...Virginia Campbell
Mrs. Sawters...Mary Morris
Julie...Martha Sleeper
Mr. Sawters...Ralph Theadore
Opal Dunham...Perry Wilson
Gard Dunham...Myron McCormick
Clabe...Leif Erickson
Blocky Lockhart...Harry Bratsburg

Act I.—Scene 1—Living Room, Sawters' Farm Home on Big Lake, Near Verdigris Switch, Indian Territory. 2—Clabe's Bedroom. Act II.—Living Room.

Staged by Martin Gabel; settings by Jo Mielziner; costumes by Rose Bogdanoff.

Julie Sawters, possessed of an unholy love for her brother Clabe, drives him from the Oklahoma farm which is the Sawters' home. Clabe's desertion preys upon the mind of his father and makes him miserable. The neighbor girl Clabe loves, unhappily married to another, is driven to suicide by the still vengeful Julie, who marries the husband and drives him to drink. Clabe, dishonorably discharged from the Navy, comes home to face Julie with the evil she has done. Julie, in further misery, throws herself in the lake. Clabe decides to stay home and run the farm.

(Closed February 8, 1941)

LADY IN THE DARK

(162 performances)

A play with music in two acts by Moss Hart; lyrics by Ira Gershwin; music by Kurt Weill. Produced by Sam H. Harris at the Alvin Theatre, New York, January 23, 1941.

Cast of characters—

Dr. Brooks...Donald Randolph
Miss Bowers...Jeanne Shelby
Liza Elliott...Gertrude Lawrence
Miss Foster...Evelyn Wyckoff
Miss Stevens...Ann Lee
Maggie Grant...Margaret Dale
Alison Du Bois...Natalie Schafer
Russell Paxton...Danny Kaye
Charley Johnson...Macdonald Carey
Randy Curtis...Victor Mature

Joe.......................................Ward Tallmon
Tom.......................................Nelson Barclift
Kendall Nesbitt..............................Bert Lytell
Helen.....................................Virginia Peine
Ruthie.....................................Gedda Petry
Carol.....................................Patricia Deering
Marcia....................................Margaret Westberg
Ben Butler.................................Dan Harden
Barbara...................................Eleanor Eberle
Jack......................................Davis Cunningham

The Albertina Rasch Group Dancers: Dorothy Byrd, Audrey Costello, Patricia Deering, June MacLaren, Beth Nichols, Wana Wennerholm, Margaret Westberg, Jerome Andrews, Nelson Barclift, George Bockman, Andre Charise, Fred Hearn, Yaroslav Kirov, Parker Wilson.

The Singers: Catherine Conrad, Jean Cumming, Carol Deis, Hazel Edwards, Gedda Petry, June Rutherford, Florence Wyman, Davis Cunningham, Max Edwards, Len Frank, Gordon Gifford, Manfred Hecht, William Marel, Larry Siegle, Harold Simmons.

The Children: Ann Bracken, Sally Ferguson, Ellie Lawes, Joan Lawes, Jasqueline Macmillan, Lois Volkman, Kenneth Casey, Warren Mills, Robert Mills, Robert Lee, George Ward, William Welch.

Act I.—Scenes 1 and 3—Dr. Brooks' Office. 2 and 4—Liza Elliott's Office. Act II.—Scenes 1 and 3—Liza Elliott's Office. 2—Dr. Brooks' Office.

Staged by Hassard Short and Moss Hart; settings by Harry Horner; costumes by Irene Sharaff and Hattie Carnegie; choreography by Albertina Rasch; music directed by Maurice Abravanel.

See page 131.

(Closed June 15, 1941)

TANYARD STREET

(23 performances)

A drama in three acts by Louis D'Alton. Produced by Jack Kirkland at the Little Theatre, New York, February 4, 1941.

Cast of characters—

Mosey Furlong...............................Barry Fitzgerald
Mrs. McMorna...............................Zamah Cunningham
Nanno Deasy................................Aideen O'Connor
Hessy McMorna..............................Margo
Hugh McMorna...............................Lloyd Gough
Davey Deasy................................Art Smith
Father Conn................................Hale Norcross
Kevin McMorna..............................Arthur Shields

Acts I, II and III.—Room in Mrs. McMorna's House in Tanyard Street in the Midland Town of Annakill, Ireland.

Staged by Arthur Shields; setting by Mercedes.

Hessy McMorna is eagerly awaiting the homecoming of her husband, Kevin McMorna, who has been fighting with Franco in Spain. When Kevin arrives he is crippled, his legs paralyzed. He has also turned from his wife. In his dreams he has seen visions of the Madonna and knows he is to be cured. The morning he finds a bouquet of flowers moved mysteriously from the shrine in his bedroom to his pillow he accepts it as a miracle and walks again. In gratitude he wants to become a priest. The church agrees to take him if Hessy will sacrifice herself to a life of celibacy. Despite the protest of Kevin's brother, Hugh, who loves her, Hessy makes the sacrifice.

(Closed February 23, 1941)

LIBERTY JONES

(22 performances)

An allegory in two acts by Philip Barry; music by Paul Bowles. Produced by The Theatre Guild at the Shubert Theatre, New York, February 5, 1941.

Cast of characters—

Liberty Jones....................................Nancy Coleman
Liberty's Uncle....................................William Lynn
Liberty's Aunt....................................Martha Hodge
Commander Tom Smith....................................John Beal
Dick Brown....................................Tom Ewell
Harry Robinson....................................Howard Freeman
Nurse Cotton....................................Katherine Squire
Nurse Maggie....................................Ivy Scott
The Two: Don Glenn, Crahan Denton
The Three: Victor Thorley, Louis Polan, Richard Sanders
The Four: Norman Lloyd, Murray O'Neill, Allan Frank, William Mende
The Seven: Lew Christensen, Joseph Anthony, Vincent Gardner, Craig Mitchell, William Castle, Roy Johnston, Jack Parsons
The Eight: Elise Reiman, Bedelia Falls, Caryl Smith, Honora Harwood, Ellen Morgan, Helen Kramer, Barbara Brown, Constance Dowling
The Singers: Eva Burton, Ruth Gibbs, Alyce Carter

Act I.—Bedroom-Sitting Room in Samuel Bunting's Roof Apartment Overlooking Rock Creek Park, Washington, D. C. Act II.—Scene 1—The Park. 2—The Roof Terrace.

Staged by John Houseman; dances directed by Lew Christensen; settings and costumes by Raoul Pene Du Bois; production under supervision of Theresa Helburn and Lawrence Langner.

Liberty is dying on a couch of luxury. Drs. Education, Letters, Divinity and Law can do nothing for her. She is menaced by the Three Shirts from abroad and a quartet of quacks at home. Her cry for help reaches Tom Smith, a young American Liberal assigned to the aviation division of the Navy. Tom orders Liberty to throw out all the phony medicines the quacks have been feeding her and to get up and walk. Later he drives off the Three Shirts and the evil influences at home and Liberty is made well and strong.

(Closed February 22, 1941)

BOUDOIR

(11 performances)

A comedy in three acts by Jacques Deval. Produced by Jacques Chambrun at the Golden Theatre, New York, February 7, 1941.

Cast of characters—

Doris Williams....................................Jane Donner
Cora Ambershell.................................Helen Twelvetrees
Culver..Richard Irving
Phillips..Curtis Cooksey
Phoebe Massuber...............................Josephine Stanton
Ethel Shannon ....Jeraldine Dvorak
Enrico Palfieri ....Henry Brandon
Edgar Massuber..................................Taylor Holmes
Gaylord..Staats Cotsworth
Oriane..Else Argal

Acts I, II and III.—Boudoir of Cora Ambershell's House, Madison Avenue, New York.
Staged by Jacques Deval; setting by Raymond Sovey.

Cora Ambershell, living under the protection of aging Edgar Massuber, turns for diversion to Enrico Palfieri. Before her new friendship can be sealed she engages a new butler and maid. In the butler, Gaylord, she recognizes a man she had formerly married and divorced, after he had taken to drink and crime. Gaylord also recognizes in Enrico a murderer he had met in Leavenworth prison. Enrico's passion was that of choking to death the women he loved. Gaylord decided to let Nature and Enrico follow their bent.

(Closed February 15, 1941)

POPSY

(4 performances)

A comedy in three acts by Fred Herendeen. Produced by Theodore Hammerstein and Denis Du-For in association with Hugh Skelly at The Playhouse, New York, February 10, 1941.

Cast of characters—

Nancy..Eva Condon
Mortimer...Raymond Cape
Professor Henry Tibbs...............................Al Shean
Mary Tibbs.......................................Edith King
Jane Tibbs...................................Natalie Thompson
Jed Prout...John Adair
Bob Hatch ....Herbert Evers
Dr. Thomas Lorett...............................Robert Harrison
Florence Tibbs Benson.............................Sylvia Field
Marie Antoinette Benson.........................Joyce Van Patten
Henry Wadsworth Benson.......................Lachland Campbell

Ruth Tibbs Brown....................................Nancy Evans
Western Union Messenger.............................Judson Pratt
Thaddeus T. Burns...................................Percy Helton
Dr. Mac...John McKee
William Brown.......................................Robert Allen
Acts I, II and III.—Home of Henry Tibbs in Madison, Wisconsin.
Staged by Rowland G. Edwards; setting by Tom Adrian Cracraft.

For many years Prof. Henry Tibbs has looked forward to the time he can retire and devote himself to the writing of a book. Finally the time arrives. In the midst of the Professor's preparations new problems arise. His youngest daughter breaks her engagement to marry. His two older daughters return to the parental home, after having had husband trouble. Retirement seems out of the question. Still, there are adjustments.

(Closed February 12, 1941)

OUT OF THE FRYING PAN

(104 performances)

A comedy in three acts by Francis Swann. Produced by William Deering and Alexander Kirkland at the Windsor Theatre, New York, February 11, 1941.

Cast of characters—

George Bodell.......................................William W. Terry
Mrs. Garnet...Mabel Paige
Norman Reese..Alfred Drake
Muriel Foster.......................................Florence Macmichael
Kate Ault...Nancy Douglass
Marge Benson..Louise Snyder
Tony Dennison.......................................Sellwyn Myers
Dottie Coburn.......................................Barbara Bel Geddes
Mr. Coburn..Henry Antrim
Mr. Kenny...Reynolds Evans
Mac...Arthur Holland
Joe...George Mathews
Acts I, II and III.—Living Room of Brownstone Front Apartment in New York City.
Staged by Alexander Kirkland; setting by Cirker and Robbins.

A group of six ambitious stage novices, led by Norman Reese, rent an apartment in New York and live in platonic contentment while they are storming the doors of the play producer living in the apartment below. The producer's current hit on Broadway is a murder mystery. The six young players cast themselves in its principal rôles, rehearse the play and scheme to get the producer to watch them play it. He is finally roped and eventually agrees to include the importunate six in a road company.

(Closed May 10, 1941)

* CLAUDIA

(144 performances)

A comedy in three acts by Rose Franken. Produced by John Golden at the Booth Theatre, New York, February 12, 1941.

Cast of characters—

Mrs. Brown....................Frances Starr
David Naughton....................Donald Cook
Claudia Naughton....................Dorothy McGuire
Bertha....................Adrienne Gessner
Fritz....................Frank Tweddell
Jerry Seymoure....................John Williams
Madame Daruschka....................Olga Baclanova
Julia Naughton....................Audrey Ridgwell

Acts I, II and III.—Living Room of the Naughtons' House in the country, Seventy Miles Out of New York.
Staged by Rose Franken; setting by Donald Oenslager.

See page 270.

THE TALLEY METHOD

(56 performances)

A comedy in three acts by S. N. Behrman. Produced by The Playwrights' Company at the Henry Miller Theatre, New York, February 24, 1941.

Cast of characters—

Avis Talley....................Claire Niesen
Philip Talley....................Dean Harens
Cy Blodgett....................Hiram Sherman
Enid Fuller....................Ina Claire
Mary....................Lida Kane
Manfred Geist....................Ernst Deutsch
Dr. Axton Talley....................Philip Merivale

Acts I, II and III.—Upstairs Living Room of Dr. Talley's Office Residence in the East Sixties, New York City.
Staged by Elmer Rice; setting by Jo Mielziner.

Dr. Axton Talley, a preoccupied specialist in surgery, decides to marry Enid Fuller, one of his attractive patients. The Doctor's children, Avis and Philip, are moderately resentful. Avis, an ardent member of the American Youth Congress, resents Enid because Manfred Geist, refugee, whom Avis hopes to marry, falls immediately in love with her. Philip, at first doubtful, is won over when Enid does not oppose his affair with a fan dancer. But when Dr. Talley himself grows jealous of the refugee, Enid decides she had better wait awhile before taking the matrimonial plunge.

(Closed April 12, 1941)

BROOKLYN BIARRITZ

(4 performances)

A comedy in three acts by Beatrice Alliot and Howard Newman. Produced by Clarence Taylor and Marie Louise Elkins at the Royale Theatre, New York, February 27, 1941.

Cast of characters—

Milton Berger....................................Herbert Ratner
Blossom..Mildred Price
Bill Boyle.......................................Thomas Hume
Elliot Berger....................................Milton Karol
Siggy..Elvin Field
Herman...Michael Artist
John Floherty....................................Ralph W. Chambers
Myrtle...Victory Abbott
Mickey...Sam Main
Natalie Valia....................................Ann Loring
Alice Stone......................................Dorothy Libaire
Fred Andrews.....................................Bertram Thorn
Ice Cream Vendor.................................Arthur Marlowe
Josie..Jean Ashworth
Rosie Berger.....................................Clara Langsner
Vincent Baretta..................................James La Curto
Butch..Angi O. Poulos
Alec Thompson....................................Owen Lamont
Peter Stone......................................James Todd
Life Guard.......................................Randolph Wade
A Solicitous Lady................................Ruth Conley
Mollie Floherty..................................Guerita Donnelly
Harry..Arthur Marlowe
Pretzel Man......................................Walter Rhodes

Acts I, II and III.—Extreme Uptown End of Coney Island Beach.
Staged by J. B. Daniels; setting by Frederick Fox.

Alice Stone, discovering that Fred Andrews had no intention of keeping his promises, was so embarrassed when her husband came home that she killed herself. Peter Stone, the husband, thereupon choked the life out of Fred Andrews, tossing his body in the ocean. After that Peter Stone, having no further use for life or the $390 in his wallet, gave the money to Alec Thompson and disappeared. This gave Alec a chance to marry Natalie Valia and go on studying art. There was real sand on the stage beach at Coney Island.

(Closed March 1, 1941)

* THE DOCTOR'S DILEMMA

(112 performances)

A comedy in three acts by George Bernard Shaw. Revived by Katharine Cornell at the Shubert Theatre, New York, March 11, 1941.

Cast of characters—

Redpenny....................Stanley Bell
Emmy....................Alice Belmore Cliffe
Sir Colenson Ridgeon....................Raymond Massey
Dr. Schultzmacher....................Clarence Derwent
Sir Patrick Cullen....................Whitford Kane
Dr. Cutler Walpole....................Ralph Forbes
Sir Ralph Bloomfield Bonington....................Cecil Humphreys
Dr. Blenkinsop....................Colin Keith-Johnston
Jennifer Dubedat....................Katharine Cornell
Louis Dubedat....................Bramwell Fletcher
Minnie Tinwell....................Margaret Curtis
The Newspaper Man....................Leslie Barrie
A Secretary....................David Orrick

Act I.—Ridgeon's Consulting-Room, Queen Anne Street, London. Act II.—Scene 1—Terrace of the Star and Garter, Richmond. 2—Dubedat's Studio. Act III.—Scene 1—The Studio. 2—Picture Gallery in Bond Street.

Staged by Guthrie McClintic; settings by Donald Oenslager; costumes by Motley.

The first American production of "The Doctor's Dilemma" was staged by Harley Granville-Barker at Wallack's Theatre, New York, in November, 1916. Lillah McCarthy was the Jennifer, Nicholas Hannen the Louis Dubedat, Ian Maclaren the Sir Colenson, O. P. Heggie the Sir Ralph and Ernest Cossart the Newsman. In 1927 the New York Theatre Guild revived the play with Lynn Fontanne the Jennifer, Alfred Lunt the Dubedat, Ernest Cossart the Sir Ralph, Baliol Halloway the Sir Colenson and Dudley Digges the Sir Patrick. It was also included in the Pasadena Playhouse repertory the season of 1926-27.

THEY WALK ALONE

(21 performances)

A drama in three acts by Max Catto. Produced by Ben A. Boyar at the Shubert Theatre, New York, March 12, 1941.

Cast of characters—

Julie Tallent....................Olive Deering
Bess Stanforth....................Carol Goodner
Robert Stanforth....................John Moore
Mr. Tallent....................A. P. Kaye
Larry Tallent....................Martin Manulis
Emmy Baudine....................Elsa Lanchester
Saul Trevithick....................Erford Gage

Acts I, II and III.—Living Room of Tallent Farm, Near Lincoln, Eng.

Staged by Berthold Viertel; setting by Lemuel Ayers.

The Stanforths of Lincolnshire engage a maid who hails from Yorkshire named Emmy Baudine. Emmy shortly develops queer habits. Organ music, for one thing, seems to change her personality completely. Now she is a Mrs. Jekyll. Again she is a Miss Hyde. During her spells she is devilishly fascinating to men.

Shortly the neighbors begin to find their sons scattered over the moors and in the haylofts, dead and mangled. With the help of the menfolk and a hound Emmy is run down. She is caught in a near-by organ loft playing a fugue.

(Closed March 29, 1941)

FIVE ALARM WALTZ

(4 performances)

A comedy in three acts by Lucille S. Prumbs. Produced by Everett Wile at the Playhouse, New York, March 13, 1941.

Cast of characters—

Brooke March....................Louise Platt
Adam Boguris....................Elia Kazan
Mme. Constantina....................Helen Zelinskaya
Jerry Manning....................Robert Shayne
May....................Ann Thomas
Theodore....................Howard Freeman
Dave Dorham....................Roman Bohnen
Young Man....................Curt Conway
Boy....................Harold Lui

Acts I, II and III.—Boguris Apartment on Sutton Place, New York City.
Staged by Robert Lewis; setting by Harry Horner.

Adam Boguris is an eccentric novelist. Brooke March, his wife, is a more normal writer and a successful playwright. Adam says Brooke is a fake. Brooke says Adam is a freak, and dares him to write a play. Adam does and his play is a success. Whereupon Adam and Brooke adjust their temperaments and start work as collaborators.

(Closed March 15, 1941)

MY FAIR LADIES

(32 performances)

A comedy in three acts by Arthur L. Jarrett and Marcel Klauber. Produced by Albert Lewis and Max Siegel at the Hudson Theatre, New York, March 23, 1941.

Cast of characters—

Helen Gage....................Mary Sargent
Philip Gage....................Vincent Donehue
Joyce Gage....................Toni Gilman
Griggs....................Henry Vincent
Lady Keith-Odlyn....................Celeste Holm
Lady Palfrey-Stuart....................Betty Furness
Richard Tolliver....................Russell Hardie
Henry Gage....................Herbert Yost
Ned Tate....................Tom Coley
Tony Stiles....................Alfred Etcheverry

Mrs. Belden S. Stiles.............................Ethel Morrison
Max.......................................Charles Furcolowe
Miss Grumley..............................Jacqueline Susann
Driscoll "Happy" Felton.............................Otto Hulett
Finnegan..................................Randolph Preston
Captain Lake...................................Lionel Ince
Acts I, II and III.—Home of Henry Gages, Willowbrook, Mt. Kisco.
Staged by Albert Lewis; setting by Watson Barratt.

Lady Keith-Odlyn and Lady Palfrey-Stuart, European refugees, cross on the Atlantic clipper plane and are taken to the home of the Henry Gages in Mt. Kisco, N. Y. There it is shortly revealed that their ladyships are a couple of American chorus girls who have made the crossing on phoney passports. Meantime the girls have been taken up and exploited by Mt. Kisco snobs and have found themselves a couple of possible mates.

(Closed April 19, 1941)

*NATIVE SON

(97 performances)

A drama in ten scenes by Paul Green and Richard Wright from Richard Wright's novel of the same name. Produced by Orson Welles and John Houseman in association with Bern Bernard at the St. James Theatre, New York, March 24, 1941.

Cast of characters—

Bigger Thomas.......................................Canada Lee
Hannah Thomas.....................................Evelyn Ellis
Vera Thomas.......................................Helen Martin
Buddy Thomas.....................................Lloyd Warren
A Neighbor.........................Jacqueline Ghant Andre
Miss Emmett..Eileen Burns
Jack...J. Flashe Riley
G. H. Rankin...................................Rodester Timmons
Clara...Rena Mitchell
Gus Mitchell...................................Wardell Saunders
Ernie Jones...................................C. M. Bootsie Davis
Mr. Dalton......................................Erskine Sanford
Mrs. Dalton.......................................Nell Harrison
Britten...Everett Sloane
Peggy..Frances Bavier
Mary Dalton...Anne Burr
Jan Erlone.......................................Joseph Pevney
Buckley...Philip Bourneuf
Paul Max..Ray Collins
A Newspaper Man..................................Paul Stewart
Judge..William Malone
A Reporter..John Berry
Newspaper Men.........Stephen Roberts, George Zorn, Don Roberts
Scene 1—The Thomas Room. 2—Chicago Street. 3 and 5—Dalton Home. 4—Mary Dalton's Bedroom. 6—Clara Mears' Room. 7—Basement of Dalton Home. 8—Room in Deserted House. 9—Courtroom. 10—Prison Cell.
Staged by Orson Welles; settings by James Morcom.

See page 29.

GABRIELLE

(2 performances)

A comedy in three acts by Leonardo Bercovici based on Thomas Mann's "Tristan"; incidental music by Rudi Revil. Produced by Rowland Leigh at the Maxine Elliott Theatre, New York, March 25, 1941.

Cast of characters—

Fleming....................................Byron McGrath
Rieman....................................John McGovern
General Hobein....................................Martin Wolfson
Detlev Spinell....................................John Cromwell
Frau Spatz....................................Frieda Altman
Fraulein von Osteloh....................................Grace Coppin
August Schulz....................................Wilton Graff
Holm....................................Whitner Bissell
Doctor Leander....................................Frederic Tozere
Anton Kloterjahn....................................Harold Vermilyea
Gabrielle Kloterjahn....................................Eleanor Lynn
Maid....................................Charlotte Acheson
Patients....................................Elaine Eldridge, Dwight Marfield

Acts I, II and III.—Drawing Room of Einfried in the Swiss Alps.
Staged by Randolph Carter; setting by Peggy Clark; costumes by Kenn Barr.

In the play version of Thomas Mann's "Tristan," adapted from the novel by Leonardo Bercovici, Anton Kloterjahn leaves his frail and sensitive wife, Gabrielle, at a sanitarium in the Swiss Alps. There is, insists Anton, little or nothing the matter with Gabrielle. In the sanitarium Gabrielle meets a brilliant but erratic young novelist, Detlev Spinell, who for the time wields a devastating influence over her. Detlev insists Gabrielle should walk when the physicians say she should rest. Also that she should play furiously upon the piano when she has been told to leave the piano alone. Gabrielle weakens and dies. To Spinell death brings release to her soul. To Anton it is a useless sacrifice.

(Closed March 26, 1941)

*WATCH ON THE RHINE

(87 performances)

A drama in three acts by Lillian Hellman. Produced by Herman Shumlin at the Martin Beck Theatre, New York, April 1, 1941.

Cast of characters—

Anise....................................Eda Heinemann
Fanny Farrelly....................................Lucile Watson
Joseph....................................Frank Wilson

David Farrelly....................................John Lodge
Marthe De Brancovis..........................Helen Trenholme
Teck De Brancovis............................George Coulouris
Kurt Muller...Paul Lukas
Sara Muller...................................Mady Christians
Babette Muller....................................Anne Blyth
Joshua Muller.................................Peter Fernandez
Bodo Muller..Eric Roberts

Acts I, II and III.—Living Room of Farrelly Country House, About Twenty Miles from Washington. 1940.

Staged by Herman Shumlin; setting by Jo Mielziner; costumes by Helene Pons.

See page 64.

YOUR LOVING SON

(3 performances)

A comedy in three acts by Abby Merchant. Produced by Jay Richard Kennedy in association with Alfred Bloomingdale and Joseph F. Loewi at the Little Theatre, New York, April 4, 1941.

Cast of characters—

Lulu...Rachel Sewall
Dorcas Winslow.............................Jessie Royce Landis
Joshua Winslow......................................Jay Fassett
Caroline Bradley.................................Kate Warriner
Joshua Winslow, Jr............................Frankie Thomas
Rosamond Payne..................................Charita Bauer
William Hollinger.................................Eddie Nugent
Muriel Payne..Ruth Lee
A Maid..Julann Coffrey
Keith Evans...Edwin Gordon
Horace Payne...............................Raymond Greenleaf

Acts I, II and III.—Drawing Room of Mrs. Joshua Winslow's Duplex Apartment Near the East River, New York City.

Staged by Arthur Sircom; setting by Raymond Sovey.

Dorcas and Joshua Winslow drift apart. Mama loves papa, but not very much. Each Winslow becomes interested in another partner and is working industriously toward a series of crises when Junior Winslow comes home and discovers how things are. With the help of Rosamond Payne, whose parents also are involved, Junior manages to break up the affairs in which his parents are engaged and to convince them that, after all, it takes a heap of livin' to make a New York duplex apartment seem like home.

(Closed April 5, 1941)

THE NIGHT BEFORE CHRISTMAS

(22 performances)

A comedy in three acts by Laura and S. J. Perelman. Produced by Courtney Burr at the Morosco Theatre, New York, April 10, 1941.

Cast of characters—

Madame Rochelle....................................Ruth Weston
Bigelow....................................John Ravold
Endicott....................................St. Clair Bayfield
Sam Bachrach....................................Louis Sorin
Denny Costello....................................Phyllis Brooks
Flora....................................Shelley Winter
Byron Schofield....................................Herbert Nelson
Fred Finch....................................George Petrie
Otis J. Faunce....................................Forrest Orr
Ruby....................................George Mathews
A Window Shopper....................................Ellen Hall
A Casualty....................................Frank Greigenhofer, Jr.
A Fuss-Budget....................................John Junior
A Sophomore....................................Carl Gose
Smitty....................................Owen Martin
Gentleman in Black....................................Charles Furcolowe
Bellhop....................................Kenneth Forbes
Policemen....................................Marshall Bradford, Charles Holden
Victor Immature....................................Dean Norton
Paranoiac....................................Jean Norwood
A Moviegoer....................................Muriel Campbell
Truckman....................................Pete Cusanelli
Aspinwall....................................William David
Leo....................................Harry Bratsburg
The Shield....................................Donald McClelland
Sergeant....................................Lew Eckels

Acts I, II and III.—A Sixth Avenue Luggage Shop, New York City.

Staged by Eomney Brent; setting by Boris Aronson.

Otis J. Faunce and his tough pal, Ruby, are working on a plan evolved by Otis and a couple of boys in Sing Sing. They plan to rent a Sixth Avenue luggage shop and tunnel through the basement wall into the bank vaults next door. Hurdling all interruptions, including the romance of Denny Costello, a former gun moll who wants to go straight for the apothecary in the corner drugstore, and the surprise arrival of Leo, the chief crook, from the Big House, they get their chiseling done only to find that they have broken into the storage room of a delicatessen instead of a bank vault. And also into a vat of potato salad.

(Closed April 27, 1941)

* THE BEAUTIFUL PEOPLE

(64 performances)

A fantastic comedy in two acts by William Saroyan. Produced by William Saroyan at the Lyceum Theatre, New York, April 21, 1941.

Cast of characters—

Owen Webster....................................Eugene Loring
Harmony Blueblossom....................................Fredrica Slemon
Agnes Webster....................................Betsy Blair
Jonah Webster....................................Curtis Cooksey
William Prim....................................E. J. Ballantine

Dan Hillboy.......................................Farrell Pelly
Father Hogan.....................................Edward Nannary
Harold Webster...................................Don Freeman
Steve ....Peter Xantho

Acts I and II.—Living Room and Yard of an Old House on Red Rock Hill near Quintara Woods in Sunset District of San Francisco, Calif.

Staged by William Saroyan; setting by Samuel Leve.

Jonah Webster, indigent and religious, lives with his two children, Owen and Agnes, in a decaying mansion on the side of a hill overlooking San Francisco Bay. Jonah believes in brotherly love and the practical beneficence of the Creator. He forges the name of a former inhabitant of the house to a monthly annuity check and manages to keep his family together. Agnes, the saint-like daughter, loves the mice that swarm the house and believes it is they, and not her brother, who spell out her name in flower blossoms they bring from the field. Owen is a sympathetic brother who plays along with Agnes, even climbing the steeple of the nearby Catholic church to recover one of the mice that has strayed from home. Various friends wander in, wander, and wander out. In the end Harold, an older son who has gone to New York with his cornet, comes home. He still has the cornet which, on still nights, the Websters can in their imaginations hear him playing 3,000 lonesome miles away.

THE HAPPY DAYS

(23 performances)

A comedy in three acts by Zoe Akins adapted from "Les Jours Heureux" by Claude-André Puget. Produced by Raphael and Robert Hakim at Henry Miller's Theatre, New York, May 13, 1941.

Cast of characters—

Francine Gassin..................................Barbara Kent
Marianne Gassin..................................Diana Barrymore
Oliver Faber.....................................Frederick Bradlee
Pernette Faber...................................Joan Tetzel
Bernard Gassin...................................Peter Scott
Michael Trent....................................Edward Ashley

Acts I, II and III.—Living Room in the Gassin Home on an Island in the St. Lawrence River.

Staged by Arthur Ripley; supervised by Raphael Hakim; setting by Raymond Sovey.

Marianne Gassin loves Oliver Faber, but Oliver, being a Harvard man, must appear superior and not let her know that he cares for her. While Marianne and Oliver, with three of their friends, are alone on an island in the St. Lawrence, Marianne and Pernette Faber decide to manufacture a story of adventure that will make Oliver jealous. They invent an aviator, and a furiously romantic tale. As they complete their story Michael Trent, aviator, appears in the doorway. He has been forced down. Now Oliver is very jealous. And all the girls believe they are in love with Michael. Pernette is ready to kill herself when she sees Michael kissing Marianne. Adjustments follow when Michael flies away.

(Closed May 31, 1941)

SNOOKIE

(15 performances)

A farce in three acts by Thomas A. Johnstone; jingles by William B. Friedlander. Produced by Olsen and Johnson at the Golden Theatre, New York, June 3, 1941.

Cast of characters—

Balmy...John McCauley
Tommy...Eddie Nugent
Jerry...Roy Johnson
Home James...Daniele Porise
El Galio...Angi O. Poulos
Sue...Julie Stevens
Quigley...William Harrigan
Quincy...John Hetherington
Old Bill...Florenz Ames
Gallup...John Kirk
Stupid Stella...Betty Jane Smith
Jim Jones...Lawrence Weber
Sam Tucker...Jack Hartley
Ten Percent...Lou Lubin
Mr. West...J. C. Nugent

Acts I, II and III.—Comic Art Department of the New York Press.
Staged by William B. Friedlander; setting by Frederick Fox.

Jim Jones from Ashtabula is trying to get a job in the comic strip department of a New York newspaper. The other artists play jokes on him. Among the jokes is one in which they send him back to Ashtabula to become the scientific father of a test tube baby that is to inherit the New York paper and thus save them their jobs. If there isn't an heir by the third act the paper will go to the managing editor who hates the comics. As it happens there is an heir produced according to custom and all Jim Jones is called upon to contribute is a blood transfusion to help sustain the plot.

(Closed June 14, 1941)

DANCE DRAMA

The Ballet Russe de Monte Carlo opened its third New York season at the 51st Street Theatre, New York, October 14, 1940. Included in the three week season were the following ballets:

"Vienna 1814" (world première), by Leonide Massine; Carl Maria von Weber music assembled by Russell Bennett; costumes and scenery by Steward Chaney.

"Poker Game," choreography by George Balanchine; music by Igor Stravinsky; costumes by Irene Sharaff.

"Rouge et Noir," by Leonide Massine; music from Shostakovitch First Symphony; conducted by Efrem Kurtz.

"The New Yorker," by Massine; music assembled from works of George Gershwin, orchestrated by David Raksin; conducted by Franz Allers; libretto by Rea Irwin; décor and costumes by Carl Kent.

"Serenade," by George Balanchine from score by Tchaikowsky; conducted by Efrem Kurtz; costumes by Jean Lurcat; settings by Gaston Longchamp.

"The Nutcracker," choreography by Petipa Fedorova; from Tchaikowsky; scenery and costumes by Alexander Benois.

"Bacchanale," with Wagner's Venusburg music, "Giselle," arranged by Serge Lifar, "Capriccio Espagnol," "Swan Lake," "The Afternoon of a Swan," "Spectre de la Rose," "Schéhérazade," "Petouchka," "Gaite Parisienne," "Fantastic Flower Shop," "Les Sylphides," "Boutique Fantasque" and "Coppelia."

Principals—Leonide Massine, Alice Markova, Alexandra Danilove, Milada Mladova, Nathalie Krassovska, Frederick Franklin, André Eglevsky, Igor Youskevitch, Marc Platoff, Chris Volkoff, Tatiana Chamie, Rosella Hightower, George Zoritch, Anna Scarpora, Robert Steele, Lubov Roudenko, Ian Gibson, Mia Slavenske, Roland Guerard, Lubov Rostova, Sonia Woicikowska, George Tomin, Tassia Semenova and Marie Jeanne.

The Ballet Russe de Monte Carlo closed November 3, 1940.

Colonel de Basil's Original Ballet Russe opened at the 51st Street Theatre, New York, November 6, 1940. Included in repertoire were:

"Cinderella," by Michel Fokine; music by Frederic d'Erlanger; decor and costumes by Natalie Gontcharova.

"Paganini," by Michel Fokine; set to Sergei Rachmaninoff's

own arrangement of his "Rhapsody on a theme of Paganini," decor and costumes by Sergei Soudeikine.

"Graduation Ball," by David Lichine; to music of Johann Strauss; decor and costumes by Alexander Benois.

"Protée," by David Lichine; to Debussy's "Danse Sacrée" and "Danse Profane"; decor by Georges Chirico.

"The Prodigal Son," by David Lichine; music by Serge Protofieff; settings and costumes by Georges Rouault.

"Pavane," by Serge Lifar; music by Maurice Ravel; decor and costumes by José Maria Sert.

"The Eternal Struggle," by Igor Schwezoff; to the symphonic etudes of Robert Schumann; decor and costumes by Kathleen and Florence Martin.

"Aurora's Wedding," "Coq d'Or," "The Hundred Kisses," "Prince Igor," "Ballet School," "Schéhérazade," "Cotillon," "Symphony Fantastique," "Les Sylphides," "The Good-Humored Ladies," "The Prodigal Son," "Afternoon of a Faun," "Cimarosiana," "Carnaval," "Choreartium," "Swan Lake," "Les Presaged," "Jeux d'Enfants," "Petrushka," and "Francesca da Rimini."

Seven post-season performances were given. January 22, 1941, the première of George Balanchine's "Balustrade" was danced to the music of Igor Stravinsky's violin concerto. The principal parts were danced by Irina Baranova, Tamara Toumanova and Tatiana Riabouchinska. Decor was by Paul Tchelitcheff. A single performance was given of "Union Pacific" by Leonid Massine with music by Nicholas Nabokoff, libretto by Archibald MacLeish, settings by Albert Johnson and costumes by Irene Sharaff.

Principals—Irina Baranova, Tamara Toumanova, Tatiana Riabouchinska, David Lichine, Nina Verchinina, Olga Morosova, Tamara Grigorieva, Sono Osato, Roman Jasinsky, Paul Petroff, Yura Lazovsky, Dimitri Rostoff, Harcourt Algeranoff, Marian Ladre, Borislav Rumanine, Michel Panaieff, Yura Skibine, Oleg Toupine, Alexandra Denisova, Marina Svetlova, Genevieve Moulin, Tatiana Stepanova and Tatiana Leskova.

The Original Ballet season closed January 12, 1941, the two ballets setting a record for New York with 106 performances.

The Ballet Theatre opened its second New York season February 11, 1941, at the Majestic Theatre. The repertoire included:

"Three Virgins and the Devil," by Agnes de Mille; music by Respighi; scenario by Ramon Reed; setting by Arno Lundborg and Peggy Harris; costumes by Motley.

"Gala Performance," by Anthony Tudor; music from Prokofieff orchestrated by Paul Baron; scenery and costumes by Nicolas de Molas.

"Billy the Kid," by Eugene Loring; music by Aaron Copland; decor and costumes by Jared French.

"Capriccioso," by Anton Dolin; music by Cimarosa; decor and costumes by Nicolas de Molas.

"Pas de Quatre," by Anton Dolin, after Jules Perrot; music by Pugni.

"The Great American Goof," by Eugene Loring; music by Henry Brant; libretto by William Saroyan; settings and costumes by Boris Aronson.

"Quintet," by Anton Dolin; music by Raymond Scott; settings and costumes by Lucinda Ballard.

"Peter and the Wolf," "Judgment of Paris," "Dark Elegies," "Swan Lake," "Carnaval," "Jardin aux Lilas," "Giselle" and "Les Sylphides."

Principals—Anton Dolin, Antony Tudor, Eugene Loring, Nana Gollner, Katherine Sergava, Alicia Alonso, Miriam Golden, Nina Stroganova, Hugh Laing, Annabelle Lyon, Karen Conrad, Leon Danielian, Vera Nemchinova, Alicia and Fernando Alonso, Tania Dokoudovska, Jerome Robbins, Agnes de Mills, David Nillo, Donald Saddler, Lucia Chase, Nora Kaye, Edward Caton, Dimitri Romanoff and Maria Karniloff.

The Ballet Theatre closed March 9, 1941.

OFF BROADWAY

The season's productions outside of regular Broadway openings included Gilbert and Sullivan revivals by the Light Opera Company at the Provincetown Theatre where "Trial by Jury" and "Iolanthe" opened June 17, alternating with "Princess Ida." Toward the end of the season this same company produced Gilbert and Sullivan revivals at the Cherry Lane Theatre for an engagement of a fortnight starting March 10. The operettas were staged by John F. Grahame.

Labor Stage gave two performances of a two hour pageant called "Labor Sings," a program which included "I Hear America Singing" based on a Walt Whitman poem, at Madison Square Garden, October 5. Louis Schaffer and Brett Warren directed the presentation. Music by George Kleinsinger, script by Alfred Hayes, dances by Lily Mehlmann and sets designed by Sointu Syrjala.

Another unusual production was "No for an Answer," a musical play by Marc Blitzstein, staged by W. E. Watts at Mecca Temple, January 5, 12 and 19, as an experiment under an agreement between the Dramatists Guild and Actors Equity. There was no scenery and music was provided by Mr. Blitzstein on the piano. The cast included Lloyd Gough, Olive Deering, Martin Pitt, Norma Green, Curt Conway and others.

"The Way," a dramatization by Martha Cabanne (Mrs. Robert Lee Kayser) of her novel "Faith," was produced by Olive Productions at the Cherry Lane Theatre, October 11. It was directed by Frank Lea Short and Wendell Phillips Dodge. In the cast were Eva Casanova, Jean Brewster, Betsy Knudsen, Georgia Harvey, Anne Shay, Jean Lawrence, Philip Arthur, Hal Clarendon, Garrett Arthur, Walter Curley and Leonardo La Mori. It ran for 10 performances.

At the Provincetown Playhouse, October 23, 1940, Ben Levinson produced and staged his own play, "Injury Sustained," with the author, Ed Hussey, William Calvert and Margaret Dickenson in the cast. This was followed November 16 by A. A. Milne's "Sarah Simple," presented for the first time in New York by the Hilltop Theatre of Maryland. The play was staged by Walter Rooney, the scenery designed by Forrest Thayr and the cast included Guy Spaull, Helen Riggs, Joy Harrington, Leslie Stevens, Florence McMichel and Edward Broadley.

Following this at the Playhouse, Eugene Endrey presented four one-act plays: "Man Hunt," "Doing Nicely," "Time to Burn" and "The Reaper," by Helen Gholson Kittredge, December 3, under the direction of the author. January 24, Ben Levinson again presented one of his own plays, "I.Q.," with much the same cast as that in "Injury Sustained." Also at the Provincetown, February 21.

The Theatre Associates produced "A Man's Reach," by Irwin Rowan and Martin J. Devon. The play, which was about the painters, Van Gogh and Gauguin, was staged by Harry Kessler. February 26, "Grand Opening," a farce by David Dargin, directed by Harrison Gladstone was presented by Michael Glade. Sanford Bickart played the leading rôle. The Popular Theatre revived "Johnny Johnson" by Paul Green at the Provincetown, May 2, in a modified form. Peter Heywood played the name part. Paul Petroff designed the scenery and Helene Smith the costumes. "Sing Before Breakfast," a farce by Peter Levins and Warren Murray, was presented May 19, and "When Differences Disappear," written and directed by Leonard Black, was given June 2. The settings were by Edna Mundson.

"The Fiddler's House," by Padraic Colum, was presented for the first time in America by Wendell Phillips Dodge in association with the Irish Repertory Theatre at the Cherry Lane Theatre, March 27. The play was staged by J. Augustus Keogh and the cast included Judith Magee, Gerald Buckley, Augustin Duncan, John Ireland, Margaret McCarthy and James Murray.

Sir James Barrie's last play "The Boy David" was produced by Theodore Komisarjevsky at the Studio Theatre with Marjorie Tas in the name rôle, April 20.

The American Actors Company produced a three act play by Horton Foote called "Texas Town," April 28, staged by Mary Hunter, with settings designed by Joseph Anthony. "American Legend," a revue which included Paul Green's one-act play "Saturday Night" and E. P. Conkle's "Minnie Field," was given in a program of early American songs and dances for which Agnes de Mille did the choreography, Baldwin Bergensen directed, and John Pratt and Hugh Laing designed the settings.

The Experimental Theatre, Inc., formed by Actors Equity and the Dramatists Guild, produced three plays late in the season. The first was "The Trojan Women" by Euripides, translated by Gilbert Murray, with a modern prologue by Robert Turney and music by Lehman Engel. Margaret Webster directed the play and Felicia Sorel designed the dance movements. The cast included Miss Webster, Dame May Whitty, Florence Williams, Frederic Tozere, Tamara Geva, Walter Slezak, Lorna Lynn, Charles Francis, Joanna Roos and Grace Coppin.

"Steps Leading Up," a drama in three acts by George Harr, directed by Paul Foley, was the second presentation April 8, at the Cort. James Gregory, Adele Harrison, Sanford Bickart, Mark Lea, Jack Effrat, Ralph Chambers and William Bock, Jr., were in the cast.

"Not in Our Stars," a play in three acts, by George H. Corey, was given at the Biltmore, April 25. In the cast were Walter Burke, Leo Needham, Frances Reid, John Ireland, Harold Vermilyea, Hallam Bosworth, Loring Smith and Ruth Thane McDevitt.

Studio Theatre, a group of professional players affiliated with the Dramatic Workshop of the New School for Social Research, presented three plays during the season. Shakespeare's "King Lear," modernized into two acts by Erwin Piscator, who did the staging with incidental music by Henry Cowell and a prologue by Colin Craig and Seymour Milbert was revived December 14. The cast included Sam Jaffe, Margaret Curtis, Roger de Koven, Lysbeth Lynn, Erford Gage, Ross Matthew, Rachel Adams and Herbert Berghof.

"The Circle of Chalk," a Chinese fantasy in five acts, adapted by Klabund (Alfred Henschke) and translated by James Laver, opened March 24. James Light did the staging, the settings were by Cleon Throckmorton and the costumes by Rose Bogdanoff. Dolly Haas played the lead. Others were Rose Quong, Zachary Scott, Anthony Randall, Richard Odlin and Ralph Morrison. Jascha Horenstein wrote the songs.

"Any Day Now," a comedy in three acts, by Philip Yordan, opened June 3, was directed by Robert Klein, supervised by Piscator and the settings were by Herbert Andrews. John Randolph played the lead.

The Davenport Free Theatre revived "The Mollusc" and "The Way of a Woman," by Hubert Davies, "The Bells," by Erckmann-Chatriace, "Louis XI" from "Quentin Durward," Ibsen's "The Master Builder," Sophocles' "Oedipus Rex," "Grumpy," by Hodges and Percival, "The Goal" and "A Builder of Bridges," by Henry Arthur Jones, and "The Swan Song," by Anton Chekov. New productions were "The Father's Sons" and "Blind Law," by Butler Davenport.

The Lighthouse Players' annual presentation was a revival of "Personal Appearance" January 5, and the annual show of the Snarks was vaudeville called "Done on a Shoestring" at the new theatre of Hunter College, March 26. S. Wesley McKee staged the show and John Sacco directed the music.

"Everyman," a morality play as dramatized by Hugo von Hofmannsthal and translated by George Sterling, was produced by the Theatre Friendship House, a refugee theatrical group directed by Walter Firner, May 8. The cast of professional American and Austrian actors included Walter Slezac, Maurice Burke, Cyrilla Dorne, Margrit Wyler and others.

Monodrama

Ruth Draper and her nephew, Paul Draper, appeared at the Booth Theatre, New York, where they gave 22 performances of sketches and dance drama, starting December 26, 1940. Miss Draper's monologues included "At a Children's Party in Philadelphia," "On a Porch in a Maine Village," "In a Church in Italy" and others. Paul Draper danced "drama" dances to the music of Scarlatti, Bach, Handel and DeBussy.

College Plays in New York

The Princeton Triangle Club produced "Many a Slip," its fifty-second annual presentation, at the Al Jolson Theatre, New York, January 3, 1941. Robert H. Coleman of Greenwich, Conn., was author of the show and also played the leading rôle. Others in the cast were Carl E. Davis, Jr., Benedict J. Duffy, Jr., John B. Green, Kenneth E. Folsom, etc. The production was staged by D. Kennedy Fox and S. Wesley McKee and the settings were by William D. Compton and Simeon Hyde, Jr. Additional dialogue was written by Henry Frielinghaus.

"One on the House," the ninety-fifth annual production of the Harvard Hasty Pudding Club, was produced in the Grand Ballroom of the Waldorf-Astoria, March 29, 1941. The book was by Bancroft G. Davis, Jr., William B. D. Putnam and Lemuel Banister, Jr.; music by Sherwood Rollins, Jr., Philip Kadison and Robert H. Coleman; lyrics by Franklin J. Tyler, Edward J. P. Zimmerman, Bancroft Davis, Charles H. Stern and Sherwood Rollins; staged by Ted Fetter, dances directed by William R. Holbrooke, music directed by Leroy Anderson.

STATISTICAL SUMMARY

(Last Season Plays Which Ended Runs After June 15, 1940)

Plays	*Number Performances*	
Du Barry Was a Lady	408	(Closed December 12, 1940)
Keep Off the Grass	44	(Closed June 29, 1940)
Ladies in Retirement	151	(Closed August 3, 1940)
Louisiana Purchase	444	(Closed June 14, 1941)
Pins and Needles	1,108	(Closed June 22, 1940)
The Male Animal	243	(Closed August 3, 1940)
There Shall Be No Night	181	(Closed November 2, 1940)
Tobacco Road	3,182	(Closed May 31, 1941)
Walk with Music	55	(Closed July 20, 1940)

LONG RUNS ON BROADWAY

To June 15, 1941

(Plays marked with asterisk were still playing June 15, 1941)

Plays	*Number Performances*	*Plays*	*Number Performances*
Tobacco Road	3,182	Student Prince	608
Abie's Irish Rose	2,327	Broadway	603
Lightnin'	1,291	Adonis	603
*Hellzapoppin	1,181	Street Scene	601
Pins and Needles	1,108	Kiki	600
The Bat	867	Blossom Time	592
White Cargo	864	Brother Rat	577
You Can't Take It with You	837	Show Boat	572
Three Men on a Horse	835	The Show-Off	571
The Ladder	789	Sally	570
The First Year	760	Rose Marie	557
*The Man Who Came to Dinner	707	Strictly Dishonorable	557
Seventh Heaven	704	Good News	551
Peg o' My Heart	692	The Music Master	540
The Children's Hour	691	What a Life	538
Dead End	687	The Boomerang	522
East Is West	680	Blackbirds	518
*Life with Father	674	Sunny	517
Irene	670	Victoria Regina	517
Boy Meets Girl	669	*Separate Rooms	517
The Women	657	The Vagabond King	511
A Trip to Chinatown	657	The New Moon	509
Rain	648	Shuffle Along	504
The Green Pastures	640	Personal Appearance	501
Is Zat So	618	Bird in Hand	500
		Sailor, Beware!	500
		Room Service	500

DRAMA CRITICS' CIRCLE AWARD

For the second time since it amended its constitution to permit its members to select the best play of the season of American authorship by a majority rather than a three-fourths vote, the New York Drama Critics' Circle was forced to abide by such a decision this year. Under the three-fourths rule five ballots were taken without a choice. Plays receiving votes included Lillian Hellman's "Watch on the Rhine," William Saroyan's "The Beautiful People," Paul Green's and Richard Wright's "Native Son," S. N. Behrman's "The Talley Method," Elmer Rice's "Flight to the West," Joseph Kesselring's "Arsenic and Old Lace," Rose Franken's "Claudia," and Moss Hart's "Lady in the Dark." On the seventh and deciding ballot "Watch on the Rhine" was given twelve votes, "The Beautiful People" six, and "Native Son" one. The Circle voted unanimously for Emlyn Williams' "The Corn Is Green" as the best play of the season of foreign importation. This is the second majority vote Miss Hellman has won from the Circle, her "The Little Foxes" topping Robert Sherwood's "Abe Lincoln in Illinois" by one vote in 1939. Previous Circle awards have been:

1935-36—Winterset, by Maxwell Anderson
1936-37—High Tor, by Maxwell Anderson
1937-38—Of Mice and Men, by John Steinbeck
1938-39—No decision. ("The Little Foxes" and "Abe Lincoln in Illinois" led voting.)
1939-40—The Time of Your Life, by William Saroyan
1940-41—Watch on the Rhine, by Lillian Hellman.

PULITZER PRIZE WINNERS

"For the original American play performed in New York which shall best represent the educational value and power of the stage in raising the standard of good morals, good taste and good manners."—The Will of Joseph Pulitzer, dated April 16, 1904.

In 1929 the advisory board, which, according to the terms of the will, "shall have the power in its discretion to suspend or to change any subject or subjects . . . if in the judgment of the board such suspension, changes or substitutions shall be conducive to the public good," decided to eliminate from the above paragraph relating to the prize-winning play the words "in raising the standard of good morals, good taste and good manners."

The committee awards to date have been:

1917-18—Why Marry? by Jesse Lynch Williams
1918-19—None
1919-20—Beyond the Horizon, by Eugene O'Neill
1920-21—Miss Lulu Bett, by Zona Gale
1921-22—Anna Christie, by Eugene O'Neill
1922-23—Icebound, by Owen Davis
1923-24—Hell-bent fer Heaven, by Hatcher Hughes
1924-25—They Knew What They Wanted, by Sidney Howard
1925-26—Craig's Wife, by George Kelly
1926-27—In Abraham's Bosom, by Paul Green
1927-28—Strange Interlude, by Eugene O'Neill
1928-29—Street Scene, by Elmer Rice
1929-30—The Green Pastures, by Marc Connelly
1930-31—Alison's House, by Susan Glaspell
1931-32—Of Thee I Sing, by George S. Kaufman, Morrie Ryskind, Ira and George Gershwin
1932-33—Both Your Houses, by Maxwell Anderson
1933-34—Men in White, by Sidney Kingsley
1934-35—The Old Maid, by Zoe Akins
1935-36—Idiot's Delight, by Robert E. Sherwood
1936-37—You Can't Take It with You, by Moss Hart and George S. Kaufman
1937-38—Our Town, by Thornton Wilder
1938-39—Abe Lincoln in Illinois, by Robert E. Sherwood
1939-40—The Time of Your Life, by William Saroyan
1940-41—There Shall Be No Night, by Robert E. Sherwood

PREVIOUS VOLUMES OF BEST PLAYS

Plays chosen to represent the theatre seasons from 1909 to 1940 are as follows:

1909-1919

"The Easiest Way," by Eugene Walter. Published by G. W. Dillingham, New York; Houghton Mifflin Co., Boston.

"Mrs. Bumpstead-Leigh," by Harry James Smith. Published by Samuel French, New York.

"Disraeli," by Louis N. Parker. Published by Dodd, Mead and Co., New York.

"Romance," by Edward Sheldon. Published by the Macmillan Co., New York.

"Seven Keys to Baldpate," by George M. Cohan. Published by Bobbs-Merrill Co., Indianapolis, as a novel by Earl Derr Biggers; as a play by Samuel French, New York.

"On Trial," by Elmer Reizenstein. Published by Samuel French, New York.

"The Unchastened Woman," by Louis Kaufman Anspacher. Published by Harcourt, Brace and Howe, Inc., New York.

"Good Gracious Annabelle," by Clare Kummer. Published by Samuel French, New York.

"Why Marry?" by Jesse Lynch Williams. Published by Charles Scribner's Sons, New York.

"John Ferguson," by St. John Ervine. Published by the Macmillan Co., New York.

1919-1920

"Abraham Lincoln," by John Drinkwater. Published by Houghton Mifflin Co., Boston.

"Clarence," by Booth Tarkington. Published by Samuel French, New York.

"Beyond the Horizon," by Eugene G. O'Neill. Published by Boni & Liveright, Inc., New York.

"Déclassée," by Zoe Akins. Published by Liveright, Inc., New York.

"The Famous Mrs. Fair," by James Forbes. Published by Samuel French, New York.

"The Jest," by Sem Benelli. (American adaptation by Edward Sheldon.)

"Jane Clegg," by St. John Ervine. Published by Henry Holt & Co., New York.

"Mamma's Affair," by Rachel Barton Butler. Published by Samuel French, New York.

"Wedding Bells," by Salisbury Field. Published by Samuel French, New York.

"Adam and Eva," by George Middleton and Guy Bolton. Published by Samuel French, New York.

1920-1921

"Deburau," adapted from the French of Sacha Guitry by H. Granville Barker. Published by G. P. Putnam's Sons, New York.

"The First Year," by Frank Craven. Published by Samuel French, New York.

"Enter Madame," by Gilda Varesi and Dolly Byrne. Published by G. P. Putnam's Sons, New York.

"The Green Goddess," by William Archer. Published by Alfred A. Knopf, New York.

"Liliom," by Ferenc Molnar. Published by Boni & Liveright, New York.

"Mary Rose," by James M. Barrie. Published by Charles Scribner's Sons, New York.

"Nice People," by Rachel Crothers. Published by Charles Scribner's Sons, New York.

"The Bad Man," by Porter Emerson Browne. Published by G. P. Putnam's Sons, New York.

"The Emperor Jones," by Eugene G. O'Neill. Published by Boni & Liveright, New York.

"The Skin Game," by John Galsworthy. Published by Charles Scribner's Sons, New York.

1921-1922

"Anna Christie," by Eugene G. O'Neill. Published by Boni & Liveright, New York.

"A Bill of Divorcement," by Clemence Dane. Published by the Macmillan Company, New York.

"Dulcy," by George S. Kaufman and Marc Connelly. Published by G. P. Putnam's Sons, New York.

"He Who Gets Slapped," adapted from the Russian of Leonid Andreyev by Gregory Zilboorg. Published by Brentano's, New York.

"Six Cylinder Love," by William Anthony McGuire.

"The Hero," by Gilbert Emery.

"The Dover Road," by Alan Alexander Milne. Published by Samuel French, New York.

"Ambush," by Arthur Richman.

"The Circle," by William Somerset Maugham.

"The Nest," by Paul Geraldy and Grace George.

1922-1923

"Rain," by John Colton and Clemence Randolph. Published by Liveright, Inc., New York.

"Loyalties," by John Galsworthy. Published by Charles Scribner's Sons, New York.

"Icebound," by Owen Davis. Published by Little, Brown & Company, Boston.

"You and I," by Philip Barry. Published by Brentano's, New York.

"The Fool," by Channing Pollock. Published by Brentano's, New York.

"Merton of the Movies," by George Kaufman and Marc Connelly, based on the novel of the same name by Harry Leon Wilson.

"Why Not?" by Jesse Lynch Williams. Published by Walter H. Baker Co., Boston.

"The Old Soak," by Don Marquis. Published by Doubleday, Page & Company, New York.

"R.U.R.," by Karel Capek. Translated by Paul Selver. Published by Doubleday, Page & Company.

"Mary the 3d," by Rachel Crothers. Published by Brentano's, New York.

1923-1924

"The Swan," translated from the Hungarian of Ferenc Molnar by Melville Baker. Published by Boni & Liveright, New York.

"Outward Bound," by Sutton Vane. Published by Boni & Liveright, New York.

"The Show-off," by George Kelly. Published by Little, Brown & Company, Boston.

"The Changelings," by Lee Wilson Dodd. Published by E. P. Dutton & Company, New York.

"Chicken Feed," by Guy Bolton. Published by Samuel French,

New York and London.

"Sun-Up," by Lula Vollmer. Published by Brentano's, New York.

"Beggar on Horseback," by George Kaufman and Marc Connelly. Published by Boni & Liveright, New York.

"Tarnish," by Gilbert Emery. Published by Brentano's, New York.

"The Goose Hangs High," by Lewis Beach. Published by Little, Brown & Company, Boston.

"Hell-bent fer Heaven," by Hatcher Hughes. Published by Harper Bros., New York.

1924-1925

"What Price Glory?" by Laurence Stallings and Maxwell Anderson. Published by Harcourt, Brace & Co., New York.

"They Knew What They Wanted," by Sidney Howard. Published by Doubleday, Page & Company, New York.

"Desire Under the Elms," by Eugene G. O'Neill. Published by Boni & Liveright, New York.

"The Firebrand," by Edwin Justus Mayer. Published by Boni & Liveright, New York.

"Dancing Mothers," by Edgar Selwyn and Edmund Goulding.

"Mrs. Partridge Presents," by Mary Kennedy and Ruth Warren. Published by Samuel French, New York.

"The Fall Guy," by James Gleason and George Abbott. Published by Samuel French, New York.

"The Youngest," by Philip Barry. Published by Samuel French, New York.

"Minick," by Edna Ferber and George S. Kaufman. Published by Doubleday, Page & Company, New York.

"Wild Birds," by Dan Totheroh. Published by Doubleday, Page & Company, New York.

1925-1926

"Craig's Wife," by George Kelly. Published by Little, Brown & Company, Boston.

"The Great God Brown," by Eugene G. O'Neill. Published by Boni & Liveright, New York.

"The Green Hat," by Michael Arlen.

"The Dybbuk," by S. Ansky, Henry G. Alsberg-Winifred Katzin translation. Published by Boni & Liveright, New York.

"The Enemy," by Channing Pollock. Published by Brentano's,

New York.

"The Last of Mrs. Cheyney," by Frederick Lonsdale. Published by Samuel French, New York.

"Bride of the Lamb," by William Hurlbut. Published by Boni & Liveright, New York.

"The Wisdom Tooth," by Marc Connelly. Published by George H. Doran & Company, New York.

"The Butter and Egg Man," by George Kaufman. Published by Boni & Liveright, New York.

"Young Woodley," by John Van Druten. Published by Simon and Schuster, New York.

1926-1927

"Broadway," by Philip Dunning and George Abbott. Published by George H. Doran Company, New York.

"Saturday's Children," by Maxwell Anderson. Published by Longmans, Green & Company, New York.

"Chicago," by Maurine Watkins. Published by Alfred A. Knopf, Inc., New York.

"The Constant Wife," by William Somerset Maugham. Published by George H. Doran Company, New York.

"The Play's the Thing," by Ferenc Molnar and P. G. Wodehouse. Published by Brentano's, New York.

"The Road to Rome," by Robert Emmet Sherwood. Published by Charles Scribner's Sons, New York.

"The Silver Cord," by Sidney Howard. Published by Charles Scribner's Sons, New York.

"The Cradle Song," translated from the Spanish of G. Martinez Sierra by John Garrett Underhill. Published by E. P. Dutton & Company, New York.

"Daisy Mayme," by George Kelly. Published by Little, Brown & Company, Boston.

"In Abraham's Bosom," by Paul Green. Published by Robert M. McBride & Company, New York.

1927-1928

"Strange Interlude," by Eugene G. O'Neill. Published by Boni & Liveright, New York.

"The Royal Family," by Edna Ferber and George Kaufman. Published by Doubleday, Doran & Company, New York.

"Burlesque," by George Manker Watters. Published by Doubleday, Doran & Company, New York.

"Coquette," by George Abbott and Ann Bridgers. Published by Longmans, Green & Company, New York, London, Toronto.
"Behold the Bridegroom," by George Kelly. Published by Little, Brown & Company, Boston.
"Porgy," by DuBose Heyward. Published by Doubleday, Doran & Company, New York.
"Paris Bound," by Philip Barry. Published by Samuel French, New York.
"Escape," by John Galsworthy. Published by Charles Scribner's Sons, New York.
"The Racket," by Bartlett Cormack. Published by Samuel French, New York.
"The Plough and the Stars," by Sean O'Casey. Published by the Macmillan Company, New York.

1928-1929

"Street Scene," by Elmer Rice. Published by Samuel French, New York.
"Journey's End," by R. C. Sherriff. Published by Brentano's, New York.
"Wings Over Europe," by Robert Nichols and Maurice Browne. Published by Covici-Friede, New York.
"Holiday," by Philip Barry. Published by Samuel French, New York.
"The Front Page," by Ben Hecht and Charles MacArthur. Published by Covici-Friede, New York.
"Let Us Be Gay," by Rachel Crothers. Published by Samuel French, New York.
"Machinal," by Sophie Treadwell.
"Little Accident," by Floyd Dell and Thomas Mitchell.
"Gypsy," by Maxwell Anderson.
"The Kingdom of God," by G. Martinez Sierra; English version by Helen and Harley Granville-Barker. Published by E. P. Dutton & Company, New York.

1929-1930

"The Green Pastures," by Marc Connelly (adapted from "Ol' Man Adam and His Chillun," by Roark Bradford). Published by Farrar & Rinehart, Inc., New York.
"The Criminal Code," by Martin Flavin. Published by Horace Liveright, New York.
"Berkeley Square," by John Balderston. Published by the Macmillan Company, New York.

"Strictly Dishonorable," by Preston Sturges. Published by Horace Liveright, New York.

"The First Mrs. Fraser," by St. John Ervine. Published by the Macmillan Company, New York.

"The Last Mile," by John Wexley. Published by Samuel French, New York.

"June Moon," by Ring W. Lardner and George S. Kaufman. Published by Charles Scribner's Sons, New York.

"Michael and Mary," by A. A. Milne. Published by Chatto & Windus, London.

"Death Takes a Holiday," by Walter Ferris (adapted from the Italian of Alberto Casella). Published by Samuel French, New York.

"Rebound," by Donald Ogden Stewart. Published by Samuel French, New York.

1930-1931

"Elizabeth the Queen," by Maxwell Anderson. Published by Longmans, Green & Co., New York.

"Tomorrow and Tomorrow," by Philip Barry. Published by Samuel French, New York.

"Once in a Lifetime," by George S. Kaufman and Moss Hart. Published by Farrar and Rinehart, New York.

"Green Grow the Lilacs," by Lynn Riggs. Published by Samuel French, New York and London.

"As Husbands Go," by Rachel Crothers. Published by Samuel French, New York.

"Alison's House," by Susan Glasgow. Published by Samuel French, New York.

"Five-Star Final," by Louis Weitzenkorn. Published by Samuel French, New York.

"Overture," by William Bolitho. Published by Simon & Schuster, New York.

"The Barretts of Wimpole Street," by Rudolf Besier. Published by Little, Brown & Company, Boston.

"Grand Hotel," adapted from the German of Vicki Baum by W. A. Drake.

1931-1932

"Of Thee I Sing," by George S. Kaufman and Morrie Ryskind; music and lyrics by George and Ira Gershwin. Published by Alfred Knopf, New York.

"Mourning Becomes Electra," by Eugene G. O'Neill. Published by Horace Liveright, Inc., New York.

"Reunion in Vienna," by Robert Emmet Sherwood. Published

by Charles Scribner's Sons, New York.

"The House of Connelly," by Paul Green. Published by Samuel French, New York.

"The Animal Kingdom," by Philip Barry. Published by Samuel French, New York.

"The Left Bank," by Elmer Rice. Published by Samuel French, New York.

"Another Language," by Rose Franken. Published by Samuel French, New York.

"Brief Moment," by S. N. Behrman. Published by Farrar & Rinehart, New York.

"The Devil Passes," by Benn W. Levy. Published by Martin Secker, London.

"Cynara," by H. M. Harwood and R. F. Gore-Browne. Published by Samuel French, New York.

1932-1933

"Both Your Houses," by Maxwell Anderson. Published by Samuel French, New York.

"Dinner at Eight," by George S. Kaufman and Edna Ferber. Published by Doubleday, Doran & Co., Inc., Garden City, New York.

"When Ladies Meet," by Rachel Crothers. Published by Samuel French, New York.

"Design for Living," by Noel Coward. Published by Doubleday, Doran & Co., Inc., Garden City, New York.

"Biography," by S. N. Behrman. Published by Farrar & Rinehart, Inc., New York.

"Alien Corn," by Sidney Howard. Published by Charles Scribner's Sons, New York.

"The Late Christopher Bean," adapted from the French of René Fauchois by Sidney Howard. Published by Samuel French, New York.

"We, the People," by Elmer Rice. Published by Coward-McCann, Inc., New York.

"Pigeons and People," by George M. Cohan.

"One Sunday Afternoon," by James Hagan. Published by Samuel French, New York.

1933-1934

"Mary of Scotland," by Maxwell Anderson. Published by Doubleday, Doran & Co., Inc., Garden City, N. Y.

"Men in White," by Sidney Kingsley. Published by Covici, Friede, Inc., New York.

"Dodsworth," by Sinclair Lewis and Sidney Howard. Published by Harcourt, Brace & Co., New York.

"Ah, Wilderness," by Eugene O'Neill. Published by Random House, New York.

"They Shall Not Die," by John Wexley. Published by Alfred A. Knopf, New York.

"Her Master's Voice," by Clare Kummer. Published by Samuel French, New York.

"No More Ladies," by A. E. Thomas.

"Wednesday's Child," by Leopold Atlas. Published by Samuel French, New York.

"The Shining Hour," by Keith Winter. Published by Doubleday, Doran & Co., Inc., Garden City, New York.

"The Green Bay Tree," by Mordaunt Shairp. Published by Baker International Play Bureau, Boston, Mass.

1934-1935

"The Children's Hour," by Lillian Hellman. Published by Alfred Knopf, New York.

"Valley Forge," by Maxwell Anderson. Published by Anderson House, Washington, D. C. Distributed by Dodd, Mead & Co., New York.

"The Petrified Forest," by Robert Sherwood. Published by Charles Scribner's Sons, New York.

"The Old Maid," by Zoe Akins. Published by D. Appleton-Century Co., New York.

"Accent on Youth," by Samson Raphaelson. Published by Samuel French, New York.

"Merrily We Roll Along," by George S. Kaufman and Moss Hart. Published by Random House, New York.

"Awake and Sing," by Clifford Odets. Published by Random House, New York.

"The Farmer Takes a Wife," by Frank B. Elser and Marc Connelly.

"Lost Horizons," by John Hayden.

"The Distaff Side," by John Van Druten. Published by Alfred Knopf, New York.

1935-1936

"Winterset," by Maxwell Anderson. Published by Anderson House, Washington, D. C.

"Idiot's Delight," by Robert Emmet Sherwood. Published by Charles Scribner's Sons, New York.

"End of Summer," by S. N. Behrman. Published by Random House, New York.

"First Lady," by Katharine Dayton and George S. Kaufman. Published by Random House, New York.

"Victoria Regina," by Laurence Housman. Published by Samuel French, Inc., New York and London.

"Boy Meets Girl," by Bella and Samuel Spewack. Published by Random House, New York.

"Dead End," by Sidney Kingsley. Published by Random House, New York.

"Call It a Day," by Dodie Smith. Published by Samuel French, Inc., New York and London.

"Ethan Frome," by Owen Davis and Donald Davis. Published by Charles Scribner's Sons, New York.

"Pride and Prejudice," by Helen Jerome. Published by Doubleday, Doran & Co., Garden City, New York.

1936-1937

"High Tor," by Maxwell Anderson. Published by Anderson House, Washington, D. C.

"You Can't Take It with You," by Moss Hart and George S. Kaufman. Published by Farrar & Rinehart, Inc., New York.

"Johnny Johnson," by Paul Green. Published by Samuel French, Inc., New York.

"Daughters of Atreus," by Robert Turney. Published by Alfred A. Knopf, New York.

"Stage Door," by Edna Ferber and George S. Kaufman. Published by Doubleday, Doran & Co., Garden City, New York.

"The Women," by Clare Boothe. Published by Random House, Inc., New York.

"St. Helena," by R. C. Sherriff and Jeanne de Casalis. Published by Samuel French, Inc., New York and London.

"Yes, My Darling Daughter," by Mark Reed. Published by Samuel French, Inc., New York.

"Excursion," by Victor Wolfson. Published by Random House, New York.

"Tovarich," by Jacques Deval and Robert E. Sherwood. Published by Random House, New York.

1937-1938

"Of Mice and Men," by John Steinbeck. Published by Covici-Friede, New York.

"Our town," by Thornton Wilder. Published by Coward-McCann, Inc., New York.

"Shadow and Substance," by Paul Vincent Carroll. Published by Random House, Inc., New York.

"On Borrowed Time," by Paul Osborn. Published by Alfred A. Knopf, New York.

"The Star-Wagon," by Maxwell Anderson. Published by Anderson House, Washington, D. C. Distributed by Dodd, Mead & Co., New York.

"Susan and God," by Rachel Crothers. Published by Random House, Inc., New York.

"Prologue to Glory," by E. P. Conkle. Published by Random House, Inc., New York.

"Amphitryon 38," by S. N. Behrman. Published by Random House, Inc., New York.

"Golden Boy," by Clifford Odets. Published by Random House, Inc., New York.

"What a Life," by Clifford Goldsmith. Published by Dramatists Play Service, Inc., New York.

1938-1939

"Abe Lincoln in Illinois," by Robert E. Sherwood. Published by Charles Scribner's Sons, New York and Charles Scribner's Sons, Ltd. London.

"The Little Foxes," by Lillian Hellman. Published by Random House, Inc., New York.

"Rocket to the Moon," by Clifford Odets. Published by Random House, Inc., New York.

"The American Way," by George S. Kaufman and Moss Hart. Published by Random House, Inc., New York.

"No Time for Comedy," by S. N. Behrman. Published by Random House, Inc., New York.

"The Philadelphia Story," by Philip Barry. Published by Coward-McCann, Inc., New York.

"The White Steed," by Paul Vincent Carroll. Published by Random House, Inc., New York.

"Here Come the Clowns," by Philip Barry. Published by Coward-McCann, Inc., New York.

"Family Portrait," by Lenore Coffee and William Joyce Cowen. Published by Random House, Inc., New York.

"Kiss the Boys Good-bye," by Clare Boothe. Published by Random House, Inc., New York.

1939-1940

"There Shall Be No Night," by Robert E. Sherwood. Published by Charles Scribner's Sons, New York.

"Key Largo," by Maxwell Anderson. Published by Anderson House, Washington, D. C.

"The World We Make," by Sidney Kingsley.

"Life with Father," by Howard Lindsay and Russel Crouse. Published by Alfred A. Knopf, New York.

"The Man Who Came to Dinner," by George S. Kaufman and Moss Hart. Published by Random House, Inc., New York.

"The Male Animal," by James Thurber and Elliott Nugent. Published by Random House, Inc., New York, and MacMillan Co., Canada.

"The Time of Your Life," by William Saroyan. Published by Harcourt, Brace and Company, Inc., New York.

"Skylark," by Samson Raphaelson. Published by Random House, Inc., New York.

"Margin for Error," by Clare Boothe. Published by Random House, Inc., New York.

"Morning's at Seven," by Paul Osborn. Published by Samuel French, New York.

WHERE AND WHEN THEY WERE BORN

(Compiled from the most authentic records available.)

Abba, Marta .... Milan, Italy 1907
Abbott, George .... Hamburg, N. Y. 1895
Abel, Walter .... St. Paul, Minn. 1898
Adams, Maude .... Salt Lake City, Utah 1872
Addy, Wesley .... Omaha, Neb. 1912
Adler, Luther .... New York City 1903
Adler, Stella .... New York City 1904
Aherne, Brian .... King's Norton, England ... 1902
Akins, Zoe .... Humansville, Mo. 1886
Allgood, Sara .... Dublin, Ireland 1883
Anders, Glenn .... Los Angeles, Cal. 1890
Anderson, Judith .... Australia 1898
Anderson, Maxwell .... Atlantic City, Pa. 1888
Andrews, A. G. .... Buffalo, N. Y. 1861
Andrews, Ann .... Los Angeles, Cal. 1895
Anglin, Margaret .... Ottawa, Canada 1876
Anson, A. E. .... London, England 1879
Arling, Joyce .... Memphis, Tenn. 1911
Arliss, George .... London, England 1868
Ashcroft, Peggy .... Croydon, England 1907
Astaire, Fred .... Omaha, Neb. 1899
Atwater, Edith .... Chicago, Ill. 1912
Atwell, Roy .... Syracuse, N. Y. 1880
Atwill, Lionel .... London, England 1885

Bainter, Fay .... Los Angeles, Cal. 1892
Baker, Lee .... Michigan 1880
Bankhead, Tallulah .... Huntsville, Ala. 1902
Banks, Leslie J. .... West Derby, England 1890
Barbee, Richard .... Lafayette, Ind. 1887
Barrett, Edith .... Roxbury, Mass. 1904
Barry, Philip .... Rochester, N. Y. 1896
Barrymore, Diana .... New York City 1921
Barrymore, Ethel .... Philadelphia, Pa. 1879
Barrymore, John .... Philadelphia, Pa. 1882
Barrymore, Lionel .... London, England 1878

Barton, James	Gloucester, N. J.	1890
Baxter, Lora	New York	1907
Behrman, S. N.	Worcester, Mass.	1893
Bell, James	Suffolk, Va.	1891
Bennett, Richard	Cass County, Ind.	1873
Bergner, Elisabeth	Vienna	1901
Berlin, Irving	Russia	1888
Best, Edna	Sussex, England	1900
Binney, Constance	Philadelphia, Pa.	1900
Boland, Mary	Detroit, Mich.	1880
Bolger, Ray	Dorchester, Mass.	1906
Bondi, Beulah	Chicago, Ill.	1892
Bordoni, Irene	Paris, France	1895
Bowman, Patricia	Washington, D. C.	1912
Brady, William A.	San Francisco, Cal.	1863
Braham, Horace	London, England	1896
Brent, Romney	Saltillo, Mex.	1902
Brian, Donald	St. Johns, N. F.	1877
Brice, Fannie	Brooklyn, N. Y.	1891
Broderick, Helen	New York	1891
Bromberg, J. Edward	Hungary	1903
Bruce, Nigel	San Diego, Cal.	1895
Bryant, Charles	England	1879
Buchanan, Jack	England	1892
Burke, Billie	Washington, D. C.	1885
Byington, Spring	Colorado Springs, Colo.	1898
Byron, Arthur	Brooklyn, N. Y.	1872
Cabot, Eliot	Boston, Mass.	1899
Cagney, James	New York	1904
Cahill, Lily	Texas	1891
Calhern, Louis	New York	1895
Cantor, Eddie	New York	1894
Carlisle, Kitty	New Orleans, La.	1912
Carminati, Tullio	Zara, Dalmatia	1894
Carnovsky, Morris	St. Louis, Mo.	1898
Carpenter, Edward Childs	Philadelphia, Pa.	1871
Carroll, Earl	Pittsburgh, Pa.	1892
Carroll, Leo G.	Weedon, England	1892
Carroll, Nancy	New York City	1906
Catlett, Walter	San Francisco, Cal.	1889
Chandler, Helen	Charleston, N. C.	1906
Chaplin, Charles Spencer	London	1889

Chase, Ilka	New York	1900
Chatterton, Ruth	New York	1893
Christians, Mady	Vienna, Austria	1907
Churchill, Berton	Toronto, Can.	1876
Claire, Helen	Union Springs, Ala.	1908
Claire, Ina	Washington, D. C.	1892
Clive, Colin	St. Malo, France	1900
Coburn, Charles	Macon, Ga.	1877
Cohan, George M.	Providence, R. I.	1878
Cohan, Georgette	Los Angeles, Cal.	1900
Colbert, Claudette	Paris	1905
Collier, Constance	Windsor, England	1882
Collier, William	New York	1866
Collinge, Patricia	Dublin, Ireland	1894
Collins, Russell	New Orleans, La.	1901
Colt, Ethel Barrymore	Mamaroneck, N. Y.	1911
Colt, John Drew	New York	1914
Conklin, Peggy	Dobbs Ferry, N. Y.	1912
Conroy, Frank	London, England	1885
Cook, Donald	Portland, Ore.	1902
Cook, Joe	Evansville, Ind.	1890
Cooper, Gladys	Lewisham, England	1888
Cooper, Violet Kemble	London, England	1890
Cornell, Katharine	Berlin, Germany	1898
Corthell, Herbert	Boston, Mass.	1875
Cossart, Ernest	Cheltenham, England	1876
Coulouris, George	Manchester, England	1906
Courtleigh, Stephen	New York City	1912
Coward, Noel	Teddington, England	1899
Cowl, Jane	Boston, Mass.	1887
Craig, Helen	Mexico City	1914
Craven, Frank	Boston, Mass.	1880
Crews, Laura Hope	San Francisco, Cal.	1880
Cronyn, Hume	Canada	1912
Crosman, Henrietta	Wheeling, W. Va.	1865
Crothers, Rachel	Bloomington, Ill.	1878
Cummings, Constance	Seattle, Wash.	1911
Dale, Margaret	Philadelphia, Pa.	1880
Davis, Donald	New York	1907
Davis, Owen	Portland, Me.	1874
Davis, Owen, Jr.	New York	1910
De Cordoba, Pedro	New York	1881

Name	Birthplace	Year
Digges, Dudley	Dublin, Ireland	1880
Dinehart, Allan	Missoula, Mont.	1889
Dixon, Jean	Waterbury, Conn.	1905
Dowling, Eddie	Woonsocket, R. I.	1895
Dressler, Eric	Brooklyn, N. Y.	1900
Dressler, Marie	Cobourg, Canada	1869
Dudley, Doris	New York City	1918
Duncan, Augustin	San Francisco	1873
Dunn, Emma	England	1875
Dunning, Philip	Meriden, Conn.	1890
Dupree, Minnie	San Francisco, Cal.	1875
Durante, Jimmy	New York City	1893
Edney, Florence	London, England	1879
Eldridge, Florence	Brooklyn, N. Y.	1901
Ellerbe, Harry	Georgia	1905
Emery, Gilbert	Naples, New York	1875
Emery, Katherine	Birmingham, Ala.	1908
Erickson, Leif	California	1917
Errol, Leon	Sydney, Australia	1881
Ervine, St. John Greer	Belfast, Ireland	1883
Evans, Edith	London, England	1888
Evans, Maurice	Dorchester, England	1901
Farley, Morgan	Mamaroneck, N. Y.	1901
Farmer, Frances	Seattle, Wash.	1914
Farnum, William	Boston, Mass.	1876
Fassett, Jay	Elmira, N. Y.	1889
Ferber, Edna	Kalamazoo, Mich.	1887
Ferguson, Elsie	New York	1883
Ferrer, Jose	Puerto Rico	1909
Field, Sylvia	Allston, Mass.	1902
Fields, W. C.	Philadelphia, Pa.	1883
Fischer, Alice	Indiana	1869
Fitzgerald, Barry	Dublin, Ireland	1888
Fletcher, Bramwell	Bradford, Yorkshire, Eng.	1904
Fontanne, Lynn	London, England	1887
Forbes, Ralph	London, England	1905
Foster, Phœbe	New Hampshire	1897
Foy, Eddie, Jr.	New Rochelle, N. Y.	1906
Fraser, Elizabeth	Brooklyn, N. Y.	1920
Friganza, Trixie	Cincinnati, Ohio	1870

Gahagan, Helen	Boonton, N. J.	1902
Gaxton, William	San Francisco, Cal.	1893
Geddes, Norman Bel	Adrian, Mich.	1893
George, Grace	New York	1879
Gerald, Ara	New South Wales	1902
Gershwin, Ira	New York	1896
Gielgud, John	London, England	1904
Gillmore, Frank	New York	1884
Gillmore, Margalo	England	1901
Gish, Dorothy	Massillon, Ohio	1898
Gish, Lillian	Springfield, Ohio	1896
Gleason, James	New York	1885
Golden, John	New York	1874
Gordon, Ruth	Wollaston, Mass.	1896
Granville, Charlotte	London	1863
Granville, Sydney	Bolton, England	1885
Green, Martyn	London, England	1899
Green, Mitzi	New York City	1920
Greenstreet, Sydney	England	1880
Groody, Louise	Waco, Texas	1897
Gwenn, Edmund	Glamorgan, Wales	1875
Haines, Robert T.	Muncie, Ind.	1870
Hall, Bettina	North Easton, Mass.	1906
Hall, Natalie	North Easton, Mass.	1904
Hall, Thurston	Boston, Mass.	1882
Halliday, John	Brooklyn, N. Y.	1880
Halliday, Robert	Loch Lomond, Scotland	1893
Hampden, Walter	Brooklyn, N. Y.	1879
Hannen, Nicholas	London, England	1881
Hardwicke, Sir Cedric	Lye, Stourbridge, England	1893
Hargrave, Roy	New York City	1908
Harrigan, William	New York	1893
Harris, Sam H.	New York	1872
Haydon, Julie	Oak Park, Ill.	1910
Hayes, Helen	Washington, D. C.	1900
Hector, Louis	England	1882
Heflin, Van	Walters, Okla.	1909
Heineman, Eda	Japan	1891
Heming, Violet	Leeds, England	1893
Henie, Sonja	Oslo, Norway	1912
Hepburn, Katharine	Hartford, Conn.	1907
Hernreid, Paul	Trieste, Italy	1905

Hobart, Rose	New York	1906
Hoey, Dennis	London, England	1893
Holm, Celeste	New York City	1916
Hopkins, Arthur	Cleveland, Ohio	1878
Hopkins, Miriam	Bainbridge, Ga.	1904
Holmes, Taylor	Newark, N. J.	1872
Howard, Leslie	London, England	1890
Hull, Henry	Louisville, Ky.	1893
Hunter, Glenn	Highland Mills, N. Y.	1896
Huston, Walter	Toronto	1884
Hutchinson, Josephine	Seattle, Wash.	1898
Inescort, Frieda	Hitchin, Scotland	1905
Ingram, Rex	Dublin, Ireland	1892
Jagger, Dean	Columbus Grove, Ohio	1904
Joel, Clara	Jersey City, N. J.	1890
Johann, Zita	Hungary	1904
Jolson, Al	Washington, D. C.	1883
Johnson, Harold J. (Chic)	Chicago, Ill.	1891
Joslyn, Allyn	Milford, Pa.	1905
Joy, Nicholas	Paris, France	1892
Kane, Whitford	Larne, Ireland	1882
Karloff, Boris	Dulwich, England	1887
Kaufman, George S.	Pittsburgh, Pa.	1889
Kaye, A. P.	Ringwood, England	1885
Keith, Ian	Boston, Mass.	1899
Keith, Robert	Scotland	1899
Kelly, Gene	Pittsburgh, Pa.	1912
Kerrigan, J. M.	Dublin, Ireland	1885
Kerr, Geoffrey	London, England	1895
Kilbride, Percy	San Francisco, Cal.	1880
King, Dennis	Coventry, England	1897
Kingsford, Walter	England	1876
Kingsley, Sydney	New York	1906
Kirkland, Alexander	Mexico City	1904
Kirkland, Muriel	Yonkers, N. Y.	1904
Kruger, Alma	Pittsburgh, Pa.	1880
Kruger, Otto	Toledo, Ohio	1895
Landi, Elissa	Venice, Italy	1904
Landis, Jessie Royce	Chicago, Ill.	1904

Larimore, Earl	Portland, Oregon	1899
Larrimore, Francine	Russia	1898
Lauder, Harry	Portobello, Scotland	1870
Laughton, Charles	Scarborough, England	1899
Lawford, Betty	London, England	1904
Lawrence, Gertrude	London	1898
Lawson, Wilfred	London, England	1894
Lawton, Frank	London, England	1904
Lawton, Thais	Louisville, Ky.	1881
Lederer, Francis	Karlin, Prague	1906
Lee, Canada	New York City	1907
Le Gallienne, Eva	London, England	1899
Lenihan, Winifred	New York	1898
Leontovich, Eugenie	Moscow, Russia	1894
Lillie, Beatrice	Toronto, Canada	1898
Locke, Katherine	New York	1914
Loeb, Philip	Philadelphia, Pa.	1892
Loftus, Cecilia	Glasgow, Scotland	1876
Logan, Stanley	Earlsfield, England	1885
Lord, Pauline	Hanford, Cal.	1890
Love, Montagu	Portsmouth, Hants	1877
Lukas, Paul	Budapest, Hungary	1895
Lunt, Alfred	Milwaukee, Wis.	1893
Macdonald, Donald	Denison, Texas	1898
March, Fredric	Racine, Wis.	1897
Margo	Mexico	1918
Marshall, Everett	Worcester, Mass.	1902
Marshall, Herbert	London, England	1890
Massey, Raymond	Toronto, Canada	1896
Matthews, A. E.	Bridlington, England	1869
Mature, Victor	Louisville, Ky.	1916
McClintic, Guthrie	Seattle, Wash.	1893
McCormick, Myron	Albany, Ind.	1906
McGuire, Dorothy	Omaha, Neb.	1918
Menken, Helen	New York	1901
Mercer, Beryl	Seville, Spain	1882
Meredith, Burgess	Cleveland, Ohio	1909
Merivale, Philip	Rehutia, India	1886
Merman, Ethel	Astoria, L. I.	1909
Mestayer, Harry	San Francisco, Cal.	1881
Miller, Gilbert	New York	1884
Miller, Marilyn	Findlay, Ohio	1898

Mitchell, Grant	Columbus, Ohio	1874
Mitchell, Thomas	Elizabeth, N. J.	1892
Mitzi (Hajos)	Budapest	1891
Moore, Grace	Del Rio, Tenn.	1901
Moore, Victor	Hammonton, N. J.	1876
Moran, Lois	Pittsburgh, Pa.	1909
Morley, Robert	Semley, Wiltshire, England	1908
Morgan, Claudia	New York	1912
Morgan, Helen	Danville, Ill.	1900
Morgan, Ralph	New York City	1889
Morris, Mary	Boston	1894
Morris, McKay	San Antonio, Texas	1890
Moss, Arnold	Brooklyn, N. Y.	1910
Muni, Paul	Lemberg, Austria	1895
Nagel, Conrad	Keokuk, Iowa	1897
Natwick, Mildred	Baltimore, Md.	1908
Nazimova, Alla	Crimea, Russia	1879
Nolan, Lloyd	San Francisco, Cal.	1903
Nugent, J. C.	Miles, Ohio	1875
Nugent, Elliott	Dover, Ohio	1900
O'Brien-Moore, Erin	Los Angeles, Cal.	1908
O'Connell, Hugh	New York	1891
Odets, Clifford	Philadelphia	1906
Oldham, Derek	Accrington, England	1892
Olivier, Laurence	Dorking, Surrey, England	1907
Olsen, John Siguard (Ole)	Peru, Ind.	1892
O'Malley, Rex	London, England	1906
O'Neill, Eugene Gladstone	New York	1888
Ouspenskaya, Maria	Tula, Russia	1876
Overman, Lynne	Maryville, Mo.	1887
Pemberton, Brock	Leavenworth, Kansas	1885
Pennington, Ann	Philadelphia, Pa.	1898
Philips, Mary	New London, Conn.	1901
Pickford, Mary	Toronto	1893
Pollock, Channing	Washington, D. C.	1880
Powers, Leona	Salida, Colo.	1900
Powers, Tom	Owensburg, Ky.	1890
Price, Vincent	St. Louis, Mo.	1914
Pryor, Roger	New York City	1901

Quartermaine, Leon	Richmond, England	1876
Rains, Claude	London, England	1889
Rambeau, Marjorie	San Francisco, Cal.	1889
Rathbone, Basil	Johannesburg	1892
Raye, Martha	Butte, Mont.	1916
Reed, Florence	Philadelphia, Pa.	1883
Rennie, James	Toronto, Canada	1890
Revelle, Hamilton	Gibraltar	1872
Ridges, Stanley	Southampton, England	1891
Ring, Blanche	Boston, Mass.	1876
Robinson, Edward G.	Bucharest, Roumania	1893
Robson, May	Australia	1868
Roos, Joanna	Brooklyn, N. Y.	1901
Ross, Thomas W.	Boston, Mass.	1875
Royle, Selena	New York	1905
Ruben, José	Belgium	1886
Sanderson, Julia	Springfield, Mass.	1887
Sands, Dorothy	Cambridge, Mass.	1900
Savo, Jimmy	New York City	1895
Scheff, Fritzi	Vienna, Austria	1879
Schildkraut, Joseph	Bucharest, Roumania	1896
Scott, Cyril	Ireland	1866
Scott, Martha	Jamesport, Mo.	1914
Segal, Vivienne	Philadelphia, Pa.	1897
Selwyn, Edgar	Cincinnati, Ohio	1875
Shannon, Effie	Cambridge, Mass.	1867
Shean, Al	Dornum, Germany	1868
Sherman, Hiram	Boston, Mass.	1908
Sherwood, Robert Emmet	New Rochelle, N. Y.	1896
Sidney, Sylvia	New York	1910
Skinner, Cornelia Otis	Chicago	1902
Skinner, Otis	Cambridgeport, Mass.	1857
Smith, Ben	Waxahachie, Texas	1905
Smith, Kent	Smithfield, Me.	1910
Sondergaard, Gale	Minnesota	1899
Starr, Frances	Oneonta, N. Y.	1886
Stenuf, Hedi	Vienna, Austria	1922
Stickney, Dorothy	Dickinson, N. D.	1903
Stoddard, Haila	Great Falls, Mont.	1914
Stone, Fred	Denver, Colo.	1873
Stone, Dorothy	New York	1905

Strudwick, Sheppard ....North Carolina 1905
Sullavan, Margaret ....Norfolk, Va. 1910

Taylor, Laurette ....New York 1884
Tearle, Conway ....New York 1878
Tearle, Godfrey ....New York 1884
Terris, Norma ....Columbus, Kansas 1904
Thomas, Frankie ....New York 1922
Thomas, John Charles ....Baltimore, Md. 1887
Thorndike, Dame Sybil ....Gainsborough, England ...1882
Tobin, Genevieve ....New York 1901
Tobin, Vivian ....New York 1903
Toler, Sidney ....Warrensburg, Mo. 1874
Tone, Franchot ....Niagara Falls, N. Y. 1907
Tracy, Lee ....Atlanta, Ga. 1898
Travers, Henry ....Berwick, England 1874
Truex, Ernest ....Red Hill, Mo. 1890
Tynan, Brandon ....Dublin, Ireland 1879

Ulric, Lenore ....New Ulm, Minn. 1897

Vallée, Rudy ....Island Pond, Vermont 1902
Varden, Evelyn ....Venita, Okla. 1893

Waldron, Charles ....New York 1877
Walker, June ....New York 1904
Warfield, David ....San Francisco, Cal. 1866
Waring, Richard ....Buckinghamshire, England.1912
Warwick, Robert ....Sacramento, Cal. 1878
Waters, Ethel ....Chester, Pa. 1900
Watkins, Linda ....Boston, Mass. 1908
Watson, Lucile ....Quebec, Canada 1879
Watson, Minor ....Marianna, Ark. 1889
Webb, Clifton ....Indiana 1891
Weber, Joseph ....New York 1867
Webster, Margaret ....New York City 1905
Welles, Orson ....Kenosha, Wis. 1915
Westley, Helen ....Brooklyn, N. Y. 1879
Weston, Ruth ....Boston, Mass. 1911
White, George ....Toronto, Canada 1890
Whorf, Richard ....Winthrop, Mass. 1908
William, Warren ....Aitkin, Minn. 1896
Williams, Emlyn ....Mostyn, Wales 1905

Wiman, Dwight Deere	Moline, Ill.	1895
Winwood, Estelle	England	1883
Witherspoon, Cora	New Orleans, La.	1891
Wood, Peggy	Brooklyn, N. Y.	1894
Worlock, Frederick	London, England	1885
Wright, Haidee	London, England	1868
Wycherly, Margaret	England	1883
Wynward, Diana	London, England	1906
Wynn, Ed.	Philadelphia, Pa.	1886
Young, Roland	London, England	1887
Yurka, Blanche	Bohemia	1893

NECROLOGY

June 15, 1940—June 15, 1941

Bickel, George L., actor, 78. Comedian of stage and screen for fifty years; began career as circus clown; later appeared with Watson and Wrothe in "Me, Him and I" which ran for three years; with Anna Held and in several Ziegfeld Follies. Born Saginaw, Michigan; died Los Angeles, California, June 5, 1941.

Blau, Bela, producer, 44. Co-producer with Marc Connelly of "Having Wonderful Time" and "The Two Bouquets"; also produced "Week End," "Overture," "The Mad Hopes" and "Everywhere I Roam." Born Hungary; died New York City, October 21, 1940.

Bradbury, James H., actor, 83. More than half century on American stage and screen; first appeared Boston Museum (1882); in original cast of George M. Cohan's "Fifty Miles from Broadway"; last seen on Broadway with the Astaires in "Lady Be Good" (1924). Born Old Town, Maine; died Clifton, Staten Island, New York, October 12, 1940.

Cameron, Beatrice (Mrs. Richard Mansfield), actress, 72. First appearances with Cora Urquhart Potter in "A Midnight Marriage" and with Robert Mantell in "Called Back"; with Mansfield company (1886) playing leading parts in nearly all Mansfield plays until 1898 when she retired; since 1932 had been reading and directing plays at Christodora House, New York. Born Troy, New York; died New London, Connecticut, July 12, 1940.

Chapman, Blanche (Mrs. H. C. Ford), actress, 90. Chapman family pedigree runs back to 1733; debut 82 years ago as child actress; 22 years under management of George C. Tyler; first Josephine in "H.M.S. Pinafore"; last appearance (1936) in "Latchstrings" at Skowhegan, Me.; widow of Henry K. Ford, owner of Ford's Theatre, Washington, D. C. Born Covington, Kentucky; died Rutherford, New Jersey, June 7, 1941.

Churchill, Berton, actor, 64. Prominent in Keith and Orpheum stock; toured with his own company in vaudeville playing "And There Were Actors Then"; first appeared on Broadway in "The World and His Wife" with William Faversham (1908); started film career in 1929 with "Nothing But the Truth"; died four days before his return to Broadway in "George Washington Slept Here." Born Toronto, Canada; died New York City, October 10, 1940.

Clark, Marguerite, actress, 53. Star of silent pictures (1915-1920); first New York appearance in "The Belle of Bohemia" (1900); played in "The Burgomaster," "Babes in Toyland," "Wang," "Happyland," "Merely Mary Ann," etc.; toured the United States with De Wolf Hopper; screen hits included "Wildflower," "The Pretty Sister of José," "The Prince and Pauper" and "Baby Mine." Born Cincinnati, Ohio; died New York City, September 25, 1940.

Collison, Wilson, playwright, 49. Author of many film scenarios, novels and farces; first success "Up in Mabel's Room" coauthored by Otto Harbach (1919); others "The Girl in the Limousine," "The Vagabond," "Getting Gertie's Garter"; since 1928 had been writing film plays, including the Maisie series. Born Gloucester, Ohio; died Beverly Hills, California, May 25, 1941.

Conness, Robert, actor, 73. Appeared with James O'Neill in "The Virginian" and "Monte Cristo"; starred with Janet Beecher in "Courage"; married Helen Strickland, actress, who died in 1938. Born La Salle County, Illinois; died Portland, Maine, January 15, 1941.

Cook, Charles Emerson, agent, author, producer and director, 71. Fifteen years agent for David Belasco, four years with H. H. Frazee; managed stock companies in Montreal, Milwaukee, Baltimore, Washington, D. C., and Martha's Vineyard, Massachusetts; wrote lyrics for "Red Feather" (1904); authored "The Rose of Alhambra," "The Koreans," "Mr. Pickwick" (in collaboration with Charles Klein); drama editor Boston *Transcript,* Boston *Herald;* founder Friars Club and member of Lambs. Born Parsonville, Maine; died New York City, June 8, 1941.

Courtney, Fay, singer, comedienne, 45. Favorite vaudeville actress and singer of the 20's as one of Courtney Sisters; appeared in musical comedy on Broadway; last appearance in "Off to Buffalo" (1939). Born Clay County, Texas; died New York City, February 14, 1941.

Cushing, Tom (Charles C. Strong Cushing), playwright, 61. First play produced on Broadway "Sari" (written with Percy Heath), 1912; adapted "Blood and Sand" and (with David

Belasco) "Laugh, Clown, Laugh"; wrote "Thank You" (with Winchell Smith), "The Devil in the Cheese" and "La Gringa." Born New Haven, Connecticut; died Boston, Massachusetts, March 6, 1941.

Danforth, William, actor, singer, 73. Appeared in more than 5,000 light operas; famous as comedian in Gilbert and Sullivan revivals; eight years with De Wolf Hopper and eight years with Frank Daniels; appeared in "Wang," "Robin Hood," "The Idol's Eye," "The Yankee Consul," "Blue Beard," etc.; last New York appearance (1936) as Dick Deadeye in "H.M.S. Pinafore"; married Norma Kopp, singer. Born Syracuse, New York; died Skaneateles, New York, April 16, 1941.

Dolly, Jenny (Yansci), actress, 48. Of dance team, "The Dolly Sisters"; internationally famous for twenty years; successes in "Ziegfeld's Follies," "Babes in the Woods," "Greenwich Village Follies," etc. Born Hungary; died Hollywood, California, June 1, 1941.

Eltinge, Julian (William Dalton), actor, 57. Internationally famous female impersonator; first appearance (1904) in "Mr. Wix of Wickham"; five years in vaudeville; one year with Cohan and Harris Minstrels; appeared in New York and subsequently toured in "The Fascinating Widow" and "The Crinoline Girl"; the Eltinge Theatre, N. Y., was named for him; last appearance in New York (1941) in Billy Rose's "Diamond Horseshoe." Born Newtonville, Massachusetts; died New York City, March 7, 1941.

Findlay, Thomas B., actor, 67. Under Belasco management many years; first appearance "Ticket of Leave Man" in Winnipeg, Canada (1890); appeared in "The Two Orphans" with Kate Claxton; "On Trial," "Tiger Rose," "The Spider," "Kiki," "The Little Minister," etc.; of late years in "First Lady," and "Of Mice and Men." Born Guelph, Ontario, Canada; died Aylmer, Quebec, Canada, May 29, 1941.

Fitzgerald, Cissy (Mrs. Cissy Tucker), actress, 68. Musical comedy star; said to be the original "Gaiety Girl"; known as "The Girl with the Wink"; played in motion pictures and operated her own company in Miami, Florida, and later in Hollywood; appeared with Ronald Colman in "The Masquerader." Born England; died Ovingdean, near Brighton, England, May 5, 1941.

Frohman, Daniel, producer, manager, author, 89. Prominent in theatrical production for over 60 years; manager of Madison

Square Theatre, New York (1880); produced "Hazel Kirke" under direction of Steele Mackaye; managed Lyceum Theatre, New York (1885), where E. H. Sothern and many other famous actors were first starred in Lyceum stock; director of Famous Players-Lasky Film Co.; president of Actors Fund for thirty-seven years; wrote "Memories of a Manager" and "Daniel Frohman Presents." Born Sandusky, Ohio; died New York City, December 26, 1940.

Gaites, Joseph M., producer, director, 67. Associated with the Shuberts for fourteen years; produced "The Three Twins," "Sky High," "Reflected Glory," "The Man Who Killed Lincoln," etc.; served often as member of arbitration committees. Born in a suburb of Pittsburgh, Pennsylvania; died Boston, Massachusetts, December 4, 1940.

Gatti-Casazza, Giulio, impresario, manager, 71. Prominent in opera and music for more than forty years; general manager La Scala, Milan, Italy, for ten years; general manager Metropolitan Opera, New York, for twenty-seven years; retired 1937; married Frances Alda (1910), Rosini Galli (1930). Born Udine, Italy; died Ferrara, Italy, September 2, 1940.

Gibbs, Robert Payton, actor, 81. Theatrical career from 1883 to 1926; created rôle of Gecko in the original production of "Trilby" with Wilton Lackaye and Virginia Harned; last appeared in "Caponsacchi" with Walter Hampden in 1926. Born Scranton, Pennsylvania; died Clifton, Staten Island, New York, February 22, 1941.

Goodman, Philip, producer, playwright, 55. Active in the twenties, producing "The Old Soak," "Ramblers" (with Clark and McCullough); "Poppy" (with W. C. Fields in his first speaking part); wrote "Lady at Large" and "Birth of a Hero." Born Philadelphia, Pennsylvania; died New York City, July 20, 1940.

Hartwig, Walter, producer, 61. Founder and manager of Little Theatre Tournament for ten years in New York; produced "Loose Moments," "If Booth Had Missed," etc., on Broadway; directed Manhattan Repertory Co. in Peterborough, New Hampshire, and Bristol, Connecticut; built theatre at Ogunquit, Maine; general manager for Actors Fund. Born Milwaukee, Wisconsin; died New York City, January 17, 1941.

Hawley, Dudley, actor, 62. Fifty years on American stage; debut at Proctor's, New York (1895); two seasons each with Richard Mansfield and Nat Goodwin; was in road show of "The Man Who Came to Dinner." Born England; died New York City, March 29, 1941.

Lawford, Ernest, actor, 70. Character actor for fifty years; started with Sir Ben Greet and Sir Frank Benson; London debut with Lily Langtry in "As You Like It" (1890); with Charles Frohman in America for fourteen years; first New York appearance in "Frisky Mrs. Johnson" (1903); last appearance in "The Brown Danube" (1939). Born England; died New York City, December 27, 1940.

Liebler, Theodore, producer, 89. With George C. Tyler, Liebler & Co. brought Mrs. Patrick Campbell, Eleonora Duse and Rejane to American stage; directed tours of Margaret Anglin, William Faversham, Arnold Daly, Otis Skinner, Ada Rehan, Viola Allen, Eleanor Robson and many others; retired in 1921. Born New York City; died Old Greenwich, Connecticut, April 23, 1941.

Macdowell, William Melbourne, 84. Matinee idol at the beginning of the century; began career with Adelaide Nielson in Montreal; married Fanny Davenport and appeared with her in Sardou repertory; later co-starred with Blanche Walsh; played in silent films. Born South River, New Jersey; died Decoto, California, February 18, 1941.

McCormack, Frank, actor, 65. American comedian forty years; debut with Mrs. Fiske in "Becky Sharp" (1900) and for six years thereafter her leading man. Born Washington, D. C.; died Connecticut, May 22, 1941.

McGuire, William Anthony, playwright, producer, 55. Wrote nine Ziegfeld shows, including "The Three Musketeers," "Whoopee," "Rosalie," "Kid Boots," etc.; wrote "Six Cylinder Love," "Twelve Miles Out," "Ripples," etc.; film plays include "The Great Ziegfeld" which won Academy Award for 1936, "Girl from the Golden West" and "Lillian Russell." Born Chicago, Illinois; died Beverly Hills, California, September 16, 1940.

Mix, Tom, actor, 60. Starred in three hundred and seventy films in twenty-four years; famous in Westerns and such features as "Destry of Death Valley" and his last picture "The Rustler's Round-Up"; served in Spanish-American and Boer Wars and Boxer Rebellion. Born near Dubois, Clearfield County, Pennsylvania; killed in auto accident near Florence, Arizona, October 12, 1940.

Morrison, Adrienne, actress, 57. Wife of Richard Bennett and mother of Barbara, Constance and Joan Bennett; seventh generation to follow stage career; debut in mother's arms in Joseph Jefferson's "The Cricket on the Hearth"; last played in "The Grey Farm" (1940) after thirteen years' absence from Broadway. Born New York City; died New York City, November 20, 1940.

Murray, J. Harold, actor, singer, 49. Started career as boy ballad singer in Boston theatres; in vaudeville two years; first Broadway appearance "The Passing Show of 1921"; next ten years matinee idol in musical comedy; acted in many films, including "Cameo Kirby"; retired in 1935. Born South Berwick, Maine; died Killingsworth, Connecticut, December 11, 1940.

Nevada, Mme. Emma, singer, 81. Star of the late nineteen hundreds; was signed by composer Verdi to sing at La Scala, Milan, Italy; appeared at New York Academy of Music (1884); sang "Rose of Sharon" composed for her, Covent Garden (1891). Born Nevada City, California; died Liverpool, England, June 20, 1940.

Penner, Joe (Josef Pinter), comedian, 36. Started in vaudeville and burlesque; first appearance New York, "Vanderbilt Revue" (1930); voted America's outstanding radio comedian in 1934; appeared in "College Rhythm" and "Collegiate" on screen; was starring in "Yokel Boy" in Philadelphia when he died. Born Nagechkereck, Hungary; died Philadelphia, Pennsylvania, January 10, 1941.

Porter, Edwin S., producer, 71. Film producer; associate of Thomas A. Edison in early days of film industry; developed elementary camera technics, including the closeup; assisted Adolph Zukor in organizing Famous Players; co-produced and directed "Tess of the Storm Country" with Mary Pickford and "The Dictator" with John Barrymore. Born Pittsburgh, Pennsylvania; died New York City, April 30, 1941.

Prince, Adelaide, actress, 84. Known on New York and London stage for more than forty years; stage debut Portland, Maine (1888); member Augustin Daly Co. (1889 to 1893); co-starred with husband, Creston Clarke, in Shakespearean and classical drama from 1893 to 1900; last Broadway appearance in "Mr. Samuel" (1930). Born London, England; died Shawnee-on-Delaware, Pennsylvania, April 4, 1941.

Rial, Louise, actress, 90. Character actress for 60 years; debut as Eliza in "Uncle Tom's Cabin"; played in "Fortune's

Fool," "Too Many Cooks," "A Woman's Way," etc.; last appearance "The Cinderella Man" (1917). Died New York City, August 9, 1940.

Richman, Charles, actor, 75. Prominent leading man; Broadway debut "Hands Across the Sea"; played leads for Lily Langtry, Annie Russell, Ada Rehan; remembered in "Bought and Paid For," "Rose of the Rancho," "Strictly Dishonorable," "Biography," etc.; last appearance in "And Stars Remain" (1936). Born Chicago, Illinois; died the Bronx, New York, December 1, 1940.

Slavin, John C., actor, 71. Known in musical comedy and vaudeville for 60 years; in original cast of "Jack and the Beanstalk"; with Lillian Russell Opera Co.; appeared in "The Wizard of Oz," "Singing Girl," "The Belle of New York," etc. Born New York; died New York City, August 27, 1940.

Spottswood, James, actor, 58. Started with Columbia Theatre (Washington) and New Orleans stock companies; played in several "Potash and Perlmutter" comedies; supported Julian Eltinge on the road; appeared in "Close Harmony," "Excess Baggage," "June Moon," etc.; pictures included "Thunderbolt." Born Washington, D. C.; died New York City, October 12, 1940.

Tinney, Frank, comedian, 62. Famous blackface comedian; debut New York in "Follies of 1910"; remembered in "Watch Your Step," "The Century Girl," "Tickle Me" and "The Music Box Revue"; served in army (1918) as Captain in Quartermaster's Corps. Born Philadelphia, Pennsylvania; died Northport, Long Island, New York, November 28, 1940.

Turpin, Ben, actor, 71. Screen, burlesque and vaudeville comedian; with Sam T. Jack's burlesque in Chicago; played a Happy Hooligan rôle in vaudeville for seventeen consecutive years; first film appearances with Charlie Chaplin and Mack Sennett; last picture "Saps at Sea." Born New Orleans, Louisiana; died Hollywood, California, July 1, 1940.

Underwood, Franklyn, actor, film executive, 63. Began career as actor at Elitch's Gardens, Denver, Colorado; later male lead in Western stock companies; played opposite Mrs. Leslie Carter, Nance O'Neill, Marjorie Rambeau and others; was general manager for Oliver Morosco; last years with film department of 20th Century-Fox. Born Denver, Colorado; died New York City, December 22, 1940.

Vonnegut, Walter, actor, director, 56. Manager for many years of Stuart Walker Stock Co., Louisville, Kentucky; appeared on Broadway in "Strange Interlude," "Mourning Becomes Electra," "Grand Hotel," etc.; last appearance "You Can't Take It with You" (1936). Born Indianapolis, Indiana; died Culver, Indiana, December 23, 1940.

Walker, Stuart, actor, playwright, producer, 53. With David Belasco for six years as actor, director, play reader and stage manager; founded Portmanteau Theatre (1915) and produced his own plays in Cincinnati, Indianapolis and Dayton; directed motion pictures; wrote "The Trimplet," "The Medicine Show," "Six Who Pass While the Lentils Boil," etc. Born Augusta, Kentucky; died Hollywood, California, March 13, 1941.

Wilke, Hubert, singer and actor, 85. Received medal from Emperor Franz Joseph of Austria for performance in "Tales of Hoffmann"; brought to New York by Heinrich Conreid (1882); co-starred with Lillian Russell in "The Grand Duchess"; with Francis Willard in "The Oolah" and with Marie Tempest in "The Fencing Master." Born Stettin, Germany; died Yonkers, New York, October 22, 1940.

Williams, John D., producer, director, 55. Associate of Charles Frohman and A. L. Erlanger; produced "The Copperhead" (1918), "Rain," "Our Betters," "Erstwhile Susan," "Justice" and Eugene O'Neill's "Beyond the Horizon." Born Boston, Massachusetts; died Riverdale, New York, March 22, 1941.

THE DECADES' TOLL

(Persons of Outstanding Prominence in the Theatre Who Have Died in Recent Years)

	Born	*Died*
Aborn, Milton	1864	1933
Ames, Winthrop	1871	1937
Anderson, Mary (Navarro)	1860	1940
Baker, George Pierce	1866	1935
Belasco, David	1856	1931
Benson, Sir Frank	1859	1939
Bernhardt, Sarah	1845	1923
Campbell, Mrs. Patrick	1865	1940
Crabtree, Charlotte (Lotta)	1847	1924
De Koven, Reginald	1861	1920
De Reszke, Jean	1850	1925
Drew, John	1853	1927
Drinkwater, John	1883	1937
Du Maurier, Sir Gerald	1873	1934
Duse, Eleanora	1859	1924
Fiske, Minnie Maddern	1865	1932
Frohman, Daniel	1851	1940
Galsworthy, John	1867	1933
Gorky, Maxim	1868	1936
Greet, Sir Philip (Ben)	1858	1936
Herbert, Victor	1859	1924
Patti, Adelina	1843	1919
Pinero, Sir Arthur Wing	1855	1934
Pirandello, Luigi	1867	1936
Rejane, Gabrielle	1857	1920
Rogers, Will	1879	1935
Russell, Annie	1864	1936
Schumann-Heink, Ernestine	1861	1936
Sembrich, Marcella	1859	1935
Shaw, Mary	1860	1929
Sothern, Edwin Hugh	1859	1933
Terry, Ellen	1848	1928
Thomas, Augustus	1857	1934
Yeats, William Butler	1865	1939

INDEX OF AUTHORS

INDEX OF PLAYS AND CASTS

INDEX OF PRODUCERS, DIRECTORS AND DESIGNERS

about the importance of the stage, a better day for the footlight endeavor would finally grow into reality. Time and again, this thought has emerged fitfully, and generally futilely; but the Noel Coward productions *did* show it to be no idle dream, and it may be that Selznick, whose daring in creating munificent cinema attractions is not to be denied, is the one to exert leadership. However, the fulfillment of his plans is beyond the purview of this review of happenings, and belongs to the 1941-42 season.

It only remains to be said that in motion pictures today, a set of conditions prevails that make stage appearances more possible than in the past. Many leading players—that is, those best qualified through experience for the stage—have more time available to enter the field of the theatre—at least for limited engagements. This is true also of certain directors, who might devote their leisure to the supervising of the plays. Authorship should not lag either in Southern California, if there seemed an outlet for the playwright's creations. It needs some salient force to weld the diversified interests together.

As a whole, 1940-41 seemed below the preceding fiscal period in initiative and purpose. Road attractions were notably conspicuous by their absence. The playhouse reserved for the touring productions, namely, the Biltmore, was dark much of the time. After the Coward plays few ambitious activities of Coast origin took form and character. Cheap endeavors were more manifest than usual. Efforts were made by various promoters to secure a musical show to follow up "Meet the People," which ran for nearly a year, ending its sojourn about the middle of the season, but these ended quickly in defeat.

Most important of premières was William Saroyan's "Across the Board on Tomorrow Morning," which took place at that old-reliable of institutions, the Pasadena Community Playhouse. This really stirred the lethargic show-going world of the Southland.

Because of the brevity of the play, two performances were put on of an evening, and owing to the opaque nature of the Saroyan novelty, a number viewed it a second time.

"Across the Board on Tomorrow Morning" is probably the author's most expressionistic manifestation—a far-away descendant of "The Adding Machine," and such like. Most prominent figure is the interlocutor, who functions in a night club setting, expounding ideas and explaining characters as they appear on the scene, many of whom become symbols of the various social complexities of today. Oliver Prickett, regularly identified with

Palo Alto Community Playhouse staged a variety of excellent productions that helped fill the void in weeks of darkened houses in the leading legitimate theatres.

And the summer theatre made its debut in Northern California with the conversion of a gymnasium on the grounds of Hotel Del Monte, Monterey, under the aegis of Charles O'Neal. The first productions were "Constant Wife," starring Helen Gahagan; Oliver H. P. Garrett's "The Hunters," with Mary Servoss as star; Judith Anderson in "Family Portrait" and later in a première of Robinson Jeffers' poetic drama, "Tower Beyond Tragedy," staged in the near-by Carmel Forest Theatre.

THE SEASON IN SOUTHERN CALIFORNIA

BY EDWIN SCHALLERT

Drama Editor of the *Los Angeles Times*

THE 1940-41 theatrical season in Southern California, which started with a verve and brilliance surpassing past precedents, went into a practical eclipse before the end of the twelve-month period. In August and September of last year, it looked for a time as if the motion picture colony had finally crystallized all its best ambitions to imbue play-giving with new life and fervor. For the sake of charity (British War Relief) the Noel Coward "Tonight at 8:30" series was presented, with casts unrivaled in their glamour, attracting large and enthusiastic audiences. The belief was generated that these productions at last spelt a new day for drama in the Los Angeles and Hollywood area.

However, the inspiration which gave birth to the elaborate events was short-lived. The "Tonight at 8:30" series was followed by a revue staged by Andre Charlot, which had many merits, and then the one or two other tentative projects faded into oblivion. There was no revival of the idea of offering attractions with notable movieland casts during the season, though toward its close David O. Selznick, choosing Santa Barbara as the proposed locale for the undertaking, announced plans for a summer theatre, which, it was thought, might help to carry on a most promising tradition.

Many feel that if only there could be some sensitiveness on the part of the studios and the personnel connected therewith